SURVEY
OF
SOCIAL
SCIENCE

SURVEY
OF
SOCIAL
SCIENCE

SOCIOLOGY SERIES

Volume 1
1-442

A—Culture and Language

Edited by
FRANK N. MAGILL

Consulting Editor
HÉCTOR L. DELGADO
UNIVERSITY OF ARIZONA

SALEM PRESS
Pasadena, California   Englewood Cliffs, New Jersey

Library of Congress Cataloging-in-Publication Data
Survey of social science. Sociology series / [edited by]
Frank N. Magill; consulting editor, Héctor L. Delgado.
   v. cm.
   Includes bibliographical references and index.
   1. Sociology—Encyclopedias.   I. Magill, Frank
Northen, 1907-   . II. Delgado, Héctor L., 1949-   .
HM17.S86   1994   94-31770
301'.03—dc20   CIP
ISBN 0-89356-739-6 (set)
ISBN 0-89356-740-X (volume 1)

PRINTED IN THE UNITED STATES OF AMERICA

PUBLISHER'S NOTE

The *Sociology Series* is the third set in the *Survey of Social Science*. The five volumes of the *Sociology Series* have been preceded by the *Economics Series* (1991, five volumes) and the *Psychology Series* (1993, six volumes) and will in turn be followed by a series on government and politics. All are designed to provide the general reader with insight into topics in the social sciences that are often accessible only to academicians and experts in the field. Supplying information in a quickly retrievable format and easy-to-understand style, the *Survey of Social Science* provides the nonspecialist with views of essential areas that are increasingly important to the layperson as well as the specialist.

Averaging six pages in length, the 338 articles of the *Sociology Series* follow the familiar Magill format. They begin with ready-reference information stating the type of sociology and particular field (or fields) of study to which the article's topic belongs. Next, a brief summary describes the topic's significance; key terms are then listed and defined. To aid the reader in finding information, the main text of each article is divided into three sections: "Overview," "Applications," and "Context." The "Overview" section introduces and explains the topic. "Applications" then describes how the topic is put into practice, including how it has been explored in sociological studies and how the principles involved may be applied to everyday life. "Context" locates the subject within sociology as a whole, relates it to relevant historical or cultural currents, and notes its implications. An annotated "Bibliography" follows these sections; it directs the reader to other sources that have been selected for their accessibility to the nonspecialist—the student and the general reader. Finally, the "Cross-References" section lists related articles (giving their page numbers) that appear elsewhere in the *Sociology Series*.

Like the field itself, the *Sociology Series* is broad in scope. Articles examine diverse topics from fifteen subfields of sociology, and a list of these areas demonstrates the comprehensive nature of the material covered: aging and ageism, collective behavior and social movements, culture, deviance and social control, origins and definitions of sociology, population studies or demography, racial and ethnic relations, sex and gender, social change, social institutions, social stratification, social structure, socialization and social interaction, sociological research, and urban and rural life. Coverage ranges from overviews of major theories and selected subfields to articles that focus directly on specific topics such as "middleman" minorities, crowd behavior, and nontraditional families. The basics of the sociological perspective are outlined in a core group of articles that discuss the history of the discipline and explain such major theoretical frameworks as functionalism, conflict theory, and interactionism. Another group of articles (such as "The Family: Functionalist versus Conflict Theory Views") specifically relates these perspectives to such areas of study as deviance, social stratification, education, and the family. The techniques of sociological research are examined in twenty-one articles from which the reader gains an appreciation of the challenges of studying human activity and interaction. These articles cover such topics as unobtrusive and qualitative research, as well as the procedures that social scientists use to ensure the validity and reliability of their data.

The study of social institutions was one of the earliest focuses of sociology, and the major social institutions are thoroughly covered here: the economy, education, the family, medicine, politics, and religion. The twenty articles that focus on the economy, for example, discuss such topics as preindustrial and industrial economic systems, corporations and economic concentration, the effects of automation and computers on the economy, and deindustrialization in the United States. Articles on education examine differing theoretical viewpoints on education as well as alternative education, academic freedom and free speech, educational inequality, "credentialism," and controversies over standardized testing and tracking.

The family, the essential institution of all societies, is viewed from traditional and new perspectives, including articles on nuclear and extended families, day care, divorce, remarriage and "reconstituted" (blended) families, nontraditional families, and two-career families. Another institution that has interested sociologists since the earliest days of the discipline is religion; included here are examinations of churches, denominations, sects, and cults as well as religious beliefs and symbols, millenarian religious movements, religious socialization, secularization in Western society, and political influence by religious groups. The institution of medicine and its increasing power in society is discussed in twenty articles on such topics as the medicalization of society, the germ theory of medicine, health care and gender, the environment and health, and epidemic disease. Articles on politics and the state include explanations of types of governments, the nation-state, the military-industrial complex, and party politics in the United States.

Deviance and social control are covered from both theoretical and practical perspectives in twenty-nine articles ranging from "Anomie and Deviance" to "White-Collar and Corporate Crime." The criminal justice system is examined, as are juvenile delinquency, drug use and addiction, the societal functions and dysfunctions of deviance, organized crime, and victimless crime. Theoretical coverage includes articles on the anomie, conflict, cultural transmission, and structural-strain theories of deviance.

Social stratification and social mobility are discussed in articles that range from an overview of the concept of social stratification to specific examinations of the power elite, inequalities in health and political power, and the ways inequality is legitimized by various social institutions, including the mass media. A number of articles tackle the subject of poverty, examining such concepts as the culture of poverty and the relationship between poverty and race. Issues of racial and ethnic relations have been of crucial importance in the United States. Included are articles that explore such central topics as race and ethnicity, minority versus majority groups, cultural and structural assimilation, and the complicated relationship between prejudice and discrimination.

The areas of gender and aging, including the issues of sexism and ageism, represent two of the newer fields to be studied extensively by sociologists. Gender socialization, gender inequality, and violence against women are examined, as are age inequality, the graying of America, and social gerontology. Among the types of discrimination included are discrimination against children and adolescents, discrimination against gays, ageism, and sexism. Articles on collective behavior and social movements cover crowds and crowd dynamics, rumors and urban legends, mass hysteria, and thirteen other topics. Culture, its components, and its relationship to society are discussed in eight articles. From studies of social structure come articles on industrial and postindustrial societies and on statuses and roles. Eight articles examine theories of social change, and the field of population studies (demography) is represented by twelve articles. Seventeen articles explore how socialization occurs in the family and other social institutions and how various aspects of social interaction affect a person's development and personality. Finally, the sociological study of urban and rural life is viewed in nine articles that range from rural societies to models of urban growth, suburbanization, and urban renewal.

Readers can locate information on a particular topic in a number of ways. The series is arranged alphabetically by article title, so looking for "deviance," for example, will bring the reader to the article "Deviance: Analysis and Overview"; the cross-references at the end of that article refer the reader to related articles, such as "Cultural Transmission Theory of Deviance." Each volume begins with a contents list of the volume and ends with an alphabetical listing of the contents of the entire set, followed by a listing of the entire contents grouped by category. Two other features that will aid the reader in understanding and locating information are found at the end of volume five. A glossary defines more than 450 important terms, and a comprehensive, cross-referenced index directs the reader to topics, personages, and concepts.

Salem Press gratefully acknowledges all the academicians and professionals who contributed their time, talents, and expertise to *Survey of Social Science: Sociology Series*. A list of these individuals and their affiliations appears on the following pages. We would especially like to thank Consulting Editor Héctor L. Delgado of the University of Arizona for his contributions to the series.

CONTRIBUTORS

Anna M. Heiberger Abell
Loyola University of Chicago

Steven C. Abell
University of Detroit Mercy

Joseph K. Adjaye
University of Pittsburgh

Richard Adler
University of Michigan, Dearborn

Olusoji A. Akomolafe
LeMoyne-Owen College

Joseph George Andritzky
Concordia University

Bryan C. Auday
Gordon College

James A. Baer
Northern Virginia Community College

Bruce E. Bailey
Stephen F. Austin State University

Nancy Balazadeh
Rust College

Gregg Barak
Eastern Michigan University

Russell J. Barber
California State University, San Bernardino

Garlena A. Bauer
Otterbein College

Alan J. Beauchamp
Northern Michigan University

Ralph Bell
Governors State University

Jon L. Berquist
Independent Scholar

John Braeman
University of Nebraska, Lincoln

John A. Britton
Francis Marion University

Robert D. Bryant
Georgetown College

Evelyn Buday
University of Illinois at Chicago

David P. Caddell
Belmont University

Malcolm B. Campbell
Bowling Green State University

Michael Candelaria
California State University, Bakersfield

Richard K. Caputo
Barry University

Arlen D. Carey
University of Central Florida

Sharon Carson
University of North Dakota

Jack Carter
University of New Orleans

H. B. Cavalcanti
University of Richmond

Kathleen A. Chara
Gannon Mental Health Center

Paul J. Chara, Jr.
Loras College

Jiajian Chen
Wright State University

Denise Kaye Davis
Independent Scholar

James M. Dawsey
Auburn University

Héctor L. Delgado
University of Arizona

Richard A. Dello Buono
Rosary College

Michael Delucchi
Loras College

Manisha Desai
Hobart and William Smith Colleges

Thomas E. DeWolfe
Hampden-Sydney College

Jackie R. Donath
California State University, Sacramento

Marjorie Donovan
Pittsburg State University

SOCIOLOGY

Charlotte Chorn Dunham
Texas Tech University

Sharon Elise
California State University, San Marcos

Susan Ellis-Lopez
Heritage College

James Feast
Baruch College of the City University of New York

Mario D. Fenyo
Bowie State University

John W. Fiero
University of Southwestern Louisiana

James H. Fisher
Wright State University

Karen Anding Fontenot
Southeastern Louisiana University

Michael J. Fontenot
Southern University, Baton Rouge

Donald R. Franceschetti
Memphis State University

Carol Franks
Portland State University

Roger G. Gaddis
Gardner-Webb University

Steven Garasky
Iowa State University

Roberta T. Garner
DePaul University

Gerald R. Garrett
University of Massachusetts at Boston

Stephen D. Glazier
University of Nebraska at Kearney

Robert F. Gorman
Southwest Texas State University

Roy Neil Graves
The University of Tennessee, Martin

Laurence G. Grimm
University of Illinois at Chicago

Lonnie J. Guralnick
Western Oregon State College

Larry D. Hall
Spring Hill College

Maureen T. Hallinan
University of Notre Dame

Sue Hammons-Bryner
Abraham Baldwin Agricultural College

Roger D. Haney
Murray State University

William John Hanna
University of Maryland, College Park

Mazharul Haque
University of Southern Mississippi

Dean Harper
University of Rochester

Hill Harper
Troy State University

Joan Hashimi
University of Missouri, St. Louis

Margaret Hawthorne
South Hadley High School

Robert M. Hawthorne, Jr.
Unity College

Donald M. Hayes
Sam Houston State University

Louis D. Hayes
University of Montana

JoAnn W. Haysbert
Hampton University

Arthur W. Helweg
Western Michigan University

Howard M. Hensel
Air War College

Stephen R. C. Hicks
Rockford College

Gunilla Holm
Western Michigan University

Donna Frick Horbury
Bennett College

Fumiko Hosokawa
California State University, Dominguez Hills

Marita Inglehart
University of Michigan, Ann Arbor

Charles C. Jackson
Northern Kentucky University

CONTRIBUTORS

Robert Jacobs
Central Washington University

Joseph E. Jacoby
Bowling Green State University

Frank H. Jurden
Boise State University

Charles L. Kammer III
The College of Wooster

Barbara C. Karcher
Independent Scholar

Charles J. Karcher
Clayton State College

Basil P. Kardaras
Georgetown University

Debra A. King-Johnson
Clemson University

Terry J. Knapp
University of Nevada, Las Vegas

Nathan R. Kollar
St. John Fisher College

Joann Kovacich
University of Maine at Orono

Sai Felicia Krishna-Hensel
Auburn University at Montgomery

Douglas L. Kuck
University of South Carolina at Aiken

Lisa Langenbach
Middle Tennessee State University

Jerry M. Lewis
Kent State University

Joseph A. Loya
Villanova University

Emma T. Lucas
Chatham College

Richard D. McAnulty
University of North Carolina at Charlotte

Nancy E. Macdonald
University of South Carolina at Sumter

Salvador Macias III
University of South Carolina at Sumter

Susan Mackey-Kallis
Villanova University

Paul Madden
Hardin-Simmons University

Paul D. Mageli
Independent Scholar

Ali Akbar Mahdi
Central State University

Cynthia Keppley Mahmood
University of Maine at Orono

Krishna Mallick
Bentley College
Salem State College

Henry W. Mannle
Tennessee Technological University

John Markert
Cumberland University of Tennessee

Grace M. Marvin
California State University, Chico

A. R. Maryanski
University of California, Riverside

Donna Maurer
Southern Illinois University at Carbondale

Linda Mealey
College of Saint Benedict

Linda J. Meyers
Pasadena City College

Diane Teel Miller
Liberty University

Laurence Miller
Western Washington University

Liesel A. Miller
Mississippi State University

Rowland Miller
Sam Houston State University

William Nelles
Northwestern State University of Louisiana

Byron Nelson
West Virginia University

Steve A. Nida
Franklin University

Charles H. O'Brien
Western Illinois University

O. A. Ogunseitan
University of California, Irvine

SOCIOLOGY

Kathleen K. O'Mara
State University of New York College at Oneonta

Patrick M. O'Neil
Broome Community College

Donald R. Ortner
Hampden-Sydney College

Robert J. Paradowski
Rochester Institute of Technology

Kate Parks
West Georgia College

William A. Pelz
DePaul University

Nis Petersen
Jersey City State College

Richard V. Pierard
Indiana State University

Stephanie Pierrotti
Independent Scholar

Marjorie J. Podolsky
Pennsylvania State University, Erie
Behrend College

Judith Primavera
Fairfield University

Ronald G. Ribble
University of Texas, San Antonio

Gregory P. Rich
Fayetteville State University

Lanzhen Q. Rich
Fayetteville State University

Hernán Vera Rodríguez
Pontifical Catholic University of Puerto Rico

Mícheál D. Roe
Seattle Pacific University

Andrew L. Roth
University of California, Los Angeles

Sunil K. Sahu
DePauw University

Robert C. Schehr
Colgate University

R. Baird Shuman
University of Illinois at Urbana-Champaign

Sanford S. Singer
University of Dayton

Rejoice D. Sithole
University of Wisconsin Centers, Waukesha

James Smallwood
Oklahoma State University

Charles Vincent Smedley
Charleston Southern University

William L. Smith
Georgia Southern University

M. F. Stuck
State University of New York College at Oswego

Susan A. Stussy
Independent Scholar

Shengming Tang
Western Illinois University

Curt Tausky
University of Massachusetts at Amherst

David R. Teske
Russell C. Davis Planetarium

Harry A. Tiemann, Jr.
Mesa State College

Leslie V. Tischauser
Prairie State College

Joseph Tloczynski
Bloomsburg University

Evelyn Toft
Fort Hays State University

I. Peter Ukpokodu
University of Kansas

Daniel E. Vasey
Divine Word College

Milton D. Vickerman
Bloomfield College

Bruce H. Wade
Spelman College

Theodore C. Wagenaar
Miami University

Donald B. Walker
Kent State University

Jana L. Wallace
Middle Tennessee State University

Jichuan Wang
Wright State University

CONTRIBUTORS

M. C. Ware
State University of New York
College at Cortland

Ira M. Wasserman
Eastern Michigan University

Ann L. Weber
University of North Carolina at Asheville

Mark W. Weigand
University of Colorado, Denver

Marcia J. Weiss
Point Park College

Richard Whitworth
Ball State University

Howard Wineberg
Portland State University

Deborah McDonald Winters
Boise State University

Karen M. Wolford
State University of New York College at Oswego

Katherine van Wormer
University of Northern Iowa

Clifton K. Yearley
State University of New York at Buffalo

CONTENTS

SOCIOLOGY

SURVEY
OF
SOCIAL
SCIENCE

ACADEMIC FREEDOM AND FREE SPEECH IN THE SCHOOL

Type of sociology: Major social institutions
Field of study: Education

Academic freedom and free speech in the school involve the right of teachers to determine course content and reading material without government interference. Also involved is the right of students for free expression in the classroom or school newsroom. The courts have granted some rights of expression, but not others, to students depending on their age and the circumstances of the expression.

Principal terms

ACADEMIC FREEDOM: the right of teachers to teach and use instructional materials in the manner that they see fit

CENSORSHIP: the procedure of suppressing or changing material that the government or another group finds objectionable

CLEAR AND PRESENT DANGER: the principle, developed by Justice Oliver Wendell Holmes, that speech in disagreement with government actions is protected unless it incites actions that the government has a compelling interest to prevent

FIRST AMENDMENT: the first article of the Bill of Rights, which states Congress shall pass no laws abridging freedoms of speech, press, or religion

FOURTEENTH AMENDMENT: the "due process" amendment to the Constitution that prevents states from passing legislation denying equal protection to individuals

INDECENT SPEECH: expression that is offensive to a community because it is vulgar or profane

OBSCENITY: sexual material that is not protected because it is patently offensive to community standards and has no serious literary, artistic, political, or scientific value

POLITICALLY CORRECT SPEECH: speech that is not offensive to any minority, ethnic group, or women and recognizes the value of cultural and ideological diversity

Overview

The First Amendment to the Constitution states that Congress shall pass "no law" restricting freedom of expression. Court cases since World War I have made it clear, however, that Congress and the states do have the right to prohibit expression that endangers the state or that threatens something (primarily lives or property) which the state has a right to protect. The education of children is of primary importance to the state because ultimately its survival depends upon such education.

Essential to education are two rights: the right to teach and the right to learn. Each of these rights has been contested at times by those who disagree with how they have been implemented. Teaching methods have been under scrutiny since the time of Socrates. Teachers clearly have an important trust and responsibility. Parents also have an important trust and an important responsibility; they are society's first and most important teachers. Sometimes, however, parents and other involved citizens come into conflict with teachers. At best, this conflict leads to enlightened instruction and to the betterment of the educational process. Sometimes the conflict leads to restrictions on teaching and on learning. Sometimes teachers are fired. Sometimes books are removed from reading lists and from school libraries; sometimes books are burned. At times, people—teachers, students, and protesters—are shot.

The Supreme Court has allowed certain restrictions on the freedom of expression. In *Schenck v. United States* (1919), Justice Oliver Wendell Holmes articulated the "clear and present danger" principle of restriction: If speech constitutes a danger to the state or the community, the state has a right to prevent that expression. The government also has the right to place restrictions on certain kinds of content and on the time, place, and manner in which that content is expressed. Individuals are not allowed to say whatever they want whenever they want. Words that are likely to lead to a fight are not protected. Material that has been found to be obscene is not allowed. Content that may be allowable in one format, such as print, may not always be allowed in another format, such as broadcast media. Speech that is considered indecent by the courts is not allowed to be broadcast when children are likely to be in the audience. Children do not have all the rights of expression that adults have.

Within this context, freedom of expression in the schools is sometimes restricted and is sometimes protected by the courts. In *Tinker v. Des Moines Independent Community School District* (1969), the Supreme Court ruled that the free expression rights of students were not vastly different from those of adults. Members of the Tinker family had worn black armbands to their elementary and high schools to protest United States military involvement in Vietnam. They were suspended from school for doing so. Since there was no evidence of disruption in the schools, however, the Supreme Court found that this was an unconstitutional infringement of their freedom of expression. The majority opinion of the Court said, "It can hardly be argued that either students or teachers shed their constitutional rights of freedom of speech or expression at the schoolhouse gate."

Later cases, however, have placed restrictions on high school students. In *Bethel School District No. 403 v. Fraser* (1986), a student delivered a speech nominating a fellow student for student elective office. In the speech, the student made a number of sexual innuendoes. The student was suspended for three days, and the suspension was upheld. The Court ruled that the speech could be considered disruptive in that naïve fourteen-year-olds were in the audience.

In *Hazelwood School District v. Kuhlmeier* (1988), the Court found that administrators have a right to regulate content in a school newspaper. The issue is not an easy one, since this constitutes direct government restriction of the press, and freedom of the press is generally considered sacrosanct by the Court. In this case, students had prepared the paper with two articles the principal believed would be inappropriate for the high school audience. The articles dealt with the impact of divorce on children and on student pregnancy and abortion. The principal deleted them on the grounds that the subjects were not suitable for adolescents, and the Court upheld his right to do so. The argument was that the paper was produced as part of a class and the school has control over instruction.

The most controversial and volatile aspect of freedom of expression in the classroom involves the issue of control over instruction. Academic freedom generally refers to the right of teachers to choose instructional content and to choose the manner of discussing it. Citizens in general and parents in particular also have an interest in instructional content and how it is expressed. School boards are elected officials who work with parents, teachers, and school administrators to ensure the highest quality education possible. Sometimes these groups are in disagreement, and that disagreement may even become violent.

Applications

On March 12, 1974, a five-member teacher committee submitted a list of 325 language arts textbooks for approval to the Kanawha County school board. West Virginia law had mandated that literature representing different cultures and ethnicities be available to students. High schools needed a large number of supplemental texts to satisfy students' diverse learning needs and to promote interest in a multicultural and multiethnic society. All the books were selected from state-approved lists. The committee had worked with education experts and publishing houses and believed that they had accomplished their task. The school board approved the list. A month later, however, the battle began. A school board member, the wife of a local minister, raised objections to several of the books. The board delayed adoption pending further study. By June, 1974, out-of-state groups had provided synopses of many of the books. The board voted (three to two) to purchase all the books but eight.

Other protesters joined the fray, protesting the use of objectionable language, the treatment of Christianity, or the depiction of objectionable behavior such as drug use. Some objected to the inclusion of controversial writers such as Eldridge Cleaver and Gwendolyn Brooks. *Jack and the Beanstalk* was objected to on the grounds that it taught children to steal and to kill. By summer, violent confrontations had occurred and shots had been fired. In September the violence escalated. Strikes and pickets took place; buses and schools were fire-bombed. The superintendent was arrested for contributing to the delinquency of minors. During the first week of school, parents kept an average of nine thousand of the district's forty-five thousand students out of school. One minister prayed for the death of school board members who approved the books.

In November, the board passed new selection guidelines that included a screening committee, 75 percent of whose members would be parents. The board also voted to return all the controversial books to the classroom with the exception of two series. The superintendent resigned. The new superintendent asked the board to return all the books to the classroom, which it did, calling for parental consent for the use of controversial texts.

In *Board of Education Island Trees Union Free School District No. 26 v. Pico* (1982), the Supreme Court ruled that books cannot be removed from high school libraries simply because school authorities object to their philosophical themes. Chief Justice Warren Burger, joined by Justices Lewis Powell, William Rehnquist, and Sandra Day O'Connor, dissented because they did not believe that the Court should interfere with school administrators. The Eighth Circuit Court of Appeals ruled in *Pratt v. Independent School District No. 831* (1982) that films could not be removed from a school because the board wished to prevent certain religious and ideological content from being expressed in the school.

The issue is not resolved, however; the Student Press Law Center estimates that at least three hundred cases of censorship occur each year on high school and college campuses. In 1986, a parent complained to the Graves County School Board in Kentucky that his son was being forced to read William Faulkner's *As I Lay Dying* for a sophomore-level English class. He read several passages, which contained words such as "bastard," "goddamn," and "son of a bitch," to the board. He complained that abortion was one of the topics discussed in the novel and demanded that the book be removed from the required reading list. The board voted to do so. This led to complaints from a number of other parents and to a threat of litigation by the American Civil Liberties Union (ACLU). The board then voted to rescind its action. Similar incidents occur each year throughout the United States.

James Moffett, author of *Storm in the Mountains: A Case Study of Censorship, Conflict, and Consciousness* (1988) and an education expert who directed the compilation of one of the series selected for the Kanawha County school system, argues that a "chilling effect" has taken place among teachers and textbook publishers. Teachers are afraid to select materials that might cause controversy. Publishers, largely for financial reasons, are reluctant to provide texts that might not be adopted. The result is less controversy but also less diversity in materials.

Another issue involving the right of students to receive information arose in 1991. U.S. high school students tend to score among the lowest of students from developed countries on tests of cultural awareness, political information, and geography. This led Whittle Communications to offer middle and high schools the opportunity to add television equipment to their schools if they agreed to broadcast the company's *Channel One* to their students. The program is a ten-minute news show, containing information about significant issues of the day. The goal is to improve students' cultural literacy and critical thinking. By 1992, twelve thousand schools carried *Channel One*, and it was available to eight million students. The program also carries two minutes of commercials, however, a source of objections that were contested in the courts. One court found that the program could be carried but that students could not be required to watch it.

Context

The democratic process requires the open and robust discussion of all issues of public interest. That is why true democracies prize freedom of speech and freedom of the press as essential parts of their heritage. Censorship is to be avoided, but it does exist when necessary to protect the state or its citizens. The government has a right to protect itself from speech that directly incites citizens to lawless action. Criticism of the government is allowed as long as it does not present a "clear and present danger." Expression that is found to be obscene is prohibited. Speech on radio or television that is "indecent" and is likely to be heard by children can also be prohibited.

The banning of books has occurred in the United States since before the American Revolution, beginning with the banning of John Cleland's *Fanny Hill: Memoirs of a Woman of Pleasure*. Mark Twain's *The Adventures of Huckleberry Finn*, now considered a classic of American literature, was banned from the library of Concord, Massachusetts, because of a letter from Louisa May Alcott: "If Mr. Clements cannot think of something better to tell our pure minded lads and lassies, he had best stop writing for them," she wrote. Alcott expressed an opinion that school boards across the country, at various times, have taken to heart.

Works of nearly every major writer have been censored at one time or another. The list includes Theodore Dreiser's *An American Tragedy*, D. H. Lawrence's *Lady Chatterly's Lover*, Aldous Huxley's *Brave New World*, George Orwell's *1984*, Richard Wright's *Black Boy*, Harper Lee's *To Kill a Mockingbird*, J. D. Salinger's *Catcher in the Rye*, Kurt Vonnegut's *Slaughterhouse-Five*, James Dickey's *Deliverance*, and Ken Kesey's *One Flew over the Cuckoo's Nest*. Works by William Shakespeare, Charles Dickens, Honoré de Balzac, Alexandre Dumas, Upton Sinclair, William Faulkner, Ernest Hemingway, John Steinbeck, Martin Luther, John Stuart Mill, Gottfried Wilhelm Leibniz, Blaise Pascal, Galileo, Baruch Spinoza, and Jean-Paul Sartre, as well as the Bible, have all been banned.

The Supreme Court ruled in 1957 that obscene material does not have First Amendment protection. The Court's definition of obscenity was revised in *Miller v. State of California* (1973). A work can be ruled obscene only if, taken as a whole by the average person, applying contemporary community standards, it appeals to the prurient interest and describes sexual conduct in a patently offensive way. What this means in practice is that none of the above works, or any like them, is obscene. Hence, all the above works are protected. Nevertheless, they are not always appropriate for all students. The courts have generally supported the rights of teachers to make decisions as to what is appropriate for their students. University professors have also been supported by the "Statement of Principles of Academic Freedom and Tenure" issued by the American Association of University Professors (AAUP) in 1941. Schools found in violation of these tenets are censured by the AAUP. High school teachers are not so protected. Nevertheless, they can draw the support of parents who agree with their views on educational materials, as well as the support of the ACLU.

In the late 1980's and early 1990's, the problem of "hate speech" became an issue on college campuses. Colleges were faced with the dilemma of whether to restrict speech that directed prejudicial or racist remarks at minorities. Ironically, the issue involved many liberals, traditionally the most vocal supporters of free speech, calling for the suppression of such speech in order to protect minorities. Hiring practices, harassment, and course content have all been involved in the debate over hate speech. The hate speech issue is extremely difficult to resolve. As many free speech issues have, it involves a clash between the protection provided by the First Amendment (freedom of expression) and that of the Fourteenth Amendment (protection of individuals) as well as the debate over the fine distinction between thought and action.

Bibliography

Coop, David, and Susan Wendell, eds. *Pornography and Censorship*. Buffalo, N.Y.: Prometheus Books, 1983. This is an excellent collection of philosophical essays, social scientific studies on the effects of pornography, and reviews of major obscenity cases. Bibliography but no index.

Cox, Archibald. *Freedom of Expression*. Cambridge, Mass.: Harvard University Press, 1981. The former special prosecutor in the Watergate scandal provides a useful discussion of the regulation of content, time, place, and manner within the context of relevant First Amendment cases. This is a good overview of First Amendment law. Notes, but no index or bibliography.

Hurwitz, Leon. *Historical Dictionary of Censorship in the United States*. Westport, Conn.: Greenwood Press, 1985. This book has an excellent introduction that categorizes types of censorship. Key legal terms, such as "clear and present danger" and "community standards," and state and federal cases are presented in a dictionary format.

Ingelhart, Louis E. *Freedom for the College Student Press: Court Cases and Related Decisions Defining the Campus Fourth Estate Boundaries*. Westport, Conn.: Greenwood Press, 1985. Several hundred college press cases are included in this comprehensive compilation. Lower court decisions are included.

Jenkinson, Edward B. *Censors in the Classroom: The Mind Benders*. Carbondale: Southern Illinois University Press, 1979. A very readable review of instances of school book-banning across the U.S. in the 1970's. The book includes an excellent section on the student's right to know and the teacher's right to teach. Notes, index.

Lewis, Felice Flanery. *Literature, Obscenity, and Law*. Carbondale: Southern Illinois University Press, 1976. This is an excellent review of First Amendment cases involving books. The review begins with the Hicklin Rule of English common law, covers the *Fanny Hill* case of 1821, and proceeds through the *Miller v. State of California* decision of 1973. Notes, index.

Moffett, James. *Storm in the Mountains: A Case Study of Censorship, Conflict, and Consciousness*. Carbondale: Southern Illinois University Press, 1988. The author was the director of the Houghton Mifflin series of readings for elementary and high school texts that led to parent protests in West Virginia. The book is his compelling personal account of the crisis. References, notes, and index.

Rogers, Raymond S., ed. *Free Speech Yearbook: The Meaning of the First Amendment*,

1791-1991. Carbondale: Southern Illinois University Press, 1991. This is a collection of essays that examine several First Amendment issues, including flag-burning, hate speech on campuses, and underlying philosophical positions.

Roger D. Haney

Cross-References

Discrimination Against Children and Adolescents, 225; Education: Conflict Theory Views, 579; Education: Functionalist Perspectives, 586; Education: Manifest and Latent Functions, 593; Educational Vouchers and Tax Credits, 614; The Free Speech Movement, 767; School Socialization, 1693; The Sociology of Education, 1939.

ACQUIRED IMMUNE DEFICIENCY SYNDROME

Type of sociology: Major social institutions
Field of study: Medicine

Acquired immune deficiency syndrome (AIDS) is a fatal disease whose incidence has reached epidemic proportions in the United States and much of the rest of the world. Aside from the individual tragedies caused by AIDS, AIDS has had a profound impact on various social organizations that must respond to and cope with the many dimensions of this crisis in a responsible but effective manner.

> *Principal terms*
> ACQUIRED IMMUNE DEFICIENCY SYNDROME (AIDS): a pattern of opportunistic diseases that are fatal because of a weakening of the body's immune system by the human immunodeficiency virus (HIV)
> AT RISK: certain individuals or ethnic groups especially susceptible to or vulnerable to contracting AIDS
> EPIDEMIC: the unarrested and rapid spread of a disease in a population
> ETHNIC GROUP: a group characterized by a unique, shared cultural heritage
> PREJUDICE: a preconceived judgment or opinion in the absence of just grounds or sufficient evidence

Overview

Because so many people have contracted and died from diseases related to it, acquired immune deficiency syndrome (AIDS) qualifies as an epidemic with major implications at all levels and within all groups of society. The first known cases of AIDS in the United States were reported in 1981. Fewer than a hundred people are known to have died from AIDS in that year; in 1986 only about 2 percent of Americans knew a person with AIDS. By March, 1992, however, more than 141,000 people had died; by July, 1993, 194,344 had died. By 1990 about 21 percent of the population knew someone with AIDS.

Early 1990's estimates placed the number of infected Americans at about 1.5 million; an estimated 11 million were infected worldwide, with 40 million worldwide projected by the year 2000. Since the latency or incubation period for AIDS ranges from a few months to ten years or more, the incidence of reported cases and deaths will continue to grow for many years after the incidence of infection has leveled off or declined (this is expected to occur around the middle 1990's in the United States).

The specter of AIDS presents numerous problems and challenges for society. To give one example, in the early 1990's, women were the fastest growing at-risk group. This fact means that children as well as women were (and are) being infected: About 30 percent of infected pregnant women infect their children in utero. Moreover, as AIDS occurs increasingly in the heterosexual population, reports indicate that parents are dying and leaving orphaned children. It has been estimated that about 18,500 children were orphaned by AIDS from 1981 to 1991; this number can be expected to increase dramatically. The situation has been referred to as "an unavoidable social catastrophe."

Another area of concern is the presence and spread of AIDS in the correctional system. The Centers for Disease Control (CDC) estimated in 1992 that about 8 percent of men and 15 percent of women entering prison may have the AIDS virus. In 1990, 4,519 cases of AIDS were reported in federal and state prisons and 2,466 cases in local and county jails. These numbers are forcing correctional institutions to deal with a number of issues. For example, adequacy of health care for prison inmates, both in terms of caring for inmates who become sick and in terms of decreasing the health risks for others, has become a serious problem. AIDS predisposes people to tuberculosis, which is facilitated by crowded conditions and poor ventilation in prisons. Homosexual behavior and drug use also facilitate the spread of AIDS to others in the prison population. Other problems include assaults by infected inmates on guards and the legal and moral issue of mandatory testing of inmates for AIDS.

Prejudice and discrimination against people with AIDS is also a concern. Some discrimination derives from attitudes toward and beliefs about AIDS (such as fear of contamination or a belief that AIDS is God's punishment for immoral behavior), and some occurs because AIDS has primarily afflicted those who are most discriminated against anyway: homosexuals, ethnic minorities (especially blacks and Hispanics), drug users, and women. A number of researchers have pointed to discrimination (almost certainly unintentional) by the medical establishment regarding diagnosis and treatment of women with AIDS. For example, women frequently develop different initial symptoms than males do, among them acute pelvic inflammatory disease and cervical cancer. Yet until 1992 the CDC's indicators were based primarily on symptoms exhibited by males. A number of studies in the early 1990's showed that fewer women were diagnosed with AIDS before death; also, women were typically diagnosed later than men, lived a shorter time after diagnosis, and had fewer social support networks. In addition, distorted statistics have caused misallocation of funds for research and health care. Poor minority women with AIDS who do not qualify for Social Security disability payments have been particularly affected.

In general, discrimination against people with AIDS appears to be a chronic problem. In 1990 evidence showed that subtle but stubborn and pervasive forms of prejudice involving denial of health care were replacing overt forms of bias. Overt bias was made illegal with passage of the Americans with Disabilities Act (1990); it tends not to occur in large companies but still has been noted in smaller ones. There has been a significant increase in the number of medical personnel (doctors, dentists) and institutions (nursing homes, hospitals, hospices) that will not care for AIDS patients. The cost of medical care has led insurance companies, employers, and health care providers to cut costs through discriminating against AIDS patients.

Finally, the economic cost of AIDS needs to be addressed. Harvey V. Fineberg noted in 1988 that advances in medical care are lowering the cost of treating the condition.

The CDC has estimated the direct lifetime costs of treating AIDS patients at between $60,000 and $90,000 per patient, for a total expense of around seven to eight billion dollars per year. These figures will increase with inflation and as more AIDS cases are diagnosed. There are also indirect costs that add to this figure; included are the diversion of research funds from other fatal diseases (such as heart attacks and cancer), expenses for protective clothing, and the "worried well" seeking treatment and testing.

Fineberg states that the United States as a whole can absorb the cost of treating AIDS, although some cities such as New York and San Francisco with high concentrations of AIDS patients will suffer a heavy financial toll. The situation is much more dire in other countries—in the Caribbean and especially in Africa, where the incidence of AIDS is much higher. The World Health Organization estimates that fifty million Africans will die of AIDS-related causes by 2000. Fineberg likens the long-term impact of AIDS on these populations to the effects of a prolonged war.

Applications

The primary goal of medical research on AIDS is to find a cure or a vaccine that will be effective in preventing infection. This may be said to be the first priority in the fight against the AIDS epidemic. Yet, since it is unknown when or even if this will be accomplished, the only effective strategy to combat AIDS is through education. Since the blood supply available for transfusion is effectively monitored, the only known ways for AIDS to be transmitted (disregarding transmission from pregnant women to children in the womb) are intimate sexual contact and sharing needles during intravenous (IV) drug use. If people can be successfully educated regarding safe sex and drug use and can adapt their behavior to match this knowledge, AIDS can be controlled.

Another major problem is that there is considerable fear and anger about AIDS among much of the population. Acts reflecting prejudice toward AIDS-infected persons persist. There are also considerable misconceptions and false information about AIDS. For example, one researcher reported that two-thirds of Americans would be concerned about sharing a bathroom with someone who had AIDS. One-third said that they would not lend their tools to an infected coworker. Another study found that 13 percent of a sample of Caucasians and 29 percent of blacks believed it to be true or possibly true that the AIDS virus was deliberately created in a laboratory to infect black people. All of these issues will also have to be dealt with through education.

Sara Glazer reported in 1990 that the incidence of AIDS in teenagers is low; the CDC counted only 539 cases in 1990 but estimates that the true number is much higher. Most school districts offer some form of AIDS education, and teenagers are generally knowledgeable about AIDS transmission. Unfortunately, however, much of this education is ineffective in influencing or changing teenage sex practices. A 1989 survey by the CDC found that 58 percent of high school students had had intercourse, 21 percent had had four or more sexual partners, and about 3 percent had used intravenous drugs. Yet only about 25 percent had used condoms when having intercourse. Teenagers at high risk (sexually active runaways and homosexual males) are knowledgeable about AIDS, but most still engage in sex with multiple partners and do not use condoms. The problem is that merely presenting necessary information is not sufficient. Teenagers need to be taught the social skills that can be translated into appropriate behavior. A number of educators have argued that the best way to change behavior is to have teenagers role-play sexual situations that put them at risk for AIDS so they can learn how to respond properly. Such efforts often encounter opposition from parents, community groups, and administrators. Role-playing, they argue, assumes an acceptance of teenage sex rather than stressing abstinence. It also involves open discussion of sensitive subjects such as condoms and homosexuality. Although the AIDS epidemic has made explicit public discussion of sexual issues much more common and acceptable, there is still significant opposition that prevents maximally effective confrontation of the dilemmas that AIDS poses to teenage sexuality.

According to Ron Stodghill in a 1993 study, if AIDS is to be effectively managed in the workplace, employers must do more than provide medical benefits and maintain confidentiality. It is also necessary to institute employee education programs to eliminate fears and misconceptions about AIDS and foster sensitivity among workers to the plight of affected coworkers. Part of this concern is humanitarian, and part is good business. Employees with AIDS are protected by several federal laws (including the Americans with Disabilities Act, the Hill-Burton Act, and the Rehabilitation Act). A hostile workplace environment therefore not only has a negative effect on employee morale and ultimately on productivity but also makes employers liable to discrimination lawsuits.

If education programs are to be successful, certain guidelines need to be followed. Phillip Yam noted in 1991 that a majority of programs lasted no more than forty-five minutes and consisted of a brochure and/or a presentation by an outside expert. In general, these brochures and presentations emphasize how to reduce the risk of infection but do not discuss how to be supportive or understanding of people with AIDS. Employees often come away from presentations with a "Now-I-know-how-you-get-it, why-should-I-help-you" attitude. Such programs may actually be harmful in that they may make workers less tolerant.

Important factors in a successful program include length of presentation, presentation content, and the identity of the person presenting the program. Longer programs (lasting more than two hours) that address issues of attitudes, sympathy, and support; programs presented by speakers who are best able to address the fears and misconceptions specific to that workplace; and programs that allow employees to ask questions and express their true feelings seem to have the best chance of changing and improving attitudes. The effects of educational programs may be limited, however, by certain attitudes of employees that are very resistant to change. One study reported that attitude changes only occurred in individuals who were not negatively disposed toward homosexuals. Those who held negative attitudes may be unwilling or unable to change their view of AIDS as a symbol of homosexual promiscuity and moral decadence.

Education can also be effectively served by knowledgeable and experienced professional organizations whose mission is to provide accurate information and increase public awareness and understanding of AIDS. An example is the Health Information Network (HIN) in Seattle, Washington. HIN continually seeks to provide innovative ways to access and distribute such information. HIN provides health education about AIDS through various modalities (such as lectures, panels, teleconferencing, and informational videos) to a wide variety of audiences, including the general public, women, pharmacists, religious groups, health care providers, businesses, teens, and government agencies.

Context

As any epidemic runs its course, it is significantly affected by social institutions. In turn these social institutions are changed as the epidemic proceeds. That is, epidemics are intertwined with social life and interpersonal behavior. Transmission of the venereal disease syphilis, for example, was facilitated by the military buildup during World War I and by the way the military was organized. Also, fear of syphilis influenced sex education in schools, the treatment of female juvenile delinquents, welfare legislation, and attitudes toward prostitution, immigration, cleanliness, health, and morality.

Sociologist Richard A. Berk argues that the AIDS epidemic is no different from previous epidemics. The rate of infection and who is infected are influenced by a number of widely divergent social entities. Berk lists as examples formal organizations or businesses such as blood banks, massage parlors, and public baths as well as less formal groups of individuals in social situations such as dating, meeting other single people, or using intravenous drugs. If effective agendas are to be set and programs put in place to cope with AIDS, many institutions, such as government, schools, prisons, businesses, the military, and the church must become involved as active participants.

Berk also emphasizes that, just as social organizations create and influence the course of the AIDS epidemic by providing opportunities for transmission and prevention, these same social entities are affected by the epidemic. Affected are the delivery of medical services; health insurance; direct medical expenses; prisons; the courts (the legal tangles concerning cases of discrimination, the need to safeguard the rights of AIDS-infected persons, and the resolution of ethical issues such as mandatory testing); the schools and teenage sexuality; the social consequences for at-risk groups in terms of infection; civil rights; access to treatment; and public attitudes. The list of social institutions could no doubt be expanded to include nearly every organization and sector within society.

The impact of AIDS on individuals is both direct and indirect, and the behavior of individuals has both a direct and indirect impact on AIDS. This reciprocity occurs within the broader context of groups and communities, each of which is distinctly affected and also has a distinct impact. This ongoing and evolving relationship between AIDS and the social order will raise questions about public policy, will change public policy, and will be a prominent political issue in the years ahead.

The enormous problems and dislocations produced by AIDS are in some ways reminiscent of an earlier epidemic, the polio epidemic, also caused by a viral infection.

During the first half of the twentieth century, repeated outbreaks of polio occurred throughout the United States and spread quickly. By the early 1950's, about thirty thousand new cases of polio were reported each year. By 1955 there were fifty-eight thousand new cases. Pools and beaches were closed, people avoided crowded places and parks, and motion picture showings were canceled. Then Jonas E. Salk (in 1954) and Albert B. Sabin (in 1961) introduced successful vaccines. In 1963 only four hundred people died, and by the 1970's polio had practically disappeared in the United States. The history of epidemics also suggests that AIDS is not the last epidemic that humankind and its social institutions will have to face.

Bibliography

Bayer, Ronald. *Private Acts, Social Consequences: AIDS and the Politics of Public Health.* New York: Free Press, 1989. As with the other books cited that were written in the late 1980's, more accurate statistical data and estimates on projected costs will be found in more recent works. This volume, however, like the others cited, does an excellent job in identifying and discussing the many complex social issues brought about by the AIDS crisis. Bayer's well-written and thoughtful book discusses such topics as compulsory screening, isolating AIDS patients, politics, and education.

Berk, Richard A., ed. *The Social Impact of AIDS in the U.S.* Cambridge, Mass.: Abt Books, 1988. This brief volume (143 pages) presents a thorough and interesting account of the impact of AIDS on a number of social organizations (such as the pornography industry, hospitals and physicians, the Catholic church) as well as gender issues and a cross-cultural perspective.

Fee, Elizabeth, and Daniel M. Fox, eds. *AIDS: The Burdens of History.* Berkeley: University of California Press, 1988. AIDS is put in the perspective of past epidemics and the information they can provide to help cope with AIDS. The authors emphasize that failure to pay serious attention to historical analysis leads to crude and inaccurate generalizations about AIDS (for example, there is a long historical record of public health workers protecting the confidentiality of people they screen and test).

Flanders, Stephen A., and Carl N. Flanders. *AIDS.* New York: Facts on File, 1991. The book provides an especially good explanation of what AIDS does and how it does it. It also nicely and concisely summarizes a number of the social issues AIDS has raised. Additionally, the book presents a detailed chronology of the significant events in the first decade of AIDS.

Hyde, Margaret O., and Elizabeth H. Forsynth. *AIDS: What Does It Mean to You?* Rev. ed. New York: Walker, 1992. A brief but informative nontechnical and easy-to-read presentation on AIDS. There is a good discussion of statistical data and there are chapters on the social impact of AIDS.

Miller, Norman, and Richard C. Rockwell, eds. *AIDS in Africa: The Social and Policy Impact.* Lewiston, N.Y.: Edwin Mellen Press, 1988. The AIDS epidemic has wreaked its most devastating toll upon the African continent. This book presents a detailed and vivid account of the effect of AIDS on economic and social development in Africa.

Pierce, Christine, and Donald VanDeVeer, eds. *AIDS: Ethics and Public Policy.* Belmont, Calif.: Wadsworth, 1988. This excellent volume discusses in detail the ethical issues arising from the social impact of the AIDS epidemic. Topics include restricting liberty, law and public policy, and sexual autonomy.

Sabatier, Renee. *Blaming Others: Prejudice, Race, and Worldwide AIDS.* Washington, D.C.: Panos Institute, 1988. This book forcefully demonstrates the insidious effects of scapegoating and casting blame for the AIDS epidemic, especially as it pertains to ethnic minorities and drug users.

The Science of AIDS: Readings from Scientific American Magazine. New York: W. H. Freeman, 1989. A collection of articles reprinted from *Scientific American.* Much of the volume discusses biomedical aspects of AIDS, but there are also excellent selections on epidemiology and the social dimensions of AIDS.

Laurence Miller

Cross-References

Endemic and Epidemic Diseases, 640; Discrimination Against Gays, 806; Health and Society, 852; Health Care and Gender, 858; The Medical Profession and the Medicalization of Society, 1159; Medical Sociology, 1166; Sexually Transmitted Diseases, 1742; Social Epidemiology, 1793.

ADULT EDUCATION

Type of sociology: Major social institutions
Field of study: Education

Adult education is a specialized aspect of education that includes a variety of programs involving the instruction of persons over legal age or outside the system of formal education. From its beginning in Great Britain in the 1800's, the movement for adult instruction has become worldwide.

Principal terms
ADULT: a person of legal age
ADULT EDUCATION: the tutelage, usually structured, given to individuals over the traditional age of formal education; most often given to individuals above either secondary school or college level
ANDRAGOGY: the art and science of helping adults learn
EDUCATION: the formal and informal acquisition of knowledge
FORMAL EDUCATION: educational instruction for which an individual registers and, frequently, pays a fee
LITERACY: the ability to read and write

Overview

The term "education" is difficult to define, since it is used in both general and specific situations to connote learning and may pertain to both formal and informal acquisition of knowledge. The term "adult education" is almost as complex, but it is often used to mean any structured learning engaged in by adults, usually over the age of traditional education. This definition may be modified according to the type of learning in which the individual participates. For example, a high school dropout of age sixteen in a remedial reading program may be defined as being in adult education, as might a mature student returning to a degree program. One significant feature of adult education is that individual involvement is voluntary; there are no legal regulations requiring the adult to participate in the educational process.

The phrase "adult education" was first used by Thomas Pole, an English physician, in his book *A History of the Origin and Progress of Adult Schools* (1816). Pole was concerned that adults be able to read and write in order to read the Bible. From this beginning in Britain, adult education has spread throughout the world. It has developed along several different lines, coalescing into four broad categories: adult literacy, training and retraining programs, returning students, and continuing education. The actual process of teaching adults is a subdiscipline of education called andragogy.

Adult literacy is the area of adult education concerned with teaching basic reading and writing skills to those people who are out of the formal education system. This includes individuals beyond the age at which they may legally leave the public school system, usually between fourteen and sixteen years of age, depending upon the country. In the United States, much of the emphasis of adult literacy has been on individuals for whom English is a foreign language. One of the earliest goals of adult education classes in the United States was to prepare immigrants for U.S. citizenship. This aspect of adult education remains strong.

Training or retraining programs are those types of classes designed to teach new skills, whether these are job development classes designed to improve one's skills at existing employment or technical training to enable an individual to change position or occupation. These programs are increasingly important as technology changes rapidly, eliminating some types of jobs and creating others.

Returning students are those adults who are returning to formal education, usually at the college or university level, after a break of several years. These students generally have the goal of obtaining a degree or professional certificate. This group includes large numbers of women and ethnic minorities who are able to avail themselves of hitherto restricted opportunities for education. Both changing attitudes of society and family needs contribute to this influx of older students into higher education.

Continuing education, a term which may be applied to all the above categories, also suggests educational programs designed for older students who are seeking learning simply for the sake of broadening their educational base, with no external goals such as employment benefits or degree programs. Early in the history of adult education, this type of education was called "leisure learning," implying a vacationlike atmosphere. Leisure learning was not considered serious education, and it was commonly considered to be the prerogative of wealthy or retired individuals.

With the return of adults to an educational setting, difficulties may arise because instructors are frequently younger, sometimes much younger, than their students. In addition, the older student has a wealth of practical knowledge and experience that colors his personal philosophy and educational experience. These realizations have caused the development of the field of andragogy. Malcolm S. Knowles and his coauthors describe the andragogical model in *Andragogy in Action* (1984). This model emphasizes that adult learners direct their own study and that the life experiences of the older learner are both qualitatively and quantitatively different from those of a younger person. It also assumes that adults are personally motivated to learn.

Societies throughout the world are entering the industrial age, some rapidly, others more slowly. As information increases (and almost as quickly becomes outdated), the need for education to be a continuing process becomes apparent. Education, however, is still frequently a prerogative of the wealthy. People of lower socioeconomic levels tend to have lower levels of education, with a resultant less positive attitude about adult education and therefore a lower level of participation. Efforts are being made throughout the world to reverse this trend. Government programs, religious groups, and the United Nations Educational, Scientific, and Cultural Organization (UNESCO) are attempting to make educational programs available to all who are willing to listen and participate.

Applications

Because of the changing needs of societies throughout the world, adult education has developed from a luxury into a necessity. The four aspects of adult education—adult literacy, training and retraining, returning students, and continuing education—reflect the current goals and values of society in the United States and throughout the world.

Illiteracy among adults is a growing concern throughout the world. There are many reasons why a person may reach maturity unable to read or write. It has been argued that in the United States this may be caused by inadequacies in the public school system. Elsewhere in the world, illiteracy may result from lack of opportunity for education, especially for females, and especially in Third World countries. Approximately 70 percent of the illiterate people in the world are women. Among educational societies in the world, UNESCO has been a forerunner in helping women to learn. The goal of female education frequently includes the need to change societal attitudes regarding the value and role of women.

Illiteracy for both genders is prevalent in rural areas. Access to resources (teachers and books) is the main difficulty. This problem has been addressed in Nicaragua by the implementation of "school" farms, which give technical assistance to the population along with teaching new agricultural techniques, as described by John Lowe in *The Education of Adults: A World Perspective* (1975). Two key factors in achieving success in adult literacy classes, as in other adult education settings, are respect of the instructor for the students and the maintenance or development of student self-esteem. Many people in adult literacy classes come from a long tradition of educational failure; this chain must be broken and replaced with a tradition of success.

Job training and retraining is a segment of adult education that is crucial in industrial societies. Industrial and technological change promotes two educational outcomes: the necessity for workers to stay current with advances in their field, and the necessity of changing occupations when certain jobs become obsolete. Maintaining proficiency on the job frequently requires additional formal education; at other times, it may be achieved by attendance at seminars relating to one's area of expertise. Retraining may occur when a worker is no longer suited for a particular occupation because of the developing technical aspects of that occupation. For example, auto mechanics with thirty years of experience have had to upgrade their skills through classwork in order to keep up with new automobile technology that includes more computerization in cars.

An increasing sensitivity of society to the needs of minorities has expanded learning opportunities for people in ethnic groups, older people, people with disabilities, women, and the prison population. Many adaptations in the educational system have centered on the special difficulties faced by the above-mentioned populations. Expanded time schedules provided by many institutions have aided returning students. Evening courses and weekend modules allow adults with daytime employment or children to attain a college degree. Along with this, the acceptance of part-time students by colleges and universities permits more people to attain a higher education.

Another adaptation was the acceptance by institutions of higher learning of college credit achieved by correspondence (or "distance") courses. These courses benefit students who are place-bound because of family ties and responsibilities, including American Indian people. Previously correspondence courses were considered to be unfit for credit because at the time many were managed by commercial enterprises whose business was to make a profit rather than to maintain academic standards. Correspondence courses are especially useful to people with disabilities that impair mobility and to prisoners.

One of the greatest obstacles to achieving a college degree in the United States today is the mobility of society. Women traditionally have been susceptible to being uprooted from their activities by the business move of a husband. Also, members of migrant families have frequently found it difficult to obtain a degree from a single institution. At one time institutions did not like to accept transfer students or to grant extensive credit for work done at another institution. These dilemmas have been moderated by colleges beginning to accept more transfer credits and to accept college courses taken at earlier times in an individual's life. In addition, the growing number of local and community colleges and the proliferation of off-campus branches of major universities have enabled place-bound people (such as many working people, housewives, and ethnic minorities such as American Indians of various tribes) to become involved in higher education.

Continuing education still plays an important role in adult education. As mentioned previously, this term is widely used to describe the phenomenon of "learning for the sake of learning." While more people are beginning to enjoy this type of education, it is still frequently people who are retired or close to retirement who participate. These classes are especially important in a society in which many of the elderly have no rewarding social function. Continuing education returns to many retirees a new self-identification and fulfillment.

Context

Adult education formally existed as early as 1814 in Great Britain. Early instruction was directed toward the lower classes of society, and it included both a literacy educational forum (including writing, arithmetic, and geography) and trade schools. World interest in adult education coalesced with the organization of the World Association of Adult Education in 1919; in 1929 this body held an international conference in Cambridge, England.

After World War II, UNESCO sponsored the International Conference on Adult Education, held in Elsinore, Denmark, in 1949. Twenty-nine representatives attended, coming mainly from Western Europe and other industrialized countries. The focus of the conference was the role of volunteers in adult education. The second International Conference on Adult Education was held in Montreal, Canada, in 1960. Fifty-one countries had delegates in attendance, including many specialists in the field of adult education. During this conference the role of adult education was expanded to include organized activities of any nature that attempted to educate adults. The third international conference was held in Tokyo, Japan, in 1972. Attendance included almost four hundred delegates from eighty-two countries and thirty-seven organizations. Many of these delegates were from the political and administrative sectors. The variety of attendees reflected the changing image of adult education; it was increasingly coming to be seen as a tool to prepare for employment.

Adult education is influenced by societal factors. With increased political concern for minorities and people of Third World nations, for example, the diffusion of education is being praised as a means of bringing opportunity to oppressed people. Although literacy alone will not guarantee success in any setting, the education of adults opens more doors of opportunity through which they may walk.

Bibliography

Adult Education Quarterly, 1950-   . Published in the United States, this journal is dedicated to research in the area of adult education. The articles are scholarly but understandable by the general reader. The topics are diverse and include both method and theory. Each article is well documented, and the references are extensive.

Adults Learning, 1989-   . A British journal (called *Adult Education* from 1935 to 1989) (1934-1989) devoted to the education of adults. A wide variety of topics are covered. Articles range from the scholarly, including references, to informal with no references. It provides good insights into the British view of adult education.

Boone, Edgar J., et al., eds. *Serving Personal and Community Needs Through Adult Education*. San Francisco: Jossey-Bass, 1980. A collection of essays defining the evolution of adult education and the assortment of needs addressed by the field. Essays also examine the contribution that adult education makes back to the community. A good work for its broad application. Includes extensive references and index.

Jones, R. Kenneth. *Sociology of Adult Education*. Brookfield, Vt.: Gower, 1984. Jones presents the topic of adult education in its relationship to sociology. His perspective is worldwide, and this book contains many good examples of application of adult education in a variety of countries and settings. An extensive bibliography is included.

Knowles, Malcolm S., et al. *Andragogy in Action*. San Francisco: Jossey-Bass, 1984. This collection presents thirty-six cases of practical applications of andragogy. It also discusses the successes and weaknesses of such teaching, and effectiveness in various settings. Since it is a book of practical application, the references are somewhat limited.

Lowe, John. *The Education of Adults: A World Perspective*. Paris: Unesco Press, 1975. UNESCO has several publications on the topic of adult education. Lowe's book includes a good history of UNESCO's involvement with adult education and the changing focus of the discipline. This volume, as with other UNESCO books, presents many examples of the worldwide application of adult education.

Pole, Thomas. *Pole's History of Adult Schools*. Reprint. Washington, D.C.: Adult

Education Association, 1967. Originally published in 1816 as *A History of the Origin and Progress of Adult Schools*, this is the earliest known work on adult education. Pole presents the state of the subject in its early years. Serious students of the study of adult education should consult this work because of its historical value.

Susan Ellis-Lopez

Cross-References
Aging and Retirement, 47; Education: Conflict Theory Views, 579; Education: Functionalist Perspectives, 586; Education: Manifest and Latent Functions, 593; Educational Credentials and Social Mobility, 600; Functional Illiteracy, 780; Higher Education: Colleges and Universities, 877; Higher Education: Community Colleges, 884; The Sociology of Education, 1939.

AFFIRMATIVE ACTION

Type of sociology: Racial and ethnic relations

Affirmative action refers to a series of actions that constitute a strategy to secure equal opportunities, particularly in education and employment, for racial minorities and women. This strategy, in turn, is designed to achieve parity for racial minorities and women in areas where they are underrepresented.

Principal terms

RACIAL DISCRIMINATION: behavior, practices, and/or policies that cause harm to individuals on the basis of their racial group membership

RACIAL GROUP: a social group for which membership is based on a combination of cultural heritage, historical circumstance, and/or the presence of distinguishable physical features such as skin color

RACIAL PREJUDICE: dislike and/or fear of others based on real or perceived physical characteristics, nationality, and ethnicity

SOCIAL CLASS: a category of group membership generally based on economic resources, income, occupational prestige, and educational attainment

SOCIAL INSTITUTIONS: social arrangements and interactions that order family relations, religion, governance, economic relations, education, and culture in society

SOCIAL STRATIFICATION: a hierarchical ranking system with differences in access to social resources; individuals at the top ranks have more access, while those at the bottom lack social resources

Overview

Affirmative action has been the focus of spirited debate in scholarly circles, among government policy makers and legislators, and—perhaps more than any other racial issue—among the public. Although many people have strong opinions on affirmative action, the debate can become quite confusing, since the term "affirmative action" refers to a broad range of activities. In his 1992 publication *The Constitution and Race*, Donald Lively says that affirmative action can refer to examining recruitment and promotion activities for obstacles to minorities, and to practices designed to assure a broader base of candidates for positions by race. It can also refer to policies and actions that give extra consideration, or preference, to racial minority and/or women candidates. Basically, as stated by Daniel Maguire in his *A Case for Affirmative Action* (1992), affirmative action is composed of two core elements: remedial affirmative action and preferential affirmative action. It is the latter that has sparked the debate, according to Maguire.

Generally, under remedial affirmative action, steps are taken to increase the pool of minority candidates by contacting and recruiting schools that are predominantly attended by racial minorities, by using minority recruiters and community contacts, and by offering special training to help minorities become qualified to apply for those positions. Preferential affirmative action, however, requires that employers examine the characteristics of the labor pool to find the proportion of available minorities and white women, and then compare that with the makeup of their own labor force. Based on this workforce utilization figure, they should then set goals for change and create strategies and a timetable for meeting those goals.

Affirmative action was developed in order to combat racial and sexual discrimination in the labor force, although debates over affirmative action are largely focused upon its racial dimension. The major targets for affirmative action policies have been professional schools and places of employment. The legal basis for affirmative action is found in the Fourteenth Amendment, which requires "equal protection under the law"; in several Executive Orders; and in the Civil Rights Act of 1964. Legal experts, however, notably those sitting on the Supreme Court, have been quite varied in their interpretations of legislation related to affirmative action.

Generally, the debate over affirmative action policies concerns the issue of whether efforts to abolish race discrimination must include measures to overcome the ongoing effects of historical injustice. Furthermore, questions arise concerning whether governance should be "color-blind," therefore rendering any race-specific policies questionable. Some say that people arguing for a color-blind approach ignore the historical dimensions of institutionalized racism.

Proponents of affirmative action argue that neither American society nor the U.S. Constitution has ever been color-blind. For example, as James E. Jones argues in *Race in America: The Struggle for Equality* (Herbert and Jones, 1993), in the 1857 case of *Dred Scott v. Sandford*, which held that a slave who had moved with his master to a nonslave state could not be granted his freedom, the Supreme Court justified its decision by claiming that, by design, the Constitution clearly considered that African Americans were a "subordinate and inferior class of beings" with no rights. Jones says that a kind of affirmative action was first developed to assist African Americans following the abolition of slavery in the United States. While the Fourteenth Amendment to the U.S. Constitution provides for equal protection, not special protection, it did provide the constitutional basis for the 1866 Freedman's Bureau Act. This act provided racially specific assistance to African Americans during the Reconstruction Era that followed the abolition of slavery.

Other supporters of affirmative action argue that a form of preference is warranted in order to break down the prominence that white males have in governance, business, education, and other social institutions. They say that this prominence is the result not of merit but of historical preference for white males. One example is given by Joe R. Feagin in *Racial and Ethnic Relations* (1978). He says that the 1862 Homestead Act was a form of "affirmative action" for white immigrants, giving them a chance to develop landed wealth which was denied to the vast majority of black people. Maguire states in *A Case for Affirmative Action* that preference must be used as a strategy to break down old preference patterns that favored white males in order to secure racial justice.

Opponents of affirmative action claim that any racially specific preference system is a form of "reverse discrimination." Such a practice, they say, repeats the same behavior that civil rights enthusiasts condemn—discrimination by race. In the case of affirmative action, they claim that it is white males who are discriminated against by a preference system that favors racial minorities and women—hence the designation "reverse discrimination." Furthermore, they argue that rewards should be based on merit, not on group membership, and that race-specific strategies lead to quotas and/or to the placement of unqualified (undeserving) individuals into positions simply to meet those quotas.

Applications

The applications of affirmative action policies have varied, broadening and narrowing with the political climate of the nation. Generally, the 1941 Executive Order by president Franklin Roosevelt, which required defense plants to show that they were hiring African American workers, is seen as marking the first step toward affirmative action. It was under the Kennedy Administration, however, that the term "affirmative action" took hold, when all companies holding federal contracts were required to demonstrate that they were moving toward achieving racial balance in their workforce.

Title VII of the 1964 Civil Rights Act made discrimination in employment by race, sex, religion, and nationality illegal. This legislation was further expanded in 1972 to allow courts to require affirmative action efforts by those found guilty of discriminatory practices.

Some educational institutions and private organizations have not waited for court-ordered plans to correct discriminatory practices. They have reexamined admissions policies and entrance requirements or skills tests to make sure those are not impediments to minority entree. The law defines that such barriers are illegal unless it is demonstrated that they are a business necessity or that such skills are necessary for satisfactory job performance. This was the decision in the *Griggs v. Duke Power Company* (1971) case. The Supreme Court said that African American employees had experienced discrimination because their employers used their disproportionately low test scores to keep them in low-skilled positions. The decision was based on the inability of the employer to show that a certain passing grade was necessary to job performance. This decision was sustained by the legislation of the Civil Rights Bill of 1991.

Affirmative action strategies include using locator services to invite applications for positions from women and minorities, providing inducements to entice minority and/or women candidates to take positions, and a variety of policies for the retention of minority and women students or employees. The application of affirmative action is always subject to opposition, however, from those who feel slighted by policies that give preference to minorities and/or women. For example, in the case of *Regents of the University of California v. Bakke* (1978), Alan Bakke was denied admission to the University of California's Davis medical school. Bakke sued because, in his view, he was denied admission because less-qualified minority applicants were accepted.

Those arguing his case claimed that his right to "equal protection under the law"—guaranteed by the Fourteenth Amendment—had been abridged and that he was a victim of "reverse discrimination." Although Bakke was ultimately admitted to medical school, the Court's decision included the interpretation that race or sex can be used as grounds for preference. Legal scholars argue, however, that the Court has created doctrines that respond well to obvious, overt discrimination but do little to confront subtle forms of discrimination that are institutionalized in society.

Context

Sociological attention is generally given to affirmative action policies and debates by scholars of social stratification, race and ethnic relations, gender relations, and institutionalized discrimination. Because equity issues are significant to all these areas of sociological inquiry, programs designed to confront equity and the debates surrounding those programs are of interest. Generally, however, scholarly research on and discussion of affirmative action have been most pronounced in the sociology of race and ethnicity.

Sociologists in the field of race and ethnic relations are not impervious to the debates over the merits of race-conscious versus color-blind policies. Nathan Glazer, in particular, is heralded as a major opponent of affirmative action, which he views as "reverse discrimination." Generally, assimilationist scholars such as he are more inclined toward policies geared to the individual, committed as they are to the notion of the United States as a meritocratic society. By this they mean that U.S. society is an open society in which individuals who work hard will be rewarded for their hard work. Such a society would not use race, nationality, or gender as barriers to individual upward mobility.

For sociologists of this theoretical persuasion, racial discrimination is often viewed as a thing of the past, and as an aberration in a society otherwise marked by equality and openness. Their view of affirmative action is directed by the assimilationist goal/vision of a "color-blind" society in which race is unrelated to social organization. These sociologists believe that their assessment that discrimination is ended is correct because of the abolition of slavery, the incorporation of people of color as citizens, and the passage of civil rights legislation. The more subtle forms of discrimination that are embedded in institutions—which are referred to as covert institutional discrimination—are often left unaddressed in these analyses or are assumed to have disappeared. This position is common among assimilationist sociologists.

According to Michael Omi and Howard Winant in *Racial Formation in the United States* (1986), the assimilationist scholars' opposition to race-conscious policies reflects a position that "is simultaneously opposed both to discrimination and to antidiscrimination measures based on 'group rights' principles." Furthermore, the assimilationist orientation in the sociology of race relations has been the predominant one. In this instance, American sociology seems to reflect the society, with an orientation toward color-blind practices.

Sociologist William J. Wilson argues that, with the passage of civil rights legislation safeguarding the legal rights of African Americans, race discrimination is no longer the primary issue facing African Americans. Rather, he argues, it is the problem of social class, which negatively affects primarily poor, inner-city blacks, that society must remedy. In other words, Wilson, who is not opposed to affirmative action, claims (as does conservative economist Thomas Sowell) that affluent and middle-class blacks have been the principal, if not sole, beneficiaries of affirmative action. Poor blacks lack the training and education necessary to take advantage of affirmative action. For this group, *class*-specific policies, Wilson argues, are required.

It is interesting to note that scholars attacking affirmative action for a variety of reasons have tended to draw on racial, not gender-based, logic in their arguments, despite the tremendous protection given women of all races under affirmative action programs and policies. In fact, affirmative action work to achieve equity for women has involved some major policy changes, such as the notion of "comparable worth," which has tremendous implications for the way in which wage scales are established. In fact, comparable-worth programs seek to bring about equity not only through preferential hiring systems but also by changing the value accorded to work that is traditionally done by women. Given some of the far-reaching policies proposed to achieve gender equity, it is interesting that the policies for racial equity tend to be the targets for foes of affirmative action.

In his book *Two Nations: Black and White, Separate, Hostile, Unequal* (1992), Andrew Hacker presents a convincing case for the persistence of racial discrimination. Further, he documents the tremendous racial disparity that persists in wealth, income, health, and poverty, among other things. As many scholars have pointed out, he suggests that race has been fundamental to the organization of social life in America from the beginning. The notion that the white race was privileged through racial injustice—for example, by the taking of land from Native Americans and labor from enslaved Africans—is used to explain the contemporary racial disparity that exists. Other scholars, however, argue that problems of contemporary society warrant continued programs to combat ongoing discrimination. They say that patterns of preference, particularly in employment, remain geared toward whites unless the government invokes affirmative action and stringent guidelines for its enforcement. As then-president Lyndon Johnson said in 1965: "You do not take a person who for years has been hobbled by chains, and liberate him, bring him up to the starting line, and then say, 'You are free to compete with all the others.'"

Bibliography

Cherry, Robert. *Discrimination: Its Economic Impact on Blacks, Women, and Jews.* Lexington, Mass.: Lexington Books, 1989. Providing an excellent socioeconomic analysis, this book details scholarly explanations of discrimination, applying them to African Americans, women, and Jews. This book is written with the nonspecialist in mind and is understandable but detailed. Tables depicting racial, ethnic, and gender differences in income, education, and occupation are included, along with a detailed index and reference listings at the end of each chapter.

Glazer, Nathan. *Ethnic Dilemmas, 1964-1982*. Cambridge, Mass.: Harvard University Press, 1983. In this collection of scholarly essays, Glazer applies his ethnicity-based, assimilationist theory of race relations to varying social issues. Principal among these is affirmative action, to which Glazer devotes an essay on what he calls "affirmative discrimination," in which he decries affirmative action policies as reverse discrimination.

Hacker, Andrew. *Two Nations: Black and White, Separate, Hostile, Unequal*. New York: Charles Scribner's Sons, 1992. In this clearly written book, Hacker provides detailed evidence for his thesis that race remains critical to the maintenance of the United States as a dual society in which African Americans are subordinated to their white counterparts at every level of society.

Hill, Herbert, and Jones, James E., Jr., eds. *Race in America: The Struggle for Equality*. Madison: University of Wisconsin Press, 1993. This collection features a multidisciplinary approach to racial equity issues in America, including historical and legal overviews. Of particular significance is an article by James E. Jones, "The Rise and Fall of Affirmative Action."

Maguire, Daniel. *A Case for Affirmative Action*. Dubuque, Iowa: Shepherd, 1992. In this book, Maguire passionately argues the case for affirmative action based on his interpretation of the history of race relations in U.S. society. This is an excellent resource for scholars on either side of the issue, for Maguire painstakingly presents the arguments on both sides and systematically examines each legal case that is relevant to the issue. Of particular importance is Maguire's view of the distinction between "equality" and "justice"; he explains the problems of a literal application of "equality under the law" prior to securing social justice.

Omi, Michael, and Howard Winant. *Racial Formation in the United States*. New York: Routledge & Kegan Paul, 1986. This text offers a critical assessment of the major race relations theories. The authors propose that race be addressed as an independent force in U.S. society; they then apply this thesis to an analysis of the role that the state plays, and then to an analysis of political contention among divergent racial groups.

Wilson, William J. *The Declining Significance of Race*. Chicago: University of Chicago Press, 1978. Surveys major epochs of race relations in American society, detailing the influence of race historically and discussing the contemporary emergence of class stratification among African Americans and of an entrenched underclass.

Sharon Elise

Cross-References

AGE GRADING AND AGE STRATIFICATION

Type of sociology: Aging and ageism

Age grading is the assignment of social roles to certain chronological ages. Age stratification is the unequal distribution of wealth, power, prestige, and privileges among people of different ages. Through theory development and research, social gerontologists attempt to understand how these two phenomena are interrelated.

Principal terms

ASCRIBED CHARACTERISTIC: a characteristic that is assigned to an individual at birth and that cannot be changed

COHORT: a category of people born at about the same time who enter various stages of the life cycle together and experience historical events at the same approximate ages

DEMOGRAPHY: the scientific study of human populations, with an emphasis on the age, sex, racial/ethnic, and socioeconomic structure of society and how the structure changes

SCAPEGOATING: the practice of unfairly blaming a person or category of people for the troubles of others

SOCIAL INSTITUTION: a major structural part of society that addresses one or more basic activities

SOCIAL ROLE: patterns of expected behavior attached to a particular status

SOCIAL STRATIFICATION: a system by which categories of people in a society are ranked in a hierarchy

SOCIOECONOMIC STATUS: a composite social ranking based on various dimensions of social inequality

STEREOTYPE: a set of characteristics assigned to a category of people; stereotypes are based on prejudice and often have no basis in reality

SUBCULTURE: a group of people who hold many of the values and norms of the larger culture but also hold certain beliefs, values, or norms that set them apart from that culture

Overview

Age grading and age stratification are two very closely related but different concepts. The former refers to the assignment of social roles based on approximate chronological ages, while the latter examines the impact of age grading on the position of the elderly in the social stratification system.

Age grading establishes age-related prescriptions and proscriptions for behavior: It defines "normal behavior" at various ages. For example, age grading tells people approximately when they are expected to begin their formal education, to marry, to become economically independent, to retire, and much more. Nearly all societies, no matter how simply they are socially and economically organized, recognize the three basic age grades of childhood, adulthood, and old age. In relatively simple societies, there is a single age grading system so that as one moves into a given category, roles relating to important social institutions are simultaneously affected so that one's family, economic, political, and religious roles are altered at the same time. In complex societies such as American society, there are multiple age grading systems; in effect, there are separate timetables for the assumption and relinquishment of roles relating to different social institutions. For example, in the contemporary United States, people are adults in the political system when they can vote at eighteen, but they are not adults in the economic sphere until gainfully employed (often some years later). They are not adults in the family system until marriage and parenthood (often later still). Some institutional domains' age grades are formalized, while others are implied.

It is a mistake to assume that even the basic age categories—infancy, childhood, adolescence, adulthood, middle age, and old age—that Western society institutionalized were assigned similar age grades or even recognized in other historical eras. For example, the modern concept of childhood as a life stage in which individuals are protected, isolated, nurtured, and socialized at great expense of time and resources was unknown before the nineteenth century. Similarly, adolescence as a transition stage between childhood and adulthood is of fairly recent origin, having developed in response to the demands of industrialization and urbanization (there is some evidence that it existed in ancient times and was abandoned in Europe in the Middle Ages).

Age grading regarding the life stage category of old age has become very complex because demographic changes have not only dramatically increased the size of the elderly population but also made it more heterogeneous than ever before. Marital, residential, health, economic, employment, and age ("young-old" versus "old-old") status must now be considered in any analysis of the age grading system's impact on this age group. These changes in the characteristics, and thus the roles, of the elderly have been dramatically transformed in a relatively short period of time. Sociologist Judah Matras offers a thorough examination of age grading in his 1990 book *Dependency, Obligations, and Entitlements: A New Sociology of Aging, the Life Course, and the Elderly*.

Age grading leads to age status distinctions that affect the distribution of wealth, status, and power, and thus age grading creates social stratification based on age. In addressing the topic of age as a determinant of social ranking, one must consider how old age affects levels of Max Weber's three dimensions of socioeconomic status— wealth, status, and power—and how age per se influences social prestige. The class, or wealth, dimension, which is arguably of primary importance, must be viewed differently for the elderly compared to younger age groups because many elderly are outside the paid labor force. Therefore, their economic ranking is based on work histories (past economic productivity), savings, and accumulation of assets or on transfers of wealth from younger age groups.

The status dimension of socioeconomic ranking is of special interest because age itself is a basis for ranking. Many societies, including that of the United States, place varying values on different age categories. Negative images of the elderly held by younger age groups (such as the idea that the elderly are dramatically less vigorous, attractive, healthy, sexually capable, and intelligent), regardless of whether they are based in fact, directly contribute to their loss of status. The most important factor of all in this respect may be the indisputable fact that the elderly are closer to death than their younger counterparts. As Gordon Streib asserts in his chapter in the 1985 *Handbook of Aging and the Social Sciences*, "Social Stratification and Aging":

> The inescapable fact of human mortality forces all other aspects of ranking to fade when evaluated in relation to life itself. Stating it boldly and simply, almost all people when asked to rank the dimensions of stratification—income, possessions, education, prestige, political power, honor—would choose extension of life over these other traits. And some persons who are most hostile to the aged as a category . . . have not come to terms with their own mortality and shun contact with anyone who might remind them of their future condition.

The area of age stratification is further complicated by the fact that the effects of characteristics such as gender and race on the social ranking of the elderly must be considered. Sociologist Erdman B. Palmore includes articles examining elderly women, widows, and the elderly from major racial/ethnic groups in detail in his 1984 book *Handbook on the Aged in the United States*.

Applications

There are numerous real-life consequences of age grading and age stratification. Among them are the legislation and government programs that formalize society's age-based norms, intergenerational conflicts over social resources, and proposed changes in government elderly support programs to bring about "intergenerational equity."

Laws and programs that codify age-related social expectations are a direct reflection of age grading and age stratification. American society has come to take for granted legislation that associates activities or social relationships to exact ages. Among these are laws addressing the responsibilities of parents toward their children, child labor, mandatory education, automobile driving licensing, becoming sexually active, eligibility for marriage, registration for the military draft, registering to vote, age requirements for holding some public offices, and programs providing old age pensions and health care for the elderly. These laws and programs and many others formalize the age grading and stratification systems at every stage of the life course.

One of the most serious societal ramifications of institutionalized age grading and stratification has been the emergence of intergenerational competition for society's resources. Given the historically recent extensions of longevity that have produced dramatic increases in the proportion of people at the oldest ages, the increase in competition between age groups for public revenues seems inevitable. Some authors assert that, while at one time the idea of elderly entitlements was almost universally endorsed, society has entered an era in which perceived public program favoritism toward the elderly has created a backlash in the form of a social movement aimed at bringing about an age-based redistribution of public moneys.

The call for "intergenerational equity" has grown as statistical analyses indicating that the proportion of elderly Americans living below the poverty line is slightly lower now than for the rest of the population have become widely publicized. Even though the same analyses showed that the poverty rate for the elderly would be higher than 50 percent were it not for government elderly support programs, the tone set by demographer Samuel Preston in his 1984 presidential address to the Population Association of America seemed to be finding acceptance with increasing numbers of working-age Americans. He argued that transfers of money from people in the labor force to elderly support programs directly mitigated against the ability of the former to take care of the nation's children. The same year, in what was possibly an even more emotionally charged statement, Governor Richard Lamm of Colorado suggested that Americans should seriously consider allowing the seriously ill elderly to die rather than continue the policy of dedicating enormous public expenditures to medical care in the last few years of their lives at the expense of younger generations. This theme has been echoed by authors from various disciplines.

The small but significant trend of more people shifting from embracing the stereotype of the elderly as needy to one that depicts them as greedy has given rise to some extreme positions on the periphery of the intergenerational equity debate. Some observers have gone so far as to argue that general economic problems and fiscal malaise have largely been caused by the elderly; such arguments link increases in the poverty rates of children to decreases in those rates for the elderly. Others have strongly disputed such ideas, holding that more conventional economic explanations for the growing ranks of the impoverished, such as changes in the economic base from high-paying industrial jobs to lower-paying service sector positions as well as losses in revenue because of tax reductions for the wealthiest individuals and corporations, are far more important.

One proposal for achieving intergenerational equity that has emerged in this debate is that eligibility for publicly funded elderly pension and health care programs be shifted from age-based to need-based criteria. The argument has been made that no other age group can claim public entitlements on the basis of age alone. Some believe that, since the elderly have mobilized into a very effective lobby in American politics through a coalition of organizations, a counterlobby operating on the behalf of nonelderly age groups is necessary to bring about changes in elderly support programs. Groups such as Americans for Generational Equity (AGE) have been formed to do political battle with the "gray lobby."

One perception related to this debate is a negative stereotype regarding the organized political activism of older Americans. The interest groups of the elderly have come to be viewed by many as powerful lobbies that support only programs directly supporting the elderly and oppose legislation designed to benefit other age groups. This perception has been the focus of research by political scientists and sociologists. Although the results of such research are not widely known to the general public, they indicate for the most part that the elderly give their support to programs that benefit people of all ages, including children, and that most young and middle-aged Americans endorse elderly assistance programs.

Many observers of the intergenerational equity debate have felt torn between their compassion for the elderly and their concern for the young. Others hold that such a polarization may represent a false problem. They point to research which indicates that the growing disparity between the rich and the poor in the United States is at the heart of the problems of needy Americans of all ages. In this view, the issue of rich and poor is a more appropriate focus for debate than perceived generational inequities in resource allocation, which in some forums has degenerated into counterproductive scapegoating of the elderly. Nevertheless, experts generally agree that it is appropriate and necessary to consider every alternative approach to the present structure of elderly support programs so that everyone in society can be more effectively served.

Context

The nineteenth century founders of the sociological perspective on social stratification, such as Karl Marx and Max Weber, were concerned with the determinants of socioeconomic ranking during the young adult and middle-age years. They can hardly be faulted for not anticipating the ways in which changes in the size and characteristics of the elderly population in modern societies have complicated their social stratification systems. In the 1960's and 1970's, sociologists were still decrying their discipline's lack of a systematic analysis of how aging and age grading are related to social stratification. These commentaries were essentially calls for further theory development regarding age grading and stratification and criticisms of efforts up to that time. Social theorists had made some attempts to set forth systematic explanations of these phenomena, and the work was continuing; however, the global demographic revolution that produced dramatically aging societies and projections of future increases in these trends created a sense of urgency regarding the need to understand age grading and stratification systems. Responsibility fell to the field known as the sociology of aging, a relatively new area.

Since the 1940's, modernization theory had attempted to address the loss of status of the elderly as a result of industrialization and urbanization. Criticisms of this theory have included its inability to explain "modernized" societies in which the status of the elderly has remained high and those in which marked improvements occurred after an initial decline.

The aged subculture theory, which dates from the 1960's, claims that age grading and stratification have isolated the elderly from the rest of society, resulting in their identifying strongly with an age-defined subculture in which higher status is accorded for good health and physical mobility than for educational or career attainment or for wealth. Some researchers claim, however, that the elderly do not develop a subcultural identity, and at least one has asserted that age does not qualify as an ascribed characteristic, which is a requirement for the designation of a true cultural group. The aged as a minority group theory is closely related to aged subculture theory. This orientation views old age as an ascribed characteristic such as race or gender. It claims that the elderly are a minority group like racial/ethnic minority groups and women, and that they suffer from both individual and institutional discrimination. This position has been criticized as being ideological and advocacy-related and for having little supporting scientific evidence.

Some of the most promising developments in the area of age stratification stem from the pioneering work of Matilda White Riley and her associates on age stratification theory, which began in the 1960's. This marked the beginning of the movement away from unidimensional age grading and stratification theories in sociology. Age stratification theory depicts age groups as being hierarchically organized, with the relationships between these different age strata being similar to strata in the socioeconomic stratification system. Social age grading means that opportunities to play specific social roles that are accompanied by status, power, entitlements, rights, and privileges are socially determined by one's position in the age stratification system. People in the same age stratum, or cohort, are similar not only because of age grading but also because their perspectives have been affected by having shared the same historical experiences. Actual or perceived inequities may exist between different age strata, and interstrata relationships may be characterized by cooperation or conflict.

The development of this area of sociology has been dramatic, and its continuation is a high priority within the discipline. A copious amount of research is being dedicated to testing and refining existing sociological theories and developing new ones. Work on social age grading and age stratification theories of relatively recent origin involves efforts by sociologists, psychologists, and social psychologists as they attempt to incorporate multidisciplinary approaches into comprehensive frameworks.

Bibliography

Gerber, Jerry, Janet Wolff, Walter Klores, and Gene Brown. *Lifetrends: The Future of the Baby Boomers and Other Aging Americans*. New York: Macmillan, 1989. This 271-page book is an engaging examination of the intensification of intergenerational conflicts that may attend the aging of the baby boom generations. The nontechnical style makes it suitable for high school and college audiences. Contains a chapter-by-chapter bibliography and an index.

Kertzer, David I., and K. Warner Schaie, eds. *Age Structuring in Comparative Perspective*. Hillsdale, N.J.: Lawrence Erlbaum, 1989. A very well-coordinated book of readings that looks at age stratification from a global perspective. The chapters focus on both developed and less developed countries. An excellent source for those interested in an international view. Contains bibliographies and a volume index.

Matras, Judah. *Dependency, Obligations, and Entitlements: A New Sociology of Aging, the Life Course, and the Elderly*. Englewood Cliffs, N.J.: Prentice-Hall, 1990. This excellent textbook presents a different perspective on the sociology of aging. Two-thirds of this book addresses issues directly related to age grading and stratification. Written for a college audience. Contains tables, graphs, a bibliography, and an index.

Palmore, Erdman B., ed. *Handbook on the Aged in the United States.* Westport, Conn.: Greenwood Press, 1984. A substantive, well-organized book of readings. It is especially noteworthy because of its separate chapters on women, widows, and five different racial/ethnic groups, including "Europeans." Most chapters are suitable for high school and college audiences. Contains bibliographies and separate author and subject indexes.

Riley, Matilda White. "Age Strata in Social Systems." In *Handbook of Aging and the Social Sciences,* edited by Robert H. Binstock and Ethel Shanas. 2d ed. New York: Van Nostrand Reinhold, 1985. This 42-page chapter is a complete articulation of age stratification theory, of which Riley is one of the main architects. Probably not for high school students because, in all its details, this is a complex theory. Contains an extensive bibliography as well as indexes.

Streib, Gordon. "Social Stratification and Aging." In *Handbook of Aging and the Social Sciences,* edited by Robert H. Binstock and Ethel Shanas. 2d ed. New York: Van Nostrand Reinhold, 1985. This 48-page chapter is an excellent essay on aging as an important dimension of the overall social stratification system. For a college audience and possibly also for highly motivated high school students. Contains a bibliography and indexes. It should be mentioned that the *Handbook of Aging and the Social Sciences* is one of the best and most comprehensive ongoing sets of reference works in the area of aging. The 1976, 1985, and 1990 volumes are highly recommended.

Jack Carter

Cross-References

Age Inequality: Functionalist versus Conflict Theory Views, 34; Ageism and the Ideology of Ageism, 41; Aging and Retirement, 47; The Aging Process, 53; The Graying of America, 846; Social Gerontology, 1799; Social Security and Issues of the Elderly, 1832.

AGE INEQUALITY: FUNCTIONALIST VERSUS CONFLICT THEORY VIEWS

Type of sociology: Aging and ageism

Age inequality refers to an unequal distribution of society's resources across different age groups and specifically to discrimination against the elderly in the allocation of wealth, status, and power. Structural functionalism and conflict theories give quite different explanations and analyses of age-based social inequality.

Principal terms

> AGE DISCRIMINATION: the denial of opportunities and rights to people on the basis of their age
>
> AGE DISCRIMINATION IN EMPLOYMENT ACT: federal legislation initially passed in 1964 that makes it illegal to discriminate against job applicants over forty; subsequent amendments in 1978 and 1986 make mandatory retirement illegal in nearly all occupations
>
> "GRAY LOBBY": a collective term for numerous elderly interest groups, such as the National Retired Teachers Association (NRTA), the American Association of Retired Persons (AARP), and the Gray Panthers
>
> INTEREST GROUP: an organization that attempts to influence elected and appointed officials regarding a specific issue or set of issues
>
> MACRO-LEVEL: a concern with large-scale patterns that characterize society as a whole
>
> MICRO-LEVEL: a concern with small-scale, or individual-level, patterns of social interaction within specific settings
>
> SOCIAL GERONTOLOGY: the area within sociology that focuses on the study of aging and the elderly, with special emphasis on the social determinants and consequences of aging for the individual and society
>
> SOCIAL INEQUALITY: the unequal distribution of such things as wealth, income, occupational prestige, and educational attainment

Overview

Social inequality is the unequal distribution of society's resources. Age inequality refers to the unequal distribution of these resources based on stages of the life cycle and, more specifically, the loss of wealth, status, and power by the elderly caused by the structure of their society. In initiating a discussion of the functionalist and conflict theory views on age inequality, it is necessary first to outline their views on social inequality in general. Functionalists insist that social inequality is necessary because it is the basis of a differential reward system that accords the most wealth, power, and status to those who fill the positions that have the greatest importance to society and require the greatest talent. Conflict theorists claim that social inequality is a mechanism that the relatively rich and powerful use to perpetuate their own privileged positions, which often results in the wasting of talent among society's lower socioeconomic status members. Conflict theorists take the position that functionalism ignores the discrimination that results from important social divisions based on characteristics such as class, race, ethnicity, gender, and age.

For some time, aging as a substantive area within sociology has been criticized for emphasizing practical and applied foci at the expense of theory development. It is true that most social aging theories, including those that specifically address aging inequality, have been adapted fairly recently (since the 1950's) from existing functionalist and conflict perspectives. Understandably, the basic differences in these two theoretical camps' views on social inequality in general are reflected in their assertions regarding age inequality.

By the late 1940's and early 1950's, functionalist essays depicted old age as a major "social problem" because of the difficulties of social and economic adjustment by the elderly in societies in which industrialization and urbanization had brought about the decline of the extended family and compulsory retirement. The functionalist theories that emerged—role, activity, and disengagement theories—have been characterized by some scholars as being more philosophical prescriptions for later life than theories, but they are certainly theories in the sense that they can generate hypotheses to be tested empirically.

Role and activity theories represent one branch of functionalist thought on aging inequality. Role theory as applied to the elderly basically posits that old age is characterized by role ambiguity or losses, causing a major identity crisis and loss of esteem. The loss of the work role was seen as being especially problematic in this respect. A relatively recent articulation of this perspective is found in Irving Rosow's 1985 essay "Status and Role Change Through the Life Cycle." Activity theory, a logical extension of role theory, proposes that it is desirable for the elderly to maintain as many middle-age activities as possible and to substitute new roles for those that are lost through widowhood or retirement. Ernest W. Burgess, whose work since the 1940's contributed to the development of activity theory, describes this perspective in his 1960 book *Aging in Western Societies*.

Disengagement theory, by far the most influential and controversial of the functionalist theories of age inequality, is an application of the functionalist perspective on social inequality to the elderly. This theory maintains that the smooth functioning of society depends on the withdrawal of the elderly from formerly important roles and activities, including the work role. Disengagement theorists claim that this process is inevitable, necessary, and mutually desired by both the elderly and their societies and that the alternative (having older people serve in important positions until senescence or death creates a crisis) is dysfunctional for society relative to a structurally prescribed smooth generational transition. Elaine Cumming and William E. Henry formulated this theory in their 1961 book *Growing Old*.

Both Marxist and contemporary conflict theories have been used to analyze the disadvantages of the elderly regarding their diminished socioeconomic status and their employment and retirement problems in particular. Although a thorough Marxist analysis of age inequality has yet to be undertaken, authors (including William Graebner in his 1980 book *A History of Retirement: The Meaning and Function of an American Institution, 1885-1978*, which examines the history of discrimination against older workers) have applied Marx's ideas on work to the elderly.

Contemporary conflict theorists, Lewis Coser and Ralf Dahrendorf among them, have retained Marx's emphasis on inequality and conflict but view social conflict as being carried out between conflict, or interest, groups that are based on any number of social/demographic characteristics, including age. In other words, intergenerational conflict can occur between age-based conflict groups, just as gender- or race-based inequality can result in conflict scenarios. Contemporary conflict theorists point out that the elderly certainly qualify as an interest group in American society.

The need for a conflict theory that specifically addresses age inequality has given rise to much-needed theory development in the area. Prominent among these efforts is the political economy of aging. The focus of theorizing concerning the political economy of aging is the ways that societies' political, economic, and social structures under advanced capitalism affect the treatment of the elderly. Political economists assert that the "structured dependency" of the elderly results from the creation of elderly problems, such as loss of domestic and community roles, retirement, poverty, and institutionalization, by society's rules and institutions. They claim that the strategy of blaming general economic problems on the growth of the elderly population is designed to hide the fact that policy decisions under a capitalistic economy are the cause of fiscal crises and the plight of the elderly. Political economists also address the ways that age-, race-, gender-, and class-based inequities intersect to perpetuate multidimensional social inequality. Laura Katz Olson, in her 1982 book *The Political Economy of Aging: The State, Private Power, and Social Welfare* presents one of the most comprehensive articulations of this theory.

Applications

One of the most important consequences of the adaptation of functionalist and conflict theories to the area of aging inequality has been much-needed theory development in the area of social gerontology. Other, more conventional, applications of these theoretical developments in aging inequality are the impacts they have had on government programs and legislation relating to elderly support systems and age-based discrimination, and on the growth of elderly interest groups.

The controversies surrounding functionalist theories of aging inequality have given rise to a strong conflict theory response. Activity theory, for example, has been challenged for its failure to describe what happens when older people do not subscribe to the middle-age norms of activity that the theory says they should maintain. Further, it does not explain whether aging becomes less "successful" as old age progresses, making those standards of activity unreasonable. Similarly, the rationale of disengagement theory's assertions that the disengagement of the elderly is natural, inevitable, and mutually desirable and functional has been questioned. There appears to be a growing consensus that almost thirty years of empirical testing has shown that much disengagement really stems from the denial of opportunities to the elderly. The staunchest critics of disengagement theory decry it as a blatant apologist rationalization for discrimination that results in age-based inequality.

The most vocal critics of functionalism among the conflict theorists have been the political economists, whose theory of age inequality has gained considerable credence within sociology since its development. The political economy theory of aging, like functionalist aging theories, has been characterized as being more an orientation or philosophy than a true theory. The challenges of aging inequality theory development have produced renewed interest in theories such as the aged as a minority group theory, the modernization theory of aging, and the age stratification theory. The first of these is decidedly conflict oriented, while the others contain elements of both functionalism and conflict orientations. All these theories are in need of further testing and refinement.

There is no better example of "sociology as real life" than the way that the changing face of social theories of age inequality has been reflected in the nature of approaches to elderly domestic policies and political activism agendas. Government programs and legislation that address the plight of the elderly were initially developed against a backdrop of functionalist thinking. The ideas on age inequality that were formalized in disengagement theory were institutionalized in laws permitting mandatory retirement. Widespread discrimination against older workers resulted in severe economic hardships for many older Americans and gave rise to the "aging as a social problem"(meaning the problem *of* the elderly) perspective that underlay government elderly support programs throughout the early and mid-twentieth century. Programs such as Social Security and Medicare, with age-based rather than need-based eligibility requirements, are grounded in the disengagement assertions that losses of status, wealth, and power are inevitable and necessary with old age.

By the late 1960's, contemporary conflict theories had gained considerable credibility within sociology. This perspective features the image of society as an arena in which clashes between conflict groups based on any number of social/demographic characteristics, including age, occur. These theoretical assertions predicted and were reflected in the emergence of the "gray lobby" in American politics. While the framework of elderly support policy remained essentially unchanged, various elderly interest groups successfully lobbied for the expansion of existing programs and the addition of new ones.

The continued absolute and proportionate growth of the elderly population after the late 1960's in the midst of a worsening overall fiscal situation brought dire predictions of the future and a trend away from concern for the problems of the elderly and toward the view that the elderly were a problem for society as a whole. The age inequality theory of the political economists had a marked impact on changes in legislation and activism. The 1978 and 1986 amendments to the Age Discrimination in Employment Act took an openly "anti-disengagement" focus in eliminating mandatory retirement.

Important elderly interest groups, such as the National Retired Teachers Association, the American Association of Retired Persons, and the Gray Panthers (a nickname for the Consultation of Younger and Older Americans) have supported a broad-based agenda that promotes not only programs directly beneficial to the elderly but also educational reform, penal reform, and antipoverty programs for Americans of all ages. This approach is consistent with political economists' view that the problems of the elderly are part of the overall structure of institutionalized inequality that affects all the disfranchised in capitalistic democracies, including many of the aged.

Context

For decades, functionalist and conflict theories presented widely divergent perspectives on the ways human societies operate. Functionalism was dominant until the mid-to-late 1960's, when conflict theories enjoyed an upsurge in credibility within sociology, at least in part because of American social and political upheavals of the 1960's and 1970's. Social inequality and stratification was always one of the major areas of contention in the ongoing theory war involving these two macro-level (large-scale) theoretical giants. In this atmosphere, micro-level (individual-level) theories (such as symbolic interactionism, exchange theory, phenomenology, and ethnomethodology) were delegated to the periphery of the discipline. When the sociology of aging, or social gerontology, began to develop as a substantive area in sociology around the 1950's, there was a dearth of theory specifically addressing aging issues.

This need for theory development resulted in the most attention being focused on the application of these "mainstream" theories to age inequality. First were functionalist theories, with disengagement theory being by far the most influential, and then contemporary conflict theory, which already featured the idea of age-based inequality in its expansion of Marx's work. The political economy of aging, with many of its seminal sources appearing in the 1980's, was a major development in the ongoing effort to develop better theories of age inequality.

The importance of these theoretical challenges should not be underestimated, because the credibility and scientific legitimacy of an area of inquiry cannot be defended unless charges that there is no theory to provide a framework for the work can be addressed to some degree of effectiveness. The critical exchanges between functionalist and conflict theorists have generally been constructive. Their theories have been refined and expanded. Yet their dominance of the theoretical discussion of age inequality in social gerontology for twenty years led to the perception by many that there were shortcomings within both camps. This, in conjunction with the recognition of the importance of micro-level orientations in general, has opened the door to the development of micro-level theories of aging, such as symbolic interactionist, exchange, and socioenvironmental theories of aging. Furthermore, efforts combining macro- and micro-level approaches, such as age stratification theory, are now seen by many as essential to understanding the social dynamics and consequences of aging.

The recognition of the shortcomings of functionalist and conflict age inequality theories to date is not equivalent to pronouncing these orientations to be of historical interest only. All the above-mentioned theories are in their formative stages, because of the relatively recent origins of the sociology of aging. There is a growing awareness, however, that the era of the historical rivalry between functionalist and conflict camps that featured the idea that the two perspectives were mutually exclusive is over, as is the exclusion of micro-level approaches. One relatively recent promising direction in aging theory development, meta theory, involves linking macro- and micro-level theory and synthesizing several theoretical perspectives into one larger abstract model.

Bibliography

Bengston, Vern L., Neal E. Cutler, David J. Mangen, and Victor W. Marshall. "Generations, Cohorts, and Relations Between Age Groups." In *Handbook of Aging and the Social Sciences*, edited by Robert H. Binstock and Ethel Shanas. 2d ed. New York: Van Nostrand Reinhold, 1985. A very good and concise essay that not only describes the social conflict theoretical perspective but also examines the study of the relationships between age groups in the social scientific literature. Well-suited for a college audience. Contains an extensive bibliography, and the book itself has both author and subject indexes.

Burgess, Ernest W., ed. *Aging in Western Societies*. Chicago: University of Chicago Press, 1960. The first 390 pages of this book of readings (to which Burgess personally contributes three chapters) consist of a classic statement of the problems of the elderly as they attempt to function in a "roleless role." Suitable for both high school and college students, with references, author and subject indexes, and easy-to-understand tables and charts.

Cumming, Elaine, and William E. Henry. *Growing Old: The Process of Disengagement*. New York: Basic Books, 1961. This seminal articulation of disengagement theory (like the Burgess volume) is not really dated because these functionalist theories have been carried forward for decades largely unchanged. Suitable for high school and college audiences, it has references, tables, and a combined author/subject index.

Graebner, William. *A History of Retirement: The Meaning and Function of an American Institution, 1885-1978*. New Haven, Conn.: Yale University Press, 1980. A well-documented historical treatment of the development of the institution of retirement under capitalism. Suitable for college students, this book uses extensive footnotes to list references and other information and has an index. Graebner effectively applies a Marxist perspective to an analysis of elderly inequality.

Olson, Laura Katz. *The Political Economy of Aging: The State, Private Power, and Social Welfare*. New York: Columbia University Press, 1982. This volume has proved to be very important in the development of the political economy of aging and, because of the relatively recent origins of this perspective, is still current. It deals with complex issues in an engaging manner. Suitable for college students and highly motivated high school students. It contains an extensive notes section with references and other information and an index. A well-focused critique of contemporary capitalism's welfare state approach to elderly support systems that sets the parameters of the debate on these issues by posing the hard questions that must be addressed by the anticonflict-perspective participants.

Rosow, Irving. "Status and Role Change Through the Life Cycle." In *Handbook of Aging and the Social Sciences*, edited by Robert H. Binstock and Ethel Shanas. 2d ed. New York: Van Nostrand Reinhold, 1985. This 31-page chapter is a thorough examination of role theory. It is very theoretically oriented and is suitable for a senior/graduate-level college audience. The article includes a bibliography, and the volume has subject and author indexes. The *Handbook of Aging and the Social Sciences* is one of the best and most comprehensive ongoing sets of social scientific reference works in the area of aging, and the 1976, 1985, and 1990 volumes are highly recommended.

Jack Carter

Cross-References
Age Grading and Age Stratification, 27; Ageism and the Ideology of Ageism, 41; Aging and Retirement, 47; The Aging Process, 53; Conflict Theory, 340; Functionalism, 786; The Graying of America, 846; Social Security and Issues of the Elderly, 1832; Social Stratification: Analysis and Overview, 1839.

AGEISM AND THE IDEOLOGY OF AGEISM

Type of sociology: Aging and ageism
Fields of study: Basic concepts of social stratification; Dimensions of inequality;
  Policy issues and debates

*Ageism is a negative system of beliefs about individuals or groups based solely upon
age. The concept of ageism has generally been used to describe beliefs about the aged,
although it has been used to describe beliefs about other age groups.*

  Principal terms
    AGE STRATIFICATION: a system in which resources, roles, and statuses
      are allocated by age
    DISCRIMINATION: unequal treatment of an individual or group of
      individuals based upon group membership
    IDEOLOGY: a system of beliefs used to justify an existing social
      arrangement
    PREJUDICE: a negative belief or set of beliefs about an individual based
      upon that person's group membership
    SOCIAL STRATIFICATION: a system in which resources, roles, and
      statuses are allocated in society; allocation may be based on such
      characteristics as age, race and ethnicity, or gender or social class
    STEREOTYPE: a belief that certain characteristics apply to all members
      of a group, even though those characteristics may or may not be
      based in reality

Overview

The ideology of ageism refers to negative beliefs about an age group which are subsequently used to justify unequal treatment. The concept of ageism was introduced in 1969 by the first director of the National Institute on Aging, Robert Butler, when he described an incident in which residents in an exclusive area objected to plans to build a home for the aged in their neighborhood.

The lower status of the elderly is demonstrated in the language sometimes used to describe them. "Old fart," "old geezer," "old coot," "dirty old man," and "cranky old woman" are typical derogatory phrases that are used at times to refer to the aged. Jokes about the elderly often refer to their lack of sexual interest or loss of physical attractiveness. Greeting cards often lament one's bad luck for being one year older. Media images of the elderly often reflect stereotypes about the aged, both positive and negative.

Stereotypes provide the foundation for ageist ideology. Stereotypes are beliefs about an entire group of people that may or may not be based in reality. In his book *Ageism: Negative and Positive* (1990), sociologist Erdman Palmore discusses some of the major societal stereotypes about the elderly. Negative stereotypes include the belief that the elderly are in poor health, asexual, lacking in physical attractiveness, senile or mentally ill, useless, poor, and depressed. Palmore points out that these stereotypes are not true of the majority of the elderly. Most elderly people are in good health, have active sex lives (provided a partner is available), and are involved in their communities and in the lives of their families. Societies in which the elderly are held in high esteem do not believe that the physical changes that accompany aging are unattractive. If the elderly are deemed to be lacking in physical attractiveness in Western society, it is a reflection of society's devaluation of the aged rather than of an absolute standard of appearance.

Women are especially vulnerable to ageism. For example, appearance norms are especially severe for older women. As psychologist Ann Gerike points out in her essay "On Gray Hair and Oppressed Brains" in Evelyn Rosenthal's *Women, Aging, and Ageism* (1990), women are more likely to want to hide their gray hair than men are, because older men with gray hair are considered to be distinguished and still physically attractive but gray-haired women are simply considered old.

Robert Binstock, a gerontologist, in the Donald P. Kent Memorial Lecture to the Thirty-fifth Annual Scientific Meeting of the Gerontological Society of America in Boston (1983) entitled "The Aged as Scapegoat," noted that it is especially ironic that there are so many stereotypes about the elderly. The aged are the most heterogeneous of all age groups and are the least likely to have typical experiences. It is impossible to make sweeping generalizations about the aged because there is so much diversity among them. For example, there are likely to be as many differences in the experiences of a sixty-five-year-old and a ninety-year-old as there are between a thirty-year-old and a sixty-five-year-old, yet stereotypes imply that all elderly people are alike.

Binstock also pointed out that in recent years several positive stereotypes, or what he has termed axioms, about the elderly have emerged. These include a belief that the aged are prosperous and no longer at risk of poverty. He points out that even though the percentage of elderly people with incomes below the poverty level is lower than is the case for some other age groups, there are considerable numbers of elderly people who are still disadvantaged—especially women and minorities. Another stereotype holds that the elderly have an unusually strong influence on the political process. In spite of the fact that the elderly vote in higher percentages than do other age groups, they do not vote as a bloc. The aged tend to vote on the basis of interests other than those associated with age, which dilutes the influence that they actually have on the political process. The last stereotype he discusses is the belief that because of their growing numbers, the aged will pose a burden to the federal budget. It is believed that as the proportion of dependent elders to working adults increases into the twenty-first century, the burden to the federal budget will also increase. Binstock points out, however, that the proportion of the gross national product needed to finance benefits for the elderly will decline in the future. The major expenditure for benefits to the elderly is in the area of health care; therefore, health care reform is needed, not the cutting of programs for the aged.

A seemingly positive view of the elderly can sometimes have negative conse-quences. Positive beliefs have been used to justify scaling back programs for the elderly. Binstock believes that the elderly have been made scapegoats for a depletion of societal resources, which has caused a "shrinking of compassion" on the part of the American public.

Applications

There are both positive and negative consequences of ageism for the elderly. Ageism can lead to discriminatory treatment that may limit access to valued resources. Ageism has also been used in a positive way to justify the passage of legislation that favors the elderly.

One area in which the elderly have experienced discrimination is in employment. Based on the belief that the elderly are in poor health and are slower and less competent, some employers have been reluctant to hire older workers. The Age Discrimination in Employment Act (ADEA), as amended in 1986, removed the previous age limit of seventy years on the protection provided against discrimination based upon age in most parts of the private sector. The ADEA prohibits all age discrimination except when age is a "bona fide occupational qualification" of the job. As gerontologist Martin Lyon Levine discusses in his book *Age Discrimination and the Mandatory Retirement Controversy* (1988), the courts have put narrow interpretations on this legislation, and in some cases employers can still discriminate against workers based upon age alone.

Mandatory retirement was a special case of discrimination in hiring. Mandatory retirement was a policy adopted by employers that stated that after a certain age (often sixty-five years old) a worker must retire, no matter what that individual person's abilities may have been. Mandatory retirement was a relatively recent phenomenon that came into widespread practice in the United States in the 1940's. This type of retirement policy existed partly because of the growth of large-scale industry, in which it was more difficult to make decisions regarding worker capacity on a case-by-case basis, making it more efficient to adopt policies that applied to entire categories of workers. This policy had the negative consequence of keeping many workers out of the labor force who were still able to make a positive contribution. Because of changes in the law, mandatory retirement is now practiced only in a limited number of industries.

The elderly also face discrimination in medical care. Physicians and other health care professionals are also shown to hold the same negative stereotypes that are held by the general public. As a result, some health care professionals are reluctant to work with the elderly, which can reduce the quality of medical care that is available to the aged.

It is important to note, however, that stereotypes have led to the practice of positive ageism as well. The stereotypes that the elderly are economically disadvantaged and in poor health were used in public debate to justify the implementation of such forms of legislation as Social Security and Medicare, which gave special benefits to the aged. As Robert Binstock has pointed out, however, these same beliefs also have negative consequences. Arguments based upon positive stereotypes are currently being used in an attempt to reduce benefits for the elderly.

Ageism can have personal consequences. Often, people expect that stereotypes apply to themselves as well as to others, which can create a self-fulfilling prophecy (a situation that becomes real because of people's expectations). A woman who believes that because she is old she is unable to learn may decide not to take a training course to upgrade her job skills. Because of her belief that she cannot learn and her subsequent reluctance to get training, she indeed becomes less skilled than younger workers.

Reduction of ageism requires a response on both individual and societal levels. In his book *Ageism: Negative and Positive*, Erdman Palmore suggests that there are strategies that can be used to reduce individual ageism. These include educating the public concerning controversial issues as well as giving the public a more accurate understanding of the true nature of the experiences of the aged in society. Much of ageism is based on incorrect information about the elderly, and Palmore suggests using the *Facts on Aging Quiz* to test the knowledge of individuals about the aging process. He also suggests the use of slogans that provide a tool for the development of propaganda that can be used to gain public recognition of the advantages of old age. Social institutions such as churches and the media can take an active role in promoting positive images of aging. Personal contact with the elderly can also be a valuable resource for shaping people's images of what it is like to be old. Palmore also points out that it is important to change the social structure and reduce ageism in hiring, the family, government programs, housing, and health care.

Ageism has implications for all groups in society, not only the elderly. Because of ageism, older individuals are at risk of giving up meaningful activity before it is necessary. As a result, both the individual and society suffer the loss of the potential contribution of that person. For example, as a result of discrimination in hiring, society loses access to a pool of experienced, responsible, and willing workers. Segregation in housing and social activities can limit contact between generations, which is detrimental for both young and old. As a consequence, young people will have limited access to role models who can provide positive examples of successful aging.

Context

Ageism can be understood in the broader context of social stratification—the way in which valued rewards are distributed in society. Traditional stratification perspectives have examined the way in which resources are distributed in society by social category, especially by social class, gender, and race or ethnicity. The age stratification perspective proposed by sociologists Matilda White Riley and Anne Foner in their book *Aging and Society: A Sociology of Age Stratification* (1972) suggests that resources are allocated in society by age as well.

The pattern of stratification is related to the relations between age groups within societies; societies vary regarding the amount of status given to elders. In more traditional societies, elders are revered and are given a special place of honor in society and in the household. For example, in the People's Republic of China, children are bound by law to care for their elderly parents.

It has been suggested by gerontologists Donald O. Cowgill and L. D. Holmes (*Aging and Modernization*, 1972) that as societies become more modern, elders lose status. This is because they lose control of scarce resources. In traditional societies, where conditions do not change much from one generation to the next and valued social knowledge is passed down orally from one generation to the next, elders are reposi- tories of the collective wisdom of a society. This gives them a source of prestige and honor. Because of the rapid social change associated with modernization, however, in modern societies it is the younger generation that is most likely to possess valued knowledge. Thus, the elderly lose a valued source of status and prestige.

Changes in the ways in which individuals make their living also have an effect on the status and prestige of the elderly. In horticultural and agrarian societies, when people survived by means of farming and/or herding, their livelihoods depended on the land that was inherited from the older generation. Thus, elders controlled key resources that gave them considerable power and prestige in society. In Ireland, for example, the family land traditionally was passed on to the eldest son, who in return provided a home and financial support for his elderly mother and father. In modern society, people do not depend on inherited property for livelihoods to the same extent. Most people work for wages in jobs that are not obtained through the inheritance of property from the older generation.

As life expectancies increase, it is feared that elders will become a drain on scarce resources. With improvements in public health and medical technology, people are more likely to live longer and to reach a stage of dependency. Such a situation will lower the status of the elderly, because, rather than commanding key resources, they will become dependent on their families and society. The resulting resentment of the young against the old may be expressed in negative stereotypes about the elderly as a group.

Bibliography

Binstock, Robert N. "The Aged as Scapegoat." *The Gerontologist* 23 (Winter, 1983): 136-143. This journal article is the text of the Donald E. Kent Memorial Lecture to the Gerontological Society of America. Binstock outlines the argument that the elderly are being made a scapegoat for federal budget problems, when, in fact, the issues are far more complex.

Cowgill, Donald O., and Lowell D. Holmes, eds. *Aging and Modernization.* New York: Appleton-Century-Crofts, 1972. This volume sets forth the basic ideas of modern- ization theory, which has been influential in the development of social gerontology. Cowgill and Holmes suggest that as societies become more modern, the status of the elderly in society declines.

Levine, Martin Lyon. *Age Discrimination and the Mandatory Retirement Controversy.* Baltimore, Md.: The Johns Hopkins University Press, 1988. This book discusses mandatory retirement as a special case of age discrimination. The author traces the history of retirement practices in the United States and their relationship to attitudes toward the aged.

Palmore, Erdman B. *Ageism: Negative and Positive*. New York: Springer, 1990. Provides comprehensive discussions of the relevant concepts of ageism, causes and consequences, institutional patterns of ageism in the family, health, and government as well as suggestions for reducing ageism. Two appendices contain the *Facts on Aging Quiz* and examples of ageist humor.

Riley, Matilda White, and Anne Foner. *Aging and Society: A Sociology of Age Stratification*. Vol. 3. New York: Russell Sage Foundation, 1972. This work establishes the basis for the age stratification perspective that has been influential in the development of the field of social gerontology.

Rosenthal, Evelyn, ed. *Women, Aging, and Ageism*. New York: Haworth Press, 1990. This volume of essays addresses the problems of older women from the perspective of older women themselves. Included are essays on the varieties of ageism, the effects of hysterectomy on older women, and the meaning of graying hair.

Charlotte Chorn Dunham

Cross-References

AGING AND RETIREMENT

Type of sociology: Aging and ageism

Retirement brings with it new social roles and requires adaptation to a new stage of life; retirees face a number of choices and challenges as they assume new identities apart from the work that had helped define their lives. These issues are of increasing concern as the population of the United States ages, a process sometimes called the graying of America.

Principal terms

BABY BOOMERS: the 76 million babies born between 1946 and 1964

COMPULSORY RETIREMENT: forced retirement, which became illegal in 1987

EARLY RETIREMENT: retirement before the age of sixty-seven, when full Social Security benefits take effect

GERONTOLOGY: the study of the biological, psychological, and sociological implications of aging

PENSION: a financial sum paid regularly after retirement from private companies or public funds

PHASED RETIREMENT: a plan offering reduced work hours rather than full retirement

SOCIAL SECURITY: a law passed in 1935 which provided that workers would contribute throughout their working years to a federal fund paying old-age benefits

Overview

By the early 1990's, average life expectancy in the United States had surpassed seventy-five years. Both the development of life-saving medical technology and a general tendency of the population to be more health conscious have contributed to this trend. Of equal sociological significance is the fact that the large segment of the population born between 1946 and 1964—the baby boom generation—will have begun to reach retirement age by the late 1990's. The U.S. Bureau of the Census estimates that, by the year 2050, adults over sixty-five will constitute nearly 22 percent of the population. These facts mean that retirement will be increasingly examined and redefined by sociologists and the general public alike.

The concept of retirement as it is thought of today (as a life stage after the years of employment that a large group of people can be expected to experience) did not exist until the twentieth century. Fundamental in fostering the idea of retirement were the institution of old-age benefits by private companies and, in 1935, the passing of the Social Security Act by the federal government, which mandated a fund to provide all workers with a small retirement income. For most people, entering the retirement years entails significant adjustments. One's income is suddenly less than it was during the working years; additionally, there is a loss of the identity and many of the social interactions that one had while employed. Balancing this, for many older people, is the new freedom that accompanies this life stage. One has the time to pursue interests for which there was previously no time.

People are working longer than was typically the case in the middle years of the twentieth century. The once-standard retirement age of sixty-five is no longer the norm. In 1978, the age at which a company could force someone to retire was moved from sixty-five to seventy; requiring retirement on the basis of age alone was subsequently made illegal. Eligibility for full Social Security benefits was increased from age sixty-five to sixty-seven. There is another side to this, however, in that many seniors are actually encouraged to take early retirement. Companies must control their costs, and one way of doing so is to replace highly paid senior personnel with young workers, who are paid entry-level salaries. Many companies therefore offer retirement packages to senior employees. Such packages have been offered to employees as young as fifty.

With backgrounds including many years of education and experience, many seniors find full retirement to be unacceptable. Some pursue second careers, but a number of factors discourage this. While pension incentives and Social Security provisions encourage early retirement, these programs limit subsequent work hours by cutting benefits after recipients earn more than a ceiling amount. For example, if people age sixty-five earn more than $8,400, their benefits are cut fifty cents for every dollar of earnings. This fact discourages seniors from taking full-time jobs after initial retirement.

One alternative to full employment is flexible retirement. Companies often place retirees in a pool of people to be called on for particular projects. The experience of seniors provides a valuable consulting source. Another plan is phased retirement, which has been offered by a number of firms (including Tektronix and Polaroid). Seniors work reduced hours per day, work fewer days per week, or may take extended vacations during the five years preceding their actual retirement. During this phased retirement period, seniors can become accustomed to having leisure time and may find activities and associations to fill their lives. The step into full retirement is not as psychologically difficult if planning has taken place during this phased retirement period.

Second careers are not easily secured because the many years of experience possessed by retirees are expensive to an employer. As a result, many seniors have turned to jobs based in the home. Some go into real estate or cottage industries. An opportunity for home employment that grew in the 1980's and 1990's came from the development of computer networking. It became possible to perform many jobs, such as consulting, free-lance writing and editing, and offering business support services, from the home. Computer networking also allows mobility, which accommodates relocation after retirement. The home office is often an answer to remaining productive after retirement.

When financial status permits, many seniors choose routes that lead away from previous careers and into social work. For example, seniors might lead discussion groups or tours at local museums, or they might offer their skills for organizations such as the Peace Corps or Teach America. Local schools are eager to utilize senior volunteers as tutors and storytellers. Hospitals encourage senior volunteers to work with patients. Many fields benefit from senior participation, so seniors can choose to donate their time and skills in areas that give them the most satisfaction. Retirement gives seniors the time and the opportunity to be constructive citizens. Many seniors choose a creative path by pursuing the arts. The visual, performing, and literary arts let seniors produce throughout their lifetimes. The arts are individual pursuits not regulated by the age clock.

Many seniors look forward to retirement as an earned time of rest. They relish having time to devote to recreational and leisure pursuits or to educational and cultural enrichment. A number of retirement communities have been developed near college campuses so that seniors can take advantage of study groups and lecture series designed for seniors. Another option for educational pursuits is the Elderhostel program, which offers one-week to four-week programs on college campuses, where seniors may participate as students as well as guest speakers. Like the pursuit of the arts, education can be a life-long pursuit.

Applications

Seniors have a wide variety of choices, finances permitting, regarding how and when to spend their retirement years. The ramifications of retirement, however, go far beyond the choices one makes regarding activities. Older people must deal with the psychological repercussions of retirement. Dramatic changes occur in one's daily routine and relations with others. One change that many new retirees find difficult is that they are no longer identified with the occupation that had occupied so many of their waking hours.

Work provides people with a sense of identity. The first question asked of new acquaintances at many gatherings is, "What do you do?" The answer reflects a major part of a person's identity, partly because particular jobs carry particular statuses. Knowing a person's job often is sufficient to infer the person's level of education, salary range, and preferences regarding other activities. Work occupies most wakeful hours; when retired, seniors sometimes feel that they are in limbo, searching for a replacement identity. Some people will make the transition to retirement easily because they have maintained a variety of interests and activities during their working years, but others will struggle to find a replacement for their work identity.

Individuals form attachments to the work they perform. They feel important as contributors to a cause outside themselves. Employees often work as team players, knowing that their performance is needed to bring success. Self-worth is therefore tightly connected with work. Retirees are in danger of feeling worthless, no longer capable of being productive contributors. They must make a conscientious effort to find alternative channels for their productivity. Some are successful in this challenge, but others fall into the trap of believing the stereotype that aging necessarily means decline.

The work environment provides constant stimulation for employees. New thoughts, new ideas, and new experiences evolve from each day on the job. This exposure to change and this human contact keep a person alert and current. When seniors retire, this stimulation is lost. Conversations may become sterile, because new input is not being encountered each day. The newspaper or television might become the focus of mental activity. To prevent this stagnation, activities outside the home need to be explored. Courses for seniors at the local college will keep the mind challenged. Participation in community activities will provide outside exposure to change. Technology is altering the world rapidly, so seniors must participate actively in society to keep abreast of current trends. Another important aspect of work is that it provides a place of belonging. People often group themselves with others of the same profession, forming a community. For many people, the community formed at the workplace takes the place of the neighborhood-centered community. Social encounters and activities are often connected with the job. With retirement, this sense of community is taken away, leaving many seniors lonely. They must take an active step to form new associations.

Retirement might also require relocation because of economic factors, and moving may necessitate detaching from life-long relationships with friends, even family members. This change requires additional adjustment as seniors seek out new associations for recreation and emotional support. Seniors must make conscientious efforts to contact others by joining social organizations: church groups, sports or hobby clubs, art circles, discussion groups, and community support groups.

The greatest obstacle that seniors face in being retired is overcoming the stereotype that seniors are unproductive, sedentary, and eccentric. Seniors can reject those labels and can create productive and social lives for themselves. Books on aging and retirement abound on library bookshelves, offering catalogs of senior organizations that provide information about retirement, recreation, financial planning, medical care, and lifestyles. Colleges offer many courses to assist seniors in retirement choices. Communities offer seminars in financial planning for retirement. The resources and opportunities are available to make the transition into retirement smooth and productive.

Context
People are living longer: By 2030, when the last of the baby boomers will have joined the senior population, people over fifty-five will constitute one-third of the population. By sheer force of numbers, seniors will have an enormous impact on politics, value systems, and marketing. The social implications of a large senior population are enormous. To a degree that cannot accurately be predicted, the American "youth culture" will be replaced by mature culture. Sociologists have already observed a number of changes related to this. Images present in motion pictures and on television, for example, have changed as the baby boom generation has aged. This generation's likes and dislikes, as reflected in their spending habits, alter the society's social values. Images of active and productive seniors are, to a certain degree,

replacing stereotypes of sedentary, eccentric old people, and this trend will undoubtedly continue.

Marketing is already showing a great shift as it competes for the dollars of the sixty million Americans over fifty who make up one-fourth of the U.S. population. Members of this age group control 70 percent of the financial assets in the United States. Their spending power is not overlooked by perceptive business managers. For example, many seniors choose to relocate after retirement to areas that are warm and comfortable, free from harsh winters. To accommodate this trend, builders are developing many retirement communities in the sunbelt states of Florida, California, Arizona, and Texas. A number of rural communities also actively encourage seniors to move to their towns because seniors make fewer demands on expensive public services.

Another shift in marketing relates to the fact that seniors insist on "user-friendly" products. Not only have many products been designed for use by the older body, but also the directions for assembling and using those products contain larger print and graphics. Seniors also buy for comfort and security, so service businesses such as restaurants and hotels are accommodating this requirement. The medical professions are shifting emphasis from pediatrics to geriatrics, physical therapy, and visual and hearing specializations. In addition, many companies have had to develop new lines of products to tap the senior market. For example, Johnson & Johnson, successful in marketing baby oil, baby powder, and baby shampoo, has developed a division called Ortho Pharmaceutical, which produces products for seniors.

The growing number of senior citizens has brought the many problems of aging to the attention of sociologists. Studies have examined the welfare of seniors as individuals and as a group. Concern is also being given to the effects on society as a whole as the shift from youth culture to mature culture takes place. Sociologists increasingly view aging and retirement from an interdisciplinary perspective by considering economic, demographic, psychological, biological, and cultural issues.

Bibliography

Arthur, Julietta K. *Retire to Action*. Nashville: Abingdon Press, 1969. This guidebook describes options for volunteer work by seniors. The book discusses the importance of giving time to plan retirement and to set goals that are fulfilling. It concludes that seniors can be constructive citizens and can avoid boredom by contributing their wisdom and experience to the community.

Berman, Phillip L., and Connie Goldman, eds. *The Ageless Spirit*. New York: Ballantine Books, 1992. Taken from interviews with creative and productive seniors, this collection of essays demonstrates that the arts can be pursued throughout life. Serious issues such as time, feelings, and death are discussed, but a touch of humor keeps these inspirational essays from being morose. All contributors are involved in some aspect of the arts.

Cessna, Cornelia B., Mark A. Siegel, and Nancy R. Jacobs. *Growing Old in America*. Wylie, Tex.: Information Plus, 1992. Offers a comprehensive analysis of the senior population in regard to economics, education, voting habits, demographics, health factors, and medical care. An excellent chapter is devoted to trends and projections for the senior population. Included is an index of programs and organizations for the elderly.

Cox, Harold. *Annual Editions: Aging*. Guilford, Conn.: Dushkin, 1994. This annual anthology contains a wide range of articles on all aspects of aging, retirement, social attitudes toward the aged, perspectives on dying, living environments, and social programs and services for seniors. Information is scholarly.

Dychtwald, Ken, and Joe Flower. *Age Wave: The Challenges and Opportunities of an Aging America*. Los Angeles: Jeremy P. Tarcher, 1989. Gives a comprehensive analysis detailing the changes emerging throughout society as a result of the growing numbers of seniors. Marketing trends, new products and services, and demographics are altering as seniors gain political and economic power.

Knopf, Olga. *Successful Aging*. New York: Viking Press, 1975. This book discusses the psychological importance of accepting the self after aging begins its biological process. Various chapters offer options for using leisure time, choosing volunteer positions, keeping physically fit, and selecting living arrangements. A fine bibliography of books for seniors is included.

Palmore, Erdman B. *Handbook on the Aged in the United States*. Westport, Conn.: Greenwood Press, 1984. Included in this book is a wide range of definitions and explanations applied to all aspects of aging and retirement. The book also lists the addresses for many organizations that serve seniors in the United States. The list of references provides excellent sources for research about seniors and retirement.

Willing, Jules Z. *The Reality of Retirement*. New York: William Morrow, 1981. This book deals primarily with the psychological aspects of retirement. It discusses the freedom of developing an identity unrestricted and unrelated to profession and studies the psychological impact of relocation and social adaptation after retirement.

Linda J. Meyers

Cross-References

Age Grading and Age Stratification, 27; Ageism and the Ideology of Ageism, 41; The Aging Process, 53; The Graying of America, 846; Leisure, 1075; Life Expectancy, 1087; Social Gerontology, 1799; Social Security and Issues of the Elderly, 1832.

THE AGING PROCESS

Type of sociology: Aging and ageism

The aging process includes physical changes in the human body over the life course, psychological changes in personality, including emotional and cognitive capacities, and social changes in how people are perceived. Although aging has a biological basis, the consequences of the aging process are often socially defined.

Principal terms

DEMOGRAPHY: the study of the size, structure, and development of human populations; sex and age composition are two central features of population structure

IDENTITY: the image or view that individuals have of themselves and the personal classifications that individuals use to specify who they are in relation to other people

LIFE COURSE: the biological progression and social sequence of expected behaviors that individuals assume from birth to childhood, middle age, old age, and death

NORMS: guidelines that are agreed upon and shared within a society that define appropriate and inappropriate ways of behaving in a given situation

SANCTIONS: rewards for behaviors that conform to social norms and punishments for behaviors that violate norms—for example, financial reward or legal restraint

SOCIAL CHANGE: any alteration in the social behavior or institutions of a society that results in important long-term consequences

SOCIAL INSTITUTIONS: continuously repeated social practices developing around a basic social need that over time become established patterns of behavior; examples include family, education, religion, and the economic system

SOCIAL ORGANIZATION: a network of interactions among individuals and groups in society that defines their mutual rights and obligations

SOCIAL STRUCTURE: the enduring, orderly, and patterned relationships that exist among social institutions within a society

STATUS: the socially defined positions occupied by an individual throughout the life course; examples include child, student, or parent

Overview

Aging results from a lifetime of biological, psychological, and social processes interacting with one another. Sociologist Robert Atchley notes that while genetic factors play a role in predisposing individuals to certain diseases or impairments, the aging process is highly dependent on the social environment. Sociologists are interested primarily in the social factors involved in the process of becoming old.

The boundary between middle age and old age is arbitrary. Social scientists typically consider the elderly in the United States to include people who are at least sixty-five years old. This dividing line is not based on any biological, psychological, or sociological evidence. Sixty-five represents the age originally designated for citizens to receive Social Security benefits, and it continues to be used as a criterion for old age.

Sociologists specify three interrelated aging processes. First is physical aging: the internal and external physiological transformations that take place over the life course in the human body. Second is psychological aging: the developmental changes in mental functioning, including emotional and cognitive capacities. The third process is social aging: the changes in how individuals are viewed, what individuals expect of themselves, and what is expected of them from others that individuals experience over the life course.

The processes of aging do not always occur together. For example, an elder composer may produce a brilliant score of music despite the onset of hearing loss; an aging auto worker may remain physically strong yet experience lapses of memory and concentration. The failure to take into account individual differences and to respond to all people as though age were their single most important characteristic is a consequence of ageism—the belief that one age group is inferior to another. Generalizations about the capabilities of the aged are problematic, because the onset of the three aging processes can occur at different and irregular rates.

Individual variation in the rate of physical aging is great, and people of seventy or eighty may be healthier, and appear younger, than people sixty years old. Nevertheless, the human body gradually degenerates with advancing age, and many people over the age of sixty-five suffer from a chronic health problem. Most common among these ailments are arthritis, diabetes, glaucoma, hearing impairments, cancer, and heart disease. Despite the health conditions associated with aging, Linda George, in "Social Structure, Social Processes, and Social Psychological States" (1990), reports that the majority of older people experience high life satisfaction and a sense of well-being.

Senility is often associated with aging, yet the condition is rare among people under seventy-five. (Social scientists often divide the older population into "old" or "elderly"—approximately sixty-five to eighty-five—and "aged" or "old-old"—over eighty-five.) Some senility involves the gradual loss of brain cells with advancing age, but much of it is caused by Alzheimer's disease, a progressive and irreversible deterioration of brain tissue. Many people are wrongly judged senile when they are actually suffering from depression, side effects of medication, or cardiovascular conditions that impede the circulation of blood and oxygen to the brain.

Sociologist Matilda White Riley suggests that social scientists treat aging as a process that is characteristic of both individuals and society. In studying age, it is necessary to recognize that both people and society undergo change. One aim of sociology is to understand how changes in society and in the processes of the individual life course transform each other as people of different ages pass through social institutions.

Sociologists are interested in the social antecedents and consequences of the aging process. The social meanings of age influence the aging process through norms and sanctions. Age is an important social status, because it affects the relationships that people have with others of similar, younger, or older age status. Many societies celebrate rites of passage, formal ceremonies that denote a transition from one age status to another. The company retirement banquet (marking the transition from middle age to old age) is one remnant of these rites in the United States. Sociologists study these age-related transitions because they are socially created and socially recognized.

Social factors can influence processes often considered exclusively biological. For example, life expectancy is determined, in part, by the availability of effective medical care, improved standards of nutrition, and efficient sanitation. An individual born in the social environment of the United States in 1900 could expect to live, on average, for forty-seven years, whereas a person born in 1990 could anticipate an average life expectancy of more than seventy-five years.

In *Aging in Society* (1983), Matilda White Riley, Beth Hess, and Kathleen Bond offer examples emphasizing that variations in the aging process among individuals are shaped in part by historical conditions and social change. The experience and the meaning of aging differ not only from individual to individual but also from one historical context to another. Being sixty-five years old today is different from being sixty-five in the 1960's or the 1860's.

Human aging is not one process, but many processes. Aging includes physical changes in the body, psychological changes, and changes in mental capacity. Although the aging process is rooted in human genetics and physiology, the significance of aging is socially constructed. Aging not only affects what people are capable of doing but also influences what they are expected to do, allowed to do, or prohibited from doing.

Applications

Social gerontology is the study of the social aspects of aging. This subdiscipline of sociology has led to greater understanding of the process of aging. Among these contributions are research on the social aspects of time and the impact of historical influences on the aging process.

Sociologist Susan A. Eisenhandler, in "More than Counting Years: Social Aspects of Time and the Identity of Elders" (1989), studies the social aspects of time and the process of aging by exploring the relationship between health and the awareness of being old. Eisenhandler interviewed fifty elders aged sixty and older. An examination of responses to questions about health revealed that elders who rated their health as good to excellent were less likely to impart meaning to being any particular age. When asked the question, "What's it like to be [the person's chronological age]?" they did not provide sharp images or statements. This remained the case even after repeated probes. In addition, healthy elders were less likely to feel their age and to think of themselves as old.

Elders who termed their health fair to poor were likely to describe being a particular age with references to physical health and fitness. They provided qualified responses about feeling their age. When asked if they thought of themselves as old, several responded, "Yes," and expanded on their answers. There were some differences in the health state reported by men and women. Men were more likely than women to assess their health as good.

Elders reported having difficulties with a wide array of illness and disability, but all of the elders were functioning sufficiently well to participate in a variety of daily activities. Yet health problems that disrupted the usual and enjoyable round of daily activities, as well as problems that caused other people to tell elders that they had to lessen their daily activities, subtly pushed respondents into rethinking their sense of old age. Rarely did elders link old age to a specific condition. The actual limitations and adjustments imposed by uncertain health rather than any particular illness instill an identification with old age. Uncertain health was the most dramatic reminder of old age and the precipitating factor in seeing oneself as old. Ill health disrupts patterns of interaction and creates uncertainty in social relations. This begins to explain how health becomes such an important influence on individual perceptions of old age.

Eisenhandler concludes that most elders do not want to be any younger. They merely want to grow older without surrendering aspects of their identity because of misconceptions that others have regarding old age. Growing old is not so much a function of counting years and running out of time as it is of adapting to the reality of eroding health. Consequently, poor health status is synonymous with the perception of being old at any chronological age during the life course.

People who are born at roughly the same time have a common history that is unlike that of all others in their society. To study this phenomenon, sociologists use the term "cohort"—a category of people who are born within a designated time frame, such as a period of one, five, or ten years. Members of a given cohort experience the same stage of life differently than do those of other cohorts who were born earlier or later. Many college students during the 1960's, for example, were involved in demonstrations and protests against college regulations and national policies. Today's students, although many are the same age, have a different experience. Historical influence takes the form of a cohort effect when social change differentiates the life patterns of successive cohorts, such as college students of the 1960's and 1990's.

Sociologist Glen Elder, in *Children of the Great Depression: Social Change in Life Experience* (1974), traces the effects of drastic income loss during the Great Depression on individual experiences later in life. Elder studies two birth cohorts, one born at the beginning of the 1920's and the other born in 1928 and 1929. He found that the younger children were more strongly influenced by the Depression than the older children, with impairment most evident in the lives of younger boys. Though decreasing in strength over time, the difference persisted up to the middle years in work life, family relations, and psychological functioning.

Elder discovered that those who were very young during the Depression had no memory of early prosperity, so they regarded the economic improvements of later years as a steady progress from adversity to affluence. Their elders, however, who had known better times before the Depression, saw the new prosperity as a sign of a possible cycle in which affluent and meager periods might follow each other. Consequently, decades after the Depression, the younger cohort assumed that lean times were gone forever, but the older cohort remained wary of the economic future and inclined to save in anticipation of another Depression. The meaning of the Great Depression was very different for the two cohorts. These differences highlight how individual lives and societal change are related and how early events and influences persist throughout the life course.

Context

Aging has always been a part of the human experience. The systematic study of aging, however, especially of its social aspects, is relatively young. Investigating the social aspects of the aging process is almost exclusively a twentieth century United States phenomenon. Longitudinal studies of children launched in the 1920's and 1930's in the United States became studies of young adulthood and old age in the post-World War II era.

The changing demography of American society caused social scientists to assign greater importance to problems of aging and the study of them. Most theories about aging have been developed since the 1950's. The generation of theories of aging has been related to the changing perceptions of aging and to changing social policies. In 1990, for the first time in United States history, there were more people aged sixty-five and over in the population than there were teenagers. The number of older persons surpassed 31 million, whereas the teenaged population dropped to 23 million. Relatively stagnant birthrates and rising life expectancy have contributed to the growth in the older population. In addition, the enormous baby boom generation, born between 1946 and 1964—which in the early 1990's represented about one-third of the population—is moving into middle age.

Although much medical and scientific research has focused on the problems of later life, sociologists now recognize the broader significance of old age and aging. One significant social factor is the fact that age plays a fundamental role in social structure and social organization. Age is a major factor in the organization of society, affecting the distribution of resources and social roles. Many forces affect social structure and individual behavior, making it difficult to isolate the effects of any one particular factor. Isolating the effects of age and characterizing the aging process are particularly difficult, because age is inherently confounded with the effects of two other factors: cohort and time of measurement. Age refers to the time since birth, and age effects are patterns resulting from the passage of time. Cohorts refer to persons born at approximately the same time. Once individuals are placed in historical context, the personal impact of historical conditions must be considered.

The meaning of aging is flexible, with people's expectations for themselves at a particular age depending on the social assumptions unique to that time and place. People do not abruptly become old at age sixty-five. Aging is a life-long phenomenon, even though the process of aging is often associated with the elderly.

Along with sex and race, age is an ascribed status—one that cannot be voluntarily chosen. Age is unique among ascribed statuses, however, in that it changes over time, and movement across age categories results in changing expectations for behavior as well as changing personal and social responsibilities. Because of the fundamental role of age in society and in individual lives, sociologists are committed to increasing the understanding of age groups and the aging process.

Bibliography

Atchley, Robert C. *Social Forces and Aging*. 6th ed. Belmont, Calif.: Wadsworth, 1991. A comprehensive introduction to a social scientific approach to the study of human aging. The text succeeds in making complex theoretical, research, and policy issues accessible to both high school and college students. Contains a subject index, an extensive bibliography, and a glossary.

Eisenhandler, Susan A. "More than Counting Years: Social Aspects of Time and the Identity of Elders." In *Research on Adulthood and Aging: The Human Science Approach*, edited by L. Eugene Thomas. Albany: State University of New York Press, 1989. Based on interviews with fifty elders, this is an insightful portrayal of how recognition of the process of aging is linked to the perception of one's health. The volume includes additional essays on menopause, institutionalization, and other topics related to aging. Recommended for a college audience.

Elder, Glen H., Jr. *Children of the Great Depression: Social Change in Life Experience*. Chicago, Ill.: University of Chicago Press, 1974. Both high school and college students will find this an excellent example of a sociological approach to the study of aging and the life course. The book examines the experience of a single cohort and shows that the historical era shapes individual lives. Contains footnotes, a combined name and subject index, and a bibliography.

George, Linda K. "Social Structure, Social Processes, and Social Psychological States." In *Handbook of Aging and the Social Sciences*, edited by R. H. Binstock and L. K. George. 3d ed. San Diego: Academic Press, 1990. An excellent discussion of life satisfaction and sense of well-being among older people. This is one essay in a good collection on aging. The chapters on "Demography and Aging" and "Stratification and the Life Course" are also well-written and informative. Appropriate for both high school and college students.

Riley, Matilda White. "On the Significance of Age in Sociology." *American Sociological Review* 52 (February, 1987): 1-14. A scholarly article describing the interplay between aging and social change. Appropriate for a college audience; however, high school students enrolled in an introductory sociology course will find most parts accessible. Contains footnotes and an excellent bibliography.

Riley, Matilda White, Beth B. Hess, and Kathleen Bond, eds. *Aging in Society: Selected Reviews of Recent Research*. Hillsdale, N.J.: Lawrence Erlbaum, 1983. A collection of articles concerned with the social, cultural, economic, and psychological factors that affect both the process of aging and the status of older people in society. Name index and a separate bibliography for each essay.

Michael Delucchi

Cross-References

AGRARIAN ECONOMIC SYSTEMS

Type of sociology: Major social institutions
Field of study: The economy

Agrarian societies are generally considered to be preindustrial societies that employ plows and other farm equipment in the production of food. Agrarian economic systems comprise agricultural production, the ownership or control of production, and the distribution of food products.

Principal terms

CUSTOMARY TENURE: rights to land that is not on any market, usually awarded by birth or kin group membership

ECONOMIES OF SCALE: savings in production or marketing costs that are better exploited by large operations than small ones, up to some ceiling, above which there are no more gains

INDUSTRIAL AGRICULTURE: agriculture that utilizes inputs from industry, such as tractors, herbicides, and chemical fertilizers; sometimes refers to agriculture that has the division among capital, management, and labor characteristic of industry

LAND CONCENTRATION (or FARM CONCENTRATION): a trend whereby there are progressively fewer owners of land

NEO-MALTHUSIANS: population theorists who believe that population growth tends to outstrip resources and improvements in the technology of resource exploitation

POPULATION PRESSURE: the demand by a population for resources; not a simple function of population density, because resource density and technology vary

SUBSISTENCE: the production of food, fiber, and other necessities for consumption within the household structure (of agriculture); the social, economic, and political structures that control agricultural production

SUSTAINABLE: capable of being continued indefinitely without degrading nonrenewable resources, such as soil

Overview

Agriculture is any form of food and fiber production based on domesticated plants and animals. A common narrowing of the definition, to be used here, excludes pastoralism, in which the dominant activity is animal grazing, and horticulture, in which no plows (and therefore no draft animals or tractors) are used.

Agrarian systems vary in intensity. The more extensive systems are those in which inputs are few; the more intensive ones are those in which the level of inputs is high. Labor-intensive, energy-intensive, and capital-intensive systems require heavy inputs of labor, energy, and capital, respectively. An association exists between frequency and intensity of cultivation. Frequently cultivated land receives inputs in more seasons than land that is in fallow (not cultivated) much of the time, and it tends to receive more inputs during a given season of cultivation. Intensification encourages further intensification to repay investments already made.

The relationship between population and agricultural intensity is a matter of theoretical interest. In the neo-Malthusian view, increases in agricultural yields, by raising the ceiling imposed by hunger, stimulate population growth. Economist Ester Boserup inverted the logic, arguing that usually few obstacles stand in the way of intensification, even for preindustrial agriculturalists. Most could increase cropping frequency, for example, but do so only when population pressure forces it, because more frequent cultivation means more work to grow the same amount of food.

Preindustrial agriculturalists have often found ways to intensify with animal energy rather than with their own labor. Historically, this has been particularly true of European and East Asian agriculture. Grazing livestock saves humans the trouble of transporting organic matter and nutrients, as it feeds on pastures, outfields, and hay and leaves manure where it can be easily gathered.

In medieval Europe, most cultivable land was in fallow one-third to one-half the time. Farmers usually plowed fallows during the summer. They fed sheep and cattle mostly from outlying pasture and hay meadows, which were adequate to feed draft animals and other livestock. During the agricultural revolution of early modern Europe, pasture was increased and fodder crops replaced fallows. Both livestock and the manure supply increased. Yields of crops also increased, but so did the productivity of labor.

Population pressure was historically greater in East Asia than in Europe. Draft oxen or water buffalo were the main grazing animals, and there was no dairying. Much of the land was cultivated every year by the time Europe was in the late Middle Ages, and there was efficient recycling of available organic matter, including manure, onto fields. Some fertility-building techniques that were new to early modern Europe are quite old in East Asia, and in some places hillsides were regularly stripped of vegetation to make compost. Population growth in the nineteenth and twentieth centuries brought about declining labor efficiency, as hand weeding, rice transplanting, and other laborious techniques were used to raise yields.

Industrial agriculture is sometimes considered distinct from agrarian systems, as it represents a combining of agriculture and industrial technology. Industrial agriculture, which has reached nearly all farmers in developed countries and some farmers virtually everywhere, is energy-intensive and capital-intensive. Petroleum products power farm machinery, irrigation pumps, and the mining and synthesis of fertilizers and other agricultural chemicals, and the farmer must pay for all these inputs. Chemical fertilizers contribute to higher yields. Tractors do not, although they may free for food production land previously used to graze draft animals. The "green revolution," which spread in developing countries of Asia and Latin America during the 1950's and 1960's, was based on newly bred varieties of wheat and rice that give high yields but require heavy fertilizer inputs and often new sources of irrigation water.

Historically, farm machinery has replaced hired labor, and land concentration has been a trend, although the degree of concentration varies according to the country involved. Concentration developed slowly in the United States and Europe, mostly after 1930 in the United States and after 1950 in Western Europe. One reason for concentration is that large farms realize economies of scale. In particular, they are better able to afford farm machinery and new sources of irrigation water. Another suggestion, somewhat controversial, advanced by economist Willard W. Cochrane, is that farmers are on a "treadmill of technology." Large, wealthy farmers are best able to adopt new methods, because they can afford to take risks; they thereby gain a competitive advantage over other farmers. Credit policies may also favor large farmers.

Prevailing incomes affect land concentration. Farms in the United States, Canada, and Australia, in order to provide an acceptable income, are commonly larger than they need to be to realize economies of scale. European farms are smaller, and subsidies are used to maintain income. Japanese farms are mostly only three to four acres and are heavily subsidized. The green revolution has occurred mostly in low-income countries, and there has been little land concentration. Farms taking part are generally very small in the rice-growing regions of Asia, but have been competitive through the use of labor-intensive methods, including the use of draft animals or small rototillers for tillage.

A trend in developed and developing countries alike, one that reduces the pressure for land concentration, is off-farm employment, or part-time farming, as it is also called. During the farm crisis of the 1980's in the United States, it was medium-sized farms, not small farms, that declined the most. Small farms often survived by means of off-farm employment.

Applications

Research on agriculture focuses on diverse issues, including environmental impact, control of agricultural science and technology (both within countries and internationally), and the impact of various trends on farmers in developed and developing countries. All are of interest to sociologists.

Concerns over the possible impact of industrial agriculture on the environment and health have led to the growth of alternative agriculture, in forms such as "organic farming" and "biodynamic agriculture," and to research into biological pest controls and sustainable agriculture. Nonsustainable traits of industrial agriculture under particular scrutiny include increases in soil erosion, pest problems that develop from growing the same crop year after year, and the drawing down of nonrenewable aquifers. Alternative agriculture refers to both a social movement and a way to manage a farm. There have been interdisciplinary studies of the managemet of alternative farms by a Netherlands study group and by a United States Department of Agriculture team. There have been a few sociological profiles of organic farmers.

Another interdisciplinary research subject is the influence of public policy and scientific priorities on sustainability. Biologist Garret Hardin has written of the "tragedy of the commons"—that the people who share common resources have no incentive to conserve them. Yet anthropologists and geographers have not found this to be true of small communities with common property, because they are able to control individual exploiters. Modern nation-states have the responsibility of managing the commons. Critics suggest that governments do not adequately control corporate exploiters of the commons and may themselves be destructive. Another problem is that much of the commons, such as the atmosphere and the seas, extends beyond national boundaries. Agriculture can affect both national resources, such as soils, and international ones, such as bodies of water.

Land tenure, including its influence on agricultural productivity and on rural society, is a research topic in developing countries. Tenure is far from uniform. For example, customary tenure prevails in large areas of sub-Saharan Africa and on some Pacific islands, large estates in much of Latin America, smallholder sharecroppers in much of India, and small owner-operators in Taiwan.

Debate over land concentration—over whether it is desirable and what, if anything, should be done to prevent it—is a nearly global phenomenon. In the United States, concerns over the comparative numbers of corporate farms and family farms enter the debate. Research informs policy makers. Governments establish subsidies and set qualifications for them, and the issue of who benefits most from subsidies is an important one. It has been widely argued, and disputed, that United States subsidies favor large farmers. The economist J. J. Benetière has found that within the European Community, government policies toward providing subsidies to part-time farmers (those who get half or more of their income from off-farm sources) strongly affect the numbers of those farmers. Land concentration is not, however, a purely economic question but also hinges on diverse reasons people remain in farming. Most farmers in developed countries could obtain a better return on their investment and labor in other occupations if those were open to them. Accordingly, farmers' values and the social determinants of remaining in farming are major research topics.

Regarding labor, a crucial theoretical problem is how farming differs from other enterprises and occupations. Sociologist Howard Newby has found that English agricultural laborers are deferential rather than angry toward their employers, despite lower wages and poorer working conditions than in industry. Peggy Barlett has obtained similar findings regarding Georgia workers.

Small farmers in developing countries often operate in a radically different setting from that of farming in developed countries, most notably in terms of tenure and their networks of social relations. Many of them live among kin in villages. Others work under a set of nearly feudal relations with landowners. The division by gender of labor and control of farming often differs greatly from that in Europe or North America. Farmers may sell most of their produce directly to consumers or to a government marketing board that fixes prices at something other than market levels. Technical and ecological circumstances may also be distinctive. What has come to be known as farming systems research has attempted to address these differences. This is an interdisciplinary approach that has primarily focused on small farms.

Issues of so-called "north-south" relations are coming to the fore, with sociologists often cast as advocates for the south—that is, the developing countries. Biologists and plant breeders have demonstrated that most of the germ plasm (hereditary or genetic material) that is likely to be useful in future plant breeding exists in the developing countries of the tropics and subtropics, where some of the species are threatened with extinction. Yet few germ plasm collections are under the control of these countries. Sociologist Jack Kloppenburg, Jr., has argued that control of these resources will be an important determinant of the structure of agriculture at the international level.

Biotechnology, which has advanced to the point where plants with genes transferred from other species are being released to farmers, has tremendous potential to shape agriculture. Kloppenburg and sociologist Frederick Buttel, among others, have argued that private companies, located largely in developed countries, dominate biotechnology and that developing countries will become increasingly dependent on these companies.

Context

Nineteenth century sociology displayed both a strong interest in and divided attitude toward rural society. On the one hand, Auguste Comte and Herbert Spencer endorsed the idea of progress and what was considered its final expression, the Industrial Revolution. On the other hand, there was what modern sociologist Robert Nisbet has called the "unit-idea" of community, expressed in nostalgia for the preindustrial village and in Frederic Le Play's peasant studies. Yet despite these latter interests, agriculture was rarely an object of study in its own right.

Sociologists Frederick Buttel, Olaf Larson, and Gilbert Gillespie, Jr., have traced the history of rural sociology, in particular the development within it since 1975 of a "new sociology of agriculture." Community studies dominated research before 1950. During the 1950's and 1960's, studies of diffusion abounded, a social psychological approach focusing on the farmer as an adopter of introduced innovations. The three main approaches of the new sociology of agriculture are neo-Marxist, neo-Weberian, and ecological. They have generated enthusiasm and productive research initiatives, prompting both a wave of self-examination and exchanges of ideas with other disciplines. The new work is informed by political economy and is concerned with the whole structure of agriculture; for example, it has looked at the relationship of the organization of farms—farm size, ownership, and relations with labor—to such influences as off-farm employment, government policies, agricultural science and extension, and the systems through which farm commodities reach consumers.

Sociologists have a long tradition of interest in human-environmental relations, going back to the human ecologists of the University of Chicago in the 1920's. Yet the Chicago human ecologists studied almost entirely urban relations. For a long time, the relationship between agriculture and the environment was left to nonsociologists, such as agricultural geographers and agricultural historians quite often. In anthropology in the 1950's and 1960's, an approach known as cultural ecology developed, typically involving studies of environment and culture in individual communities. Sociological studies, increasingly common after 1975, sometimes share this community focus.

Sociological studies of the relations between the structure of agriculture and its environmental impact include those by Graham Cox and Philip Lowe for England and Michael Redclift for developing countries. Much of the work concerns the conservation motive or the structuring of incentives to promote or discourage control measures. William Catton and Riley Dunlap, among others, have endorsed a human ecological approach that draws strongly on biological ecology. This approach points toward complex ecological interrelations and finds many indications that present trends in industrial agriculture are not sustainable.

Bibliography

Boserup, Ester. *The Conditions of Agricultural Growth.* Chicago: Aldine, 1965. A widely cited work on population and food production. Argues that population growth alone causes agricultural intensification. Cites few case studies and relies on Boserup's experience in the tropics. The specific model of intensification does not apply to all environments.

Buttel, Frederick H., Olaf F. Larson, and Gilbert W. Gillespie, Jr. *The Sociology of Agriculture.* New York: Greenwood Press, 1990. A historical synthesis and critical analysis of rural sociology and how the sociology of agriculture developed within it. It is in part a bibliographic essay focused on the United States, with references to key work in Europe and Canada but little from elsewhere. Critical of many trends in the structure of agriculture.

Goodman, David, Bernardo Sorj, and John Wilkinson. *From Farming to Biotechnology.* Oxford, England: Basil Blackwell, 1987. The writing in this source is a curious combination in that descriptions of technical issues are generally clear, as is a historical treatment, but theoretical discussion of social issues is mostly in difficult prose. Nevertheless, it is a valuable synthesis.

Griffin, Keith. *The Political Economy of Agrarian Change: An Essay on the Green Revolution.* Cambridge, Mass.: Harvard University Press, 1974. Coming at the tail end of the phase of rapid expansion of the green revolution, this work is one of the more balanced and thoughtful social and economic critiques. The author finds evidence of unequal benefits. For readers with at least a basic knowledge of economic concepts.

Grigg, David B. *The Agricultural Systems of the World.* London: Cambridge University Press, 1974. A fairly concise survey, strong in its relating of agricultural practices to environmental variables such as rainfall and soil type, but by design lean on social associations. The time frame is mostly before the population growth and economic development of the post-World War II era. Well-chosen bibliography.

Newby, Howard. *Social Change in Rural England.* Madison: University of Wisconsin Press, 1979. Exemplary in many respects of the new sociology of agriculture. The book is about land concentration, the adoption of new technology, and social change, in particular the restructuring of social class relations. Theoretically informed but ordered historically, which helps its readability.

Redclift, Michael. *Sustainable Development*. London: Methuen, 1987. A persuasive demonstration that sociologists have a role to play in the promotion of sustainable agriculture. Well illustrated with case studies, mainly, but not exclusively, from developing countries.

Westley, John R. *Agriculture and Equitable Growth: The Case of Punjab-Haryana*. Boulder, Colo.: Westview Press, 1986. A more favorable view of the green revolution than that of Griffin, but one drawn from a single showcase region. Finds that benefits have been widely shared. Abundant documentation from primary sources.

Daniel E. Vasey

Cross-References

The Agricultural Revolution, 67; Communal Societies, 297; Culture and Technology, 443; Horticultural Economic Systems, 903; Hunting and Gathering Economic Systems, 909; The Industrial Revolution and Mass Production, 946; Multinational Corporations and the Third World, 1268; Population Size and Human Ecology, 1428.

THE AGRICULTURAL REVOLUTION

Type of sociology: Major social institutions
Field of study: The economy

The agricultural revolution transformed agricultural technology in early modern Europe. Along with the growth of empire, the development of modern science, and the Industrial Revolution, it marked the restructuring of European society and the emergence of Europe as the center of empire and the global economy.

Principal terms
ENCLOSURE: the division of open lands managed in common into hedged, walled, or fenced individually managed plots
FALLOW: a period during which the cultivation of land is discontinued
GENTRY: in England, persons—traditionally, country people—of substantial means and with many of the manners of the upper classes, but not of noble birth
HOLDING: land managed by a single household or enterprise
PEASANTRY: in the broadest sense, small-scale farmers living under the control of a state; often associated with strong collectivist institutions, especially those based on kinship
STRUCTURE OF FARMING: the totality of allocation of land, labor, and other agricultural resources; farm size, land tenure, terms of rent and labor, and access to markets are some of its important components
USUFRUCT: the right to use land, short of ownership
WORLD SYSTEM: according to Immanuel Wallerstein, the modern system of nations and their economies, which is dominated by wealthy capitalist economies

Overview

The agricultural revolution in Europe brought about a large increase in farm production between the sixteenth century and the early nineteenth century, before chemical fertilizers and other industrial inputs were in use. Farmers, not professional scientists, were the innovators, improving their management of the old inputs of soil, water, seed, stock, and labor. Gains in yields were slow before 1800 in most of Europe but were substantial in Flanders and The Netherlands as early as the sixteenth century. In England, which became the leader in commercial agriculture, livestock production grew early, but not so certainly grain production. Some economic historians infer from population trends that the greatest increases in English grain yields occurred after 1750. Mark Overton and Gregory Clark, however, have found evidence in, respectively, probate land assessments and records of labor costs that yields per acre rose dramatically before 1700.

The agricultural revolution came mostly before the Industrial Revolution, but commerce and agriculture stimulated and complemented each other, particularly in

Flanders, The Netherlands, and England. These changes in turn helped foster the growth of industry.

New crops played a part. These included introductions from the New World, notably the potato, the ideal staple crop in the cool summers of the Atlantic fringe, and maize, which is well-suited where summers are hot and rainfall or irrigation are ample. Many "new" crops were familiar plants that were being put to new uses, fodder (animal feed) in particular. With new crops came new systems of farming.

In the most common of the previous farming systems, one or two years of crops alternated with a year of fallow. Farmers plowed the fallow fields in the summer. Pastures and meadows (for hay) were usually located in outlying areas.

The new systems were varied. Fodder crops tended to replace fallows. Many farmers, encouraged by an expanding market for meat, milk, and wool, put prime land into "leys"—that is, intensively managed grass or clover pasture. Often, leys and crops alternated as prices for grain and animal products fluctuated, and some farmers alternated them by design, the so-called "convertible husbandry."

There was increased drainage of wet land and irrigation of dry land. Drainage included the reclamation of land from the sea by diking and drainage, notably in The Netherlands. Irrigation expanded not only near the Mediterranean and in rice lands in northern Italy but also in the damp climates of northern and central Europe, in what the English called "floating meadows." This was done to imitate "water meadows," grasslands that flooded naturally in winter and supplied abundant, high-quality hay or pasture in summer.

The changes had sound ecological bases. Farmers recognized that legume fodder crops—clover, alfalfa, sainfoin, and vetches—benefited the crop that followed them, though they could not have known that these crops added nitrogen to the soil. The new methods supported greater numbers of livestock, which contributed more manure to spread on cropland.

Other important advances occurred in animal breeding, new uses for farm products, and greater use of long-known fertilizers. The latter included urban nightsoil, peat, seaweed, sea sand, lime, and marl, a lime-rich clay.

Fodder crops replaced fallows and leys replaced crops as early as the thirteenth century in Flanders. These techniques spread slowly but, along with the planting of clover, were in general use in Flanders, The Netherlands, and the northwest German coast by the seventeenth century, and they turned up then or a little later in Pfalz, in Alsace, and in isolated pockets in central Germany, northern Italy, and Catalonia. Adoption on the Continent was otherwise slow, however, until well into the nineteenth century. In the meantime, the English widely adopted leys in the sixteenth century, the floating of meadows in the next century, and the planting of clover and turnip by the eighteenth century. Historian Eric Kerridge dates convertible husbandry to the six-teenth century.

"Enclosure" was another trend. The late medieval northern European landscape had included large tracts of open fields—that is, pasture grazed in common and cropland worked in unfenced strips under individual usufruct. Enclosure put these lands in private hands. From the sixteenth century to the early 1800's, most of England's open fields were enclosed. The stimulus in the sixteenth century was the high price of wool, which also led many landlords in Spain, northern France, and western Germany to enclose.

The new technology and enclosure speeded a breakdown of community controls over land use. Traditional controls had been ubiquitous, but they were strongest over open fields. Operators who were free of traditional constraints were best able to make needed investments and gain high profits. Inevitably, some succeeded better than others, increasing differences of wealth among villagers. Some historians have argued that the close-knit peasant community died when the new technology was most successful, as competition replaced cooperation.

Rural society evolved quite differently in the various regions, and technical innovation was not the only cause of change. By the fifteenth and early sixteenth centuries, little remained of the old feudal order of the Middle Ages, whereby warrior lords had controlled land and serfs. Depopulation that had begun with the Black Death of 1346 to 1351 created a chronic labor shortage and improved the peasants' bargaining position. In East Prussia, Poland, and much of Russia, a lucrative grain export trade to western Europe encouraged landowners to coerce peasants into a new serfdom. The population was particularly thin, and large grain surpluses were produced with the old methods. At another extreme, smallholders, many of them owner-operators, were the main innovators in densely populated Flanders and The Netherlands. Tenants on small farms predominated in much of France and the western German states, but in most places traditional relations among peasants and between them and their landlords provided little incentive for innovation, which until the nineteenth century took place mainly in the few locales already noted and in France in such specialized undertakings as the production of wine or produce for urban markets.

English farming developed a unique structure that encouraged capital-intensive undertakings. Great landowners enlarged their holdings at the expense of smallholders and became mostly collectors of rents. The main innovators of the new technology were from a new class of farmer-entrepreneurs, who typically rented much of their land from the great landowners and hired landless laborers and cottagers.

Landless persons, many of whom were paupers, were a widespread feature of Europe in this early modern era. Their existence often has been attributed to the agricultural revolution itself, but while some of the new technology required less labor on a given area of land, other techniques required more. Other historians have blamed pauperization on population growth, first from 1550 to 1650 in much of Europe, and again after 1750. Wars were often another factor. Whatever their origins, these landless persons were part of a growing population that was fed by the agricultural revolution, and they would eventually form the labor force of the Industrial Revolution.

Applications

The agricultural revolution is a source of several lessons for the present. The lessons relate to issues of technology and environment and to matters of farm and economic policy. One lesson, both ecological and economic, is that much was achieved without tractors, fossil fuels, or modern agrochemicals. Present-day farmers in developing countries may be able to raise yields through better biological management, even if they cannot afford industrial inputs. This may possibly be done without straining the environment: Most of the land use of the agricultural revolution was sustainable. To this lesson should be attached the caution that gains made without the use of industrial inputs are not always environmentally benign. Cultivation and overgrazing in the agricultural revolution sometimes led to soil loss, and soil fertility was not always carefully maintained. Wetlands were drained on a scale that would be unthinkable in many countries today.

For many developing countries, a lesson is that the structure of farming during the agricultural revolution offers alternative models to that of, say, industrially based agriculture in North America. Many farmers in developing countries own or have rights to only two to four acres where land use is intensive, or five to ten acres where they fallow some part of the holding each year. To change these farms to the North American model, whereby a single family works hundreds of acres with the help of heavy machinery, would mean throwing far more people off the land than was ever done in Europe during the agricultural revolution, even judging by the darkest accounts.

While there is no good reason to believe that only European precedents are worth following, it is nevertheless encouraging to know that the innovators of the agricultural revolution were a varied lot. Historian J. V. Beckett has compiled estimates of the size of English landholdings in the 1750's. About 300 owners had holdings of 9,000 acres and up, 12,000 families were on 300 to 3,000 acres, and 210,000 families had holdings of fewer than 300 acres. A few great landowners were among the innovators, not only in England but also in Prussia and Italy. Some specialized horticultural operations in The Netherlands were only two or three acres, and many Dutch or German farms successfully combined plant and animal husbandry on only twenty to fifty acres. Relations between ownership and labor also varied greatly during the agricultural revolution. Many English farmers combined ownership with rental and their own labor with that of landless laborers or part-time smallholders. Small farms were generally family farms.

The diverse structures that were established during the agricultural revolution survived for a long time the adoption of industrial inputs in agriculture. Only since World War II have the pressures mounted to consolidate smallholdings. Only then did subsidies swell to keep profits competitive with the high wages and returns on capital investment paid by industry. For developing countries, the wage competition at least is not nearly so great.

Not all forms of tenure and labor, however, are equally favorable. Debate persists regarding the desirability of land reform in countries wherein large holdings now prevail and landless laborers or sharecroppers do the work. In the agricultural revolution, besides having a favorable market for their goods, the innovative farmers were those who had reasonably secure tenure and prospects of keeping the greater share of the rewards of innovation and investment. Most large landowners were content to collect rents or shares until fairly late. A common criticism of sharecropping, that it stifles investment and innovation, is well borne out by the late progress made in southern France and southern Italy, where sharecropping predominated.

The priority, or lack thereof, that developing countries ought to give agriculture is the subject of an old controversy. During the late 1940's and the 1950's, many newly independent countries favored industry over agriculture, for example, by concentrating scarce capital in industry and by fixing food prices at low levels, so that urban workers could be fed at low cost. Since then many countries have given a greater priority to agricultural development, though some observers also point to the economic success of the nearly farmless city-states of Hong Kong and Singapore.

Although the agricultural revolution largely preceded the Industrial Revolution, agricultural and industrial growth were complementary. In England, industry had been growing for centuries before the beginning of the Industrial Revolution, which is usually put at about 1760 to 1780, when factories and the use of artificial power began to increase rapidly. Agriculture continued to grow in the nineteenth century and began to make use of industrial inputs. Domestic agricultural products helped feed England's growing industries. Profits from agriculture and the trade in wool and other farm products fed English prosperity and presumably helped to finance the Industrial Revolution. Whether the cause was enclosure, done to expedite the new farming, which supplied the urban workforce, or the growth of population, which the higher yields fed, the agricultural revolution helped create an industrial proletariat.

Context

Most research into the technological, ecological, and economic changes of the agricultural revolution has been conducted by agricultural historians, but their works have found a wide audience. A classic contribution, Lord Ernle's *English Farming Past and Present*, went through six editions. Much recent work has been based on econometric analyses, and there are connections with work on the history of population and social structure (for example, by the French Annales School and the Cambridge Group for the History of Population and Social Structure).

Among the founders of sociology or those social thinkers who most influenced sociology were several who held an interest in the agricultural revolution. The founder of classical economics, Adam Smith, saw in England's success with the new farming proof of the power of the free market. Thomas Robert Malthus, the founder of demography, knew well that farm productivity and population had long been growing in tandem. In the first edition of his *Essay on Population*, Malthus seemed to say that population growth inevitably cancels gains made in agriculture, but in later editions he was more optimistic. To Karl Marx and Friedrich Engels, enclosure was an integral part of the development of capitalism, as landlords drove peasants from the land to become a disenfranchised proletariat. Max Weber was inclined to see the English farmer-entrepreneurs as a progressive force, in contrast to the landlords of central and eastern Europe.

Much modern social thought is concerned with the reasons for the rise of the West. In 1400, Europe had neither technological and economic advantage nor political hegemony over the rest of the world. The scientific, agricultural, and industrial revolutions represent the technological and economic rise of Europe, in the same way that the Age of Exploration began with Prince Henry the Navigator and that Columbus represents the start of global empire. Anthropologist Alan Macfarlane has suggested that England in the late Middle Ages did not have the close-knit, peasant communities that other scholars have suggested; the English were individualistic and already well-suited to the kind of entrepreneurial activity that would bring their agriculture and industry to the fore in the following centuries. Sociologist Immanuel Wallerstein begins his chronicle of the rise of what he calls the capitalist world system with enclosure and the trade in English wool in the sixteenth century. Like Marx, he sees this as a process of exploitation, first of English peasants, later of much of the world.

Bibliography

Blum, Jerome, ed. *Our Forgotten Past: Seven Centuries of Life on the Land*. London: Thames & Hudson, 1982. A wide-ranging series of essays on rural life throughout Europe before, during, and after the agricultural revolution. Several of the essays present the dark side of peasant life in the past. For a general audience, with well-chosen illustrations and a limited bibliography.

Campbell, Bruce M., and Mark Overton, eds. *Land, Labour, and Livestock: Historical Studies in European Agricultural Productivity*. Manchester, N.Y.: Manchester University Press, 1991. A specialized collection of essays that emphasize quantitative economic indicators of change. Several of the essays form a valuable update on research into the agricultural revolution (and other periods) in England and on the Continent. A good source of updated bibliography as well.

Finberg, H. P. R., and Joan Thirsk, eds. *The Agrarian History of England and Wales*. 8 vols. London: Cambridge University Press, 1967-1981. A collection of expert essays that make up the comprehensive and often detailed work on English agriculture before, during, and after the agricultural revolution. Of the volumes already published, the fourth (1967) covers 1500 to 1640, and the sixth (1989) covers 1750 to 1850. Thoroughly referenced and indexed.

Kerridge, Eric. *The Agricultural Revolution*. London: Allen & Unwin, 1967. The best descriptions in any general source of the new techniques that constituted the agricultural revolution. Argues that the main changes of the agricultural revolution took place before the eighteenth century. Still the basic source on the agricultural regions of England in the period. Excellent and useful maps.

Laslett, Peter. *The World We Have Lost*. London: Methuen, 1965. A highly readable, popular yet authoritative evocation of life in preindustrial rural England. Laslett is more upbeat than most social historians of the period, particularly in his unusual claim that it was a "one-class" society, though he does not neglect poverty, high mortality, and other ills.

Mingay, G. E. *A Social History of the English Countryside*. London: Routledge, 1990.

Another aging treatment of England—still a fine synthesis, but subject to revision from a large literature on English social history, both periodicals and more specialized books. This volume's greatest strengths are its historical depth—from medieval times through the agricultural revolution to the modern era—and its integration of technological, economic, and social change. A scholarly presentation that is accessible to general readers.

Slicher van Bath, B. H. *The Agrarian History of Western Europe,* A.D. *500-1850.* Translated by Olive Ordish. London: E. Arnold, 1963. Particularly good regarding postmedieval changes on the European continent. Essentially an economic history, this work includes good detail on tenure and on farm management, often put in an ecological context, all in a volume of moderate length. A mine of quantitative data, though readers might wish to consult Campbell and Overton (1991) and recent periodicals for more information.

Wallerstein, Immanuel. *The Modern World-System: Capitalist Agriculture and the Origins of the European World-Economy in the Sixteenth Century.* New York: Academic Press, 1976. Gives agriculture a central role in the early development of capitalism and imperialism. The book's political-economic treatment of the subject is strong on the context and broad consequences of agriculture change, but the author is inclined to make sweeping generalizations about the changes themselves.

_____ . *The Modern World-System II: Mercantilism and the Consolidation of the European World-Economy, 1600-1750.* New York: Academic Press, 1980. Continues Wallerstein's 1976 work. These works have been so highly influential in recent sociological thought that it will be difficult from now on for anyone to treat any socioeconomic changes, including those in agriculture and agrarian society, as isolated local or even national phenomena. Both books are exhaustively footnoted.

Daniel E. Vasey

Cross-References

Agrarian Economic Systems, 60; Culture and Technology, 443; Horticultural Economic Systems, 903; The Industrial Revolution and Mass Production, 946; Population Size and Human Ecology, 1428; Rural Societies, 1673; Social Change: Sources of Change, 1786; Technology and Social Change, 2043.

ALCOHOLISM

Type of sociology: Deviance and social control
Field of study: Controlling deviance

Alcoholism has been called the number one health problem in the United States, and alcohol abuse and its related problems take a tremendous toll on society. Sociologists have conducted various types of research on alcoholism, an illness that plays a major role in many significant contemporary social problems.

Principal terms
ADDICTION: a pattern of compulsive substance abuse or other harmful behaviors over which there is a lack of control
BIOPSYCHOSOCIAL MODEL: an approach to human phenomena that takes into account biological, psychological, and social factors
DISEASE: a condition of the body in which there is incorrect or impaired function
RECOVERING ALCOHOLIC: an alcoholic who abstains from drinking, often by "taking one day at a time"
SOCIAL LEARNING THEORY: an approach that views behavior as socially influenced through observing and learning behavior from others
TWELVE-STEP PROGRAM: the organizing principles of Alcoholics Anonymous, which involves acknowledging the unmanageability of one's life because of an addiction and admits the need to look to a "Higher Power" for strength

Overview

Alcohol is probably the most widely used painkiller of all time. Historically, alcohol has been used to alleviate the pain of disease and injury and to sedate patients prior to surgery. It also has strong psychological effects; it can elevate or depress one's emotional state, or do both in rapid succession. Above all, it dulls the senses. Alcohol use has profound effects on individual lives and on society at large. A leading cause of death for adolescents is alcohol-related automobile accidents. Alcohol abuse is often combined with abuse of other drugs, and the combination may be unexpectedly fatal. Yet in spite of the widely known problems involved with alcohol use, its lure is powerful. Many people are able to drink alcohol in moderation, but one in ten drinkers of alcoholic beverages in the United States develops an addiction.

An alcoholic is a person who is not able to control his or her drinking. A recovering alcoholic is a person who recognizes this inability to control drinking and who therefore abstains from the use of alcohol. Sociologically, dependence on alcohol is seen as a social problem and as a form of deviance. Alcohol abuse is one of the most destructive and widespread drug-linked forms of deviance in the industrialized world. Because of alcohol's inhibition-reducing qualities, heavy drinking is closely associated with a host of other deviant and illegal behaviors such as assault, child abuse, sexual offenses, and reckless driving.

The term "alcoholism" was introduced in Sweden in 1849, and the concept of alcoholism as an illness began to gain ground in the late nineteenth century in both Europe and the United States. In 1960, a landmark work by biometrician Elvin M. Jellinek, *The Disease Concept of Alcoholism*, likened alcoholism to a disease. This scholarly work was consistent in its ideology with the influential but somewhat controversial teachings of the group Alcoholics Anonymous (AA). Through the combination of new scientific research and the efforts of AA, the concept of alcoholism was revolutionized in the 1960's. In 1966, the American Medical Association officially used the term "disease" for alcoholism for the first time.

The disease concept, however, does not provide an explanation of causation. It is more an approach to a phenomenon that is seen as having diseaselike characteristics: Alcoholism is primary, chronic, often progressive, and fatal if unchecked. For an understanding of the development of alcoholism, one must turn to sociology, biology, psychology, or all three. The sociological study of alcohol consumption and of alcoholism places considerable stress on cultural value orientations and socialization processes. Government policies, laws, and individual drinking behavior patterns can all be viewed against the context of culture.

While some cultures and ethnic groups ritualize the use of alcohol (examples include Italians and Orthodox Jews), others have a live-and-let-live attitude (for example, the French and their descendants in New Orleans), and still others restrict the consumption of alcohol through taxation (as is the case in Norway and Sweden). Punitive after-the-fact treatment of drunkenness is meted out in Russia. In the United States, several elements are combined at once—prevention, taxation, leniency, and mandated jail time. This is a reflection, no doubt, of the cultural contradictions that exist within a large, heterogeneous society.

Social scientists have used occurrence rates of cirrhosis of the liver (a disease caused by alcoholism) country by country to make cross-cultural comparisons. Countries and cultural groups with clear-cut and traditional drinking customs tend to have low rates of alcoholism. In contrast, social systems characterized by ambivalent or contradictory attitudes about drinking tend to have high alcoholism rates. A philosophy supporting moderation of lifestyle seems most conducive to a healthy appreciation of alcohol. A philosophy condoning excess, on the other hand, is consistent with alcohol abuse and alcoholism.

Microlevel sociological explanations point to factors responsible for excessive drinking in the immediate social milieu. Family drinking practices and attitudes, religious affiliations, and peer group influences might be explored. Macrolevel sociology conceives of deviant substance use as a product of the general social structure. The role of community stability, of social legislation, or of the mass media in determining drinking patterns might be considered. Sociologist Richard Stephens places the key emphasis on set and setting. In his model, set refers to the expectations of the physical experience of chemical use. Setting refers to the context in which the drug (alcohol, in this case) is taken. The act of drinking is given meaning through association and learning in the social context.

In addition to such sociocultural factors, human behavior is also influenced by biological and psychological variables. Textbooks and other works on alcoholism often take a holistic or "biopsychosocial" approach for a multidimensional understanding of the problem. Concerning the individual alcoholic, the notion of pain is a key concept. A cycle of pain, pain relief through self-medication (drinking), and then more pain caused by the drinking is the classic cycle of addiction. The pain is most often psychological, caused by early childhood trauma, perhaps, or by overwhelming emotions such as feelings of guilt or loss. A person may seek relief from the pain through alcohol. There may also be a biological susceptibility to excessive drinking. The perceived intensity of the pain (physical or psychological) the person is trying to alleviate may itself be biologically based. For whatever reason, some individuals seem far more sensitive to pain than others and are more inclined to be drawn to various avenues of escape.

The social aspect of the biopsychosocial model has already been mentioned. In short, social factors relevant to alcoholism are embodied in laws and customs and enforced by peer groups; they create the climate in which alcohol (or other drugs) may be chosen as a remedy for problems or as an end in itself.

The concept of the "alcoholic personality" or "addictive personality" is debated in the literature. These terms are often used to describe personality variables conducive to the development of addiction. The fact that some individuals move from one addiction to another (as from alcoholism to workaholism to spending addictions) seems to indicate a generalized tendency toward extreme behavior rather than a singular vulnerability to any one substance. An overwhelming number of alcoholics and recovering alcoholics, for example, are chain smokers. Although researchers generally agree that there is no single alcoholic personality, systematic studies do indicate high instances of depression, sociopathy, and hyperactivity as forerunners of alcoholism. Early childhood trauma, especially in the form of sexual abuse, is highly correlated with substance abuse in adolescence and adulthood. The relatively high rate of alcoholism among lesbians and gay males, estimated by some to be about 25 percent, is considered a result of the identity crisis caused by being homosexual in a society that has been termed "heterosexist."

Elements of biology, psychology, and social life all come into play in the etiology and tenacity of alcoholism. A multifaceted biopsychosocial approach is necessary for attaining a full understanding of alcoholism and for designing effective approaches to prevention and treatment.

Applications

Cultural and historical forces form a large part of any society's understanding and treatment of alcoholism. These forces are reflected in a society's norms, sanctions for violations of norms, legislation, and medical treatment.

The alcoholic beverage most consumed in early America was beer. According to historians Mark Lender and James Martin, more beer than water was carried across the Atlantic on the Mayflower. The Puritans drank, and, contrary to popular belief, drunkenness was widely tolerated by the Puritans and only occasionally punished. When distilled liquor replaced beer as the beverage of choice (there were obvious transportation advantages to distilled liquor—smaller amounts were needed for one to achieve the same level of intoxication), moderation gave way to intemperance. The years between 1725 and 1825 were characterized by hard drinking and an increase in the kind of bellicose behavior associated with this practice.

James Royce has traced the "temperance to abstinence" movement that grew from 1825 to 1919. Calvinist clergymen aligned with concerned citizens to condemn the wasteful and debaucherous behavior that was characteristic of the day. The focus of attention went from the sinner to the substance itself, "demon rum." A strong women's movement, exemplified by the Women's Christian Temperance Union, helped with a relentless propaganda effort until the Prohibition laws (the Volstead Act, in force from 1920 to 1933) took effect.

Along with changes in sanctions and social control, there are always changes in the definition or conceptualization of deviant behavior. Sociologists Peter Conrad and Joseph Schneider trace the conceptualization of what is now called alcoholism from sin to weakness, crime, and, most recently, illness. The title of Conrad and Schneider's textbook, *Deviance and Medicalization: From Badness to Sickness* (1980), summarizes their basic theme: The hospital has replaced the church and parliament as the symbolic center of Western society. The social response to deviance has therefore become therapeutic rather than punitive.

The conceptualization of alcoholism as a disease, which had its birth in the Alcoholics Anonymous movement in the 1930's, emphasized the fact that alcoholism was treatable but not curable. This conceptualization helped to render alcoholism a respectable subject of scientific research and of professional attention. Eventually, medical insurance coverage was provided for treatment of this disease. In the United States, 95 percent of all alcoholism treatment programs utilize the twelve-step approach to treatment. Through the 1980's, most of these programs were administered in inpatient treatment centers at hospitals. Business trends in the 1990's began to favor an outpatient, community-based setting.

The disease model and the twelve-step approach are essentially synonymous. A basic tenet of this approach is that alcoholism is a disease, a progressive disease that is fatal if unchecked. Step one, admitting that one is powerless over alcohol, is the step of giving oneself the label "alcoholic." This identity becomes a way of life. Strength is attained through a fellowship of persons who carry the same label and look to a "Higher Power" for spiritual guidance. Another tenet is that total abstinence from all mood-altering substances is required. In addition, sobriety is held to be achieved one day at a time. It is estimated that, worldwide, more than one million people are members of AA. College communities and college campuses often have AA groups and other self-help groups to which students may belong. Typical examples of other twelve-step programs are Overeaters Anonymous, Narcotics Anonymous, Gamblers

Anonymous, and Al-Anon (for families of alcoholics).

Because of knowledge that the leading causes of death for college-age youth are alcohol-related accidents and suicide, most colleges and universities offer information programs and treatment opportunities directed by their counseling center. In addition, fraternities and sororities have instituted strict recruitment and recreational policies intended to reduce alcohol abuse. Athletes are monitored closely for use of mood- and performance-altering drugs. Moreover, alcoholism research and treatment courses are frequently offered as a part of health or social work curricula. Internships at substance abuse treatment centers are available in these and related fields.

For every trend there is a countertrend; the countertrend regarding alcoholism is a stress on individual responsibility and willpower to resist temptation rather than on a blanket abstinence from drinking. The writings of Stanley Peele and Herbert Fingarette in the late 1980's both reflect and helped shape this trend. These approaches emphasize individual responsibility and accountability. According to Fingarette, "No longer is the heavy drinker viewed as a victim of disease, a passive patient who will be treated by an expert." Moderate drinking, rather than total abstinence, is an alternative possibility recommended by these iconoclastic but thought-provoking writers.

Context

In studies of addictive behavior, sociologists have tended to focus on addiction of the illegal variety, especially drug addiction. Drinking problems, alcoholism, and alcoholic family issues have not generally been the subjects of sociological discourse. Alcohol consumption is often viewed as prescribed or accepted by society, whereas other drug consumption is seen as proscribed. Sociological theories of deviant behavior as applied to alcohol use and abuse all view such behavior as socially patterned. Differences in rates and manner of drinking are viewed in a sociocultural perspective. Variations in group and societal customs as well as in the social setting determine the form that drinking behavior will take.

The best known of the sociological theories with relevance to alcoholism is Robert K. Merton's anomie theory, first introduced in the 1930's and refined in the 1950's. Anomie theory locates the source of deviant behavior in a discrepancy between the goals of society—high achievement—and a person's or group's means of achieving them. When goals cannot be achieved, according to this view, some people retreat into drug abuse or alcoholism. The theory suggests that efforts to prevent addiction should be made at the societal level, providing opportunity for everyone.

Ronald Akers, a sociologist who has researched drinking behavior, offers in *Drugs, Alcohol, and Society* (1992) a revised sociological orientation to drugs and alcohol that focuses on social structure, process, and policy. Social learning theory is the theoretical framework; individual drinking behavior is shown to be the result of a social learning process involving group and cultural associations. Primary groups such as family and peer groups provide the most important immediate environments in which the social learning process operates. The publication of Akers' comprehensive textbook acknowledges that drug and alcohol use and abuse constitute an enormous social problem and that these areas need further sociological investigation.

Bibliography

Akers, Ronald. *Drugs, Alcohol, and Society*. Belmont, Calif.: Wadsworth, 1992. This popular introductory text offers a rare sociological perspective on the world of substance abuse, the theoretical approaches, and the treatment industry. The physiological, psychological, and social factors in drinking and alcoholism are reviewed. Particularly well suited to a college audience. Contains an extensive bibliography.

Conrad, Peter, and Joseph Schneider. *Deviance and Medicalization: From Badness to Sickness*. St. Louis: Mosby, 1980. The focus on the politics of reality is a theme of this informative, theoretically based view of the medicalization of social problems. Provides a history of thought concerning alcoholism as an example of the gradual transformation of deviance designations. Insightful reading.

Fingarette, Herbert. *Heavy Drinking: The Myth of Alcoholism as a Disease*. Berkeley: University of California Press, 1988. This iconoclastic work challenges most of the major beliefs of the disease model. Fingarette also exposes the power of the alcoholism and addictions treatment industry. Should be read in conjunction with other works because of the controversial nature of the presentation.

Jellinek, Elvin M. *The Disease Concept of Alcoholism*. New Haven, Conn.: Hillhouse Press, 1960. This is the classic study in alcoholism, a book that made history by using the disease metaphor for alcoholism. The stages of addiction were first set forth in this work, and varieties of alcoholism were defined. Recommended as a reference resource.

Lender, Mark, and James Martin. *Drinking in America: A History*. New York: Free Press, 1982. From Plymouth Rock to the early 1980's, this comprehensive book traces the American love/hate relationship with alcohol. Well indexed and highly readable.

Merton, Robert K. *Social Theory and Social Structure*. Glencoe, Ill.: Free Press, 1957. This book is of historical value and shows grand theory in its purest form. Anomie theory is spelled out in detail in this work. Anomie theory was widely discussed following this book's publication.

Royce, James. *Alcohol Problems and Alcoholism: A Comprehensive Survey*. Rev. ed. New York: Free Press, 1989. A concise and well-written survey of the nature, causes, and prevention of alcoholism. Includes a bibliography of more than eight hundred entries and reading lists at the end of each chapter.

Katherine van Wormer

Cross-References

ALIENATION AND WORK

Type of sociology: Major social institutions
Field of study: The economy

The concept of alienation helps to provide a critical perspective on the social relations of work. Alienated work results from the structural separation of laborers from their product and from control over their labor process.

Principal terms
 BUREAUCRACY: an organization that is administered by a set of hierarchically arranged positions, with formal regulations governing a
   carefully designed set of specialized work tasks
 CAPITALISM: an economic system in which the institution of wage labor
   prevails, with private ownership controlling the means of production
 CLASS STRUGGLE: the pervasive range of social conflict that emerges
   from the antagonistic relationship between social classes that
   exploit and the classes being exploited
 EXPLOITATION: a social relationship involving dominance and subordination, brought about by an imbalance in the distribution of power
 SOCIOLOGY OF WORK: a subfield of sociology that focuses on
   occupational processes and variables in human societies
 STRUCTURAL: the level of human reality that is directly attributable to
   the patterns of social organization and that is not reducible to the
   level of the individual
 TAYLORIZATION: the process of applying scientific management to the
   labor process as pioneered by Frederick W. Taylor
 WAGE LABOR: a legally sanctioned, institutionalized form of organized
   work under capitalism that pays money (wages) to workers in
   exchange for completing tasks as specified by an employer

Overview

The concept of alienation is employed in a variety of fields in addition to sociology, including literature, psychology, and philosophy. It invariably refers to a difficult or problematic human condition, although the nature and source of the problem depends upon the particular academic context in which the concept is used. As a sociological concept, it provides a useful means of analyzing the exploitive dynamics of work in modern societies. Human beings are characterized by their capacity for creative, conscious activity in which their nature can be expressed through their work. The word "alienation" literally means separation or "estrangement." In alienated work relations, people become, to some degree, separated from their creative human nature and compelled to expend their labor for the benefit of others.

The concept of alienation was introduced to the sociological tradition by Karl Marx, the radical nineteenth century social theorist who was highly critical of capitalism. Marx was primarily concerned with analyzing the exploitive character of work in class societies. He argued that alienation is the separation of human beings from control over their social lives. This loss of control is experienced in virtually every social institution including the economy, religion, and the political sphere.

Marx's analysis of alienation in the economic sphere became extremely influential in the sociology of work. According to Marx, the worker's product becomes "alien" to the worker because of the particular nature of property relations in class societies. Marx shows that, under capitalism, wage workers lose control over their product. The legally sanctioned arrangement of the capitalist workplace leaves workers with only their wages following the end of the working day, with capitalists remaining in full possession of the product created by the workers. Moreover, wage workers are compelled to labor in accordance with the dictates of their capitalist employers, whose demands are constrained only by the established legal regulations that emerge from the protracted class struggle between workers and capitalists.

The contemporary sociological concept of alienation has both a "quantitative" and "qualitative" dimension. In work, human beings create products that have value. Because of the institutionalized patterns of exploitation found in class-stratified societies, workers are not entitled to keep the full value of those products which they produce. Rather, they become separated from the full value of their product through various social mechanisms and remain in possession of only a portion of the value they have produced. The quantitative dimension of alienation therefore relates to the amount of value that becomes separated from workers in the course of their social production. The qualitative aspect of alienation, in contrast, involves the issue of control over work. Although workers have the potential to be in full control of their own labor activity, they become estranged from that control in a variety of ways. Qualitative alienation therefore refers to the social manner and degree to which workers lose control over their work in production.

Together, the qualitative and quantitative aspects of alienation provide the basis for contemporary antagonisms within the workplace. Workers strive to reclaim a larger share of the value of their product, as represented in the struggle for higher wages. At the same time, workers seek to maximize their control over the actual labor process so as to lessen their exploitation by capitalist employers. This struggle for control can take the form of demands for better working conditions, organized protests over persistent occupational hazards, and even calls for workers' participation in manage-ment. Management, on the other hand, seeks to maximize its profits, providing a generalized drive to reduce wages. Similarly, the search for higher profits results in the continuing attempt of management to control all aspects of the labor process.

Many sociologists have attempted to demonstrate the social harm that alienation in work inflicts upon the working class. Robert Blauner's *Alienation and Freedom: The Factory Worker and His Industry* (1964) exemplifies this thrust in the sociological literature. Blauner's thesis suggests that alienation as a social structural concept results in social harm that becomes empirically observable in the occurrence of social-psychological problems.

According to Blauner, alienation in work causes a pervasive tendency toward feelings of meaninglessness, powerlessness, isolation, and self-estrangement among industrial laborers. These social-psychological outcomes, despite their origin in the social structural phenomenon of alienation, are frequently regarded as the personality problems of "weak" or dysfunctional individuals who are unable to cope with the pressure of hard work. To the extent that social authorities redefine the harmful consequences of alienated work as "pathologies" or illnesses of a strictly psychological (individual) nature, the larger social structures of work remain insulated from legal blame or social scrutiny.

Applications

Employed as a sociological critique of work, the concept of alienation has provided the basis for numerous contemporary studies. Harry Braverman's seminal study *Labor and Monopoly Capital: The Degradation of Work in the Twentieth Century* (1974) detailed the way in which workers in modern capitalist societies become qualitatively alienated in their work. Preferring the term "degradation" to alienation, Braverman as a Marxist analyst convincingly shows how the rise of capitalist management has led to the progressive alienation of industrial workers.

Braverman's "degradation thesis" is rooted in an analysis of the specific institutional character of work in capitalist social relations. Under capitalism, a worker is not wholly responsible for producing a product per se. This would imply that the laborer retains control over the labor process. Yet in actuality, the worker is responsible for obediently following the dictates of his or her employer for the duration of a wage period. The design of the labor process in the capitalist workplace ultimately rests in the hands of the capitalist. The worker generally agrees to work as directed for a specified time period and amount of wages.

Braverman's study shows how industrial capitalists have progressively developed more effective ways of "getting the most" out of the "labor time" they purchase when wage labor is hired. Based on the pioneering work of Frederick W. Taylor, an industrial engineer, capitalist management became transformed into a science in which technology was employed as a tool for assuming full control over the labor process. The rise of "scientific management" ultimately created the assembly line style of work responsible for the rise of mass production. For example, Henry Ford's application of Taylor's principles revolutionized the automobile industry.

As Braverman points out, the basic principles of "Taylorism" (or "Fordism," as it is sometimes called) are more or less universal and can be summarized in a three-step process. First, management must gather meticulous knowledge about all aspects of the production process, down to the smallest detail, with particular emphasis upon the labor process. Second, management subjects this accumulated information to a careful analysis, examining all aspects of the labor process in which workers exercise any sort of discretionary power in their work. Management must conceptualize how such operations could be broken down into simpler, more mechanical activities. Finally, management uses the results of its ongoing analysis to reformulate the production process, implementing a design for the workplace that removes all possible control over the labor process from the worker. This results in a virtual separation of conception from execution in modern work: The "brainwork" in production is placed in the hands of management, while the laborer is left to implement a "mindless" series of tasks.

Braverman points out that there is no intrinsic end to the process of Taylorism. In other words, once these three steps have been accomplished, management begins to gather further knowledge about its newly reconstituted labor process and proceeds to analyze it once again. Thus, the gathering of knowledge concerning the production process, with the aim of exerting ever greater control over the laborer, became an ongoing and permanent feature of modern, scientific management. This process progressively "de-skilled" the assembly-line workforce, increasing the qualitative alienation of production workers.

With the growth of mass production throughout capitalist industries during the twentieth century, the associated explosion of data collection within the production process made the growth of white-collar and managerial occupations inevitable. Braverman's study showed that Taylor's principles ultimately proved quite applicable to white-collar as well as blue-collar work. Clerical occupations were among the first to become Taylorized, leading to the progressive alienation of "office work." Virtually all service and retail trade occupations soon underwent the process.

Many case studies were published in the decades following Braverman's work. One such study, Richard Edwards' *Contested Terrain: The Transformation of the Workplace in the Twentieth Century* (1979), argued that Braverman's study was pathbreaking but incomplete. Edwards' study demonstrated Braverman's failure to account for the persistent role of worker resistance to Taylorization, thus overlooking how class struggle constrained capitalist management, in turn pushing managers to look for more effective means of increasing their control over the workplace.

Edwards shows that one increasingly common managerial strategy involves the creation of "artificial" distinctions within an increasingly bureaucratic workplace, with workers being assigned a large number of occupational positions that are carefully differentiated by rights and responsibilities. The result is a seemingly diverse set of occupational positions with a "pecking order" that is actually based on minuscule differences in wages and responsibilities. Creating divisions between workers renders it more difficult for them to organize around their common interests.

Context

Karl Marx's influential nineteenth century analysis of alienation was a reformulation of an earlier conceptualization advanced by the German philosopher Georg Wilhelm Friedrich Hegel. Hegel's philosophical approach to alienation viewed humanity as an incomplete realization of the human potential. Throughout history, he said, the human spirit as the essence of humanity became progressively able to realize its potential, gradually bringing it closer to perfection. Hegel's work represented an idealist approach to alienation in that it focused upon the "human spirit" rather than on the practical work of human actors.

Marx sharply critiqued the Hegelian concept of alienation for being too abstract and divorced from the social relations of everyday life. Influenced by another German philosopher, Ludwig Feuerbach, Marx reinterpreted Hegel's work through a materialistic perspective. Rather than look at the separation of human spirit from its potential, Marx looked at the alienation posed by social patterns of human labor in which workers are prevented from realizing their full potential as creative human actors.

Once Marx derived his distinctive approach to alienation, he applied it to the field of classical political economy as represented by Adam Smith, David Ricardo, and others, resulting in a far-reaching critique of economic theory. First, Marx rejected the notion that the pursuit of "self-interest" is rooted in human nature (as was argued by Smith). Marx instead showed how the propensity to act according to one's self-interest is itself the historical product of capitalistic social relations and is therefore not "natural" but amenable to historical transformation.

Second, Marx's analysis uncovered the conflictual nature of social classes. The pervasive existence of class struggle, a point largely overlooked by classical political economy, provides a basis for explaining historical social change. This aspect of Marx's analysis would later become extremely influential upon radical social movements because it tends to undermine conservative arguments that oppose social change.

Finally, it was Marx's materialist critique of classical political economy that proclaimed the impossibility of analyzing economic activity as divorced from the larger social relations that govern it. This point has influenced generations of critical thinkers who have rejected claims made by many modern economists that their analyses are politically neutral or "value free."

Bibliography

Blauner, Robert. *Alienation and Freedom: The Factory Worker and His Industry.* Chicago: University of Chicago Press, 1964. Sociologist Blauner shows how alienation fits into the sociological mainstream. He argues that alienation causes social-psychological problems that can be studied independently of the political framework advanced by Marxists.

Braverman, Harry. *Labor and Monopoly Capital: The Degradation of Work in the Twentieth Century.* New York: Monthly Review Press, 1974. Written from a Marxist perspective, Braverman's renowned study shows how the rise of scientific management intensified the laborer's loss of control over the industrial labor process. Virtually no form of wage labor, the author argues, remains immune from the monopoly capitalist trend toward growing managerial control.

Edwards, Richard. *Contested Terrain: The Transformation of the Workplace in the Twentieth Century.* New York: Basic Books, 1979. Edwards presents a sympathetic yet highly critical view of the "degradation thesis" advanced by Harry Braverman's

Labor and Monopoly Capital: The Degradation of Work in the Twentieth Century (1974). Building upon a Marx-Weber synthesis, Edwards uses empirical data to argue that modern management increasingly relies upon bureaucratic management techniques as a response to the ongoing class struggle that results from the alienation of wage laborers.

Marx, Karl. *The Economic and Philosophic Manuscripts of 1844*. Translated by Dirk J. Struik. Reprint. New York: International Publishers, 1986. This English translation of Marx's manuscripts contains one of his most important discussions of alienation. Particularly evident is Marx's critique of classical political economy.

Ollman, Bertell. *Alienation: Marx's Concept of Man in Capitalist Society*. 2d ed. New York: Cambridge University Press, 1976. In this frequently cited work, Ollman, a Marxist, explores the overall meaning and implications of Marx's concept of alienation. In doing so, the author shows the continuing relevance of alienation for a critical understanding of modern capitalist society. Ollman's academic work provides a general, college-level introduction to alienation.

Rinehart, James W. *The Tyranny of Work: Alienation and the Labor Process*. Don Mills, Ontario: Longman Canada, 1975. This study surveys the various managerial schemes that have been employed in modern industry, particularly those supposedly aimed at improving the quality of life of alienated workers. The author's critical approach shows how alienation remains a central problem in these reformed labor processes.

Schroyer, Trent. *The Critique of Domination: The Origins and Development of Critical Theory*. Boston: Beacon Press, 1975. This comprehensive study in social thought contains a useful account of the evolution of alienation as a critical concept, from its Hegelian roots to its development by Marx and its later reformulation by critical theorists. Dense and difficult to understand in places, the work is not recommended for beginning students.

Zimbalist, Andrew, ed. *Case Studies on the Labor Process*. New York: Monthly Review Press, 1979. This collection of articles explores alienation and work in the tradition pioneered by Harry Braverman. Managerial control strategies are examined in various industries, including computer programming, clerical work, carpentry, and coal mining.

Richard A. Dello Buono

Cross-References

Capitalism, 191; Class Consciousness and Class Conflict, 271; Conflict Theory, 340; The Industrial Revolution and Mass Production, 946; Industrial Societies, 953; Industrial Sociology, 960; Marxism, 1127; Workplace Socialization, 2202.

ALTERNATIVES TO TRADITIONAL SCHOOLING

Type of sociology: Major social institutions
Field of study: Education

The education of children is mandated by law in the United States, but the law does not require that children be educated in a particular type of institution or given manner; indeed, a significant number of parents, for a variety of reasons (including religious ones), have chosen alternatives to traditional public education.

Principal terms
> FREE SCHOOL: a school designed to foster noncompetitive, nonauthoritarian attitudes in students; they use open classrooms and emphasize individualized instruction
> HOME SCHOOLING: providing educational instruction to children in a home setting; home schooling usually offers services to elementary children or individuals with special needs
> PAROCHIAL SCHOOL: a school, usually an elementary school, that is supported by the parish of a church
> POPULACE: the body of the common people; the "masses"
> PUBLIC SCHOOL: a school maintained by public funds for the free education of children in the community, usually covering elementary and secondary grades

Overview

Life, liberty, and the pursuit of happiness are considered inalienable rights guaranteed to each citizen of the United States by the Constitution. The right to an education, perhaps surprisingly, is not found among the Constitution's guarantees. Nevertheless, free public education is offered by all fifty of the United States. The ideal of American public education, as it became institutionalized in the nineteenth century, was that it would provide young people with the information and values they needed to participate in a democratic society. The three R's formed the basis of the curriculum; basic reading, writing, and arithmetic skills were considered necessary for people to function effectively as adult citizens. As immigrants from many countries arrived in large numbers in the late nineteenth and early twentieth centuries, it was believed that the public schools would help "Americanize" their children. Public education has therefore played a significant role both in the American belief that anyone can get an education and improve his or her lot in life and in the concept of the American "melting pot."

There have always been groups that have, for various reasons, not subscribed to the belief that public education was the ideal way to teach their children. Often the reason has been religious; Roman Catholic churches, for example, established a system of parochial schools for Catholic children. Other religious groups developed their own schools as well. In addition, some immigrant parents with deep ties to their traditional cultures worried that public education would cause their children to turn away from their own culture. Often their solution was simply to teach children their ethnic traditions in the home in an attempt to balance the socialization into American culture that occurred at school.

More recently, parents have had other reasons for considering alternatives to traditional education. The deep problems, even crises, in public education have received considerable attention; parents are aware of falling student achievement scores and of the presence of drugs and violent behavior in the schools. The methods of traditional schooling have been questioned. Moreover, one of the benefits of traditional schooling was considered to be its function in socializing children into their culture. Many parents and educators had begun to wonder, however, into what sort of culture modern schools, with their deep problems, were socializing children. Other reasons that parents have chosen to pursue nontraditional methods of education for their children involve individual concerns regarding particular children, ranging from a child having disciplinary or other psychological problems to a child being too constricted—unable to express himself or herself creatively—by the traditional school setting.

A number of nontraditional schooling approaches have been tried. Among the earliest were the hiring of private tutors and sending children to private academies (frequently all-girl or all-boy schools) or parochial schools. The concept of "free schools" developed in the 1960's; at that time there was also an increase in schools designed for students with particular needs—such as children with disabilities. The other major alternative to traditional public schooling is home schooling. In 1987, the National Association for the Legal Support of Alternative Schools reported that more than 75,000 families had children being educated through home schooling. Arguments have been made for and against various forms of nontraditional education. Such education can often provide students with considerable individual attention and with unique experiences not available in public schools; however, teachers do not need to meet the same requirements that public school teachers do, and alternative schooling (notably home schooling) often does not provide the exposure to different viewpoints and cultures that public education can.

Parents undeniably share with the state both the right and the responsibility to obtain a good education for their children. Parents, in fact, have significant legal rights in the education of their children. They have the right to choose the type of education, the place for education, and the educational process they desire for their children. In deciding what type of education they want for their children, parents weigh factors such as the relative importance of family life and the schooling process, the development of individual potential, the preservation of cultural heritage, the value of religious beliefs, and the complexities of the social environment surrounding today's schools.

Parents' rights to choose alternative forms of education for their children have been established by Congress, protected by the United States Supreme Court, and, in many states, promoted by legislative action. In their book *The Law of Public Education* (1976), E. Edmund Reutter, Jr., and Robert R. Hamilton discuss the judicial background for alternatives to traditional schooling. Early in its history, the United States established public, tax-supported schools and expected all children to attend. In 1922 the state of Oregon went so far as to pass a law requiring all children to attend public schools. In the landmark case *Pierce v. Society of Sisters* (1925), however, the Supreme Court said that a state may not "standardize its children by forcing them to accept instruction from public teachers only." Thus the Court unanimously invalidated the Oregon law and firmly established the right of parents to send their children to the school of their choice. *Wisconsin v. Yoder* (1972) further clarified this right to choose when the Court held that "the primary role of the parents in the upbringing of their children is now established beyond debate as an enduring American tradition." In *People v. Levisen*, the Illinois Supreme Court sustained the right of parents to educate their children at home. The court stated that the law mandated that "children shall be educated; not that they shall be educated in a particular manner or place." The court held that the law should only punish the parent "who fails or refuses to properly educate his child." As a result of these cases, parents have the opportunity to influence and guide the education of their children.

Applications

Historically, the alternatives to public education have been parochial schools, private academies, and hired tutors. Since the 1960's, other alternatives to public education have been found in the establishment of schools for students with disabilities, schools for delinquents, schools for the gifted, schools for pregnant girls, and schools for students who wish to pursue the performing arts. A variety of independent schools (such as Marva Collins West Side Preparatory School in Chicago) have also been established. Many alternative schools have been criticized because of a lack of quantifiable data to substantiate and support their claims regarding student progress. Yet the pattern of growth in alternative education has continued, and new alternatives have developed in response to the criticisms of public schools. Alternative schools provide learning opportunities and experiences that are not available in the average public school. They tend to allow greater individualization, more independent study, and freedom from external control. Some research suggests that the most effective alternative to traditional schooling can be found in home schooling and free school programs.

Home schooling, simply stated, is the act of providing educational instruction to children in a home setting. Parents may choose home schooling for a number of reasons. The reason most often cited is that home schooling allows parents to ensure that children will receive an education that is consonant with the family's religious beliefs; however, parents also seek this alternative form of education for philosophical, pedagogical, political, psychological, social, moral, and academic reasons. Some parents choose home schooling as a short-term solution to a temporary problem.

A 1981 study profiled parents who chose to educate their children at home as typical professional or semiskilled workers who earned $15,000 to $20,000 annually. They lived in small towns and had an average family size of four (that is, they had two children). The mother usually provided the instruction for the children. In Cheryl Gorder's book *Home Schools: An Alternative* (1987), she describes home schooling families as "politically conservative but individualistic law-abiding church-goers with one to three years of college education."

In *Family Matters* (1992), David Guterson argues that home schooling allows instructors to express "neglected truths" and that it reaffirms the bond between parents and children. He also provides an awareness of the academic success of home-schooled children regardless of their parents' educational background. Home schooling is characterized by a wide variety of contexts and styles: How home schooling is approached depends on the parents and their reasons for selecting this type of alternative education. David Colfax and Micki Colfax, in *Homeschooling for Excellence* (1987), suggest four areas of "governance" allowed by the home schooling process: It allows control over content, methods, timing, and personnel; it is more efficient than most forms of formal education; it encourages autonomy; and it promotes creativity.

The Colfaxes also offer a number of suggestions to parents considering home schooling. These include carefully designing the curriculum (beginning with the basics) and selecting instructional materials (either homemade or commercially purchased), analyzing the entrance requirements of the schools in which children will continue their education, and devoting specific space in the home for the schooling process. As these suggestions indicate, successful home schooling requires a significant investment of parental time and energy; the process cannot be undertaken lightly.

As previously noted, critics of home schooling (and other forms of alternative education) have argued that they may not follow curricular practices that have proved effective across a large spectrum of students. These schools also cannot offer multifaceted programs because of funding limitations. The teachers are often parents who have no formal training as educators. Moreover, students have fewer opportunities to explore values different from their own, and their school experiences therefore often inhibit cultural diversity.

Free school programs represent another major alternative to traditional schooling. Allen Graubard, in *Free the Children* (1972), states that free schools are designed to foster noncompetitive, nonauthoritarian attitudes in pupils. These schools are often antibureaucratic, using "open classrooms" and emphasizing individualized instruction. The curriculum in the free school is designed to fit the child. Free schools typically try to develop political awareness, sensitivity to the feelings of others, and antiracist sentiments. Although the concept of the free school dates from the mid-twentieth century (Summerhill, in England, was one pioneering institution), the American movement came into its own in the mid-1960's.

The free school movement represents an effort to free schools from bureaucratic constraints by establishing a network of schools outside the public school system. Such schools are free from the dictates of state-imposed regulations; free from rules about appropriate credentials for teachers, lesson plans, and subject requirements; and free of traditional detailed behavioral controls over student conduct. Decisions about curriculum, class attendance, and even grading practices are made by students as well as teachers, and by parents as well as administrators.

In most free schools the teacher, as Herbert Kohl suggested in *The Open Classroom* (1969), is asked to become a "human being" and show his or her emotions. Teachers are often expected to reveal something of their personal lives, and they must not cut themselves off from students by the use of titles or by hiding behind a mask of professional anonymity. In many free schools teachers are called by their first names, and they form personal relationships with students outside school. There is a quest for a genuine relationship based on the "natural authority of adults over children." Children are often free to choose whether to attend class and are permitted substantial freedom within the classroom (to move around or to leave the room, for example). In sum, free schools attempt to redefine the nature of schoolwork and its evaluation by teachers. Evaluation is for the purpose of providing the child with "feedback" on his or her progress.

Context

Historically, parents throughout the world have made the choice as to how to equip their children with necessary survival skills. This pattern of informal education began in preliterate societies and extended into ancient Greek society. For many centuries afterward, only a tiny minority of people received a formal education. Whether someone received an education was largely a matter of wealth; schooling was reserved for the wealthy and their offspring.

Before the nineteenth century, American education followed that exclusionary model, but as that century progressed, the call for widespread public education grew. Massachusetts was the first state to enact a compulsory school attendance law. Reformers in the "common school" reform movement such as Horace Mann were instrumental in this shift. In the early nineteenth century there was a class-based division between the academies for children of the well-to-do and the elementary (common) and high schools for poor children. Schooling was intended to help inculcate in all children a belief in the value of capitalism, Protestantism, and republicanism.

A second round of compulsory school legislation occurred after the Civil War; the earlier common school movement was replaced by the bureaucratic school movement. Compulsory attendance laws became more widespread; they were established partly to protect young children from exploitive labor in factories. Laws were enacted that mandated the correct way for children to be educated; there were laws that prohibited home schooling. It was in the late nineteenth century that provisions began to be made for educating children deemed "incorrigible" or unmanageable in normal classroom situations. It was also at this time that the system of Catholic parochial schools was created.

By the late twentieth century, a number of problems with American public education had become evident. Institutionalized educational practices were questioned, and alternatives to public education began to be viewed as viable choices. The role of parental responsibility and parental choice in response to this situation has been reiterated as a part of the dual responsibility of the state and parents to educate children.

Bibliography

Colfax, David, and Micki Colfax. *Homeschooling for Excellence.* Philo, Calif.: Mountain House Press, 1987. This book is for parents interested in pursuing home schooling. The Colfaxes successfully taught their children at home, then sent them to prestigious universities for their continued education.

Gorder, Cheryl. *Home Schools: An Alternative.* Columbus, Ohio: Blue Bird, 1987. This resource book is a helpful manual, providing guidance and aiding in decision making for the home schooler. The book is filled with supporting statistics and examples.

Graubard, Allen. *Free the Children.* New York: Pantheon Books, 1972. This essay provides the lay reader with a practical description of the free school program.

Guterson, David. *Family Matters.* New York: Harcourt Brace Jovanovich, 1992. *Family Matters*, written by a teacher and father, presents a thoughtful and clearly articulated discussion of home schooling issues and practices in the early 1990's.

Kohl, Herbert. *The Open Classroom.* New York: New York Review Books, 1969. Kohl provides a chronology of the free school movement and offers a model for those interested in free schools. The work is representative of an experimental approach to education.

Reutter, E. Edmund, Jr., and Robert R. Hamilton. *The Law of Public Education.* Mineola, N.Y.: Foundation Press, 1976. Provides basic knowledge of the law directly affecting public education in the United States. The ninety-four principal cases included provide readers with an opportunity to examine the reasoning of the courts in deciding educational issues.

JoAnn W. Haysbert

Cross-References

ANNIHILATION OR EXPULSION OF RACIAL OR ETHNIC GROUPS

Type of sociology: Racial and ethnic relations
Field of study: Patterns and consequences of contact

Annihilation and expulsion are two of six basic patterns of intergroup relations; the others are assimilation, pluralism, legal protection of minorities, and subjugation of one group by another. Annihilation and expulsion have been studied primarily since the 1960's, and scholars continue to debate how to define the concepts as well as how to understand them.

Principal terms

DOMINANT GROUP: the group that is at the top of a society's racial or ethnic hierarchy

ETHNIC GROUP: a group distinguished principally by its distinctive cultural heritage

EXCHANGE OF POPULATIONS: mutual expulsion of populations, such that two ethnic minorities are compelled to exchange countries

EXPELLEES: persons forced to flee their country because of the ethnic group to which they belong

HOLOCAUST: the attempt of Nazi Germany, during World War II (1939-1945), to exterminate the Jews of Europe

MINORITY GROUP: any group that receives fewer of society's rewards because of its physical or cultural characteristics; it need not be a numerical minority

PLURAL SOCIETY: a society rigidly divided along ethnic lines

REFUGEES: persons forced to flee their country for any reason, be it ethnic or ideological

Overview

Annihilation of racial or ethnic groups is also called genocide (although other types of mass killing are sometimes included under that term); the expulsion of racial or ethnic groups is also called population transfer. Although these two phenomena are distinct, one can fade into the other. A government determined to expel a particular ethnic group at any cost may resort to genocide if expulsion becomes impractical, and the process of ethnic expulsion can lead to massive deaths from heat, cold, or hunger when it is carried out too abruptly.

Expulsion of an ethnic minority can assume three variants. One is the unilateral expulsion of an ethnic minority group across an international frontier. Classic examples are the expulsion of ethnic Finns from the part of Karelia annexed by the Soviet Union after the 1939-1940 Russo-Finnish War and the forcible transfer of ethnic Germans from Poland and Czechoslovakia after World War II. Yet another example is dictator Idi Amin's peremptory ouster of all individuals of South Asian descent from Uganda in August, 1972.

In another variant, called the exchange of populations, two states agree to accept the minorities expelled by the other. The classic example is the expulsion of ethnic Greeks from Turkey and of ethnic Turks from Greece following the Greco-Turkish War of 1922-1923. When British India was partitioned in 1947, violence forced many Muslims to flee what became India and many Hindus to flee what became Pakistan. This process, too, could be called exchange of populations (although many Muslims remained in the new Republic of India).

In still another variant of ethnic expulsion, a government forcibly uproots a minority ethnic group and resettles it within the same state, but far from the group's homeland. Examples from American history are the deportation of the Five Civilized Tribes from Georgia to what is now Oklahoma in the 1830's and the rounding up of Japanese Americans of the Pacific Coast states into internment camps during World War II. Under Joseph Stalin, dictator of the Soviet Union between 1929 and 1953, many Estonians, Letts, and Lithuanians, from the Baltic states acquired by Stalin in 1940, were deported eastward to Siberia. During the German invasion of the Soviet Union (1941-1945), the Volga Germans, the Chechens, the Kalmyks, and the Crimean Tatars were also deported eastward; because so many of these deportees died, this particular deportation is sometimes seen as an example of genocide.

During World War II, nearly six million Jews (German, Russian, Polish, Hungarian, Dutch, and French) were murdered by the Nazi regime. This mass extermination, called the Holocaust, differed from other acts labeled genocide: It aimed not merely to ethnically purify a single nation-state (as did the Turkish killings of Armenians in 1915-1923) but to eliminate an entire people, wherever in the world they lived. Reputable scholars agree that Nazi Germany was trying to exterminate all the Jews. The Nazis also targeted other groups for destruction; among them were the Gypsies.

Yet the lists of cases of genocide compiled by various social scientists do not always agree with one another. It is difficult both to define genocide and to determine when it has occurred. The massive death toll among the Armenians of Turkey between 1915 and 1923, which reduced their numbers from a million to a little less than fifty thousand, is regarded as genocide by Armenians throughout the world and by many American social scientists (including sociologists Leo Kuper and Helen Fein and political scientist Robert Melson), but not (at least as of the early 1990's) by the Turkish government. Kuper also regards as genocide the bloody repression in Bangladesh during that country's 1971 struggle for freedom from Pakistan and the mutual killings of Hutus and Tutsis in Rwanda and Burundi in the early 1970's; Melson, however, sees both events as examples of massacre rather than genocide. The famine that struck the Ukraine during the agricultural collectivization of 1932-1933 is seen as anti-Ukrainian genocide by some Western experts (including both Kuper and Melson and historian James Mace); none of the governments of the pre-1985 Soviet Union saw it that way. Between 1975 and 1979, the Khmer Rouge of Cambodia slaughtered many of their fellow Cambodians. Since the basis for killing was ideological rather than ethnic, some scholars do not see this atrocity as genocide (although both Kuper and Melson do).

Many scholars regard as genocide only those mass killings undertaken by governments; many also argue that the intention to exterminate a group must exist. Such a definition would exclude many cases of the decimation of aboriginal peoples in North America; here, excess deaths often resulted from exposure to European diseases or from the violent acts of individual European settlers; governments did not always intend to exterminate the native peoples. All scholars agree that ethnocide—the deliberate destruction of aboriginal culture—was practiced. Melson carefully distinguishes between killings of members of a group with intent to intimidate and killings with intent to exterminate the group; the former, he argues, is not genocide. Scholars also argue about how innocent an ethnic group must be of secessionist aims or violent rebellious activity if it is to be seen as a victim of genocide rather than of arguably justifiable repression. Finally, some scholars, such as Judaic studies professor Steven Katz, insist that only the Holocaust deserves the label of genocide.

It is also sometimes difficult to determine if a dominant group is expelling an ethnic minority. After the Arab-Israeli War of 1948-1949, many Arabs fled Israel, and many Jews emigrated from the Arab states to Israel. Israel and the Arab states each accused the other of ethnic expulsion. Another ambiguous case is the exodus of the ethnic Chinese boat people from Vietnam in 1979. Although the Vietnamese government outlawed their livelihood as traders, it never explicitly ordered them to leave the country. Hence, some foreign scholars deny that ethnic expulsion occurred.

The causes of genocide are disputed. Kuper, who has studied ethnicity in Africa, sees the plural society, rigidly divided along ethnic lines, as a seedbed of genocide; it is difficult, however, to fit the German case into this theoretical framework. Sociologists of ethnicity Pierre Van den Berghe and Walter Zenner see so-called middleman (trader) minorities as especially likely victims of genocide; Kuper, seeing no utility in the middleman minority concept, disagrees. Political scientist Robert Melson sees war and revolution as necessary preconditions for genocide. Political sociologist Irving Horowitz sees totalitarian regimes as the most likely to commit genocide; such a view, however, ignores all centuries prior to the twentieth.

Applications

With the collapse of Communism in eastern Europe in 1989-1991, ethnic expulsion and genocide, believed by some in the early 1980's to be a thing of the past, seemed to be returning. Toward the end of 1989, Bulgaria tried to expel to Turkey, or to compel to Slavicize their names, all of Bulgaria's ethnic Turks. With the collapse of Yugoslavia in 1991-1992, Serbs and Croats each tried to expel the other group from territory that they claimed, and both tried to expel Bosnian Muslims from Bosnian towns and villages. These actions became so vicious that journalists and opinion leaders in the United States raised the cry of genocide.

Many of the governments that carry out either genocide or ethnic expulsions are dictatorships. Such actions are often carried out either during a war or in the immediate aftermath of a war. Although a United Nations declaration against genocide was drawn up in 1948, the United Nations can do nothing effective to prevent genocide unless warring ethnic groups truly want peace or unless a repressive regime truly values the good opinion of the rest of the world.

If a country is both democratic and at peace, some form of restitution for past acts of genocide or ethnic expulsion is possible although by no means inevitable. The government of the Federal Republic of Germany, created in 1949, decided to offer reparations payments to surviving Jewish victims of Nazism, wherever they happened to live; these payments, however, have been extremely modest. In the late 1980's, the United States Congress finally offered restitution payments to the survivors of the forced internment of Japanese Americans during World War II. Once a genocidal regime is gone, those who helped perpetrate genocide can be punished; in the early 1960's, Israel kidnapped, tried, and executed Nazi bureaucrat Adolf Eichmann.

Even if a country in which genocide or ethnic expulsion seems likely to occur is not completely democratic, worldwide publicity can sometimes deter a government from carrying out either of these two violations of human rights, especially if the government depends heavily on the outside world for economic aid or business investment. By the early 1990's, a notable development in telecommunication—the creation of the Cable News Network (CNN) by American entrepreneur Ted Turner—made the searchlight of such publicity brighter and more powerful than in previous eras. Thus, in the aftermath of the Soviet crackdown of January, 1991, in Vilnius, Lithuania, in which thirteen people were killed, pressure from American and Western European governments (which involved the threat to reduce economic aid) persuaded Soviet leader Mikhail Gorbachev to ease up on the repression.

Human rights groups and other voluntary nongovernmental organizations can conduct letter-writing campaigns either to persuade repressive regimes to change their policies or to persuade the United States government or other democratic governments to exert pressure on such regimes. In 1985, a pioneer in the sociology of genocide, Leo Kuper, helped to found a nongovernmental organization dedicated to the prevention of genocide: the International Alert Against Genocide and Mass Killing. In the late 1980's, the organization concerned itself with violations of human rights in Uganda, Sri Lanka, and Burundi; its precise contribution to the eventual easing of repression in these countries is difficult to measure. A notable victory for the nongovernmental approach was the success, in the early 1980's, of the efforts of American chapters of the Baha'i faith to persuade the Iranian government to stop persecuting their Iranian coreligionists.

Some efforts to prevent genocide are directed at individuals rather than at governments. The American psychiatrist Vamik Volkan, born of Turkish stock on the ethnically divided island of Cyprus, has tried to devise a cure for the kind of hatred that leads to genocide and ethnic expulsion. Volkan was aware, from the history of his native Cyprus, how acts of genocide or ethnic expulsion could instill in the victims an unquenchable thirst for revenge. Such a desire for revenge can be seen in the behavior of Latvians and Estonians, who, having achieved freedom in 1991, imposed severe restrictions on the ethnic Russians living in their midst. In 1993, aided by foundation grant money, Volkan held, in a remote Estonian town, a four-day interethnic group therapy session for members of the Latvian, Lithuanian, Estonian, and Russian elites. He hoped that the ventilation of painful, repressed memories would promote interethnic reconciliation.

Another means of combatting in individuals the prejudice that leads to genocide is to introduce genocide education programs in high schools and colleges. In the 1980's, efforts to introduce such curricula in the schools were made in several states; in California and New York, such efforts were deemed successful. The state boards of education, in attempting to draw up such curricula, sought the advice of sociologists and historians who had studied genocide, such as Leo Kuper and Helen Fein. Efforts to have the schools teach about genocide, however, have run into the same obstacle that bedevils sociologists who study genocide: the difficulty of deciding which particular atrocity deserves the label genocide. In shaping the curricula, and in deciding which events to include as examples of genocide, the activities of ethnic pressure groups and the desire of education bureaucrats to avoid offending anyone seem to have had as much influence as the advice of scholars.

Context

The first to use the term genocide, and to try to define it, was the American legal scholar (himself a European Jewish refugee) Raphael Lemkin. In *Axis Rule in Occupied Europe* (1944), Lemkin described policies carried out by Nazi Germany in German-occupied Europe during World War II. At the end of the war, Allied soldiers discovered the extermination camps in which Germans had killed Jews solely for the crime of being Jewish. In 1948, a United Nations Convention on Genocide was adopted; the United States did not become a signatory to this convention, however, until November, 1988.

Although Americans first became aware of the Holocaust in 1945, serious research by sociologists on the subject of genocide did not begin until the 1970's; before that decade, the topic was largely left to historians, who concentrated their attention on the Holocaust (the first full-scale history of the Holocaust, by political scientist Raul Hilberg, did not appear until 1961). To many sociologists of the immediate post-World War II period, genocide must have seemed too emotionally charged an issue for objective social research; it may also have appeared to be an inexplicable aberration, characteristic of a thoroughly defeated European tyranny (Nazi Germany), rather than a normal and recurrent social phenomenon.

One thing that reawoke interest in genocide among sociologists was the recurrent ethnic conflicts in post-World War II Africa and Asia, which seemed to worsen as the decolonization process accelerated in the 1960's. Another stimulus to research on genocide, particularly for younger sociologists, was the social and political turbulence in the United States in the 1960's and early 1970's, which shattered the illusion that violence and repression were faraway aberrations. Interest in the themes of ethnic conflict and the role of violence in politics was aroused by the Civil Rights movement, the urban riots, and the war in Vietnam. Among young Jews, the Arab-Israeli War of 1967 awoke both a new sense of ethnic pride and a new interest in the history of the Holocaust.

In 1976, in *Genocide: State Power and Mass Murder*, Irving Horowitz scolded his fellow sociologists for neglecting the study of genocide. In the 1970's and the 1980's, this challenge was answered. In *Accounting for Genocide* (1979), sociologist Helen Fein, who would later become chair of the Institute for the Study of Genocide (in New York City), tried to explain variations in the percentage of Jews killed among the different countries of German-occupied Europe during World War II. Illuminating comparisons between the Holocaust of 1939-1945 and the massacre of Armenians in Turkey in 1915-1923 were pointed out by Fein herself, in the 1979 book and in her later writings; by the Armenian American sociologist Vahakn N. Dadrian; and by Robert Melson, an American political scientist of Jewish refugee origin. Leo Kuper, in his 1981 work *Genocide: Its Political Use in the Twentieth Century*, compared the Armenian and German cases not only with each other but also with post-World War II atrocities in Africa and Asia. Other students of genocide included sociologists Pierre Van den Berghe and Kurt Jonassohn and political scientist Barbara Harff. The participation of Jewish sociologists in the comparative study of genocide blunted the charge, made by adherents of the particularist approach to the Holocaust, that the comparative, or universalist, perspective minimized the horrors of Nazism.

The study of ethnic expulsion per se has not attracted much attention from sociologists, except where a particular instance is seen as genocidal. The phenomenon of refugee flight (both ethnic and ideological) has been studied by demographer Michael S. Teitelbaum, historian Michael Marrus, and political scientist Aristide Zolberg.

Bibliography

Charny, Israel W. , ed. *Genocide: A Critical Bibliographic Review.* Vol. 2. New York: Facts on File, 1988-1991. The editor is a psychologist; contributors include a professor of law, two sociologists, three political scientists, two historians, and a professor of education. The Holocaust and the Armenian genocide receive the most attention. Especially interesting are two essays on genocide education and one on humanitarian intervention. Annotated bibliography after each essay; index.

Fein, Helen. "Genocide: A Sociological Perspective." *Current Sociology* 38 (Spring, 1990): 1-126. An excellent survey and critique of the growing social science literature on genocide written by one of the pioneers in the sociology of genocide. Includes three tables; references (abbreviated in text; complete in bibliography). For both college undergraduates and graduate students.

_____ , ed. *Genocide Watch.* New Haven, Conn.: Yale University Press, 1992. Includes an introduction by the editor; two insightful essays on theory (by sociologist Kurt Jonassohn and political scientist Barbara Harff); two essays examining, respectively, refugee accounts and the Western press regarding atrocities in Asia and Africa; and several essays (including one by Leo Kuper) on prevention. Tables; footnotes.

Horowitz, Irving L. *Genocide: State Power and Mass Murder.* New Brunswick, N.J.: Transaction Books, 1976. In this slim (60 pages of text) but tightly reasoned essay, a sociologist evaluates various governments of the twentieth century according to their willingness to commit mass killing. Little attention is paid to interethnic conflict as a cause of genocide. References (abbreviated in text; complete in bibliography) and an index of names.

Kuper, Leo. *Genocide: Its Political Use in the Twentieth Century.* New Haven, Conn.: Yale University Press, 1981. Kuper provides new perspectives not only on the Holocaust and the Armenian genocide but also on a variety of post-World War II interethnic conflicts and atrocities unknown to the average American. The sheer number of examples, however, can overwhelm the reader. Offers penetrating insights into the genocidal mentality. Footnotes; appendices; bibliography; index.

Marrus, Michael Robert. *The Unwanted: European Refugees in the Twentieth Century.* New York: Oxford University Press, 1985. A survey of refugee movements from 1880 to 1970. Devotes much attention to the Jews' flight from Nazism; also provides information on the victimization of non-Jews by frontier shifts and on the flight of Europeans from decolonizing African countries. Maps; endnotes; index. For the general reader.

Melson, Robert. *Revolution and Genocide: On the Origins of the Armenian Genocide and the Holocaust.* Chicago: University of Chicago Press, 1992. Melson's point-by-point, analytical comparison of the two genocides is illuminating; other atrocities are treated in passing. The discussion of universalist versus particularist perspectives on the Holocaust is sensitive and fair. The well-written introductory and concluding chapters, and four tables, make the book especially easy to follow. Richly informative endnotes; bibliography; index.

Teitelbaum, Michael S. "Forced Migration: The Tragedy of Mass Expulsions." In *Clamor at the Gates: The New American Immigration,* edited by Nathan Glazer. San Francisco: Institute of Contemporary Studies Press, 1985. A demographer treats three mass expulsions of the period 1970 to 1985: the Ugandan, the Vietnamese, and the Cuban. Teitelbaum, who ascribes the first two cases to government hostility toward ethnic minorities, discusses ways the international community could deter regimes from practicing mass expulsion. Notes and contributor information at end of book.

Wallimann, Isidor, and Michael N. Dobkowski, eds. *Genocide and the Modern Age: Etiology and Case Studies of Mass Death.* New York: Greenwood Press, 1987. Thirteen original essays. Most deal with the Holocaust and the question of its uniqueness; one discusses the Armenian genocide, and another treats the decimation of the Australian aborigines. Walter P. Zenner's comparative essay on middleman minorities and genocide is especially interesting. Annotated bibliography; index.

Zolberg, Aristide, et al. *Escape from Violence: Conflict and the Refugee Crisis in the Developing World.* New York: Oxford University Press, 1989. A survey of refugee flows (ethnically and ideologically motivated) in Africa, South Asia, East Asia, and Latin America. The expulsion of Uganda's Asians and the flight of Vietnam's ethnic

Chinese are treated in detail; the authors do not regard the latter event as ethnic expulsion. Tables; informative endnotes; index.

Paul D. Mageli

Cross-References

Anti-Semitism, 114; Conquest and Annexation of Racial or Ethnic Groups, 353; Ethnic Enclaves, 682; Immigration and Emigration, 921; Internal Colonialism, 1015; "Middleman" Minorities, 1200; Minority and Majority Groups, 1219; Racial and Ethnic Stratification, 1579; Racism as an Ideology, 1586.

ANOMIE AND DEVIANCE

Type of sociology: Deviance and social control
Fields of study: Social implications of deviance; Theories of deviance

Robert K. Merton's theory of anomie is a popular and influential sociological perspective on the origins of deviance. Merton's theory helps explain how a society's social structures create and influence the forms of deviant behavior in social groups.

Principal terms
ANOMIE: a state of normlessness in society stemming from social change and a society's inability to control the behavior of its individual members
CULTURAL UNIVERSALS: beliefs, values, and norms held in common by all members of a society
NORMATIVE SYSTEMS: a society's collection of norms
NORMS: rules generated by society that specify acceptable and unacceptable behavior
SOCIAL STRUCTURE: relatively stable patterns of social relationships organized around statuses and roles
SOCIALIZATION: process through which individuals learn to become members of a social group by assimilating the group's norms, values, and beliefs

Overview

In *Social Theory and Social Structure* (1949), sociologist Robert K. Merton examines the role that social structures play in promoting deviant behavior. Merton criticizes traditional psychological and sociological theories that attribute deviance to conflicts between humankind's biological drives and the need for social order, arguing instead that variations in the amounts of deviance experienced by human societies are a consequence of differences in social structures.

Merton argues that two essential components of all social structural systems are culturally defined goals that specify objectives to which individuals should aspire and culturally defined means that regulate how those goals are to be attained. The culturally defined means of attaining goals reflect the values of a given society. Consequently, culturally prescribed means of attaining goals are not always technically efficient. For example, while control of population growth might be efficiently achieved by legally limiting family size, public sentiment and the value structure of a given group might prohibit such action. Additionally, a society may place differential emphasis on the goals for which its members should strive and the means by which they achieve them.

Culturally prescribed goals and culturally prescribed means of attaining goals are part of a society's normative system. Norms are rules, sometimes codified as laws, that regulate conduct. Anomie, or normlessness, occurs when the norms governing a particular aspect of behavior become weak and fail to regulate human conduct. A state of anomie reduces social order and increases opportunities for the occurrence of previously prohibited behavior. Merton believes that deviance is likely to occur when a society places great emphasis on its culturally defined goals and places less emphasis on (and provides unequal access to) the culturally defined means to achieve them.

Merton illustrates his theory of anomie by applying it to American society. Merton argues that contemporary American society places great emphasis on the acquisition of material wealth (a culturally prescribed success goal). Merton claims, however, that the culturally prescribed means of attaining wealth are not as strongly emphasized and are not equally available to all members of society. Merton believes that individuals respond in one of five ways to the resulting state of anomie: conformity, innovation, ritualism, retreatism, and rebellion.

Individuals are most likely to conform when a society places equal emphasis on its culturally prescribed goals and means and provides all members equal access to the legal means of achieving success goals. For example, if material wealth is a culturally prescribed goal, conformity occurs when legitimate avenues for achieving wealth are emphasized and all members of the group have equal opportunities to receive an education, to work, or to own a business, and so on. Consequently, Merton argues, conformity is most common in the middle and upper classes of American society, where individuals have realistic opportunities to achieve wealth by conventional means.

Innovation involves the use of illegitimate means (crime) to achieve society's success goals. Innovation is most likely to occur when individuals have internalized the success goals of society but are denied equal access to the institutionalized means of achieving them because of their position in the class structure. Innovation, Merton holds, is most common in the American lower class, because members of the lower class have limited opportunities to achieve wealth by conventional means and have not completely assimilated society's value of conformity to the law.

Ritualists conform to social dictates but have accepted the belief they will never achieve society's success goals. Ritualists reduce the status anxiety produced by the competitive nature of modern society by lowering their aspirations and engaging in routinized behavior. Ritualism is most likely to occur in the American lower middle class where conformity is stressed but opportunities to succeed are limited.

Merton views retreatism as the least common mode of adaptation to anomie. Retreatists (such as alcoholics, drug abusers, hermits, and the mentally ill) have assimilated the success goals of society and the socially prescribed means of attaining them but have been unable to achieve success. Because of their failure to succeed, retreatists eventually withdraw from society. Rebels seek to create a new social structure. They regard the current normative system as arbitrary and seek to establish a new system of norms. Merton believes that rebellion is likely to occur when individuals believe the current social structure is a barrier to positive social change and when allegiance to the current social order is transferred to groups that possess "new myths." These new myths are ideologies that blame the present social structure for societal ills and propose alternative social orders that offer hope of constructive change.

Merton believes that the family plays a critical role in the creation of deviance. Merton notes that the family, through socialization, instills in children the value system of society. Additionally, parents frequently project their own ambitions onto their children. The pressure exerted on children by the family and the limited opportunities for reaching goals, create the foundation for deviance.

While Merton's theory of anomie has been influential, it has not been without its critics. Some sociologists question Merton's claim that all members of society share the same success goals (cultural universality). For example, many Americans who are capable of material success place a higher value on helping others and enter occupations that are less well paid, becoming religious leaders, social workers, or teachers, for example.

Other critics note that Merton's theory does not address the problem of white-collar crime. Merton implies that crime is primarily located in the lower classes, yet white-collar criminals cost American taxpayers billions of dollars each year. Similarly, Merton's theory is unable to explain violent crime, except in cases in which violence is used as a means to achieve financial gain. Other critics have noted that a substantial amount of juvenile delinquency involves nonutilitarian acts (petty vandalism, for example) that have no financial motivation. Further, some types of retreatism may best be explained by genetic factors that predispose individuals to engage in certain behaviors.

Finally, Merton's theory is unable to predict precisely which individuals are likely to engage in deviant behavior. Many individuals who have internalized the success goal of wealth and who are denied equal access to the legitimate means of achieving wealth conform. Some individuals who have internalized the success goal of wealth and who have access to the legitimate means of achieving wealth break the law anyway. Because it is unable to differentiate satisfactorily between potential deviants and potential conformists, Merton's theory has limited predictive and explanatory value.

Applications

Richard A. Cloward and Lloyd E. Ohlin modified Merton's theory of anomie and used it to explain the formation of delinquent gangs. Cloward and Ohlin argue that gangs form when a disjunction exists between culturally based aspirations for achievement (wealth) and the availability of legitimate means to realize them. Cloward and Ohlin claim that cultural and structural barriers deny some individuals the opportunity to achieve wealth by conventional means. Gangs subsequently form as a mode of adaptation to anomie. Unlike Merton, Cloward and Ohlin argue that innovation is likely to occur only when individuals have access to illegitimate opportunities to achieve financial gain. Specifically, they argue that opportunities must exist to learn, practice, and perform acts of innovation before innovation can occur.

Cloward and Ohlin distinguish among three types of delinquent gangs: criminal, conflict, and retreatist. Criminal gangs form when a criminal subculture exists that provides criminal role models and role preparation by age-level integration. Cloward and Ohlin argue that successful criminal activity involves learned skills that are passed on from one generation to the next. In addition, opportunities must exist for the inexperienced innovator to learn these skills by exposure to criminal role models and by practical application. Criminal gangs indoctrinate younger members into the group by providing them with opportunities to learn criminal skills. They exert control over their members and actively discourage nonutilitarian acts of violence. Like other economic enterprises, gangs seek to maintain social order and stability internally and within the community in which they operate. Social disorganization and nonconforming members are bad for business, and they represent potential threats to the normal operations of the gang. Consequently, gangs pressure members to conform to the norms of the gang and punish divergent behavior.

Conflict gangs occur when individuals have limited access to conventional and unconventional (criminal) opportunities to achieve wealth, no access to criminal role models, and no opportunity for age-level integration into criminal subcultures. In the absence of social control exerted by the larger community and by criminal subcultures, and because of limited opportunities to achieve culturally based success goals, individuals engage in violence as a means of status attainment. Cloward and Ohlin believe that conflict gangs disappear when opportunities for achieving wealth by conventional or unconventional means become available to their members.

Retreatist gangs use drugs as a way of escaping the realities of everyday life. Retreatist gangs emerge when individuals have internalized both the success goals of society and societal prohibitions against using illegal means to achieve them or when individuals have attempted to achieve success but have failed. In a sense, retreatist gangs act as a psychological defense mechanism to reduce status anxiety and guilt resulting from feelings of personal failure.

In another study of gangs, Martin Sanchez Jankowski found that urban street gangs exhibit an "entrepreneurial spirit" similar to that found in the American business community. Jankowski notes that gang members are competitive, believe in their ability to achieve success through personal effort, and possess a desire to accumulate material wealth to improve the quality of their daily lives. Additionally, gang members seek social status and share material possessions to gain prestige and power within the group. Gang members also develop extensive plans for the future and are willing to take calculated risks to achieve a desired end.

Jankowski argues that the entrepreneurial spirit of gangs stems from four primary sources. First, Jankowski believes gang members are individualists who distrust others and believe that "only the strongest survive." The individualism of gang members promotes competitiveness and risk-taking behavior that form the basis of the entrepreneurial spirit. Second, Jankowski notes there is a disjunction between the lifestyle of mainstream American culture and the resources available to gang members in low-income neighborhoods to achieve a similar lifestyle. Gang members believe material goods are a key to success and happiness, yet have limited legitimate means of earning money. The desire for money encourages creativity, strategic planning, and calculated risk-taking to achieve financial gain.

Third, gang members believe that they are "one good idea" away from success. For the gang member, lack of a good idea, not individual liabilities and deficiencies, accounts for failure. This attitude promotes strategic planning and the cultivation of personal relationships. As in any business enterprise, contacts enable the gang member to put his or her plan into action by providing logistic and financial support.

Finally, Jankowski argues, the entrepreneurial spirit of the gang stems from its members' desire to avoid failure and poverty. Gang members typically believe that their parents have resigned themselves to a life of economic deprivation. Gang members reject these self-defeating attitudes and seek to maintain a belief that success is possible through individual effort and achievement.

In general, Jankowski's study supports many of Merton's claims concerning American culture. Jankowski suggests that gang members have assimilated the success goal of wealth yet are denied access to the legitimate means of achieving wealth. Gang members innovate to achieve goals unattainable through conventional means. Despite differences in the techniques used to realize their ends, gangs and conventional businesses share a similar set of core values. Like business organizations, gangs believe competition leads to economic success, and they mobilize resources to attain these ends. Gangs also act as a psychological buffer, protecting individual self-esteem and maintaining goal aspirations in the face of adversity.

Context

Merton's theory of anomie is an outgrowth of functionalism, a dominant theoretical perspective in modern sociology. Functionalism can be traced to the writings of Auguste Comte, Herbert Spencer, and Émile Durkheim and is a reaction to the social turmoil of late eighteenth century Europe.

The French Revolution and the Industrial Revolution produced massive social change and instability in Western Europe. Comte, a French intellectual, sought to examine the question of social order and identify the underpinnings of social organization through scientific investigation. Comte viewed society as a collective organism whose parts work toward common ends through action and reaction among its constituent parts and its environment. Comte believed that social progress consists of increased specialization that promotes harmony of structure and function and greater integration in society. Increased specialization, however, can result in social disorganization if society's sense of unity and identity is lost. Consequently, Comte believed that government must regulate specialization to promote social unity.

Herbert Spencer, the English social philosopher, argued that social systems become more differentiated as they increase in size. Spencer believed that the increasing complexity of modern society produces mutual interdependence and social integration. More important, Spencer noted that societies must fulfill certain needs (such as the production and distribution of goods and services and the maintenance of social control) if they are to survive. Spencer believed that the institutions that make up society function to fulfill these needs and enable a society to adapt to its environment.

French sociologist Émile Durkheim focused on the problem of how societies create and sustain social integration. Durkheim believed that crime is beneficial to society because punishing rule breakers reinforces a society's normative system and thus reaffirms group identity. According to Durkheim, norms function to create and maintain social order. A society without a properly functioning normative system runs the risk of social disorganization.

Other theorists have expanded Durkheim's theory. For example, Kai Erikson argues that social groups increase their enforcement of norms when their identity is threatened. Punishing deviants reaffirms a society's values and serves to reinforce group integration and identity. In a similar vein, Philip Jenkins argues that British perceptions of rampant increases in crime are a reaction to social change in British society. Specifically, Jenkins believes that rapid social change in Britain in the 1980's threatened group identity. Subsequent public reaction to perceived social problems served to reaffirm social identity and reinforce order.

Merton's theory of anomie is firmly grounded in the functionalist tradition. For example, he assumes that norms form the basis for social order and examines how disruptions in a society's normative system produce social deviance. Merton locates the origins of deviance in the social structure of society and suggests that it is a poorly functioning normative system, not the individual per se, that creates that foundation for deviant behavior. Deviance occurs because norms fail to regulate behavior and social institutions fail to meet the needs of society and its members.

Bibliography

Cloward, Richard A., and Lloyd E. Ohlin. *Delinquency and Opportunity: A Theory of Delinquent Gangs*. Glencoe, Ill.: Free Press, 1960. Claims that gang formation is a response to anomie. Presents the view that gangs innovate when gang members have the opportunity to learn, practice, and perform criminal acts. Stresses the role of social inequality in creating delinquent subcultures.

Durkheim, Émile. *The Rules of Sociological Method*. Translated by Sarah A. Solovay and John H. Mueller. 8th ed. New York: Free Press, 1938. Outlines Durkheim's views on the science of sociology and his theory that crime serves to reinforce a society's belief system, thereby preserving social order and identity.

Erikson, Kai T. *Wayward Puritans: A Study in the Sociology of Deviance*. New York: John Wiley & Sons, 1966. Uses Durkheim's theory of crime to examine anomie in the seventeenth century Massachusetts Puritan colony. Argues that increased identification and persecution of deviants is related to social stress and perceived threats to group identity.

Jankowski, Martin Sanchez. *Islands in the Street: Gangs and American Urban Society*. Berkeley: University of California Press, 1991. Outlines Jankowski's theory of gang formation. Argues that gangs are economic organizations that innovate to achieve financial gain and that they hold values that are similar to those found in the corporate world.

Jenkins, Philip. *Intimate Enemies: Moral Panics in Contemporary Great Britain*. New York: Aldine de Gruyter, 1992. Argues that British exaggerated beliefs (moral panics) in the existence of rampant crime are a consequence of changes in British society. Suggests that moral panics serve to reintegrate society and promote social organization and identity.

Merton, Robert K. *Social Theory and Social Structure*. Rev. ed. New York: Free Press, 1968. Originally published in 1949 and expanded in 1968, this work contains the original statement of Merton's theory of anomie. Expanded version presents review of relevant writings and research on anomie by others. Extremely readable.

Charles Vincent Smedley

Cross-References

Cultural Norms and Sanctions, 411; Cultural Transmission Theory of Deviance, 424; Deviance: Analysis and Overview, 525; Deviance: Functions and Dysfunctions, 540; Social Stratification: Analysis and Overview, 1839; The Structural-Strain Theory of Deviance, 1990; Values and Value Systems, 2143.

ANTIPOVERTY PROGRAMS

Type of sociology: Social stratification
Field of study: Poverty

Antipoverty programs refer to the cluster of income support programs targeted primarily toward economically disadvantaged individuals and families.

Principal terms

CASH BENEFITS: payments that the recipient can determine how and where to use; AFDC payments are an example

IN-KIND BENEFITS: assistance designated for certain specific uses, such as medical or housing expenses

MEANS-TESTED PROGRAM: a program for which a person's or family's income is assessed in order to determine eligibility

STANDARD OF NEED: the dollar amount that a state determines is essential for a family to maintain a minimum standard of living

VOUCHER BENEFITS: payments designated for a specific purpose that give a recipient choice within that specification; food stamps are an example

Overview

The United States has a variety of income support programs for its economically disadvantaged citizens. Targeted or selective antipoverty programs include Supplemental Security Income (SSI), Aid to Families with Dependent Children (AFDC), food stamps, Supplemental Food Program for Women, Infants, and Children (WIC), school lunches, Low-Income Home Energy Assistance, General Assistance (GA), public and other subsidized housing, and the Earned Income Tax Credit (EITC). Such programs are "means tested," which means that a family's or person's income is assessed to determine eligibility. Other means-tested programs that supplement antipoverty efforts include Head Start (preschool education) and Medicaid (medical assistance).

For specific programs, legislation or regulations determine whether a program uses the official federal poverty income guidelines or uses a modification of the guidelines (for example, 130 percent or 185 percent of the guidelines) as one of several eligibility criteria or for purposes of targeting assistance or services. The official federal poverty income guidelines vary by family size. They are adjusted each year to account for changes in the cost of living. The February, 1992, federal poverty income guidelines for the forty-eight contiguous states were $6,810 for an individual, $9,190 for a family of two, $11,570 for a family of three, and $13,950 for a family of four. Some programs, such as rental assistance, use a geographic area's median income to determine a family's eligibility. Families whose incomes do not exceed 50 percent of the median income for the area are eligible for rental assistance.

Assistance or services come in two basic forms: cash and in-kind. There are advantages and disadvantages associated with each type of social provision. Proponents of cash benefit programs, such as AFDC, GA, and EITC, argue that individual consumers are in the best position to obtain the maximum amount of satisfaction for a given outlay of public funds. This position assumes that the welfare recipient as consumer will make choices just as any other consumer would and will thereby contribute to the common good. In other words, in seeking to maximize their satisfaction in the marketplace, participants in cash-related programs will also enhance the common welfare. Proponents of in-kind benefits, however, place a higher premium on ensuring state control of public spending. For example, medical care and school lunches can be targeted to those specifically in need of these services, thereby ensuring that the legislative and public intentions are fulfilled. A third type of social provision, vouchers, balances the social control and consumer choice functions. The food stamp program uses vouchers. Eligible citizens either receive or, for a nominal fee, buy food stamp coupons with a designated value that may then be used to purchase food at supermarkets.

Other income support programs, such as the social insurance programs, are more broadly based than the means-tested programs are. These universal programs are not ordinarily considered antipoverty programs; nevertheless, over the years they have prevented many people from falling into poverty. Old-Age, Survivors, and Disability Insurance (OASDI), commonly referred to as Social Security, for example, provides many elderly and widowed Americans with a monthly cash income that has kept them from falling below the poverty line during their retirement years. Unemployment Insurance assists those temporarily removed from the labor force. About half of the federal government's social welfare expenditures go into the social insurance programs, while the means-tested programs, including Medicaid, receive 14 percent.

In general, the federal government shares the costs of the means-tested antipoverty programs with states and local governments. The major exception is SSI, the federal program that in 1972 replaced the federal-state programs for the needy aged, blind, and disabled. For other means-tested programs, however, states use federal guidelines to set their own eligibility standards. Since states vary in wealth, per-capita income, and revenue enhancing capabilities, eligibility standards and public assistance payments differ across the country. For example, in 1990, the monthly average AFDC payment per family was $118.35 in Mississippi, $365.85 in North Dakota, $559.19 in Massachusetts, and $619.95 in California. Although education and social insurance payments account for sizable shares of most state expenditures, increased numbers of poor individuals and families, combined with the rising costs of Medicaid payments throughout the 1980's and 1990's, disproportionately added to the fiscal burdens of state and local governments.

Applications

SSI and AFDC are the two major cash assistance programs for the economically disadvantaged; the lesser-known EITC found favor with the Clinton Administration in the early 1990's. Under the SSI program, each eligible aged, blind, or disabled person living in his or her own household and having no other income is provided with a monthly cash payment. The amount established in January, 1993, for example, was $434 ($652 for a couple if both members were eligible). The federal benefit level is reduced by formula if the individual or couple lives in another's household and if there is countable income. Individuals are considered disabled if they are unable to engage in any substantial gainful activity by reason of any medically determinable physical or mental impairment that can be expected to result in death or that has lasted (or can be expected to last) for a continuous period of twelve months. Individuals are considered blind if they have a central visual acuity of 20/200 or less in the better eye with the use of correcting lenses, or if they have tunnel vision of 20 degrees or less. States may supplement federal payments, which are adjusted automatically to reflect Social Security cost-of-living increases. States may not reduce their supplemental payments to offset any increases in the federal amount. In December, 1991, 5.1 million persons received federal SSI payments averaging $321 per month. Applications for SSI payments are taken at the Social Security Administration (SSA) district offices throughout each state. The SSA is part of the U.S. Department of Health and Human Services (DHHS).

The AFDC program authorizes federal matching grants to assist states in providing cash and in-kind services to economically disadvantaged families with dependent children. The federal share of AFDC payments is determined in a way that provides a higher percentage of federal matching to states with lower per-capita incomes and a lower percentage to states with higher per-capita incomes. In addition, the federal government pays a certain percentage of administration-related costs. Federal administration is the responsibility of the Administration for Children and Families in the DHHS. To qualify for grants, states must comply with federal guidelines set forth in Title IV, Part A, of the Social Security Act. The most important guidelines are that anyone wishing to apply will be given an opportunity to do so; assistance will be confined to need; an applicant's income and resources must be considered in determining eligibility and payment levels; the AFDC program must be statewide and either administered by a single state agency or, if locally administered, supervised by a single state agency; and assistance must be provided promptly and an opportunity for a fair hearing must be given to anyone whose application is denied or whose payment is reduced or terminated. States may not exclude eligible individuals from participating in the program on the basis of citizenship or residency requirements. Within these guidelines, states determine eligibility requirements and the amount of assistance to be given.

Each state computes its own need standard—the dollar amount that a state determines is essential to meet a minimum standard of living in that state for a family of a specified size. In computing the need standard, states include allowances for food, clothing, shelter, utilities, and other necessities. Theoretically, a family's need is equal to the difference between the determined need standard for a family of a given size and the actual income and resources available to the family. States, however, are not required to provide the full amount of this difference. They have statutory and administrative ceilings on the amount that may be paid; in most cases, the ceilings result in assistance payments below the need standards.

In fiscal year 1990, 4.0 million families—consisting of 11.6 million recipients, of whom 7.9 million were children—received average monthly AFDC payments of $392 each ($136 per recipient). For families to receive assistance, children must be economically disadvantaged and deprived of parental support or care by reason of death, continued absence from the home, physical or mental incapacity of a parent, or unemployment of a parent who is a principal wage earner. The children must be living in the home of a parent or other relative. Determination of need, income, and resources is a complex matter that entails calculation of the resources of all those living in the same "assistance unit" as the dependent child, with an upper limit of $1,000 or less on the equity value of the resources that an assistance unit may own.

Less widely known than SSI and AFDC is the EITC program, targeted to the nation's nearly 12 million working poor families. They include some 30 million people, nearly three times the AFDC population at any given time. Minimum wage legislation and the EITC are the primary antipoverty efforts for low-wage workers. The minimum wage ($4.25 an hour in 1993) falls short of the amount necessary for self-sufficiency for a full-time worker to support a family. In 1975, Congress enacted the EITC, a special tax credit to supplement the earnings of low-wage workers, and it has enlarged the tax credit several times since. According to political scientists John E. Schwarz and Thomas J. Volgy in *The Forgotten Americans* (1992), in 1990, the EITC granted a 14 percent credit to workers for each dollar of earnings, up to annual earnings of $6,810 for a family, thereby providing a maximum additional supplement of $953 to the family. The credit remained at $953 until the family's annual earnings reached $10,730, after which it declined at a rate of 10 percent for each additional dollar earned. The credit returned to zero when family earnings reached $20,264. The EITC raises some full-time working poor families' annual income above the official poverty line, but evidence by sociologists Susan Meyer and Christopher Jencks in "Poverty and the Distribution of Material Hardship," *Journal of Human Resources* 24 (Winter, 1989), suggests that as many as one-third of families with incomes up to 200 percent of the official poverty line are still unable to afford food, clothing, or medical care at some time during the year. President Bill Clinton called for an expansion of the EITC. Opponents fear that the EITC, like AFDC, may ultimately become part of a mix of benefits that encourages dependency on government beneficence rather than on market forces to enhance labor force participation. Proponents counter that government intervention is appropriate to compensate for the economy's proliferation of low-wage jobs.

Context

For most of their nation's history, Americans responded to people in economic need through relief efforts provided by cities, towns, and counties as well as through private, charitable (often church-related), and philanthropic efforts. During the 1920's, the states increasingly accepted the idea that certain categories of the poor, such as the aged and the blind, could not reasonably be expected to provide for themselves on the same basis as the young and able-bodied; by 1929, nearly half the states had some kind of cash assistance program. The Great Depression of the late 1920's and 1930's resulted in nearly 12 to 14 million unemployed Americans in 1933, and nearly 19 million—almost 16 percent of the population—were on state relief rolls.

In 1933, Congress passed the Federal Emergency Relief Act to help alleviate the burden on the states. The act authorized $500 million in grants to the states for relief purposes. Over the next two years, the federal government channeled $2.5 billion to the state relief administrations. By 1934, twenty-eight states provided old-age assistance and twenty-four provided aid to the blind. The Social Security Act of 1935 established two categorical federal-state grant programs. The first, Old-Age Assistance and Aid to the Blind, was extended in 1950 to include Aid to the Permanently and Totally Disabled, and in 1972, the programs were replaced by the federally administered SSI program. The second categorical federal-state program, AFDC, has undergone many revisions since passage of the Social Security Act of 1935.

In 1962, the Social Security Act was amended to add a social services component to AFDC, but this strategy to make welfare recipients self-sufficient and thereby to reduce the welfare rolls was abandoned in 1967. In that year, Congress, partly because it was unhappy about the results of the Johnson Administration's 1964 War on Poverty efforts, enacted the first federal work program, the Work Incentive (WIN) Program. Congress expanded its definition of the able-bodied poor to include mothers with children six years of age or younger, required their mandatory registration in the WIN program, changed the focus of the program from education and institutional training to employment services and subsidized employment, and provided tax incentives to prospective employers.

The Reagan Administration's 1981 Omnibus Budget Reconciliation Act provided an opportunity to design a set of experiments in several types of work programs for AFDC recipients in eight states. On the basis of research done by the Manpower Demonstration Research Corporation, Congress incorporated lessons learned from these demonstration projects into the JOBS program of the Family Support Act of 1988.

Paradoxically and inexplicably, the War on Poverty launched by the Johnson Administration as the Economic Opportunity Act of 1964 bypassed AFDC recipients, who were increasingly women of color with out-of-wedlock children, and focused instead on mobilizing and employing inner-city black men. The War on Poverty is survived primarily by programs such as Head Start and Volunteers in Service to America (VISTA). Many, if not most, of the Community Action Programs launched by the now nonexistent Office of Economic Opportunity (OEO) had fleeting histories. They were operated by an assortment of grass-roots organizations as well as by joint city-level public and private sector initiatives. Such organizations provided entry for many poor black males and others into more stable jobs and into political office. With the American economy facing increasing unemployment and inflation in the 1970's, the fiscally conservative Ford Administration and Congress moved away from big-spending items for the poor and enacted EITC legislation to assist the working poor.

Bibliography

Axinn, June, and Herman Levin. *Social Welfare: A History of the American Response to Need*. 3d ed. New York: Longman, 1992. This book combines original source documents and scholarly commentary as it traces the history and philosophy of antipoverty programs in the United States. It reads easily and contains a thorough index.

Caputo, Richard. *Welfare and Freedom American Style: The Role of the Federal Government, 1900-1940*. Lanham, Md.: University Press of America, 1991. This text traces the formative years of contemporary antipoverty programs. It highlights the relationship between ideology and programs. Includes a bibliography and index.

Ellwood, David T. *Poor Support: Poverty in the American Family*. New York: Basic Books, 1988. This book examines the relation of poverty to changing social and economic factors associated with changing family structures in the United States. It offers lucid programmatic modifications to the current array of antipoverty programs. Contains detailed footnotes and an index.

Levitan, Sar A. *Programs in Aid of the Poor*. 6th ed. Baltimore: The Johns Hopkins University Press, 1990. This book provides the most descriptive summary of existing antipoverty programs. It clearly and concisely identifies and discusses cash assistance programs, provisions of goods and services, and programs for the working poor. Also discusses the dimensions of poverty in the United States and the scale of antipoverty programs. It is a standard in the field.

Levitan, Sar A., and Robert Taggart. *The Promise of Greatness*. Cambridge, Mass.: Harvard University Press, 1976. Levitan and Taggart provide cogent perspectives and retrospectives on the programs and policies of the Johnson Administration's War on Poverty and Great Society programs. This is an invaluable source for anyone interested in the promises, challenges, and performance of the War on Poverty. Contains more than two dozen easily readable tables and figures. Index.

Schwarz, John E., and Thomas J. Volgy. *The Forgotten Americans*. New York: W. W. Norton, 1992. This book highlights the plight of the American working poor. It contains a full explication of the workings of the EITC in straightforward, nontechnical language. The book has extensive notes gathered at the end. Includes a bibliography and index.

Wilson, William Julius. *The Truly Disadvantaged: The Inner City, the Underclass, and Public Policy*. Chicago: University of Chicago Press, 1987. An important and influential work on poverty and poverty programs in the 1980's. President Bill Clinton mentioned the influence of this text on him when he introduced Wilson during the economic summit held shortly before Clinton assumed the presidency. An extensive bibliography and thorough index are included.

Richard K. Caputo

Cross-References

ANTI-SEMITISM

Type of sociology: Racial and ethnic relations
Field of study: Basic concepts

Anti-Semitism is defined as discrimination or hostility by non-Jews against Jews as a group, whether expressed in words or in actions. Anti-Semitism has waned in the United States since the 1940's, but it still exists; the question of how serious a problem it remains has been the source of controversy.

Principal terms
DISCRIMINATION: the denial of opportunities and rights to certain groups on the basis of race or ethnicity
ETHNIC GROUP: a group distinguished principally by its distinctive shared cultural heritage
HOLOCAUST: the attempt of Nazi Germany, during World War II, to annihilate the Jews of Europe
POLITICAL ANTI-SEMITISM: the belief that Jews have too much power in the government
PREJUDICE: arbitrary beliefs or feelings about an individual of a certain ethnic or racial group or toward the group as a whole
SOCIAL DISTANCE: the degree of intimacy that people are willing to establish with members of a different ethnic group
STEREOTYPE: a sweeping generalization about a particular racial or ethnic group

Overview

Anti-Semitism can be defined as hostility toward Jews, based on a belief in negative stereotypes concerning Jews. Anti-Semites commonly stereotype Jews as avaricious, excessively wealthy, overly aggressive, dishonest, hungry for power, clannish, and unpatriotic. Some anti-Semites see these characteristics as ineradicable racial traits. It is important to note that an individual may believe in one stereotype but not in others and that many non-Jewish Americans have positive stereotypes about Jews, seeing them as hardworking and intelligent. The term "anti-Semitism," which is not strictly accurate (Arabs as well as Jews possess a Semitic language), was coined in the 1870's to distinguish between the traditional Christian animosity toward Jews on grounds of religious difference and the newer animosity toward Jews on grounds of alleged racial difference.

Anti-Semitism can be expressed in words, in violent deeds, in political activism, or in discriminatory behavior. The political anti-Semite believes that Jews are excessively powerful and ascribes nearly all problems in the country to a Jewish conspiracy. Such a belief can be held by individuals who do not compete directly with Jews and who may have never even seen a Jew. The German Nazis, who killed six million

European Jews during the Holocaust, represent the most extreme expression of political anti-Semitism. The White Aryan Resistance and the 1980's version of the Ku Klux Klan are American examples. Most individuals who accept one or more anti-Semitic stereotypes never join such extremist movements.

The refugee social scientist Theodor Adorno and his American colleagues, in the pathbreaking *The Authoritarian Personality* (1950), argue that anti-Semitism and antiblack racism go together. The pioneering researchers Bruno Bettelheim (a psychologist) and Morris Janowitz (a sociologist), writing in the 1950 work *Dynamics of Prejudice*, disagree with that viewpoint. Antiblack racism, they find, is more prevalent among white non-Jews than is anti-Semitism. (The same point is made in the 1979 work *Anti-Semitism in America*, by sociologists Harold E. Quinley and Charles Y. Glock.) Anti-Semitic stereotypes, Bettelheim and Janowitz find, differ significantly from antiblack stereotypes. Jews are stereotyped as crafty, overly ambitious, and dishonest; blacks are most often stereotyped as lazy and sexually immoral.

It has traditionally been the more educated and affluent anti-Semites who have discriminated against Jews in employment, housing, and admission to universities and social clubs; even some college-educated people who are not especially anti-Semitic, sociologists Gertrude Selznick and Stephen Steinberg found in the mid-1960's, still condone social club discrimination. Discrimination against Jews was much rarer by 1990 than it had been in the period between 1920 and 1945. Yet in the 1980's, sociologists G. William Domhoff and Richard L. Zweigenhaft still detected a pattern of exclusion from certain elite social clubs and underrepresentation in certain industries. Industrial psychologist Abraham K. Korman has seen a tendency among some large corporations to avoid recruiting at predominantly Jewish colleges and to confine Jewish hires to technical and scientific research jobs, and demographer Gary Tobin, sampling Jewish opinion in sixty American communities, heard some reports of discrimination on the job or in housing.

Because Jews are both a religious and an ethnic group, precisely what constitutes anti-Semitism is not always clear. For example, some American Christians want their city governments to allow or sponsor creches (nativity scene displays) on public property and want public schoolchildren to sing Christmas carols at Christmastime. Especially in parts of the United States that have almost no Jews (Jews were about 3 percent of the total population in 1980), such Christians are not necessarily anti-Semitic, although they are insensitive to Jewish feelings. Some Christians do not like Judaism as a religion but welcome individual Jewish converts to their own religions; such an attitude, while understandably offensive to many Jews, differs from the virulent racial anti-Semitism of Nazi Germany.

Sociologists Charles Y. Glock and Rodney Stark, in the 1966 work *Christian Beliefs and Anti-Semitism*, see a strong connection between adherence to Fundamentalist Protestant beliefs and acceptance of anti-Semitic stereotypes, but this conclusion is controversial. Two experts in public opinion polling, Gregory Martire and Ruth Clark, argue in *Anti-Semitism in the United States: A Study of Prejudice in the 1980's* (1982) that no relationship between Fundamentalism and anti-Semitism exists if differences in educational levels are taken into account. Nevertheless, many American Jews, in the 1980's and 1990's, feared the identification of Americanism with Christianity that they detected among some Fundamentalist Protestants.

The reasons for anti-Semitism are disputed. The emotive theory, propounded by Adorno in 1950, argues that individuals become anti-Semitic to cope with the psychological frustrations engendered by a rigid and authoritarian upbringing. According to the cognitive theory, voiced by Selznick and Steinberg, lack of education leads individuals to accept the anti-Semitic stereotypes already found in the culture; psychological frustration, they argue, is beside the point.

In the 1980's, incidents of vandalism of Jewish synagogues revived the debate about how dangerous anti-Semitism is. Journalist Charles E. Silberman, in *A Certain People: American Jews and Their Lives Today* (1985), saw the threat as nearly nonexistent. Martire and Clark, in 1982, saw a decline in anti-Semitic attitudes since 1964 but conceded that much prejudice still existed. Gary Tobin reported, in *Jewish Perceptions of Anti-Semitism* (1988), that one out of every four interviewees claimed to have experienced some anti-Semitic incident in the year the survey was conducted; nevertheless, he viewed the danger of anti-Semitism as a controllable one. A public opinion survey released by the Anti-Defamation League in November, 1992, revealed that one-fifth of all Americans still harbored anti-Semitic beliefs or attitudes.

Applications

In 1945, many medical schools and Ivy League universities severely limited their enrollment of Jewish students by a quota system. Certain wealthy suburbs barred Jews from becoming residents; many resorts refused to admit Jews; and many corporate employers and elite law firms would not knowingly hire Jews. Nearly one-fifth of all Americans regarded Jews as a major threat to the United States, while fully one-half thought that Jews had too much power. In the decades since then, both anti-Jewish discrimination and anti-Jewish attitudes (as revealed to pollsters) have declined sharply.

The brunt of the effort to combat anti-Semitism was borne by such Jewish "defense" organizations as the Anti-Defamation League, the American Jewish Committee, and the American Jewish Congress. As late as the 1980's, they carefully monitored all anti-Semitic incidents. They sponsored much of the sociological research on anti-Semitism. Partly because of the pressure exerted by the Jewish defense organizations on the nation's colleges and schools of medicine, all quota restrictions on the admission of Jewish university students had been eliminated by the late 1960's. As the pressure of publicity was exerted on resort hotels, they too gradually opened up to Jews; access did not become a matter of law, however, until the passage of the Civil Rights Act of 1964. A Supreme Court decision of 1966 forced city clubs and service clubs to drop provisions excluding Jews by threatening to revoke the clubs' tax exemption; private country clubs were untouched by the ruling.

Coalition-building was key to the Jewish organizations' strategy. Laws and court decisions that would benefit all minorities, not merely Jews, were pursued. Partly because of the organizations' lobbying, the New York state legislature passed a law in 1945 banning discrimination in state hiring based on race, creed, or national origin; twenty-one states had passed such laws by 1961. A 1948 Supreme Court decision banned the use of the courts to enforce restrictive real estate covenants. In the late 1950's, the cities of New York and Pittsburgh and the states of Colorado, Massachusetts, Oregon, and Connecticut passed fair housing laws.

The post-World War II decline of anti-Semitism was only partly attributable to the efforts of Jewish organizations. The defeat of Nazi Germany and certainly revelations about the Holocaust helped discredit the United States' most rabid political anti-Semites. In the 1950's and 1960's, a booming economy that demanded technically trained workers reduced non-Jewish employers' motivation to discriminate. The rapid expansion of higher education during those years probably made it easier for universities to end discrimination against Jewish students and applicants for college teaching positions. Growing Jewish affluence even blunted the effect of housing discrimination: The leading suburban real estate developer of the 1950's, William Levitt, was himself Jewish. Finally, the steady migration of African Americans to Northern cities provided an alternative target for white bigots.

In the United States, unlike in some other countries, the national government has never encouraged anti-Semitism. After 1945, federal and local law enforcement dealt effectively with those extreme anti-Semites who resorted to violence. In the late 1960's, the Federal Bureau of Investigation (FBI) solved a case of Ku Klux Klan terror against Jews in Mississippi. In the 1980's, the FBI succeeded in smashing a shadowy racist sect, the Aryan Nations, which had murdered an outspoken Jewish radio talk-show host. By 1983, thirteen states had passed laws explicitly against the vandalism of synagogues.

American anti-Semitism can be compared both with the prejudice and discrimination suffered by other American ethnic and racial minorities and with the anti-Semitism found in other countries of the world. American Jews who used the first standard of comparison could be lulled into a sense of security. If they looked at the larger history of Jews elsewhere in the world, however, in which periods of acceptance were followed by persecution, they could never feel completely secure. Jews were, in 1990, the only white American ethnic group specifically targeted by white racist hate groups. The fact that these hate groups had, in 1990, little appeal to American voters would not reassure the historically minded American Jew: The German Nazis, the perpetrators of the Holocaust, had likewise once been an insignificant political sect.

Hence, Jewish individuals and organizations have tried to make both adults and schoolchildren in the United States more aware of the Holocaust and have labored to counter the efforts of the so-called historical revisionists who deny that the Holocaust ever took place. In April, 1993, a U.S. Holocaust Memorial Museum was opened in Washington, D.C. Jewish organizations have persuaded leaders of various Christian denominations, also mindful of the lessons of the Holocaust, to remove any derogatory references to Jews from their religious educational materials.

Another method of fighting anti-Semitism, one inspired perhaps by research linking such prejudice with low educational levels, is through spreading information and correcting misconceptions. One such myth is the notion of the Jews as conspiratorial rulers of the international financial system. In the mid-1980's, when anti-Semitic political extremists began using this myth to win a following among financially distressed Midwestern farmers, representatives of Jewish defense organizations visited the farmers to show their sympathy with the farmers' plight.

Context

Although the most extreme expressions of anti-Semitism have occurred in Europe, most sociological research on anti-Semitism has taken place in the United States. Social psychologist Emory Bogardus, in his 1926 experiment on social distance using college students as subjects, found that Jews were the white ethnic group to which Americans of Northern European Protestant background then felt most averse. After the Nazi takeover of Germany in 1933, further research (this time using subjects from beyond the campus) was stimulated by the arrival of Jewish refugee social scientists from Germany and the determination of American Jewish defense organizations to help prevent any Nazi-like movement from taking over the United States. In addition, various opinion research agencies, during the years from 1937 to 1962, regularly polled Americans on their attitudes toward their Jewish fellow citizens.

The first fruits of the new social science research of the 1940's, largely funded by Jewish defense organizations, appeared in 1950: *The Authoritarian Personality*, by Theodor Adorno and others; and *Dynamics of Prejudice: A Psychological and Socio-logical Study of Veterans*, by Bruno Bettelheim and Morris Janowitz. The former was based on a sample from the San Francisco Bay area; the latter, on interviews of a random sample of 150 white, male, non-Jewish World War II veterans who were residents of the Chicago area.

Another research project sponsored by Jewish defense organizations was begun in response to a rash of synagogue vandalism incidents; it lasted from 1963 to 1975. Six volumes were published by the project, with the final volume coming out in 1979. Most of the research relied on surveys in which non-Jews were asked their opinions about Jews. Volumes in the series treated the relationship between Christian religious belief and anti-Semitism, anti-Semitism among blacks, anti-Semitism among teenagers, the American reaction to the trial of Nazi bureaucrat Adolf Eichmann, and the intrusion of anti-Semitism into a school board election in 1967.

In the 1980's, further research on anti-Semitism was published by Richard L. Zweigenhaft and G. William Domhoff; Gregory Martire and Ruth Clark; Abraham Korman; and Gary Tobin. Yet such research, although substantial, was dwarfed by the volume of sociological work on racism and discrimination against blacks. Many sociologists who were interested in American Jews studied other aspects of Jewish life. By 1990, American Jews enjoyed an above-average economic and educational status, and the rate of Jewish-Christian intermarriage was so high as to strike some Jews as a threat to group survival; yet many Jews remained worried about anti-Semitism. Important insights into anti-Semitism have been provided by European and

American theologians, journalists, historians, and novelists as well as sociologists. Without some knowledge of European as well as American history, the non-Jewish reader will comprehend neither the full significance of anti-Semitism nor the anxiety it arouses.

Bibliography

Korman, Abraham K. *The Outsiders: Jews and Corporate America.* Lexington, Mass.: Lexington Books, 1988. Uses interviews, analysis of a published list of corporate executives, and a comparison of recruiting behavior at six different colleges. Pointing to a looming oversupply of independent professionals, Korman stresses the need to overcome discrimination against Jews. Includes tables, appendices, references, and name and subject indexes. Suitable for undergraduates.

Marger, Martin N. *Race and Ethnic Relations: American and Global Perspectives.* Belmont, Calif.: Wadsworth, 1991. One chapter in this textbook, "Jewish Americans," offers undergraduates a good introduction to the subject and a wealth of bibliographical references. Examining social mobility, prejudice and discrimination, and intermarriage, Marger compares Jews with Italian Americans. Sketchy information on European anti-Semitism. References and index.

Martire, Gregory, and Ruth Clark. *Anti-Semitism in the United States: A Study of Prejudice in the 1980's.* New York: Praeger, 1982. The authors' optimistic conclusions concerning trends in anti-Semitism, based on analysis of a 1981 opinion survey commissioned by a Jewish organization, are somewhat controversial. Some knowledge of basic statistical reasoning is helpful in reading this book. Chapter notes, tables, methodological appendices, bibliography, and index.

Quinley, Harold E., and Charles Y. Glock. *Anti-Semitism in America.* New York: Free Press, 1979. The last volume produced by a twelve-year (1963-1975) research project summarizes the research results for all the topics pursued during the project, including those of a 1964 nationwide survey. The endnotes help guide the reader to the earlier social science literature. For both the scholar and the general reader.

Sachar, Howard M. *A History of the Jews in America.* New York: Alfred A. Knopf, 1992. This long book (936 pages of text alone) includes much detail on the discrimination and prejudice Jews faced in the pre-World War II era and on Jewish defense organizations' struggle against anti-Semitism after World War II. The rich bibliography includes works by sociologists and historians.

Selznick, Gertrude, and Stephen Steinberg. *The Tenacity of Prejudice: Anti-Semitism in Contemporary America.* New York: Harper & Row, 1969. This study, based on interviews of a nationwide sample of nearly two thousand non-Jews, was produced during the 1963-1975 research project. Differences in anti-Semitism by race (black and white) and education are investigated; differences among white ethnic groups, and between Hispanics and non-Hispanics, are not.

Silberman, Charles E. *A Certain People: American Jews and Their Lives Today.* New York: Summit Books, 1985. Written by a journalist who understands sociological methods. Anti-Semitism is treated as only one aspect, and a minor one at that, of the American Jewish experience in the 1980's. Silberman's rosy view of American anti-Semitism as a nearly extinct phenomenon is controversial. Index; richly informative endnotes. For the general reader.

Stember, Charles Herbert, et al. *Jews in the Mind of America*. New York: Basic Books, 1966. Seventeen essays by sociologists, social psychologists, and historians. The introduction summarizes all the essays, thereby aiding the busy reader. The most useful essay, by Stember, traces the post-World War II decline in anti-Semitism through poll data collected between 1937 and 1962. Includes appendices, figures, tables, notes at end of each essay, and an index.

Tobin, Gary. *Jewish Perceptions of Anti-Semitism*. New York: Plenum Press, 1988. Tobin, who interviewed Jews across the U.S. in 1987, argues that anti-Semitic incidents (such as verbal slurs and discrimination) occur more often than is generally believed. The informative chapters on Jewish defense organizations and the Jewish press are only loosely connected with the rest of the book. Endnotes, list of interviews, methodological appendices, and bibliography.

Zweigenhaft, Richard L., and G. William Domhoff. *Jews in the Protestant Establishment*. New York: Praeger, 1982. Relying on both personal interviews and statistical data gleaned from biographical dictionaries, the authors of this slim but tightly reasoned book offer profound insights into the ambiguous status of wealthy Jews in American society and the lingering discrimination against them. Index, appendices. For both the scholar and the general reader.

Paul D. Mageli

Cross-References

Assimilation: The United States, 140; The Authoritarian Personality Theory of Racism, 159; Individual Discrimination, 547; Ethnicity and Ethnic Groups, 689; The Frustration-Aggression Theory of Racism and Scapegoating, 773; Judaism, 1029; Prejudice and Discrimination: Merton's Paradigm, 1498; Prejudice and Stereotyping, 1505.

ANTIWAR MOVEMENTS

Type of sociology: Collective behavior and social movements
Field of study: Sources of social change

Antiwar movements are a particular type of social movement; the primary goal of antiwar movements is the prevention or halting of armed state conflict. The anti-Vietnam War movement was the most effective American antiwar movement of the twentieth century.

Principal terms

CONSCIENTIOUS OBJECTOR: a status held by a person who, by virtue of his or her objection to war because of religious, moral, or political reasons, does not serve in the armed services but instead often performs alternative government service

PEACE MOVEMENT: a social movement with the primary goal of preventing armed conflict between states rather than opposition to a particular war

RELATIVE DEPRIVATION: a theoretical perspective on social movements which states that social movements occur when there is a gap between expectations and objective conditions experienced by members of society

RESOURCE MOBILIZATION THEORY: a perspective on social movements that places the emphasis on understanding the characteristics of the organizations involved

SOCIAL MOVEMENT: ongoing attempts by an outside organization to change society or some aspect of society

Overview

Antiwar movements are organized and ongoing groups that have the goal of preventing or stopping armed conflict within or between states. There has been organized opposition to most American wars since the early nineteenth century, including opposition to the War of 1812, the Civil War, World War I, World War II, the Vietnam War, and the Persian Gulf War. In the 1950's, there also developed an active antinuclear movement. Antiwar movements generally have two major foci: opposition to the goals of a particular war and/or opposition to war itself. Some people opposed the Spanish-American War, for example, because it was seen as imperialistic and represented an undesired expansion of American influence in world affairs. Other groups, such as the American Peace Society, were established with the general goal of abolishing war.

Peace groups have traditionally drawn their constituency from such segments of society as women's organizations, pacifist religious groups, and intellectuals. Historian Berenice Carroll, in her essay in *Women and Peace: Theoretical, Historical, and*

Practical Perspectives (1987, edited by Ruth Roach Pierson), discussed the way in which women have relied upon traditional sex roles to promote peace. During the Victorian era of the late nineteenth and early twentieth centuries, women were seen as having higher moral authority than men and therefore as responsible for promoting peace. Women's status as mothers was seen to give them a special concern about the consequences of war. Women's early peace groups included such groups as the Women's Peace Party and the Women's International League for Peace and Freedom (WILPF). Both groups were an outgrowth of the International Congress of Women, which met in 1915.

There are religious groups that have a long history of pacifism. One of the most well known is the American Society of Friends, or Quakers; the antiwar Quaker organization is called the American Field Service Committee (AFSC). The AFSC was active in World War II in committees created to aid conscientious objectors and to arrange alternative service. During the Vietnam War, the AFSC was actively involved in organizing antiwar activity including lobbying, organizing mass rallies and demonstrations, and counseling draft resisters.

Historically, intellectuals have also had an important role in antiwar movements. Henry David Thoreau, in his book *Walden* (1854), discussed his opposition to the Mexican-American War and subsequent refusal to pay taxes which would be used to support that war. The antiwar treatises of Leo Tolstoy influenced many early American peace activists. Much of the antiwar debate in the 1960's occurred on college campuses among intellectuals.

One of the most influential antiwar movements in the twentieth century was the anti-Vietnam war movement in the United States. American involvement in Vietnam began during the Eisenhower Administration in the 1950's. U.S. involvement slowly escalated, so that by the summer of 1965 the Johnson Administration had sent 125,000 men to fight in Vietnam; by 1969, there were 550,000 troops in Vietnam.

From the beginning, an antiwar movement emerged in response to U.S. involvement in Vietnam. In the early years, the AFSC set up an information service for legislators. As the war escalated, so did the antiwar movement. Several major events occurred in response to the war, including a march on the Pentagon in 1967, riots at the Democratic Convention in Chicago in 1968, and a huge demonstration in Washington, D.C., in 1969. In 1970, it was estimated that as many as a million college students participated in demonstrations on campuses around the country against President Richard Nixon's bombing of Cambodia.

The anti-Vietnam War movement was composed of a loose confederation of groups organized to oppose the war. These groups drew from existing peace groups such as the AFSC as well as newer student groups such as the Students for a Democratic Society (SDS). These groups formed a coalition called the National Mobilization Committee to End the War in Vietnam ("Mobe"). The decade of the 1960's was also a time of broad cultural change; there were other social movements that were also concerned about the war in Vietnam. The Civil Rights movement was making important gains during this period in history. Author Ronald Frazier, in the book *1968*

(1988), noted that the Civil Rights movement was involved in the antiwar movement but only in a low-key manner. That movement's priority was the problem of racial injustice at home. Martin Luther King, Jr., however, did release a statement opposing the war in Vietnam.

Student groups emerged during this time period as well. The free speech movement launched a period of student unrest and a social movement for student rights in 1964. Students were also involved in civil rights organizations. These groups provided a natural organizational structure for the emergence of an antiwar movement. The SDS, which was originally organized to confront domestic issues of student rights and economic equity, became one of the more important organizations in the antiwar movement.

Applications

Various sociological perspectives that address social movements can be used to understand antiwar movements. For example, Anthony Oberschall, in his book *Social Movements: Ideologies, Interests, and Identities* (1993), applies the resource mobilization perspective to the understanding of social movements including the anti-Vietnam War movement. There are two major classes of theories used to understand the way in which social movements emerge. The first comprises solidary theories, which view social movements as emerging from organizations; included here is resource mobilization theory. Conditions of discontent may exist, or a specific precipitating event may create a situation that people want to change. In order to understand the mechanism by which they achieve that change, it is important to understand the organizations they create to achieve their goals. In the case of the anti-Vietnam War movement, the precipitating event was the war itself, especially the escalation of that war over the years. The war provided a sufficiently important source of discontent to serve as a catalyst for the movement.

According to Oberschall, there are several challenges faced by social movement organizations that are unique to these types of organizations. Social movement organizations, for one thing, work toward collective good rather than individual good. As a result, it is important that they be able to convince potential participants that belonging to the organization will provide enough benefit to justify the costs of involvement. A sense of personal benefit can be created, however, by providing other valued resources such as a sense of contributing to a moral and ethic good, and a community of like-minded people with whom to associate. The Vietnam War was considered by its opponents to be an unjust war in which people were fighting and dying needlessly. Frazier, in *1968*, discusses the way the antiwar movement adopted the ways of the counterculture, which provided an alternate lifestyle and culture that often accompanied activism.

Social movement organizations are also led by members who are self-appointed rather than being elected or appointed. Sociologist Todd Gitlin argues that the leaders who emerged were often those who were most appealing to the media; they were therefore sought out as spokesmen. Organizations also have the challenge of relying on what Oberschall terms "transitory teams." They are people who participate on a part-time basis and must have a flexible schedule in order to be able to participate. The antiwar movement of the 1960's had a ready-made constituency in the large number of college students who were involved in antiwar activity. College students have more free time and flexible schedules than do most other members of the community.

There were some inherent weaknesses in the movements of the 1960's, including the antiwar movement, that led to their eventual decline. The organizations involved were never able to produce sufficient solidarity among themselves to create an enduring social movement. For example, some black groups did not trust white groups. Groups such as the SDS had leadership that constantly changed. Groups were vulnerable to factions; the most famous faction that broke away from SDS was the Weathermen, created in 1969. Nevertheless, the antiwar movement had some measure of success. Lyndon Johnson did not run for reelection, and by the administration of Gerald Ford troops were almost completely withdrawn from South Vietnam. The immediate injustices that people perceived were thus removed.

The other class of theory that has been used to explain social movements is breakdown theory. Breakdown theories say that social movements occur when there is rapid social change or when social conditions are disappointing to the point that people create social movements to promote change. One type of breakdown theory is relative deprivation theory. As sociologist Ted Gurr states in his book *Why Men Rebel* (1970), revolution happens when there is a gap between expectations and reality. This is a perspective that accounts for the role of anger, discontent, and frustration in providing the mechanism by which social movements are organized. In the case of the Vietnam War, especially in the later stages of the war, many Americans decided that the war was not worth the disruption to American life that was created by the divisiveness caused by the war.

Understanding that is derived from applying sociological theory to social movements such as antiwar movements can have practical applications. Such theories and studies help provide an understanding of the mechanism by which people form organizations as well as the characteristics of organizations that are successful and able to endure. Policy makers and activists can apply this information to create organizations that can work effectively to achieve collective good.

Context

Antiwar movements are as old as war itself. For example, there are references to antiwar movements in Greek literature. Aristophane's play *Lysistrata*, which was first performed in 411 B.C.E., tells the story of Athenian and Spartan wives who successfully end a war between their two cities by denying sex to their husbands until a peace treaty is negotiated.

Antiwar movements have been influential in the history of the United States, and the peace movement has a long history in the United States as well. The first peace associations were the New York Peace Society and the Massachusetts Peace Society, both founded in 1815. The American Peace Society was founded in 1828. These early organizations were founded by community religious leaders and had a strong foundation in Christian principles. They formed the core of opposition to many U.S. wars. Between wars, an ongoing peace movement was maintained that worked for world peace by trying to prevent the conditions that create war. The focus on international peace included advocating the creation of an international organization to promote peace. A more recent peace movement was the antinuclear movement that was strong in the 1980's. Other antinuclear groups include Physicians for Social Responsibility, the Council for a Liveable World, and the Union of Concerned Scientists. One of the more visible efforts was the Nuclear Weapons Freeze campaign in the 1970's.

The opposition to the war in Vietnam was part of a climate of social upheaval and social change that occurred during the 1960's. In order to understand the anti-Vietnam War movement, it is important to understand the social climate of the times. People were questioning the way things should be in terms of the relations between races and student relations in the university. This provided a natural constituency when the war in Vietnam was escalated.

Because of changes in world events, antiwar and peace movements are likely to change in focus from past movements. From the 1950's to the 1980's, the emphasis for achieving peace was on nuclear disarmament and preventing war between the two superpowers. With the breakup of the Soviet Union and the end of the Cold War, the focus will change to an emphasis on civil wars and wars between smaller states. The reemergence of American antiwar movements will depend on the United States' future role in world affairs.

Bibliography

Chatfield, Charles. *The American Peace Movement: Ideals and Activism*. New York: Twayne, 1992. An overview of peace movements in the United States from the first associations created in 1815 to the antinuclear movement in 1987. Provides a historical analysis of the role of various organizations and people involved in peace movements in American history.

Fraser, Ronald, ed. *1968*. New York: Pantheon Books, 1988. An edited volume that provides in-depth coverage of the history-making events that occurred in and around the year of 1968, both in the United States and in Europe, often from the point of view of individual actors. The book also provides a list of important organizations and a chronology of events.

Gitlin, Todd. *The Whole World Is Watching: Mass Media in the Making and Unmaking of the New Left*. Berkeley: University of California Press, 1980. Gitlin provides an analysis of the relationship between the media and antiwar and activist groups in the 1960's. Contains an in-depth bibliography.

Gurr, Ted. *Why Men Rebel*. Princeton, N.J.: Princeton University Press, 1970. An important book in the literature of social movements that describes the role of social breakdown and relative deprivation in the emergence of political violence.

Oberschall, Anthony. *Social Movements: Ideologies, Interests, and Identities*. New

Brunswick, N.J.: Transaction, 1993. One of the most current volumes explicating the resource mobilization theory of social movements. It provides an analysis of several social movements in U.S. history, including the anti-Vietnam War movement.

Pierson, Ruth Roach, ed. *Women and Peace: Theoretical, Historical, and Practical Perspectives*. New York: Croom Helm, 1987. A publication of the proceedings of a conference entitled "Women and Education for Peace and Non-Violence." Includes essays on the role of women in peace movements including peace movements in the nineteenth and twentieth centuries in Canada, the United States, France, and Japan.

Zaroulis, Nancy, and Gerald Sullivan. *Who Spoke Up?: American Protest Against the War in Vietnam, 1963-1975*. New York: Holt, Rinehart and Winston, 1984. Provides an analysis in a chronological format of the Vietnam antiwar movement from 1963 to 1975.

Charlotte Chorn Dunham

Cross-References
The Civil Rights Movement, 265; The Cold War, 284; Deprivation Theory of Social Movements, 512; The Gay Liberation Movement, 799; Social Movements, 1826; The Structural-Strain Theory of Social Movements, 1997; War and Revolution, 2164; The Women's Movement, 2196.

APARTHEID

Type of sociology: Racial and ethnic relations
Field of study: Policy issues and debates

Apartheid refers to the rigid system of total racial segregation, or, literally, "apart-ness," that evolved in South Africa between 1948 and the early 1980's. It involved "separate development" of the races and supported the ideology of white supremacy. An intricate system of oppressive laws ensured minority white domination of South Africa's majority black population.

   Principal terms
      AFRIKAANS: the language spoken by the European South Africans
         descended from the early colonialists
      AFRIKANER: a descendant of the early Dutch, French, and German
         settlers whose ancestors arrived in South Africa as early as the
         seventeenth century
      BLACKS: under apartheid, the government designation for the majority
         population in South Africa
      COLOUREDS: under apartheid, the designation for South Africans of
         racially mixed backgrounds
      HOMELANDS: areas to which blacks were legally restricted; these areas
         reserved 13 percent of South Africa's land for 73 percent of the
         population
      WHITES: under apartheid, the designation for South Africa's caucasian
         minority population

Overview

Apartheid can be defined briefly as the stringent policy of racial segregation and oppression that existed in the Republic of South Africa between the late 1940's and mid-1990's. Under apartheid, the government officially divided the country's population into "whites," "coloureds" (the South African spelling will be used here), and "blacks." The country was completely under the control of the white minority; other groups were restricted to certain areas of the country and had to obey an elaborate set of laws that mandated virtually every aspect of life, including where and how they could work.

In many ways, the concept of rigid segregation as embodied in apartheid was already a historical anachronism when it was instituted in South Africa. The United States had allowed segregation since the late nineteenth century, but the social forces that set the Civil Rights movement in motion and overturned segregation laws were already gathering strength. South Africa, dominated by a white minority and occupy-ing a status somewhere between a Western country and a developing nation, was perhaps the only place such a policy could, or would, have been newly instituted at the time. The rigid caste system of India, for example, had been outlawed—although its effects are still felt—shortly after India became independent in 1947.

The apartheid system, designed to solidify white control of the country's resources, engendered immediate opposition both within the country and internationally. Protest, then violence, resulted in South Africa. As the years went on, the racist, even brutal conduct of the white government seemed increasingly indefensible to the world community. Economic sanctions were put in place in an attempt to make South Africa change its policies. Eventually, in the early 1990's, even South Africa's newly elected president, Frederik W. de Klerk, realized that maintaining apartheid was an untenable position.

How the apartheid system came into being can only be understood within the context of South African history following European contact. The first European settlement, Cape Town, was established by the Dutch in 1652. In 1820, some five thousand English colonists joined them, settling in Port Elizabeth. In 1836, an event often called the "great trek" occurred; twelve thousand Boers (Dutch farmers) moved into the interior to escape from the cultural influences of the British. They claimed land and resources in the interior of what was to become South Africa. The Union of South Africa was formed in 1910 as the British colonists joined with the Boer republics to form one country (it officially became the independent Republic of South Africa in 1961, withdrawing from the British Commonwealth). African resistance began as early as white governments were formed, and organized movements were soon created. The first major opposition movement, the African National Congress (ANC), was formed in 1912.

Apartheid as an all-encompassing system of racial stratification began after the election to power of the National Party in 1948. Yet it is important to realize that black South Africans had been subject to a wide variety of oppressive measures since Europeans arrived. They were displaced from some of their lands almost immediately, a situation which only grew worse as the years went by. After slavery was outlawed in 1833, blacks were still required to obey pass laws and carry identification cards. Blacks were prohibited from owning lands in white residence areas by the Native Lands Acts of 1913 and 1936. Although the most rigid restrictions were those on black South Africans, Asians and people of mixed ancestry also faced discrimination and were held to lower positions in society than those of the dominant whites.

South African society experienced significant population shifts in the 1930's and 1940's because of accelerating capitalist growth that attracted tens of thousands of blacks to the urban centers in search of jobs. Black slum areas resulted, as did militant struggles around the country. The expanding capitalist economy required adjustments in the overall system of white control. Believing that the increasing black urban population presented a threat to that control, the National Party institutionalized and extended white supremacy and black oppression more than any previous regime had.

Applications

White South Africans began to draft and pass new laws to codify and implement the policy of apartheid soon after the National Party gained control in 1948. There was some opposition within the government itself, as a significant number of white lawmakers did not favor the imposition of apartheid. Among the leaders of the opposition was Jan Christian Smuts, leader of the United Party, which had been in power prior to the National Party victory (although it should also be noted that the Smuts government was by no means integrationist). Nevertheless, enough national leaders and legislators favored apartheid to turn the policy into law.

Prime Minister Daniel François Malan, the leader of the National Party, delineated four initial components of the apartheid program. Black representation to the House of Assembly would end; blacks would have limited self-government in their reserved lands; coloured voters would be removed from the voter rolls in Cape Province; and all schools and universities would be racially segregated. A law was quickly passed that made it illegal for blacks to use first-class railroad cars. This type of law—and there were soon many—became known as a "petty apartheid law." In 1949, the Prohibition of Mixed Marriages Act forbade marriage between persons of different races. The Immorality Act of 1950 made sexual relations between the races illegal and punishable by up to seven years in prison.

The Group Areas Act of 1950 established separate geographical areas for use by whites, coloureds, and blacks. Provisions were included for the forcible removal of blacks from areas where they were not wanted. The Population Registration Act required registration at birth as white, coloured, or African; an Asian category was added later. The Suppression of Communism Act made the expression of a number of ideas illegal, including anything that would promote hostility between people of European and African descent; in 1982, this was strengthened by the Internal Security Act. Pass laws and "influx control" laws mandated that all blacks sixteen years of age or older obtain a passbook (later called a "reference book"), which was to be carried at all times.

The Bantu Authorities Act was passed in 1951; it was a central part of a program that was put forward by Hendrik Verwoerd, the new minister of internal affairs. This program included the concept of granting black South Africans tribal autonomy and was intended to further segregation by providing an overall plan of "separate development" for the different groups in the country. This act provided for the reinforcement of traditional tribal authority and the tribal election of regional representatives. Black "homelands" were established as the only areas where black South Africans could reside. Only within certain isolated and poor rural areas could blacks exercise any political freedom. For many males in the homelands, migrating to work in white parts of the country was the only source of income. Many migrant workers signed one-year contracts and were required to return to their homeland before being re-employed. Women, mostly domestic servants, were employed in the cities, and contact with their families was restricted. Violators were fined or imprisoned.

The repressive acts and policies of the apartheid program engendered controversy and protests, both inside and outside South Africa, but opposition was insufficient to keep apartheid from maintaining and strengthening its grip in the ensuing years. In the

1980's, limited apartheid reforms were initiated by the white government. By 1983, a tricameral legislative proposal allowed one house each for whites, Indians, and coloureds but none for black Africans. The exclusion of blacks from these reforms caused violent protest in black townships. In 1986, South African president Pieter W. Boetha predicted an end to the system of apartheid by proposing changes to the homeland policies and the pass laws.

Organized movements were resisting segregation and oppression before the 1950's. In addition to the early activities of the African National Congress, in the 1920's, black trade unions also organized. Organized protest began in earnest at the ascendence to power of the National Party in 1948; among the leaders of the ANC at the time were Albert John Lutuli and Nelson Mandela. Other groups also formed to fight domination and control by the white authorities. The ANC decided to use strikes and civil disobedience to protest and to attract international attention. Church groups condemned apartheid, but it had no effect on government policies. Membership in the ANC soon grew to more than 100,000. In the "defiance campaign" of 1952, ANC leaders wrote to Prime Minister Malan requesting the repeal of the Bantu Authorities Act; they were rebuffed and were told essentially that the government would use any means necessary to enforce its new policies.

Indeed, through the years, protests and their violent, deadly suppression became a regular part of life for black South Africans. The infiltration of police informers led to arrests and the banning of the ANC's leadership. ANC leaders and other black leaders were thrown in jail for years; one, Steven Biko, died in jail under questionable circumstances. Nelson Mandela was sentenced to life imprisonment in 1964. In 1969, the Sharpeville massacre left dead sixty-nine people who were protesting the pass laws; most were shot in the back. In its wake, the ANC and the Pan-African Congress, another anti-apartheid protest group, were outlawed. The ANC went underground and into exile (it eventually emerged with full force in the 1980's, with huge popular support). In 1976, the Soweto riot saw many more black South Africans killed in the putdown of a protest begun by students over being required to use the Afrikaans language as their means of expression in school. In August, 1983, the United Democratic Front was formed as an umbrella organization of more than six hundred groups across racial and functional lines; it pressured the government to dismantle apartheid.

By 1990, even as violence and brutality continued, change was slowly beginning to occur. Mandela was released from prison in 1990 by the government of Frederik W. de Klerk. The ban on the ANC was lifted that same year. Describing the ANC, activist Oliver Tambo noted that "the organization is a child of Africa's determination to achieve and enjoy human dignity, freedom, and national independence. It is at once the life, national awareness and the political experience of the popular masses of Africa. As the people cannot be liquidated, neither can the ANC."

Context

Frederik W. de Klerk became president of South Africa in August, 1989, and shortly thereafter began work to dismantle the apartheid laws. Originally viewed as a moderate with Afrikaner lineage who would uphold the system of apartheid, President de Klerk surprised many when he began advocating reconciliation instead of confrontation. One year after taking office, de Klerk made another bold announcement: He would lift the ban on the African National Congress, and Nelson Mandela, a leader of the ANC, would be released from prison, where he had been confined for twenty-seven years. These actions and others started South Africa on a course that would change its history forever. The decision to attempt to bring an end to apartheid was the outgrowth of mounting internal, international, and global opposition.

Pressure to end apartheid continued, and on September 24, 1993, before the United Nations Special Committee Against Apartheid, Nelson Mandela declared that the "countdown to democracy" had begun. Mandela never relented in his advocacy for a democratic, nonracist South Africa. After his release from prison in 1990, Mandela and President de Klerk began a series of talks, the first of which took place in May, 1990, to move toward a democratic system of inclusion. In June, 1991, de Klerk ordered that the major apartheid laws be repealed, and formal negotiations to end apartheid began in December, 1991. Throughout the process, violent confrontations between South Africa's blacks and whites continued, with black leaders accusing the white government of continuing brutality. Negotiations were plagued by numerous roadblocks, but early in 1993, Mandela, President de Klerk, and twenty-six other parties began the negotiating forum that set April 27, 1994, as the date for South Africa's first multiracial national democratic election based on adult suffrage and the "one person, one vote" principle.

Numerous world governments had had economic sanctions in place against South Africa for many years, and many investment companies and corporations had divested themselves of their interests in South African ventures or pulled out of South Africa. Sanctions and divestment were intended to pressure the government into repealing apartheid. By late 1993, because of the progress toward ending apartheid, Mandela and the ANC had called for the removal of sanctions and called for new planning regarding investment in South Africa. On September 24, 1993, Mandela stated, "To strengthen the forces of democratic change, and to help create the necessary conditions for stability and social progress, the time has come when the international community should lift economic sanctions against South Africa."

On November 17, 1993, South African negotiating parties ratified the proposed new constitution which would bring an end to white domination by renouncing the country's racist past. Fundamental rights include such democratic basics as free speech, fair trials, prohibition against torture, a promise that people can live where they choose, an assurance that citizens cannot be stripped of their citizenship, and limitation on the president's power to declare a state of emergency. Discrimination based on race, gender, sexual orientation, physical disability, or age is also prohibited. The ten self-governing homelands that were established as reservations for blacks are abolished. In December, 1993, the last white-dominated South African Parliament voted overwhelmingly to approve the new constitution.

Yet as was the case in the United States when the Civil Rights movement of the

1950's and 1960's was instrumental in ending legally sanctioned segregation, real change will be undoubtedly be slow and plagued by further problems and confrontations. Ending apartheid will not immediately reverse the deep-rooted domestic, social, economic, and political inequalities in South Africa. The struggle for social justice and economic security will continue. Laws can state that all citizens are equal, but they cannot erase the scars of apartheid or eliminate racially based economic stratification.

In recognition of their efforts to bring an end to apartheid and to end the bloody violence in South Africa, Nelson Mandela and Frederik W. de Klerk were awarded the 1993 Nobel Peace Prize. Symbolizing the difficulties still ahead, however, relations between the two men remained cool; Mandela, for example, stated that he and de Klerk simply had "no alternative but to work together" in ending apartheid.

Bibliography

Bunting, Brian. "The Origins of Apartheid." In *Apartheid: A Collection of Writings on South Africa by South Africans*, edited by A. La Guma. New York: International Publishers, 1971. This article traces the origins of apartheid and the political and economic conditions which subjected the majority population to the worst forms of colonial oppression.

Carter, Gwendolen. "The Republic of South Africa: White Political Control Within the African Continent." In *Africa*, edited by Phyllis Martin and Patrick O'Meara. 2d ed. Bloomington: Indiana University Press, 1986. In addition to an overview of the historical developments of apartheid, responses to major policy enforcements and organized freedom struggles are discussed.

Grundy, Kenneth. *South Africa: Domestic Crisis and Global Challenge*. Boulder, Colo.: Westview Press, 1991. A very good book that examines apartheid as an international affairs issue and discusses the role of international coalition-building in the struggle against it.

Harsch, Ernest. *South Africa: White Rule, Black Revolt*. New York: Pathfinder Press, 1980. This book focuses on South Africa's black majority and their struggle for citizen rights. It details the organized efforts of black resistance groups and movements. The role of industrialization as an oppressive force which led to the creation of a working class is traced.

Mahoso, Tafataona. "South Africa's Reforms Are a Sham." In *Problems of Africa: Opposing Viewpoints*, edited by Janelle Rohr. St. Paul, Minn.: Greenhaven Press, 1986. This concisely written article discusses South Africa's system of apartheid and compares it with racial segregation in the U.S. The self-determination of the South African black majority and their response to declared states of emergency are analyzed.

Omer-Cooper, J. D. *History of Southern Africa*. Portsmouth, N.H.: Heinemann Educational Books, 1987. An in-depth analytical interpretation of the systematic racial discrimination, repression, and exploitation created by apartheid; traces the development of the racial hierarchy which gave whites economic advantage and social status.

Tambo, Oliver. "Armed Struggle Is the Way to Eliminate Apartheid." In *Problems of Africa: Opposing Viewpoints*, edited by Janelle Rohr. St. Paul, Minn.: Greenhaven Press, 1986. The tactics and goals of the ANC are highlighted in this view of the ANC's armed struggle against apartheid.

Emma T. Lucas

Cross-References

Annihilation or Expulsion of Racial or Ethnic Groups, 92; Caste Systems, 198; Conquest and Annexation of Racial or Ethnic Groups, 353; Prejudice and Stereotyping, 1505; Racial and Ethnic Stratification, 1579; Racism as an Ideology, 1586; Segregation versus Integration, 1707.

ARRANGED MARRIAGES

Type of sociology: Major social institutions
Field of study: The family

An arranged marriage refers to a situation in which marriage partners are chosen primarily by someone other than the partners themselves. These other persons are usually parents, but they may also be other kin, a matchmaker, or an agency. Because the marriage partners may or may not be consulted, this situation implies a strong sense of family loyalty.

Principal terms

ENDOGAMY: a societal expectation that individuals should marry partners very much like themselves in terms of race, ethnicity, and class

EXOGAMY: a societal expectation that individuals should marry partners different from themselves in terms of lineage

MATE SELECTION: a process by which a male and a female are brought together for the purpose of marriage

MODERNIZATION: a process of social change in which new political, cultural, economic, and social practices are being created

TRADITIONAL SOCIETIES: societies with strong cultural beliefs and practices that sometimes endure for centuries

Overview

An arranged marriage is a type of mate selection in which the individual getting married has little or no choice in selecting a spouse because family members—usually parents—are more influential in the process. Most contemporary Americans have virtually no experience with arranged marriages, at least in the strictest sense of the term, yet arranged marriages do occur in the United States among many ethnic groups. They can exert a powerful cultural influence that continues for generations.

Arranged marriages are a standard practice in many parts of the world, and most studies of arranged marriages have been undertaken in countries where the tradition is more universally practiced than in the United States. Ashraf U. Ahmed, for example, studied arranged marriage in Bangladesh and listed a number of functions that arranged marriages serve. He noted that they help to maintain social stratification, to affirm and strengthen parental power over children, to keep family traditions and value systems intact, to consolidate and extend family property, to enhance the value of the kinship group, to maintain the tradition of endogamy, and to aid young people in finding mates.

In looking at China's modern-day society, it is possible to see how the communist government attempted to eradicate such aspects of traditional society by declaring arranged marriages to be invalid in 1950. Individuals were encouraged to select their own mates without parental consent, thus ensuring greater loyalty to the state than to the family. China's policy was not accepted by many of the older generation. They maintained control over their children's marriages because they had the economic resources to do so. The children could legally win the right to select their own spouse, but it was difficult to disobey parents with whom they might have had to live after marriage.

The authority of parents in traditional societies cannot be overemphasized. When the young live close to their parents and are dependent on them, parental power remains strong. If parents can arrange their children's marriages while they are still young, children will have fewer resources with which to oppose their parents. They are also more likely to be molded into a family culture with strict requirements, as in the caste system of India.

In traditional families, there is also a concern about maintaining class distinctions and social boundaries. The upper classes, as in modern societies, will attempt to emphasize these distinctions more to their children than the lower classes. As another example of parental authority, maintaining class and social boundaries helps to keep family values and property intact. For example, a suitable marriage during the early American colonial period was one entered into as an economic and social alliance that would ensure the son or daughter remaining in the station in which he or she was reared. At the same time, it would secure and perhaps enhance the status and fortune of the family as a whole.

In the Middle Ages, the kinship unit was very important in the transmission of property and the protection of the individual and family. The bride and groom were the least important unit in the forming of a marriage because parents, other kin, the church, and the community all played major roles and even competed with one another. Accordingly, marriages could be contracted in order to implement an alliance between feuding families. Not only would this practice continue to enhance the value of the kinship group, but also it would help keep the tradition of endogamy.

Marriage in traditional Japan meant that a couple became permanent members of an extended household and were expected to fulfill familial obligations. They were providing a vital link to ancestors by bringing infants into the world and taking care of elders soon to leave the world. Because of these important cultural mandates, it made sense that parents, rather than sons and daughters, would select marriage partners.

In American society, arranged marriages were common before the twentieth century. Parents in earlier eras had more authority over their children, and marriages involved more practical considerations than they do today. When the institution of dating came into existence in American society, it enabled young men and women to make their own choices in mate selection. Becoming popular in the 1920's, dating replaced the earlier custom of a man "calling" on a young woman at her house and under the supervision of her parents. A number of factors—the automobile, the telephone, and the existence of coeducational schools and colleges, for example— gave young men and women greater mobility and more opportunities to meet and communicate on their own.

In this way, American youths became free to select any mate they desired. It can be argued, however, that there are limits to this freedom. Implicit norms within socioeconomic classes and within ethnic, racial, and religious groups define who a suitable mate would be. These norms go along with endogamous beliefs that one should marry a person within one's ethnic group, race, religion, or class. Exogamous rules still operate in American society, as well, prohibiting marriage between close relatives. In addition, there are laws governing the permissible age for marriage and, in some states, laws prohibiting the marriage of those defined as mentally incompetent.

Although the overwhelming majority of American parents do not, strictly speaking, arrange marriages for their children, both parents and society at large influence the choices that young people make in selecting mates in a number of subtle ways. For one thing, they influence the opportunities available for mate selection. Individuals within the same social class are more likely to go to similar social functions and the same schools, and to live in the same neighborhoods. Parents also may show strong disapproval of dating partners selected by their children. In general, the control of parents is likely to be stronger the higher the social class of the family and the more traditional the ethnic culture is. The fact that between 50 and 80 percent of all American marriages are between people of similar religious and class groups indicates that some sort of "arranging" is involved in marriages of all cultures.

Applications

Knowledge gained from the study of arranged marriages is useful in understanding and comparing the degree of satisfaction found among marital partners and the success of marital unions. In many cases, the arranged marriage is compared with a marriage based on romantic love or free choice by the marital partners. Those who support arranged marriages would say that these marriages are likely to last longer than love matches, be more satisfying in the long run, be more realistic and practical, and create more partner compatibility. In comparison with arranged marriages romantic unions do result in a higher divorce rate, which may indicate more intense involvements, idealization of the marital partner, and subsequent disillusionment, leading to marital dissolution.

On the other hand, arranged marriages are scrutinized by those who favor free choice in mate selection. This group argues that romantic unions result in greater marital happiness than in family arranged unions because the attraction is more immediate and the compatibility more realistic. Xu Xiaohe and Martin King Whyte provide support for this argument in their article "Love Matches and Arranged Marriages in China," published in the *Journal of Marriage and the Family* 52 (August, 1990). Their study of Chinese women, both in arranged marriages and free-choice marriages, showed that women in free-choice marriages are consistently more satisfied with their marital relationships and rate their marriages higher than the women in arranged marriages.

While this finding supports the Western view of mate selection, it does not indicate that arranged marriages are becoming extinct. Arranged marriages are being examined by younger generations of various ethnic populations as much as ever, both in the United States and in other, more traditional societies. These young, single individuals will be deciding whether to follow their parents' tradition of arranged marriages or to follow the Western way of selecting their own spouse. The decision is not always easy, so studying the benefits of an arranged marriage as well as its costs is very important to this population.

Unfortunately, the United States does not have marriage and family counselors who specialize in explaining the pros and cons of arranged marriages. This service would be helpful to tradition-socialized youth in the same way that premarital counseling has been helpful for Western couples. Currently there are many ethnic immigrants in the United States who are already in arranged marriages. If these individuals have a negative overall experience in their arranged marriages, they are less likely to force an arranged marriage on their own children. Their children are more likely to have a choice either to follow the tradition or to select their own spouse.

Some individuals may prefer to steer a middle course between having completely free choice and having a mate chosen for them; in this way they can seek their own mate yet obtain family approval to avoid the risks of opposing their parents entirely. Individuals may also want more free choice in seeing and communicating with prospective mates before the actual marriage. In V. V. Prakasa Rao and V. Nandini Rao's book *Marriage, the Family, and Women in India* (1982), college students in India were asked about their preferences for arranged versus free-choice marriages. The most popular response was that the students would like to consult with their parents about a spouse but make the final choice themselves.

The study of arranged marriages can also be applied to societies going through transitions in which they are influenced by Western practices. The study of arranged marriages makes it possible to see whether cultural traditions are being maintained or lost. In highly traditional societies such as those of India, many Muslim countries, China, and Japan, filial piety is strong, and females have long been dependent on their families for economic and social support. As these countries become industrialized, educational levels for both women and men rise, as do their opportunities for employment. These two factors are associated with a decrease in arranged marriages. Consistent with this trend, one finds that areas that are more urbanized have higher rates of free-choice marriages, while rural areas have a predominance of arranged marriages.

A patriarchal form of authority with emphasis on the extended family is also found in traditional societies. Family unity is emphasized, as opposed to individual goals. In China and Japan, the arranged marriage ensures family continuity and a direct link to ancestors. It redefines a household with a new generation of permanent members who will carry on the traditions of the family. As the family system becomes weaker because of Western cultural influences and industrialization, the younger generation is more likely to have options in mate selection. This helps explain why countries undergoing westernization that have had a strong tradition of arranged marriages develop competing systems of mate selection.

While it is likely that industrialized nations will have a weaker system of arranged marriages and a greater prevalence of marriages by choice, this does not mean that the system of arranged marriages will completely disappear. More research is needed to determine how and why arranged marriages persist and even increase at certain periods of time when there are many forces opposing their continuation. Countries such as China and Japan show modernization trends together with unchanging (or very slowly changing) cultural beliefs and traditions about marriage.

Context

Sociologists study arranged marriages as a particular form of mate selection. Arranged marriages are considered, by American standards, to be unacceptable in principle when compared to choices available based on romantic love. Arranged marriages are certainly not rare, however, in that a large percentage of the world's population currently engages in this practice.

The subject of arranged marriages is relatively new to sociology, though it has been studied for a long time in the field of cultural anthropology. Textbooks on the family that were written since the 1980's are likely to have a section on mate selection within a chapter that may include arranged marriages; books written in the 1970's and earlier generally do not single out this topic or even mention it. Perhaps the subject was deemed too "foreign" and exotic to merit coverage earlier in sociology textbooks that basically addressed the American family. Now that American society has become more multicultural than ever before, however, and particularly since immigration from Asia has increased significantly in the 1980's and 1990's, it would be a serious omission to leave this topic out of textbooks.

As an area of study within sociology, arranged marriages add to the understanding of the functions of marriage, types of social authority, and the nature of families in traditional societies. This focus on traditional societies allows comparison with modern societies, helping elucidate factors in both systems that perpetuate certain behaviors and values. As the United States continues to receive a heavy influx of immigrants, this information should be useful in understanding ethnic diversity as it persists despite the forces of assimilation.

Bibliography

Croll, Elisabeth. *The Politics of Marriage in Contemporary China*. Cambridge, England: Cambridge University Press, 1981. China's system of arranged marriages was basically abolished on May 1, 1950, by the government of the People's Republic of China. This book explores the conflicts between parents and children that resulted when the younger generation challenged the tradition of arranged marriages. Rather than eliminating this tradition, the ban created strong social resistance from both the family and the community. Arranged marriages still dominate in rural areas of China.

Gies, Frances, and Joseph Gies. *Marriage and the Family in the Middle Ages*. New York: Harper & Row, 1987. This book provides a fascinating account of what marriages were like during the Middle Ages among various classes. The general audience will find this information from medieval scholars to be a good way to see how arranged marriages can take place in a non-Eastern, non-Muslim context.

Goode, William J. *World Revolution and Family Patterns.* New York: Free Press, 1963. An excellent text on traditional societies that practice arranged marriages. The author covers the marriage and family patterns of the Arabic Islamic nations, sub-Saharan Africa, India, China, and Japan. Even the West is included to show how parents at one time controlled their children's choice of spouse through the inheritance of land.

Hendry, Joy. *Marriage in Changing Japan: Community and Society.* New York: St. Martin's Press, 1981. The historical and cultural context of arranged marriages in Japan is presented in great detail. The importance of the arranged match can be seen in how it integrates not only families but also the community and society. Provides a good societal perspective of a form of mate selection that has not died out in Japan.

Prakasa Rao, V. V., and V. Nandini Rao. *Marriage, the Family, and Women in India.* New Delhi: Heritage, 1982. The chapter on arranged marriages in this book goes into detail about the effects of modernization on this tradition in India. The rest of the chapters complement the subject of arranged marriages by looking at various aspects of culture and the position of women in society.

Tepperman, Lorne, and Susannah J. Wilson, eds. *Next of Kin: An International Reader on Changing Families.* Englewood Cliffs, N.J.: Prentice-Hall, 1993. The series of articles in this volume nicely address the issue of family changes in cultures around the world. The concept of arranged marriages is mentioned throughout the book as various authors discuss how traditional families are having to adapt their marital and familial expectations to societal changes.

Fumiko Hosokawa

Cross-References

The Family: Functionalist versus Conflict Theory Views, 739; Interitance Systems, 989; Types of Marriage, 1120; Nuclear and Extended Families, 1303; Patriarchy versus Matriarchy, 1349; Residence Patterns, 1635; Socialization: The Family, 1880.

ASSIMILATION: THE UNITED STATES

Type of sociology: Racial and ethnic relations
Field of study: Theories of prejudice and discrimination

Assimilation refers to the process by which individuals or groups take on the culture of the dominant society, including language, values, and behavior, as well as the process by which groups are incorporated into the dominant society. The "melting pot" and "Anglo-conformity" are two models of assimilation. The first implies that the society is one to which all groups have contributed their values, norms, and behaviors; the second implies that all groups who are not Anglo must accommodate themselves to Anglo culture before assimilation takes place.

> *Principal terms*
> ACCULTURATION: the process by which culturally distinct groups understand, adapt to, and influence one another
> ASSIMILATION: the process by which individuals take on the language, behavior, and values of another culture, as well as the process by which outsiders are incorporated into a society
> ETHNIC GROUP: a group bound by a common and distinctive cultural heritage and history
> INTEREST GROUP: a group that is bound together by a common interest, generally working together to maintain or advance a common agenda; society is pluralistic, composed of competing groups among whom social power is divided
> RACIAL PREJUDICE: a dislike and fear of others based on real and perceived physical differences

Overview

Assimilationist theories have dominated the sociology of race and ethnic relations. Such theories suggest that the outcome of race and ethnic relations in society is assimilation: the ultimately harmonious blending of differing ethnic groups into one homogeneous society. A key question that emerges among assimilationist theorists concerns what the basis of that homogeneity will be. Will distinct groups each contribute to the building of a new culture and society that is a "melting pot" of all their differing values and behaviors, or will one group (such as the Anglo-Saxons) come to dominate the process of assimilation? Assimilation based on the adoption of Anglo-Saxon values has been termed "Anglo-conformity."

According to Milton Gordon in his book *Assimilation in American Life* (1964), assimilation involves both acculturation and structural assimilation, wherein groups are fully incorporated into, and indistinguishable from, the larger society. Cultural assimilation, or acculturation, however, can go in one of two directions, following either a "melting pot ideal," the process of either developing a blended, or "melting pot" culture, or an "Anglo-conformity ideal" under which other ethnic groups acculturate to the Anglo-Saxon culture.

Gordon, who attributes the "Anglo-conformity" thesis to Stewart Cole, states that this ideal requires that immigrants completely abandon their cultural heritage in favor of Anglo-Saxon culture. According to Gordon, those who propose Anglo-conformity as a viable ideal of assimilation view the maintenance of the English language, institutions, and culture as desirable. Such views, in his estimation, are related to nativist programs that promote the inclusion of those immigrants who are most like the English as well as to programs that promote the acceptance of any immigrants willing to acculturate on the basis of Anglo-conformity. Furthermore, Gordon maintains, this is the ideal which guided assimilationist ideology throughout American history. For example, in his book *The Ethnic Myth* (1981), Stephen Steinberg quotes Benjamin Franklin saying, in part, "Why should Pennsylvania, founded by the English, become a colony of aliens, who will shortly be so numerous as to Germanize us, instead of our Anglifying them . . .?" Yet the "founding fathers" were not opposed to immigration; at best, they were ambiguous. They needed immigrants for the growing labor demands of the new society, but they were also concerned that these immigrants and their differences might be a source of conflict.

According to Gordon, those espousing the Anglo-conformity ideal cannot be automatically heralded racist although, as he puts it, all racists in the United States can be heralded Anglo-conformists. Furthermore, Anglo-conformists tend to assume that English ways and institutions are better than others. Even those who do not support that view argue that, whether they are better or not, they do predominate in existing American society. Therefore, newcomers must adapt to what is already in place. Anglo-conformists also assume that once immigrants have acculturated based on Anglo-conformity, they will be found acceptable and will no longer be the targets of prejudice and discrimination.

While the Anglo-conformity ideal has been the prevalent form of assimilation proposed, the melting pot ideal has also been an important and influential aspect of assimilationist thought. Particularly in the early twentieth century, those who viewed American society as a new experiment in which diverse peoples came together to forge a new culture saw Americans as a new "race" of people. In this view, the United States was a giant melting pot that received all immigrants, melting them—and their cultures—down into one homogeneous and unique group.

The "melting pot" model of assimilationist theory was implied by sociologist Robert Park's theory of the race relations cycle, suggested in the 1920's. In that theory, Park presented the idea that assimilation involves both cultural and biological processes. In other words, Park conceived of assimilation as accomplished both by the "interpenetration" of distinct cultures, in which each group takes on some of the other's culture, and by amalgamation, or biological mixing through intermarriage and reproduction.

Gordon criticizes melting pot idealists for failing to discuss whether all groups can contribute equally to the final mixture. Furthermore, since Anglo-Saxons arrived chronologically before other immigrants, they were able to establish the social order into which newer immigrants are expected to "melt." Because of this difference in group influence on the American character and society, Gordon claims that the melting pot ideal masks the fact that non-Anglo-Saxons are the ones expected to change. Furthermore, while some differences, such as nationality, can be melted down among whites, other differences, such as race and religion, are either not willingly given up or cannot be melted away. So, white Protestants who wish to can melt into the Anglo society relatively easily, while Jews and Catholics must melt into their respective religious pots. Blacks and other people of color, however, do not melt down, according to Gordon; they are prevented from doing so by racial discrimination.

In their book *Beyond the Melting Pot* (2d ed., 1970), Nathan Glazer and Daniel Patrick Moynihan review the "melting pot" thesis in the light of continuing ethnic diversity and conflict in New York City. Glazer and Moynihan believed that ethnic groups could join society if they were willing to change, to acculturate. Unlike Gordon, Glazer and Moynihan do not view prejudice as the major obstacle to assimilation. They view internal group weaknesses as the major obstacle; they also cite the lack of a single American identity for immigrants to adopt. Glazer and Moynihan think that American society does melt away the old ethnic culture; however, a new ethnic identity emerges, so the ethnic group remains distinct—neither melted down nor conforming to the Anglo model.

Applications

The melting pot and Anglo-conformity models are used both to analyze assimila- tionist trends in American society and to propose the most desirable direction for assimilationist efforts. Generally, Anglo-conformity assimilation, in practice, is asso- ciated with nativist efforts. Melting pot assimilation has been related to reformist efforts to "Americanize" new immigrants, purportedly easing their adjustment to American society.

According to Stephen Steinberg, the early rise of nativism in the United States implies that Anglo-conformity dominated assimilationist views. Nativism refers to the desire to maintain the given ethnic character of society or particular social institutions. Generally, nativists see themselves as the real Americans and are xenophobic, or fearful and hateful of foreigners. Anglo-Saxon settlers wished to preserve their cultural legacy in the face of massive immigration that labor shortages forced them to tolerate. Perhaps one of the greatest instruments for Anglo-conformity has been the centralized system of public education that was developed in the United States. Immigrants were and are taught English language skills, as well as citizenship, and are thus American- ized. According to Gordon, other forms of Anglo-conformity assimilation include political movements by nativists to exclude "foreigners" from social institutions, favoring immigration only by people similar in background and culture to Anglo- Saxons, and basing social inclusion on the adoption of Anglo-Saxon culture by immigrants. Nativist political movements flourished throughout the nineteenth cen- tury, including programs to exclude Catholics and foreign-born persons from holding public office as well as programs to make naturalization (gaining American citizenship) more difficult. During World War I an "Americanization" movement led to efforts by public institutions to have immigrants learn English, become naturalized, and become fully Americanized in values and behavior. In the 1920's immigration quotas, spurred by nativist sentiments, restricted immigration from southern and eastern Europe.

According to Joe R. Feagin and Clairece Booher Feagin, American social scientists also promoted Anglo-conformity through their reification of the English impact on U.S. social institutions. These social scientists believed that English culture was the most civilized of all cultures, and that the powerful influence on American culture and social institutions would make the United States home to the greatest Anglo-Saxon culture in the world.

The nativist sentiments which are popular manifestations of the Anglo-conformity model of assimilation remained significant in the early 1990's. According to Feagin, the California English campaign pushed programs to prohibit bilingual education programs, arguing that immigrants should be made to adapt to their adopted country quickly by being forced to speak English only in school. English-only advocates also argue that voting ballots should be printed only in English so that potential voters would have to be literate in English before they could fully enjoy the rights of citizenship.

Robert Park was the leading theorist of assimilation based on a melting pot ideal. In his conception, groups might differ in the amount of time it would take them to acculturate, but they eventually would. He also held that the melting pot would emerge through amalgamation—accomplished through intermarriage across lines of ethnicity. For melting pot theorists, then, intermarriage is an important measure of the extent to which groups are merging into one homogeneous group. Steinberg, however, offers a different version of the melting pot that does not require full homogeneity but rather the absence of substantive differences by ethnicity. In other words, those who—like Glazer and Moynihan—argue that ethnic groups have not melted down base their argument on the visibility of divergent ethnic groups in society. According to Steinberg, however, these "different" ethnic groups have more in common with one another than they have differences from one another.

Studies of intermarriage reveal that ethnic groups, in particular, are marrying across group lines, though not always across religious or racial lines. For example, intermarriage has increased substantially between Jews and non-Jews, although in-marriage is still strong for Italian Americans and Irish Americans. Ruby Jo Reeves Kennedy's 1944 study reported intermarriage within three pools: Protestants, Catholics, and Jews. Intermarriage still tends to be culturally prohibited across racial lines, reflecting important differences between race and ethnicity which melting pot theorists tended to downplay in their analyses.

Israel Zangwill's 1908 play *The Melting Pot* presented one of the most influential and emotional depictions of the melting pot ideal. In Zangwill's play, a Russian Jew immigrates to the United States, which he proclaims the "great melting pot." Generally, however, later assimilationist theorists abandoned the melting pot thesis in favor of either Anglo-conformity or cultural pluralism, in which ethnic groups retain some of their distinctive features while sharing in the dominant social institutions.

Context

The melting pot and Anglo-conformity models are two variants developed in the context of assimilationist theories of race relations, pioneered by Robert Park in the 1920's. As variants of the same general theory of race relations, both models are embedded in a theoretical framework that focuses on ethnic groups and their incorporation into the larger society, predicting that ultimately ethnicity will cease to be of importance and that social status and achievement will be the primary markers for an individual's identity. Generally, these assimilationist theories assume that the United States is a basically egalitarian and open society. Exclusionary practices, prejudice, and discrimination, in this view, will diminish over time—though more rapidly for some groups than for others. Assimilationist theorists generally have not distinguished race from ethnicity. They have not ignored the significant differences between the levels of assimilation of white ethnic groups and groups of other races; they explain them either as a product of the greater prejudice held against people who look different or as a product of the failure of nonwhite minorities to conform to and embrace the dominant culture. Assimilationist theorists view prejudice as the product of the differences that minority group members present to the dominant society. As group members acculturate, these differences diminish, and the people are accepted by the dominant society. They then no longer experience discrimination.

The melting pot ideal is the precursor to Anglo-conformity, and it was implicit in the development of Park's race relations cycle theory, as it was considered a result of the ultimate trend toward the amalgamation of ethnic groups. Steinberg comments on the remarkable development of the melting pot thesis at a time, in the early twentieth century, when ethnic groups were, perhaps, more entrenched and numerous than at any other time. The melting pot theorists, however, found it astounding that immigrants from diverse cultures were able to embrace and acculturate to new American ways and values so rapidly. The melting pot theory of assimilation influenced many of the sociologists who followed Park, including Louis Wirth and Gunnar Myrdal. These sociologists shared the immigrant group analysis of ethnicity and race, arguing that the black experience was an aberration—or, as Myrdal put it, an "American dilemma"—in the generally egalitarian and open character of American society.

Glazer and Moynihan also used the immigrant analogy, in which all groups are viewed as cycling through the same experience of immigration, competition, conflict, accommodation, and assimilation. The melting pot ideal, however, came under attack in their book *Beyond the Melting Pot*. According to Glazer and Moynihan, ethnic groups had clung to their cultures and were not melting down into one homogeneous group. This led Glazer and Moynihan to advance the concept of ethnic (or cultural) pluralism, wherein some ethnic groups retain distinctive features as well as participating in the dominant society. Milton Gordon, however, broke with the melting pot theorists, claiming that Anglo-conformity was a more accurate description of the type of assimilation taking place in American society. While he agrees that assimilation is the outcome of race relations, he sees immigrants as forced to make a choice between retaining ethnic group identity and culture or being incorporated into American society.

Assimilationist theory enjoyed prominence in the sociology of race relations through much of the twentieth century. This began to change in the late 1960's. In the early and mid-1960's, it had seemed that the United States, driven by the Civil Rights movement, would at last begin to incorporate its racial minorities. Racial strife and rebellion, however, occurred widely in the late 1960's, demonstrating both that an acceptable level of assimilation was not occurring and that assimilation was not even a common goal of minorities. Social scientists began to look at assimilation, prejudice, and racism from new perspectives. They realized that measurable racial differences in the allocation of social resources could not be solely attributed either to the persistence of prejudice among whites or to the "pathologies" of racial minorities. Rather, it appeared to a growing number of scholars that racism was institutionalized, or embedded, in the very foundation of American society and that assimilation therefore was not possible for people of color. These developments in the sociology of race relations led to new theories, including institutional racism and internal colonial theory. These concepts reflected the realization that race and ethnicity were not melting down. The Black Power movement and other liberation movements seemed to reveal that racial minorities did not universally embrace the premise of assimilation and that other models were needed to explain the distribution of political and economic power in society according to race and ethnicity.

Bibliography

Blauner, Robert. *Racial Oppression in America*. New York: Harper & Row, 1972. Blauner begins with a criticism of predominant trends in the sociology of race relations, particularly assimilationist theories, and counters their focus on race prejudice with an analysis of racial privilege as embedded in a system of internal colonialism.

Feagin, Joe R., and Clairece Booher Feagin. *Racial and Ethnic Relations*. 4th ed. Englewood Cliffs, N.J.: Prentice-Hall, 1993. This introductory text in the sociology of race relations examines sociological theories against the background of extensive case history of both white ethnic groups and ethnic groups of other races. An excellent source on each of the ethnic groups presented, with bibliographic information at the end of each chapter.

Glazer, Nathan, and Daniel Patrick Moynihan. *Beyond the Melting Pot*. 2d ed. Cambridge, Mass.: MIT Press, 1970. This controversial book presents an ethnic overview of New York City in the 1960's, with an updated introduction in this second edition. The authors present studies of blacks, Jews, Puerto Ricans, Italians, and Irish Americans to re-examine the melting pot thesis. Although the tables in the appendices are dated, the index is useful, and the book is an important landmark in the history of the sociology of race relations.

Gordon, Milton. *Assimilation in American Life*. New York: Oxford University Press, 1964. This book presents Gordon's theory of assimilation, with chapters devoted to the Anglo-conformity model and the melting pot model. The book is thoroughly indexed, and the nonsociologist should be able to follow Gordon's clear language.

Steinberg, Stephen. *The Ethnic Myth*. New York: Atheneum, 1981. This is an important sociology text in race and ethnic relations. Ethnicity is reexamined in the light of economic organization and the class structure. Theories of race relations are presented and reviewed in the light of the specific historical overviews presented on various racial ethnic groups.

Sharon Elise

Cross-References

Cultural and Structural Assimilation, 405; Individual Discrimination, 547; Ethnic Enclaves, 682; Ethnicity and Ethnic Groups, 689; Immigration and Emigration, 921; Immigration to the United States, 928; Prejudice and Stereotyping, 1505; The Race Relations Cycle Theory of Assimilation, 1572; Racial and Ethnic Stratification, 1579.

ATHEISM AND AGNOSTICISM

Type of sociology: Major social institutions
Field of study: Religion

Atheism and agnosticism are both forms of religious unbelief: Atheists say they do not believe in the existence of God (or gods) or the supernatural, while agnostics say they have inadequate knowledge to reach conclusions on the subject. Atheism and agnosticism place individuals outside the cultural mainstream because the majority of people—even in modern, secularized societies—have some sort of religious beliefs.

Principal terms
DISCRIMINATION: treating members of a minority group (such as unbelievers) differently than others simply because they are in that group
HERESY: a doctrine contrary to official church teachings; a heretic is one who teaches or believes such a doctrine
IDEOLOGY: a philosophy, worldview, or systematic body of ideas about human life or culture
INSTITUTION: an established organization, practice, or relationship (such as the church, or marriage) in a culture
ORTHODOXY: conformity to established religious beliefs and practices
RELIGION: an institutionalized system or personal set of beliefs and practices about God (or gods) and the origins and meaning of life
RITE: a ceremony, such as a christening, baptism, marriage, or burial, often recognizing a stage of life; a rite of passage (such as the Jewish bar mitzvah) is an initiation ceremony into adulthood
SECULARISM: a lack of concern for religion and its aspects
STIGMA: a mark of shame

Overview

Atheism and agnosticism are both ideologies that profess or advocate unbelief toward god (God, gods, divinity, or deity), religion, and the supernatural. Although there are some modern organizations of unbelievers, such groups have minor social significance in comparison with the numerous churches and other powerful institutions founded on the traditional principle of shared religious belief.

Since unbelief is a matter of personal attitude, and since many people are uncertain or have mixed views, factual data about atheism and agnosticism are elusive. The *Statistical Abstract of the United States* (1991) reports that in 1989 only 10 percent of adults expressed "no religious preference"; earlier, in 1957, only 3 percent of the population had expressed that position. Such figures suggest a slight trend toward unbelief. Yet a Gallup poll in the late 1980's showed more than 90 percent of Americans still believing in miracles, which are supernatural events. *Time* magazine reported that 54 to 79 percent of adult Americans in early 1992 found religion personally "very important," and 65 to 80 percent believed that the Bible was the "'totally accurate' word of God"; the lowest percentages were for adults age eighteen to twenty-six, and the highest were for people age forty-six to sixty-four. Since many nonreligious people are merely neutral or apathetic toward religion, atheists and agnostics with carefully thought-out philosophies of unbelief make up a very small minority group in modern society—probably numbering below 5 percent in 1993.

The Encyclopedia of Unbelief (1985) points to the difficulty of defining "unbelief"—a term some sources prefer to "nonbelief" or "disbelief." The nearest synonym may be "heterodoxy," the opposite of religious orthodoxy. "Atheism" and "agnosticism" are also difficult to define. Each term begins with the previx *a-*, meaning "not." Since "theism" is a belief in God, "atheism"—first used in 1571—suggests "without a belief in God." Despite customary dictionary definitions, however, many atheists do not deny the existence of God. Rather, they think that the term "God" has no meaning and say they cannot "disbelieve" in an idea they do not acknowledge.

"Agnosticism" is a term invented in 1869 by Thomas Henry Huxley, an advocate of science; it suggests an ideology based on "not knowing"—with its Greek root, *gnosis*, meaning "knowledge" or "recognition." Huxley used the term to describe an approach that involves following reason only as far as it will go and not stating that something is true if it cannot be demonstrated. Thus "agnosticism" had an original meaning similar to "rationalism." The Victorian evolutionist Herbert Spencer first used "agnostic" to mean one who believes that God is unknowable. Popularly, an agnostic is one unsure about whether God exists. Some atheists view agnosticism as a subtype of atheism. Many atheists and agnostics would also call themselves materialists, positivists, existentialists, objectivists, humanists, or skeptics. These ideologies are quite diverse, and defining each one of them is complicated; all, however, tend to reject orthodox religion and supernaturalism. When unbelievers speculate about cosmic origins, they are likely to focus on scientific rather than supernatural phenomena.

To believers, whose value systems are founded in religion, the terms atheist and agnostic carry negative connotations and suggest being against something good and sacred. Unbelievers themselves, however, often see themselves as affirmative, rational, and independent in their views. Though believers often see unbelievers as people without morals, many atheists and agnostics are consciously ethical, law-abiding, humane, altruistic, and socially conventional. Society is somewhat more tolerant of "skeptical" agnostics than "heretical" atheists. Atheists are generally more vocal and dogmatic than agnostics, thus setting themselves up for active disapproval by the orthodox majority.

Atheists and agnostics of all ages share certain aspects, but positions of unbelief are always relative to the popular religious views that unbelievers appear to be rejecting. The playwright George Bernard Shaw commented that "All great truths begin as blasphemies," suggesting that the unbelievers of one cultural epoch open the way for new ideologies in the next. A newly converted Roman Christian in the second century

C.E., for example, would have been an unbeliever in the Roman gods.

The sociological effect of unbelief in the United States is defined against the backdrop of a predominantly Christian country. Despite widely acknowledged secularism and materialism, a diversity of religious views that tend to conflict with one another, and widespread apathy toward (or merely routine participation in) religious belief or activity, modern society still expects either religious orthodoxy or silence on the subject. There are no fully satisfactory ways for the unbeliever to join comfortably with a wide range of social peers in celebrating important rites; group sanction to marriages, christenings, and deaths still occurs mostly within religious institutions. Despite the feeling among some unbelievers that such services are outdated and irrelevant, many participate in them rather than accept the social isolation and stigma that go with rejecting them. In many ways, then, unbelievers are socially excluded by their ideological views and tend to suffer social inconvenience or even ostracism to the extent that they insist on making open issues of their unbelief.

Applications

While modern unbelievers exist at all social strata, many atheists and agnostics are well educated, and the articulate ones are often academicians or social reformers. Training in either the humanities or the sciences is often in the background of unbelieving individuals. The "ivory tower" of academia allows free thinking, whereas the world of business and social exchange exerts pressure to be orthodox in religion (or at least to appear to be), to fit in, and to be normal. Usual channels of social connection include not only churches and synagogues but also service clubs, such as Boy Scouts and Rotary International, which tend to assume religious belief.

In the United States—especially among conservative Protestants, in small towns, and in the "Bible Belt" South—patriotism and religious faith have been closely intertwined through the twentieth century. The coins of the nation proclaim "In God We Trust"; the Pledge of Allegiance mentions "one nation, under God"; sports teams sometimes have locker room prayers before games; public meetings and sporting events may open with prayer; and a new president (or witness in court) is sworn in on a Bible, a symbol of the country's Judeo-Christian heritage. In such a context, the election of an avowed agnostic or atheist to public office in any locale in the United States has been almost unheard of. Though the United States Constitution guarantees freedom of religion, unbelievers wishing to teach in public schools or otherwise maintain public status have almost always kept their views private.

The negative public image of atheists has been at least partly shaped by militant activists such as Madalyn Murray O'Hair, who in 1962 won a suit in the United States Supreme Court against the Baltimore schools, where her son was enrolled. The Court interpreted the constitutional ban on government-established religion to mean that Bible readings and prayer in schools were unconstitutional religious exercises. That decision helped start a persistent public debate over the proper role of "religious" activities in publicly funded institutions. O'Hair moved to Austin, Texas, and founded the Society of Separationists, later called American Atheists; she eventually obtained a tax-exempt status for the group, the same legal privilege given to churches. O'Hair sued unsuccessfully to stop U.S. astronauts from reading the Bible in space, but she did get a Texas law overturned that required holders of public office to believe in God. Her outspoken, unpopular fight to outlaw "religion in schools" and to stop legal and social discrimination against the unbelieving minority seemed to many religious conservatives to show the dangerous, "un-American" character of atheism.

The story of writer George H. Smith, as he tells it in his essay "My Path to Atheism" (1991), offers a less sensational example of modern atheism. Smith grew up in a somewhat religious family and lived on various Air Force bases. He went to Sunday school, "believed in the Bible, heaven, and hell," and got a "God and Country" merit badge in the Boy Scouts by helping maintain churches and learning about the Bible. Gradually he stopped going to church; he experienced disillusionments with individual Christians but kept a vague sense of faith. At one stage in high school he studied the Bible closely and was bothered by what he found in the Old Testament. Soon he started analyzing how the Bible was put together. He also read freethinking American writings, including Thomas Paine's 1794 *The Age of Reason*. For awhile he thought of himself as a Deist—a "rational theist" of the sort that some of the United States' founders were. Smith challenged conservative Christians in debates and began to identify himself as an atheist, never going through the stage of agnosticism. Seeing author Ayn Rand—an atheistic writer and leader in the Objectivist movement—on a television interview program brought Smith under her spell. Soon, however, Rand's ideology, including a dislike of social benevolence and a strong pro-American stance, seemed inadequate to Smith. He lost faith in her movement when he saw a photograph of three American soldiers in Vietnam holding the decapitated heads of their victims like hunting trophies. Further reading led him toward a new belief system that included internationalism and anarchy.

Trying to attain a sense of what atheism and agnosticism mean in real life by using examples of social protesters or writers and academicians certainly does not give a full picture. Unbelief is often a private matter that may not generate predictable public or group behavior patterns, though it can sometimes lead to behavior that appears antisocial. Most atheists and agnostics simply ignore aspects of belief in their daily lives to the extent that society allows. Many choose not to make a public issue of their attitudes, since society in various ways generally disapproves of unbelief.

Context

Sociologists of religion, whose main interests are the normal cultural effects of institutionalized religion, generally have not discussed unbelief much at all. For example, Max Weber's classic work on religion that forms a part of *Wirtschaft und Gesellschaft* (1922; *The Sociology of Religion*, 1964), Thomas F. O'Dea's *The Sociology of Religion* (1966), *The International Encyclopedia of Social Sciences* (1968), and Michael Hill's *A Sociology of Religion* (1973) all omit both atheism and agnosticism, which are more likely to be discussed by philosophers, psychologists, or even literary critics than by sociologists.

The famed sociologist Max Weber concluded, as anthropological studies have also shown, that all human societies have religions which include a belief in a god or gods or in supernatural forces that govern human life and give it meaning in ways that go beyond rational understanding. Religions have strong power over social order and change, and they generate ideas of normal and forbidden behavior. Religious concepts are thus powerful forces for controlling people's lives and providing values and goals. Major breakthroughs in religious thought, Weber hypothesized, have been accompanied by major social changes throughout history. Weber believed, in fact, that the major patterns in the development of industrialized Western society have complex, selective origins in religion. Talcott Parsons notes that since Weber wrote, the value systems of Protestant, Catholic, and Jewish faiths have been institutionalized in a generalized way in the culture of the United States, calling into question some of Weber's specific points but not his main thesis. In this view of history, nonbelievers stand outside the mainstream and seem not to have clear, positive roles in a society whose ethics and value systems are rooted in religion.

A counter view, expressed in 1951 by famed writer C. S. Lewis, is that many moderns see the twentieth century as a "post-Christian" age, rejecting supernatural views and embracing secularism or naturalism. To such nonbelievers, the world's meaning lies within human experience—within the world itself. In this sense, the modern nonbeliever appears to be not a social outcast but rather a reasonably typical social specimen and perhaps a prototype of future humans. He or she is unlike both the earlier Christians and earlier "pagans," for both groups interpreted the world as having origins in a divine, transcendent reality that also operated in human history.

As author James Thrower points out in his *Short History of Western Atheism* (1971), there have been instances of individuals and schools since classical antiquity who have held naturalistic rather than supernaturalistic views; particularly, Thrower argues, the rise of modern secularism and nonbelief dates from the late Middle Ages, when a scientific view first started to replace conventional attitudes based on faith. Charles B. Upton has underscored the relativistic position of the unbeliever in religion: "The history of [atheism] is little more than a collection of instances in which doubt and negation in regard to some essential element in theism have arisen." That is, disbelief rejects aspects of whatever theism is currently dominant in a given culture. Thus an agnostic in modern times and one in ancient Greece might have few ideas in common. Thrower says, however, that the tendency to reject supernatural explanations of things also represents one absolute polarity in human thinking.

In past ages, when conventional theism controlled practical aspects of human life, the nonbeliever not only was a social outsider but also was physically at risk. "Heretics" could be put to death, and many others who inwardly harbored doubt or disbelief were forced into outward conformity for the sake of self-preservation. The modern context of religious liberty, granting freedom to believe or not believe, makes the life of the modern atheist or agnostic relatively secure, but it does not remove the social stigma of unbelief.

Bibliography

Henderson, Charles P., Jr. *God and Science: The Death and Rebirth of Theism*. Atlanta: John Knox Press, 1986. A Christian minister examines the works of such thinkers as Marx, Darwin, Freud, Einstein, and Tillich to trace a history of what he calls the "rise and fall" of scientific atheism. Argues that a new kind of biblical faith can arise out of the doubt generated by science.

Masterson, Patrick. *Atheism and Alienation: A Study of the Philosophical Sources of Contemporary Atheism*. Notre Dame, Ind.: University of Notre Dame Press, 1971. Traces the historical evolution of atheism, showing how it has repudiated theism and other belief systems (such as Marxism and Positivism) that are religion's "secular substitutes." Argues finally that the "affirmation of god" is a hopeful cure for the modern sense of futility.

Smith, George H. *Atheism, Ayn Rand, and Other Heresies*. Buffalo, N.Y.: Prometheus Books, 1991. A diverse collection of essays by Smith, who was influenced by novelist Ayn Rand's atheistic philosophy, Objectivism. Smith knows his views are unorthodox and says "there should be something in this book to offend everyone."

Stein, Gordon, ed. *The Encyclopedia of Unbelief*. 2 vols. Buffalo, N.Y.: Prometheus Books, 1985. A large work comprising items by 101 scholars. Includes discussions of atheism and agnosticism, along with biographies of prominent unbelievers, summaries of philosophical movements, and discussion of such topics as "unbelief in literature," ". . . in Australia," and ". . . in the concept of the devil." Though the work seeks to popularize unbelief and fight bias against it, the entries are informative and reasonably objective.

Strem, George G. *Agnosticism Is Also Faith*. San Diego, Calif.: Libra, 1986. A critic of religion here makes the case for taking an agnostic position, which, he argues, is reasonable, life-affirming, and self-assertive—not passive and reactive.

Thrower, James. *A Short History of Western Atheism*. London: Pemberton Books, 1971. Traces patterns of unbelief since ancient Greece in individuals and groups, with an emphasis on the replacement of the mythological view of life with the modern scientific view. Sees the process as incomplete and ongoing. Chronologically organized and readable.

Roy Neil Graves

Cross-References

AUTHORITARIAN AND TOTALITARIAN GOVERNMENTS

Type of sociology: Major social institutions
Field of study: Politics and the state

Since the beginnings of civilization, authoritarian rule has been the norm. It has assumed various forms and has acquired an even greater variety of names.

Principal terms

ABSOLUTE MONARCHY: a system of government in which the monarch, or ruler, has considerable power in her or his hands

AUTHORITARIANISM: a form of rule in which one person or a small group has a monopoly of political power

AUTHORITY: refers to an interpersonal relationship in which one person looks upon another as superior

AUTOCRACY: rule by one person

DESPOTISM: authoritarian rule in which power is used to the detriment of most subjects

DICTATORSHIP: another term for authoritarianism, or a form of authoritarian government in which power is concentrated in the hands of a single person or a small group of rulers

MONARCHY: a system of government in which at least some power is in the hands of the ruler

OLIGARCHY: government by a small group

TOTALITARIANISM: a government that exercises nearly total control over individual citizens—a relatively recent and extreme form of authoritarianism

TYRANNY: arbitrary power, unrestricted by law, wielded in the interest of the ruler and, usually, hostile to the interests of the governed

Overview

Practically every culture has developed its own set of titles indicative of hierarchy, its own terminology for authoritarian rule. Thus, the distinctions between dictatorship, totalitarianism, autocracy, despotism, tyranny, and so forth are matters of degree and of culture, if they are true distinctions at all. For example, the term "oriental despotism" points to Asia, although there have been ruthless authoritarian regimes or systems on other continents as well. *Caudillismo* is a term used with reference to military dictatorships in Latin America, but such dictatorships became equally common in African countries in the decades following independence. Phalangism is a Spanish (and Lebanese) adaptation of fascism that developed during the regime of Francisco Franco in the middle third of the twentieth century, whereas "fascism" is a generic term describing a form of totalitarianism originally associated with Italy under Benito Mussolini.

Many terms for authoritarianism have a Greek etymology, which merely means that the Greek language has had a profound impact on English and Western languages, particularly in the realm of terminology; it need not imply that these forms of government were first practiced in Greece. For example, oligarchy—a Greek term— can take the form of aristocracy or plutocracy, which are also words of Greek derivation. Whereas aristocracy means rule by the "best," or the government of the nobility, plutocracy means rule by the wealthy. These forms of oligarchy existed in ancient China, in ancient Peru, and elsewhere around the globe.

Although such terms have negative connotations if viewed from the modern "democratic" perspective, they seldom represent unmitigated evil. There are many examples of enlightened or benevolent despots, of good tyrants or dictators who saved the nation or sided with the people. For example, the Athenian tyrant Pisistratus is described by the Greek historian Herodotus as administering the state according to established practice and resorting to "wise and salutary" arrangements. Although they were despots, Frederick the Great of Prussia and Catherine the Great of Russia were, according to the consensus of distinguished contemporaries as well as modern historians, both great and enlightened. The monarchy, wrote Bertrand de Jouvenel (1962), which "is but one solitary individual, stands far more in need of the general support of society than any other form of government."

Throughout most of history, authoritarianism was the standard form of government. Alternative perceptions did not exist. The institution of monarchy, a legitimate ruler's right to rule, was seldom challenged; it was the manner in which that authority was exercised that was either appreciated or deplored by the ruler's subjects and, for that matter, by historians.

Acceptance of and respect for authority are instilled in people from the moment of birth; authority is implied in any parent-child relationship. This must have been the case even before the beginnings of civilization, when rulers and authoritarianism were not yet the norm. Schoolchildren in the United States take political authority, centered on or exclusively represented by the president, for granted. The president becomes a father figure, at least for children.

It is only in recent times that alternative forms of government have come to the fore. Although in the nineteenth century Europe as well as much of the rest of the world was still dominated by authoritarian government, it appeared that time was on the side of democracies and constitutional monarchies, that "democracy was the wave of the future."

In the aftermath of World War I, however, it appeared that democracy and parliamentary government had been discredited, at least in some countries. The very name social democracy was rejected by the leaders of the Bolshevik Revolution in Russia, although they had joined in the "movement" as militant Social Democrats. Partly because of the war itself and partly because of the ensuing depression, right-wing or left-wing totalitarian regimes arose in Italy, Germany, the Soviet Union, and many other countries, whereas in Latin America military dictatorships seemed to prevail. Although totalitarian regimes became discredited in their turn, dictatorships and one-party rule proliferated after the war, especially in areas that had undergone decolonization. By the eve of the twenty-first century, however, a number of authoritarian and one-party governments once again gave way to democracies.

Under authoritarian regimes, political activity is restricted; there is no legal political opposition. Economic and cultural activities, insofar as they can be dissociated from politics, may be given free rein. Totalitarian regimes, however, have sought to exercise economic as well as cultural control.

Applications

The foregoing discussion might lead one to assume that authoritarian governments and democracies are antithetical. There is, however, no clear dividing line between democracy and certain forms of authoritarianism. Representative democracy, parliamentary democracy, and bourgeois democracy invariably result in government by a small group—that is, oligarchy. Such small groups have been identified in modern times as the ruling class (Vilfredo Pareto), the leisure class (Thorstein Veblen), the power elite (C. Wright Mills), and so forth. Whatever the term, it means that relatively few people rule or dominate the political process. These include, and are limited to, "the warlords, the corporation chieftains, the political directorate" (Mills, 1956). The members of this oligarchy may or may not be replaced at regular intervals. If the replacement takes place in an orderly fashion—that is, as a result of elections rather than through revolution or coup d'état—it is likely that the new administration, while possibly claiming a different party allegiance, still represents the same social forces or class.

Furthermore, democracy and authoritarian government are points on a continuum. Democracy falls next to dictatorship by one person or a single party. At times, the public may have difficulty differentiating between political reality and mere slogans. One might wonder whether the people of Indonesia were misled when their first president after independence, Sukarno, declared that "what Indonesia needs is not parliamentary democracy, but democracy with guidance, with leadership . . . Guided democracy is not dictatorship." Even typical cases of totalitarianism, such as fascism in Italy or national socialism in Germany, can be viewed as forms of democracy or at least as dictatorships of the masses. There is no question that the leader in both cases enjoyed widespread popularity until near the end of his regime. It is also not true that mass support in these cases was a result of ignorance or brainwashing; for while Hitler and his bureaucracy enjoyed power over the German masses, the masses themselves were taught or encouraged to enjoy power over other nations. So-called populist regimes also enjoy wide support, as the term indicates; in these, the charismatic leader often exercises power without the destructive component associated with fascism.

"Men make their own history, but they do not make it just as they please; they do not make it under circumstances chosen by themselves," wrote Karl Marx in *Der achtzehnte Brumaire des Louis Bonaparte* (1852; *The Eighteenth Brumaire of Louis Bonaparte*, 1852). Even the most authoritarian or absolute rulers have to heed certain principles of justice, rely on grassroots support, bend with socioeconomic pressures.

Rulers who completely disregard the interest of the people, Niccolò Machiavelli's precepts notwithstanding, seldom die a natural death. Ancient and modern history are replete with examples of assassinations of dictators (under whatever name) who paid no heed to public opinion.

The Bolshevik regime in the Soviet Union termed itself the dictatorship of the proletariat—that is, the dictatorship of a majority—while defining democracy in economic terms as the control exercised by the people over the means of production. Indeed, at least initially, the regime aimed at a maximum of social justice, but it was also an "exclusive pattern of social existence." According to the Soviet constitutions, the legislature did remain supreme, and their members may indeed have believed that they had meaningful authority. A system of democratic centralism—not very different from the practice in parliamentary or "bourgeois" democracies—remained in place. Actually, the power of the people went through a series of simplifications; it was reduced to the power of the soviets, which was then reduced to the power of the Communist Party, which in turn was reduced to the power of the "Politburo" or general secretariat, and eventually to the power of one man, Joseph Stalin. Of the "dictatorship of the proletariat" only the dictatorship remained. Subsequent efforts to restore the original concepts of the Bolsheviks or to backtrack to the road leading to the construction of true socialism have resulted in the disintegration of the Soviet Union. "There is no doubt," wrote Hannah Arendt (1966), "that Lenin suffered his greatest defeat when, with the outbreak of the civil war, the supreme power that he originally planned to concentrate in the soviets definitely passed into the hands of the party bureaucracy." As Vladimir Ilich Lenin himself noted, even though he argued that revolutions use their force against the might of the state, "to destroy it or blot it out," yet they tend "to buttress Power," to improve "the government machine" (Jouvenel, 1962). The process proved irreversible, and the Bolshevik revolution itself was an apparently wasted process.

Thus, in democracies as well as in authoritarian regimes, decisions are made by the few rather than the many. Democracy turns into a kind of authoritarian system in which individual citizens have scant means of influencing the decision-making process. "The English," wrote Montesquieu, "think they are free but they are quite wrong; they are only free when Parliamentary elections come around" (Jouvenel, 1962). Thus, the antithesis of authoritarian government is not democracy but "primitive" communism (communalism), or anarchy, which is no government at all. As Julius Nyerere, the former leader of Tanzania, put it: "to the ancient Greeks, 'democracy' meant simply government by discussion. Discussion is the one thing that is as African as the tribal sun." In traditional African communities the elders "talk until they agree." That is "traditional African democracy."

Context

Although authoritarian governments are commonly viewed as negative by members of presumably democratic societies, they are often interpreted as fulfilling a psychological urge. Authoritarian government, in modern times, is yearned for by millions.

A sizable minority, or even a majority, may in fact yearn for and vote for a powerful authority. Traditional cultures have been shaken by modernization, rural life has given way to urban life, and therefore "the individual feels helpless and alone." As Arendt put it, "what prepares man for totalitarian domination in the non-totalitarian world is the fact that loneliness, once a borderline experience usually suffered in certain marginal social conditions like old age, has become an everyday experience of the ever growing masses of our century." In an authoritarian system such as the military, the rigid chain of command and system of beliefs relieve the individual of the burden of having to make decisions, providing a measure of escape from painful perplexities. In Fyodor Dostoevski's terms, freedom is too much of a burden for the individual.

There may also be other psychological factors at play. Since the time of Thomas Hobbes, at least, the desire for power and domination has often been assumed to be a component of "human nature." "The perpetual and restless desire of power after power that ceaseth only in Death," wrote Hobbes, "is the general inclination of all mankind" (quoted in Fromm, 1941). On the contrary, others argue, it is the general yearning for submission to authority that prevails among humans. Under fascism, there was not even a pretense of party elections. The "Fuhrerprinzip" (leadership principle) prevailed in Germany. According to Rudolf Hess, "Adolf Hitler is the Party. The Party is Adolf Hitler." Thus, in psychological terms, the need for security may match the need for self-respect or self-esteem—to use H. Maslow's terms—on the part of the would-be leader. In Hitler's terms, "the masses love the ruler . . . like a woman who will submit to the strong man" (quoted in Fromm, 1941).

Bibliography

Arendt, Hannah. *The Origins of Totalitarianism*. New York: Harcourt, Brace, and World, 1966. Part of a three-volume work on political power, this essay or treatise on contemporary politics was basically a response to the national socialist regime in Germany, which affected the author personally. It also includes comments on other totalitarian regimes such as the Soviet Union under Stalin, which, though deplored, is given more sympathetic treatment.

Burch, Betty Brand, ed. *Dictatorship and Totalitarianism*. Princeton, N.J.: Van Nostrand, 1964. In addition to providing an anthology of texts by dictators and commentators on dictatorship, the editor has included extensive and lucid introductory remarks to the various sections of the collection containing a wealth of valid definitions and analysis.

Fromm, Erich. *Escape from Freedom*. New York: Farrar and Rinehart, 1941. This treatise, like Arendt's work, was a response to the national socialist regime in Germany, from which Fromm managed to escape. Its approach to the topic, however, is often at the level of individual and mass psychology, with a tip of the hat to Sigmund Freud.

Hobbes, Thomas. *The Leviathan*. New York: Cambridge University Press, 1991. A classic of political philosophy from seventeenth century England which provides an explanation of the need for government, particularly for strong government in the form of monarchy and even absolute monarchy.

Jouvenel, Bertrand de. *On Power, Its Nature and the History of Its Growth*. Boston: Beacon Press, 1962. Although this work was written under the influence of World War II and the Nazi regime that had been imposed on France, its level of analysis is far above merely contemporary and topical issues. De Jouvenel makes ample use of the "classics" and of the historical lessons offered by Western civilization to show how leaders assume and maintain their leadership. This is the book a somewhat mellowed Machiavelli might have written, had he lived four centuries later.

Machiavelli, Niccolò. *The Prince*. New York: Knopf, 1992. A classic of political philosophy from early sixteenth century Florence, Italy. Although the author seems to have favored republicanism and Italian independence, this treatise was nevertheless written as a "how-to" book for a member of the princely Medici family. Its precepts have been widely adopted by well-meaning leaders and despots alike.

Meinecke, Friedrich. *Machiavellism: The Doctrine of Raison d'État and Its Place in Modern History*. New Haven, Conn.: Yale University Press, 1957. A perceptive analysis of power by a well-known German historian who stood in opposition to the national socialist regime.

Mills, C. Wright. *The Power Elite*. New York: Oxford University Press, 1956. Provides an analysis of social conditions in the United States and debunks certain cherished myths. Mills wrote descriptive rather than quantitative sociology—not to make an inventory but to "discover meanings"—which left his work open to attacks by conservatives.

Mario D. Fenyo

Cross-References

Democracy and Democratic Governments, 483; Legitimacy and Authority, 1055; Marxism, 1127; The Military-Industrial Complex, 1207; Power: The Pluralistic Model, 1484; The Power Elite, 1491; Social Stratification: Analysis and Overview, 1839; Traditional, Charismatic, and Rational-Legal Authority, 2064.

THE AUTHORITARIAN PERSONALITY
THEORY OF RACISM

Type of sociology: Racial and ethnic relations
Field of study: Theories of prejudice and discrimination

The theory that an identifiable personality type, termed the authoritarian person-ality by Theodor Adorno and his colleagues, was especially susceptible to racism gained popularity in the early 1950's. The study that produced the theory was trying to account for the rise of Nazism and the perpetration of the Holocaust in 1930's and 1940's Germany.

Principal terms
AUTHORITARIANISM: a syndrome of personality characteristics that predispose a person to hold extreme views and act on them
DOGMATISM: Milton Rokeach's term for a more general form of authoritarianism than that originally theorized, one that is independent of political ideology
D-SCALE: Rokeach's test for dogmatism; a more general measure than the F-Scale
F-SCALE: the classic test for authoritarianism
HIGH AUTHORITARIAN: a person who scores very high on the F-Scale, usually in the top 5 to 7 percentiles
PERSONALITY THEORY: a framework proposed to explain the organization and interaction of characteristics in a person

Overview

The idea of the authoritarian personality was conceived by a group of social scientists and was developed to try to explain behavior of extraordinary social importance. The behavior, a widespread German willingness, prior to World War II, to embrace an extreme form of fascism, was of intensely personal importance to two of the researchers: They had fled Germany and come to the United States to protect their lives. Many fellow social scientists, as well as others who directed and supported the National Jewish Committee's "Social Science Series" of publications, agreed that the topic was important and helped to develop it.

The personality that Theodor Adorno and his colleagues described in *The Authori-tarian Personality* (1950) is a prefascist personality. Their choice of the label "authori-tarian" could have been better made, since a dictionary definition such as "charac-terized by or favoring absolute obedience to authority, as against individual freedom" (from *The American Heritage Dictionary of the English Language*) covers only a small part of the personality syndrome (collection of characteristics) they revealed. Through questionnaires and scales that they devised, Adorno's group studied their subjects' anti-Semitic ideology, politico-economic ideology, ethnocentrism, religious attitudes and practices, and other related topics. Through clinical interviews and projective testing, they evaluated their subjects' personalities in considerable depth. The personality type they came to call authoritarian is a complex one. Those people who display it are troubled individuals, often coping with society's demands in ugly and dangerous ways.

Adorno and his colleagues developed what they called the F-Scale to measure the degree to which respondents display authoritarianism. The person who measures high on the scale is extreme on many, if not all, of the following characteristics. The person may exhibit "conventionalism," a rigid adherence to conventional middle-class values. The person may show both "authoritarian submission," a submissive, uncritical attitude toward idealized moral authorities of the in-group, and "authoritarian aggression," a tendency to look for and condemn, reject, and punish people who violate conventional values. "Anti-intraception" is opposition to the subjective, the imaginative, and the tender-minded. "Superstition and stereotypy" are the belief in mystical determinants of an individual's fate and a disposition to think in rigid categories. "Power and toughness" refer to a preoccupation with the dominance-submission, strong-weak, leader-follower dimension. This aspect of the authoritarian personality includes identification with power figures and an exaggerated assertion of strength and toughness. "Destructiveness and cynicism" mean a generalized hostility and vilification of the human. "Projectivity" is the disposition to believe that wild and dangerous things go on in the world; it represents the projection of unconscious emotional impulses. Finally, the authoritarian personality may show an exaggerated concern with the sexual activities of others.

The "high authoritarian" is an anxious, often confused person who sees threats where others would see only minor concerns and who favors drastic actions to protect against those threats.

Researchers investigating the authoritarian personality in the 1950's found people in the United States who displayed the same authoritarian characteristics that were found among Nazis, a situation that prompted considerable concern. Individuals that test high on the authoritarian scale, in fact, can be found in virtually every society. It was the Jewish population that was the prime target of high authoritarians in Nazi Germany. In the United States, various forms of racism overshadow anti-Semitism, but the model is nevertheless applicable. Blacks, Hispanics, Asians, and any other racial or ethnic group that can be identified may be the target of the high authoritarian.

Critics of the related concepts of authoritarianism and dogmatism (developed by Milton Rokeach) have called attention to a seemingly simpler concept that may explain the behaviors of those who score high on the F-Scale. Most, perhaps all, of the characteristics identified in the early research on the authoritarian personality can be found in highly anxious people. Two of the characteristics or aspects of them— projectivity and identification—are identical to ego defense mechanisms stated by Sigmund Freud to be ways people combat anxiety. Although the terminology is a bit different, several of the other characteristics also accomplish the basic purpose of Freudian defense mechanisms.

Probably the most reasonable way to relate anxiety to authoritarianism is to suggest that developing these personally protective but societally damaging characteristics is but one of several ways people may cope with anxiety. Some resolve anxiety-producing conflicts directly; this is presumed by most psychologists to be the healthiest approach. Some develop neurotic, perhaps even psychotic, patterns of behavior. Probably a few withdraw from society or from life itself as suicides. Developing an authoritarian personality protects a person well, but at a high and often hidden cost to society.

Applications

Authoritarian personality theory offers an interesting, research-based explanation of racism to complement the many other explanations that the behavioral sciences have offered. Unfortunately, it provides few suggestions of how racism may be reduced or eliminated; those that have been proposed work in conjunction with other explanations of the phenomenon. The theory can offer a few suggestions because, at least in its original form, it indicates that individuals who can be identified as high authoritarians have developed their dysfunctional personalities over a lifetime. They are very unlikely to change, even with extended counseling. Further, they are unlikely to feel a need to change; their barely rational beliefs protect them to a much greater degree than they cause them discomfort. It is other people who experience the discomfort.

Most of the identified characteristics of high authoritarianism become more extreme under stress, and high authoritarians are likely to be seriously stressed by many circumstances that other people can tolerate. Some of the ways in which an understanding of the nature of the authoritarian personality can be used to moderate racism rely on minimizing stress in the potential racist. Too often, however, nothing can be done about the sources of the stress; at best, behavioral scientists can suggest ways to limit its consequences.

Because high authoritarians think in rigid categories, they especially need reassurance and rational direction by strong leaders during unsettling times to minimize the likelihood of their becoming involved in extreme actions. For example, during bad economic times for which there are no easy-to-understand causes, leaders ideally should state that the bad times will not last forever, that they are caused by factors that the nation can discover and correct, and that no villains are responsible—no one should be sought out and attacked. Such statements would offer some stress reduction and would discourage people from seeking scapegoats. All people would benefit from such leadership; high authoritarians require it. Unfortunately, agitation or irrational, emotional direction can prompt high authoritarians to extreme action. Some leaders have gained considerable power by taking advantage of high authoritarians' vulnerability; Adolf Hitler is the prime example.

The syndrome labeled "the authoritarian personality" was identified originally as a basis for the development of fascism, but it soon became evident that political ideology was a coincidental factor. Racism, sexism, ethnocentrism, and other fanatical forms of behavior can flourish within almost any political framework. Milton Rokeach proposed an apolitical variation of authoritarianism, which he called "dogmatism," to address this issue.

Rokeach had noticed that members of Communist Party cells in the United States, at a time when communism was seen as the ultimate evil, scored low on authoritarianism. Seeking a reason for this counterintuitive finding, Rokeach concluded that because the communist political system was in many ways opposed to the fascist system, the extremism of the U.S. communists was concealed. Political references on the F-Scale had pushed respondents toward nonauthoritarian choices. Rokeach developed a test, the D-Scale, to measure a more general, apolitical version of authoritarianism he called "dogmatism." He found, as he expected, that communist extremists scored high.

Senator Joseph McCarthy, during the 1950's in the United States, launched senate hearings to uncover communists within the government and the entertainment industry and on college campuses. Many careers and lives were ruined. The damage he caused serves as a vivid example of how authoritarian thinking may be directed at targets other than races. The mechanics of the process remain the same: Irrationality within a part of the population is exploited to gain power or fame or to shift blame away from a leader's own shortcomings. McCarthy's followers found political identity the key factor. Being black, or Jewish, or female was unimportant; being a communist or a communist sympathizer made a person the target.

The fact that research has demonstrated that high authoritarians' extremism extends beyond racism may require modification of the original theory to deal with selectivity of targets. Perhaps the selectivity of targets that some high authoritarians demonstrate can be used to moderate their actions. If, for example, within an area where the norm was to use blacks as scapegoats, religious norms were also strong, high authoritarians' hatred for a racial group might be softened by appeals to religious values of equality. Since the rigid thinking of high authoritarians allows them to compartmentalize thoughts, the incompatibility of "I hate them!" and "They're children of God, along with me" might not spontaneously be noticed, but effective religious leaders might force recognition and might be able to encourage rationality.

Psychologist Leon Festinger's theory of cognitive dissonance is a formal expression of this idea. He proposed that a recognized lack of consistency (dissonance) between individual beliefs, or between belief and behavior, is uncomfortable and that people are motivated to reduce the dissonance.

Context

The concept of the authoritarian personality was developed at a time of deep concern over what had occurred in Nazi Germany in the late 1930's and early 1940's. World leaders and social scientists alike sought new explanations for racism and anti-Semitism; they were driven by the discovery of the unimaginable horror of the Holocaust, in which six million Jews as well as members of other groups, such as Gypsies, were murdered by the Nazis. Leaders worldwide sought ways to ensure that such a tragedy would never occur again. It was during this time, for example, that a number of scientists put forth the idea that the term "race" should be abandoned altogether, arguing that it was scientifically indefensible and had been terribly misused.

An interesting question within authoritarianism theory remains unanswered: Do high authoritarians' dysfunctional personalities influence all that they do, or are they capable of dealing with some topics with average rationality? For example, is the racist whose actions are heavily influenced by authoritarianism capable of political or religious rationality? Research that correlates average F-Scale or D-Scale scores with measures of racism conceals individual differences of this sort. Anecdotal accounts and informal observation often suggest that some people can display strongly authoritarian characteristics in one circumstance and virtually none of them in another. The fanatical racist may have moderate religious views, the political fanatic may show no animosity toward minorities, and so on.

The question of whether authoritarianism is general or topic-specific may be of importance both for explaining origins of the syndrome and for reducing the impact it has on racism and other forms of fanaticism. If it is general—that is, if the characteristics are displayed no matter what the topic—it is likely that authoritarianism is, indeed, a dysfunctional personality pattern. On the other hand, if it is topic-specific, it is possible that authoritarianism which leads to racism (for example) is a set of undesirable learned behaviors that are activated in a particular situation. In other words, the characteristics (conventionalism, authoritarian submission, authoritarian aggression, and so on) that define the syndrome may be demonstrated only during encounters with other races. Modern personality theory increasingly incorporates interactions of individual characteristics with environmental forces as determinants of behavior. Revising the authoritarian theory of racism along such lines may enhance its value.

Bibliography

Adorno, T. W., E. Frenkel-Brunswick, D. Levinson, and R. Sanford. *The Authoritarian Personality*. New York: Harper Brothers, 1950. The original source of the concept of the authoritarian personality, and of the F-Scale devised to measure it, this book contains material essential to understanding the prefascist personality that the authors believed contributed to the perpetration of many of the atrocities in Nazi Germany. Some of the material is too specialized for the average reader but most can be read and understood by anyone who is willing to make the effort.

Katz, Irwin, and Patricia Gurin, eds. *Race and the Social Sciences*. New York: Basic Books, 1969. This is a collection of chapters by eight authors—political scientists, psychologists, and sociologists—examining several aspects of race relations. The book, which should be found in many college libraries, covers a range of topics related to racism, effectively illustrating that no single explanation of the problem can begin to be sufficient.

O'Reilly, Kenneth. *Racial Matters: The FBI's Secret File on Black America, 1960-*

1972. New York: Free Press, 1989. A very unpleasant reminder that racist actions which one might expect to be found in Nazi Germany or some other "evil society" have recently been a part of American society. The parallel between governmental treatment of German Jewish citizens and black Americans is chilling.

Rokeach, Milton. *The Open and Closed Mind*. New York: Basic Books, 1960. Documenting a decade of research since the publication of *The Authoritarian Personality*, Rokeach's book provides broad coverage of extremist behavior, heavily overlapping that of Adorno and his colleagues. A major point of Rokeach's research is that extremist thought and the behavior it promotes may focus on a variety of topics, from anti-Semitism to other forms of religious intolerance, to general racism, to political extremism.

Steinfield, Melvin, comp. *Cracks in the Melting Pot: Racism and Discrimination in American History*. Beverly Hills, Calif.: Glencoe, 1970. A fascinating and often disturbing collection of short segments drawn from many sources. Chapter topics include racism and discrimination in other countries, anti-Indian policies, the Mexican War, and presidential racism (of Abraham Lincoln, among others). Although the historical perspective seldom offers explanations for what is reported, students of sociology or psychology can browse through the segments and apply various theoretical perspectives quite readily.

Harry A. Tiemann, Jr.

Cross-References

Anti-Semitism, 114; Individual Discrimination, 547; The Frustration-Aggression Theory of Racism and Scapegoating, 773; Prejudice and Discrimination: Merton's Paradigm, 1498; Prejudice and Stereotyping, 1505; Race and Racial Groups, 1552; Race Relations: The Race-Class Debate, 1566; Racial and Ethnic Stratification, 1579; Racism as an Ideology, 1586.

BUDDHISM

Type of sociology: Major social institutions
Field of study: Religion

To believers, Buddhism identifies and removes the fundamental causes of human suffering. Its promise of enlightenment and release from a constant cycle of birth, pain, and death has attracted numerous devotees throughout East and Southeast Asia for more than a thousand years, and its emphasis on meditation and compassion has created increasing interest in Buddhism in contemporary Western societies.

Principal terms

BODHISATTVA: an enlightened individual who delays entry into nirvana in order to inspire others to seek enlightenment

BRAHMANISM: the early Aryan religion; also called early Hinduism and located historically in the Vedic age

EIGHTFOLD PATH: the fourth Noble Truth, the method by which release, or nirvana, is achieved

FOUR NOBLE TRUTHS: insights that summarize the nature of existence and the path to enlightenment; they look at the causes of suffering and at the way to end it

HINAYANA: the Lesser Vehicle, a variety of Buddhism stressing individual discipline through monastic practice; also called Theravada, the Doctrine of the Elders

KARMA: the consequences, good or bad, that are carried into the next life because of actions taken in this one

MAHAYANA: the Greater Vehicle, a variety of Buddhism stressing compassion and altruism at the expense of monastic discipline; it has incorporated many foreign religious elements

NIRVANA: the release from the cycle of births and deaths that is arrived at through enlightenment

SAMSARA: the cycle of births and deaths to which the unenlightened are condemned, the major feature of which is suffering; sometimes called the Great Wheel of Being

SANGHAS: early associations of devout Buddhists that evolved into monastic orders

Overview

The Buddhist faith, which first appeared in northern India in the sixth century B.C.E., was an offshoot of an early form of Hinduism called Brahmanism. The original beliefs of Buddhism are somewhat unclear, for the earliest surviving Buddhist text, the Pali canon, dates only from the first century B.C.E. The Pali canon and later texts identified Siddhartha Gautama as the founder of Buddhism and showed that he was strongly affected by the religious climate of the time. For example, he accepted the Brahmanic notion of karma, which holds that conduct in this life determines the circumstances of the next, as well as a modified version of reincarnation, or samsara. Gautama also adopted the Hindu belief that enlightenment leads to nirvana, or ultimate release from earthly existence. He repudiated the authority of the Brahmanic priesthood and its sacred literature, however, claiming that truth must be discovered individually and cannot be transmitted through pronouncement or scripture.

Since Gautama thought that truth is reached only through meditation upon personal experience, he rejected the graded spiritual levels of the Hindu caste system. Opportunities for experience and reflection are available to all, so enlightenment is within reach of all. He also turned against the extreme asceticism practiced by some Hindu holy men, the yogis. He had tried physically harmful exercises himself and decided that productive meditation required good health. Because Gautama's deeper meditative states produced feelings of personal absence or emptiness rather than a sense of constant being, he opposed the Hindu belief in the existence of the individual soul, the *atman*. In its place, he advanced the doctrine of no-self, or *anatman*, arguing that living beings are impermanent combinations of separate elements and that their "souls" do not exist apart from those combinations.

These beliefs came together into a new religious system around 528 B.C.E., when Gautama believed that he suddenly understood the workings of the Great Wheel of Life, the essential process of existence. He then became the Enlightened One, or the Buddha. His insights became the Four Noble Truths, the fundamental principles of Buddhism. Buddhism's antiworldly temper was revealed by the first Noble Truth, which held that all life is caught in a perpetual cycle of suffering, death, and rebirth into renewed suffering. In describing that agonizing cycle, the Buddha used the customary Brahmanic term "samsara," although he changed its meaning by equating life with suffering and replacing the Hindu idea of the pilgrim soul with his own concept of no-self.

The second Noble Truth identified two basic causes of suffering: ignorance of the illusory nature of the world and craving, defined as the desire to cling to these illusory things. It also offered an explanation for samsara—that perpetual desire is the motor that drives life onward, creating long chains of causes and consequences that trap beings in karmic webs. Incessant craving even explains rebirth in the absence of a soul, for it is the impulse that allows an old set of elements at the point of collapse to kindle life in a newly assembled one. Desire is the guardian of being, passing life from individual to individual as a flame leaps from candle to candle.

The third Noble Truth stated that the quelling of desire breaks the cycle of suffering and leads to nirvana. Early Buddhism did not clarify the nature of that transcendence, although it was imagined as awareness within a mysterious vastness. While it was left largely undefined and assumed to be beyond human understanding, later Buddhists described it as union with all existence, or all "suchness."

The fourth Noble Truth described the Eightfold Path and revealed the internal logic at the heart of Buddhist practice. Sometimes called the Middle Way, the Eightfold Path steers a prudent course between self-indulgence and austerity. Its eight precepts fall naturally into three major groups. The first is morality, or shila, which includes right speech, right conduct, and right livelihood. The second is mental discipline, or samadhi, which comprises right effort, right mindfulness, and right concentration. The final group is wisdom, or prajna, which includes right views and right intentions.

The Eightfold Path offers a carefully planned and mutually supporting series of steps to enlightenment. The moral demands of right speech, conduct, and livelihood condemn lying, slander, stealing, promiscuity, murder, and unethical employment. Conversely, it encourages virtues such as compassion, modesty, courtesy, honesty, and friendship. Once undesirable behavior is controlled, the precepts involving mental discipline can produce results. Their exercise, which includes meditative techniques borrowed from Hindu yogis, reduces cravings, allows intuitive insights, strengthens virtues such as patience and compassion, and reveals the underlying reality behind appearances. Finally, the understanding, mental strength, and emotional detachment drawn from meditation are focused on the transient nature of reality and the uselessness of desire. The wisdom gained from these right views and right intentions extinguishes all craving. That extinction produces enlightenment and, upon death, permanent release in nirvana.

Many early believers agreed that anyone could benefit from Buddhist practice and gather merit for the next existence, but they also thought that the Eightfold Path required a level of dedication incompatible with the demands of ordinary life. Accordingly, the truly devout formed religious communities, or *sanghas*, hoping to reach enlightenment within one life span. The first *sanghas* were informal associations, but as time passed they ritualized practices, became religious orders, and served as institutional centers of Buddhism.

Applications

Buddhism's distinctive approach to the basic problems of human existence changed the religious climate of India. It greatly reduced psychological dependence upon the supernatural, for Buddhists believe that the gods are also trapped in the Great Wheel of Being. The gods do not need pacifying, for they are not really deities in the Brahmanic sense; the universe is full of spirits, but it is a universe in which karma and the effects of the Eightfold Path act independently.

The Buddhist view of reality also produced a unique ethical system. In this transient universe, things are always becoming rather than being. Existence is not a state; it is a constantly changing process that fails to form enduring relationships. As Nagarjuna, a second century Buddhist theologian, expressed it:

> The result is cause-possessor,
> But causes are not even self-possessors.
> How can result be cause-possessor,
> If of nonself-possessors it be a result?

Since the constant flux of existence makes consequences unpredictable, the moral value of a given action has to be determined subjectively. Buddhists judge actions to be good or bad strictly in terms of intentions. This produces a kind of moral relativism; two individuals can take completely opposite, but equally exemplary, actions in the same circumstances.

The constantly changing nature of things also shifts moral emphasis to the present. Contrary to appearances, Buddhism holds, moments are not connected to each other. Each one is separate and, because it is dissociated from other moments, timeless. In a special sense, Buddhists live and act in the present and deal with each present as it presents itself. The Buddhist focus on immediacy gives their values and attitudes a distinctly practical, and usually apolitical, cast.

While the Buddhist view of time determines how its ethical system functions, its benchmark characteristic is a benign, empathetic attitude toward others. This is an outgrowth of the first Noble Truth, which defines existence as suffering. All life is painful, so no distinction can be made with regard to individual traits such as beauty, intelligence, and health or on the basis of gender, race, ethnicity, or social status. In a universe where moments of pleasure are always preceded, followed, and outweighed by pain, and where all life is awash in suffering, the proper response is one of sympathy and compassion. Envy and jealousy always reflect ignorance of the underlying nature of appearances.

Since Buddhism (along with a contemporary religious movement, Jainism) addressed problems that had been largely ignored by Brahmanism, it also forced adjustments in the parent religion. The resulting series of shifts in Brahmanic practice away from sacrificial and ritualistic matters toward moral concerns marked the transition to mature Hinduism and turned it into one of the world's major religions. The forced evolution of Hinduism also permitted it to remain competitive with Buddhism. By the tenth century, after centuries-long political rivalries favored preservation of the caste system, Hinduism reconverted all but a remnant of its great competitor. By about 1200, that remnant vanished from India under the double impact of continued absorption and the Moslem invasions. Long before Buddhism disappeared in India, however, it spread to neighboring areas such as Ceylon, Burma, Nepal, Thailand, and Tibet. Through northwestern India it reached central Asia, then China in the first century C.E., Korea in the fourth century, and Japan two centuries later.

Buddhism tended to develop rival sects, and its most serious split occurred over the degree to which believers had to withdraw from ordinary life in order to achieve release. Two major schools appeared: the Hinayana, or Lesser Vehicle (also called Theravada, or the Doctrine of the Elders), which preserved the Pali canon's monastic stress on individual discipline; and the Mahayana, or Greater Vehicle, which emphasized social virtues such as compassion and altruism. Mahayana drifted furthest away from the nondeistic universe of early Buddhism, portraying the Buddha as an eternal being that saved believers and popularizing the concept of the bodhisattva, the enlightened individual who postpones entry into nirvana in order to serve others.

While variants of Hinayana dominated much of Southeast Asia, most of central and East Asia followed the Mahayana pattern. The spread of Mahayana into non-Indian cultures increased its tendency to invoke the magical, and it eventually accepted the gods, demons, hells, and heavens of numerous foreign cults. Its most extreme varieties, called Esoteric Buddhism, are Tibetan Tantrism, whose collections of spells, called tantras, contain magical formulas (mantras) designed to give its users superhuman powers, and the Japanese Shingon sect, which uses mystical chants, signs, and symbols to reach union with the cosmos. One of the less cryptic and more important forms of Mahayana is the Pure Land sect, which deifies the Buddha Amida, emphasizes his compassion, and promises paradise to all who call upon his name. Another is Ch'an, or Zen, Buddhism, which uses meditation to locate an interior Buddha nature, prizes intuition, and views rationality as an obstacle to enlightenment.

Even in emigration, after long exposure to different cultural traditions and values, both the Mahayana and Hinayana schools preserved their basic orientation. Whether the faithful lived as celibate monks or in the midst of families, they carried traditional Buddhist attitudes and values into the wider society.

Context

While Buddhism began as a specific reaction to the caste system and Brahmanic ritualism, it became part of a broad ethical movement that swept through much of the Asian land mass and reached into Europe. The sixth century B.C.E. saw the rise of mature Hinduism alongside Buddhism in India, the appearance of Taoism and Confucianism in China and Zoroastrianism in Persia, the development of Jewish monotheism, and the rise of salvation cults such as the Pythagorean brotherhood in the eastern Mediterranean. In one way or another, these religious and ethical systems grappled with growing differences within their societies and increasing links between different populations. Buddhism was one of the more successful responses to these changing conditions. Its emphasis on empathy and compassion blunted group and class antagonisms, and its promise of release into nirvana promoted optimism as well as toleration.

Buddhism was also a socially stabilizing force. Its emphasis on the present did not lead to individual inaction, for Buddhists were urged to use every day to the fullest. Yet its view that moments are disconnected, that existence is a never-completed process, and that karmic consequences are created by intentions instead of results prevented it from acting as an agent of political or social change. Buddhists saw themselves as belonging to a religious, not a political, institution. Nevertheless, their general indifference to political issues made it a bulwark of tradition. To nineteenth and twentieth century liberals and radicals, Buddhism was a synonym for social and political inertia.

That close association with tradition has placed Buddhism at a disadvantage in many contemporary Asian societies, where it is often viewed as an obstacle to modernization. It is well-established in Japan, has a considerable following in South Korea, and is the dominant religion in Burma. Nevertheless, twentieth century assaults on Buddhism in China, Indo-China, Mongolia, Tibet, and North Korea have seriously reduced its influence. While retreating in large parts of Asia, however, the major types of Buddhism have had some success in Europe and the Americas. Prospects for a mass following in those areas are poor, for Buddhist ideas of reincarnation and no-self contradict deeply rooted Western religious traditions, and Buddhism's social conservatism clashes with the political dynamism typical of the Western world. Yet certain aspects of Buddhism have enjoyed success. A growing number of westerners, including psychologists and physiologists, appreciate its meditative techniques. Also, the timelessness and serenity of its art has attracted a large audience.

In industrialized countries, Buddhism's most promising feature is its accent on altruism, kindness, and toleration. Technological societies are complicated, and their parts have grown indifferent to one another. Since the 1970's, waves of immigration into Western countries have increased cultural fragmentation, reviving nationalist, racial, and ethnic disputes and sharpening already serious class divisions. Under conditions of social isolation and group antagonism, attitudes of toleration, empathy, and compassion are extremely important. Buddhist ethics may fill a vital place in the value system of the Western world if it can reduce tribal tendencies, promote civility, and help repair the damaged social fabric of modern life.

Bibliography

Blofeld, John. *The Wheel of Life: The Autobiography of a Western Buddhist.* 2d ed. Boulder, Colo.: Shambhala Press, 1978. Describes one person's spiritual journey into Mahayana Buddhism. Interesting on many levels, it reveals the interplay of different Buddhist sects with other religions and describes Chinese Buddhism before the Communist takeover of that country. Includes illustrations and an index.

Dumoulin, Heinrich, ed. *Buddhism in the Modern World.* New York: Macmillan, 1976. A strong collection of articles on the background and status of Buddhism in various countries. Concentrates on Asia, but includes an article on Buddhism in the West. A good bibliography and index.

Hamilton, Clarence H., ed. *Buddhism: A Religion of Infinite Compassion.* New York: Liberal Arts Press, 1952. An excellent survey of Indian, Chinese, Japanese, and Tibetan Buddhist literature. Provides a general introduction and prefaces for each section. Contains a glossary and a bibliography.

Pilgrim, Richard B. *Buddhism and the Arts of Japan.* Chambersburg, Pa.: Anima Books, 1981. A good introduction to the impact of Buddhism on art forms, concentrating on the visual arts. Offers illustrations, an annotated list of audiovisual resources, a bibliography, and a glossary.

Saddhatissa, H. *The Buddha's Way.* New York: George Braziller, 1971. A good general introduction to Buddhism with references to Christian thought. Discusses different types and techniques of meditation. Appendices, illustrations, a short glossary, a bibliography, and a subject index.

Tatz, Mark, trans. *Asanga's Chapter on Ethics with the Commentary of Tsong-Kha-Pa; The Basic Path to Awakening, the Complete Bodhisattva.* Lewiston, N.Y.: Edwin Mellen, 1986. Contains two important Buddhist documents: a third or fourth century Indian work on ethics, and a medieval Tibetan guide to enlightenment. Notes, a bibliography, and an index.

Watts, Alan W. *The Way of Zen.* New York: Pantheon Books, 1957. An excellent treatment of the origins and characteristics of Zen Buddhism, Watts's book is divided into two roughly equal parts: background and history, and principles and practice. It contains illustrations, a bibliography, and an index.

Wright, Arthur F. *Buddhism in Chinese History.* New York: Atheneum, 1965. A very useful introduction to the impact of Buddhism on the course of Chinese history by a noted Chinese specialist. Stresses the changes in Buddhism as it spread into a radically different culture. Bibliography and index.

Michael J. Fontenot

Cross-References

Christianity, 231; Confucianism and Taoism, 347; Islam and Islamic Fundamentalism, 1022; Judaism, 1029; Religion: Beliefs, Symbols, and Rituals, 1598; Religion: Functionalist Analyses, 1603; Religion: Marxist and Conflict Theory Views, 1610; Socialization: Religion, 1894; The Sociology of Religion, 1952.

BUREAUCRACIES

Type of sociology: Social structure
Field of study: Key social structures

Evolved to enhance the authority and operational effectiveness of modern organizations—governments, businesses, trade unions, and political parties—bureaucracies have become a worldwide phenomenon. Their defenders perceive them as efficient, essential, and flexible; their critics see them as disinterested, impersonal, and self-serving manufacturers of paper work and red tape.

Principal terms

AD-HOCRACY: a temporary work group of skilled persons designed to solve specific, nonroutine problems

AUTHORITY: power accepted as legitimate by the people over whom it is exercised

BUREAUCRATIC PERSONALITY: the tendency for bureaucrats to adhere strictly and impersonally to regulations beyond the point at which these regulations cease to serve organizational objectives

IDEAL TYPE: a logical, exaggerated model used as a methodological tool for the study of specific phenomena

INFORMAL SYSTEM: an organization within supposedly rational and impersonal bureaucracies which is composed of personal and closely knit social groups

OLIGARCHY: a small group of people who control an organization's or system's power

PARKINSON'S LAW: the observation that the work of bureaucracies expands to fill the time required for its completion; in other words, self-serving bureaucracies "make work"

PETER PRINCIPLE: explains the incompetence of bureaucrats by suggesting that in a hierarchy every employee tends to rise to his or her own level of incompetence

RATIONAL-LEGAL AUTHORITY: the legitimization of power by law, rules, and regulations rather than by tradition or personality

Overview

Bureaucracies have developed throughout societies in which complex tasks must be placed under centralized control and administered efficiently. Millennia ago, Egyptian dynasties established bureaucracies to collect taxes, facilitate irrigation, and carry through massive dynastic works; for example, tomb and pyramid construction. Similarly, beginning roughly two thousand years ago in order to collect taxes over a vast area, to control rivers, to maintain armies, and to assist in canal building, China created a sophisticated bureaucracy that was staffed and controlled by mandarins, a scholarly elite. It is the bureaucracies that have evolved since the 1780's within modern industrial and postindustrial societies, however, that have captured the attention of sociologists and other social scientists.

In eighteenth century France, for example, during an era when the absolutist monarchy was not only engaged in international wars but also attempting to regulate the national economy more closely, the word "bureaucracy" first appeared as the collective designation for groups of administrative officials. In Prussia soon thereafter, bureaucracy meant government by officials, while in 1860 in Great Britain, political economist John Stuart Mill defined the essence of bureaucracy as the placement of government work in the hands of "governors by profession."

These casual definitions were given scholarly substance by the German sociologist and political economist Max Weber (1864-1920). Weber recognized that modern society had become increasingly rational, so much so that humans were being caught in an "iron cage." Moreover, no aspect of modern society more completely embodied this rationality than did bureaucracies. Because of the importance of this phenomenon, Weber formulated an abstract, logical, ideal type of bureaucracy in comparison with which further study of real bureaucracies could proceed. Although they were subsequently refined and embellished, Weber's criteria of what constitutes bureaucracies have remained valid and continue to be employed by sociologists.

Bureaucracies, therefore, are understood to be organizations displaying at least a half-dozen common characteristics. Labor is divided among members of bureaucracies according to written prescriptions of responsibilities and functions. Authority, flowing from the top down, is allocated among their memberships according to well-defined rank order. Detailed, written rules and regulations subsequently determine the rights and duties applicable to every position. Likewise, specified procedures and regulations govern the handling of tasks. As is the case in the large, impersonal (*Gesellschaft*) societies that bureaucracies serve, impersonality or neutral attitudes mark relationships among bureaucrats and between bureaucrats and their clients. Finally, the selection, recruitment, and employment of bureaucrats, as well as their promotions within their bureaus, are based on demonstrable competence—usually measured by formal examinations—and expertise.

Weber's theoretical or ideal type of bureaucracy is a formal organization designed to achieve definite goals with maximal efficiency, but the authority under which it operates is described by sociologists as rational-legal authority. That is, the legitimization of bureaucracies stems from the law and a social system's basic rules rather than from the influences of personality, charisma, idiosyncratic decision making, or tradition.

Weber's abstraction, although a classic one, is only one of several. In 1911, Robert Michels supplemented Weber's work by including not only governments but also political parties in his concept of bureaucracy. Bureaucracies in Michels' study derived from the administrative necessities confronting all modern organizations; not least, he argued, they strengthened the oligarchic power of a handful of party leaders. Almost at the same time, and in a similar vein, Gaetano Mosca insisted that bureaucracies were fundamental to the governance of all major political systems. Moreover, those societies in which bureaucracies had not developed, he declared, could be classified as feudal.

As the twentieth century progressed, such theories allowed sociologists increasingly to study the ways in which bureaucracies functioned in reality. The yields of these studies have sharpened definitions of bureaucracy just as they have tended to divide sociologists and other social scientists over the efficiency as well as the effects of bureaucratization.

By the 1950's, for example, many sociologists were demonstrating that in reality bureaucracies were far from the efficient, goal-oriented organizations that classic models had proposed. Empirical study instead shows that in many cases bureaucratic operations were quite inefficient and even counterproductive. Conclusions from these studies, which examined governmental, private corporate, and political organizations, tended to confirm the idea prevalent in nearly all developed countries that bureaucracies had introduced vexatious, sometimes nightmarish, burdens into people's daily lives.

To begin with, while bureaucrats often handle routine tasks capably, they frequently appear to be paralyzed by unusual or nonroutine tasks as well as by unexpected changes (war, natural disasters, and so forth)—to the chagrin of their clients and at considerable cost to everyone. Like Max Weber (who was the subject of one of Bendix's studies), Reinhard Bendix worried about a world filled with people who clung to little jobs and struggled like careerists toward bigger ones.

Other sociologists described the formation of a "bureaucratic personality": the bureaucrat's inclination to follow rules beyond the point at which their organizational goals ceased to be served. Having noted that bureaucracies continuously sought bigger budgets and larger workforces, C. Northcote Parkinson posited a "law" that bureaucratic work seemed to expand with the time available for its completion, while Laurence Peter's famed "Peter principle" suggested that in every hierarchy each employee is likely to rise to the level of his or her own incompetence. To these impressions still other sociologists have added details on the inner world of forms, memos, studies, and regulations that characterize bureaucracies.

There are sociologists, however, who address the question of why, despite their unpopularity, rigid routines, and red tape, bureaucracies persist as one of the major institutional characteristics of modern society. A number of studies have supplied partial answers by noting what appear to be bureaucratic virtues. For example, although red tape and elaborate procedures anger some citizens, they can be shown to protect the rights of others. Similarly, bureaucratic impersonality and neutrality sometimes play positive roles. Thus, students seeking government-subsidized grants or loans and private builders seeking government contracts often prefer that personal or political influence—indeed, any type of discrimination—be excluded from decisions concerning their applications.

Other studies suggest that some bureaucracies may be less mechanical in their operations and bureaucrats often may be less hidebound in their reactions than is commonly assumed. Sociologist Melvin Kohn, for example, indicates that bureaucracies can and do encourage open-mindedness, imagination, and creativity among their employees. Moreover, according to test results, bureaucrats demonstrate high levels of intellectual performance. They likewise place heavy demands on themselves, value self-direction and nonconformity, and are more likely to favor change than are nonbureaucrats.

Applications

One hallmark of modernity is the pervasiveness of bureaucracies. In developed nations, they have grown steadily in size and number both in the public and private spheres since the late nineteenth century. In the 1990's, despite continuing complaints about their inefficiencies, their erosive effects on individualism, and their inhumanity, they remain expansive and wield enormous authority. Small wonder that German sociologist Henry Jacoby was able to title one of his major works *The Bureaucratization of the World* (1973). Small wonder, too, that like Jacoby and Weber, sociologists Hans Gerth, C. Wright Mills, Michel Crozier, and Robert Merton, among many others, asked what forces might be found to control "this monstrous system" and how liberal democracy might be preserved in the face of it.

Undoubtedly, there is a close fit between the operations of bureaucracies and Weber's ideal model of them. When the evolution of bureaucracies and their mature functions have been studied closely and comparatively by social scientists, however, these key institutions have been found to display their own unique characteristics.

These distinctions frequently appear within the bureaucracies of specific nations. For example, over long periods, the bureaucratic organization of American Telephone and Telegraph (AT&T), International Business Machines (IBM), Eastman Kodak, and Minnesota Mining and Manufacturing (3-M Company)—all at one time models of effectiveness—have differed significantly from those of American steel, railroad, and automotive companies.

In addition, such distinctions also differentiate the bureaucracies of one nation from those of another. Comparatively, for example, America's federal bureaucracies are readily distinguishable from China's collectivist state bureaucracies, just as American corporate bureaucracies often reveal unique characteristics when compared with many corporate organizations in Japan. More specifically, China's collectivist models emphasize greater ideological commitment and higher technical competence among an organization's members than is true in the United States. They likewise strive for egalitarianism, minimize the range of rewards, and entrust authority to the collectivity as a whole. To motivate workers, the Chinese stress comradeship, personal appeals, and the diffusion of skills. In addition, they deemphasize the division of labor and tend to favor ad hoc decision making by formal groups.

By comparison, American corporate bureaucracies frequently reveal salient features that are quite different from those of Japan's corporate bureaucracies. Unlike many American corporations, in which managers are expected to show results quickly and thus concentrate on short-term rather than on long-term goals, risking their jobs if they fail, the opposite tends to be true in Japan. In fact, until Japan's lengthiest and deepest economic recession (which entered its third year in 1994) raised questions about prevalent practices, Japanese managers and workers could count on lifetime employment with their organizations.

Sociological studies have also proposed other comparisons, such as those advanced by Stephen Skowronek in 1982 and Bernard S. Silberman in 1993. Both specialists have examined the development of America's federal bureaucracy as well as the development of its major political parties. Silberman, in particular, has compared the evolution, structure, and functions of the U.S. bureaucracy and political parties by applying his focus to related developments in France, Japan, and Great Britain. To generalize, what has been learned is that distinct cultures produce their own unique brands of bureaucracy. To be sure, features of the ideal type proposed by Weber and by other classic sociological studies are in varying degrees detectable in the structuring and goal-setting of all bureaucracies. Differences between their organization, functioning, and objectives in relation to their cultural contexts, however, frequently appear to be as significant as their similarities.

America's federal and state bureaucracies, for example, historically seemed to be assembled in defiance of rationality when contrasted with Weber's ideal bureaucratic model. Satisfying demands for patronage upon which political parties relied for much of their strength during most of the nineteenth century took precedence over administrative efficiency and effectiveness. Recruitment to administrative posts was not selective, based on technical or professional competence, or intended to place administrators and bureaucrats beyond the reach of political influence. On the contrary, selections were based on favoritism, pull, and bureaucrats' willingness to heed the wishes of the politicians and party that chose them.

Federal enactment of the Pendleton Act in 1883 and subsequent civil service acts (shortly followed by similar state laws) gradually eroded patronage but failed to depoliticize America's governmental bureaucracies. In fact, control over the federal bureaucracy during the twentieth century shifted from the Executive branch of government to the Congress, and Congress has tightened and formalized bureaucratic recruitment, rank orders, technical competence, and its bureaucrats' rewards. Nevertheless, bureaucratic autonomy and depoliticization have not occurred. Thus, in the 1980's, federal bureaucracies paid nearly five hundred full-time lobbyists to plead their cases—most of which were related to budget and personnel—with the Congress. In this and many other respects, government bureaucracies in the United States contrast sharply with those of Great Britain, France, and Germany.

Context

Auguste Comte (1798-1857), one of the founders of sociology, in common with other of sociology's early pioneers, used the term "organization" in referring to bureaucracies. Not only did those scholars consider bureaucracies to be essential organizations, their references to them also were usually positive ones. Later in the nineteenth century, however, when industrialization was in full swing and the power of Western governments was rapidly expanding, the perspectives of sociologists changed. They continued to view bureaucratic organizations in the abstract as essential components of rational, modern societies, but bureaucracy nevertheless posed a dilemma for them. Although no one could suggest a substitute for these apparently indispensable organizations, the cold, mechanical, inhumane, often inefficient, and inflexible character of public and private bureaucracies in action were worrisome.

Weber's classic depiction of an ideal type of bureaucracy manifested this ambivalence. From a purely technical view, bureaucracies, he believed, represented the most rational of all organizations and therefore were capable of bringing the greatest efficiency and precision to bear in pursuit of their objectives—and of doing so cheaply. It was the effects of bureaucratization and the consequences of the modern passion for rationality which the process reflected that drove Weber to despair. Without knowing what to do about such problems (Alvin Toffler's concept of "ad-hocracies" lay half a century in the future), Weber feared the dehumanization of bureaucrats and their clients alike, as well as a general loss of individual freedom. Just how much Weber's negative perceptions of bureaucracy stemmed from his own bitter conflicts with his bureaucrat father remains conjectural. What is certain, however, is that hundreds of additional sociological studies of bureaucratic organizations have not dissipated anxieties and fears such as Weber's.

Weber died in 1920, but those sociologists who have pursued his interests in bureaucracies have sharpened their definitions of these organizations and directed their analytical focus toward the major institutional changes and problems of their times. Because professional sociology was largely a Western European and an American enterprise, sociologists have concentrated their attention, insofar as bureaucracies are concerned, on the structure and operations of important new institutions as well as on significant changes in older ones.

One of these new institutions of transcendent importance is the private business corporation, the activities of which since the end of the nineteenth century have played vital roles in the social and economic lives of Americans and Europeans. The older institution is government, which during the twentieth century has not only taken on novel forms but also has assumed vastly more intricate and expanded authority. Both new and changed organizations function by virtue of their bureaucracies.

Taking different tacks from those of earlier twentieth century sociologists such as Mosca and Crozier, for example, Jerald Hage and Wolf Heydebrand have studied the adaptations of bureaucracies to technical change, stressing their inner working, their informal groups, and their flexibility. Peter Blau and Marshall Meyer similarly have examined adjustments between bureaucracies and modern society with more sanguine results than Weber's, while Alvin Toffler concentrated on the efficacy of ad-hocracies, which he viewed as replacements for bureaucracy. Fresh analyses of the expansion of American administrative capacities, meantime, appear in the work of Herbert Simon, Gordon Tullock, Bernard Silberman, Reinhard Bendix, Paul DiMaggio, and Robert Skowronek, while organizational and bureaucratic elites have been analyzed by Robert Presthus, C. Wright Mills, Robert Dahl, Charles Lindblom, and Paul Goldman.

Bibliography

Crozier, Michel. *The Bureaucratic Phenomenon*. Chicago: University of Chicago Press, 1964. A clear, precise, and jargon-free survey of the subject by a French sociologist. Crozier's view is that modern bureaucracies are distinguished by their inability to correct their errors and hence are detrimental organizations. Includes a brief bibliography and an index.

Jacoby, Henry. *The Bureaucratization of the World*. Translated by Eveline L. Kanes. Berkeley: University of California Press, 1973. Surveys the bureaucratic origins of modern governments, the advent of the administered world, and the rule of bureaucracy and its problems. A clear, reflective work intended for the nonspecialist. Contains footnotes, a valuable bibliography, and a useful index.

Ritzer, George. *Sociological Theory*. New York: Alfred A. Knopf, 1983. This is a clear, effective book. Chapter 5, which discusses Weber and his views on bureaucracy, is first-rate and essential. Ritzer succeeds in explaining theory without using jargon. Includes photographs and biographical sketches of sociological theorists, a valuable bibliography, and an index. A good starting point for understanding bureaucracies.

Silberman, Bernard S. *Cages of Reason*. Chicago: University of Chicago Press, 1993. A fine, detailed survey of the rise of rational (bureaucratized) states in France, Japan, the United States, and Great Britain. Silberman convincingly adduces evidence to contradict Weber's pessimism about bureaucratization. Contains tables, a superb bibliography, and an index.

Weber, Max. *From Max Weber*. Edited and translated by H. H. Gerth and C. Wright Mills. New York: Oxford University Press, 1946. This book consists of well-chosen excerpts, with annotations, from Weber's influential sociological essays. Weber always makes exciting reading. Notes and an index are included.

Clifton K. Yearley

Cross-References

Industrial and Postindustrial Economies, 940; Industrial Societies, 953; Institutions and Total Institutions, 1003; Legitimacy and Authority, 1055; Organizations: Formal and Informal, 1316; Postindustrial Societies, 1446; Socialism and Communism, 1873; Traditional, Charismatic, and Rational-Legal Authority, 2064.

BUSING AND INTEGRATION

Type of sociology: Racial and ethnic relations
Field of study: Policy issues and debates

Busing to achieve integration of schools began in the late 1960's in Berkeley, California, and appeared to be a feasible way to end continuing segregation (de jure or de facto) in public schools. Opposition on the part of many white Americans and some African Americans, however, has disrupted and blunted the effectiveness of the busing experiment.

Principal terms
DISCRIMINATION: the denial of opportunities and rights to certain groups on the basis of race or ethnicity
INSTITUTIONAL RACISM: the way society's institutions operate so as systematically to favor some groups over others with regard to opportunities and resources; often such racism is unintentional, but the discrimination is nevertheless real
MINORITY GROUP: any group that, on the basis of physical or cultural characteristics, receives fewer of society's resources and rewards
PREJUDICE: arbitrary beliefs or feelings about an individual of a certain ethnic or racial group or toward the group as a whole
RACISM: the denial of rights and/or opportunities to certain groups because of race or ethnicity
SEGREGATION: the physical separation of groups, usually imposed by one on another

Overview

Transporting children from one area to another to get them to school was nothing new in the late 1960's. Indeed, a full century before, in 1869, Massachusetts set aside money to pay for carriages and wagons to bring students to and from school. Within fifty years, all states in the union made public money available for the transporting of students.

Until the controversies of the 1960's and 1970's, busing was seen as a progressive educational innovation: Children could be moved from poorly funded and equipped one-room "country" schools to new consolidated schools that generally had more funding, more equipment, and a larger library. Further, in consolidated institutions teachers were allowed to specialize and could deliver better education in their major fields of study. By 1970, more than eighteen million children rode buses to school, representing about 40 percent of all public school students in the United States.

No public outcry against busing surfaced until the issue of school integration became a priority, as mandated by the United States Supreme Court. Passions against busing to achieve integration first arose in the South. For decades, busing had been used there to maintain segregation and discrimination in the public schools. Often, once a bus had picked up white students, that bus would drive right by an African American school to get to an all-white school that was farther away. The reverse was also true; once a bus had picked up a group of black students, that bus would drive by an all-white school but continue on until, perhaps many miles away, the bus finally arrived at an all-black school. For example, in Selma, Alabama, some African American youngsters traveled more than 50 miles by bus to Montgomery to reach a segregated black trade school. Selma had an all-white trade school. In Oklahoma City, Oklahoma, some African American children were bused up to 70 miles a day until they reached their segregated black school, even though several white schools were closer to their neighborhood.

One of the first major crises over busing to achieve racial balance occurred in the early 1970's in the Charlotte-Mecklenburg area of North Carolina. There, more than 84,000 children attended the more than one hundred schools in the 550-square-mile school district. Although the district had a voluntary transfer policy in place, African Americans, who totaled 29 percent of the student population, still attended segregated schools and were concentrated in one section of the district. Eventually, a legal test case reached a federal district judge, who ruled that the district was not complying with various Supreme Court rulings; moreover, in 1971 the Supreme Court ruled specifically, in *Swann v. Charlotte-Mecklenburg Board of Education*, that district judges had broad authority to achieve desegregation of schools, even if busing was needed to achieve that goal.

Elected president in 1968, Richard Nixon asked Congress in 1972 to grant a moratorium on, or a restriction against, busing. Then he appeared on nationwide television to denounce forced busing, and he continued throughout his term to oppose and obstruct busing programs.

Eventually, the busing crisis reached the North and the West, where de facto segregation (as opposed to de jure segregation, or segregation "by law") of schools existed because of residential patterns. In such cities as New York, Chicago, and San Francisco, African Americans complained about the continuing segregation of schools. One center of opposition was Boston. As early as 1965, Massachusetts' laws stipulated that districts should integrate all schools that had more than 50 percent African American enrollment: Yet in 1974, 85 percent of the city's black youngsters attended institutions where they were still in the majority; more than 50 percent of them attended schools that were still 90 percent black. Consequently, in June of 1974, a federal judge demanded that busing be used to comply with Supreme Court rulings and with federal civil rights laws.

After busing was begun in the city, there were several white riots as well as white boycotts of certain schools. In one episode, national television networks captured and broadcast scenes of white middle-class mothers who rioted in the street and made a yellow school bus an object of their immediate hatred; they set it afire, then stepped back to applaud their work. Riots continued to occur in South Boston because of issues related to busing and the larger issue of integration. Eventually, because of white opposition such as that found in Boston, busing as a technique to achieve integration lost favor; to many, that development signaled that the Civil Rights movement was taking a step backward. Indeed, even as the United States has made progress on some social issues, the problem of continuing segregation of schools has not been solved.

Applications

Studies of busing and the fierce debates it has engendered have produced a number of observations. One is the argument that the busing of students per se is a false issue. Busing to achieve and maintain segregation had long been practiced, most notably in the South, and whites did not object to such busing. Another argument is that, if society were to reject busing as an approach to school integration, it would be helping to perpetuate a major form of institutional racism. In 1970, Stephen Spotswood of the National Association for the Advancement of Colored People (NAACP) labeled opposition to busing as racist, reminding some critics that they had once supported busing when it was used to enforce segregation. Spotswood mentioned a 1970 survey of three hundred Southern school districts that used busing to achieve integration. In 290 of the schools, there was actually less busing after integration than before.

Likewise, a study of the verbal, and often violent, reactions of a number of individuals and groups opposed to busing illustrates that the United States is still a racist country. For example, one irate white Bostonian complained about busing by verbally assaulting Thomas J. Cottle of the Children's Defense Fund of the Washington Research Project (headquartered in Boston). The white parent told Cottle that his son was being forced to attend an integrated school miles away while buses brought in other children to a nearby school. Finally, the parent began screaming and told Cottle that the youngsters being bused in "don't belong here."

Other negative words and actions concerning busing abound. For example, when South Boston High School first began busing to achieve integration, a white boycott saw only one hundred Anglos attend the first day of a new term, while more than fourteen hundred stayed away. As soon as the buses carrying black students arrived, white youngsters and adults started stoning the African Americans; several of their number received cuts and bruises. In the case of South Boston High, the predominantly working-class parents of the neighborhood repudiated the tolerant racial attitudes and the sense of fairness that had once accompanied the Civil Rights movement.

Responding to busing, many whites enrolled their children in private schools or moved to all-white suburban school districts. Meanwhile, civil rights activists, who knew that busing was a false issue, tried to pressure first President Nixon and then President Gerald Ford to uphold the practice. One such protester was James Farmer, longtime leader of the Congress of Racial Equality (CORE), whom Nixon had appointed assistant secretary of health, education, and welfare; Farmer's efforts achieved no success. Indeed, Nixon continued to oppose busing and threatened to seek a constitutional amendment to stop the practice. He even warned federal officials—especially those in the Department of Health, Education, and Welfare—to stop forcing the busing issue or to look for other jobs. At one point in Ford's administration, he reportedly approached his attorney general, Edward H. Levi, and suggested that Levi support busing foes in a pending Boston court case; however, aides eventually talked Ford out of such a course of action.

Even the federal courts took a step backward. In 1973 a circuit court barred a Virginia school district's attempt to bus students. The Supreme Court heard the case on appeal but ruled four to four to uphold the lower court's decision.

Although advocates of busing experienced stormy times in dealing with the Nixon and Ford administrations, at the state and local levels some victories were won. They were not usually achieved without a fight. Oklahoma City, Oklahoma, is a case in point. There, when the first debates about busing surfaced, conservative legislators passed an antibusing bill that was supposedly racially "neutral." Republican governor Dewey Bartlett signed it into law on April 15, 1970. Black educator F. D. Moon of Oklahoma City exposed the true motives of the politicians who supported the law, however, when he mentioned that he could not get too "worked up" about the busing crisis because for many years African American youngsters in the Oklahoma City metroplex had been bused up to 70 miles a day to enforce segregation. Most local whites continued to oppose the idea of busing to achieve school desegregation and heartily supported their legislature.

Federal judge Luther Bohanon did not support the legislature, however; instead, he ordered a busing policy put in place. It was known as the "finger plan" (also called the magnet schools plan) and had been drawn up by a Rhode Island educator. It called for the drawing of new attendance "zones" for senior and junior high schools and for a new network of fifth-grade centers for primary schools. Implemented in February of 1972, the plan was unpopular with many whites but was enforced, thereby creating more racial balance in many Oklahoma City schools.

Context

The antibusing "movement" was but a small part of a bigger problem—the bigger problem being the attempts of some people to try to forestall or reverse the gains of the Civil Rights movement of the 1950's and 1960's. Since the Supreme Court made its 1971 ruling in *Swann v. Charlotte-Mecklenburg Board of Education*, members of Congress, pressured by their white constituents, have introduced sundry proposals that would limit the federal courts' authority over school desegregation issues. If such proposals were to become law, the Supreme Court would lose its appellate jurisdiction in school cases as would the lower federal courts. Other proposals explicitly have sought to restrict the use of busing to achieve integration. All such proposals would return preeminent power to the states. Critics argue that the federal judiciary exceeded its authority when it immersed itself in the educational issues because it usurped legislative functions and the chief executive's policy-making functions.

Many members of Congress have echoed the white mothers in South Boston by producing a litany of the negative aspects of busing: It is a divisive issue within a community; it aggravates racial tensions and therefore disrupts the educational process; and it undermines the stability that schools need if children are going to learn effectively. Further, children lose time—time to study, time to develop friendships among their peers, and time to engage in extracurricular activities. Busing opponents say that, within forced-busing programs, parents also suffer. Parents do not have the opportunity to participate in parent-teacher associations and to visit teachers and classes, nor can they engage in school functions if the schools are remote from their homes.

Opponents of busing also point out that busing costs money, money better spent on educational programs. Finally, critics mention that busing is counterproductive; as a tool to achieve racial balance, they argue, the practice is a failure because it often leads to "white flight" to white suburbs, to rural schools, or to private schools. When whites leave, part of the school district's tax base leaves with them. Nevertheless, integrationists still insist that congressional bills to "regulate" the Supreme Court and arguments over jurisdiction are only subterfuges designed to void the Court's decisions on busing. Indeed, most antibusing proposals embody racial classifications and are therefore suspect. They attempt to shift governmental power and then to make decisions on busing that would burden a racial minority. Such action would violate *Washington v. Seattle School District No. 1* (1982), wherein the Supreme Court ruled unconstitutional a state policy that prohibited school administrators from requiring a child to attend a school if it was not the one closest to his or her residence. The state policy effectively stopped busing in the district, but the Supreme Court ruled that the policy violated the Constitution's equal protection clause.

Bibliography

Feagin, Joe R., and Clairece Booher Feagin. *Discrimination American Style: Institutional Racism and Sexism*. Englewood Cliffs, N.J.: Prentice-Hall, 1978. This volume is more up-to-date than Knowles and Prewitt's *Institutional Racism in America* (listed below). It is a handy reference that, in comparing racism and sexism, adds to the understanding of both forms of discrimination. The volume has no bibliography but does include footnotes.

Formisano, Ronald P. *Boston Against Busing: Race, Class, and Ethnicity in the 1960's and 1970's*. Chapel Hill: University of North Carolina Press, 1991. Formisano's effort is a detailed account of foes of busing in Boston. Bringing a human touch to his work, the author remains critical of the movement, but he paints a sensitive portrait of many of the antibusers—middle- and working-class whites, many of whom were moderates or liberals on many issues of the day but who believed that forced busing was unjust and that it greatly interfered with their children's education.

Keynes, Edward, with Randall K. Miller. *The Court vs. Congress: Prayer, Busing, and Abortion*. Durham, N.C.: Duke University Press, 1989. This book is an excellent piece of in-depth research into three of the most controversial political, social, and judicial issues in the modern United States. Moreover, its first five chapters give a sweeping historical overview of the struggles between Congress and the judiciary from the Federalist era to modern times.

Knowles, Louis L., and Kenneth Prewitt, eds. *Institutional Racism in America.* Englewood Cliffs, N.J.: Prentice-Hall, 1969. While it is now a dated study, this volume nevertheless has excellent essays on various kinds of institutional racism, including its existence in education. The essay by Harold M. Baron shows the interrelatedness of the various types of institutional racism.

Sears, David O., Carl P. Hensler, and Leslie K. Spears. "Whites' Opposition to 'Busing': Self-Interest or Symbolic Politics?" *American Political Science Review* 73 (June, 1979): 369-384. The authors maintain that direct, obvious racial hatred is definitely of times gone by but that a more indirect, sophisticated symbolic form of racial hatred has taken its place, with the new form arriving after the decline of the Civil Rights movement.

Smallwood, James, and Crispen Phillips. "Black Oklahomans and the Question of 'Oklahomaness': The People Who Weren't Invited to Share the Dream." In *The Culture of Oklahoma*, edited by Howard F. Stein and Robert F. Hill. Norman: University of Oklahoma Press, 1993. This book chapter summarizes the contributions of black Oklahomans. It notes how their contributions were largely overlooked or ignored by the white majority in the state, largely because of racial biases. Part of the chapter focuses on school desegregation, busing, and the successful "finger plan" used in Oklahoma City.

Wellman, David T. *Portraits of White Racism*. Cambridge, England: Cambridge University Press, 1977. The author examines many cases of racism, including institutional racism in schools. He deflates the belief that working-class bigots are the only racists in American society. Wellman shows that most whites benefit from institutional arrangements that place African Americans in a subordinate position. He concludes that racism is "characteristically" American and is found among all social and economic classes.

James Smallwood

Cross-References

CAPITAL PUNISHMENT

Type of sociology: Deviance and social control
Field of study: Controlling deviance

Capital punishment is the state-ordered execution of an offender who has been convicted of a crime that is punishable by death. Capital punishment has engendered considerable controversy, and it has both staunch supporters and opponents.

Principal terms

AGGRAVATING CIRCUMSTANCES: any condition that accompanies the commission of a capital crime which adds to the severity of the crime and increases the likelihood that the death penalty will be invoked

BIFURCATED TRIAL: a two-stage trial in which guilt or innocence is first determined, followed by a second stage in which the appropriate penalty is recommended if guilt is established

DETERRENCE: punishment that is intended to prevent further occurrences of the crime

MITIGATING CIRCUMSTANCES: any condition related to the background of the offender which decreases the likelihood that the death penalty will be invoked

MORATORIUM: a period during which the execution of offenders was suspended

RETRIBUTION: a philosophy which rests on the argument that the offender must pay for his or her crime with a penalty equal to the seriousness of the act

Overview

The execution of Gary Mark Gilmore by a Utah firing squad on January 17, 1977, marked the end of a ten-year moratorium on the use of capital punishment in the United States. At the end of 1991, the number of persons executed since 1977 was 157. Of those executed, 60 percent were white and 40 percent were black. In 1993, thirty-six states and the federal government retained the death penalty. Although sixteen of those thirty-six states carried out at least one execution between 1977 and 1991, the majority occurred in the Southern states, with Texas, Florida, Louisiana, and Georgia leading the list. At the end of 1991, the capital punishment states were holding 2,482 persons on their death rows.

Although the method of execution varies by state, the usual methods have been hanging, firing squad, electrocution, and lethal gas. Throughout the years, states have experimented with more "humane" means of carrying out the death sentence. Lethal gas was first used by the state of Nevada in 1921. One refinement came in 1982 in Texas when Charlie Brooks, Jr., became the first person to be executed by lethal injection. Following that execution, a number of states revised their death penalty statutes to provide for lethal injection as either the prescribed form of execution or as an option for the condemned prisoner. Twenty-two of the thirty-six states now include lethal injection as a means of execution.

The debate over the use of capital punishment in the United States began shortly after the American Revolution ended and has continued in various forms to the present. During colonial days the criminal code of Great Britain, which provided for the death sentence in more than two hundred offenses, also applied to the Colonies. The first attempt to revise the use of capital punishment was undertaken by the Society for Alleviating the Suffering of Public Prisoners, a Philadelphia-based Quaker group (its most famous member was Benjamin Franklin) in 1787. The overall goal of this organization was penal reform. While the society did not succeed in abolishing capital punishment in any of the former colonies, it did succeed in reducing the use of the death penalty in Pennsylvania to cases involving first-degree murder only.

The most significant event in the early movement to abolish the death penalty came in 1846, when the state government of Michigan became the first anywhere in the world to ban the use of capital punishment completely. Michigan's prohibition on the death penalty was a direct response to the discovery that an innocent man, Patrick Fitzpatrick, had been publicly hanged for the rape of a nine-year-old girl in Windsor, Ontario, Canada. Fitzpatrick was hanged in 1837; the error was discovered three years later, when another man, Maurice Sellers, confessed to the crime on his deathbed. The close proximity of Ontario to Michigan created a widespread public outcry in Michigan based on the fear that such a mistake could be made in their state. The states of Rhode Island and Wisconsin followed Michigan's lead in 1852. These three states continue to be among the states that do not have capital statutes.

Very little further progress was made by the abolition movement prior to the Civil War, although Illinois and Minnesota did halt public executions. Following the Civil War, Maine abolished the death penalty, and a number of other states, most notably Iowa, Colorado, and Kansas, experimented with abolition but eventually reinstated it. During the period just preceding the entry of the United States into World War I, seven more states abolished the death sentence, bringing the total at that time to twelve states without a death penalty. The outbreak of World War I found eight more states with legislation to abolish the death penalty pending in their legislatures. The war effort intervened, however, and no action was taken.

Efforts to abolish capital punishment in the United States can be divided into two distinct phases. From 1790 to 1960, the focus was on individual states in an attempt to convince the legislators to repeal capital punishment statutes. The second phase, beginning in the early 1960's, has been directed toward a constitutional attack on the death penalty, primarily under the Eighth Amendment to the Constitution, which prohibits the use of "cruel and unusual" punishment. Early efforts had some limited success in that fourteen states abolished capital punishment, public executions were entirely eliminated, and the use of the death penalty was restricted to convictions for first-degree murder only.

Applications

With the rise of the Civil Rights movement in the 1960's, with its focus on expanding the protection of the Constitution to minority groups, those opposed to capital punishment shifted their focus to the national level in an attempt to have capital punishment declared unconstitutional by the U.S. Supreme Court. Their efforts were encouraged by the nature of the Supreme Court at that time, which consisted of a liberal majority under Chief Justice Earl Warren. These conditions led the states to impose a voluntary moratorium on executions in 1967. A number of cases were slowly moving their way through the appellate structure toward the U.S. Supreme Court. The states agreed to halt executions until the Court could examine and decide the issue of the constitutional status of the death penalty statutes which were then in place.

The first of a series of significant Supreme Court cases, *Furman v. Georgia*, was decided in 1972. In this case, the Court relied on social science data which showed that the death penalty had been applied disproportionately to poor people, black people, and those without private counsel. The Court held that the death penalty as then being applied did constitute cruel and unusual punishment, since it was being used in a capricious and discriminatory manner. As a consequence of this decision, 629 persons who were then under the death sentence had their sentences commuted to life in prison.

The apparent victory of the abolition movement in *Furman v. Georgia* was short-lived. The Court did not find that capital punishment in and of itself was cruel and unusual punishment. It was cruel and unusual only as it was then being applied by state courts. The decision did render existing death penalty statutes in forty states unconstitutional. At about the same time that the Court rendered its decision in *Furman v. Georgia*, a number of significant and influential events occurred in American society. The homicide rate began to climb, violence associated with the Civil Rights movement and the Vietnam War protest movement escalated, and, in the late 1960's, a series of riots broke out in major urban areas. All these events contributed to a rising fear of crime throughout the country. A Gallup Poll taken at the time of the moratorium indicated that fewer than 50 percent of the population favored the use of the death penalty. This figure also began to climb to a point where, today, more than 75 percent of the people favor its use. These events placed pressures on state legislators to pass new death penalty legislation. Of the forty states that had their capital punishment laws overturned by *Furman v. Georgia*, thirty-seven introduced new legislation. The moratorium remained in effect as new convictions were obtained under these revised statutes. Finally, in 1976, following a review of the new laws in five states, the Supreme Court handed down decisions that permitted the resumption of executions. Of those five cases, *Gregg v. Georgia* and *Woodson v. North Carolina* are the most significant.

Recognizing that the Supreme Court had based its decision principally on the discriminatory application of the death penalty, the states seeking to restore capital punishment followed two patterns. Some states, including Georgia, Utah, and Texas, provided for a two-stage or bifurcated trial process. The first stage was to determine the guilt or innocence of the person charged. The second stage, or penalty phase, was initiated if the jury returned a finding of guilt. In this stage, the prosecution introduced aggravating conditions which made the death penalty appropriate, while the defense introduced mitigating circumstances in arguing for a sentence less than death. The jury was then instructed to weigh these conditions and return with a sentence recommendation of either death or life in prison.

Other states, including North Carolina and Ohio, passed legislation which made the death sentence mandatory in any conviction for first-degree murder. The mandatory imposition of the death sentence was an attempt to eliminate any discretion on the part of the jury and hence to limit discriminatory treatment of offenders. In *Woodson v. North Carolina*, the Supreme Court struck down all mandatory statutes as unconstitutional. At the same time, it upheld all statutes which provided for the two-stage trial approach in the *Gregg v. Georgia* case. Since Utah's statute was modeled after the Georgia legislation, it was that decision which paved the way for executions to resume with the execution of Gilmore.

Since the resumption of executions in 1977, the Supreme Court has been asked to review and decide a number of constitutional questions connected with capital punishment. First, is capital punishment "cruel and unusual" if applied to crimes other than first-degree murder? The Supreme Court answered this question in the affirmative in the case of *Coker v. Georgia* (1977), which struck down the Georgia statute providing the death penalty for rape. Second, what is the minimum age at which an offender might receive the death penalty? The Supreme Court addressed this question in two separate cases. In 1988, the Court held in *Thompson v. Oklahoma* that a death sentence applied to a juvenile who was fifteen or younger at the time he or she committed the crime for which he or she was sentenced is unconstitutional. One year later, in the case of *Stanford v. Kentucky* (1989), the same Court ruled that the death penalty for persons who were at least sixteen at the time of their crime is not cruel and unusual punishment. Hence it would appear that the minimum age for which capital punishment could be the appropriate penalty is sixteen. Third, is racial discrimination a sufficient factor in ruling the death penalty unconstitutional? Despite evidence presented in the case of *McCleskey v. Kemp* (1987) that indicated a strong statistical correlation between the race of the offender and the race of the victim in applying the death sentence, the Court held that the offender must show that racial discrimination was intended in that particular case. In short, deliberate racial discrimination must be shown on a case-by-case basis. Finally, what role does the physical or mental condition of the condemned person play in decisions to carry out an execution? Since the restoration of capital punishment in 1976, the mental and physical condition of the condemned prisoner has been a key issue in the debate over the death sentence. Although the Court has held that the execution of an obviously mentally ill prisoner does constitute cruel and unusual punishment, the Court has refused to halt executions of both mentally retarded prisoners and prisoners with severe disabilities. The latter was revealed when the Court refused to halt the execution of Charles Stamper in January, 1993. Stamper, a paraplegic, had to be carried to the electric chair in Virginia by three correctional officers.

Context

The debate over the use of capital punishment has continued in the United States from the time of the American Revolution to the present. During this period, many other nations have resolved the issue by eliminating the death penalty from their criminal codes. In the early 1990's, the United States was the only Western industrial nation to retain capital punishment.

Proponents of capital punishment have argued that it serves as a deterrent both for the individual offender and for others in the community. Research carried out over the years has generally failed to support the deterrent argument. The continuing high rate of homicide despite the reinstatement of the death penalty suggests that it fails to deter others from committing crimes for which they could receive the death sentence. Moreover, the substitution of life sentences without the possibility of parole indicates that individuals who commit murder can be successfully isolated from the community and prevented from committing future crimes. The major remaining argument for the continued use of the death sentence is retribution. Those who favor this position maintain that the death penalty and execution is the only just sentence for those who take the life of another person. This position is based on the "deserved" penalty according to the crime committed and is the modern counterpart of the "eye for an eye" philosophy. Since this argument is fundamentally an emotional one, grounded in personal values, it is difficult to refute.

Those who oppose capital punishment do so on several grounds. The "cruel" nature of the death sentence is alleged to be demonstrated by both the conditions of confinement of death row prisoners, which are demonstrably different from those of all other offenders, and by the methods of execution itself. It is the latter which has led legislators to search for more humane methods of execution over the years. The "unusual" nature of the penalty is based both on the extensive power of discretion held by the prosecutor in deciding to charge a person under a capital statute and the option of the prosecutor to engage in plea-bargaining. Discretion is further extended to the jury in deciding whether to recommend the death sentence and to the judge, who decides either to accept or to reject the jury's recommendation. Finally, since the entire structure of review and appeals is based on the concept of reversibility of error, the argument that the death sentence is "unusual" contends that this penalty is the only sanction in American criminal codes that is not subject to correction in the event of error once the sentence has been executed.

Bibliography

Bohm, Robert M., ed. *The Death Penalty in America: Current Research*. Cincinnati, Ohio: Anderson, 1991. This edited volume reports research conducted since the decision in *Gregg v. Georgia* in 1977. The chapters address the critical issues of racial discrimination, prosecutorial discretion in asking for the death penalty, and a follow-up study of convicted murderers who were released on parole following the *Furman v. Georgia* decision. A particularly interesting chapter provides a comprehensive collection of information on the characteristics of offenders executed in the

United States between 1608 and 1987.

Frank, Jerome, and Barbara Frank. *Not Guilty*. Reprint. New York: Da Capo Press, 1971. This highly readable volume was written by one of America's most eminent jurists and his daughter. It focuses entirely on one of the most vexing issues in capital cases—the possibility of convicting and executing an innocent person. The authors report in detail on eighteen cases (and eighteen more in lesser depth) in which errors led to the conviction of innocent persons.

Isenberg, Irwin, ed. *The Death Penalty*. New York: H. W. Wilson, 1977. This book examines the central issues in the debate over capital punishment. Included among the articles are those written by both staunch supporters and vocal opponents of the death penalty. Although somewhat dated, it does present a thorough review of the arguments presented by both sides.

Johnson, Robert. *Condemned to Die*. New York: Elsevier, 1981. Johnson looks at the death sentence from the viewpoint of condemned prisoners living on death row in Alabama. The major portion of the book provides the reader with an insight into the conditions of confinement of inmates living under the threat of death.

_____ . *Death Work*. Pacific Grove, Calif.: Brooks/Cole, 1980. This book can be considered a companion volume to the Johnson work discussed above. As Johnson notes, "*Death Work* is about executions." The primary focus in on the impact of capital punishment on those who work on death rows and who carry out the executions. It examines the execution process from life on death row to the execution itself. It also details the impact on witnesses, the warden, the executioner, and the death team in the hours following the execution.

Donald B. Walker

Cross-References

CAPITALISM

Type of sociology: Major social institutions
Field of study: The economy

Capitalism refers to an economic system in which the means of production are privately owned and production decisions are made by firms in response to market conditions in order to realize profits. This concept is used to understand labor markets, global inequalities, and the culture and class structure of contemporary societies.

Principal terms

CAPITAL: wealth used to produce further wealth or accumulated goods used to produce further goods

CORPORATE CAPITALISM: a form of economy characterized by large firms

LABOR: productive activity; in capitalism, labor power is bought and sold as a commodity in a market

MARKET: a self-regulating mechanism of economic production in which goods are produced and distributed in response to supply and demand

POLICY: a purposive course of action undertaken to solve or cope with a social problem; public policy is undertaken by government

PRIVATE OWNERSHIP: a system in which the means of production are held by individuals and firms and are freely disposable in a market

Overview

Capitalism is a type of economy that is based on private ownership of the means of production and on the market as the regulating mechanism of production and distribution. Decisions about what to produce and how much to produce are made by private firms in response to conditions of supply and demand in markets; the point of economic activity for firms is maximization of profit.

This definition of capitalism is associated with distinct social characteristics. First, capitalism is a system based on free labor: Workers are paid wages or salaries for their labor power in a contractually limited relationship that is entered into freely. In this respect, capitalism differs from slavery and serfdom, in which labor is coerced, and from "primitive" and "household" economies in which custom and kinship ties, along with necessity, induce people to engage in economic activities. In capitalism, labor power as a factor of production is available in a labor market as a commodity.

Second, capitalism is an expanding system, in both technological innovation and geographical horizons. Driven by competition and the search for profitable investments and markets, capitalist firms introduce new machinery and expand operations globally. Capitalism is characterized by accumulation, by expansion of investment, and by buildup of machinery and material culture. Investments can shift quickly, bringing about rapid social change. Third, in capitalist society, the political system is relatively autonomous from the economy, unlike under feudalism, in which the state is formed directly by the landed nobility itself. Although the ideology of laissez-faire (minimal government intervention in the economy) has been more an ideal than a reality, there is a considerable degree of separation between economy and government in most capitalist nations. In the twentieth century, these two institutions have drawn closer together, with governments taking steps to regulate the economy, integrate economic production with national priorities, and undertake "countercyclical measures" to reduce the magnitude of economic crises.

Fourth, capitalism is associated with distinct forms of culture and ideology. Capitalism has historically been associated with rational calculation, impersonal norms, and individualism. People see themselves as individuals "freed" from traditional ties and obligations. Advertising creates new wants and needs to make possible the realization of profit on new products; acquisition of commodities is a central value, and desire for material goods escalates.

Marxist and non-Marxist social scientists differ in their evaluation of capitalism as a system. The former tend to emphasize inherent inequalities and limitations, while the latter are more inclined to "take it for granted" or to point to positive features. For Marxist social scientists, capitalism contains a fundamental split between those who own the means of production and buy labor power (capitalists) and those who do not own the means of production and must therefore sell their labor power (the working class). For Marxists, these two groups form two classes with opposed interests. Workers depend on capitalists for employment, but in a larger perspective, the potential of workers as human beings cannot be realized within the capitalist system. Non-Marxist social scientists point to the fluidity of these class categories, since capitalist classes are not hereditary or castelike; they see the sale and purchase of labor power as an even exchange rather than as an exploitive mechanism by which surplus value is extracted from labor. They emphasize that liberal-democratic states associated with capitalism have been responsive to mass pressures for improved living standards and social services. They suggest that capitalism is a necessary (though not sufficient) condition for democracy.

Marxist and non-Marxist social scientists differ in their view of the origins of capitalism. They agree that capitalism emerged as land, labor, and capital became commodities in Western Europe in the period between 1500 and 1800. Prior to that period, commerce and markets had existed, and money had circulated as a medium of exchange. Land, however, could be obtained only through inheritance or feudal obligations. Labor was coerced (as slavery and serfdom) or embedded in kinship relations; money did not circulate in a capital market, nor was it viewed as the basis of investment. Capitalism in its modern form emerged with several institutional changes. Modern systems of banking and credit were established; money relations replaced serfdom, and monetary land rents sped development of commercial agriculture. National and international markets in raw materials, land, and finished products expanded, and factory production using wage labor replaced guild manufactures and cottage industries.

Marxists explain the decline of feudalism in terms of class conflict between landholders and other social forces (such as peasants and merchants) or emphasize structural problems in the feudal economy. Marxists also examine the role of European expansion and point to wealth produced by African and American Indian slaves as an accelerant of capital accumulation in Europe. Non-Marxist historical sociologists put more emphasis on changes in values, especially the role of the Protestant Reformation in creating preconditions for "the spirit of capitalism." The German sociologist Max Weber theorized that Protestant values such as frugality and a strong work ethic accelerated practices associated with the accumulation of capital. The differences between Marxist and non-Marxist sociologists have been exaggerated and oversimplified; Marxists do not deny the role of ideas and values in history, and Weber did not neglect changes in class structure and the economy as elements in the advent of capitalism.

Marxists and non-Marxists differ in their view of the centrality of capitalism in "modern" society. For Marxists, capitalism defines "modern" society. Capitalist relations of production shape and limit all other practices in the society. Non-Marxists see a looser connection between economic, political, and social institutions and often give theoretical priority to political, cultural, or technological practices. For example, non-Marxists point to "technological imperatives" that come with the introduction of computers; machinery itself, they say, induces certain kinds of behavior regardless of its social context. Marxists emphasize that computers are introduced by capitalists in order to reduce labor costs, increase output, beat the competition and widen profit margins; the capitalist socioeconomic context limits how machinery is used.

Marxists and non-Marxists also differ in their views of the trajectory of capitalism. Non-Marxists see no internal contradictions in the system that might lead to a final economic collapse or to political crisis. While they acknowledge that capitalism is associated with poverty in underdeveloped regions and inequality even in the most developed countries, they believe that these conditions can be alleviated by a variety of policies pursued within the framework of capitalism. Marxists identify "contradictions" within capitalism that revolve around the tension between capitalism's enormous productive potential and the limited and alienated condition that it imposes on human beings in terms of poverty, exploited labor, unemployment and underutilization of human talent, and the hollowness of consumer culture. Impending crisis is signaled by rising unemployment and falling rates of profit. Poverty and regional wars in the capitalist periphery are warning signs of the system's lack of viability: "Socialism or barbarism," say Marxists.

While Marxists see capitalism as a revolutionary and positive step forward from feudalism, they do not see it as a desirable end result. Non-Marxist sociologists are less inclined to think that capitalism should or will be replaced by another type of society and economy.

Applications

The most important application of the concept "capitalism" is to draw attention to the systemic nature and economic determinants of social behavior and social problems. Using this concept is a way of indicating that certain problems or issues are unlikely to be resolved unless a major political and economic change takes place. For many non-Marxist social scientists, this change involves a more active relationship between the state and the capitalist economy. In their view, when the source of problems is an institution as large and pervasive as the capitalist economy, only government is a sufficiently powerful institution to represent the interests of those who do not own capital and to implement policies designed to solve or reduce social problems. For Marxists, the problems can only be solved by a global transition to socialism. Most Marxists support public policy to improve conditions in the short run, but they believe that as long as capital operates globally, national public policy is limited in its effectiveness. Some sociologists favor less government intervention, asserting that freer markets lead to better functioning societies on both a national and a global scale.

One major issue of capitalist societies is the class structure, whether conceived as sharply polarized or more minutely stratified. As long as capitalism generates class inequality, it is likely that many social problems will persist, especially in the view of Marxist sociologists. For example, poverty and street crime are direct results of these inequalities. A related problem is the social effect of unemployment, which is both a systemic feature of capitalism and a result of shifts in investments. Sociologists point to individual effects of unemployment, such as suicide and domestic violence, and to the effects of high rates of unemployment on communities and ethnic groups (such as African Americans). Marxist and non-Marxist sociologists tend to agree that a full-employment economy would reduce inequality and associated problems. Many sociologists call for strategies of government intervention in the capitalist economy, such as job training, tax credits for employers who expand jobs, and stimuli for the economy as a whole, to reduce its tendency to function with high levels of unemployment. A higher minimum wage, access to health care, and better education are seen as supportive measures. Government can intervene directly in labor markets by policies such as affirmative action to reduce high levels of unemployment among minorities. Keynesian "countercyclical" measures are seen as a way of reducing cyclical unemployment and inflation characteristic of capitalist economies.

Sociologists use the concept of capitalism to study changes in developing nations, sometimes said to be on the "periphery of capitalism." Replacement of traditional economies by the global capitalist economy has produced new inequalities, disruption of village life, and the formation of urban shantytowns of the underemployed. Sociologists try to understand what public policies and-or grass-roots movements can do to make this transition less traumatic; for example, they look at conditions that facilitate producer cooperatives, community organizations, and labor unions. Sociologists study how peasant populations enter industrial wage work in "newly industrializing nations." Since the paid labor force is increasingly female, sociologists also look at connections between the changing nature of work in the capitalist economy and traditional gender systems.

The changing nature of capitalism has stimulated new perspectives in sociology, notably in the 1970's and 1980's. The "stagflation" of the 1970's gave way to restructuring in the 1980's. Corporate mergers increased, unions became weaker, government involvement was cut back, layoffs included managers as well as production workers, a service economy replaced manufacturing, and the middle class came under economic pressure. Non-Marxist as well as Marxist sociologists gave renewed attention to labor markets. They demonstrated that there was not a single labor market; rather, there were "segmented" markets, differentiated by ethnicity and gender. They also looked at the social impact of rising unemployment. Some studies focused on how African Americans and other urban populations were affected by deindustrialization and by a loss of manufacturing jobs in central cities as investment shifted to other locations and activities. Sociologists also studied the impact of labor force participation on women, families, and the gender system.

The globalization of capitalism has also stimulated sociological analysis. Capitalism has been a global and transnational system from the start, but these tendencies accelerated in the late twentieth century with several trends: the rise of multinational corporations; the establishment of integrated regional economies such as the European Community; and the movement of industries into "underdeveloped" regions that offer lower labor costs. Sociologists study how work, culture, ethnic relations, and everyday life are affected by the mobility of capital and labor.

Sociologists study the internal workings of corporations, giving attention to bureaucratic decision making; work satisfaction; the roles of gender and ethnicity; and the process of technological innovation. Capitalist technological innovation also changes behavior and culture. For example, sociologists look at the impact of computerization and "video culture." They are exploring the relationship between postmodern culture and trends in capitalism such as globalization, media monopolies, and the service economy.

Context

Since the middle of the nineteenth century, when capitalism became discernible as the prevailing form of economy, sociologists have directed their attention to explaining it and understanding its social effects. All four of the great classical sociological theorists—Karl Marx, Émile Durkheim, Max Weber, and Georg Simmel—used capitalism as a central concept. Marx devoted his life to an analysis of capitalism. Durkheim was interested in how capitalism affected social integration. He believed that it weakened traditional types of solidarity, only partially replacing these bonds with an "organic solidarity" based on a complex division of labor and economic interdependence. Max Weber examined preconditions of capitalism in religious thought, specifically the Protestant Reformation. He explored the relationship between capitalism and rational calculation characteristic of modern societies. Unlike Marx, Weber did not see much hope for socialism as an alternative to capitalism; he believed that all modern societies tend toward bureaucratic organization and impersonal rationality. Simmel looked at capitalism in terms of social forms and types of individuals created by a money economy. The metropolis is the site of the money economy and is characterized by a fast pace of activity, impersonal and objectified treatment of human beings, diversity in fashion and lifestyle, and social types that are defined by money, such as the miser, the spendthrift, and the prostitute.

In the period from World War I to the 1950's, interest waned in capitalism as a leading concept in non-Marxist sociology, especially in the United States. Exceptions were Robert S. Lynd and Helen Lynd's *Middletown: A Study in Contemporary American Culture* (1930) and *Middletown in Transition: A Study in Cultural Conflicts* (1937), examinations of life in a Midwestern city that emphasized the economic context of social behavior and identified socioeconomic class as a major force in everyday life. By the 1950's, C. Wright Mills reawakened the interest of sociologists in the capitalist economy with his concept of the power elite, which included the top ranks of large corporations and the "military-industrial complex." In *White Collar: The American Middle Classes* (1951), Mills looked at how the shift from small-scale business to corporate capitalism was transforming the American middle class; he noted that all types of white-collar work, from sales to intellectual production, were increasingly carried out within corporations. William H. Whyte reached similar conclusions in *The Organization Man* (1956), a study of corporate employees and their emerging suburban lifestyles. Because the 1950's was a period when labor unions became bureaucratized, sociologists explored conditions under which unions retained internal democracy, rank-and-file participation, and militancy.

With the changes in capitalism that occurred in the 1970's and 1980's, capitalism has remained a central sociological concept for non-Marxist as well as Marxist researchers and theorists. As long as most of the globe is involved in a capitalist economy, capitalism will persist as a topic of the social sciences; since capitalism itself is a dynamic and changing system, it is likely to stimulate new research and theory continuously.

Bibliography

Braverman, Harry. *Labor and Monopoly Capital*. New York: Monthly Review Press, 1974. A Marxist analysis of the de-skilling of workers in capitalist firms. An influential and controversial contribution to the sociology of work, organizations, and technology.

Eitzen, D. Stanley, and Maxine Baca Zinn. *Social Problems*. 5th ed. Boston: Allyn & Bacon, 1992. A textbook that uses capitalism as an explanatory concept and presents a clear introductory overview. Excellent, balanced bibliographies.

Giddens, Anthony. *Capitalism and Modern Social Theory*. Cambridge, England: Cambridge University Press, 1971. A leading non-Marxist sociologist discusses the importance of the concept "capitalism" to the foundation of modern sociology. A clearly written guide to the work of Marx, Durkheim, and Weber; scholarly but not narrowly technical.

Heilbroner, Robert. *The Making of Economic Society*. 8th ed. Englewood Cliffs, N.J.: Prentice-Hall, 1989. A clear, comprehensible textbook that introduces economic concepts and issues; treatment of the material is historical and sociological. Includes helpful chapter glossaries and study questions. A good beginning for understanding market economies.

Hobsbawm, Eric. *The Age of Revolution, 1789-1848*. London: Weidenfeld & Nicolson, 1962.

_____ . *The Age of Capital, 1848-1875*. London: Weidenfeld & Nicolson, 1975.

_____ . *The Age of Empire, 1875-1914*. London: Weidenfeld & Nicolson, 1987. Hobsbawm's three volumes present a social history of the growth of capitalism, including excellent coverage of cultural and political changes. Illustrated.

Marx, Karl. *Selected Writings*. Edited by David McLellan. Oxford, England: Oxford University Press, 1977. The definitive one-volume collection. Part I of the *Communist Manifesto* remains an excellent overview of the dynamics of capitalism from a Marxist perspective.

Polanyi, Karl. *The Great Transformation*. Boston: Beacon Press, 1957. A classic work of social history that analyzes the onset and impact of the market economy in England and western Europe; difficult reading but influential in social thought.

Wilson, William J. *The Truly Disadvantaged*. Chicago: University of Chicago Press, 1987. A pioneering study of poverty among African Americans. Wilson proposes full employment policies to reduce class and racial inequality in the United States.

Roberta T. Garner

Cross-References

Corporations and Economic Concentration, 360; Industrial and Postindustrial Economies, 940; The Industrial Revolution and Mass Production, 946; Industrial Societies, 953; Marxism, 1127; Multinational Corporations and the Third World, 1268; Social Stratification: Functionalist Perspectives, 1845; Social Stratification: Marxist Perspectives, 1852; Unemployment and Poverty, 2083; Unionization and Industrial Labor Relations, 2096.

CASTE SYSTEMS

Type of sociology: Social stratification
Field of study: Systems of social stratification

A caste system is a hierarchy of social categories in which movement from one category to another is highly restricted by custom and law. Caste systems represent a particularly rigid example of how social stratification can be based on the status that one obtains at birth.

Principal terms

APARTHEID: the type of segregation that developed in South Africa; separateness was the principle guiding contacts between whites, blacks, and "coloureds"

BURAKUMIN: a social group in Japan that is discriminated against because its ancestry can be traced to outcastes in feudal Japan

ENDOGAMY: marriage between members of the same social category

OUTCASTE: the lowest social category in a caste system

POLLUTION: an Indian ideology that the higher castes can be polluted if coming into contact with the outcaste

REINCARNATION: the Hindu religious belief that human souls are reborn after death

SEGREGATION: a principle of separation that guides contact between the higher castes and lower castes in a caste system

UNTOUCHABILITY: an Indian concept according to which the lower caste and outcaste are regarded as impure and untouchable; contacts with them lead to pollution and should be avoided

Overview

The word "caste" has a Portuguese origin. In Portuguese, *casta* means breed, race, or kind. The present meaning of caste, according to John Henry Hutton, did not begin until the sixteenth century.

Modern definitions of caste contain many layers of meanings. Herbert Hope Risley, a scholar of Indian tribes and castes, defines it as

> a collection of families or groups of families bearing a common name; claiming a common descent from a mythical ancestor, human or divine; professing to follow the same hereditary calling; and regarded by those who are competent to give an opinion as forming a single homogeneous community.

Sociologist W. Lloyd Warner adds other aspects to this definition. Caste exists "where marriage between two or more groups is not sanctioned and where there is no opportunity for members of the lower groups to rise into the upper groups or of members of the upper to fall into the lower ones."

In a caste system, the castes are interdependent social phenomena. A caste system, first of all, is entirely based on ascribed status—the status that one obtains at birth. Just as one is born a male or a female, one is born into a certain caste (or into the outcaste) in a caste society. Rigid ranking exists among the different castes.

Discussion of the Indian caste system presents the problem of whether to consider it a historical or ongoing phenomenon. When India drafted its democratic constitution in 1948, discrimination against the lower castes was made illegal. Moreover, a type of affirmative action program reserved a significant number of government jobs for people from the lower castes. In that sense, the system is historical and may be discussed as such. Regardless of official policy, however, the system is deeply ingrained and still permeates Indian life and culture. Each person knows the caste into which he or she is born, and caste still limits social advancement and affects job opportunities and marriage choices.

There are four main castes in the Indian caste system. The highest caste is that of Brahmans, followed by the Kshatriyas, Vaishyas, and Shudras. Beyond these four castes are the lowest of the low—the outcastes. In this system, once a person was born into a certain caste (or the outcaste), he or she would remain in that caste (or the outcaste) for life.

Caste identification can be based on perceived physical differences, most often on skin color, but that is not always the case. In India, physical differences do not play an important part in distinguishing among castes. Social descent forms the most important and most prominent criterion for distinction. The difference between castes is largely a difference of social status.

Segregation was the rule that governed contact between a higher caste and a lower caste or outcaste. The Shudras and outcaste people in Indian society, for example, were often considered "untouchable." Traditionally, a member of a higher caste could be polluted by the slightest physical contact with a member of the Shudras or outcaste. In some extreme cases, a mere glance from an untouchable at a cooking pot could defile the food and make it uneatable. In certain regions, even the shadows cast by untouchables represented a potential danger to others; untouchables were therefore not allowed to walk in the villages during early morning or late afternoon.

Two important features of the Indian caste system helped sustain the ranking system. The first feature was the association of the castes with occupations. The Brahmans were either priests or scholars; the Kshatriyas, nobles or warriors; and the Vaishyas, merchants or skilled artisans. The lowest caste, the Shudras, were common laborers. The second feature was the enforcement of endogamy. In a caste society, a person is not allowed to marry outside his or her caste. A Brahman had to marry another Brahman, a Shudra another Shudra. The purity of the hereditary line was thus maintained, and the possibility of moving up in social status by way of marriage or occupation was ruled out.

A caste system must be supported by social institutions. Segregation between the higher castes and the lower castes, enforcement of endogamy, and association of occupation with caste cannot be achieved without the backing of social institutions.

A caste system is also perpetuated by wide acceptance on the people's part. In India, the Hindu religion provided a necessary justification for enforcement of caste duties and obligations.

The Hindu religion maintains a belief in reincarnation; according to Hinduism, the soul will be reborn after death. Traditionally, if a person had sinned seriously in a previous life, he or she would be reborn as an untouchable. This belief in reincarnation carries two implications. On the one hand, it suggests that the caste into which a person is born is a reflection of the deeds he or she has done in a previous life. On the other hand, a person is given the hope that he or she can move up in the caste system at rebirth. Whether one will move upward or downward in the caste system at rebirth depends on how well one respects one's caste duties and obligations.

Caste systems are similar to class systems in that both are systems of stratification. Just as the class system is characterized by unequal access to resources in the society, the caste system is characterized by unequal access to prestige, privilege, and higher social status. The basic difference between the class and caste systems lies in the fact that the former is based at least partly on achieved status, whereas the latter is based solely on ascribed status. In this sense, a class system is an open system, while a caste system is a closed one.

Applications

The caste system is not limited to India, and it is not a phenomenon only of ancient times. In the postindustrial society of Japan, for example, the influence of the caste system can still be observed.

From the early seventeenth century to the late nineteenth century, during what is called the Tokugawa period in Japan, Japanese rulers established a very rigid system of closed caste ranks. At the top of the caste structure were warriors, the samurai (the military elite), and the higher aristocracy. This top caste was followed by peasants and artisans, with merchants at the bottom. The outcastes in Japan's caste system were called "eta," meaning "abundant filth."

The eta faced discrimination in every aspect of their lives. Laws were passed to stipulate their inferior status, and they were restricted to occupations such as butchers, executioners, and grave tenders, commonly regarded to be the dirtiest, most defiling, and least desirable tasks. Although their legal status as outcastes was eliminated in 1871, the stigma of having been eta continues for their descendants.

Today it is estimated that there are about one to three million Japanese having eta lineage. Commonly referred to as "burakumin," they have met extensive discrimination in modern Japanese society. Burakumin are physically indistinguishable from other Japanese, so one must look very hard to find that a person has this background; however, people do look very hard. It is common practice to undertake exhaustive investigations to check the background of a person for burakumin ancestors before agreeing to marriage or even offering jobs. Sociologist Mikiso Hane points out that this is a primary reason that the rate of intramarriage for burakumin is still as high as 90 percent. According to the Japanese sociologist Hiroshi Wagatsuma, the burakumin continue to be viewed by most Japanese as "mentally inferior, incapable of high moral behavior, aggressive, impulsive, and lacking any notion of sanitation or manners." They are often the "last hired and first fired."

Apartheid, the rigid system of racial segregation that existed in South Africa between the late 1940's and the mid-1990's, provides another modern example of a caste system. This system did not originate until the National Party of South Africa won a political victory in the 1948 elections. Apartheid (which literally means "separateness") had four major castes: whites, coloureds (the South African spelling will be used here), Indians, and Africans. "Coloureds" were people of mixed ancestry. "Indians" referred to the Asian population in South Africa. Since coloureds and Indians, like Africans, were both people of color, this caste system could be seen as a dichotomy, with whites over nonwhites.

Sociologist Pierre L. Van den Berghe distinguishes between "microsegregation" and "macrosegregation" under apartheid. "Microsegregation" refers to the dozens of laws and mandates passed between the early 1950's and the mid-1980's to maintain ethnic separation. In accordance with this legislation, restaurants, hotels, means of transportation, restrooms, hospitals, theaters, parks, schools, and many other places in which ethnic contact might be possible were segregated. The separate public facilities were invariably unequal in quality and quantity. "Macrosegregation" refers to the intention and practice on the part of South African authorities to assign geographical areas to different ethnic groups. Africans were not allowed to leave the assigned areas unless permitted by the white authorities. This policy was by nature one of exclusion.

Mere segregation or exclusion, however, does not sufficiently assure white supremacy. Since Africans were needed as a workforce in South Africa, discrimination against them in the workplace was also deemed necessary. Laws stipulated that blacks and whites should receive different wages, and they guaranteed that whites would get the higher-ranking jobs. In fact, no blacks could be promoted to a position higher than a white in the same occupational area.

Some social scientists argue that a variety of caste system exists in the United States; those who say this are generally referring to black and white relations. African Americans today still suffer from racism and racial discrimination. Segregation is characteristic of the residential patterns of African Americans and white people. Interracial marriages between African Americans and whites are rare occurrences, and African Americans as a whole are still a subordinate social group. Based on these facts, social anthropologist Gerald D. Berreman suggests that the American class system is complicated by caste features in the form of racial differentiation, segregation, endogamy, and hierarchy and that therefore the United States should be viewed as both a class and a caste society. This view is supported by sociologists W. Lloyd Warner, Charles Vert Willie, and many others. While acknowledging the emergence of a class structure among African Americans, they point out that a "caste line" exists between whites and African Americans in the United States. As Warner has put it: "Although [a person] is at the top of the Negro class hierarchy, he is constantly butting his head against the caste line."

Context

Caste systems, especially that of India, have been the object of considerable study by anthropologists and sociologists. The earliest study of the caste system, however, was done by some European "Orientalist" scholars. They brought to the attention of the Western intellectual world the key features of the caste system: the hierarchical ordering of castes, the importance of pollution and untouchability, the practice of endogamy, and the occupational feature of castes. The early Orientalists believed that the religious power enjoyed by the Brahmans was also a political power, and they explained the origins of the caste system as a process of evolution of occupations. It was not until 1908 that the French sociologist Celestin Bougle distinguished the two kinds of power. Bougle also noted that although caste occupations are important, the hierarchy of castes is not so much a hierarchy of skills as a hierarchy of pollution.

Western views of caste systems present differing perspectives. On the one hand, the inequities and injustices of caste systems are emphasized. In his *Population of India and Pakistan* (1951), the American sociologist Kingsley Davis refers to the caste system as "the most thoroughgoing attempt known in human history to introduce absolute inequality as the guiding principle in social relations." Berreman also speaks out against the "life sentence" that birth hands out to the member of a caste. On the other hand, the caste system is seen as performing social functions. Hutton suggests that the caste system is particularly suited to continuing culture patterns and helping to integrate different social groups while making it possible for them to retain their own distinctive character and separate individual life. Similarly, the French social anthropologist Louis Dumont contends that although all castes are not equally rewarded, all are integrated into the system. According to Hindu ideals, all are cared for; the system exists for the benefit of all.

As it is a product of the preindustrial period, scholars disagree as to whether the caste system is an obstacle to modernization. In *Hinduismus und Buddhismus* (1921; *The Religion of India: The Sociology of Hinduism and Buddhism*, 1958), the influential German sociologist Max Weber argued that the caste system, supported by Hindu beliefs in rebirth and rewards for virtuous or sinful behavior, serves as an obstacle to modern capitalism and industry. His opinion was shared by the Swedish economist Gunnar Myrdal. In contrast, the anthropologist Milton Singer and the historical sociologist Barrington Moore, Jr., have argued that the caste system is flexible and adaptive.

So far, available evidence seems to point to the breaking down of the traditional caste system, marked by specialized occupation, with modernization. It is difficult, however, to predict when the caste system will thoroughly disappear, if indeed it will. In the final analysis, it is unlikely that a social system that has had a history of more than a thousand years could be totally expunged within a few decades. The dying out of a caste system, whether in India, Japan, South Africa, or (as some social scientists would argue) the United States, is likely to be a slow and gradual process.

Bibliography

Berreman, Gerald D. *Caste and Other Inequities*. Meerut, India: Folklore Institute,

1979. This book consists of a series of essays that cover twenty years of research and thinking by Berreman about social inequality and social justice both in India and cross-culturally. Although many are reprints from articles first appearing in sociology and anthropology journals, they are readable for college students.

Cox, Oliver Cromwell. *Caste, Class, and Race: A Study in Social Dynamics.* New York: Monthly Review Press, 1959. Cox discusses a large variety of subjects relating to caste, class, and race; each discussion is given a subheading that can be found in the table of contents. An index and bibliography are also included.

Davis, Allison, Burleigh B. Gardner, and Mary R. Gardner. *Deep South: A Social Anthropological Study of Caste and Class.* Chicago: University of Chicago Press, 1941. Written before the Civil Rights movement of the 1950's and 1960's, this book gives a thorough account of the life of blacks and whites as well as a view of the class and caste structures in a community in the American "deep South." Contains a good index but no bibliography.

De Vos, George, and Hiroshi Wagatsuma. *Japan's Invisible Race: Caste in Culture and Personality.* Berkeley: University of California Press, 1966. One of the few books written in English about the outcaste in Japan. The authors have taken historical, psychological, and comparative perspectives in their study of the buraku-min. Includes a bibliography and subject index as well as pictures of Japan's outcastes and their living conditions.

Dumont, Louis. *Homo Hierarchicus: The Caste System and Its Implications.* Translated by Mark Sainsbury, Louis Dumont, and Basia Gulati. Rev. English ed. Chicago: University of Chicago Press, 1980. This book is an English translation of the French original. It is considered an important work on the caste system, and the translation is fairly readable for the general public. Contains both bibliography and subject index.

Hutton, John Henry. *Caste in India: Its Nature, Function, and Origins.* 4th ed. London: Oxford University Press, 1963. As its title suggests, this book studies the caste system at various places in India—its structures, its sanctions, its functions, and the theories and factors in the emergence of caste. Recommended for students with a special interest in the caste system in India.

Marger, Martin N. "South Africa." In *Race and Ethnic Relations: American and Global Perspectives.* 2d ed. Belmont, Calif.: Wadsworth, 1991. In this chapter, Marger discusses the development of ethnic inequality, the emergence of apartheid, and the forces of stability and change in South Africa. Highly readable and well documented; both the index and references are very useful.

Willie, Charles Vert. *The Caste and Class Controversy.* Dix Hills, N.Y.: General Hall, 1979. This book addresses one of the most controversial issues of the late 1970's: Is the significance of race increasing or decreasing? The collection of essays included in the book will help students understand why some social scientists claim that a caste system exists in the United States.

Shengming Tang

Cross-References

CAUSAL RELATIONSHIPS

Type of sociology: Sociological research
Fields of study: Basic research concepts; Data collection and analysis

Determination of cause and effect relationships requires controlled experimentation. Since this is rarely possible when studying large-scale human interactions, the findings of most sociological studies are subject to more than one interpretation.

Principal terms

ALPHA ERROR: an error that occurs when a researcher seems to have found a causal relationship but has actually observed a statistical fluke or artifact (also called a type 1 error)

BETA ERROR: an error that occurs when a true causal relationship is not identified, either because of a statistical fluke or because it is masked (also called a type 2 error)

CONFOUND: an uncontrolled variable in research which causes either an alpha error (artifact) or a beta error (masking effect), leading to misinterpretation of the study results

CORRELATIONAL RESEARCH: observational studies which seek statistical patterns among variables but which cannot determine whether those patterns are attributable to cause and effect relationships

DEPENDENT VARIABLE: a variable which is observed in an experiment because it is thought to be dependent upon (an effect of) changes in another variable

ECOLOGICAL FALLACY: an error in logic that occurs when a researcher tries to apply a conclusion drawn from one level of analysis (such as social systems) to another level (such as individuals)

EXPERIMENTAL RESEARCH: studies which manipulate an independent variable, observe its effects on a dependent variable, and control confounds, thus allowing the discovery of cause and effect relationships

INDEPENDENT VARIABLE: a variable which is manipulated in an experiment because it is thought to cause change in another (dependent) variable

PANEL CORRELATION: a special type of long-term correlational study which produces the only type of correlation that can be used to sort out cause and effect relationships

PATH ANALYSIS: a complex mathematical model of the possible cause and effect relationships between multiple interacting variables

Overview

Although philosophers continue to debate the meanings of "cause" and "effect," most people, including sociologists, have fairly straightforward conceptions of these terms. Causes are events or phenomena that occur at a certain point in time (or develop over a certain period of time) and that have a direct consequence or result; that is, they lead to a change in something else. That consequence or result is called the "effect." Causal events, therefore, always precede their effects, so to be able to demonstrate that one phenomenon causes another, it must be shown that the event thought to be the cause preceded the event thought to be the effect.

Causal relationships are not necessarily one-to-one. Some causes can have many effects; for example, smoking can lead to lung disease, throat cancer, and heart disease. Likewise, some effects can result from more than one cause: Lung disease can be an effect of smoking, exposure to radon, or genetic inheritance. Causal relationships can also occur in chains, like a series of dominoes, each of which, in the act of falling, leads to the fall of its neighbor. When such a cascade occurs, the immediately preceding causal event is called the "proximate cause," and the original causal event is called the "ultimate cause."

Because causal relationships can be so complicated, it is difficult to draw conclusions about causality only by looking at the temporal or statistical relationship between two events; simply knowing that one event commonly precedes another is not enough to know whether the first event actually causes the second. To be sure that an event causes another event, all other possible causes must be ruled out; in order to do this, it is necessary to run a controlled experiment.

In a controlled experiment, the experimenter allows only one event or process to change at a time. This change is the "independent variable"; it is what the experimenter suspects might be a cause of something else. The experimenter looks for an effect by observing the "dependent variable"—whatever the researcher thinks will be changed as a result of the change in the independent variable. Presumably, if the dependent variable changes, then it must have changed because of the change in the independent variable; that is, the independent variable must have caused the change in the dependent variable.

This logic will work, however, only if the experimenter can be sure that nothing else was changing at the same time as the independent variable; if there was something else changing at the same time, then it might have been the cause of the change in the dependent variable. Such uncontrolled events are called "confounds," and whenever there is a confound in a research study there will be more than one possible interpretation of that study's results. If the dependent variable changed because of the confound rather than because of the independent variable, scientists say that the change in the dependent variable was "spurious." If the experimenter does not notice the confound and mistakenly believes that the independent variable caused the change in the dependent variable, the experimenter has made an "alpha error" or "type 1 error." On the other hand, if the independent variable really did have an effect on the dependent variable, but the confound had the opposite effect, so that there was no overall change in the dependent variable, scientists say that a "masking effect" has occurred. In this situation, if the experimenter does not notice the confound and mistakenly believes that the independent variable had no effect on the dependent variable, he or she has made a "beta error" or "type 2 error."

There are basically two ways to control possible confounds. First, the experimenter can ensure that a possible confound literally does not vary through the course of the experiment; in an educational setting, say, the researcher would want to ensure that the subjects (students) do not get a new teacher halfway through the study. Many confounds cannot be truly controlled, however; for example, all students will get older as a study goes on. To be able to differentiate the effects of the independent variable from the effects of aging, the experimenter must have a "control group" of students who go through the experiment in exactly the same way as the experimental group, except that the independent variable is not changed for them. The experimental group will experience the effects of the independent variable and of aging, while the control group will experience only the effects of aging. The two groups can then be compared to isolate the effect of the independent variable. Subjects must be assigned to the control group and to the experimental group at random; otherwise, the groups might be different to start with, and these existing differences would be a confound.

In sociological research, for both practical and ethical reasons, it is often impossible to control confounding variables or to randomize subjects to experimental and control groups. Most sociological data come not from experiments but from large-scale correlational studies—that is, surveys and other kinds of observational research in which statistical patterns are observed but no variables have been manipulated or controlled. Thus, the results of most sociological studies have more than one possible cause-effect interpretation. The goal of a good researcher, therefore, is to design a study which minimizes the number of possible confounds and thus minimizes the number of possible interpretations of the results.

Applications

One important area of sociological (and psychological) research is the search for causes of violence. Since violent behavior has been increasing in the United States for several decades, it is likely that some other change that also began a few decades ago is causing this increase. One possible candidate is the spread of television viewing and the subsequent exposure of children to televised violence.

To test whether exposure to televised violence causes violent behavior, it is possible to design an experiment in which some children see a violent television show and other children see a nonviolent show; subsequent behavior of the children could then be compared between groups. Any such experiment, however, could only assess the effect of short-term television exposure on immediate behavior, when what researchers really want to know is whether long-term television exposure has any long-term effects.

Since it is neither practical nor ethical to assign children randomly to high versus low levels of television violence over a long period, one could do a correlational study looking for statistical relationships between television viewing and patterns of violence. (Such studies have found that children who watch a considerable amount of television are more violent than children who watch little television.) There are, however, two problems with such studies. One is that, since both behaviors are observed at the same time, it is not possible to show that one preceded the other; thus, it is impossible to know whether one caused the other. The second problem is that since children are not randomly assigned to be frequent viewers versus infrequent viewers, there may be uncontrolled factors that cause some children to watch much television and be violent and others to avoid television and be nonviolent. For example, children with violent parents may become violent themselves and may also watch much television because they do not get quality parenting, whereas children with nonviolent parents may not become violent and may also watch less television because their parents provide more alternative activities. Simple correlational studies always have confounds, making it impossible to know which variables are causes and which are effects.

One kind of correlational study, however, a "panel correlation," allows researchers to make educated guesses about causal relationships. In a panel correlation, the researcher measures both the presumed causal variable (in this case, amount of television viewing) and the presumed effect (in this case, violent behavior), twice— once at an early age (say, six) and once at a later age (say, thirteen). Then it can be discovered whether television viewing at age six is related to violent behavior at age thirteen and whether violent behavior at age six is related to television viewing at age thirteen. Since causes must precede effects, if the first relationship is much stronger than the second relationship, the researcher can safely guess that the television viewing was the cause of the violent behavior, rather than vice versa. (This is indeed what such studies have found.) A panel correlation cannot rule out other possible causal inter-pretations, since it is not a controlled experiment, but it is better than a simple correlation of two variables measured only once at the same time.

Another area in which it is difficult to sort out causal relationships is the study of social stratification. An example is trying to determine the causes of the patterns of differential wages for men versus women and for whites versus minorities. Do women make less money than men do because they have different interests and seek different jobs (which happen to be lower-paying), or are women discriminated against when they apply for higher-paying jobs? Alternatively, could it be that once women break into a field that has been traditionally male-dominated, wages in that field start to drop? Since it is impossible to do controlled experiments to sort out the cause and effect relationships in this area, how can researchers deduce causal interpretations from analysis of statistical (correlational) patterns?

There are ways to make educated guesses about cause and effect relationships, even when there are a multitude of variables involved in a complex interaction. In such "multivariate" situations, a technique called "path analysis" can be used to try to diagram visually and mathematically the cause and effect relationships interconnect-ing a set of related phenomena. To begin, the researcher must have a good initial guess (model) about which variables come first, which come later, which are causes, and which are effects. The model is fed into a computer, along with actual statistical data on all the relevant variables; the result is a set of numbers describing the relative strength of each of the "paths" (causal relationships) between each pair of variables in the set. The researcher can run as many path analyses as desired, each time giving the computer the same data but a different model. When all the possible models have been run, the researcher can compare the results to find which model had the best fit to the data. Models with a good fit are more likely to have correctly specified the true cause and effect relationships than models with a poor fit. Although path analyses are better than simple correlations, they are not controlled experiments, so researchers still cannot be sure that they have made the correct interpretation. It is always possible that the researcher missed some important variables that were never included in the model-testing process.

Context

As computer modeling techniques become more complex and more advanced, it is likely that the findings of sociologists will be given more weight and will be increasingly incorporated into the political decision-making process. Still, the application of sociological research will always be controversial because the inability to be certain about cause and effect relationships means that there will always be the potential for mistakes in the interpretation of research. Making mistakes in socially sensitive areas can have severe consequences. If research suggests that exposure to televised violence, for example, is one of the causes of later violence in viewers, is it therefore a good idea for government to regulate television viewing or television content? Is it acceptable for government to restrict individual choices in order to effect social change? One problem is that even if television viewing increases violence in general, that does not mean that every person who watches considerable television will become violent. Moreover, it could be that the relationship really is not causal after all. No matter how much sociologists can refine their methods to sort out cause and effect relationships, how their conclusions are applied to public policy will continue to require ethical, as well as scientific, discussion.

Sociologists must also be able to integrate their findings and interpretations with those of scientists in related fields such as management, psychology, history, political science, and anthropology. It is tempting to draw causal conclusions at one level (for example, individuals or families) based on research findings at another level (communities or countries), but such conclusions are often in error. Just because there is a statistical relationship, say, between parenting practices and rates of violent behavior in families across different societies, that does not mean that the same relationship would necessarily exist across families in a single society. This is a common error of logic (called the "ecological fallacy"), and the only way to prevent it is to ensure ongoing cross-disciplinary discussion.

Finally, some people criticize sociology (and the other social sciences) as being "soft" science (as opposed to the "hard" science of physics, chemistry, and biology). Yet even though sociologists are less able than other scientists to do controlled experiments on their subject matter, there are many methods available to sociologists that are not available to others. Chemists, after all, cannot interview the subjects of their study. Sociologists utilize a variety of methods and then draw conclusions from the convergence of evidence derived from these methods. In this way, sociology is like any other science: It uses observation, statistics, and logic to arrive at ever better educated guesses about causal relationships in the world.

Bibliography

Cole, Stephen. *The Sociological Method.* Chicago: Markham, 1972. This short (136-page) book covers the kinds of questions sociologists ask, how they answer them, and how they use their results; includes a very simple introduction to complex (multivariate) causal relationships. Full of fun, interesting examples and very basic statistics, which can easily be skipped if so desired.

Cook, Thomas D., and Donald T. Campbell. *Quasi-Experimentation: Design and Analysis Issues for Field Settings.* Chicago: Rand McNally, 1979. This classic text is written for graduate students in the social sciences. Chapter 1, however, "Causal Inference and the Language of Experimentation," provides an excellent background on various philosophical approaches to the analysis of cause and effect relationships, including summaries of the positions of John Stuart Mill and Karl Popper.

Homans, George C. *The Nature of Social Science.* New York: Harcourt, Brace & World, 1967. This brief book (109 pages) was written at about the same time as the Platt article mentioned below and has the same basic message. The difference is that it is less technical, as it was written for a lay audience rather than from one scientist to another.

Huck, Schuyler W., and Howard M. Sandler. *Rival Hypotheses: Alternative Interpretations of Data Based Conclusions.* New York: Harper & Row, 1979. This wonderful book consists of brief summaries of 100 flawed research studies. It is up to the reader to figure out the logical flaw in each. Answers are provided at the end, along with an appendix summarizing the most common types of logical errors in interpretation of cause and effect.

Platt, John R. "Strong Inference." *Science* 146 (October 16, 1964): 347-353. This classic article discusses "scientific falsification," the process whereby different causal hypotheses are ruled out one by one, leaving the strongest, presumably best hypothesis, as the sole survivor of rigorous attempts at disproof. Platt believes that the social sciences will remain unacceptably "soft" until this approach is used more regularly.

Smelser, Neil J. *Essays in Sociological Explanation.* Englewood Cliffs, N.J.: Prentice-Hall, 1968. The first essay in this book, "Sociology and the Other Social Sciences" (42 pages), does a wonderful job of describing the kinds of variables and relationships that sociologists study and the methods they use to do so. Compares sociology with economics, political science, anthropology, history, and psychology.

Linda Mealey

Cross-References

Experimentation in Sociological Research, 721; Hypotheses and Hypothesis Testing, 915; Inferential Statistics, 983; Logical Inference: Deduction and Induction, 1093; Paradigms and Theories, 1328; Quantitative Research, 1546; Surveys, 2030; Triangulation, 2071; Validity and Reliability in Measurement, 2136.

CENSUSES AND CENSUS DATA

Type of sociology: Population studies or demography

A census is an enumeration of the population in a territory and the compilation of demographic, social, and economic information pertaining to that population at a given time. Information tabulated from a census is referred to as census data.

Principal terms

BUREAU OF THE CENSUS: a branch of the Department of Commerce that is responsible for the taking of the United States Census every ten years; it also compiles and distributes the census data

CONTENT ERROR: inaccuracy in the census data owing primarily to an error in reporting, editing, or tabulating

COVERAGE ERROR: an error in the census count owing to some people being missed by the census

DE FACTO POPULATION: a count of the people who are actually in a given territory on the census day

DE JURE POPULATION: a count of the people who "belong" to a given area in some way or another, regardless of whether they are in this area on the census day

LONG-FORM QUESTIONNAIRE: the census form that one in six United States households receives; it contains all the questions on the short form as well as twenty-six additional questions about individuals and nineteen additional questions about housing conditions

REAPPORTIONMENT: the process through which the seats in the United States House of Representatives are apportioned every ten years based on the population counted in the census

SHORT-FORM QUESTIONNAIRE: the census form that five out of every six United States households receive; it asks seven questions pertaining to individuals and seven questions pertaining to housing conditions

Overview

A census is taken to count and characterize the population of a given territory at a given time. Virtually every country has conducted a census since 1950, although the frequency of census-taking varies substantially among countries. In most countries, as in the United States, one adult in a household usually answers questions about all the people living in that household. A national census is a primary source of data on population size and distribution, as well as on structure and characteristics of the population. The level of detail provided by a census varies tremendously among countries, since some countries ask numerous questions and others ask only a few questions of its population.

There are at least two different estimates of population size that can result from a census: the de facto population and the de jure population. For countries with few foreign workers and in which working in another area from where one lives is rare, the distinction makes little difference. For some countries, however, such as Switzerland, with large numbers of alien workers, the de facto population is much larger than the de jure population. Americans are enumerated on the basis of "usual residence," which is roughly defined as the place where a person usually sleeps. This is closer to the concept of de jure than de facto, as people with no usual residence (such as migratory workers, vagrants, and homeless people) are counted where they are found.

A national census has been taken every ten years in the United States since 1790. Mandated by the U.S. Constitution, the decennial census is the basis for reapportionment of the House of Representatives. Census data are also used to ensure proportional representation of numerous elected state and local offices, such as state representatives and school district boards.

Although a census is supposed to count everyone, some people are missed. The United States Census tends to undercount a relatively high percentage of minorities and poor persons, owing to the greater difficulty in locating them and in getting those that are found to complete their questionnaires. The Bureau of the Census conducts an intensive public relations campaign to increase awareness of the national census, and it works with corporations, schools, religious and national minority organizations, and local governments to persuade people to answer the census. A toll-free telephone number is listed on the questionnaire for those having difficulty in completing their questionnaire. In areas where a substantial proportion of the population may speak a language other than English, the census questionnaire is printed in both English and this other language. The Bureau of the Census tries to assure everyone that personal identities are kept confidential, that answering the census questionnaire is in the public interest, and that no one will be punished based on his or her responses on the questionnaire. Numerous undocumented aliens, however, still do not complete a questionnaire for fear this information will be used to deport them.

In addition to missing people, there can also be problems with the accuracy of the census data owing to errors of reporting, editing, or tabulating. Numerous field checks and data processing methods are built into the United States Census procedures to ensure that the census is accurate, in terms of both the data and the population count; these efforts also make the census quite expensive. The census bureau estimates that the United States population was undercounted by about 1.6 percent in 1990. In general, the more highly developed a country is, the more accurate is its census.

The 1990 census, for the vast majority of Americans (about 86 percent), involved a census questionnaire being delivered to their residences. This form was to be completed and returned by mail. For another 11 percent of the nation's housing units, where addresses did not specify housing units precisely enough for mailing-list purposes, enumerators visited every housing unit before census day, and left a census questionnaire to be completed and returned by mail.

The Bureau of the Census enumerated residents of group quarters, such as college dormitories, jails, nursing homes, and boardinghouses, separately from household residents, using individual census forms instead of the household questionnaires. Attention was also paid to including the homeless in the census count. The census bureau conducted two operations specifically designed to locate selected components of the homeless and include them in the 1990 enumeration.

For the 1990 census, the short-form questionnaire that was distributed to approximately five out of every six households in the nation asked for such basic information as age, sex, race, and marital status of the individuals in the household. It took people an average of fifteen minutes to complete the questionnaire. A random sample of approximately one in six households received a long-form questionnaire that asked every question on the short form plus other questions covering a wide range of areas, such as education, income, mobility, languages spoken at home, disability status, and occupation. Some of the questions were quite detailed and provided data, for example, on whether a person served in the military during the Vietnam War, the length of time it took residents to travel to work, and the mode of transportation used to travel to work. It took an average of fifty minutes to complete the long-form questionnaire. The information obtained from this questionnaire provides a detailed picture of the United States population on census day.

Applications

Census data are used to allocate billions of dollars of government benefits to states, cities, and counties. Many government assistance programs use census data as part of their allocation formulas. The Older Americans Act of 1965, for example, requires age data at the state level for planning community programs for the elderly. United States law specifies that the Job Training Partnership Act will use decennial census data on income and poverty to make decisions about funding training programs. For some programs, funds are distributed throughout the decade based on the census data. For other programs, government agencies use estimates in noncensus years to distribute funds; the census data are used as the benchmark for these estimates. The tremendous amount of money that is distributed based on the census makes it important to have an accurate census.

A census of population, especially in the United States or another highly developed country, is an incredibly rich reservoir of information about human society. In its charting of the characteristics of the American people, each census is a snapshot of society at a single point in time. The fact that much of the data from the long-form questionnaire are not estimated in noncensus years makes this information very important to many government agencies and private corporations who use the data for efficient planning, marketing, and forecasting of consumer demand. Because the deletion of certain questions may create problems for government programs, the census bureau tries to keep the new census questionnaire as similar as possible to the previous questionnaire, thus ensuring consistency in the census data over time. Questions have changed over time, however, with the new questions reflecting what is occurring in the United States at census time. For example, in 1920, when interest in immigration was at its peak, the census added numerous questions on migration, whereas in 1970, a question was added on disability status to reflect interest in the casualties associated with the Vietnam War.

The 1990 census data are easily accessible to the general public, as the data are available in printed reports and on computer tapes, compact disks (CD-ROM), and microfiche. In addition to the availability of census products directly from the Bureau of the Census, census data are available in numerous libraries throughout each state. Further, there are several data centers in each state designated by the bureau that provide census data to state agencies, private corporations, and the general public and that offer assistance in answering questions and in interpreting census data.

Printed reports are quite useful for obtaining data for states, counties, and cities, whereas computer tapes and disks are the primary source of data for smaller geographic areas. The availability of census data varies by geography, with less detailed subject matter available for smaller geographic areas. Even for small geographic units such as census tracts, which contain about four thousand people, there is an abundance of available data. There are some data available for individual blocks: the population under age eighteen and the population ages eighteen and older, race, whether a person is of "Hispanic Origin," and housing counts. Information at the block level is used for the reapportionment of congressional representatives.

Numerous companies use census data in deciding where to locate a particular business. A company that specializes in clothing for teenagers, for example, may use the census data to find out how many teenagers and preteens are in a specific area. Programs or services tailored to the elderly would find it useful to know the number of elderly in a particular area as well as the number of elderly with disabilities; the census contains this information.

Census data may also be used for planning purposes. For example, school districts may use census data to determine how many children in their area are ages 0, 1, 2, 3, 4, and 5 years, thus providing them with advance notice of how many children may be expected in each of the elementary school grades in the next few years. This information may be used to help ensure that there will be adequate facilities in the school district in the coming years to accommodate the school population, both in terms of the total number of students and the number of students in each grade.

The standard reports, tapes, and disks contain tables of census data which cannot be combined with one another. To allow researchers to manipulate the data, the Bureau of the Census has created two Public Use Microdata Sample Tapes. The first tape comprises 1 percent of the U.S. population, and the second tape comprises 5 percent of the population. These tapes contain a sample of responses to individual questionnaires from residents of cities or groups of counties that contain more than 100,000 people. No information is contained about household addresses or identities of residents, thus ensuring the confidentiality of the census.

Although current census questionnaires are confidential, they become available to the public seventy-two years after the census is taken. In 1992, the general public had access to the responses to individual questionnaires from the 1920 census. Because the questionnaires contain names and addresses, people often use census data to trace their ancestry. Old census questionnaires can also be used by researchers to document the marriage and fertility patterns occurring in the United States a hundred years ago.

Context

Throughout time, governments have desired information about their populations. In addition to determining population, censuses were initially used as a way to identify a country's taxpayers as well as potential laborers and soldiers. The earliest governments to undertake censuses of their populations are believed to have been those in the ancient civilizations of Egypt, Babylon, China, Palestine, and Rome. For about eight hundred years, citizens of Rome were counted every five years for tax and military purposes.

After the demise of the Roman Empire, there were only sporadic censuses until the eighteenth century, when censuses once again were conducted on a regular basis. Countries in Europe began the practice of taking regular censuses, with Sweden starting in 1749, followed by Norway and Denmark in 1760. By the mid 1900's, many countries were conducting regular censuses; questions were asked about various subjects, such as marital status, whether people were employed and what their occupation was, literacy, place of birth, and so forth. The fact that over time national censuses have asked more detailed questions has resulted in an increased reliance on the census as a source of data by both government agencies and private corporations. There has also been increased pressure for censuses to be as accurate as possible.

The taking of a national census has become more than only a counting of the population, and it is often quite controversial. In numerous countries, such as England, Switzerland, and Germany, there has been public concern that the census asks for too much private information about its residents. Some censuses have even been postponed because of public outcry. Other countries have been pressured into not asking certain questions that the public deemed too sensitive. In the United States, numerous lawsuits are associated with each census, since various jurisdictions feel that the census has undercounted their population, thus resulting in their receiving less than their fair share of funds from the federal government.

The census has charted the United States' growth, beginning in 1790, with a country containing about 4 million people clustered along the eastern seaboard whose economy was heavily dependent on agriculture. By 1890, the population had increased sixteenfold to about 63 million people spread across the entire continent, although with a substantial proportion of the population still along the East Coast. The economy was less dependent on agriculture, with greater numbers of people employed in manufacturing, transportation, mining, and services. The census taken in 1990 showed that the population had grown to 250 million, with a substantial proportion of the population residing in the West. The economy had become extremely diverse, and the once-dominant agricultural industry employed only about 2 percent of the workforce.

The definition of who is counted for congressional reapportionment purposes has changed over time. For congressional representation based on the 1790 census, for example, a slave counted as three-fifths of a free person, and American Indians were counted only if they were taxed. In 1990, undocumented immigrants were counted for reapportionment purposes.

Bibliography

Abramowitz, Molly. *Census '90 Basics*. Washington, D.C.: U.S. Dept. of Commerce, Bureau of the Census, 1990. A brief report that presents a good overview of the taking of the 1990 census. Data users will appreciate the section describing each of the census products expected to be released and its date of release, including the level of detail available by various geographic units and the format of the data (in printed reports, on computer tapes, or on compact disks).

Anderson, Margo J. *The American Census: A Social History*. New Haven, Conn.: Yale University Press, 1988. A historical account of the taking of the U.S. Censuses that includes the controversies associated with many of the censuses. Focuses on the changes in census data over time and the relevance of the census in U.S. history.

Citro, Constance F., and Michael L. Cohen, eds. *The Bicentennial Census: New Directions for Methodology in 1990*. Washington, D.C.: National Academy Press, 1985. An extensive report by the Panel on Decennial Census Methodology which explored ways to improve the accuracy of the 1990 census and future censuses. Begins with an overview of the census. The remainder of the book, however, focuses on new approaches for taking upcoming censuses and requires a solid background in statistics.

Robey, Bryant. *Two Hundred Years and Counting: The 1990 Census*. Washington, D.C.: Population Reference Bureau, 1989. An excellent overview of the United States Decennial Census with the focus on the 1990 census. Includes a copy of the 1990 census questionnaire. The bibliography includes the address and telephone number of the lead agency in each state that works with the Census Bureau to distribute census data to the public and to provide assistance in interpreting census data and answering census questions. Well suited for the general audience.

United States General Accounting Office. *Federal Formula Programs: Outdated Population Data Used to Allocate Most Funds*. Washington, D.C.: U.S. General Accounting Office, 1990. This report documents, in tabular form, the federal programs that allocated funds for fiscal year 1989 based on decennial census counts and those programs that allocated funds based on current population estimates. Although this guide contains little analysis, it is a good source for showing the variety of government branches that distribute funds and the amount of money distributed by each program based on census data.

Howard Wineberg

Cross-References

CHILD ABUSE AND NEGLECT

Type of sociology: Aging and ageism
Fields of study: The family; Forms of deviance

Child abuse refers to nonaccidental harm that is inflicted on children by their parents or other adults, while child neglect describes the failure of adult caregivers to provide children with such basic necessities as food, clothing, shelter, or supervision. Both child abuse and child neglect are serious social problems that often have a lasting negative impact on the development of minors.

Principal terms

CHILD MALTREATMENT: a catchall phrase used to refer simultaneously to all forms of child mistreatment, such as physical, sexual, and emotional abuse, as well as child neglect

CHILD NEGLECT: a failure on the part of adult caregivers to provide a child with adequate supervision, nourishment, shelter, education, medical treatment, or emotional and intellectual stimulation

EMOTIONAL ABUSE: an extreme attempt on the part of an adult to terrorize, berate, or humiliate a child

PHYSICAL ABUSE: the inflicting of physical harm or inordinately severe pain upon a child by an adult

POST-TRAUMATIC STRESS DISORDER: a mental disorder in which symptoms such as flashbacks, impaired concentration and memory, and excessive anxiety occur after the experience of a highly traumatic event

PRIMARY PREVENTION: preventive efforts intended to establish conditions that will prevent the occurrence of mental disorders or social problems

SECONDARY PREVENTION: prevention techniques that typically involve emergency or crisis intervention, with efforts focused on reducing the impact, duration, or spread of a problem

SEXUAL ABUSE: any type of inappropriate sexual contact between a child and an adult

Overview

The term "child abuse" is used to describe the physical, emotional, and sexual abuse of minors by adults. In cases of physical abuse, children may be slapped, kicked, hit, pushed, or burned. Bruises, wounds, broken bones, or other injuries are common results of physical child abuse. In the most severe cases, physical child abuse can result in permanent physical damage or even in death. Children who suffer from physical abuse generally develop psychological problems as well, because their feelings of security and well-being have been severely compromised.

While emotional abuse does not leave the telltale scars or injuries of physical abuse, the long-term psychological effects of emotional abuse can also be quite devastating. Unfortunately, it is often difficult for child welfare authorities to agree on what constitutes emotional abuse. While most authorities agree that normal criticism and discipline are acceptable, an extreme effort to humiliate, berate, or terrorize a child is often said to constitute emotional abuse. For example, few child welfare experts would object if, after a five-year-old has written on the walls, a parent reacts by telling the child to stop the behavior and taking away the child's crayons. If the same parent, however, were to dangle the unruly five-year-old by the feet from a sixth-story window and threaten to drop him or her if the behavior did not end, then such a parent would surely be guilty of emotional child abuse. Such treatment can do long-term damage to a child's sense of safety and self-esteem. While physical symptoms may not be immediately apparent, pediatrician Howard Dubowitz has noted that the stress of psychological maltreatment will also often result in such symptoms as stomachaches, chest pain, headaches, and problems with bowel and bladder control.

In the same way that emotional child abuse can seriously damage a child's physical and psychological welfare, sexual abuse also tends to have long-term negative effects on a child's condition. Sexual abuse consists of a wide range of inappropriate sexual behaviors between an adult and a child, such as fondling, masturbation, or intercourse. Sexual abuse also occurs when children are involved as subjects in the production of pornography.

Unlike child abuse, child neglect occurs not when adults deliberately harm children but rather when adult caregivers fail to provide children with their basic needs. Inadequate supervision, improper nourishment, insufficient shelter, or a failure to provide children with appropriate schooling, medical care, or emotional nurturance can all constitute child neglect. Like other forms of child maltreatment, child neglect often results in lasting damage to a child's physical and emotional welfare.

Since the early 1960's, social scientists have attempted to determine the incidence of child maltreatment in the United States. Estimates of child maltreatment have varied widely, from a low of several hundred thousand cases per year to a high of two to three million. Although these numbers are widely divergent, nearly all researchers agree that child maltreatment is a prevalent and serious problem in the United States.

There is also some evidence that the problem is growing. A report issued by the Department of Health and Human Services in 1990 indicated that the number of minors reported as abused and neglected rose 64 percent from 1980 to 1988 to reach an alarming total of 2.2 million yearly cases of child maltreatment by 1988.

In the past, most social scientists believed that such child maltreatment was the result of defects in the abusive adult's personality. This theory continues to have some credibility, since research suggests that many abusive adults were themselves reared in chaotic and emotionally insensitive homes in which violence and neglect were common. In his seminal book on child maltreatment, *Somewhere a Child Is Crying* (1973), pediatrician and social theorist Vincent J. Fontana has described how a cycle of abuse can pass from one generation to the next:

Just as the majority of yesterday's maltreated children are the maltreating parents of today, so the maltreated children of today will become the maltreating parents of tomorrow. We see this acted out from generation to generation: abuse breeds abuse, and violence breeds violence, and one horror breeds another. If we are subjected to abuse, we either disintegrate under pressure or learn from our aggressors to become aggressors ourselves.

While the parents' emotional history can be a crucial determinant, a mounting body of evidence has suggested that child abuse and neglect are also related to a number of social and economic problems, such as poverty, unemployment, and drug abuse.

Influential research in this area was conducted by social psychologist Leroy Pelton, who studied the occurrence of abuse and neglect in New Jersey during the 1970's. Pelton found that child neglect was particularly prevalent among impoverished lower-class families. Whereas more affluent parents could obtain adequate child care services, poor parents were often forced to neglect their children when they had to work or attend to other business.

Research such as Pelton's suggests that psychological intervention alone will not remedy the problem of child maltreatment. The social and economic problems that lead to child abuse and neglect must also be addressed if the frequency of this problem is to decline.

Applications

Knowledge of child maltreatment must be used to prevent the future occurrence of child abuse and to offer treatment for the victims of this social malady. Medical, legal, and mental health professionals have taken steps to prevent the abuse and neglect of children. In the United States, laws have been enacted in every state requiring teachers, pediatricians, nurses, social workers, psychologists, and other professionals who work with children to report cases of suspected child abuse and neglect. As long as such professionals report a case of child maltreatment in good faith, they are immune from legal action associated with the report. Most developed nations have similar laws designed to protect children from abuse.

In addition to mandatory reporting laws, every state in the United States has developed a child protective service that investigates reported cases of child maltreatment and takes steps to protect a child's welfare when abuse has occurred. These child protective services also provide evidence of child mistreatment to law enforcement officials, since child abuse is a crime in every state and abusers are sometimes prosecuted.

Unfortunately, the child protective services of many states are underfunded and understaffed. The National Committee for the Prevention of Child Abuse and Neglect, a Chicago-based advocacy group, has issued guidelines recommending that child protective workers have no more than twenty to twenty-five cases to investigate and monitor at any given time. In many states, however, caseworkers must often attempt to monitor fifty or more reportedly abusive families at one time. Such conditions make it difficult for child protective services to investigate and supervise abusive families in a productive fashion.

A different approach to preventing child maltreatment has come from abusive parents themselves who are seeking to find less destructive ways of rearing their children. In 1970, Parents Anonymous was formed; it is a self-help group in which troubled parents attempt to provide one another with emotional support and better parenting skills. Professionals often volunteer to lead local Parents Anonymous groups in order to provide additional assistance. Parents Anonymous has grown rapidly, and by the early 1990's more than a thousand chapters existed nationwide.

Other efforts to prevent child maltreatment include the establishment of regional hotlines that allow potentially abusive adults to call for help on a twenty-four-hour basis. Various state, municipal, and private agencies have also funded educational programs to reduce the incidence of child maltreatment. Educational programs focus on increasing public awareness about the gravity of this problem, striving to teach basic parenting skills to abusive mothers and fathers, and attempting to teach children about their basic rights. In this last category are a number of educational efforts that attempt to prevent sexual abuse by teaching children about the difference between "good touching" and "bad touching" and that encourage children to tell an appropriate adult if they have been victimized.

While educational efforts and other preventive measures have met with some success, they come too late for children who have already been abused or neglected. These children require treatment from a number of different professionals so that they can be safe and begin to recover from their negative experiences. If a child has suffered physical harm, he or she must first receive the attention of a pediatrician or family practitioner who is sensitive to child abuse issues. Child protective workers may need to place the child in a shelter, residential treatment center, or foster home if the child's home environment is too dangerous to warrant his or her return. Most maltreated children also need to receive mental health services in order to address the emotional ramifications of their abuse. In some cases family therapy may be helpful, while in other situations individual treatment may be more appropriate. With young children, play therapy can be an effective way to help them express their thoughts and feelings.

If a child's abuse is severe or prolonged, some clinical psychologists and psychiatrists believe that the child may be at risk for the development of post-traumatic stress disorder (PTSD), a serious form of mental illness. Individuals with post-traumatic stress disorder generally have recurring thoughts or repetitive nightmares about the traumatic event; they also suffer from such symptoms as increased tension and irritability, insomnia, impaired concentration and memory, and a general avoidance of social contact. Children who fit this pattern after an abusive experience usually require intense assistance from mental health professionals.

While such efforts can help individual children, many social theorists have argued that work with individual children and deviant parents will not alone resolve the problem of child maltreatment. These authors, such as sociologist Richard Gelles, have argued that child abuse is really a symptom of other social problems, such as poverty, unemployment, the deterioration of the family structure, and drug and alcohol addiction. Gelles believes that these problems can push even well-intentioned parents to the breaking point so that they lash out against their children. Advocates of this position suggest that most programs for child abuse are merely secondary prevention, since they attempt to reduce the impact and spread of the problem without eliminating its source. Authors who take a sociological view of child maltreatment generally argue for primary prevention, which would need to focus on the numerous social problems that are thought to be the basic causes of abuse and neglect.

Context

The problem of child maltreatment has existed throughout human history. Scholars have found evidence that abuse and neglect were common in a number of ancient civilizations. For example, historian Evaline Feucht has found that in ancient Egypt, unwanted children were sometimes abandoned in the desert, while other children were disciplined by being thrown against a stone wall. To their credit, the Egyptians did have strong social sanctions against this type of behavior and considered abusive adults to be morally bereft. In ancient Greece, on the other hand, certain aspects of child abuse were considered socially acceptable. Unwanted or sick infants were frequently killed by their parents to prevent children from becoming an economic burden on the family. Although this practice represents an extreme example of socially sanctioned child abuse, few early civilizations gave children the rights and protection that are now considered normal.

Only in recent times have child abuse and neglect been recognized as important social problems. In 1962, American pediatrician C. Henry Kempe coined the term "battered child syndrome." Kempe established a nonprofit center for the study of child abuse and neglect and did much to increase public awareness of the problem. Kempe's research promoted a number of legal changes designed to protect children from abuse. Between 1963 and 1967, all fifty states and the District of Columbia passed child abuse reporting laws. These laws were often modeled on existing statutes that required medical personnel to report the presence of certain infectious diseases. In 1974, the U.S. Congress, in an almost unanimous vote, passed the Child Abuse Prevention and Treatment Act, which created the National Center for Child Abuse and Neglect (NCCAN). The NCCAN is now part of the Department of Health and Human Services, and it funds projects across the country to study and prevent child abuse.

Despite such efforts, the number of children reported as abused and neglected continues to grow. The causes of this troubling phenomenon are not entirely clear. Some theorists have argued that the United States is facing a child protection emergency because it has failed to commit the necessary resources to protect and treat abused children. Others, such as social worker Elizabeth Hutchinson, have suggested that the country is really facing a family support emergency. Hutchinson argues that child abuse would best be prevented by social initiatives that support families, such as affordable child care, universal health insurance, drug treatment programs, improved family leave policies, and adequate low-income housing. No matter what the causes of child maltreatment may be, nearly all child welfare experts agree that it is a pervasive and growing problem in our society.

Bibliography

Breiner, Sander J. *Slaughter of the Innocents: Child Abuse Through the Ages and Today.* New York: Plenum Press, 1990. An excellent and easy-to-read reference for anyone interested in the history of child abuse or in a cross-cultural study of child maltreatment. The author examines the problem of child abuse in five ancient civilizations and then compares these groups to contemporary Western society.

Carson, Robert C., and James Butcher. *Abnormal Psychology.* 9th ed. New York: HarperCollins, 1992. This textbook provides an excellent overview of child abuse and neglect as well as a description of what can be done to prevent and treat the problem. Recommended for the reader who seeks a brief description of child abuse and its possible solutions.

Fontana, Vincent J. *Somewhere a Child Is Crying.* New York: Macmillan, 1973. Fontana's book has come to be considered a classic in the field of child abuse and neglect. It is strongly recommended for the high school student, college student, or lay reader who seeks a well-written overview of the field. The author illuminates his discussion of the topic with a number of fascinating case studies.

Mann, Eberhard, and John McDermott, Jr. "Play Therapy for Victims of Child Abuse and Neglect." In *The Handbook of Play Therapy,* edited by Charles Schaefer and Kevin O'Connor. New York: John Wiley & Sons, 1983. This chapter explains clearly how abused and neglected children can begin to recover with the help of individual play therapy. The authors provide a concise description of play therapy as well as case histories of abused and neglected children who benefited significantly from this type of treatment.

Miller, Alice. *For Your Own Good: Hidden Cruelty in Child-Rearing and the Roots of Violence,* translated by Hildegarde Hannum and Hunter Hannum. 2d ed. New York: Farrar, Straus & Giroux, 1984. For the college student or lay reader who is interested in the emotional ramifications of child abuse, this insightful book is likely to be quite helpful. Swiss psychoanalyst Miller provides the reader with a detailed account of the ways in which an abusive childhood can produce an adult who is prone to violence.

Starr, Raymond H., Jr., and David Wolfe, eds. *The Effects of Child Abuse and Neglect.* New York: Guilford Press, 1991. This collection of essays contains scholarly discussions of many issues that pertain to child maltreatment. While the reading level is challenging, the book will provide the college student or general reader with a wealth of empirical information about the consequences of child abuse.

Wolfe, David. *Preventing Physical and Emotional Abuse of Children.* New York: Guilford Press, 1991. This book is a detailed description of steps that social welfare agencies can take to prevent child abuse. The book is recommended for those who are interested in learning both about direct services for troubled families and about social policy issues.

Steven C. Abell

Cross-References

Discrimination Against Children and Adolescents, 225; Day Care and the Family, 450; Delinquency Prevention and Treatment, 476; The Feminization of Poverty, 754; The Incest Taboo, 934; Parenthood and Child-Rearing Practices, 1336; Poverty: Women and Children, 1466; Violence in the Family, 2157.

DISCRIMINATION AGAINST CHILDREN AND ADOLESCENTS

Type of sociology: Aging and ageism

Modern industrial societies treat individuals below the age of legal maturity differently from the way they treat adult individuals. Since the early twentieth century, children and adolescents have been viewed as needing certain protections that adults do not; ironically, however, the very belief that such safeguards and protections are necessary has led to discrimination against minors.

Principal terms

ADVOCACY: the use of argument to support a point of view in order to influence policy making

AGE DIFFERENTIATION: the process of assigning different roles to members of groups based on relative age

AGEISM: discrimination systematically directed toward groups based on age

CIVIL RIGHTS: legal rights that have been accorded to all citizens within a political state

DISCRIMINATION: the denial of opportunities and rights to certain groups on the basis of some identifiable characteristic

PARENS PATRIAE: a legal doctrine by which the state can intervene to protect a citizen with some disability

TERMINATION OF PARENTAL RIGHTS: the legal process by which a parent is relieved of the right to custody and the right to make decisions concerning a child

Overview

Discrimination is the denial of opportunities and rights to certain groups on some arbitrary basis. It is generally used in referring to racial or ethnic minorities, but it can apply to other groups as well. When discrimination is systematically directed toward groups defined by age, it is called ageism. There is much interest in the United States in ageism in terms of discrimination against the elderly, but ageism also denies opportunities and rights to children and adolescents. The study of discrimination against children and adolescents has come about relatively recently, since they are not normally considered "minority groups." Yet they can be considered minority groups in terms of their dependence on adults and their relative powerlessness. They are dependent on adults to meet the basic needs of life. In general, people assume that parents and social institutions will operate for the benefit of young people, but in fact children and adolescents sometimes suffer various forms of discrimination.

Societies normally operate on the basis of age differentiation. Distinctions are made between the young, the mature, and the old in terms of different roles assigned to each.

Age differentiation will almost certainly lead to inequalities. There are social attitudes that go along with the different roles that people are allowed to have, and these attitudes become associated with the people who occupy those roles. For example, people below a certain age in the United States must go to school; they cannot vote; and they cannot obtain a driver's license. They are not considered mature enough for the last two activities. The social attitude is that young people lack knowledge, skills, and the experience necessary to function independently in society. This attitude has led to laws intended to protect young people from their own immaturity and to protect property and other people from the actions of children and adolescents.

The suggestion that there is institutionalized discrimination against children and adolescents at first seems quite strange, since young people are often counted as among the great treasures of society. In his influential book *L'Enfant et la vie familiale sous l'Ancien Régime* (1960; *Centuries of Childhood*, 1962), the historian Phillippe Aries showed that children have been treated in many different ways in different societies throughout history. For much of history, children were simply treated as miniature adults. It was not until the nineteenth century that children came to be recognized as individuals with extraordinary needs. Sociologists and psychologists have repeatedly pointed out that youth reach physical and mental maturity long before they are accorded "social maturity." A number of social scientists argue that young people are not given status commensurate with their capabilities because of social attitudes concerning their immaturity. Some adolescents are able to see the discrepancy and consequently feel victimized by what they see as authoritarianism and regimentation. It is very difficult for most people to see discrimination against youth in the last part of the twentieth century, however, because almost everything parents and social institutions do (or so it is thought) is intended to protect, help, or rehabilitate children and adolescents. Such discrimination is an example of what sociologists call institutional discrimination, as opposed to individual discrimination. Institutional discrimination is a consequence of policy and actions rather than rationale or intentions. In many respects, children and youth are not faring well under the present system. The frequency and intensity of social problems such as runaways, physical and sexual abuse, and delinquency compel questions about the treatment of minors by parents and social institutions.

As classes of people, children and adolescents seem to have special, restrictive statuses that pervade every area of their lives. Discrimination may be seen by an examination of laws that regulate the lives of young people. Law is a social mechanism to resolve conflicts among people, and it is a formal indication of the norms of a society. American law is based on precedent as a means to promote stability and fairness. The common law is the body of customs and law, based on decisions of common-law courts in England, which formed the basis of American law. Under the common law, for example, children were bracketed together with those of "unsound mind" that had no personal or legal rights. Therefore, they were subject to guardianship: They did not have any control over their lives or property. Hence, based on common law and legal precedent, children and youth in the United States are subject to unique restrictive rules because of their age. Discrimination in general is often indexed by forced segregation and lack of money and power, and there is evidence that children and adolescents have been victims of discrimination.

Applications

Before the Industrial Revolution, children were considered economic assets to the family, and children were put to work at a variety of tasks from a very young age. With the advent of factories and urbanization, however, the nature of childhood and adolescence changed. Children in the United States were seen as vulnerable to abuse in the workplace and as needing protection; they were also seen as needing formal schooling. Child labor laws, compulsory education, and special legal provisions for juveniles changed the nature of childhood and adolescence. After these events, children became a drain on a family's resources. The effects of these events persist to the present day. In general, the only place that children and adolescents are supposed to be for most of the week is in school. If a minor wants to work, he or she must obtain a "work permit" from a government office. If a minor gets in serious trouble with authority figures (school officials, police officers, or even parents), juvenile court officials will almost certainly become involved. Although laws concerning children were passed with benevolent intentions, they set apart a class of people for differential and possibly discriminatory treatment.

Discrimination against children and youth has many practical implications, especially for young people who grow up in environments that are not conducive to their health and well-being. There are three major arenas in which minors may encounter demonstrable discrimination: in the schools, in court, and in the home. Minors are required to attend school, and violation of this requirement can subject a person to legal penalties. The 1960's and 1970's saw students win a number of rights through litigation. In *Tinker v. Des Moines Independent Community School District* (1969), the Supreme Court held that students do not "shed their constitutional rights to freedom of speech or expression at the schoolhouse gate." Since then there have been victories in freedom of dress and assembly. In addition, gains have been made in securing due process in disciplinary matters. Questions concerning the constitutionality of search and seizure and drug testing as applied to juveniles have also been raised. Of great importance to students have been changes in the use of corporal punishment in schools. Challenges to the use of corporal punishment have been mounted on the basis of the section of the Eighth Amendment forbidding cruel and unusual punishment. The Supreme Court has refused to disallow the use of corporal punishment as a means for teachers to maintain order in schools. Some states have disallowed corporal punishment within their schools, but other states have passed specific legislation affirming its use.

The second arena in which some analysts have seen discrimination against minors is in juvenile court. All states have established juvenile courts or family courts to handle the legal offenses of minors. These courts were established in acknowledgment that young people were different from adults and that they deserved special treatment.

Originally, juvenile court was set up not for punishment but for treatment purposes. The idea was to help youngsters "recover" so that they could proceed toward productive maturity. Unfortunately, according to political scientist Judith Baer, the system of juvenile justice has not lived up to its promise. Juvenile courts enforce laws relating to runaways, truancy, and incorrigibility (which generally consists of unco-operative, rebellious, and disobedient behavior). Minors have fewer rights than adults do in criminal court; for example, they may be arrested without a warrant. They do not have the right to a jury trial or to a speedy public trial. Before the Supreme Court decided *In re Gault* (1967), juveniles had virtually no rights in juvenile court. In that case, the Court declared that juveniles had the right to written notice, to be informed of the right to an attorney, and to confront and cross-examine accusers. The Court did not, however, accord juveniles full adult rights. Even after *In re Gault*, children and adolescents remain accountable to someone—parents, teachers, juvenile authorities—until they reach the age of maturity.

The third and by far most problematic arena of concern is the home. The 1980's saw the beginning of an explosion of reports of physical and sexual abuse of children in American homes. Every state has statutes concerning neglect and abuse of children and has set up mechanisms for intervening when reports of child abuse are filed. Yet under American law, parental rights and rights to privacy in the home often outweigh concern for the child. In general, according to child advocate Jack Westman, parents have the right to custody of the child and the right to the child's service and earnings. They can discipline the child and determine where the child lives, what the child eats, and how the child dresses. Children, on the other hand, have almost no rights. Courts presume that parents are loving and wise. "Keeping the family together" is a primary goal of the judicial system. The family is almost sacrosanct under American law. When things do go wrong in families, as they often do, the state may intervene. It does so under the legal doctrine of *parens patriae*—the concept of the state acting as a good parent to protect citizens who suffer from a disability. Foster care, adoption, and institutionalization are among the options under the *parens patriae* doctrine. In extreme cases, social workers may try to terminate the rights of the parents, a process which is complicated and often unsuccessful. The minor has very few legal rights in comparison with those of adults. Many child advocates see this area as the most glaring example of discrimination against minors.

Context

Sociologists have a long history of involvement in issues relating to discrimination. The Supreme Court's landmark decision in *Brown v. Board of Education* (1954) concerning the impossibility of "separate but equal" schools was informed by the findings of sociologists and other social scientists. Discrimination, whether based on race, ethnicity, sex, or age, is anathema to the principles of the United States Consti-tution. If that discrimination is somehow tacitly permitted by the court system (as was the case before *Brown v. Board of Education*), there may be an outcry for reform. Discrimination against children and adolescents, a form of ageism, has been the subject of increasing scrutiny since the early 1970's.

Courts have responded to the needs of children, although at a much slower rate than many advocates have desired. Courts have used various doctrines in dealing with issues concerning the welfare of children. Based on the common law, early American courts acceded to the idea that what a father decided to do with his children was his own business. Children were doubtless neglected and abused routinely. In the nineteenth century the courts used the "tender years doctrine," which was based on theories from psychology and other social sciences about the importance of childhood to the development of the individual. Specifically, in custody disputes, the mother was the preferred caretaker. With the advent of no-fault divorce, that doctrine was abolished on the grounds that it was gender-specific and therefore discriminatory. Today the most prevalent doctrine is the "best interests of the child." Politicians, scholars, public interest groups, attorneys, and child advocates all wish to have a say in how those interests are defined. The doctrine is, in reality, little more than an aspiration. There are not adequate resources to provide for the best interests of children who come before judges. There is not sufficient public acceptance of the need for the community to care for its children to bring voters to the point of supporting taxes to help the children.

Reform movements of the 1960's and 1970's did much to bring issues concerning child welfare to the public's attention. Reformers such as Paul Goodman, A. S. Neill, John Holt, Paul Adams, Maxine Greene, David Gottlieb, Robert Burt, Hillary Rodham (Hillary Rodham Clinton), and Richard Farson represented a wide variety of interests and contributed to a wider understanding of the issues. The 1969 Joint Commission on the Mental Health of Children and the 1970 White House Conference on Children were precursors to the increasing support of government. Despite the general federal reductions of programs for children in the 1980's, interest in children's issues has remained high.

One unique difficulty in formulating policies opposing discrimination against minors is the fact that there is a continuum of mental and emotional development from early childhood through adolescence. Fifteen-year-olds have very different levels of intellectual, emotional, and physical maturity than eight-year-olds do; in addition, individual levels of maturity vary widely within age groups. It is difficult, therefore, to create policies that deal fairly with children and adolescents while providing the protection that some younger individuals undeniably need. Nevertheless, many voices are saying that policies and laws need to be thoroughly examined and reevaluated. Some supporters of children's rights advocate an antidiscrimination movement that would parallel earlier civil rights movements, hoping to emulate the gains that other groups have been able to win at the national level.

Bibliography

Aries, Phillippe. *Centuries of Childhood*. Translated by Robert Baldick. New York: Vintage Books, 1962. This is a classic analysis of family life and the status of children through the ages. This is one book that is cited in almost every academic discussion of children.

Baer, Judith. *Equality Under the Constitution: Reclaiming the Fourteenth Amendment.* Ithaca, N.Y.: Cornell University Press, 1983. This is an excellent legal analysis of the equal protection clause of the Constitution. There are chapters on children, people with disabilities, and homosexuals. Includes an extensive bibliography and an index of cases.

Farson, Richard. *Birthrights.* New York: Macmillan, 1974. A critical book that challenges naïve assumptions of American life. Farson argues for equality in the treatment of children with reasoned allowance for their developmental stage.

Forer, Lois G. *Unequal Protection: Women, Children, and the Elderly in Court.* New York: W. W. Norton, 1991. This was written by a trial judge who has handled more than four thousand cases. Forer discusses cases involving "others," her name for anyone except adult males. She describes real-life people from the vantage point of the judicial bench.

Vardin, Patricia, and Ilene Brody, eds. *Children's Rights.* New York: Teachers College Press, 1979. A book of readings concerning different aspects of the children's rights movement. It includes an article on children's rights by Hillary Rodham (Hillary Rodham Clinton).

Westman, Jack, ed. *Who Speaks for the Children: The Handbook of Individual and Class Child Advocacy.* Sarasota, Fla.: Professional Resource Exchange, 1991. This is an excellent resource containing a number of articles written by analysts of the social movement. The issue of family as a part of a political agenda is most useful. Includes an extensive bibliography.

Zimring, Franklin. *The Changing Legal World of Adolescence.* New York: Free Press, 1982. A discussion of the marginal world of the adolescent in the legal arena. Considers the problem of semi-autonomy in adolescence. Includes an appendix on legal reasoning.

Roger G. Gaddis

Cross-References

Academic Freedom and Free Speech in the School, 1; Age Grading and Age Stratification, 27; Age Inequality: Functionalist versus Conflict Theory Views, 34; Ageism and the Ideology of Ageism, 41; Child Abuse and Neglect, 218; The Criminal Justice System, 380; Individual Discrimination, 547; Juvenile Delinquency: Analysis and Overview, 1036; Female Juvenile Delinquency, 1043.

CHRISTIANITY

Type of sociology: Major social institutions
Field of study: Religion

Christianity is a religion that is based on the belief that salvation can be achieved only through faith in Jesus Christ. Christians believe that Jesus Christ was crucified by the Romans until he died, that after his crucifixion he rose from the dead, that he is the lord and savior, and that those who believe in him will receive eternal life.

Principal terms
CONFORMITY: behavior by members of a society or group that is compatible with the norms, values, and folkways of that society or group
MORAL AUTHORITY: norms that are highly valued or are considered sacred by a society
SOCIAL GOSPEL: a movement that attempted to apply Christian principles to social problems and to reform society on the basis of Christ's charity, justice, and mercy
SOCIALIZATION: the process by which individuals learn the roles, norms, and values of the society to which they belong
VALUE: a hypothetical construct based on observable positive or negative behavior toward objects or symbolic representations of persons, situations, and objects; provides socialized individuals with bases for making judgments and choices

Overview

The Christian religion, which grew out of the Jewish tradition, is based on a belief that Jesus, a Jewish teacher who promoted an ethic based on love for all people, rose from the dead after he was crucified by the Romans, thereby demonstrating that he was the Christ, the son of God. Christians believe that having sincere faith in Jesus Christ is the route to personal salvation.

When it came into the Greco-Roman world in approximately 29 C.E., Christianity competed with many different religions and cults. Some scholars of religious history express surprise that Christianity outlasted its competition. Jesus' public career spanned only three years, and he met staunch opposition from the leaders of the religion of his own people—Judaism. Ultimately, he died like a common criminal, by crucifixion.

Many religions of Jesus' day had to do with a god (or gods) who met death at the hands of enemies but who was raised from the dead. Believers in such religions thought that they shared in the god's death and acquired immortality because of the god's resurrection. Christianity differed from such religions, however, in that it focused not on a mythical god but on a historical figure. Christians believed that, in Christ, God had become man, had died, and had been resurrected.

For centuries, Christians were intermittently persecuted by Jews, by the general public in the Roman Empire, and by the Roman emperors themselves. Yet such was Christ's message that, within five hundred years, a majority within the Roman Empire converted. The emperor Constantine began the mass conversion in 312 C.E., when he embraced Christianity. Later, his three sons—each of whom later served as emperor—converted. By the fifth century, Christianity had not only swept the Roman Empire but had also won converts in Persia, India, and Armenia in addition to gaining followers among the Germanic tribes on Rome's northern frontier.

Christianity gained its remarkable following for several reasons: First, the apostles (the original followers of Jesus) became missionaries, with Peter apparently the most prominent; second, the movement's martyrs exhibited remarkable heroism—the heroes included some of the original apostles, including Peter, as well as thousands of "common" believers; third, Greco-Roman culture progressively disintegrated and Christianity was there to fill the void; fourth, Christianity was not an "ethnic" religion (such as Judaism), but embraced people of all classes and all nationalities; fifth, leaders such as Paul, who followed the apostles, were firm in their adherence to the Church's convictions; sixth, the conversion of Constantine and his sons was extremely influential; and, finally, Christ himself promised the faithful a joyous immortality in fellowship with God. He carried a message that captured the imaginations of his followers.

As Christianity grew and developed, all believers became, in theory, members of one "universal" body—the Catholic church—which was organized into "dioceses," each of which was headed by a bishop. Bishops in the larger cities were deemed the most important leaders; among such cities were Jerusalem, Antioch, Constantinople, Alexandria, Carthage, and Rome. Because he was located in the empire's capital, the bishop of Rome was regarded early on as being particularly important. Furthermore, many believed that Peter had been designated by Jesus to head the church, and Peter is acknowledged by most authorities as being the first bishop of Rome, the city in which he later became a martyr.

Although the early Church stood in danger of being absorbed by Judaism as a variant of that religion and of thus becoming an "ethnic" religion, the early work of Paul and other missionaries among the Greeks and Romans precluded that outcome. The early Church was also threatened with a number of heresies, including Gnosticism, which seemed to deny that Christ was human and held that he was spirit only, and Marcionism, whose leader Marcion rejected the Old Testament and believed in two gods—one evil, one good.

Probably the most serious threat to "orthodox" Christianity came from Arius, a priest in Alexandria who lived from 256 to 336. Basically, Arius preached that there was never a time when God did not exist, but that there was a time when Jesus did not exist, since he was created by God. Thus Jesus was subordinated in Arianism. Controversy over Arianism became so divisive that in 325 Constantine (who was afraid that such divisions could destroy his empire) convened a Church council in

Nicaea. After much debate, the council condemned Arianism and adopted the Nicene Creed, the doctrine of the Trinity, which held that God, Jesus, and the Holy Spirit were all of the same substance and were joined, not separate. Because questions about Jesus' status still remained, a council assembled at Chalcedon in 451 and ruled that Jesus was not only of the same substance as the Father but was also of the same substance as humankind. Therefore, Jesus was simultaneously completely human and completely God.

By the time the council at Chalcedon had made its rulings, another important influence on the early Church was felt in the life and works of Augustine of Hippo (354-430), who had experienced a remarkable spiritual odyssey and an equally remarkable conversion. Augustine stressed that humanity, which was sinful because of the fall of Adam, the first man, could not simply voluntarily turn to God for salvation. Instead, an act of grace on the part of God allowed some believers to repent and thus be given eternal life.

Applications

Christianity, like other religions, has appeal because individuals have psychic needs and because social groups need solidarity and a common set of values. Such solidarity and norms are most effective when they carry the force of moral authority.

Christianity helps believers to overcome specific fears and general anxiety. To the extent that the world is a dangerous place where many "unknowns" exist, faith in the Christian God helps many people find ease and peace. Second, Christianity helps many people "make sense" of an otherwise incomprehensible cosmos. Most Christians find the Bible's religious answers to cosmic questions (the Book of Genesis on creation, for example) soothing. Third, individuals confront a chaotic world and look for some meaning in their existence. Christianity answers believers' questions, gives them a sense of purpose, and helps them develop an orderly "worldview." Christianity teaches its followers that they are only "visiting" this earthly realm. Their real home is in heaven, so long as they acknowledge the divinity of Jesus. Fourth, when a Christian inevitably suffers calamaties—the death of relatives, physical sickness, grievous losses at the hands of evil people, or unjust losses of any kind—faith in God gives the suffering believer something to hold on to, for in heaven all will be perfect. Fifth, many people fear death, and Christianity offers believers immortal life in the world to come.

Christianity also satisfies many other common needs. The United States, for example, needs willing cooperation and a degree of conformity from its people, and the majority's common belief in Christianity helps to meet those ends. Although the United States observes the separation of church and state, its paper money bears the words "In God We Trust." Cooperation might well be gained through the ordinary processes of socialization, but if Christianity gives society's values divine sanction, believers are more likely to embrace those values. Émile Durkheim maintained that shared religious beliefs were so important for group cohesion that he once averred that society was the "soul" of Christianity—in other words, society was the real object of religious devotion. Durkheim maintained that any society needs moral authority behind its values, and Jesus' sanctions help to substantiate that authority.

Over the centuries, however, the trend in Western civilization has, in part, led to secularization and the elimination of Christianity as a force that provides for social integration; indeed, religion has declined so much that some modern sociologists maintain that it no longer meets the criteria for being called an "institution." First, the power of Christianity in American life stems from firm belief, but many Americans now do not believe that Christianity has any relevance in this world. Consequently, the power of church functionaries to control other institutions of society is lost. Second, when it becomes necessary to force a wayward believer to conform to "correct" behaviors and beliefs, coercion or sanctions may be needed; yet modern Christian leaders in the United States and elsewhere have access to very few sanctions as compared, say, to the famous Catholic inquisition in Europe that allowed the Catholic church to torture and kill victims who were charged with unbelief. Third, Christianity has lost its "interconnectedness" with other social institutions, which are, in turn, more interested in the affairs of this world.

As early as the nineteenth century, however, reformers tried to reestablish the primacy of Christianity by giving more attention to the problems of this world. They practiced an early version of "liberation theology." For example, Germany saw the beginnings of the Inner Mission, while England saw the birth of the Young Men's Christian Association (YMCA) and the Young Women's Christian Association (YWCA), organizations that soon spread to other nations, including the United States. Christian pacifism arose to counter warmongering, while the Red Cross was founded to help cope with it. Earlier, some Christians in both England and America united in opposing slavery, while England's government passed many statutes to help solve the ills caused by the Industrial Revolution. An intellectual precursor of such Christian activism was F. E. D. Schleiermacher (1768-1834).

Compatible with the above-mentioned activism was the Social Gospel movement that grew up in the United States in the 1870's and remained influential until approximately the 1920's. In the Social Gospel movement, liberal Protestant congregations made efforts to reform the rapidly industrializing cities in Europe and America and to combat social inequalities and evils by applying biblical principles— particularly those of charity, justice, and mercy. Prominent among the Social Gospel's reform goals were the following: a desire to end child labor; a drive for a shorter work-week for all industrial laborers; a demand for higher wages for the working poor; a call for greater safety regulations in factories; and, finally, a demand that working conditions for women be improved. Indeed, those who preached the Social Gospel ultimately were successful: In the United States, many of their reform goals were realized during the Progressive era, and other reforms followed in the 1930's when Franklin D. Roosevelt and his Democratic Party passed their "New Deal" programs.

Still, despite the aforementioned positive efforts to attend to this world and to help believers cope with its evils, Christianity seemed to decline in the twentieth century; the general worldwide trend (except perhaps for some countries in the Middle East) was toward the adoption of a thoroughly antireligious secularism. In part, religion appeared to decline because of the horrors seen in World War I and World War II. The civilized world blamed Germany for the great destruction that the European phases of both those wars caused—the same Germany that had once been home to the Protestant Reformation and the highest cultural achievements in Europe. Unfortunately, Goethe's home was also Hitler's. The home of the Inner Mission was also the home of the Nazis, who murdered millions of people. Some thinkers gave up on the high ideals of religion after noting how short the step was from civilization to barbarism and how readily some Christians would kill.

Still, even amid international wars, doubt, and decline, Christianity did not disappear as a force. Instead, it experienced a revival after World War II. Increasingly, Protestants and Catholics turned to secular problems and tried to reassure people with Christian values. For example, Christians sought higher standards in the education and health fields, along with reforms in the economic sector that were intended to alleviate poverty. Christians also called for peace in a world of increasing violent crime. African American ministers in the United States provided much of the leadership in the Civil Rights movement. Furthermore, Catholic priests in Latin America attacked the world's problems by means of "liberation theology."

Some philosophers have averred that a person can discern the values of civilizations, past and present, by observing architecture. Certainly, for example, the architecture of the Middle Ages and High Middle Ages demonstrated that Christianity was at "flood-tide." Massive cathedrals dominated most European cities and the larger towns as well. Furthermore, the common people gave the greater part of their "allegiance" to their religious leaders, from archbishops and bishops on down to parish priests. Everyday life revolved around not only the feudal manor but also the Church. Secular rulers tended to "bend the knee" to the ecclesiastical leaders.

In the modern United States, massive cathedrals exist but are not ubiquitous. Instead, twentieth century American architecture has celebrated the secular. Massive high-rise business buildings (such as the Empire State Building) dominate the urban landscape, and they indicate what Americans deem most important.

Context

In its early growth and development, the new Christian religion seemed to be definitely otherworldly. The Church appeared to be unconcerned about the problems of this world. The focus was on the Trinity, and all thought was of heaven. Over time, critics began to complain that Christianity was somewhat beside the point because humans have to live in this world, not the next. Some even argued that Christianity was unhealthful for humankind, especially after the Protestant Reformation occurred and religious wars followed in its wake, with thousands of Catholics killing thousands of Protestants, and vice versa. All the deaths were supposedly "justified" in the name of Christianity. Furthermore, during the early Protestant era, the popularity of the Catholic church declined as a succession of immoral men served as popes, their number including Rodrigo Borgia and Giovanni Medici.

The Catholic world began to stabilize during the Counter-Reformation of the sixteenth century. New crusading orders were formed, the most famous being that of the Jesuits, which was founded by Ignatius of Loyola (1491-1556). The Council of Trent, which met from 1543 to 1563, adopted reforms that were intended to purify the Catholic church from within.

The Enlightenment of the seventeenth and eighteenth centuries provided new criticisms of both Catholic and Protestant bodies. Such thinkers as John Locke of England, Gotthold Ephraim Lessing of Germany, and the French Encyclopedists adopted the skeptical doctrine of Deism and an impersonal God, a doctrine that seemed fitting for the rationalist scientific and philosophic views of the era.

Into the nineteenth century, threats to the Christian churches continued. The French Revolution, which lasted from 1789 to 1815, was decidedly anticlerical and also anti-Christian in part. Next came the revolutions of 1830 and 1848, which continued to cause turmoil within the Christian community. Then, as the Industrial Revolution accelerated and gave rise to economic inequities, Marxist socialism made its appearance. Openly atheist and anti-Christian, Marxists criticized all religions, and the movement's founder called religion the "opiate of the masses." The German philosopher Friedrich Nietzsche openly attacked Christianity and proclaimed that "God is dead." Clearly, in a changing, turmoil-filled world, many people began to agree that Christianity was irrelevant.

The study of Christianity is as old as the religion itself. Yet early study was difficult because Jesus left no written records, no body of work. Nevertheless, some years after the crucifixion, new Scriptures began to appear—including the Gospels of Matthew, Mark, and Luke, in addition to some of the writings of Paul. Still, it took the early Church until the fourth century to collect and verify the documents that are now called the New Testament. Furthermore, the written records were kept by the Ecumenical Councils, which provided interpretation on critical issues and tried to keep Christians from committing heresy. As time passed, scholars such as Augustine, Thomas Aquinas, and Jerome also left written bodies of work.

Modern studies of Christianity abound. The work of Reinhold Niebuhr is well known, as is that of Karl Barth. Barth developed a "Christocentric" philosophy that held that only with the help of Jesus Christ is an "unknowable" God made known. Niebuhr developed a school of philosophy that studied Christianity in connection with the social, economic, political, and international problems of the modern era.

Bibliography

Barth, Karl. *Christ and Adam.* Translated by T. A. Smail. New York: Harper & Row, 1957.

_____ . *Ethics.* Edited by Dietrich Braun. Translated by Geoffrey W. Bromiley. New York: Seabury Press, 1981.

_____ . *God Here and Now.* Translated by Paul M. van Buren. New York: Harper & Row, 1964.

_____ . *The Humanity of God.* Richmond, Vir.: John Knox Press, 1960. Karl Barth (1886-1968) was one of the most intellectual and prolific researchers on the subject of religion. In Protestantism, he was probably the most influential theologian since Schleiermacher. Managing to earn the respect of both Protestant and Catholic scholars, Barth rejected the liberal theology of his own era and developed a Christocentric philosophy, in which only Jesus Christ could make the "unknowable" God known.

Durkheim, Émile. *The Elementary Forms of the Religious Life.* Translated by Joseph W. Swain. 2d ed. New York: Free Press, 1912. Durkheim's work is still considered classic. He believed that religion was of primary importance because it was the glue that held society together.

Marcel, Gabriel. *Being and Having: An Existentialist Diary.* New York: Harper & Row, 1965.

_____ . *The Existential Background of Human Dignity.* Cambridge, Mass.: Harvard University Press, 1963.

_____ . *The Philosophy of Existence.* Translated by Manya Harari. New York: Philosophical Library, 1949. Like his contemporary Albert Camus, Gabriel Marcel (1889-1973) examined existentialism and its relationship to faith. Like Camus, he examined the religious crises that existentialists face and tried to determine why some embraced Christianity and some turned toward atheism.

Niebuhr, Reinhold. *Christian Realism and Political Problems.* New York: Scribner's, 1953.

_____ . *Christianity and Power Politics.* New York: Scribner's, 1940.

_____ . *Moral Man and Immoral Society: A Study in Ethics and Politics.* New York: Scribner's, 1960. Reinhold Niebuhr (1892-1971) was the founder of a school that profoundly analyzed the relationship of Christianity to the social, economic, and international problems of his day. He stressed the sinfulness of humankind, but held that, although human perfection is not possible, men and women might still be saved because of the "impossible possibilities" set forth by the Bible.

Weber, Max. *The Protestant Ethic and the Spirit of Capitalism.* Translated by Talcott Parsons. New York: Scribner's, 1976.

_____ . *The Sociology of Religion.* Translated by Ephraim Fischoff. Boston: Beacon Press, 1963. Max Weber (1864-1920) opposed Karl Marx. Influenced by Marx and to an extent building on Marx's work, Weber nevertheless emphasized the "one-sidedness" of Marxism and its materialistic core. Weber stressed the importance of ideas, particularly religious ideas, in history and sociology. Weber did agree with Marx about the class struggle between capitalists and workers; unlike Marx, however, Weber was alarmed by the prospect of socialism because he believed that with its extensive bureaucracy, socialism would only extend many of the abuses of capitalism.

James Smallwood

Cross-References

Buddhism, 165; The Church and African American Life, 239; Churches, Denominations, and Sects, 246; Confucianism and Taoism, 347; Islam and Islamic Fundamentalism, 1022; Judaism, 1029; Liberation Theology, 1081; The Protestant Ethic and Capitalism, 1533; Secularization in Western Society, 1700; Socialization: Religion, 1894; The Sociology of Religion, 1952.

THE CHURCH AND AFRICAN AMERICAN LIFE

Type of sociology: Major social institutions
Field of study: Religion

The term "black church" refers collectively to the many autonomous denominations of African American Christian churches. Although these denominations are varied, the church provides a critical center for religious expression and social activism according to values defined within African American culture. The black church evolved as a highly visible social institution in response to white racism in American society and racism in white-defined Christianity.

Principal terms

BLACK SOCIOLOGY: a subfield in which sociological study is conducted under terms and methods that reflect values and perspectives which have evolved from black experience

INSTITUTIONS: ongoing social structures that allow for organized activities in society; for example, churches enable social expression of religious experience and provide a place for social identity

LIBERATION THEOLOGY: theology that makes explicit connections between religious experience and struggles for social justice

RELIGION: a matrix of belief and practice within a society in which the center of focus is whatever that society identifies as "the sacred"

SOCIAL MOVEMENT: an organized effort among people within a society who work together under shared principles or beliefs in order to alter social conditions within that society

Overview

From a sociological perspective, religion can be defined as a matrix of belief and practice that has as its center whatever a particular society deems as "sacred." Religion, in this sense, must be understood as existing within particular social and cultural contexts. Religion evolves from social experience and, when institutionalized, creates social structure within communities.

Although African American religious experience is diverse and social forms of religious life vary greatly, the black church has historically been the most visible religious institution in African American culture. As a visible institution controlled from within the black community, the black church has played a central role in African American social and political history. This history has evolved within the broader historical context of American racism and racial politics. The church, also evolving within that broader context, has been an important center for the development of African American Christian theology and for community identity. In fact, the black church originated as a formal institution when African American religious leaders in Philadelphia were forcibly removed from worshiping on the main "whites only" floor of St. George's Methodist church. When Richard Allen and Absalom Jones were evicted from the church in 1787, they and their fellow black Christians concluded that the racism of white-defined Christianity precluded full Christian expression for blacks in white-controlled congregations. Their formation of the Free African Society that year paved the way for the later creation of the fully autonomous African Methodist Episcopal (AME) church, one of the earliest black churches in the United States. An institutionalized form of distinct African American Christian theology began to emerge.

The role of the black church in African American culture has been debated within the black community since its earliest days. As Vincent Harding emphasizes in his social and religious history of black struggle, *There Is a River: The Black Struggle for Freedom in America* (1981), it is important to remember that the social movement that came to be known as the Civil Rights movement in the twentieth century had its origins in African resistance on the shores of Africa in the earliest days of slavery. Many of the ongoing debates about the political and theological nature of the church crystallized during the period of the Civil Rights movement and remain important. The controversy within black communities over the social role of black churches illustrates the powerful impact that the church continues to have as a primary social and religious institution.

In their expansive sociological study entitled *The Black Church in the African-American Experience* (1990), C. Eric Lincoln and Lawrence H. Mamiya propose a dynamic model for interpreting the sociology of black churches in their diversity and complexity. Lincoln and Mamiya identify the major black denominations as the African Methodist Episcopal (AME) church, the African Methodist Episcopal Zion (AMEZ) church, the Christian Methodist Episcopal (CME) church, the National Baptist Convention, U.S.A., Incorporated (NBCA), the Progressive National Baptist Convention (PNBC), and the Church of God in Christ (COGIC). These denominations, as well as many other smaller ones and local churches, provide institutional structure for the religious (and often political) life of millions of African American Christians.

While sociologists and political historians debate the nature of the black church and its political role (or, as some argue, its lack of a political role), Lincoln and Mamiya offer a "dialectical model of the Black Church" that encourages an open and ongoing analysis. Because it permits many possible interpretations, the Lincoln/Mamiya model is a useful way to approach sociological analysis of any of the many forms of the black church.

The Lincoln/Mamiya model offers a way of analyzing the ongoing tensions, both theological and political, within African American Christianity as those tensions are embodied in the structure of the black church. The model proposes the following six "dialectically related" pairs, or opposites. With these pairs the focus is on the ways that human experience shifts back and forth between the two opposites, sometimes tending more toward one idea, sometimes tending more toward the other. In other words, the dialectic approach shows that much of human experience involves a middle ground or synthesis between what seem to be opposing ideas.

For example, the first dialectic is that between "priestly" and "prophetic" functions of the church. In other words, it concerns how the church balances its role as the center for worship (priestly) in relation to its role as an agent for social change in the community (prophetic). Second, there is a dialectic tension in the black church between the "other-worldly" and the "this-worldly." Does the church focus on individual spiritual salvation for the "life to come" or does it focus on social justice in the here-and-now? Obviously, it can do both, but this issue has been debated since the earliest days of African American Christianity. The third dialectic proposed by Lincoln and Mamiya is between "universalism" and "particularism": how the black church negotiates its role in Christianity, broadly speaking, and its very particular role in African American history. The black church is part of a universal religious institution but is also a very particular response to white racism in American Christianity. A fourth dialectic is between the "communal" and the "privatistic": How does the church address individual spiritual life in the context of the social realities of African American experience? The fifth dialectic is especially important politically; it is between the "charismatic" and the "bureaucratic." This involves how the church uses the power of personalized and local leadership in relation to developing larger-scale institutional structure and national leadership as well as how it handles the tensions inherent in doing both. Finally, Lincoln and Mamiya join many African American historians and cultural critics when they identify the dialectical tension between "accommodation" and "resistance." Given the realities of white racism and African American history's origins in the experience of slavery, how has a primary social institution such as the black church moved between accommodating and resisting white mainstream culture in the United States? As Lincoln and Mamiya put it: "The crucial axis of black history, according to Manning Marable [*How Capitalism Under-developed Black America: Problems in Race, Political Economy, and Society*, 1983], has consisted of two political options, that of resistance versus accommodation. Every black person and every black institution has participated in making compromises between these two poles."

It is in this final dialectic that much of the debate over the role of the black church in the twentieth century Civil Rights movements evolved. It is debated, for example, whether the church served as an accommodationist spiritual escape that diluted the intensity of its members, whether the church served as a fundamental source of activism and militancy, or whether the black church did both.

Applications

During the 1950's and the 1960's, the African American Civil Rights movement accelerated and moved to the center of the national political stage. Beginning with efforts to integrate schools following the Supreme Court's *Brown v. Board of Education* decision in 1954 and continuing through the Montgomery bus boycott (1955-1956), the formation of the Southern Christian Leadership Conference (1957), the Freedom Rides summer (1961), and the March on Washington (1963), hundreds of

thousands of African Americans confronted American racism and fought for fulfillment of the United States' stated commitment to freedom for all its people. The black
church played a central role during these years, providing people and resources for
grassroots organizing while cultivating leadership for the national movement.

During this period, tensions arose in the black community that illustrate the
sociological complexity of the church as a social institution. From the perspective of
the emerging Black Power movement, the church was suspect in its adherence to
Christian principles of nonviolence in the face of white racial violence and was
deluded in its emphasis on integration into mainstream American society. For black
nationalists, this mainstream society remained white-dominated and white-controlled.
Some nationalists argued that African American Christianity itself was flawed because
of its origins as a religion of enslavement.

From another perspective, political and religious leaders such as Martin Luther
King, Jr., proposed that African American Christianity provided both the spiritual and
material bases for a militant liberation theology, one that posed a radical challenge to
the white-supremacist status quo of the mid-twentieth century United States. King was
a nationally recognized Christian leader, but with him were thousands of African
American Christian women and men who argued that the black church provided the
path of most, rather than least, resistance to white racism. As Lincoln and Mamiya
point out, the fact that white racists bombed several hundred black churches during
the civil rights period indicates that the threat posed to white supremacy by the black
church was substantial.

A second debate that highlights some of the issues from the Lincoln/Mamiya model
concerns the role of women in the black church. During the Civil Rights movement,
women provided the "rank and file" of many organizing efforts, working together with
men to form the core of the movement. In the church, however, men still maintained
a monopoly in terms of formal congregational leadership. On the national level, this
trend was even more pronounced; the nationally recognized black leadership of the
Civil Rights movement was almost exclusively male. Women such as Rosa Parks,
Fannie Lou Hamer, and Mamie Bradley (Emmett Till's mother) were recognized on
a national level, but the political leadership of black women in many key political
battles, especially on the local level, went unacknowledged both in the national media
and in the formal leadership structure of the church. Historian Jacqueline Jones, in
*Labor of Love, Labor of Sorrow: Black Women, Work, and the Family from Slavery to
the Present* (1985) documents in detail the extent of women's involvement in the
church and the movement as a whole. Jacquelyn Grant's *White Women's Christ and
Black Women's Jesus: Feminist Christology and Womanist Response* (1989), while
primarily a challenge to white feminist theologians, also outlines an emerging black
feminist theology that challenges the institutionalized gender bias in the black church
itself. Her emphasis is on a feminist "Christology" that is constructive within the
broader black community—a political theology that recognizes the unique oppression
of black women without separating their interests from those of the African American
community as a whole.

Gender politics are significant because they highlight tensions within the church when issues that are often expressed in secular political terms (such as women's oppression) are also engaged in theological and spiritual terms. This can result in significant structural change within a social institution such as the black church. In the case of women and the church, the political becomes religious and the religious becomes political, bringing into play the dynamic tensions between the "this-worldly" and the "other-worldly," between the "priestly" and the "prophetic."

Context

It is difficult to document the nature of religious experience, especially in traditional sociological terms. For example, religious institutions represent only one socially visible structure of religious life. Individuals bring their religious beliefs into the realms of history and community in many other ways that are harder to trace. In African American history, the black church has been central to African American politics and the long struggle for civil rights. Religiosity in African American experience, however, is much more complex. The black church, as one social institution, provides an important source of knowledge, but religious history in black America is varied in form and content. The twentieth century challenge to African American Christianity posed by African American Islam is only one example of this diversity.

In the late 1960's and early 1970's, black studies emerged as a formal intellectual discipline in American universities. At about the same time, black sociology was proposed as a theoretical and methodological stance within the broader field of sociology. Following earlier work by sociologists such as W. E. B. Du Bois and E. Franklin Frazier and challenging white racism in previous sociological work related to African American culture, sociologists and cultural theorists such as Robert Staples, Joyce Ladner, and Maulana Karenga proposed that the sociology of the African American experience be approached from "Afrocentric" theoretical perspectives—in other words, from perspectives rooted in black history, including the history of Africa as it relates to African American culture. Given the long history of racial inequality in American society, proponents of black sociology argue that the black church can only be accurately interpreted from this Afrocentric perspective. They state that traditional sociological methods are rooted in presumptions based on white-defined values and modes of thought and will thus inevitably distort the nature of black experience. Black sociology as a discipline has developed a range of sociological methodologies based in an always emerging (and quite diverse) Afrocentric philosophy.

While not all sociologists of African American experience embrace Afrocentric theory, formal study of the black church in all its periods expands in scope as sociological inquiry opens further to the perspectives of diverse African American theorists, especially in regard to the political implications of activity in the church. Sociology offers insight into structural dynamics that occur within the church and in African American culture as a whole. Additionally, sociology of the black church offers insights into the dynamics of American society. Any sociological critique of the black church must account for a complex set of relationships between religious experience (broadly defined), social institutions, and social action; it must also consider the cultural and historical contexts in which these relationships develop.

Bibliography

Cone, James H. *A Black Theology of Liberation*. 20th anniversary ed. Maryknoll, N.Y.: Orbis Books, 1990. This edition of Cone's now classic study in African American liberation theology includes a set of critical essays by other writers who address the ongoing political implications of Cone's work. Cone develops a challenging synthesis of political theory and theology. His work is important for anyone interested in the social role of African American religions.

Frazier, E. Franklin, and C. Eric Lincoln. *The Negro Church in America: The Black Church Since Frazier*. New York: Schocken Books, 1974. An important sociological study that offers the comparative perspectives of two important scholars of the black church. Frazier's thesis about the radical break from African tradition in African American experience is no longer widely accepted, but his work here is still an important part of sociological discussion of the church. Lincoln's portion of the book offers good detail on the Nation of Islam during the Civil Rights period and addresses the effects of the Black Power movement on the church.

Karenga, Maulana. *Introduction to Black Studies*. Los Angeles: University of Sankore Press, 1982. Karenga's introduction to black sociology in this volume is an important starting point for any reader interested in the field. Similarly, his chapter on black religion highlights key issues in African American religious history. Both chapters have good bibliographies for publications up to 1982. Karenga offers a black nationalist perspective on African American studies.

Lincoln, C. Eric, and Lawrence H. Mamiya. *The Black Church in the African-American Experience*. Durham, N.C.: Duke University Press, 1990. An essential text for sociological work related to the black church. Covers theoretical and historical issues as well as providing in-depth denominational histories and useful statistical data. Excellent and extensive bibliography.

Paris, Peter J. *The Social Teaching of the Black Churches*. Philadelphia: Fortress Press, 1985. A very good source for more detailed discussion of the ways that the black church, as a social institution, has participated in African American culture. Paris engages many of the key issues and controversies regarding the social role of the church, and readers holding various opinions on the issues will find his discussion challenging.

Wilmore, Gayraud S., ed. *African American Religious Studies: An Interdisciplinary Anthology*. Durham, N.C.: Duke University Press, 1989. This excellent source offers both a wide range of readings in the subject of African American religion and an introduction to many important scholars in the field. Of special interest are the historical essays and the essays by Jacquelyn Grant and Cheryl J. Sanders on women in the church. Individual essays have useful bibliographies related to their subjects.

_____ . *Black Religion and Black Radicalism*. 2d ed. Maryknoll, N.Y.: Orbis Books, 1983. This study offers a historical overview of the relationship between religion (including the black church) and the evolution of black political radicalism. An important introduction to the subject. Notes for the book provide an extensive bibliography.

Sharon Carson

Cross-References

Christianity, 231; Churches, Denominations, and Sects, 246; The Civil Rights Movement, 265; Gender and Religion, 813; Legitimation of Inequality: Religion, 1068; Liberation Theology, 1081; The Nation of Islam, 1275; Political Influence by Religious Groups, 1394; Socialization: Religion, 1894.

CHURCHES, DENOMINATIONS, AND SECTS

Type of sociology: Major social institutions
Field of study: Religion

Churches, denominations, and sects are types of religious organizations. The distinction between them makes it possible to analyze various church bodies and to comprehend their varying relationships to society and to one another.

Principal terms
CHURCH: a religious body, usually related to the state, occupying a
   position of privilege and generally devoid of tension with the society
   in which it exists
DENOMINATION: a religious body generally at peace with its
   environment that serves the middle and upper strata of society
ECCLESIA: another name for a church that is closely tied to the state
ESTABLISHED SECT: a sect that has survived for several generations
   without changing into a denomination
SECT: a religious body at tension with its environment, rarely
   cooperating with other religious groups, and serving mostly the
   blue-collar working class

Overview

Sociologists consider religion a major social institution; nearly all societies have some form of religion, and it has been studied by sociologists since the nineteenth century. Religious organizations have been categorized according to a number of factors, including their size, their relationship to the state, and the tension that exists between the group and the larger society. The categories most often used are churches, denominations, sects, and cults. Churches are the largest of the groups, and they are frequently tied to the state in some way. Denominations are generally considered to be less centrally placed in society than churches are; they are also sometimes considered to be smaller in size. Sects and cults are smaller and less inclusive, and they usually exist in a state of tension (be it great or small) with the larger society.

The essential defining characteristics of a church are that it is relatively large and it exists in an influential and central position in society. Some countries have official state churches (Norway and Sweden have state-established churches), others have churches closely allied with the state (as in Iceland or Spain), and others have one church that, although not officially sanctioned, is strongly dominant or occupies a privileged position (as in England). Rarely is a church in a state of tension with the secular world. A church is an umbrella-like organization that seeks to serve the religious needs of all people within its geographical territory. Members are often "born into" the church in that their parents are members; children are socialized into the church at a young age and join when they are old enough. Churches have a hierarchy of authority, but the way this is organized varies from church to church. Serving in the clergy is usually a full-time occupation and involves specialized education and formal religious training.

The United States, founded by people with a belief in religious freedom and the separation of church and state, does not have a state or national church. Nevertheless, Christianity is the overwhelmingly dominant religion in the country. In one common typology, Christianity in the United States is divided into two major churches, Roman Catholic and Protestant, with Protestants being divided into denominations such as Presbyterian, Methodist, Lutheran, and Baptist.

Denominations are generally considered to be religious organizations that are not affiliated with the state and that are relatively equal in their place in a society. The United States has been called a "denominational society" in that a large number of religious organizations, from huge ones to tiny ones, are able to coexist. In this sense of "denomination," both Catholicism and Judaism could be considered denominations in the United States, but in practice, the term usually refers to Protestant religious groups. (Judaism, in fact, has its own divisions—Conservative, Orthodox, Reform, and Reconstructionist—that are in some ways akin to denominations but are not usually considered as such.) Some sociologists have simply made membership in the National Council of Churches a criterion for being considered a denomination. This distinction seems objective and has much to recommend it; however, others point out that some non-National Council of Churches groups (such as the Lutheran church and the Missouri Synod) may exhibit more of the characteristics of a denomination than of a sect.

Many denominations began their activities as sects; these include the United Methodists and the American (northern) Baptists. Others did not have a sectlike origin but, rather, are transplanted European state churches. Examples include the Episcopalian and Lutheran churches. A denomination has made its peace with society. It cooperates with other denominations, often through an overarching organization like the National Council of Churches. Worship services in denominational congregations are usually formal and are not spontaneous. Clergy typically have had four years of undergraduate college education and three or four years of theological school. Many eventually do additional graduate work and earn advanced degrees. The members come from the middle, upper-middle, and upper classes.

The line that divides churches and denominations from sects is somewhat more clearly distinguishable. Sects are smaller than churches and are not as integrated into society at large as either churches or denominations are. Sects often begin when a group breaks away from a larger, established religious organization. The founders frequently are attempting to return to the principles of the church's original founders, believing that the church as it exists has strayed from those principles or beliefs. As a sect progresses, its early history often becomes mythologized, a process that can make it more difficult to maintain adherence to the earlier principles. In their worship services, sects are usually more informal than churches, and the clergy of a sect often serve only part time and have less formal education and training than the clergy of a church or denomination. A sect expresses tension with the dominant society by warning its members against the "sins of the world," which are usually reflections of the lifestyle of the dominant society and may include such activities as drinking alcohol, wearing makeup, and dancing. Although members usually have low-paying jobs, a large number of them tithe (pay an automatic percentage of their incomes to the sect) to provide the group with sufficient funds. For many, the sect is the locus of social as well as religious life. Attending two or three services a week is common. Some sects remain stable in size, whereas others grow and eventually evolve into denominations or churches themselves. Examples of sects in the United States include the Amish, the Mennonites, and such holiness and Pentecostal groups as the Church of God and Church of God of Triumph.

An established sect is one that has existed for some generations without becoming a denomination even though it has gained acceptance in the community. Established sects include the Assemblies of God, Jehovah's Witnesses, and the several Churches of Christ. Some scholars include the Amish, Latter-day Saints (Mormons), and Jewish Hasidim in this category.

Applications

A look at the fastest-growing church body in the United States is instructive in understanding the nature of sects and established sects. The Assemblies of God was founded in 1914 at Hot Springs, Arkansas. In the beginning, it attempted to be nondoctrinal, allowing freedom of belief. When, however, it appeared that there were great doctrinal differences, especially that one large group was unitarian rather than trinitarian in its beliefs about God, about one-fourth of the original membership seceded. The remaining group has grown to more than two million members in ten thousand churches with twenty-two thousand ministers in the United States. World-wide membership stands at fifteen million.

The Assemblies of God emphasizes emotion and charismatic healing. It distrusts science and stresses personal experience. These are considered more important than theological teaching. Typically the Assemblies of God rejects denominations as proclaimers of the rational, evangelical God of the intellect. It emphasizes a God one can feel, respond to, and love—one who cares about people's present and their future. Seventy-nine percent of the members are in church every Sunday, and another 11 percent miss only once a month. Church governance is local and is said to rely on divine guidance.

An example of a denomination is the Presbyterian church (USA), a transplanted national church. Presbyterianism traces its roots to French-born John Calvin, who converted to Protestantism in 1533 or 1534. He became the spiritual and political leader in Geneva, Switzerland, where he was pastor of St. Peter's Church. It was a Scot, however, John Knox, who eventually returned to his native land from Europe to become the father of the Scots' reformation.

The largest group of Presbyterians to come to the United States were Scots-Irish immigrants from Northern Ireland, who settled along the mid-Atlantic. In the United States, this ecclesia became a denomination marked by typical denominational characteristics. It serves the middle, upper-middle, and upper strata of society, conducts formal services, insists upon a highly educated clergy, cooperates with other denominations and sects, and generally expresses little tension with its environment, although it has taken a moral and social stance in a number of matters. Doctrinally, it accepts the Bible as written by persons who were inspired by God. Emphasis is on the teachings shared with most Christians. Thus Presbyterianism clearly serves as a model for the religious organizations called denominations.

There are no state religions in North America. Therefore it is instructive to consider a small but typical state church, the Evangelical-Lutheran National Church of Iceland. Norwegians settled Iceland late in the ninth century; at the instigation of the Norwegian king, the Icelandic parliament adopted Christianity in the year 1000. Many farmers owned the churches built on their land and paid the salaries of the priests. At the time of the Protestant reformation in the sixteenth century, Iceland became Lutheran by royal fiat of the king of Denmark (of which kingdom Iceland had become a part). The church exchanged its farms for salaries of priests in perpetuity, allowing it to claim that it is a national, rather than a state, church. The titular head of the church, formerly the king of Denmark, has been, since independence, the president of Iceland; the functional head is the bishop, who is elected chiefly by the clergy.

As is typical of national churches, clergy are highly educated. Salaries of priests are paid by the state, and their homes are furnished either by the state (in small towns and in the countryside) or by the congregations (in the cities). Services are conducted with great dignity, observing ancient liturgical niceties, paraments, vestments, and ceremonies. Sermons are in the form of literary essays. The liturgy is chanted by priests whose performance shows their professional training. Hymns and liturgical responses are sung by choirs with a high level of musical ability. Ninety-four percent of the population belongs to the national church, and another 3 percent belongs to a Lutheran Free Church, whose only difference from the national church is that congregations pay their pastors' salaries and are free to dismiss them. Other religions are permitted, and there are a few Roman Catholic, Seventh-day Adventist, and Salvation Army congregations as well as a Pentecostal sect called Filadelfia. The national church practices no exclusivity toward the dissenters: They are included by the office of the bishop in such things as the Sunday morning national radio broadcast. The state-church bishop personally ordains priests who are called by Lutheran Free Churches and is frequently called upon to settle differences or arbitrate in their congregational matters. Clergy move freely between the national church and the Lutheran Free Church. Thus inclusivity is a distinct mark of this national church, which seeks to be an umbrella serving all in its territory. Yet it remains confessionally Lutheran in teaching and practice. Despite its attempts to serve all in its territory, the leadership seems to gravitate to members of the upper classes (this in a country which claims to have no social classes). There is clearly no tension between the church and the state, and a number of priests have served as members of the parliament, one also becoming his country's representative to the United Nations. Although the bishop is not a cabinet officer of the Icelandic government, he is consulted regularly on religious, moral, and other questions. Citizens of Iceland support the national church through their taxes; if they wish, however, they may divert their tax money to one of the other recognized religious groups or to the University of Iceland.

Sociologists have long spoken of the tendency of sects to turn into denominations despite the fact that they originally opposed them. In order to visualize how such movement takes place, one might imagine a continuum—a line with the number 1 at the far left and 7 at the far right. Along this continuum, sects would be placed at 1, established sects at 3, denominations at 5, and churches at 7. As sects move toward becoming denominations, their sociological characteristics change. For example, one could rank characteristics such as "tension with society" at 1, and "no tension with society" at 7. "Uneducated membership and clergy" might be placed at 1, and an educated membership at 7; a very informal service of worship could be placed at 1, and a formalized, liturgical service at 7. As a sect moves toward denominationalism, its characteristics gradually change to move closer to the higher numbers along the continuum.

Context

It was German theologian Ernst Troeltsch who, in 1912, first alerted the theological and sociological world to the great dichotomy between what he called churches and sects. His work was not translated into English until 1931, and was then entitled *The Social Teaching of the Christian Churches*. Subsequently, other scholars have enlarged his scheme to differentiate between sects and established sects and between denominations and churches. Notable among these are J. Milton Yinger, Howard Becker, Richard Niebuhr, and Colin Clark.

It was Yinger's contention that Troeltsch did not provide as many categories as were needed to describe the various religious bodies. His categories included the universal church, the ecclesia (which is a universal church that has become "settled in"), the class church or denomination, the established sect, the sect, and the cult. Richard Niebuhr used the relationship of religious bodies to their culture to differentiate among them. He identified groups marked by Christ against culture, Christ of culture, Christ above culture, and Christ and culture in paradox. Colin Clark analyzed sects and found seven types: pessimistic (or adventist) sects, perfectionist (or subjectivist) sects, charismatic (or Pentecostal) sects, communistic sects, legalistic (or objectivist) sects, egocentric (or new thought) sects, and esoteric (or mystical) sects.

The tension between sects and denominations in the United States is clearly seen in sociologists Roger Finke and Rodney Stark's 1992 book *The Churching of America, 1776-1990: Winners and Losers in Our Religious Economy*. They contend that mainline denominations in early New England, namely the Presbyterian and Congregational churches, crumbled badly in the face of (then sectarian) aggressive Methodist and Baptist activity in the period from 1776 to 1850. (Their chapter for that time period is called "The Upstart Sects Win America.") In their concluding chapter, "Why 'Mainline' Denominations Decline," they summarize their conclusions, noting that established religious bodies gradually become more worldly until their religious rewards are few; at that point, people begin to switch to other groups. Some join very high tension movements, while others move to "the newest and least secularized" denominations.

Bibliography

Finke, Roger, and Rodney Stark. *The Churching of America, 1776-1990: Winners and Losers in Our Religious Economy.* New Brunswick, N.J.: Rutgers University Press, 1992. A highly readable, well-documented approach to the history of religion in the United States by two noted sociologists of religion. It takes a market approach to religious bodies and also shows the many errors in early religious statistics.

McGuire, Meredith B. *Religion: The Social Context.* 3d ed. Belmont, Calif.: Wadsworth, 1992. In a chapter on the dynamics of religious collectivities, the author examines the transformation of sects and cults into other types.

Moberg, David O. *The Church as a Social Institution: The Sociology of American Religion.* 2d ed. Grand Rapids, Mich.: Baker Book House, 1984. Chapter 4 is an excellent, thorough discussion entitled "Church—Sect and Other Typologies." Especially valuable is the author's evaluation of the various typologies. Discusses Clark's seven types of sects. Although the volume has gone out of print, many university libraries have a copy.

Petursson, Petur. *Church and Social Change: A Study of the Secularization Process in Iceland 1830-1930.* Helsingborg, Sweden: Plus Ultra, 1983. Written entirely in English, this work by the son of the former bishop of Iceland is as valuable for a history of religion in that country from 860 to 1830 as it is for the century it purports to cover.

Poloma, Margaret M. *The Assemblies of God at the Crossroads: Charisma and Institutional Dilemmas.* Knoxville: University of Tennessee Press, 1989. This work emphasizes the fact that the Assemblies of God's growth is related to its emphasis on emotion and charismatic healing. Since it has not made its "peace with the world," it remains a sect, although it is an established one.

Theissen, Gerd. *The Sociology of Early Palestinian Christianity.* Translated by John Bowden. Philadelphia: Fortress, 1978. Since many sects try to return to the earliest Christian practices, it is useful and instructive to see how a sociologist reconstructs those times.

Troeltsch, Ernst. *The Social Teaching of the Christian Churches.* Translated by Olive Wyon. Reprint. Louisville, Ky.: Westminster/John Knox Press, 1992. This is the landmark book, first published in German in 1912, in understanding the difference between churches and sects; all subsequent work is in its debt.

Winter, J. Alan. *Continuities in the Sociology of Religion: Creed, Congregation, and Community.* New York: Harper & Row, 1977. This once-popular text is especially useful for the fifth chapter, which traces the rise of sects and discusses clearly the Niebuhr-Pope hypothesis of sects turning into churches.

Donald R. Ortner

Cross-References

Christianity, 231; The Church and African American Life, 239; Cults, 399; Religion: Beliefs, Symbols, and Rituals, 1598; Religion: Functionalist Analyses, 1603; Religion: Marxist and Conflict Theory Views, 1610; Secularization in Western Society, 1700; The Separation of Church and State, 1714; Socialization: Religion, 1894; The Sociology of Religion, 1952.

CITIES: PREINDUSTRIAL, INDUSTRIAL, AND POSTINDUSTRIAL

Type of sociology: Urban and rural life

The large, densely populated areas known as cities have undergone transformations since ancient times; preindustrial, industrial, and postindustrial cities have been observed to have differing types of social and economic organization as well as differing uses of space.

Principal terms

ANOMIE: a condition in which social norms are absent, as during times of overwhelming social change

COMMUNITY: a territorially based, interdependent social organization

ECOLOGY: the relationship between populations and their physical environments

MEGALOPOLIS: a "supercity" resulting from uncontrolled expansion that lacks a central core

MODERNIZATION: the process of social change by which traditional societies acquire the characteristics of developed societies

SUBURBANIZATION: the expansion of communities beyond a city

TECHNOLOGY: cumulative skills and knowledge applied in environmental adaptation, including such processes as food production

URBANIZATION: the process of expansion of urban areas and culture through rural-urban population shifts

Overview

Cities are large, densely settled communities whose populations are engaged in a variety of highly specialized nonagrarian activities. The first cities, which emerged during the urban revolution of 4000-3000 B.C.E., were preceded by the development of extensive agriculture, which provided the surpluses consumed by the urban populations. As a result of this progress in subsistence farming, achieved through advances in technology, urban populations were able to turn their attention to a range and variety of nonagricultural specializations that continue to be characteristic of cities.

Cities developed economic and political institutions; social class divisions; ruling military, political, and religious elites; intercity trade; and municipal services including transportation, water supply, law enforcement, and recreational facilities. Cities were spatially distinguished by the presence of monumental public structures, a street system, residential neighborhoods, and, in many instances, defensive walls that also served to control urban expansion beyond these boundaries.

An overview of cities from their earliest beginnings reveals a range and diversity that has eluded easy categorization. Each phase in the history of urbanization has produced unique examples of collective living, ranging from the impressive centers of the first civilizations to the cities of the classical, medieval, and Renaissance periods. Some of this diversity is attributable to cultural and geographical factors, as cities developed in response to the limitations or advantages of terrain, and reflected design and aesthetic preferences that were culturally based. Other cities, however, were products of careful thought and design, such as those of classical Greece. Plato's and Aristotle's concepts of ideal communities, as well as Hippodamian ideas of spatial organization, influenced the design and location of these cities. Deriving inspiration from these and other examples, the Romans utilized urbanization as an instrument of imperial expansion, founding cities based on a uniform formula in the distant corners of their vast empire. Urbanization underwent a decline following the disintegration of the Roman Empire, and despite some activity in subsequent historical periods, it was not until the eighteenth century that a dramatic increase in urbanization occurred.

The fundamental social change that was brought about by the Industrial Revolution accompanied the growth of cities in Europe and the United States. These industrial cities provided sociologists with a dynamic and complex environment in which to examine the behavior of urban populations. As industrialization accelerated the rapid expansion of cities by providing incentives for people to migrate from their rural occupations to employment in urban factories, significant social changes took place. The rapidity of growth outpaced the cities' ability to provide basic services to the expanding population, thus creating large urban slums inhabited primarily by the newcomers. Crowding, pollution, and generally chaotic urban conditions, in conjunction with the increasingly wide gap between the city's wealthy inhabitants and the less fortunate, resulted in the expansion of population beyond the urban area in a phenomenon known as suburbanization. Suburbs grew on the peripheries of cities, providing a better standard of living because of the low cost of land and reduced levels of pollution and crowding. The transportation advances that resulted from industrial progress, such as railroads and automobiles, made it more convenient for people to live far from city centers and travel into the city to work. Beginning in the 1920's, suburban expansion has been a principal direction taken by urban growth. Despite possessing the conditions to build coherent communities, suburbs have generally been characterized by limited social interaction among their residents.

The flight to the suburbs left a vacuum in many inner-city neighborhoods, which was often filled by indigent people, thereby reducing the economic value of properties. This transformation affected law enforcement as well as the tax base of municipalities. A growing underclass, excluded from the urban economic opportunity structure, became a predictable feature of large cities. Equally characteristic of industrial cities was a loss of kinship-based interaction and the interjection of impersonal encounters that often led to a sense of alienation among the urban population. The consensus among scholars is that economic progress in itself was not a source of satisfaction for the urban resident in the absence of close community structures.

Another distinctive aspect of industrial urban growth was an inability to control expansion, attributable to the absence of planning for the future and to the loss of traditionally inhibiting features of urban design such as city walls. Observations such as these have enabled urban scholars to identify what was distinctive about cities and populations that experienced the effects of the Industrial Revolution. It also focused attention on the nature of urban life prior to this time.

A qualitative and quantitative difference existed between the city that existed before the Industrial Revolution and that which was transformed or created by this energy revolution. The most important difference was simply size. Until this time, only a small proportion of the overall population lived in cities—approximately 3 percent in the period immediately preceding the Industrial Revolution. Preindustrial cities with populations over 100,000 were rare, and the average size of preindustrial cities is estimated to have been between 10,000 and 25,000 inhabitants. Close, interpersonal relations formed the basis of social organization. Cities often performed more than one function, serving simultaneously as political, religious, economic, educational, and military centers. Capital cities, housing the ruling elite, had a special status. The reputation of cities was often based on architectural beauty, specialization in a specific craft, possession of a renowed school of learning, or reputation as a place of holy pilgrimage.

With some exceptions, the preindustrial city possessed poor drainage and water supply, narrow streets, and little differentiation of land use between commercial activities and residences. Unable to expand because of the controlling features of walls, many cities experienced crowding and close living conditions that were disadvantages during epidemics, when diseases could ravage urban populations. The preindustrial city functioned at a level of technology (such as animal-powered transportation) that determined the pace of life. Hereditary craft specialization, extended families, traditional gender roles, and a reliance on informal social control through religion and kinship relations typified the early city.

The postindustrial city represents a developing urban form that is distinguished by its enormous size and rapidly evolving functions. Representing the social and spatial evolution of economies that have already achieved industrialization and are heavily involved in consumerism, the postindustrial city retains many of the problems of its industrial predecessor. It continues to have a disproportionately large underclass whose contributions to the urban tax base falls short of its needs in the areas of health care, education, housing, and other benefits. Educated urban workers often reside in suburban areas, paying little in city taxes yet availing themselves of some of the city's services, at least during their working hours.

Applications

The typology of preindustrial, industrial, and postindustrial cities signifies the emergence of a comparativist framework in urban sociology. These categorizations of urban form are a response to the diversity of urban experience as well as to the acceleration of global urbanization that is expected to see the concentration of 60 percent of the world's population in urban centers by the year 2025. A large proportion of this growth is expected to occur in the developing societies. Urbanization in these societies diverges in many fundamental ways from the experience of Europe and North America. To interpret accurately the trends in these societies, which represent various levels of industrialization and modernization, technological adaptation, and sociopolitical change, it is necessary to have more than one set of analytic criteria.

The preindustrial city prototype accentuates cultural variables, in addition to technology, as being responsible for divergent forms and differential levels of urbanization. Thus, it explains the unique character of contemporary cities in developing societies, cities which simultaneously display preindustrial and industrial features. Industrialization in developing societies results in patterns of change that differ from the experiences of Western cities. In developing societies, urban areas retain substantial proportions of the preindustrial legacy, such as marketplaces in narrow streets dedicated to specialized production and marketing. Cities such as Istanbul, Bombay, and Cairo, among others, have specific wholesale and retail areas for silver, gold, silks, carpets, spices, and other commodities in addition to modern shopping centers. Even the days of operation differ, sometimes based on the European work week, sometimes on patterns followed locally.

The preindustrial features of cities in modernizing societies account for other deviations from the Western experience as well. The persistence of rural kinship bonds within urban communities generally prevents migrants from experiencing the extreme isolation and anomie observed in developed societies. The extended family structure continues to provide a support system and a variety of functions that are usually provided by social agencies and other urban institutions in Western cities. Sharing economic success as well as failure within the family group reduces dependence on social institutions. Modernization of traditional societies does erode the extended family over time, through increased mobility, job opportunities, and emancipation of women. As this occurs, the insufficient presence (or even absence) of urban social services is highlighted.

A notable divergence of settlement patterns between cities in modernizing societies and those of industrialized societies is seen in the location of the urban underclass. A characteristic of most large American cities is concentration of the underclass in declining inner-city neighborhoods and central city areas. In developing societies, it is usually the outskirts of cities that are characterized by large squatter settlements, as in the cases of Bombay and Mexico City.

The knowledge and experience provided by examination of the industrial city enabled urban planners and architects such as Daniel Burnham and Louis Sullivan to suggest improved models for urban communities by the early twentieth century. They recognized a need for "green-belt" areas in cities, ring roads to relieve traffic congestion on main routes, and aesthetically pleasing architecture to uplift the spirits of urban populations. Greater attention was paid to the design and location of housing for the urban poor. Ideal communities were designed and executed in various locations; government-sponsored green-belt towns were built in Ohio, Maryland, and Wisconsin during the 1920's. Later "planned communities" such as Reston, Virginia, were an outgrowth of this movement for improved urban living. Attempts had also been made in European countries, including the garden city of Letchworth in England, designed by Ebenezer Howard in 1902.

Notwithstanding such efforts, the pace of urbanization and suburbanization has overtaken the abilities of planners to control and direct the process centrally. Cities with postindustrial economies compete with suburban expansion and the growth of satellite towns for revenues as these developments continue to draw away from the central cities. As uncontrolled growth creates the phenomenon known as the mega-lopolis, in which once-discrete urban areas merge, the postindustrial city may ulti-mately represent the end of the city as it is now recognized.

Context

Urban sociologists at the University of Chicago pioneered in systematic attempts to study cities during the 1920's and 1930's. These early studies of urban institutions, populations, and spatial organization were based on the changes being observed in American cities at that time. Influenced by the work of European social theorists such as Ferdinand Tönnies, Émile Durkheim, Georg Simmel, Max Weber, and Karl Marx, American sociologists sought to explain the alienation, deviant behavior, and margin-ality they observed in sections of the urban population.

Several of these studies identified behavioral change as part of the transitional process of populations from kin-based community relationships to impersonal urban contacts. Louis Wirth wrote "Urbanism as a Way of Life" (1938), a landmark study of the social and psychological disintegration that accompanied "progress" in the cities. Other studies explored the transformation of immigrants and migrants who were exposed to the forces of urban life. Robert Park looked for the structures of spatial organization that underlay the apparent chaos of large cities. Along with his colleagues Roderick McKenzie and Ernest Burgess, he contributed the idea of the concentric zone model of urban spatial and social processes. Alternate interpretations of urban growth were provided by the sector model of Homer Hoyt, which emphasized the role played by transportation routes in influencing land use patterns, and the multiple nuclei theory of Chauncey D. Harris and Edward L. Ullman, which suggested the absence of a central focal point in some examples of metropolitan growth.

Significant as these studies were, they had limited applicability for the study of global urbanization that was beginning to capture the attention of sociologists as growth in developing countries began to outpace that in industrialized societies. With the help of increased mobility and advanced communications, populations relocated from rural to urban areas and from developing societies to industrialized countries in larger and larger numbers. Scholars such as Kingsley Davis, Burt F. Hoselitz, and Philip Hauser found existing theories increasingly unsatisfactory in analyzing non-Western cities. The appearance of Gideon Sjoberg's *The Preindustrial City: Past and Present* in 1960 provided generalizable structural and social criteria that were charac-teristic of societies that predated the Industrial Revolution yet could still be observed in the cities of modernizing societies.

The transformation of industrial economies into postindustrial economies seems to exaggerate the negative qualities of industrial urban areas, because the urban under-class is expanded by the entry of workers displaced from their occupations by global industrialization. The very relevance of communities comes into question as social forces originating at great distances influence the lives of local populations. Some studies, such as those of Constantinos Doxiadis and Melvin Webber, even envisage postindustrial urbanization as independent of the city as an urban form.

Bibliography

Davis, Kingsley, ed. *Cities: Their Origin, Growth, and Human Impact.* San Francisco, Calif.: W. H. Freeman, 1973. An excellent and comprehensive collection of essays tracing the development of cities from ancient times to the 1970's. Reprinted from *Scientific American.*

Doxiadis, Constantinos. *Ekistics.* London: Hutchinson, 1968. A visionary concept of the city of the future that has intrigued many scholars.

Mumford, Lewis. *The City in History: Its Origins, Its Transformations, and Its Prospects.* New York: Harcourt, Brace & World, 1961. An outstanding interpreta-tion of urban history that has become a classic in the field. Despite a repetitious style, it addresses fundamental questions regarding progress, technology, and human needs.

Park, Robert, Ernest W. Burgess, and Roderick McKenzie. *The City.* Chicago: Uni-versity of Chicago Press, 1967. One of the earliest works of the "Chicago school" of urban studies. Provides a good background on the kinds of issues that have confronted students of industrial cities.

Sjoberg, Gideon. *The Preindustrial City: Past and Present.* Glencoe, Ill.: Free Press, 1960. The most extensive examination of the preindustrial city. A major contribution to the field of comparative urban studies. Should not be overlooked by students interested in global urbanization.

Wirth, Louis. "Urbanism as a Way of Life." *American Journal of Sociology* 44 (July, 1938): 1-24. The generalizations presented in this essay have been challenged by later scholars as pertaining to a cultural and historical phenomenon relating only to American cities; nevertheless, this approach focuses on the relationship between urbanization and modernization as sources of change. A thought-provoking study of urban behavior.

Sai Felicia Krishna-Hensel

Cross-References

CIVIL RELIGION AND POLITICS

Type of sociology: Major social institutions
Field of study: Religion

All societies develop ideological systems that bind them together, creating unity and social cohesion through a sense of national identity. The study of civil religion analyzes these belief systems in ways equivalent to other religions; this approach provides insight into the nature of American politics and religious life.

Principal terms

CIVIL RELIGION: a religious system that concentrates on the nation or the society, serving to create social cohesion through building a national identity

LEGITIMATION: the ideological and material process of supporting a specific worldview and the institutional powers that derive from it

NATIONAL IDENTITY: the sense of who a nation is, involving symbolic and ideological notions of history, nature, and purpose, to be propagated and believed by the populace in order to support the society as a whole

RELIGION: a system of symbols and institutions that embody values and worldviews, addressing ultimate questions of human existence and cosmic reality

RITUAL: an activity that expresses certain religious or ideological beliefs, living out a certain worldview through individual and corporate symbolic action

SOCIAL COHESION: forces that bind a society together, in ideological, social, and material aspects, to produce unity and harmony

Overview

Religion refers to complex patterns of beliefs, actions, and institutions that construct a sense of meaning for humans. As such, religion can take a wide variety of forms, all of which serve to provide meaning for individual people as well as for social groups. Religion's specific focus is on the questions of ultimate meaning, and thus classic religious questions include inquiries into the existence and nature of God as well as the purpose for human existence, the reasons for death and suffering, and the nature of good and evil. Some sociological theorists argue that all human groupings are religious, in the sense that all human groups deal with such basic issues of meaning, at least at a covert level of group assumptions.

At times, the political sphere forms a realm for these religious answers to such questions of ultimate human concern. In other words, the nation (or state or government) becomes part of the answer to the questions of meaning. Some political ideologies, for example, assert that service to the state is the reason for human existence or that the nation is the proper arena in which to conduct actions of goodness and morality. Such notions represent civil religions, in which there is a strong connection between the forms of political organization and the religious beliefs about ultimate reality.

From a functionalist perspective, civil religions serve to provide social cohesion. They offer a coherent system of beliefs about reality that bind together a political community into a group within common goals, orientations, beliefs, values, norms, and assumptions. As such, civil religions tend to legitimate the social order and its systems of power and advantage. As a belief system, the civil religion explains why the people in power should be in power and why obedience to the government is a moral issue akin to obedience to God. Civil religions function to construct a rationale for the existence of the state, and thus they address the common social problem of legitimation. By asking and answering such basic questions as "What is the identity and direction of America?" the civil religion assumes the existence of the nation and then proves the value of its purpose. It constructs identity and legitimates goals and values.

Civil religions, as other religions, are rarely monolithic. Different positions exist within the belief system. Martin Marty has made a distinction between "priestly" and "prophetic" versions of civil religion. The priestly form emphasizes the nation's greatness and rightness, celebrating the past history of successes and predicting the same for the future. The prophetic form, on the other hand, concentrates on the propagation of the ideal values of the community and calls the community to accountability for the injustices and inequalities still in its midst. These two types of civil religion are closely related, but they do operate distinctly from each other.

In the United States, a further distinction exists between "conservative" and "liberal" civil religions. The conservative form emphasizes loyalty to the nation as it is, connecting God's favor with the privilege systems currently in place. Conservative civil religion tends to be more static than its liberal counterpart. The liberal form of civil religion identifies an agenda of social change, involving issues such as the avoidance of nuclear war and the desire to allow all Americans to avoid poverty and violence. In many ways, these conservative and liberal distinctions parallel the priestly and prophetic forms, but there are important differences.

Civil religion thus not only provides a commonality of assumption that creates bondedness in lived experience but also provides a set of symbols and structures for the growth of difference and the expression of dissent. It serves as a rhetorical system of symbols in which individuals can experience commitment to the social organization or can distance themselves from its functioning through commitment to idealized social values. Both responses are experiences of the civil religion.

Applications

In the United States, the American civil religion has formed a coherent belief system of surprising power and endurance. Beginning with the belief that God has chosen the United States for a specific purpose, the civil religion explains why the nation should do what it does, why the history of the nation features the events that it does, and why the nation should progress in certain directions favored by those now in power. The belief system bases itself in the notion that the United States is a place of liberty, especially religious and economic freedoms. The mythology of American civil religion also emphasizes the idea that God's favor upon the American people manifests itself in the military and economic power of the nation as well as in the prestige and affluence of individual Americans. The civil religion supports the notion that there is a particularly American way of life that involves a high level of consumption that is both a national right and a display of individual worth.

Civil religions are like all other religions in the existence of myths, doctrines, rituals, ethics, and experiences as vital analytical categories. Again, the American experience serves as a good example, but other nations' civil religions develop in much the same sort of process. A civil religion bases itself in a myth, usually a story that describes the nation's founding period. In the American example, the myth involves the stories of the "founding fathers," such as George Washington and Thomas Jefferson. The myth continues to explain how later generations came into being, and so the religion traces the development of the present through other prominent figures, such as Abraham Lincoln, Franklin D. Roosevelt, and John F. Kennedy. These personages function in much the same way that saints operate in other religions; they are symbols of the life that one should lead according to the religion's values, and they are important parts of the history that is perceived to have produced a "national character."

This national character exhibits the presence of certain doctrines or beliefs that underlie the civil religion. For example, the United States values notions such as equality, liberty, and justice. These values find expression in the civil religion's "sacred texts" (the Declaration of Independence, the Constitution, the Bill of Rights, the Gettysburg Address, and so forth) and are held to be common values throughout the society, despite the varying ways in which they are interpreted and lived. These doctrines parallel a set of ethics, which are norms for behavior, including the striving for financial independence and affluence, plus the ability to afford goods such as health care, a single-family house, automobiles, education, and entertainment.

The celebration of the civil religion involves both holidays and monuments. Americans celebrate days such as Independence Day, Memorial Day, Thanksgiving, and Presidents' Day as reminders of the national history and opportunities for the propagation of the shared values of the national civil religion. Likewise, a series of "shrines" or holy places symbolizes history and values. The system of national parks offers several places, but more specifically there are monuments in Washington, D.C., such as those for Presidents Washington, Jefferson, and Lincoln, as well as various war memorials. Elsewhere in the nation, there are locations such as Mount Rushmore, dedicated to the memory of the national past. Pilgrimages to these shrines make tourism a major industry, and many Americans desire to see these places at least once in a lifetime.

These elements of the national civil religion certainly operate within the priestly notion. Other priestly aspects in American history include the doctrine of Manifest

Destiny, which held that God desired the American nineteenth century expansion from the eastern location of the original colonies until the nation would reach "from sea to shining sea." National imagery compared the entire continent to the Old Testament idea of a Promised Land, which God had given to the chosen people if only they would lead moral lives and would expend the energy needed to conquer the territory and drive out its former occupants. This priestly version of the civil religion asserted the rightness of God's chosen Americans and insisted upon the lesser value of other peoples.

The civil religion's prophetic side has also found expression at many points throughout the history of the nation. Two examples will suffice. During his lifetime and before his admission into the pantheon of civil religion, Abraham Lincoln developed doctrines of national unity that reflected the priestly notions of protecting the status quo, but he also expressed certain prophetic ideas. Lincoln rewrote the history of the nation to emphasize the founding fathers' desire for freedom for all persons. Ignoring the fact that many of the nation's first generations of leaders were slave owners, Lincoln favored the abolition of slavery and defended the notion through appeals to the civil religion, including such masterful rhetorical pieces as the Gettysburg Address. In the 1960's, Martin Luther King, Jr., functioned as one of the national civil religion's most important prophets through his use of civil religious language to champion civil rights for African Americans. His use of metaphors drawn from the civil religion, such as "dreams" and "covenants," marked the prophetic nature of his speech, as he called the nation to renew its commitment to the "higher values" of its civil religion, such as liberty, equality, and freedom, and to change the national system of privileges to reflect better the commitments of the prophetic civil religion. The success of King's rhetoric derived in large part from the effective use of images from the civil religion.

Context

Eighteenth century French philosopher Jean-Jacques Rousseau, in his *Du contrat social* (1762; *A Treatise on the Social Contract*, 1764), emphasized the need for a widespread ideology to support a government and its social contract with the people. Such an ideology would be a civil religion—that is, a belief in the ultimate power of the society rather than in some otherworldly divine being who might at times question and challenge the political realities of the day. A civil religion would assert a beneficent deity whose interests and actions provide helpful guidance for the community. It would also be necessary to believe in some sort of life after death in order to provide proper reasoning for individuals to live in harmony with the state on this earth. Finally, such a civil religion would need to affirm the sanctity and rightness of the social order. These views were widely reflected in the movement of Deism, with strong roots in the founding philosophies of the United States.

Much later, sociologist Émile Durkheim returned to the notion of civil religion and emphasized the idea that religion, by definition, expresses social cohesion. Any society's representation of itself as a social unit is therefore a "religious" depiction and embodies itself in ritual observances such as holidays and in symbols such as flags. According to Durkheim, religion is the realization of the presence of a real and external force upon individuals' lives, and that force is society itself. Thus, every society has a civil religion, and all civil religions serve to promote social cohesion. Even though Durkheim's critics have rightly charged that there is also the potential for conflict and social opposition present in religion, including civil religion, Durkheim's connection of cohesion and religion has proved to be an insight of powerful explanatory potential.

Over the past century, scholars of religion have been less willing to recognize the influence of civil religion, but in recent years many theologians, especially among the more conservative elements of Christianity, have embraced civil religions as an analytical device. Usually these Christian scholars emphasize the differences between "correct" Christian belief and the doctrinal elements of the civil religion. This direction is likely to continue. At the same time, sociologists are also realizing the problems with overly facile equations of civil religion and standard Christian theological symbols; they are concentrating more on the civil religion's transformation of Christian symbols than on its appropriation of them. This distinction will allow the study of civil religion to recognize the increasing plurality of American religion and American political metaphor, occurring as individuals of non-Christian religions assume increasing numbers of leadership positions. As scholars in the 1950's began to recognize distinctions between Protestant, Catholic, and Jewish versions of the civil religion, so Islamic, Buddhist, and perhaps even New Age notions will make themselves felt increasingly in the future.

Bibliography

Bellah, Robert N. *The Broken Covenant: American Civil Religion in a Time of Trial.* New York: Seabury, 1975. In this classic study of civil religion, Bellah establishes the historical roots of this phenomenon and then analyzes the problems in American national self-identity created by the dissolution of this unifying concept.

Chidester, David. *Patterns of Power: Religion and Politics in American Culture.* Englewood Cliffs, N.J.: Prentice-Hall, 1988. Chidester analyzes issues such as religion and the exercise of democracy, the conflict between different minority understandings of religion, and the connections between religion and the American legal system. Provides helpful insight into the way that the rest of culture reacts and responds to religious phenomena.

Durkheim, Émile. *The Elementary Forms of the Religious Life.* Translated by Joseph W. Swain. London: Allen & Unwin, 1915. In this classic book, Durkheim's focus is on the religious practices of "primitive" societies. He concludes that religion symbolizes the society itself. He understands this view of religion to apply equally to modern societies, and thus he defines religion as the (ideological) forces of social cohesion.

McGuire, Meredith B. *Religion: The Social Context.* 3d ed. Belmont, Calif.: Wadsworth, 1992. This book provides a basic introduction to the larger context of issues in sociology of religion, allowing the placement of civil religion within its setting of other human religious experience. The author provides a helpful summary of Durkheim's theoretical development of civil religion as social cohesion.

Pierard, Richard V., and Robert D. Linder. *Civil Religion and the Presidency*. Grand Rapids, Mich.: Academie, 1988. This book documents changes in civil religion as supported by United States presidents, especially those of the late twentieth century. There is insightful and skeptical attention to the presidents' rhetorical use of civil religion for political ends, with a call for Christians to delineate between the cultural phenomenon of civil religion and the transcendent claims of "true faith."

Nederveen Pieterse, Jan P., ed. *Christianity and Hegemony: Religion and Politics on the Frontiers of Social Change*. New York: Berg, 1992. This anthology offers a series of analyses of civil religion and other types of religious influence on politics in the United States and internationally, including chapters on Iraq, Israel, the Philippines, Poland, South Africa, Western Europe, and Zimbabwe.

Rouner, Leroy S., ed. *Civil Religion and Political Theology*. Notre Dame, Ind.: University of Notre Dame Press, 1986. These essays cover issues of civil religion's influence on American politics and, more explicitly, religious and theological attempts to influence political life. Several of the articles develop the view that civil religion is a corruption of Christianity that endangers both true religion and political freedom.

Wuthnow, Robert. *The Restructuring of American Religion: Society and Faith Since World War II*. Princeton, N.J.: Princeton University Press, 1988. Wuthnow is one of the premier interpreters of religion as an American social phenomenon. In this book, he traces the development of society's religious involvement during the second half of the twentieth century. Despite an emphasis on the institutional and denominational aspects of American religion, he includes a specific chapter on civil religion, with a strong comparison of conservative and liberal forms of civil religion.

_____ . *The Struggle for America's Soul: Evangelicals, Liberals, and Secularism*. Grand Rapids, Mich.: W. B. Eerdmans, 1989. This book provides a readable account of the issues that have arisen between factions in American Christianity, with special attention to the way each group uses civil religion in its arguments and appeals.

Jon L. Berquist

Cross-References

Legitimacy and Authority, 1055; Legitimation of Inequality: Religion, 1068; The Nation-State, 1282; Political Influence by Religious Groups, 1394; Secularization in Western Society, 1700; The Separation of Church and State, 1714; Socialization: Religion, 1894; The Sociology of Religion, 1952.

THE CIVIL RIGHTS MOVEMENT

Type of sociology: Collective behavior and social movements

The Civil Rights movement was the struggle that began after World War II and continued through the 1960's to achieve equal rights for American minority groups, particularly African Americans. Tactics included demonstrations, marches, and sit-ins. The influences of the movement, both on society at large and on subsequent protest movements, has been profound.

Principal terms
  CIVIL RIGHTS: rights—economic, social, and political—guaranteed to all United States citizens by the United States Constitution, especially the protection found in the Bill of Rights and the fourteenth and fifteenth amendments
  CONFLICT THEORY: the sociological theory that some groups dominate other groups; the struggle between the "haves" and "have nots" explains most of the divisiveness found in society
  DISCRIMINATION: the withholding of equal rights and opportunities from certain groups by using race, ethnic heritage, or gender to disqualify them
  FUNCTIONALISM: the sociological perspective, sometimes called "consensus theory," that the sharing of common values holds society together and that society is a system of interrelated parts working together
  MASS MOVEMENT: a movement that occurs when a large group within society reaches a consensus that change is needed and moves to reform society to reflect the movement's norms and values
  MINORITY GROUP: any group whose individual members are denied full political, social, and economic participation in (and rewards of) the society of which they are a part
  PREJUDICE: unfavorable attitudes toward individuals or groups based on their alleged undesirable traits (prejudice is covert; discrimination is its overt manifestation)
  SEGREGATION: the physical separation of groups in society, usually imposed on minority groups by the majority group
  SOCIAL STRATIFICATION: the division of society into hierarchical groups; racial, ethnic, and gender stratification are three types of such division

Overview
Scholars have chosen various dates to begin their discussions of the modern Civil Rights movement, but the year 1941—earlier than most dates used—may be the best. That year, the United States was in the middle of a great military preparedness

campaign, for many people believed it would only be a matter of time before the country entered World War II, already raging in Europe. Even as the country geared for war, minorities were being discriminated against in the defense industry, which was receiving billions of federal dollars. Long-time black labor leader A. Philip Randolph contacted President Franklin D. Roosevelt and threatened to organize a march on Washington to protest discrimination. Needing support from a united country, Roosevelt issued an executive order that banned job discrimination in the defense industry by threatening to cancel the contracts of those industries that did not heed the order. By war's end, more than 2 million African Americans were working in the nation's defense plants.

In the later 1940's, President Harry S Truman followed Roosevelt's lead. In 1948 he became the first white presidential candidate to walk the streets of Harlem, New York, asking for black votes. Once elected, Truman established the Civil Rights Commission, a study group that compiled reports on racial segregation and discrimination. In addition, he used his power of appointment to bring more African Americans into the government. In 1948 he eliminated segregation in the armed forces. Truman wanted to do more but conservative Republicans and Southern "Dixiecrats" in Congress thwarted many of his plans.

Conservatives, however, could not thwart rulings of the United States Supreme Court, the body that took the lead in the Civil Rights movement. In a series of rulings from 1949 to 1954, the Supreme Court handed down decisions leading toward the integration of public schools. Finally, in 1954, in *Brown v. Board of Education*, the Court mandated integration. President Dwight D. Eisenhower and his successor, John F. Kennedy, were hesitant to enforce the ruling because strict enforcement would lead directly to a confrontation with many Southern whites who still believed in black inferiority and in rigid segregation. Nevertheless, the slow process of school integration began.

Shortly after the Court's 1954 ruling, a true mass movement began when the Civil Rights movement took to the streets. In 1955 Martin Luther King, Jr., led the Montgomery, Alabama, bus boycott. After a federal court ordered the Montgomery bus company to integrate, King founded the Southern Christian Leadership Conference (SCLC) to coordinate boycotts and other forms of peaceful protest all across the South. Soon came more boycotts, protest parades, and, in 1958, the sit-in movement. Slowly, in the late 1950's and early 1960's, more and more places of public accommodation integrated.

In 1961 came the "freedom rides," sponsored by the Congress of Racial Equality (CORE). Riders boarded buses in the North and rode into the South to test the ban of the Interstate Commerce Commission (ICC) on segregated public transportation. In the South, many riders were assaulted, some beaten after they went to jail; however, such events only inspired more and more people, particularly college students, to join the riders. Soon, new ICC rulings and federal court decisions cracked the wall of segregation in public transportation.

Major centers of protest included Birmingham, Alabama, where policemen and members of the Ku Klux Klan virtually went to war with civil rights protestors; Oxford, Mississippi, where state authorities, white college students, and outside agitators destroyed part of the University of Mississippi and sent more than 150 wounded or injured federal marshals to hospitals (all this to stop one African American from enrolling in the college); and Jackson, Mississippi, where civil rights leader Medgar Evers was murdered in his own front yard in the summer of 1963 after leading peaceful protests in Jackson. After Evers' death, Kennedy finally reacted; he sent his administration's civil rights bill to Congress. It was stalled there until 1964, when President Lyndon Johnson demanded passage.

Congress finally responded and passed the Civil Rights Act of 1964, the most sweeping piece of civil rights legislation in United States history. The act forbade discrimination in all public accommodations, forbade discrimination in employment and in voting, and forbade segregation of schools. The act was supplemented by the Voter Registration Act of 1965, giving the president the power to send federal voter registrars into areas where potential voters were being denied their rights. In 1968 an open housing law rounded out the civil rights legislation of the decade. For his efforts, Johnson has been called "America's civil rights president."

Just as the Civil Rights movement seemed to peak, however, it also appeared to go into decline—a decline caused by various factors: First, much of what the movement had sought had been accomplished. Second, the years from 1965 to 1968 saw increasing urban violence. More than 150 riots occurred, apparently because inner-city blacks came to believe that not enough meaningful economic reform was being implemented. Third, Martin Luther King, Jr., was assassinated in April of 1968, and that act deprived the national movement of the one leader who could hold its diverse factions together. After King's death, the movement fragmented. Fourth, the country's collective national attention increasingly turned toward the Vietnam War and away from the civil rights crusade. Finally, Richard Nixon became president in 1969, and he was no friend to the movement. In general, Nixon's election brought to an end a liberal era of reform.

Applications

Knowledge and experience gained from the Civil Rights movement have been valuable in a number of areas, both theoretical and practical. Tactics effectively used in the Civil Rights movement, such as marches and sit-ins, were adopted by other movements in the 1960's and early 1970's. Studies of the gains and shortcomings of the movement have been valuable both to government policy makers and to those seeking to motivate mass movements for other causes. If, as widely argued, the movement failed to address economic issues adequately, leaving millions in the poverty of inner cities, reformers today must develop programs to relieve that poverty. The problem of institutional racism still exists, and further attempts must be made to counter its effects.

The Civil Rights movement has provided a modern model for the study of mass movements. From the early 1950's to about 1965, it was indeed a mass movement, cutting across such dividing lines as race, class, and gender, and it achieved its considerable success precisely because it was able to do so. Its victories also attest the power of King's philosophy of nonviolence. The movement fragmented and declined partly because some leaders directed their followers toward violent confrontation, believing that nonviolence had reached a dead end. The majority in the movement feared or rejected the use of violence, and many withdrew support. This splintering in part enabled the government (particularly when Nixon was president) to suppress the movement. Moreover, race consciousness remained a powerful and volatile force in American life. As evidenced by continuing poverty and riots in urban areas in the 1980's and 1990's, the central problem of American society is probably still race relations.

The Civil Rights movement can serve as a "laboratory" for the debate between two sociological perspectives, the functionalist (consensus) viewpoint and the conflict theory perspective. Functionalists stress consensus in society—a consensus based on the voluntary sharing of norms and values. These theorists believe that society changes slowly. When political, economic, or social change does come, it is possible only because the societal consensus has changed.

Conflict theorists, on the other hand, believe that certain groups dominate other groups. Social stratification occurs when the "haves" continually defeat the "have nots" and maintain absolute control of a society. Such conflict causes most of the divisiveness found in society. Conflict theory often appeals to reform-minded individuals who seek change; they attempt to identify potential for change and identify groups that might challenge society's "establishment." Rather than stressing the supposed common values of society, they emphasize the tension and strains produced by society's authority structure.

The events of the Civil Rights movement seem to validate the ideas of conflict theorists. The movement defined existing authority in its marches and protests as well as in its essential "meaning." Individuals went to jail rather than obey what they believed to be unjust laws. Early civil rights workers were often punished and ostracized for their behavior, but that behavior eventually led to new court decisions and eventually to legislation that ended segregation—thereby changing the rules, or consensus, of society.

The Civil Rights movement is sometimes considered to have ended by the late 1960's, after reform legislation had been passed, when the segmentation of the movement decreased its effectiveness. Its continuing effects, however, can be seen in many areas, one of which is the movement toward "multiculturalism" that began in the 1980's. Under the concept of multiculturalism, a diversity of cultures and ethnicities are viewed as relevant and as valuable contributors to the texture of American society and culture.

Context

Few sociologists studied race relations until well after the beginning of the twentieth century. There were a few nineteenth century precursors, such as William Sumner and

Lester Ward, but such scholars viewed discrimination as conscious acts committed by prejudiced individuals. Many early sociologists believed that if racial prejudice could be eliminated, then racial discrimination would cease; they also viewed racial discrimination as a contradiction inconsistent with the ideals such as freedom, justice, and equality expressed in the Declaration of Independence. In *An American Dilemma: The Negro Problem and Modern Democracy* (1944), Swedish sociologist Gunnar Myrdal, provided a synthesis of the above views.

Other early twentieth century sociologists believed that minority groups, including African Americans, would eventually be assimilated by the larger society. Robert Park, in his pathbreaking work on immigration, gave voice to the above view, as did Milton Gordon—in part—when, in the 1960's, he wrote on cultural and structural assimilation. He believed that black Americans were well on their way to cultural assimilation but that achieving structural assimilation (the ability to participate legally in all aspects of American life, including entry into social cliques, clubs, and institutions) would be far more difficult.

In the 1950's and 1960's, the Civil Rights movement made tremendous gains, as chronicled by both historians and sociologists. Yet the movement did not fulfill the economic hopes of millions of inner-city blacks who continued to live in poverty. Further, the movement could not solve the problem of institutional racism.

Most accounts of the Civil Rights movement tend to focus on the African American community, but it is helpful to set the movement in a broader context. The 1960's, for example, saw many freedom movements, such as the women's liberation movement, the free speech movement, the gay rights crusade, the "good earth" ecology movement, the gray panthers, the American Indian movement, and César Chávez's farm labor movement.

Further, although the King-led Civil Rights movement focused on blacks, once civil rights laws were passed in the 1960's, those laws protected everyone. For example, Hispanics and American Indians had long been subject to the same sort of segregation and discrimination that African Americans faced. Once laws were on the books, all minorities benefited. For that matter, so did the members of the country's dominant group, many of whom took pride in the changes for the better and the fact that their country had made an effort to live up to the ideals expressed in the American Declaration of Independence and the United States Constitution.

Bibliography

Blauner, Robert. *Racial Oppression in America*. New York: Harper & Row, 1972. A very useful book, Blauner's volume contains a series of essays in which the author develops his interpretation that it is the capitalist system itself that has made minorities "internal colonies" of the United States—separate and still not equal.

Branch, Taylor. *Parting the Waters: America in the King Years, 1954-1963*. New York: Simon & Schuster, 1988. This massive study is probably the best chronicle of the early years of the movement. Well documented and well written, Branch's work takes readers behind the scenes for an in-depth look at the decision makers and their importance in guiding the movement. Branch's book also serves as a good model regarding the organization and direction of a modern mass movement.

Broom, Leonard, and Philip Selznick. *Sociology: A Text with Adapted Readings*. 6th ed. New York: Harper & Row, 1977. A good introductory sociology textbook that would appeal especially to college readers. A valuable set of "adapted readings" follows each chapter and amplifies the chapter's theme. There is good coverage of the Civil Rights movement—its successes, its failures, and its overall significance. Each chapter includes a list of references and lists supplementary readings.

Carson, Clayborne. *In Struggle: SNCC and the Black Awakening of the 1960's*. Cambridge: Mass.: Harvard University Press, 1981. The Student Nonviolent Coordinating Committee (SNCC) was most important to the movement because it provided an "umbrella" under which students and other young people could unite. Its early leadership trained youngsters in the nonviolent ways of protest and helped coordinate student participation in boycotts, sit-ins, and the like. Later leaders became more militant because they viewed change as coming too slowly.

Feagin, Joe R. *Racial and Ethnic Relations*. 3d ed. Englewood Cliffs, N.J.: Prentice-Hall, 1989. A good introductory textbook, this volume is documented, is easy to read, and has a good index. Feagin discusses minorities in a larger social context.

Forman, James. *The Making of Black Revolutionaries*. New York: Macmillan, 1972. In part autobiographical, Forman's book gives readers a first-hand look at various aspects of the Civil Rights movement and the racial injustices that made the movement necessary.

Garrow, David J., ed. *We Shall Overcome: The Civil Rights Movement in the United States in the 1950's and 1960's*. 3 vols. Brooklyn, N.Y.: Carlson, 1989. Garrow's three volumes contain the best collection of documents relevant to the Civil Rights movement.

Powledge, Fred. *Free at Last?: The Civil Rights Movement and the People Who Made It*. Boston: Little, Brown, 1991. Powledge covers much the same ground as Branch's book, but Powledge continues the story beyond 1963 and thus gives more complete information on the movement.

Sitkoff, Harvard. *The Struggle for Black Equality, 1954-1980*. New York: Hill and Wang, 1981. This volume is well documented and is an excellent single-volume study. Comprehensive in its coverage of the entire movement.

James Smallwood

Cross-References

Affirmative Action, 21; Busing and Integration, 179; The Church and African American Life, 239; Individual Discrimination, 547; Institutional Racism, 996; Minority and Majority Groups, 1219; Improving Race Relations, 1559; Race Relations: The Race-Class Debate, 1566; The Race Relations Cycle Theory of Assimilation, 1572; Racial and Ethnic Stratification, 1579; Racism as an Ideology, 1586; Segregation versus Integration, 1707; Social Movements, 1826.

CLASS CONSCIOUSNESS AND CLASS CONFLICT

Type of sociology: Major social institutions
Field of study: The economy

Class consciousness refers to the ways in which members of particular classes view their common cultural, political, and economic interests as distinctly opposed to the interests of members of other classes. Class consciousness and class struggle have been studied to understand society's changing political, economic, and cultural configurations.

Principal terms

CAPITALISM: an economic system generally defined as private ownership of the means of production (raw materials, buildings, and machinery); sociological meaning also includes the social system that encompasses capitalist social relations

CLASS: a group of people with shared political, economic, and cultural experiences who identify their interests as different from those of other classes

CULTURE: the values, norms, and material goods created by members of a particular group

DEMOGRAPHY: the study of human population that investigates the size, age, and sex composition of a population in addition to its mobility patterns

IDEOLOGY: an array of ideas actively expressing the way a group views the appropriate functioning of society's political, economic, and cultural institutions and activities

INSTITUTIONS: relatively stable arrangements designed to promote efficiency in meeting a society's goals

MODE OF PRODUCTION: the combination of the social relations of production and the sources of production; capitalism is one example of a mode of production

STRATIFICATION: a system by which categories of people in a society are ranked in a hierarchy

Overview

At a superficial level, class consciousness simply refers to a recognition that a number of classes exist in one's society and that one belongs to a certain class and not to others. This suggests an acknowledgment of differences in cultural, political, and economic characteristics of members of other classes. There are, however, degrees of consciousness. Sociologist Anthony Giddens has identified three distinct levels of class consciousness: conception of class identity, conception of class conflict, and revolutionary consciousness. A conception of class identity is the least developed of the three levels of class consciousness; all it requires is some recognition of class differentiation. This minimal level of consciousness can be further distinguished by the absence of a conflict orientation, which requires not only acknowledgment of class differentiation but also recognition of oppositional interests.

Conflict consciousness emerges with the unveiling of class structure—that is, through the identification of those qualities of capitalism that make levels of class inequality obvious. Historically this has meant the "homogenization" of the effects of industrialization on workers forced into large factory settings. While this concentration of labor was advantageous for capitalists, it had the unintended consequence of providing workers (now sharing common experiences and interests) with the ability to identify levels of inequality inherent in the production process. The product of conflict consciousness has been the emergence of unions and political parties, as well as other organizations and agencies, to promote the interests of the working class.

Conflict consciousness, however, carries working class interests only so far. A class which has attained a level of revolutionary consciousness not only identifies layers of class-based inequality but also, through heightened experiential and theoretical aware-ness, views the existing socioeconomic structure as illegitimate. A class attaining revolutionary consciousness proposes an alternative to the existing cultural, political, and economic order and identifies possible actions necessary to advance it. Many sociologists contend that the primary objectives of class struggle and class conflict are worker control over industry (centering primarily on creativity and the organization of production) and society; material and moral fulfillment; economic self-sufficiency; and freedom of self-expression. Consciousness alone will not produce a revolution. Sociological analysis suggests that revolutions are the product of both revolutionary ideology (consciousness) and institutional breakdown.

There are many institutional, associational, and demographic factors that mediate the transmission of class consciousness. Among those most readily identifiable are family, school, religion, media, peer groups, work associations, gender, and ethnicity. One goal of sociological research on class consciousness and class struggle is to unveil the apparent equality inherent in relations between capitalists and workers to show that these social relations are, in actuality, unequal. By studying the many ways in which class struggle manifests itself in structural, symbolic, and ideological confron-tation, sociologists have been able not only to understand the objective experiences of the working class with respect to the socioeconomic constraints of capitalism but also to identify counterideology expressed through revolutionary consciousness.

Applications

Theories of class consciousness and class struggle have been used to explain, among other things, the de-skilling of workers and the investments that industries and corporations have made in technology.

Sociologist Harry Braverman published a book in 1974 entitled *Labor and Monop-oly Capital* that has been widely influential among sociologists who study the organization of work and its effects on workers. Braverman emphasized the struggle taking place at the point of production over control of the productive process. He focused on identification and politicization of the division of labor as it manifested itself under the influence of scientific management.

Scientific management had been offered earlier in the twentieth century as a potential panacea for managers and owners attempting to resolve their "labor problems." More specifically, since workers at the beginning of the twentieth century were still in command of the primary skills and knowledge of how to produce specific products, attempts to increase production, reduce worker pay, or change work methods were frequently met with hostility, often disrupting production entirely. The labor problem, as Frederick W. Taylor (scientific management's major proponent) identified it, was how to get workers to produce in the most efficient manner possible without driving them to rebel or to withhold their effort.

The answer for Taylor, and other scientific managers, was a detailed division of labor. Since workers possessed the knowledge and skill needed for production, Taylor reasoned, management needed to formulate a method for separating the worker from as much "thought work" as possible. Successful application of the "separation of conception from execution," as Braverman referred to it, would begin to de-skill workers to the point where their knowledge of production would be limited solely to their own narrowly defined (by management) activity.

Taylorism consists of a process characterized by three fundamental principles. First, managers must assume the responsibility of gathering all the traditional knowledge formerly held by working men and women and reducing this knowledge to rules, laws, and formulae. No longer would managers be dependent on the craft knowledge of workers; they could rely instead on the planning of management. The second principle, related to the first, suggests that all brainwork should be removed from the shop floor and relocated in departments of planning or layout. This is what Braverman referred to as the separation of conception from execution. In the name of efficiency, it was Taylor's mission to see that the process of conceiving and implementing an idea would never again occur under the power of workers. The third principle of scientific management was to use management's new monopoly over knowledge "to control each step of the labor process and its mode of execution." This was to be accomplished through a detailed description of each job, including how to do the work, the time that should be required to complete it, and product specifications.

The direct effects of scientific management on workers were immediate and severe. The cheapening of the workforce that developed as a consequence of de-skilling not only reduced the price of labor (the wage workers could command) but also enhanced their interchangeability. Workers could no longer summon the attention of employers as effectively as they formerly had based on their ability to withhold productive effort. This made them more vulnerable to threats of dismissal and more likely to accommodate a dehumanizing work environment. The ideological significance of scientific management was its appeal to rational concerns over efficient production. Taylor's appeal to "science" masked the underlying class struggle implicit in employers' and managers' efforts to eliminate worker control over production. Braverman's contribution to the sociology of work was to expose the class struggle taking place at the point of production and to identify the efforts of managers to appropriate productive control through the implementation of scientific management. His insight into the de-skilling of workers continues to inform research on contemporary labor market characteristics.

In one of the most compelling applications of class theory, historian David Noble identifies the consequences of class struggle for the implementation of technology in the workplace. In two well-documented works, Noble applies the conceptual strengths of the concepts of class and class struggle to a historical account of the growth of industrial automation.

Noble begins by identifying the coordination of interests among the military, corporations, universities, and science establishments in the United States following the conclusion of World War II. The primary purposes, according to Noble, were to form a political and economic force capable of containing the Soviet Union abroad and controlling labor at home. Labor union strength had grown rapidly during the war, climbing from nine to fifteen million members between 1940 and 1945. The War Labor Board, however, assumed control over arbitration. Wages were frozen at 15 percent above 1941 levels and labor was forced to adhere to no-strike pledges. This occurred while prices increased 45 percent and profits increased 250 percent. Despite no-strike pledges, the war years saw 14,471 strikes involving more than seven million workers. According to Noble, the most frequent cause of strike activity was a grievance over discipline (such as harassment). Wages and working conditions constituted the remaining reasons as workers "endured speed-ups, long hours, and a hazardous environment." He cites data suggesting that between 1940 and 1945, eighty thousand workers were killed and more than eleven million were injured as a result of industrial accidents.

According to historian Neil Chamberlain, "the end of World War Two marked the beginning of the greatest industrial crisis in American history." Class struggle in the United States during the period of 1945 to 1955 led to the greatest confrontation between capital and labor in the history of a capitalist country. Noble cites more than forty-three thousand strikes involving some twenty-seven million workers. Union demands moved beyond instrumental concerns over wages to include control over working conditions, shorter hours, health and welfare funds, and the pace of production.

Faced with continued work stoppages and dependence on workers in unionized firms for most decisions concerning personnel, hours, and pay, management went on the offensive. Two crucial events served to weaken the labor movement in the 1950's: returning veterans (whose presence in firms formerly homogenized by a strong union made the labor force more heterogeneous and hence more difficult to organize), and the anti-Communist "red scare." Renewed interest in de-skilling and control led employers to pursue innovative ways to redesign the work process, avoiding the use of skilled craft workers as much as possible.

Efforts to utilize technology in increasingly sophisticated ways, thereby reducing the need for skilled workers, were widely referred to in the 1950's and early 1960's as "automation." Noble notes that among the forces encouraging factory owners to automate was the desire to "weaken the power of unions, and otherwise adjust a recalcitrant work force to the realities of lower pay, tighter discipline, and frequent layoffs." In other words, the strength of labor, as it struggled for control of production and higher wages, was among the forces that drove the combined interests of corporations, universities, the military, and scientific communities to invest in the redesign of the workplace.

Central to automation was a technological development known as the numerical control device, a predecessor of the digital computer. Engineers gathered detailed information and specifications about the operation of machinery, then coded the information in such a way that the numerical control device could control the machines. Work that formerly required ten skilled workers could now be accomplished by machines, with only one semiskilled worker needed to monitor the equipment.

Context

To many scholars, the study of class, class consciousness, and class struggle is synonymous with sociology. Initiated in the works of Karl Marx and Friedrich Engels, and later transformed by German sociologist Max Weber, theoretical analyses of class consciousness and class struggle have continued to be a source of great sociological debate.

Marx identified the emergence of class consciousness as a product of shared experiences brought on by the increasing homogenization of labor. Workers' objective experiences with capitalist production, he wrote, would lead inevitably to a revolutionary class consciousness. Later Marx clarified his earlier propositions by arguing that it was the combination of objective experiences and class struggle, producing a unity of interest, that would transform that working class from "a class *in* itself" to "a class *for* itself" (a revolutionary class). Class struggle, according to Marx, exposes the true interests of capitalists and, in the words of sociologist M. Levin, reveals "the horrific extent to which a ruling class will go to preserve its interests."

Vladimir Ilich Lenin, like Marx, believed that class-based exploitation may not be readily apparent—it must be uncovered. Lenin proposed that consciousness can only be brought to workers from without. Only activists (intellectuals) having the ability to see through the veil of ideology could generate and lead a truly revolutionary movement. Workers, after all, had only a "working class" consciousness. What was needed was a revolutionary consciousness.

Sociologist Jean Cohen suggests that class analyses since the 1940's have generally been of four basic types: theories seeking a revolutionary subject that is not a class to substitute for or spark the proletariat; "new working class theories"; structuralist Marxist class analyses; and theories of the "new intellectual class." Those theories seeking a revolutionary subject argue that it is impossible for the working class to be the force for revolutionary change since the harshness of capitalism has been mediated by the welfare state. This has resulted in some theorists, among them sociologist Herbert Marcuse, searching for other populations experiencing the severity of capitalist exploitation as the source for revolutionary change; (among those populations studied have been the underclass, blacks, students, and women). New working class theorists such as sociologists Serge Mallet and Andre Gorz argue that technological transformations in the mode of production within Western capitalist countries have placed workers once again at the forefront of class struggle and revolutionary consciousness. Technological homogenization places workers in positions of power and makes them crucial links in the productive process.

Structural Marxists such as Nicos Poulantzas and Eric O. Wright are considered the forerunners in the contemporary "boundary debate." That is, they have taken up Marx's efforts to identify clearly how many classes there are and who belongs in which ones. Finally, sociologists Ivan Szelenyi, Alvin Gouldner, and Barbara Ehrenreich, and John Ehrenreich, among others, are associated with identification and theorization of the new intellectual class. The theoretical crux of this approach is identifying the extent to which intellectuals have replaced workers as having revolutionary potential.

Bibliography

Braverman, Harry. *Labor and Monopoly Capital*. New York: Monthly Review Press, 1974. Braverman's book refocused attention on the class struggle that occurs at the point of production. His primary endeavor was to identify the de-skilling process and discuss its ramifications for workers.

Cohen, Jean. *Class and Civil Society*. Amherst: University of Massachusetts Press, 1982. Cohen offers a valuable critique of traditional Marxist, neo-Marxist, and Weberian conceptualizations of class. She then attempts to salvage the strengths of Marx's class theory to provide a more stimulating critique of stratification.

Giddens, Anthony. *The Class Structure of the Advanced Societies*. New York: Harper & Row, 1975. In this book, Giddens attempts a rearticulation of class theory. He enters a debate with both Marx and Weber, offering valuable critique and theoretical insight.

Giddens, Anthony, and David Held. *Classes, Power, and Conflict: Classical and Contemporary Debates*. Berkeley: University of California Press, 1982. This edited volume offers and invaluable look at the classical and contemporary theoretical approaches to class, state, ideology, and conflict.

Marx, Karl. *Capital: A Critique of Political Economy*. Vol. 3. New York: Penguin Books, 1990. In the last chapter of volume 3 of his classic work, Marx begins to systematize his analysis of class and class consciousness. Available in a number of editions and translations.

_____ . *The Eighteenth Brumaire of Louis Bonaparte*. New York: International, 1981. Here Marx designates the three historically relevant classes according to Marxist theory: capitalists, proletarians, and land owners.

Noble, David. *Forces of Production*. New York: Oxford University Press, 1986. A detailed account of the development and implementation of technology in industry. While focusing primarily on the development of numerical control, Noble's identification of class struggle, implicit throughout this work, serves to invigorate the "active" or subjective side of history.

Thompson, E. P. *The Making of the English Working Class*. New York: Vintage Books, 1963. Widely proclaimed as a masterpiece of historical and sociological insight, Thompson's book documents the emergence of English working class consciousness. This book is essential reading for all students of class consciousness and struggle.

Willis, Paul. *Learning to Labor*. New York: Columbia University Press, 1981. Willis' book stands as a classic ethnography of the impact of political, economic, and cultural experiences on the reproduction of class stratification. Widely credited for its cogent observation of working class "counterideology."

Wright, E. O. *Class, Crisis, and the State*. London: NLB, 1978. Wright's book expanded on the work of structuralist Marxists Althusser and Poulantzas to add new layers of class structuration. By doing so, Wright was able to identify what he called "contradictory class locations" held by individuals within society who did not seem to fit the orthodox Marxist class scheme.

Robert C. Schehr

Cross-References

Capitalism, 191; Conflict Theory, 340; Industrial Societies, 953; Inequalities in Political Power, 972; Marxism, 1127; Revolutions, 1641; Social Stratification: Analysis and Overview, 1839; Social Stratification: Marxist Perspectives, 1852; Social Stratification: Modern Theories, 1859; Unionization and Industrial Labor Relations, 2096; Workplace Socialization, 2202.

COGNITIVE DEVELOPMENT: PIAGET

Type of sociology: Socialization and social interaction
Field of study: Development, personality, and socialization

Jean Piaget's theory of cognitive development describes how children develop their understanding of the world around them. Piaget believed that the ability to know and to organize information develops with age and experience and does so in an orderly, stagelike manner. His theory of development has had a profound impact on the education of children.

Principal terms

ACCOMMODATION: the phenomenon that occurs when the acquisition of new information requires an individual to change a cognitive structure (a concept or way of viewing reality)

ADAPTATION: adjusting to a new experience; accommodation and assimilation are examples of adaptation

ASSIMILATION: the phenomenon that occurs when the acquisition of new information extends a cognitive structure to a new example but does not require changes in the way one views reality

COGNITION: the mental activities involved in the acquisition and retention of knowledge, such as thinking, remembering, understanding, perceiving, and learning

EQUILIBRIUM: a dynamic state of balance; when one's cognitive structures and the environment balance, one's methods of viewing the world are sufficient to understand one's experiences

OPERATION: in Piaget's theory, a mental activity; thinking of doing something, either with objects (a concrete operation) or in the abstract (formal operation)

QUALITATIVE CHANGE: a change in kind or style, as when one has a new way of doing or understanding something

QUANTITATIVE CHANGE: a change in amount or number, as when one can do something faster or think of more things

STAGE: a normal, prescribed pattern of development, related to age and maturation

Overview

A three-year-old is convinced that he has more juice after it is poured from a short, wide glass into a tall, thin one. A five-year-old asks her father, "What color is gravity?" An eight-year-old knows the answer to "5 times 10" but has great difficulty calculating the cost of five apples at ten cents each. A thirteen-year-old believes that everyone will notice even one hair out of place. A sixteen-year-old with boyfriend problems sobs to her mother, "You don't understand what it's like to be in love." Each of these "cognitive mistakes" portrays a style of thinking that is typical for a particular age range. Yet each also shows an increased capacity with age. How is it that we become able to understand, and how do these abilities change with age?

Children are not born "knowing how to know"; they learn to acquire knowledge. Moreover, children acquire knowledge very differently from the way adults do. In fact, much of the charm and innocence of childhood arises from the unusual ways in which children form conclusions.

The theory of cognitive development advanced by Jean Piaget from the 1930's through the 1970's explains how people's ability to understand the world grows and changes as they do, and it is this changing cognitive capacity that creates the interesting circumstances illustrated above. Piaget called the study of how individuals learn to know "genetic epistemology." This use of the word "genetic" simply refers to "origins" or "beginnings" (as in "genesis"). Epistemology is the study of knowledge. Piaget studied the origins of an individual's ability to know by observing how infants, children, and adolescents understand the world.

According to Piaget, children take an active part in their own development. The acquisition of understanding comes from interactions with the world around them. All experiences are taken in and understood according to the level of thinking that individuals are currently using. The very act of taking in new information, however, also changes the way one understands the world.

The process of taking in information through experiences is called adaptation. Often, this process is little more than using what one already knows. For example, a toddler who knows how to use a cup (however clumsily) may be trying to drink from a slightly larger-than-normal cup. The child must adapt to the larger container. This is a relatively simple task and requires only the application of what the child already knows. Still, the behavior is new and does cause the child to grow and change slightly. Such adaptation is called assimilation. On the other hand, the same child may be attempting to eat with a spoon. Because toddlers usually eat with their fingers, the changes required now are rather large and call for new abilities. The task is much more challenging; the growth is much greater. Such adaptation is called accommodation.

Piaget believed that such changes occur because of an innate drive to maintain equilibrium. Biologically speaking, human bodies maintain relatively constant temperature, weight, oxygen and hydration levels, and so on. This type of equilibrium is called homeostasis and is described as a dynamic balance. The input (of food, energy, and air) matches the output and keeps the status quo. If a person gets out of balance (for example, if one holds one's breath too long or has not eaten in a long time), he or she is in disequilibrium and is motivated to establish the proper balance.

Likewise, Piaget believed that the human cognitive capacity maintains a balance between a person's experience with the environment and system of thinking. If the experience only requires the application of knowledge one already possesses (such as drinking from a glass), one does not need to change significantly; one adapts with little cognitive growth because one's abilities can handle the challenge. If a person does not have the necessary skills (as when trying to eat with unfamiliar utensils or trying to comprehend a new conceptual system, such as algebra), he or she is in disequilibrium;

abilities and experiences do not balance. In order to regain balance, one must change the way one views the world.

Piaget called the ways we view the world cognitive structures. He believed that we all follow the same general pattern in the acquisition of new and advanced structures. He described the pattern of growth as a series of stages throughout life. Cognitive growth within a stage is slow. Generally, it involves the application of understood concepts to new situations (assimilation). Piaget described these types of changes as quantitative in nature. That is, the number of things an individual can do or understand using a particular concept will grow, but the concept itself does not change significantly. The change from one stage to another is qualitative. It involves new concepts and ways of viewing the world (accommodation). This period of change is relatively rapid. Once the new stage is reached, however, change will be fairly slow while the new concepts are applied to various aspects of life.

Piaget believed that this process of growth and change was attributable to both nature and nurture. The child's drive to experience the world in an active fashion and to maintain equilibrium is biological (nature), whereas the impact and changes caused by the experiences provided by the world is environmental (nurture).

Applications

Piaget described cognitive growth as progressing through four distinct stages: sensorimotor, from birth to about two years of age; preoperational, from years two to seven; concrete operational, from seven to eleven; and formal operational, from eleven through adulthood. There are transition periods between stages, and there is a fair amount of individual variability, so the age ranges are approximate.

In the sensorimotor stage, the infant's knowledge of the world is entirely dependent upon current sensory experience and activity. Infants have little knowledge except what is going on at the moment. They know that the toy they are playing with exists while they are playing with it, but they do not realize that it continues to exist at other times. The idea that objects exist even when one is not in contact them is called object permanence. Knowing about existence means that one has knowledge beyond sensation. Infants develop this slowly over their first two years of life. At first they do not look for an object that they dropped unless it is in plain sight. Around six months of age, infants will look for an object if they can see part of it. Generally, objects are "out of sight, out of mind."

Around nine or ten months, they may search even if they cannot see the object, but their search pattern is not like that of older individuals. They might look where the object was during a previous search rather than where they saw it go. For example, if a toy is hidden sequentially under three different blankets, they may look under the first blanket instead of the final location. They may also look where they found it on a previous search. They behave as if objects are where they look because they are looking rather than because that is where they were placed. It is not until between eighteen and twenty-four months of age that infants can reliably search for hidden objects even if they did not see them hidden. Finally, they have object permanence and are entering the preoperational stage.

In the sensorimotor stage, infants could not think of objects; now they can, but they are unable to think of acting on those objects. (This is essentially the definition of an operation, and this stage is preoperations.) Preoperational children are highly egocentric. Piaget defined this concept as a cognitive ability, not a description of personality. A child may want the last cookie, but this is because he or she does not understand that someone else may want it, too. Knowing that others have their own thoughts and desires is beyond their capacity. They are selfish because they do not understand, not because they do not care. Small children may answer questions by shaking their heads or pointing, even when they are on the telephone, not realizing that the person they are talking to cannot see them.

Preoperational children also believe that what they perceive is real; since it looks like the moon follows them at night, they conclude that it does. This perceptually ruled logic also causes small children to believe that a cookie broken into two pieces is more than a single, whole one, that tall, thin containers hold more than short, wide ones, and that a long clay snake contains more clay than the ball it came from.

The concept called conservation means that one knows that changes in appearances do not automatically mean changes in number, amount, volume, and so on. Preoperational children cannot conserve. Like object permanence in sensorimotor children, conservation develops slowly over the preoperational years. When a child can mentally "walk through" the actions of, for example, pouring liquid back and forth between two containers and can see that the amount has not changed, he or she is performing an operation and therefore is moving to the next stage.

The concrete operations stage takes up most of the school years. Children in this stage can think of doing things with objects, so they can plan strategies and consider consequences. The actions they are contemplating must be tied to the mental representation of an object; that is, they are unable to think of actions in the abstract. Though they may understand a procedure when the explanation uses examples, applying the same principle in new situations is often very difficult. That is why word problems in algebra are so perplexing; they require the application of abstract principles. The child may have understood the original example, but being able to use the concepts in new circumstances requires a deeper understanding of the principles themselves.

When a child can mentally separate the action from the object acted upon, he or she is developing abstract thinking. This is the first indication of formal operations, defined by the ability to understand abstract principles. One is able to think of ideas apart from objects. This stage lasts throughout adulthood. It should be added, however, that no one is "completely formal operational." That is, though people may use advanced thinking strategies in familiar areas of their lives, they may use a more unsophisticated, "concrete" strategy for problems with which they are not so experienced. Thus, a very capable and creative store manager who can utilize abstract principles when arranging merchandise, fixing prices, and managing personnel may have only primitive thoughts when faced with a leaky faucet. The solution may be limited to wrapping tape around the pipe and placing a bucket under the sink, a very "concrete" approach.

Context

Piaget's theory continues to have an immense impact on social science in general and on child development and education in particular. At the time his work was translated into English, the field of child psychology was mostly concerned with either Freudian concepts (Sigmund Freud's psychoanalytic theory) or behaviorism (mostly from B. F. Skinner and other learning theorists). Unlike the psychoanalytical methods or laboratory experiments used by proponents of those approaches, Piaget primarily used an observational strategy in collecting data. Occasionally he would ask questions or pose problems, but even then he allowed the child's behavior to guide his explorations. This approach led to many new and startling conclusions about how children think. His theories resulted from this technique of gathering data.

Theories are usually evaluated on two main criteria: How well they explain the data and whether they can be tested. Regarding the first, a theory should be able to organize the facts of a field and explain them. Piaget's methods led to many new facts, and his theory was an effort to organize and explain these "facts." Piaget never considered his theories to be anything but tentative explanations, and he continued to work and modify his theories even in his eighties. Nevertheless, his theory must be awarded "high marks" on this first criterion. While more modern research suggests that many features of Piaget's explanations are wrong, his organizational strategy continues to provide an excellent system for studying children.

Regarding the second criterion, evaluations have been more mixed. Testing a theory means exploring whether it leads to specific predictions and hypotheses on which a scientist can then conduct an experiment or observation. Many of Piaget's concepts (such as operation, conservation, and egocentrism) are very difficult to define in a way that lends itself to such testing and measurement. Still, even by this standard, his theory has been remarkably useful. It has led to more research in child development than any other theory has.

The field of education has been virtually transformed because of Piaget's theories. Understanding how children think and understand is tremendously important to education. Many educational reform efforts have depended on the Piagetian ideas that children actively construct knowledge, that they are participants in their own development, and that there is a logical sequence to children's conceptual development.

Bibliography

Donaldson, Margaret. *Children's Minds*. New York: W. W. Norton, 1978. Donaldson's main purpose is to show the practical application of child psychology to education and parenthood. This very readable book (even for those without education or psychology backgrounds) uses Piagetian concepts and gives an excellent summary of his theory in the appendix. Donaldson concludes, however, that modern evidence requires scientists to reject much of his theory.

Flavell, John. *The Developmental Psychology of Jean Piaget*. New York: D. Van Nostrand, 1963. This is the ground-breaking text that introduced Piaget to most English-speaking readers. Most of Piaget's work had not previously been available in English, and there was no single source describing it in its entirety. Because Piaget's work is so difficult to understand in any language, Flavell's presentation is all the more remarkable for its accessibility.

Ginsburg, Herbert P., and Sylvia Opper. *Piaget's Theory of Intellectual Development.* 3d ed. Englewood Cliffs, N.J.: Prentice-Hall, 1988. A text intended to introduce Piaget's theory to the undergraduate reader. Thus, while it presumes little background knowledge of psychology, it does require a relatively advanced college-level reader.

Miller, Patricia H. *Theories of Developmental Psychology.* 3d ed. New York: W. H. Freeman, 1993. This text presents most major developmental theories. Miller's excellent review of Piaget's theory includes a biographical sketch, Piaget's biological and philosophical approach, and a summary of the stages of cognitive development. Miller critically reviews the theory in the light of modern research, highlighting strengths and weaknesses. Accessible to readers with little background in psychology.

Piaget, Jean. *Adaptation and Intelligence.* Chicago: University of Chicago Press, 1980. This was one of Piaget's final publications, and in many ways it is a summation of his life's work. Piaget ties together his research in biology and psychology, showing how the two interact, and are (to him) different manifestations of the same phenomena. Advanced and difficult reading.

Piaget, Jean, and Barbel Inhelder. *The Psychology of the Child.* Translated by Helen Weaver. New York: Basic Books, 1969. A translation from the original 1966 French publication. It is Piaget's summary and synthesis of his own work and theorizing. While it was intended for professional and lay readers alike, it is rather difficult at times.

Salvador Macias III

Cross-References

Moral Development: Kohlberg, 1255; Moral Development: Piaget, 1262; Parenthood and Child-Rearing Practices, 1336; Personality: Affective, Cognitive, and Behavioral Components, 1356; Personality Development: Erikson, 1362; Personality Development: Freud, 1368; Socialization: The Family, 1880.

THE COLD WAR

Type of sociology: Major social institutions
Field of study: Politics and the state

The Cold War was a lengthy period of tension between the United States and the Soviet Union. The absence of normal relations between the great post-World War II powers generated ideological, political, and military competition that increased the danger of war, divided much of Europe and Asia into rival camps, and deeply influenced the course of world events.

Principal terms

BERLIN CRISIS: a major military and diplomatic crisis that occurred in 1961, when communist authorities unilaterally sealed the East German border; symbolized by the Berlin Wall, which isolated East Berlin

CONTAINMENT: the U.S. policy supporting opposition to communist expansion with material aid or armed force

CUBAN MISSILE CRISIS: 1962 military confrontation in which the United States forced the Soviet Union to withdraw nuclear missiles from Cuba in exchange for American tolerance of Cuban communism

DE-STALINIZATION: the removal of restrictive elements of Soviet totalitarianism; accompanied by governmental criticism of past Stalinist practices

DÉTENTE: the thaw in the Cold War accompanying the U.S. withdrawal from Vietnam; characterized by attempts to limit nuclear weapons

MARSHALL PLAN: the U.S. program to reconstruct the shattered economies of postwar European states; motivated by humanitarian and anticommunist considerations

PERESTROIKA: the restructuring of the Soviet state in order to reduce centralized administrative practices; the goal was increased flexibility, innovation, and productivity

TRUMAN DOCTRINE: 1947 U.S. policy to help states counter aggressive internal or external totalitarian movements with financial and military aid

Overview

The Cold War, which lasted from 1948 to 1991, included the perpetual threat of large-scale nuclear warfare between two dominant world powers, the United States and the Soviet Union. Other states, relatively weaker and less influential, were often forced to choose sides. This bipolar era was marked by ideological conflict and diplomatic antagonism. Its intensity varied as the participants softened or hardened particular stances, and its fluctuations were described as "thaws" and "freezes." The political, economic, and military competition it created strongly affected the latter half of the twentieth century.

The deepest roots of the Cold War lay in mutual distrust dating from 1917. American support for non-Bolshevik forces during the Russian revolutionary period convinced most communists that they were targets of a capitalist plot to encircle and destroy them. At the same time, many Americans saw the atheistic, socialist government of the Soviet Union as a direct threat to the central values of the Western world. That impression was aided by ineffective Soviet efforts to spread revolution abroad and by the harsh methods used to break internal resistance. The two powers opened diplomatic relations in 1933, but legal recognition did not remove the mutual suspicion of the previous fifteen years.

The wartime alliance against Nazi Germany temporarily reduced American-Soviet hostility. Germany attacked the Soviet Union in June, 1941, and the Red Army was in desperate shape when the United States entered the war six months later. The Americans had to provide immediate aid, for a Soviet collapse would mean German victory in Europe and possible Japanese victory in Asia. In order to gain popular support for the massive transfer of war material to Russia, American propaganda stressed the heroic nature of the Soviet resistance and obscured the dictatorial nature of Joseph Stalin's rule. While relatively more critical and demanding, the Soviets considered the United States to be partners in an antifascist crusade.

That relative unity broke down with the collapse of Nazi Germany. As long as the outcome of war had been in doubt, potential problems were ignored or minimized. In early 1945, however, when German forces retreated from France and most of Eastern Europe, differences reappeared. The February, 1945, Big Three meeting at Yalta between Stalin, British prime minister Winston Churchill, and the American president Franklin D. Roosevelt first examined the issues that would fuel the Cold War. That meeting produced general agreements based on false suppositions. First of all, the Americans thought that Germany could remain politically united while split into separate occupation zones. Second, the Soviets were promised heavy German reparations on the assumption that a unified German administration would distribute them. Third, the United States was sympathetic to Russian demands for a safety zone in the East, but thought that pro-Soviet governments in Eastern Europe could be formed by representative provisional governments holding free elections. Finally, Roosevelt won Stalin's agreement to enter the Pacific war in the mistaken belief that Russian aid was necessary for Japan's defeat.

By the next meeting in Potsdam in July, 1945, strains between the allies had already increased. While two of the members—British Prime Minister Clement Attlee and United States President Harry S Truman—had not been at Yalta and were unfamiliar with all of its details, it was generally realized that previous understandings had broken down. Since the western and eastern parts of Germany were treated differently and would probably evolve into two separate states, the reparations issue would have to be rethought. Also, the occupying Red Army had already prevented free elections in Eastern Europe. Even the Soviet Union's approaching entry into the Pacific war raised unexpected problems, for British and American scientists had successfully tested an atomic bomb. That new weapon, which practically guaranteed that the main Japanese armies would not have to be fought, introduced an extremely unstable element into international relations and changed Soviet intervention from an advantage into a needless complication.

Formal negotiations in 1946 and 1947 further sharpened those issues. The United States believed that Russian refusal to allow democratic governments in Eastern Europe was part of a general plan to export revolution. Other events seemed to fit into that pattern, including the attempts of the Communist Information Bureau (Cominform) to direct communist activities in Western Europe, Soviet backing for Greek and Chinese communists in their civil wars, Russian refusal to allow free elections in Korea, Soviet attempts to intimidate Turkey, Stalin's demand for increased reparations from West Germany, and Soviet resistance to nuclear control proposals.

The Americans responded with the Truman doctrine, which offered American aid to anticommunists threatened with internal subversion or outside pressure, and the Marshall Plan, aimed at restoring Europe's war-shattered economies and blunting the appeal of communism. Along with Great Britain, they then refused Russian demands for German reparations, increased German industrial production, and began German currency reforms.

Soviet leaders interpreted Western Germany's reconstruction as preparation for future aggression and Western opposition to Russia's control of Eastern Europe as an attempt to establish a beachhead close to the socialist heartland. In July, 1948, hoping to force either a Western withdrawal from Berlin or renewed negotiations on the German issue, they closed all rail and road links between Berlin and the West. The resulting Berlin blockade began the Cold War.

Applications

Although the Berlin blockade was broken by a massive American airlift, it sparked a series of reactions that divided Europe into two armed camps. Nuclear control discussions collapsed; by 1949 the Soviet Union had its own nuclear capability. In 1950 the United States formed a military alliance, the North Atlantic Treaty Organization (NATO), and the Soviet Union organized its equivalent, the Warsaw Pact. Eastern and Western Germany became separate states integrated into their respective alliances, and the United Nations became a forum for ideological rhetoric.

The Cold War also spread to the Far East. In 1949 the Chinese communists, led by Mao Zedong and supported by the Soviet Union, defeated the nationalist forces of Chiang Kai-shek and drove their remnants into exile in Taiwan. As a result, the United States became concerned about adjacent areas, especially Korea and Southeast Asia.

The Korean situation was fairly uncomplicated. Divided into rival states along the thirty-eighth parallel after Soviet and American troops disarmed the Japanese in 1945, Korea fit the pattern established in Germany. South Korea's nearness to American-occupied Japan made it strategically important, and its clear borders and peninsular shape made it reasonably defensible. When North Korea attacked South Korea in June,

1950, Truman promised to halt aggression, gained United Nations support for his policies, and reinforced the hard-pressed South Koreans with American troops and material. After initial setbacks, the American-led alliance broke the invading forces and counterattacked north across the thirty-eighth parallel. The invasion of North Korea provoked Chinese intervention. A limited conflict, which left both states in approximately their original positions, lasted until 1953.

The war resulted in stalemate, but the continued survival of the South Korean state appeared to justify the United States' policy of containment. The Korean conflict also allowed Truman to rebuild the United States' armed forces, which had largely been demobilized at the end of World War II. The large postwar American military dates from the Korean conflict.

Southeast Asia was a more perplexing problem for American policy makers, for the French were involved in a struggle with the native Viet Minh, led by Ho Chi Minh. Since the insurrectionists were both nationalists and communists, the Indochinese situation pitted the American principles of national self-determination and anticolonialism against those of anticommunism. From the late 1940's until the French withdrawal in 1954, the United States tried to solve its ideological dilemma by supplying the French with military and financial aid while refusing to take direct military action against the Viet Minh.

Stalin's death in 1953, the Korean armistice of that same year, and the French withdrawal from Indochina in 1954 began a period of diplomatic accommodation known as the era of peaceful coexistence. Started by Soviet premier Nikita Khrushchev, it was a serious effort to moderate Cold War tensions so that liberalizing reforms could be carried out within the Soviet sphere. Khrushchev's de-Stalinization programs, however, provoked sharp domestic disputes and led to unrest in Eastern Europe. After narrowly averting a Polish uprising and suppressing a Hungarian revolt, he abandoned compromise and returned to a rigid Cold War posture. In the late 1950's and early 1960's, Soviet-American tensions flared in the Middle East, Germany, and the Caribbean. In two cases—the Berlin Crisis in 1961 and the Cuban Missile Crisis in 1962—nuclear war appeared imminent. The fear generated by that prospect produced an accelerated arms race and, in a variant of the arms race, a contest to put men in outer space.

The increased competition also renewed the Indochinese conflict. Agreements reached in 1954 between the Viet Minh and France temporarily divided Vietnam into communist and noncommunist parts, with elections for a united government to be held in 1956. When the South Vietnamese government canceled the planned elections and showed misleading signs of political strength, the United States transformed it into another testing ground for containment. South Vietnam's political instability, however, combined with determined guerrilla warfare by communist forces made American intervention costly and politically divisive. In 1973, after years of acute domestic controversy over the role of the military in American society and the course of American foreign policy, U.S. forces withdrew from South Vietnam. In 1975, North Vietnam reunited the country.

The end of the Vietnamese conflict marked the transition from containment to détente. After the Soviet Union acquired a numerically superior nuclear stockpile in the late 1960's, the Soviet premier, Leonid Brezhnev, tried to moderate the nuclear arms race. Negotiations throughout the 1970's produced few results, for they were accompanied by traditional Cold War politics—Soviet support of leftist movements in Nicaragua, Angola, and Mozambique and the 1979 Soviet invasion of Afghanistan killed détente.

In 1980, President Ronald Reagan's administration opened an intense arms race at a technological level beyond the Soviet Union's capacity. In order to compete with the more dynamic West, the Soviet general secretary, Mikhail Gorbachev, called for a fundamental restructuring ("perestroika") of the Soviet state and economy. He condemned Stalinist administrative practices and relaxed social control mechanisms to spark greater creativity, innovation, and flexibility. Restructuring led to the collapse of the Soviet bloc in 1989 and 1990 and to the dissolution of the Soviet Union in 1991. When the Soviet Union fell apart, the Cold War came to an end.

Context

The Cold War was almost as global in scope and divisive in nature as the conflict that produced it; mistrustful Americans and Soviets faced each other in so many parts of the world that relatively localized events often had magnified consequences. Continued bipolarity also complicated the situation, for the attempts of weaker countries to follow nonaligned policies had little practical effect. Without the moderating influence of other powerful states, disagreements between the United States and the Soviet Union easily led to threats or hostile action. This gave the Cold War a diplomatic bluntness and ideological rigidity seldom found in peacetime. Narrowly averted superpower confrontations over the building of the Berlin Wall in 1961 and over the Arab-Israeli War of 1973 showed that regional events could quickly turn into international crises even during periods of relative tranquillity.

The financial costs were also high, for both the United States and the Soviet Union shifted badly needed funds from domestic areas in order to compete on a worldwide basis. Because of its weaker economy, the Soviet Union paid a higher relative price for its ventures into Cold War diplomacy and the arms race. As early as 1960, however, many Americans were worried about domestic imbalances, increasing foreign commitments, and the long-range effects of a growing military-industrial complex on public policy. By the 1970's, it was clear to both sides that the relentless and seemingly endless technological competition of the Cold War also carried high psychological and environmental costs. Multiplying nuclear arsenals decreased national security, and the waste products of high technology were not easily biodegradable.

Strategically placed states benefited financially from superpower rivalry; for example, the defeated Axis Powers received so much American aid after 1945 that their restored economies surpassed those of Great Britain and France. Egypt explored Cold War options in another way; alternating between the American and Soviet camps since the 1950's, it received significant financial and material support from both sides. Also, the massive military expenditures and diplomatic commitments of the United States and the Soviet Union reduced the need for allied governments to maintain expensive armed forces.

The Cold War left deep marks on the domestic politics of all participating countries. It allowed Stalin to crush reformist tendencies in Russia at the end of World War II and to open a new era of state terror that claimed millions of victims. It also perpetuated inefficient authoritarian practices in Soviet-controlled areas until the mid-1980's. In the United States, Cold War fluctuations prompted occasional outbursts of extreme anticommunism, such as Senator Joseph McCarthy's antisubversive campaign. Waged from 1950 to 1954, McCarthy's strident anticommunist crusade diminished the quality of public discourse and unfairly harmed the careers and reputations of several hundred people in academics, government, and entertainment.

Throughout its existence, the Cold War exercised a powerful influence on American politics. In some cases, it undermined attempts at domestic social reform; President Truman's Square Deal and President Lyndon Johnson's War on Poverty lost momentum because of the expense and controversy surrounding the Korean and Vietnamese conflicts, respectively.

Bibliography

Breslauer, George W., Harry Kresiler, and Benjamin Ward, eds. *Beyond the Cold War: Conflict and Cooperation in the Third World*. Berkeley: University of California Press, 1991. Includes strong articles examining Russian-American relations, from Southeast Asia to Central America. Particularly interesting on factors affecting American-Russian cooperation in the Middle East.

Clark, Michael T., and Simon Serfaty, eds. *New Thinking and Old Realities: America, Europe, and Russia*. Washington: Seven Locks Press, 1991. A good collection of essays dealing with problems raised by the end of bipolarity. Especially interesting essays on future German policy choices and the post-Cold War Third World. Contains an index.

Freedman, Lawrence, ed. *Europe Transformed: Documents on the End of the Cold War*. New York: St. Martin's Press, 1990. An excellent collection of documents covering the development of the Cold War from the end of 1945. Contains treaties, diplomatic proposals, and speeches. Most of the material dates from 1985 to 1990.

Gorbachev, Mikhail. *Perestroika and Soviet-American Relations*. Madison, Conn.: Sphinx Press, 1990. A revealing collection of Gorbachev's speeches between 1987 and 1989; provides his point of view on the end of the Cold War and his explanation for the necessity of perestroika.

Hyland, William G. *The Cold War: Fifty Years of Conflict*. Rev. ed. New York: Times Books, 1991. A good, traditional treatment of the Cold War and Russian-American relations through the Persian Gulf crisis. Written by a former Central Intelligence Agency (CIA) official and foreign policy expert. Contains a general bibliography and an index.

LaFeber, Walter. *America, Russia, and the Cold War, 1945-1984*. 5th ed. New York:

Alfred A. Knopf, 1985. A good survey of major Cold War events up to the beginning of perestroika by an excellent historian. Index, bibliography, and maps.

Larson, Deborah W. *Origins of Containment: A Psychological Explanation*. Princeton, N.J.: Princeton University Press, 1985. A fascinating interdisciplinary study of the beginnings of the Cold War. Larson applies cognitive social psychology concepts to trace attitude changes. A revisionist, multilevel approach; includes an index and bibliography.

Lynch, Allen. *The Cold War Is Over—Again*. Boulder, Colo.: Westview Press, 1992. Lynch argues that the Cold War was actually over in the late 1960's and early 1970's, when the postwar European settlement was accepted by all sides. Bibliography, index, and selected documents.

Michael J. Fontenot

Cross-References

COLLECTIVE BEHAVIOR

Type of sociology: Collective behavior and social movements

Studies of collective behavior are dedicated to explaining the presence of emerging structures in any social system, including society. Scholars of collective behavior study many subjects, including gossip, rumors and urban legends, physical and technological disasters, panic, mass hysteria, and crowd behavior.

Principal terms

COLLECTIVE BEHAVIOR: coordinated behavior between two or more persons that emerges from traditional culture

CROWD: a large temporary gathering of people in a face-to-face situation

DISASTERS: physical events that have an impact on a community, causing considerable social disruption

EMERGING BEHAVIOR: coordinated behavior between two or more persons that is new, untried, and responsive to stimuli external to the group

GOSSIP: hearsay and unverifiable statements about people with whom one is closely tied in a small group

MASS HYSTERIA: temporary delusional beliefs held by a large and scattered population of persons

PANIC: uncontrolled flight based on intense personal fear and emotional shock

RUMORS: hearsay and unverifiable statements about persons or events in society

TRADITIONAL CULTURE: established and understood social patterns that are the sources for collective behavior

URBAN LEGENDS: narrative stories that are hearsay and unverifiable that deal with contemporary urban life

Overview

Collective behavior deals with the description and explanation of emerging social structures in society. Until recent years, collective behavior scholars have also included in their studies the analyses of social movements. The study of social movements, however, has moved away from collective behavior research on emerging structures by taking an organizational approach to the subject.

Scholars of collective behavior have investigated three categories of emerging behavior. First are those activities that involve primarily talk that is hearsay and unverifiable about events or persons. This includes mass hysteria, gossip, rumors, and urban legends. Mass hysteria involves talk about events between people who are not in face-to-face contact. For example, the widespread sightings of unidentified flying objects (UFOs) are examples of mass hysteria.

Gossip occurs among intimates—people who know one another well. Rumors and urban legends differ in their complexity. Rumors are simply statements about persons or events that are passed from one person to the next in face-to-face situations; they generally do not involve people that one knows well. In contrast, urban legends are hearsay and unverifiable stories that have a narrative structure about urban life that is repeated in the same way each time the legend is told. In that they capture the essence of urban life, there is an element of truth to these legends. For example, sightings of Elvis Presley are examples of rumors, whereas reports of alligators in the sewers illustrate urban legends. The latter illustrate anxieties and fears people have of city life.

The second topic studied by collective behavior scholars is associated with panic or the sudden impact of physical disasters such as hurricanes, earthquakes, and tornadoes that involve immediate individual and organizational response. Most of the important research on social responses to disaster in the United States has been conducted by the Disaster Research Center, formerly at the Ohio State University and now at the University of Delaware. The two cofounders of the center, Enrico Quarantelli and Russell Dynes, have made significant contributions to the literature on the social impact of disasters. Quarantelli, in a series of studies, has found that there is little panic in disaster. Dynes, while researching the impact of disasters on communities, found that four types of organizations emerged to deal with the disaster. They range from organizations that change very little to those that change considerably because of emergent responses to the disaster. The first type of organization is called "established" and changes very little as a result of the disaster. For example, police and fire departments are established organizations that carry out normal emergency tasks. The second type is "expanding"; it carries out normal functions but is often called on to do emergency activities. It can perform these with little difficulty. Gas and electric utility companies are examples of expanding organizations. The third type is "extending." These are organizations that normally do not do emergency tasks because they are unfamiliar with them. They do, however, have the resources for emergency response. Local construction companies are examples of extending organizations. Finally, there are "emerging" organizations that do unfamiliar emergency tasks. An example of this type of group would be local neighborhood rescue and cleanup crews. Researchers have also examined the impact of technological disaster such as explosions in the chemical industry.

The third area of inquiry is research on crowd behavior. The central concern of most collective behavior research, both theoretically and empirically, is crowd behavior. Crowd researchers have studied a variety of subjects, including the behavior of people in ethnic, racial, and protest crowds as well as behavior at sports and music events. In addition, the long-term consequences of police violence on crowd members have been the subject of scholarly inquiry.

Applications

The core of inquiry into crowds has been directed toward emerging structures. The term "emerging structures" refers to the notion that people in groups respond in new ways to situations for which they are unprepared. These new ways become, for a short time, guidelines for behavior that results in new social forms. These emerging forms have a complex social structure and culture. Crowd behavior is a prime example of these new social structures.

In the late 1800's Gustave Le Bon, a French journalist, looked at rioters in Paris and concluded that crowds are crazy and have a "law of mental unity." Practitioners and researchers dealing with gatherings have had to reevaluate and challenge this conclusion. They have done this by looking at a crowd's complex social structure and culture. One area that has been closely examined is the roles of people in a crowd. Crowds are organized into various roles, and different behavior is associated with each role. In addition, these roles are spatially distributed. For the sociologist, a role is a set of expected behaviors carried out in a given context. A norm is a general set of guidelines that a person follows when dealing with others in their roles. For example, a police officer plays a role and follows certain norms as he or she gives instructions to automobile drivers at an intersection in a large city.

The basic structure of most crowds can be divided into three roles: the active core, the cheerleaders, and the observers. The core does different things than do the cheerleaders or the observers. The core carries out the action of the crowd; it is the crowd protagonist. The cheerleaders act in verbal support of the active core. They applaud and support the core's actions. Finally, any crowd has a set of observers who follow the actions of the active core and the cheerleaders but do not take part in core or cheerleader activities.

Crowds can come about any time and any place. They may emerge on the street, for example, created by such events as an automobile accident or a street entertainer's act. They also form in looting or celebrating situations. One can see these crowd structures when watching protesting crowds in which looting is also occurring or observing crowds in which fans are celebrating their team's championship victory.

The active core is closest to the focal point. The cheerleaders are nearby with the observers, watching the event happen and creating the arena in which it is carried out. For example, extensive rioting took place in South Los Angeles in 1992 after white police officers were acquitted of all charges in the beating of a black motorist named Rodney King. The beating had been videotaped and was widely shown on television. After the acquittal, rioting broke out and many deaths occurred. Looting of stores was widespread in the riot area. In a riot situation in which looting takes place, the active core takes commodities from stores. Cheerleaders are close to stores but not as close as the active core. Their focus is on the actions of the looters. They verbally ratify the actions of the core. Lastly, the observers simply watch the proceedings and show their approval by staying or disapproval by leaving. All this happened during the 1992 riots in Los Angeles.

At celebrating riots after championship sporting events, the active core celebrates their team's victory by vandalizing stores, signs, and other items in public areas of large cities. The cheerleaders follow the core's action closely and support the active core with cheers and chants. The observers support the core and the cheerleaders by watching and creating an arena for the activities of the core.

The notion that crowds have a role structure and culture allows one to challenge two myths about crowds. The first myth is that crowds are crazy and irrational. There is no doubt that crowds commit antisocial acts. One need look no further than the 1985 Heysel stadium soccer riot in Belgium (in which thirty-nine people died) to confirm this truth. This does not prove, however, that crowds are crazy or out of touch with reality. Most people in crowds can recall what happened and why it happened although they may not have liked what happened. Assuming that crowds are crazy leads one to the conclusion that studying a crowd is impossible because the behavior is random and unpredictable and therefore not amenable to scientific investigation. Collective behavior scholars reject this position. When it is assumed that crowds have social structures with their own cultures, then it follows that they can be studied scientifically.

The second myth is that crowds are highly suggestible. This myth derives from the "crowds are irrational" perspective, and it is widely held by the press. If crowds were as suggestible as newspapers often say they are, then crowd management would be very easy. All police would have to do is "suggest" that the crowd leave, go home, or go have a drink and unwind at the local bar. The police's problems would be solved for the day. If crowds have social structures with cultures, however, then one would not expect them to be highly suggestible. Any proposal would likely be dealt with by discussion with friends or peers. Any proposal or suggestion would be filtered through the person's relationships to others in the crowd. In other words, crowds should be seen as information processing entities rather than as emotional relay systems.

Context

Collective behavior, and particularly its approach to crowds, is a uniquely American specialty of sociology. While there have been a few European influences, notably the work of Le Bon, empirical work has come from American sociologists and has focused on problems related to the United States.

There are two theoretical approaches to crowds widely found in the scientific literature and usually presented in introductory sociology texts. The structural-functional position, with its stress on equilibrium and norms, is represented in collective behavior theory by the work of Neil J. Smelser in the early 1960's. Smelser was a student of and a collaborator with sociologist Talcott Parsons. The other theory comes from the interactionist tradition that stresses the analysis of face-to-face behavior. This theory was presented in the work of Ralph Turner and Lewis Killian (1987). The ideas of Clark McPhail (1991) build on Turner and Killian. Each theory can be illustrated with rock concert crowds.

Smelser's model is presented in his book *Theory of Collective Behavior* (1963). It is divided into six determinants, each with a set of subdeterminants. The determinants are structural conduciveness, structural strain, growth of a generalized belief, precipitating event, mobilization for action, and social control.

Structural conduciveness refers to conditions of social structure that describe social possibilities for an incident of collective behavior to happen. Structural conduciveness sets the parameters and constraints for the other components of the model, particularly structural strain. The conduciveness for rock concert violence is found in the bringing together in a small space excited people determined to have a good time in an emotionally charged environment.

Structural strain occurs within the parameters of conduciveness. The sociological researcher looks for strain in terms of uncertainty. At rock concerts the uncertainness is generally associated with the ability to reach a location in the auditorium or area that provides most enjoyment for the concert. For many rock concert fans, this is near the rock stars at the front of the hall. Smelser's model instructs the researcher to look for beliefs that guide action. Beliefs are rooted in uncertainty. Regarding rock concerts, these beliefs become shared in terms of uncertainty about access to desirable locations in the concert hall.

Regarding mobilization for action, the Smelser model encourages the investigator to look at the initial and derived phases of a crowd action. Most incidents of collective behavior change during the flow of events. Rock concerts are no exception. The Smelser model refers to this as the process of moving from the initial and derived phases. In looking at social control, the model directs one to investigate several dimensions that shape a rock concert and keep it from getting out of control. The investigator looks at issues of formal control from traditional sources, such as the police and ushers, as well as informal social control such as the rock artists themselves or the peer group.

Clark McPhail, in his book *The Myth of the Madding Crowd* (1991), has developed seven basic categories of crowd behavior including collective orientation, vocalization, verbalization, gesticulation, vertical locomotion, horizontal locomotion, and manipulation. Collective orientation usually describes where people are looking. One type of collective orientation is arcing/ringing, which refers to the process whereby small groups of people create an arc or a ring around a focal point. The arcing/ringing process at a rock concert occurs near the stage as young people attempt to get closer to the musicians. Collective vocalization is the process in which two or more persons engage in common vocal sounds. Booing and cheering are two subcategories.

Collective verbalization describes two or more people engaging in coordinated speech including singing; at rock concerts, audiences often sing along with the artists as they perform. Collective gesticulation occurs when two or more persons coordinate their physical gestures. This is often done with collective vocalization and verbalization. The categories of behavior that one often sees at rock concerts are praise or victory gestures. Fans raise their arms in these gestures while swaying back and forth to the music. This is often combined with chanting and singing.

Collective vertical locomotion refers to coordinated vertical behavior involving two or more crowd members. One type is jumping. Rock concerts begin with fans sitting. Once the music begins, fans seldom remain seated, moving into standing and jumping patterns, often combined with collective gesticulation, vocalization, and verbalization. Collective horizontal locomotion takes place when two or more people coordinate their movements in space. One example found at rock concerts is surging, which can be horizontal (side to side) or vertical (back to front). It is one major source of danger at rock concerts. Collective manipulation refers to the process of two or more people coordinating their hand activities, including synchronized clapping at rock concerts. It is coordinated with the music and dance of the performers.

Bibliography

Le Bon, Gustave. *The Crowd*. New York: Viking Press, 1960. The first study of crowd behavior, first published in French in 1895. While many sociologists disagree with Le Bon's conclusions, it is an important book because of its core idea that crowds can be studied systematically. Le Bon's "law of mental unity" remains a popular notion in the general press.

Lewis, Jerry M. "A Value-Added Analysis of the Heysel Stadium Soccer Riot." *Current Psychology: Research and Reviews* 8 (Spring, 1989): 15-29. The most detailed use of the Smelser model in the sports riot literature. It is a study of the Heysel stadium soccer riot in Brussels, Belgium, in 1985 that caused the death of thirty-nine fans and the injury of four hundred more.

McPhail, Clark. *The Myth of the Madding Crowd*. New York: Aldine de Gruyter, 1991. This is the definitive presentation on categories of gathering behavior. McPhail reviews all previous theories of crowd behavior except Smelser's, showing each model's weaknesses. He argues that students of crowds must carefully describe the behavior of crowd members before efforts are undertaken to explain it. He proposes his categories as a way to classify the actions of crowd members.

Miller, David L. *Introduction to Collective Behavior*. Belmont, Calif.: Wadsworth, 1985. Miller presents Russell Dynes's typology of established, expanding, extending, and emerging organizations, developed by field researchers to classify organizational responses to disasters. It is based on the type of task carried by organization in the wake of a natural or technological disaster.

Smelser, Neil J. *Theory of Collective Behavior*. New York: Free Press, 1963. Presents the Smelser model in detail. It shows its roots in structural-functionalist social theory of Talcott Parsons. The data that are used to illustrate Smelser's ideas are taken from secondary sources.

Turner, Ralph, and Lewis Killian. *Collective Behavior*. 3d ed. Englewood Cliffs, N.J.: Prentice-Hall, 1987. This is the most influential textbook in collective behavior. It bases its theory of the crowd on symbolic interactionism of George Herbert Mead and Herbert Blumer.

Jerry M. Lewis

Cross-References

Crowds and Crowd Dynamics, 393; Deprivation Theory of Social Movements, 512; Fads, Fashions, and Crazes, 733; Mass Hysteria, 1134; Mass Psychogenic Illness, 1141; Mobs, Riots, and Panics, 1226; Rumors and Urban Legends, 1667; Social Movements, 1826; The Structural-Strain Theory of Social Movements, 1997.

COMMUNAL SOCIETIES

Type of sociology: Social stratification
Field of study: Types of societies

Primitive communal societies continue to exist in spite of the onslaught of developed Western technology. By studying these societies, social scientists may learn much about human interactions.

Principal terms

COMMUNAL: shared by the members of a community; both responsibilities such as labor and resources such as food or property can be communal

EGALITARIANISM: human equality in social, political, and economic circumstances

MOIETY: an intermarrying kin group

POLYGYNY: a type of marriage in which a man has more than one wife

PRIMITIVE: in this context, societies that are not industrialized

SOCIETY: an organized group of people living and working together, interacting in the pursuit of common goals

Overview

Sociologists and anthropologists have extensively studied and categorized various types of societies. Among them are societies that are often termed simple, primitive, or preindustrial; these include hunting and gathering, agrarian, and pastoral societies. Some of these societies, most notably hunting and gathering societies, may be considered communal in that work and resources are pooled and shared to a significant degree by all members of the community. These societies may be contrasted with modern industralized societies, which are generally larger, have formal social controls (including governments), and have complex systems of stratification.

Traditional communal societies are also distinct from the types of communes or communal societies that sometimes appear as subcultures or countercultures within a larger complex society. To differentiate between these two types of communal societies, traditional communal societies are often called primitive communal societies. The use of "primitive" as a term to describe a society or group is somewhat controversial; it has been argued that the term carries negative connotations, implying that the society is inferior to an "advanced" society. Nevertheless, the term has been used widely to denote a nonindustrial society, and that is how it is intended in this discussion.

Characteristics of a primitive communal society are social equality, including equal or almost equal access to resources; a nebulous government; kin-centered groups; primarily monogamous marriage with occasional polygyny; and the definition of most work tasks by gender. Most primitive communal societies are hunting and gathering societies. Fishing or small agricultural groups may also contain some aspects of communalism.

A distinctive feature of primitive communal societies is social equality. While not all members of the group play the same role, access to life-sustaining resources is available to every member. The position of headman (or headwoman) does not confer any special rank, power, or wealth. The leader takes part in food collection, tool making, and dwelling construction, as do all adult members of the group. The duties of the leader may consist of advising the band where to move to find resources, suggesting discipline for a recalcitrant individual, or consenting to the admission of an individual into the band. Even if leadership is centered on the men of the band, women usually have equal influence and voice in community matters.

Access to resources is extremely important. Whether this access is for the individuals within a community or is for other communities depends upon the situation. A community is usually associated with a specific territory. The basic life-sustaining materials are communal property, although a band may "control" or "own" certain areas. In times of crisis, this access may be less restricted, and when resources are not being used by the "owning" group, they may be used by others. In a communal society, cooperative food access mitigates against temporary incapacity, adversity, or old age. This cooperation increases the chances of the survival of the individual.

Most primitive communal societies are composed of about thirteen to fifty people. This size of society is called a "band," and the need for government is minimal. The eldest person may be looked to for overall leadership. This person may also be the parent or grandparent of many members of the group. A society in which each person is intimately acquainted with every other person encourages proper social behavior. Each deed is a community occurrence. Discipline may be administered by any member of the group, who is likely to be kin to the offending party. Conformity to group norms is rewarded.

The nuclear family (parents and offspring) is a common element of societies throughout the world. The extended family is composed of several nuclear families of a common lineage. Tribal band society favors formation around kin groups, and most communal tribal societies are based on the extended family, whether of patriarchal or matriarchal lineage. This necessitates marriage outside the clan, since often all children in the group are close cousins. Marriage relationships define to whom one owes loyalty and obligations. One of the results of living in a kin-based group is that the group as a whole may bear responsibility for rearing the younger generation, rather than this task being left solely to the biological parents of the offspring. This situation reinforces the socialization of children into the group because of the number of people interested in the outcome of the child-rearing.

Marriage in these societies is primarily monogamous, with some polygyny also occuring. Polygynous marriage may indicate higher status for a man, but access to resources remains the same for all. Marriage, both monogamous and polygynous, is usually exogamous (into a group outside one's own society or kin). Polygynous marriage may be a result of a lack of males (because of such events as warfare), a long postpartum sex taboo, or delayed marriage for males. Whether groups favor monogamy or polygyny, marriage acts as a binding tie to communities outside one's own area, thereby conferring the right to exploit the resources of the group into which one marries.

One might think that in communal societies work tasks may be accomplished by anyone who wishes to do them, but this is not so. Work tasks tend to be defined by gender: Men usually fish and hunt (and make the tools for these activities), while women usually forage for vegetables and small game (and make the baskets and tools for cooking and storage of the same). There are many variations on this model. Men who are too old to hunt may make the projectile points which will kill the animal; old women may do the basket weaving. Their contribution to the group entitles them to the result of the harvest or hunt. Sometimes men will make baskets or pottery, and frequently they will gather vegetal foods. Women may fish, and they often gather shellfish. Habitation construction varies: In some societies it is in the domain of males, but in others it is in the domain of females.

There is much variation among primitive communal societies. The most important aspects of these groups are that they are basically egalitarian and that every member of society has essentially the same access to resources for survival.

Applications

A number of primitive communal societies still exist in the world. They are located in Australia, the South Pacific, South America, and Africa. Additionally, partially communal societies are found in Asia and elsewhere in the Americas.

At the core of the communal society is social equality. Decisions are made by consensus; disputes are settled by the group. Almost all achieved statuses are equally accessible in the group. The BaMbuti of Zaire, Africa, are considered to be one of the most egalitarian societies in the world. They exist without chiefs and understand that cooperation is necessary for survival. If cooperation is not forthcoming from a member of the group, the entire group assists the individual in mending his or her ways by heaping shame upon the person. If this is not successful, the offending member may be threatened with exile from the group, which would deny the individual access to the resources in the area of his band. This threat is usually strong enough to bring about the desired cooperation.

Anthropologist Marvin Harris describes access to resources among the !Kung San of Africa. He states that the water holes and hunting and gathering territories are owned by particular bands. With intermarriage among the bands quite frequent, however, sharing of the resources is common because of visiting between bands. Permission to hunt, gather, or drink is seldom denied to outsiders. Regarding personal property, Harris points out that in a primitive communal society a person's effects are limited because of the mobile lifestyle. Even so, a person's own property is considered his or her own, although property is customarily shared if one is asked. In an environment such as that in which the !Kung live, there is easy access to materials necessary to make the tools, nets, containers, ornaments, and clothing that a person needs.

In such egalitarian societies, there is little need for strong formal leadership. Leadership is accessible by any member of the society, although a male is usually

found in a headman position. Among the Dobe !Kung, both men and women participate in the decision making of the group. A serious dispute within a group may be
resolved by the group splitting up and going different ways. Any leader who emerges
does so because of his or personal qualities of wisdom; a leader possesses no formal
authority to enforce his or her own will. In such a setting, people are considered
responsible for themselves and their neighbors, who are usually kin.

Kinship is at the core of much of human behavior. Among the Rapa of French
Polynesia, a child's father and all the male relatives of his generation are called *metua
tane*. The mother and her female relatives are all called by the term *metua vahine*. This
may be compared with the United States, where one's female parent is called "mother"
but her sister is called "aunt," her brother's wife is called "aunt," her father's sisters
are called "aunt," and her father's brother's wife is called "aunt." An older female
cousin may also be called "aunt," as may "honorary" kin (those related not by birth
but by respect). The above example has the potential for at least seven separate kinship
terms. Among the Dani, kinship terms are divided somewhat by generation, gender,
and moiety, producing an increased number of kinship terms. Because of access to
resources, kinship is very important among primitive communal societies.

Marriage patterns are one manifestation of the kin-centered group. There is considerable variation in marriage patterns among primitive communal societies, much of
which results from the part that marriage plays in each society. Marriage tends to be
seen more as an alliance between groups than as a union of two people in love. Among
the !Kung San of Africa, there are no rigid postmarital rules. The family may choose
to live with either the parents of the bride or groom or to split its time between the
families. Usually the couple and their children have access to the territories of both
groups. In Australia, the Aborigines have a complicated network of kinship ties.
Through these, the men are also united politically. At their birth, female children may
be married to older men, who are then bound to their in-law family for economic and
political favors.

The division of labor among primitive communal societies has more to do with the
practicalities of human reproduction than with human capability. Since it is the female
who carries, bears, and feeds the infant, it is easier for her to do the daily gathering of
foods in a secured territory. This type of work is more compatible to a lifestyle in which
she is tied to an infant to whom she must provide food on demand. On the other hand,
males are not so encumbered by an infant or toddler, who might also cry out at an
inappropriate moment and frighten game away. As far as the worth of each job is
concerned, studies indicate that gathered food (vegetal material, small game, shellfish,
and so on) provides the bulk of the daily food for such societies, while hunting provides
the occasional "treat." This balance helps to account for the degree of social equality
in the primitive communal society.

Context

Primitive communal societies have been studied by anthropologists and sociologists
since the Enlightenment of the eighteenth century. Philosophers were concerned with

the development of human society and believed that the primitive society was the beginning step on the ladder of civilization—represented in its culmination by Europe. Primitive societies encountered by the Europeans were studied in order to explain the nature of human society. It was believed that all societies went through a period of communalism prior to their development into socialism or capitalism. This idea continued through the period of European colonialism, at its peak in the 1700's and 1800's. The popularity of Charles Darwin's theory of evolution and its subsequent application to human groups (Social Darwinism) in the late nineteenth century caused societies viewed as "primitive" to be seen even more strongly by Europeans and North Americans as existing on the bottom rung of the social evolutionary ladder.

The mid-1900's saw these societies being viewed as artifacts of past lifeways. They were studied as "frozen-in-time" examples of humankind's evolutionary development. Many societies were invaded by sociologists, ethnographers, and anthropologists who wished to record their ways of life in order to capture these examples of early hominid behavior before they disappeared. At first unrealized or ignored was the fact that the Aborigines of Australia, the bushmen of Africa, and others had already been pushed from some or all of their original territories; they were living in marginal areas and had adapted accordingly. The lifestyles existing in modern times are not those of the past when the primitive societies ranged over territory now occupied or farmed by the European colonials. The study of primitive communal societies has developed to include such marginalized groups as distinctive social categories, valid systems of living within their own sphere. With this recognition comes respect for these groups as valid and adaptive social groups.

The encroachment of the industrialized world into the territories of communal societies has affected those groups profoundly. Some have been completely destroyed, and others have been restricted to limited territories that cannot sustain the groups effectively. Contact with Western societies has caused changes in diet, health, and technology that have changed most remaining simple societies irrevocably. Environmental damage such as pollution has affected their lifeways as well. The Amazon River, for example, is being mined for gold, and the chemical products used in the process are simply dumped back into the waters of the Amazon, poisoning the local Indians and driving them from their traditional territories along the river. There is no easy answer to this dilemma. In some cases industrialized countries are, if belatedly, taking measures to protect communal societies, but there is great doubt whether such attempts will succeed in the long run.

Bibliography

Foster, George M. *Traditional Cultures and the Impact of Technological Change*. New York: Harper, 1962. An interesting early study of the effects of industrial society on other cultures. Foster draws on a wealth of experience from professionals in the fields of public health, nursing, community development, education, and engineering. Although the book deals with more than primitive communal societies, it presents many applicable ideas concerning the effects that industrialization has on developing and primitive communities.

Fox, Robin. *Kinship and Marriage: An Anthropological Perspective*. Cambridge, England: Cambridge University Press, 1967. A classic study of kinship among cultures of the world, described by the author as a good "neutral" introduction. This book contains a clear account of a variety of kinship systems. Readable by the scholar and the layperson alike. Reissued in 1983.

Harris, Marvin. *Culture, People, Nature*. 4th ed. New York: Harper & Row, 1985. An anthropology text, Harris' book contains a good selection of material about primitive communal societies. (Such information may be found in many general anthropology texts.)

Hawkes, Kristin, Kim Hill, and James F. O'Connell. "Why Hunters Gather: Optimal Foraging and the Aché of Eastern Paraguay." *American Ethnologist* 9 (May, 1982: 379-398). An interesting look at variations in hunting/gathering among primitive societies. Discusses food preferences and the cost of hunting versus gathering, providing new ideas as to why certain foods are preferred, why gathering or hunting may predominate, and so on.

Heider, Karl. *Grand Valley Dani*. New York: Holt, Rinehart and Winston, 1979. One of a series of case studies in anthropology, all of which have valuable information on their respective societies. These case studies are invaluable as a source of information on cultures which have been undergoing rapid change. Heider's book is a standard work on the Grand Valley Dani of New Guinea.

Hunter, David E., and Phillip Whitten. *A Study of Anthropology*. New York: Harper & Row, 1976. A very good text on anthropology in general, with excellent brief examples of cultures around the world, including primitive communal groups. A good text for a comparative study of cultures.

Radcliffe-Brown, A. R. *Structure and Function in Primitive Society*. New York: Free Press, 1965. Radcliffe-Brown has been a key influence in social anthropology since at least the 1940's. This book is a collection of his lectures dealing with his theory of social structure. Gives the background of the development of the study of primitive social systems.

Susan Ellis-Lopez

Cross-References

COMPARABLE WORTH AND SEX SEGREGATION IN THE WORKPLACE

Type of sociology: Sex and gender
Fields of study: Dimensions of inequality; Theories of prejudice and discrimination

The principle of comparable worth holds that women and men should be paid on the same scale not only for doing equal jobs but also for doing different jobs of equal skill, effort, and responsibility. The principle of comparable worth is used to rectify sex segregation in the workplace, where women have to take female-dominated jobs that pay consistently less than male-dominated jobs do.

Principal terms

COMMUTATIVE JUSTICE: that which is fair and proper in exchange transactions between individuals, groups, or organizations; commutative justice exists between equals

DISCRIMINATION: the denial of rights and opportunities to a group—in this case, women

JOB EVALUATION: measuring and comparing the features of a job for which a worker ought to be compensated

PAY EQUITY: equal pay for equal work

SEX SEGREGATION: the separation of jobs on the basis of sex; sex segregation devalues women's work by paying them lower wages

Overview

In the workplace, women and other minorities earn less than do white males who have comparable jobs. Over the years, most minorities' earnings have been increasing compared to what they were previously, but the remedies for the problem of wage differences between men and women have not been as effective. Advocates of women's rights have chosen another means to remedy this form of discrimination: the principle of comparable worth. According to this principle, jobs that are not similar can be compared with respect to certain features, and jobs that have the same features should have the same wage levels. For example, the job of a secretary is much different from the job of a painter, but if it can be shown that both jobs require a similar degree of skill and effort, then secretaries and painters should be paid at the same rate.

Advocates of comparable worth argue that wages should be determined by the job content. This content is usually determined by job evaluation, which measures and compares the features of a job for which a worker should be compensated. Skill, work, effort, responsibility, and working conditions are the features that are considered in job evaluation. Based on these features, each job is assigned a certain number of points and then jobs are ranked according to number. Compensation is determined according to these rankings; jobs with the same number of points are paid the same, jobs with more points are paid at higher rates, and jobs with fewer points are paid at lower rates.

Since 1920, job evaluation has been used by companies to measure the content of jobs, providing rational means for setting wages. Laws of supply and demand determine the overall level of wages for different kinds of work, but laws of supply and demand alone are not sufficient to make fine distinctions among different jobs in a large organization. Job evaluation is a very helpful tool for managers to use in determining wages, particularly for unionized employees.

Advocates of the principle of comparable worth contend that the wages that are actually paid to some workers are not the same as what would be paid if there were no discrimination. Since skill and effort are the features that enable workers to command a certain price for their labor in a free market, a comparison of jobs according to job content provides a way of determining whether discrimination exists and what wages would be without the discrimination. Comparable worth is a method for detecting discrimination in the labor market and rectifying it. Every worker has the right not to be paid lower wages simply because of membership in a certain sex, race, or ethnic group.

Two reasons behind the concern with the average wage levels of occupations and jobs are extreme job segregation by sex and the disparity in pay between men and women. Among workers who are employed full-time year-round, women on average earn about 72 percent of what men earn, and this gap is not shrinking the extent that it should. Full-time working women receive 65 to 70 percent as much as full-time working men. In 1982, the female-male earnings ratios for full-time year-round workers with a high school degree, four-year college degree, and five or more years of college were 62.6 percent, 62.2 percent, and 66.3 percent, respectively. Furthermore, sex segregation of jobs also exists. Many jobs are classified as "male" or "female." Different social science studies document that there is a correlation between average occupational wage levels and the extent of female representation in the occupation. Jobs that are done mostly by women have lower average wages. It is this connection between "femaleness" and lower wage levels that is challenged by the principle of comparable worth.

There are four different issues that must be considered with regard to this debate over comparable worth. The first is whether the difference in earnings between men and women is the result of discrimination or the result of the impersonal workings of the labor market. It can be argued that one reason why men earn more than women do is that they work more hours. Therefore, one needs to distinguish between income and wages. One of the most important factors in explaining why women earn lower wages than men is segregation of jobs according to sex. In the traditionally female occupations, there are more women, and since large numbers of women compete for different jobs, that also leads to lower wages. Opinion is sharply divided on whether women are forced into traditionally female occupations because those are the only jobs available to them or whether women freely choose these jobs because they prefer certain kinds of jobs. There are many other factors that are important. For example, different industries, age distribution in the work force, unionization, regional differences, and many other variables have to be studied to explain the wage gap between men and women.

Second, it must be determined whether it is possible to measure job content in such a way that the resulting comparisons are meaningful and reliable. Opponents of comparable worth argue that job evaluations are not objective and therefore are discriminatory. Supporters of comparable worth, however, argue that job evaluation is objective because each job has an inherent value for which it deserves a certain pay. For example, there is a similarity between a truck driver's job and a nurse's job, because in the first case there is a major responsibility involved in driving a truck, and in the second case there is a major responsibility involved in taking care of patients. It is also true, however, that there are differences between these two jobs.

Third, ignoring market forces in setting wages may undermine the ability of the market to price and allocate labor in an efficient manner, resulting in lower productivity. There are positive effects of market forces; for example, incentives are provided for workers to leave crowded areas with low-productivity jobs for which there is a declining demand and to prepare for more productive work in newer areas where the demand is greater. Such incentives might not exist if workers were paid on the basis of job content. Those who argue against comparable worth believe that comparable worth is likely to be accompanied by a complex administrative structure that will increase government interference in business decision making and lower productivity.

Finally, the cost of implementing a system of compensation based on comparable worth needs to be assessed. This involves not only the cost of reduced efficiency but also the direct cost of raising the wages of women in undervalued jobs. Because of increased payroll cost, employers may be forced to increase prices, which might produce inflation or lower the wages of men in male-dominated jobs.

Opponents of comparable worth argue that because of this extensive cost, following the principle of comparable worth is unwise. Advocates of comparable worth, however, argue that cost should not be a major factor. Fairness and equity demand that women should receive equal pay for jobs of comparable worth.

Applications

Comparable worth debate is based on two federal laws, both of which are intended to eliminate discrimination. The first is the Equal Pay Act of 1963, under which employers are required to provide men and women with equal pay for equal jobs. The second is Title VII of the 1964 Civil Rights Act, which prohibits racial and sexual discrimination. Opponents of comparable worth apply the Equal Pay Act and claim that employers are obliged to pay equal wages only for equal jobs, not for different jobs. Supporters of comparable worth claim that Title VII covers all sex-based discrimination in wages.

Minnesota is the only state that requires all its localities to develop and implement a comparable worth/pay equity plan for their employees. Of the more than 1,700 local bodies that have implemented pay equity plans nationwide, more than 1,300 are in Minnesota. Moreover, most reports from Minnesota are quite favorable, and advocates see the state as a good example of how to use pay equity efficiently.

In the late 1970's, Minnesota evaluated the state's personnel system. Hay Associates did a study of salary and benefit policies. This study included job evaluation point totals for 762 multi-incumbent job classes. The study showed that female-dominated job classes were paid less than male-dominated job classes were. For example, delivery van drivers were paid 24 percent more than were similarly rated clerk typists 2. As a result of this study, the State Employees Pay Equity Act was passed in March of 1982. According to this law, the primary consideration in establishing pay is comparability of the value of the work, which includes skill, effort, responsibility, and working conditions required in work. This act required the Department of Employee Relations (DOER) commissioner to submit, every other year, a list of the female-dominated and the male-dominated classes for which a compensation inequity exists. The commissioner submitted her first list of inequities early in 1983, and the first money began flowing to workers of underpaid female-dominated classes later that year. After implementation of this law, the pay gap in Minnesota state employment declined. About one-third of the state labor force received a pay equity increase. Sixty percent of all females and 9 percent of all males received this pay equity increase. Ninety-five percent of clerical workers and 72 percent of health care nonprofessionals received increases.

There are some problems with the comparable-worth system of Minnesota, because it has an arbitrary cutoff point for female-dominated classes. If a job class is a fraction of 1 percent above 70 percent female, it is treated as if below-the-line wages are held down artificially because of discrimination. The class is entitled to pay equity raises. If the pay of a job class is more than 10 percent below the line but the job class is only about 69 percent female (for example, social workers), it is assumed that the below-the-line pay was not a result of discrimination, and employees in this group are not entitled to pay equity raises. In addition to this arbitrariness, since the percentages of men and women in job classes are always changing, the problem is magnified further.

Comparable worth has achieved some successes at the local level. For example, the Los Angeles City Council agreed to approve pay increases of 15 percent for 3,900 employees, most of whom are female clerks and librarians. The city agreed to these increases in order to settle a sex discrimination complaint. Over a three-year period, the city planned to spend $36 million raising the wages of its female workers.

Context

Sex segregation at work is the most important cause of the wage gap between men and women in the Western world. Occupational segregation is the basis of debate over comparable worth. This is vital to the question of the place of women in the class structure as well as to the nature of class structure itself. The class structure is formed by the nature and extent of the differential barriers to the social mobility of men and women. To understand the sexual division of paid work, it is essential to understand the maintenance of gender segregation at work. Historically, employers often established separate wage scales for women and men, even though they were doing similar work. The top of the female scale was often the same as the bottom of the male scale. This practice became illegal in the United States in 1963 with the passage of the Equal

Pay Act. As a result of this act, inequities in pay for the same work have decreased, but the wage gap between women and men still remains stable.

In the early 1970's, as a result of the study of comparable pay in the state of Washington and efforts of the International Union of Electrical Workers to gain pay equity at Westinghouse, the idea of comparable worth spread rapidly among activists, who attempted to improve women's positions in the labor market. Eleanor Holmes Norton, who was the chair of the Equal Employment Opportunity Commission during that time, gave comparable worth a national presence in 1977 when she identified it as a top issue for the 1980's. She commissioned the National Research Council of the National Academy of Science to form a committee to investigate the practicality of comparable worth as a policy for establishing equal pay. The reports that came out of that committee's work were instrumental in further spreading news about comparable worth and providing an expert base for defending it.

In the federal government, states, cities, and counties of the United States, women's groups and trade unions saw the possibilities of comparable worth and began organizing to achieve it in the late 1970's. Most comparable worth efforts took place and are still taking place in the public sector, since it is more accessible to outside groups than is the private sector. By 1983, comparable worth efforts were underway in at least 143 public jurisdictions, and by 1986, comparable worth had been taken up as a policy issue in at least 156 jurisdictions.

Public sector comparable worth projects follow a certain pattern. First, through legislation or collective bargaining, a policy is established. Second, jobs are evaluated to determine the extent of wage inequity. Then, a plan for equity adjustment is formulated. Finally, politics and bargaining are used in efforts to implement the plan.

In terms of the impact and potential of comparable worth, it can be argued that the strength of the comparable worth movement shows that there is a continuing vitality of the women's movement. Joan Acker, in her book *Doing Comparable Worth: Gender, Class, and Pay Equity* (1989), says that comparable worth reveals that there are conflicts of interest between women in different occupational and class situations, and between women and men in similar class situations, but this does not mean that the reform is headed in the wrong direction. It was through comparable worth, after all, that these contradictions were brought to light in a public arena in which they could be confronted, if not resolved.

Bibliography

Acker, Joan. *Doing Comparable Worth: Gender, Class, and Pay Equity.* Philadelphia: Temple University Press, 1989. This book is a study of the effort to implement comparable worth salary settlements in the state of Oregon. Acker is an activist-scholar and a winner of the American Sociological Association's lifetime achievement award in gender studies. Contains a bibliography and an index.

Livernash, E. Robert, ed. *Comparable Worth: Issues and Alternatives.* Washington, D.C.: Equal Employment Advisory Council, 1980. This, the first book written on this subject, gives an analysis of the issue, discusses its origin, examines the practical impact of its adoption, and gives a detailed review of its legal basis. This book argues against comparable worth. Contains summaries and footnotes.

Paul, Ellen Frankel. *Equity and Gender: The Comparable Worth Debate*. New Brunswick, N.J.: Transaction, 1989. Evaluates the economic and pragmatic arguments of both sides of the comparable worth debate, providing legal background. Contains a bibliography and an index.

Rhoads, Steven E. *Incomparable Worth: Pay Equity Meets the Market*. New York: Cambridge University Press, 1993. Gives a detailed analysis of the implementation of comparable worth in the state of Minnesota, the United Kingdom, and Australia. Contains extensive endnotes and an index.

Treiman, D. J., and H. I. Hartmann, eds. *Women, Work, and Wages: Equal Pay for Jobs of Equal Value*. Washington, D.C.: National Academy Press, 1981. A good nontechnical book on the subject for the general audience.

Krishna Mallick

Cross-References

Individual Discrimination, 547; Gender Inequality: Analysis and Overview, 820; Gender Inequality: Biological Determinist Views, 826; Gender Socialization, 833; Sexism and Institutional Sexism, 1728; Women in the Labor Force, 2185; Women in the Medical Profession, 2191; The Women's Movement, 2196.

COMPULSORY AND MASS EDUCATION

Type of sociology: Major social institutions
Field of study: Education

When knowledge is transmitted by formal means and reaches large numbers of people, it is called mass education. Mass education frequently is accomplished through compulsory education laws. Sociology offers explanations for the rise of compulsory and mass education which help explain how society is structured and how it operates to place persons in jobs and to favor some groups over other groups.

Principal terms

COMPULSORY EDUCATION: school attendance required by law for youths between certain specified ages

CONFLICT THEORY: a way of understanding social phenomena in terms of conflict between groups

EDUCATION: the transmission of knowledge by either formal or informal means

ETHNIC GROUP: a group distinguished mainly by its distinctive cultural heritage

FUNCTIONALISM: the analysis of social phenomena in terms of the functions they perform for the whole society

STRATIFICATION: unequal access to scarce yet widely valued goods and services; unequal access may occur on the basis of various attributes, including age, sex, class, race, and ethnicity

Overview

Education in the United States is highly decentralized. The form, function, and content of schooling are not mandated by a national or federal political authority. These matters are left to each of the states to decide, and the states in turn delegate many of these responsibilites to local communities. This decentralization, which is unique among the industrial democracies, has permitted diversity to flourish in American educational institutions.

Education at the elementary level in colonial America took place in a variety of contexts. The skills of reading, writing, and arithmetic were taught through apprenticeship, in churches, in private schools, by tutoring, at home, and in some public schools. Public schools were only a small part of this educational structure. They often required a small fee from their students. Both in colonial America and in the newly independent United States of America, truly free public education was rare and tended to be reserved mainly for the children of families that were willing to declare themselves indigent. Therefore, attendance at public schools was fairly low.

Support for free public elementary education varied according to social-class position. In general, the urban lower classes were opposed to, or apathetic about, free public education, as were farmers, on the grounds that there was no need for it. The support of organized labor unions usually was indirect; they supported restrictions on the competition posed by child labor. In his book *The Social Ideas of American Educators* (1935), historian Merle Curti indicates that the main impetus for the foundation of free public elementary schools came primarily from reformers with upper-class and upper-middle-class, largely Protestant, professional backgrounds. For these persons, the issue of free schools was one cause among many. Persons with such backgrounds were active in crusades against slavery, intemperance, harsh penal conditions, harmful labor conditions, inhumane treatment of the insane, and imprisonment for debt; they also agitated for child-labor laws, social welfare services, public hospitals, and the establishment of the juvenile court.

Many arguments were used by these reformers to garner political support for free public elementary-school education. Claims were made that education would not only teach youth to read and write but also would increase labor productivity, promote political stability, prevent social disintegration, forestall labor uprisings, instill respect for private property and for legitimate authority, and preserve other revered values. Between 1870 and the second decade of the twentieth century, reformers proclaimed that the school was the premier agency of social change and social amelioration. Free schooling would solve social problems: Through schooling, the plight of the impoverished and the disorganization of the city would be remedied, the assimilation of the foreign born would be accomplished, and adjustments to an industrial economy would be made.

The efforts of these reformers were successful. In the first half of the nineteenth century, the basic pattern of free elementary schooling was established in the New England states. Starting around the turn of the nineteenth century, states there began to require local townships to establish free public elementary schools; somewhat later, they began to support them with financial aid. Most New England states had established free elementary school systems by 1860; this pattern was extended by Reconstruction to the Southern states after the Civil War and to the Western states and territories after they were formally organized.

The political battle for free public secondary education was waged by reformers very similar in background to those who had won the struggle for public elementary schools. As in the earlier case, all manner of benefits were alleged to accrue from publicly supported high schools.

Educators were crucial players in the diverse coalitions involved in establishing these schools. In his book *The Credential Society* (1979), sociologist Randall Collins argues that the elementary schools founded in the first half of the nineteenth century "themselves provided the major element in the growth of free secondary education in the second half of the century: an articulate and highly dedicated group of men who strongly believed in the value of education and were skilled at gaining political support for it, the administrators and state educational officials."

These coalitions succeeded in having state after state enact laws that established public high schools and made attending school between specified ages compulsory.

In his book *Origins of the Urban School* (1971), professor of education Marvin Lazerson indicates that before the Civil War, only Massachusetts had passed a compulsory education law, which was infrequently enforced. The second such law was passed by Vermont in 1867. Twenty-three additional states enacted similar laws prior to 1890. By 1900, another eight states had followed suit. Most of the remaining states, concentrated primarily in the South, had done so by 1920.

The ages specified by these laws varied. The lower age frequently was eight, and the upper age frequently was fourteen; the upper age was gradually raised to sixteen in many states. If one follows the lead of sociologist Martin Trow, in his classic article "The Second Transformation of American Secondary Education" (1966), and takes, somewhat arbitrarily, an enrollment of 15 percent of the age-grade as the beginning of the mass phase of an educational system, then one finds that secondary education passed this mark around 1910 and that higher education did so in 1940.

Applications

Sociology provides two main explanations for the expansion of schooling in modern societies: functionalism and conflict theory. The sociological perspective known as functionalism maintains that schools expand because of the services they provide for the community as a whole. In 1800, the United States was an agrarian society of individuals working on small farms or in small businesses; at least seven out of ten Americans in the labor force were small farmers or farm laborers. By 1910, however, the nation was well on its way to becoming an urbanized industrial society of salaried employees. One functionalist interpretation, then, views the growth in secondary education as a response to changes in the occupational structure that happened as part of the industrialization process: Schools expanded to train the salaried employees needed by an increasingly industrial labor force.

Similarly, the expansion of higher education that took place in the United States after World War II has been explained in terms of meeting labor-market demand. Whereas in 1940, about 15 percent of traditionally college-age persons (aged eighteen to twenty-one) were enrolled in college, by 1950 that proportion was up to 30 percent, and by 1970 it was 45 percent and still rising. Whereas 10.7 percent of the entire population of the United States had completed four or more years of college in 1970, that figure had doubled to 21.4 percent by 1991. This tremendous growth has been explained as a response to the demands of the occupational structure. Between 1940 and 1950, for example, the number of engineers in this country doubled and the number of research workers increased by 50 percent. There has been tremendous growth since World War II in the number of professional, technical, and kindred workers, and these are precisely the occupations that call for at least some college education.

Other countries have industrialized without experiencing comparable changes in their educational systems. England is a case in point. England had long been an industrial giant by the beginning of the nineteenth century, a feat that it accomplished without establishing an extensive system of free public education and without compulsory education laws. Not until after World War II did England institute a system of free secondary education; colleges and universities there did not become democratized until the mid-1960's.

In his book *Youth and the Social Order* (1965), sociologist Frank Musgrove presents a functionalist explanation for the rise of compulsory education in England. The statutes of 1870 and 1880 that introduced compulsory education there were needed not because children were at work but because increasingly they were not. Techno-logical change had displaced them economically; the economy no longer needed their labor. By some estimates, more than half of all children were neither at work nor at school. Compulsory schooling acted as a street-sweeping operation, warehousing youths who were no longer needed by an already industrialized economy.

Different explanations for the rise of compulsory and mass education are offered by conflict theory. This perspective emphasizes that various groups—for example, those defined by ethnicity, social class, occupational grouping, and religion—use education as one resource among many in their struggle to win or to retain privilege in a system of stratification. In this view, the structure and size of educational systems reflect the outcomes of struggles in which groups seek to control and to shape educational systems to their benefit.

In *The Credential Society* (1979), Randall Collins argues that in the United States both public elementary and secondary schools grew as a result of ethnic conflict. At the beginning of the republic, the American population approached ethnic homogene-ity. In 1790, about 85 percent of the population was Protestant and probably English speaking. About two-thirds of these persons were of English-Scottish background; about 10 percent were of German or Dutch ancestry; and another 8 percent were from Ireland, mainly Protestants from the north. Most of the remaining 15 percent were black Africans, mainly slaves. The 4 million people who carried the culture of the early United States were thus overwhelmingly white, Protestant, English-speaking persons.

Beginning with the influx of Irish Catholics into the New England states during the 1830's and 1840's, the previously homogenous Anglo-Protestant culture faced wave after wave of alien immigration that threatened to displace its ministers, educators, editors, and lawyers from political, economic, and cultural leadership. Randall Collins argues that public schools and their compulsory attendance laws spread precisely in those states that faced the greatest influx of alien immigration. As conflicts between native-born Protestants and immigrant ethnic groups built up, the schools were used by the former as a weapon of social control to preserve their position and interests.

Similar arguments have been presented to explain the expansion of higher education at various historical periods. Conflicts among competing regional, political, and religious groups have been proffered as explanations for the modest proliferation of colleges during the colonial days: the Congregationalists founded Harvard, Anglicans founded The College of William and Mary; Yale was founded as an orthodox alternative to the liberalism of Harvard; Baptists founded Brown, and the Dutch founded Queens College (now Rutgers University). Sociologists Christopher Jencks and David Riesman, in their book *The Academic Revolution* (1968), argue that such rivalries are generally responsible for the founding, growth, and demise of colleges in the United States before World War I.

Context

The perspective known as functionalism dominated American sociology in general, including sociological inquiry with regard to education, for the first five decades of the twentieth century. The great functionalist sociologist Émile Durkheim, in his book *Education and Sociology* (1922), traced the connections between the form and content of schools and larger social forces, such as a general trend toward individualism and the emergence of an urban middle class. One version of this perspective holds that modern societies rest on a body of technical knowledge that lies beyond the ability of the family to transmit; hence, schools expand to provide what the family cannot.

Social unrest erupted in the wake of the U.S. Supreme Court's 1954 *Brown v. Board of Education of Topeka* decision, which, by declaring racial segregation in public schools unconstitutional, ushered in the modern Civil Rights movement. Social unrest and protest spread during the 1960's and manifested itself in many ways, including protests against American military involvement in Southeast Asia, the spread of drug use among American middle-class youth, the emergence of the modern women's movement, and race riots in major American cities.

Widespread social unrest and protest frequently act as a catalyst that leads to the examination and reformulation of basic assumptions guiding social analysis. This occurred in the 1970's in the guise of a major challenge to the primacy of functionalism as an explanation for the growth of schools.

Some scholars questioned functionalism on empirical grounds. They examined the alleged link between schooling and the provision of job skills. Sociologist Ivar Berg, in his book *Education and Jobs: The Great Training Robbery* (1971), argues that the link between schooling and the provision of job skills is far weaker than previous researchers have supposed and is too weak to explain school growth. School growth, Ivar Berg maintains, far outstrips the "needs" of the economy.

Other scholars questioned functionalism on theoretical grounds. Despite the diversity within conflict theory, its basic premise is that groups at the top of the stratification system use education as a resource to secure a favored position.

Sociologists Samuel Bowles and Herbert Gintis, in their book *Schooling in Capitalist America* (1976), find that schools grew in the United States because capitalists endeavored to produce a reliable supply of docile, obedient, disciplined, dependable labor. From this perspective, education is imposed upon the mass of reluctant citizens and teaches lower-strata groups a healthy respect for dominant values, styles, and institutions. Randall Collins, in *The Credential Society* (1979), argues that elementary schools, high schools, and colleges grew as previously privileged but threatened groups used education to counteract social trends that distressed them. This relatively new way of analyzing school growth is important because it has shifted the focus from schools as instruments of skill transmission to the manner in which society itself is structured and operates so as to favor some groups over others.

Bibliography

Berg, Ivar. *Education and Jobs: The Great Training Robbery*. Boston: Beacon Press, 1971. A brief, lucid book arguing that the relationship between education and job performance is a myth. Presents much empirical data. Has a chapter on manual workers and a chapter on public service, focusing on the armed forces and on civilian employees in the federal civil service.

Bowles, Samuel, and Herbert Gintis. *Schooling in Capitalist America: Educational Reform and the Contradictions of Economic Life*. New York: Basic Books, 1976. There is much that is arguable in this book. It presents data supporting the thesis that U.S. schools mirror the inherently unequal structure of capitalist society. This provocative book should be of interest to those who are concerned about educational policy and the impact that schools have on American society.

Collins, Randall. *The Credential Society: An Historical Sociology of Education and Stratification*. New York: Academic Press, 1979. This small volume presents a strong criticism of the notion that schools expand in order to provide job skills. It also presents a readable, provocative, revisionist history of the expansion of public elementary, secondary, and higher education in the United States. It has a rich bibliography.

Edwards, Newton, and Herman Richey. *The School in the American Social Order*. 2d ed. Boston: Houghton Mifflin, 1963. Analyzes the development of schools in the United States through World War II. Has separate chapters on colonial New England, the colonial South, and the Middle Colonies (which include New York, New Jersey, and Pennsylvania). Contains black-and-white photographs, footnotes, and selected references for further reading at the end of each chapter, and it has a very good index.

Jencks, Christopher, and David Riesman. *The Academic Revolution*. Garden City, N.Y.: Anchor Books, 1969. A history of the evolution of higher education in the United States. This book is delightful, richly detailed, and larded with grace, wit, and audacity. Has separate chapters on Catholic colleges, women's colleges, Protestant colleges, and African American colleges. Has a good table of contents and an extensive bibliography.

Musgrove, Frank. *Youth and the Social Order*. Bloomington: Indiana University Press, 1965. This is more than a readable history of compulsory education laws in England. Written with insight and wit, it places school growth within a broader framework of demographic, social, cultural, and economic change.

Trow, Martin. "The Second Transformation of American Secondary Education." In *Class, Status, and Power: Social Stratification in Comparative Perspective*, edited by Reinhard Bendix and Seymour Martin Lipset. 2d ed. New York: Free Press, 1966. This article is a concise, even-handed explanation of the emergence and growth of the comprehensive public high school in the United States. It is a good introduction to the subject for a general audience.

Marjorie Donovan

Cross-References

COMPUTERS, AUTOMATION, AND THE ECONOMY

Type of sociology: Major social institutions
Field of study: The economy

Advances in computer technology and the introduction of other sophisticated machinery in the workplace have dramatically changed the nature of employment in manufacturing, stimulated the growth of the service sector of the economy, and caused widespread and ongoing social change.

Principal terms

AUTOMATION: the improvement in an industry's productivity by the introduction of self-regulating or programmable machines

BUSINESS CYCLE: the general trend in free-market economies for periods of growth to be followed by periods of recession, including temporary increases in unemployment

CAPITAL INVESTMENT: expenditures to secure the means of production, such as land, buildings, and machinery

COMPUTER: a machine that is capable of rapid information processing and is programmable to perform a wide range of information-processing tasks

CYBERNETICS: the science of communication and control; based on the principle of feedback, in which a mechanism monitors its own operation and makes appropriate changes

HUMAN CAPITAL: the skills and knowledge of a group of employees

TECHNOLOGICAL DISPLACEMENT: the elimination of jobs as the result of technological innovations

WELFARE STATE: a country in which the government provides the means for unemployed citizens to obtain the goods and services necessary for a comfortable life

Overview

The term "automation" came into widespread use in the decade following World War II to describe the introduction in factories of machinery with built-in self-regulatory and communication capability. While primitive forms of automation existed in the textile industry in the early nineteenth century, the large-scale automation of industrial plants was a direct result of the war, which required the increased production of war materiel by a reduced labor force and, at the same time, required the development of cybernetics—the theory of mechanical communication and control—for military applications.

During World War II, the term "computer," which originally referred to an individual human trained to do mathematical calculations, came to mean an electronic device capable of the rapid manipulation of symbols. Initially large, relatively slow, and so costly that only large corporations could afford to rent or buy one, computers have decreased in size and increased in power so that the vast majority of businesses and individuals can afford them. Automation and the widespread application of computers have greatly altered the conduct of business in industrialized nations. These innovations have exerted profound effects on wages, numbers of jobs, placement of factories, and social class structure. In addition, many of the concepts of cybernetics have been adopted in the social sciences, so that the vocabulary of cybernetics has entered the literature of economics and political science.

The automation of industrial processes has also had dramatic effects on the labor force. Automation allows the same level of production to be achieved with a smaller number of workers, and its introduction thus gave rise to initial fears that automation would lead to widespread unemployment as production workers were rendered "redundant" by new technology. Massive technological unemployment has not generally occurred, although many workers have had to accept new employment at reduced levels of income. Managers have not been eager to dismiss proven workers, who might well represent the valuable human capital needed for future growth. It is not, however, always to a worker's advantage to remain as long as possible in a job in which the worker has become redundant; in such a situation, a worker is more likely to be dismissed during downturns in the business cycle, when employers generally are forced to reduce labor costs where possible and when few new jobs may be available. Reduced working hours allow a greater number of workers to be retained, with some being assigned different duties. Other workers displaced by automation have found new employment opportunities in the service sector or in new industries related to automation and computers.

Even more profound, perhaps, has been the effect of the widespread availability of computers on white-collar workers. A mail-order firm that might have previously employed hundreds of clerks to compute, address, and record bills sent to millions of customers could, with the aid of computers, perform the same functions with a much smaller number of employees. Office automation likewise reduced the number of workers needed to keep and retrieve records. For example, the number of accountants required by many firms to keep track of financial transactions diminished. Fewer lower-level managers were needed, as upper-level managers began using computers to retrieve information, analyze operations, and develop new strategies for their companies.

The pace of automation in the United States diminished somewhat as many of the larger manufacturing companies acquired production facilities in countries with abundant labor available at low wages. Beginning in the 1970's, American companies increasingly turned to globally integrated manufacturing, in which the components of a product, each made where it is most economical to do so, are shipped to an assembly site in a low-wage area, then reimported into the United States or shipped directly to foreign consumers. The globalization of production has itself been made possible by advances in telecommunications and management information systems, which themselves are a consequence of improvements in computer technology. Many economists have argued that the United States in the late twentieth century is undergoing a period of deindustrialization and that industry, both automated and not, will come to play a diminished role in the economy. Instead, such experts predict, the leading component of the United States economy will be the service sector, especially the development and transmission of the information needed to operate a complex worldwide manufacturing and distribution system.

Automation and the widespread adoption of computer technology have also had profound effects on social and economic mobility. For workers and managers, there has been a reduction in middle-income opportunities. While some highly skilled workers have been able to move to positions of greater responsibility and pay in automated plants and offices, a large number have had to accept positions at reduced responsibility and income. Those moving to newer industries have generally found a lower level of pay and less job security. Entry-level management positions that might once have been open to college graduates with liberal arts degrees often now require specialized training in a business field and a graduate degree. A new type of manager, the technocrat—who combines traditional managerial skills with a knowledge of the technical details of production, finance, sales, and world markets—has increasingly come to figure in top leadership roles in business. As highly educated professionals, technocratic managers tend to identify with one another as professionals and are less likely to feel a strong allegiance to their companies. Competition for the most talented managers has worked to increase salaries, increasing the income gap and social distance between management and the average worker.

Applications

Industries in which assembly-line production (such as the aircraft or automotive industries) or continuous-flow production (such as the petroleum or chemical industries) were already in place were the first to be automated. The automation of a factory allowed the process of production to be managed with far fewer workers than previously required or, alternatively, allowed a given number of workers, once properly trained, to achieve far more production. While not all manufacturing industries have proved equally amenable to automation, the potential financial rewards of automating production have caused many manufacturers to redesign their processes and products to take advantage of new technology.

Manufacturers introduced automation into their plants in order to increase rates of production and lower the cost of producing products. The increase in productivity has in many cases allowed companies to lower the price of products and yet increase the volume of sales more than enough to substantially increase income. In the mid-1950's, one television manufacturer was able to reduce its prices by 32 percent and yet increase its sales volume sufficiently so that no workers lost their jobs. Such increased income resulting from automation is then available for distribution to a company's shareholders for capital investment in new production facilities, or even for increasing the incomes of employees. In a quantitative study conducted in the 1950's, economist Yale Brozen found that the largest part of such income was generally realized by salaried workers rather than production workers. Workers also can benefit from lower product prices resulting from increases in production.

For unemployed workers and workers who have had to accept lower-wage positions, automation is a less attractive prospect. The oil-refining industry became substantially automated in the 1950's with a loss of about ten thousand production jobs despite a 58 percent increase in productivity. At roughly the same time, the chemical industry was able to increase productivity by 80 percent while eliminating some thirteen thousand production jobs. In 1960, the Bureau of Labor Statistics reported that in the previous decade, total employment had increased by 15 percent while overall employment of production workers had remained more or less constant. Thus, the growth rate in nonproduction jobs had vastly outpaced that in production jobs, even though there were enough new production jobs to offset those lost to automation in major industries. Since the recession of 1957-1958, however, employment in production has not been strong enough to offset the combined effects of automation, foreign competition, and the increased placement of plants outside the United States. Employment in the automotive and steel industries has been particularly affected, with the loss of hundreds of thousands of U.S. production jobs.

Fear of technological unemployment was a major concern in the early days of automation. In defense of automation, it was argued that the combination of a reduced work week and the creation of new jobs by automation would be sufficient to avert widespread unemployment, although special accommodation might be needed by workers who were too old to retrain effectively or whose highly developed skills could not be transferred to new occupations. Some more utopian thinkers proposed the replacement of the traditional work ethic by that of the welfare state, in which unemployed people would be spared both hardship and social disapproval. Those who believed that the total amount of human work to be done would decrease generally advocated a reduction in the number of hours in the work week, the creation of programs to help workers make better use of leisure time, and guarantees of income and essential services for the unemployed.

Automation has contributed to some extent to a deurbanization of production. Since automated plants require fewer workers, there is less reason for production facilities to be located near large cities. In many cases, plants could also be smaller. Some of the largest American companies, including General Motors, General Electric, and U.S. Steel, began to build smaller, less centrally located plants.

The displacement of workers by technology is not limited to production industries. The development of computer programs known as "expert systems" has made it possible for computers to enhance the productivity of many kinds of service workers and has even caused technological displacement for highly trained professionals. Expert systems are programs that can accept information, ask questions, and simulate the reasoning processes of human experts. Expert systems have allowed novice repair personnel to undertake the repair of highly complex machinery and inexperienced bank personnel to evaluate the likelihood of a loan being repaid. Expert programs have even been developed to simulate the thinking of medical specialists as they diagnose ailments and prescribe treatment. The possibility of automating the work of even high-status professionals is thus very real.

Context

Preindustrial societies generally accepted as inevitable the separation of humanity into a laboring class, which provided the essentials of life, and an aristocracy, which was seen as fit to govern and produce works of art and culture. Only with the development of mechanized agriculture and industry did it become possible for broad sections of society to enjoy leisure and intellectual development. Indeed, it is only in industrialized societies that young children and the aged are generally exempt from the obligation to work.

Historians of technology generally recognize three stages in the evolution of industrial production: mechanization, or the replacement of human muscle power by machinery; mass production, or the continuous production of goods on an assembly line, with a corresponding division of labor and standardization of products; and automation, or the introduction of machinery that can monitor and adjust its own performance and communicate with other machines. Like the earlier revolution in agriculture that made it possible for the nutritional needs of an entire population to be met by the labor of a small fraction of its members, the increased productivity of automated industry reduced the number of workers needed to achieve the production of manufactured goods.

Fear of technological change, however, has frequently determined the response of one group or another to innovation, and concern about unemployment has often been associated with increases in productivity. In England, the early Industrial Revolution saw the formation of organized bands of workers called Luddites who actively sought to destroy textile machinery. The German philosopher Karl Marx, one of the founders of communist ideology, believed that the cost of improvements in production machinery would fall to levels competitive with workers' wages and would eventually result in widespread "technological unemployment," a term coined by him, and ultimately to the downfall of capitalism. Even Norbert Wiener, one of the founders of cybernetics, the science upon which modern automation technology is based, cautioned in his book *The Human Use of Human Beings: Cybernetics and Society* (1954) that automation might lead to an economic depression in the United States comparable to the Great Depression of the 1930's.

Instead, improvements in productivity have led to a diversity of new products and services and an increased variety of occupations. By the close of the twentieth century, fewer than half the workers in the United States were engaged in producing agricultural or industrial goods; the majority of workers had been moved to the service sector, although not always with comparable wages. Computer technology allowed new professions to be created to manage production and to facilitate consumption. Credit cards increased the money supply, while producers and merchants could use computer technology to monitor the exact state of their inventory at all times. According to some economic analysts, the growth of the service sector, made possible by automation—

and perhaps made inevitable by the globalization of production—was an early stage in the emergence of a new postindustrial society, one based on the generation and manipulation of information and continuing rapid, but generally beneficial, social change.

Bibliography

Asimov, Isaac. *Asimov's New Guide to Science*. New York: Basic Books, 1984. The concluding sections of this book provide an introduction to the scientific basis for automation and computing and place their development in historical perspective.

Bagrit, Leon. *The Age of Automation*. New York: New American Library, 1965. A brief and very readable set of lectures given by the author, a noted industrialist, over British radio. The author argues that the gain in living standards resulting from automation more than justifies the social adjustments that must be made as automation is achieved.

Bell, Daniel. *The Coming of Post-Industrial Society*. New York: Basic Books, 1973. The author, a Harvard University economist, analyzes the transition from agricultural to industrial to information-based societies and provides insights into the role of automation and computers in changing social and economic structures.

Brozen, Yale. "Automation's Impact on Capital and Labor Markets." In *Automation and Society*, edited by Howard Boone Jacobson and Joseph S. Roucek. New York: Philosophical Library, 1959. A brief but readable account of the impact of automation on the labor market and on the accumulation of capital.

Buckingham, Walter S. *Automation: Its Impact on Businesses and People*. New York: Harper & Brothers, 1961. The author, a professor of industrial management, discusses the impact of automation on both the labor force and the structure of business.

Einzig, Paul. *The Economic Consequences of Automation*. London: Secker & Warburg, 1957. Written for the lay reader by a professional economist, this book was an attempt to provide an understanding of the economic factors that must enter into any government policies developed in response to automation.

Feigenbaum, Edward, Pamela McCorduck, and H. Penny Nii. *The Rise of the Expert Company*. New York: Times Books, 1988. Describes how the process of automation is being extended into the service sector by computer systems to increase the productivity of managers and other professionals.

Donald R. Franceschetti

Cross-References

THE CONCENTRIC ZONE MODEL OF URBAN GROWTH

Type of sociology: Urban and rural life

The concentric zone model of urban growth, developed in the 1920's and based on studies of Chicago, attempts to explain how cities grow and develop. In this model, cities grow outward from the central business district in concentric rings or zones, with each zone representing a different type of activity and class of people.

Principal terms

CENTRAL BUSINESS DISTRICT: the center of an industrial city in which is located most or all commercial and financial operations and most or all social and cultural opportunities

CONCENTRIC CIRCLES: a series of circles of increasing size radiating out from the center circle (as a pebble dropped into a pond creates concentric circles in the water)

INVASION AND SUCCESSION: applied to human relations, invasion refers to the immigration of a group into an area occupied by a different group; succession refers to a situation in which most or all previous residents have departed and been replaced by the immigrant group

METROPOLITAN AREA OR METROPOLIS: an aggregation of many suburban municipalities and satellite cities loosely connected to or affiliated with a central city

MULTIPLE NUCLEI THEORY: a concept of urban development which asserts that urban growth takes place from a number of centers or nuclei, the central business district being only one of them

SATELLITE CITIES: neighboring municipalities of a major city that may serve as "bedroom communities" for commuting workers to the central city

SECTOR THEORY: a theory of urban growth which asserts that urban development proceeds outward from the central business district in wedge-shaped sectors, each containing a particular social class

Overview

The concentric zone model of urban growth was first articulated by Ernest W. Burgess in *The City* (1925), by Robert E. Park, Burgess, and Roderick D. McKenzie. Usually referred to as a theory or hypothesis by later students of urban growth, Burgess' model is an ideal type which attempts to describe and summarize the zones of expansion and development in a modern city. It suggests that competition for land (according to the "principle of domination," analogous to Herbert Spencer's notion of "the survival of the fittest") assumes that the richest and most powerful groups acquire the land that they require first, with successively less powerful groups acquiring land relative to their ability to compete in the market. This results in a pattern of urban growth resembling concentric circles. Each of these zones or rings can be identified by different land uses and populations.

The innermost circle is composed of the central business district or downtown center in which most of the political, cultural, and economic life of the city resides. This zone is surrounded by a zone of transition. As its name implies, this is an area in which transient populations, including new immigrants to the city (both foreign-born and domestic) reside in rooming houses, deteriorated buildings, and other low-rent units. This is a blighted area (slum) that provides an initial stopping place for new migrants to the city; it is a zone of first settlement. In addition, this transitional zone is an area in which businesses may be buying land for speculation in the hope of an expanding central business district. Thus, there is an inherent instability about this zone.

The third concentric circle is the zone of workingmen's homes. This zone is where the more settled industrial working class, frequently second-generation Americans but also some immigrants, resides. It is composed of somewhat better dwellings than the transitional zone. Included in this zone are urban ethnic enclaves such as Little Italies and Chinatowns.

The fourth zone contains primarily the homes of middle-class families, but it also includes the homes of families of those industrial workers who are most highly paid. This is a zone comprising mostly single-family dwellings occupied by economically secure families. The fifth zone is usually just beyond the city limits and is a commuters' zone of larger homes on larger lots. This suburban zone may be composed of satellite cities.

Burgess argued that as a city grows, each inner zone or ring invades the next outlying zone or ring (a process sociologists call invasion and succession), but the basic concentric zone pattern remains. According to Burgess, the description and even the actual number of zones may differ among cities, but the underlying principles remain constant. The chief idea is that the forces which create and control the central business district have a major impact on subsequent zones, and the shifting fortunes of the central business district affect the demographic growth or decline as well as the socioeconomic characteristics of an area. This concentric zone model will hold true, Burgess believed, unless discrimination or a specific topographical factor acts to block some facet of it. Rivers, mountains, railroad lines, and similar features, either natural or artificial, may affect or skew the concentric circle in particular cases.

Each circle or zone differs from the others in its incidence of poverty, juvenile delinquency, and divorce. Each zone also has a different number of foreign-born residents as well as a different percentage of families who own their own homes.

In a 1927 article using 1920 census tract data for Chicago, Burgess examined how his concentric zone theory works in the real city (Chicago). He discovered that the percentage of families owning their own homes is quite low in the innermost circle, the central business district, and in the zone of transition. The zone of workingmen's homes shows much higher incidence of home ownership, superceded by even greater rates of home ownership in the middle-class residential district and in the suburban residential district. The same pattern applies in reverse, to the incidence of poverty.

The central business district and zone of transition show relatively high poverty rates compared with far lower (to nearly nonexistent) poverty in both middle and suburban zones. Juvenile delinquency follows roughly the same pattern—the highest concentration existing close to the center, and less occurring the farther from the center one travels.

Applications

When superimposed on the maps of many large cities, the concentric circle model shows considerable accuracy in its prediction of the location of specific types of individuals and their dwellings. While no city fits the ideal of the model precisely, most show some evidence of concentric zones of growth. Particularly when one looks at maps of an earlier era, prior to the post-World War II building boom, many industrial cities of the northeastern and midwestern United States fit Burgess' theory quite well.

Burgess himself studied only the Chicago of the 1920's; what he found there formed the basis of his theory. Burgess' study found that the tendency of the city was to expand radially from "the Loop," or central business district. Encircling this area he found an area of low-income rooming houses filled with transient workers, an area that was being invaded by businesses and light manufacture. Surrounding this area, Burgess discovered a zone of industrial workers' homes composed largely of row houses and duplexes, and beyond that, single-family middle-class homes. Still beyond that, beyond the city boundaries, there existed suburban areas and satellite cities within commuting distance of the central business district.

Observing the growth of Chicago in this way, Burgess hypothesized that there is a tendency for a city to expand by invasion of the next outlying zone. This concept, known as invasion and succession, refers to the penetration and ultimate displacement of an existing group or population by a different group or population. When the process results in the complete exodus of former residents, it is termed succession. Burgess borrowed this concept from biology, where a similar ecological process is observed in plant and animal communities.

This process of expansion concerned Burgess in that he pondered how the growth of the city in its physical aspects might be matched by an adequate readjustment in its social aspects. In other words, he wondered whether the social organization would keep pace with the physical growth. Toward these ends, Burgess examined the people and social pathologies of the different zones in Chicago. In the zone of transition, he found persons whom he deemed "lost souls" as well as great numbers of newly arrived immigrants grouped into ethnic enclaves. In the zone of workingmen's homes, he found mostly second-generation Americans with skilled occupations, and beyond that the more economically successful middle classes.

Massive immigration into Chicago was taking place as Burgess wrote. This invasion of the city was of great concern to him, and he observed the new immigrants overwhelming and pushing earlier immigrants from the zone of transition. These dislodged inhabitants overflowed into the next zone, whose residents overflowed into the next, in a rapid pattern of invasion and succession. In a case such as this when mobility is great, Burgess observed that areas of demoralization, vice, and promiscuity developed. Burgess found that in these areas of high mobility the rates of juvenile delinquency, crime, gang activity, poverty, and a host of other social evils were greatest.

Burgess' concentric circle model formed the basis of several subsequent theories of urban growth, and thus it can be seen as a significant and trailblazing study in urban sociology. One of the major reactions to concentric zone theory was the empirically based criticism known as sector theory. This theory disputed the concentric zone model by asserting that development tends to take place in sectors along major transportation routes, radiating out from the central city, thus producing fairly homogeneous wedge-shaped sectors rather than concentric rings. Sector theory was developed by Homer Hoyt in his study of residential areas in the 1930's. It argues that high-rent residential areas are the primary impetus behind urban development and that there is a decline in housing value and desirability as one moves away from them. In Hoyt's theory, different income groups segregate themselves within a sector and move, within that sector, away from the central business district.

Another theory that arose in conflict with the concentric zone model of urban development was the multiple nuclei theory. This theory, first proposed by Roderick McKenzie and developed in the 1940's by Chauncy Harris and Edward Ullman, holds that cities grow not in concentric rings from the central business district, but from a series of centers or nuclei. These nuclei may include the central business district, a university, heavy industry, and a railroad terminal. The various classes of residential districts are also arranged in the form of nuclei.

Context

In the early 1920's, Chicago was a city bustling with commerce and industry. Rapid industrialization fueled massive immigration both from the rural areas of the United States and from many foreign countries. This urban growth, both in its physical proportions and in its social maladies, was startlingly rapid. Muckraking journalists of the era, such as Upton Sinclair and Lincoln Steffens, wrote extensively about the human side of this phenomenon, but it was the Chicago school of sociologists, led by the German-educated Robert Park, that first studied this phenomenon of urban physical growth and, to an extent, its social impact.

Three men, Ernest Burgess, Roderick McKenzie, and Clifford Shaw, under the direction and guidance of mentor Park at the University of Chicago in the 1920's and 1930's, developed a theoretical perspective which they called the ecological perspective. Cities such as Chicago seemed to them to be the result of unplanned forces much like the organization of natural ecological communities. The Chicago school believed that human social relations could be studied and understood by sociologists in the same way that biologists approached the study of the location and movement of plant and animal communities.

They believed that human society is natural and unplanned and that urban society generally develops, much as Chicago had, in a series of concentric rings or zones. The concentric circle model was in the forefront of studies of urban development and later spawned contrary theories such as the multiple nuclei theory and sector theory. The importance of Burgess' work lies in the fact that he initiated an empirical examination of urban development, one which (though heavily criticized) still applies in certain circumstances.

The concentric zone model of urban development was for a number of years the standard model or traditional concept of urban growth. It is widely believed now, however, that this model ceased to be particularly useful in its explanatory power sometime after the wave of growth that took place after World War II. It was during this postwar boom in housing development that the United States saw the growth of the "metropolis," an agglomeration of central city, satellite cities, and ever-expanding suburbs and their suburban municipalities as one large metropolitan area only loosely tied to the commerce of the central city. The construction of the interstate highway system, beginning in the 1950's and 1960's, and the building of ring roads connecting suburban municipalities with the central city facilitated commuting and hastened the city's decline. The development of large commercial shopping centers and malls in the suburban areas also spelled disaster for the retail sector in the central business district and led in many ways to the further decline and social dislocation of the area.

While the concentric zone model of urban growth provided early students of urban sociology with empirical observations and analyses of urban growth, the newer metropolis resembles the concentric zone model less than it does the multiple nuclei theory.

Bibliography

Glaab, Charles N. *The American City: A Documentary History*. Homewood, Ill.: Dorsey Press, 1963. A detailed history of urban development in the United States from colonial days to the growth of the metropolis. It contains many readable and informative chapters concerning various aspects of urban growth.

Gutman, Robert, and David Popenoe, eds. *Neighborhood, City, and Metropolis: An Integrated Reader in Urban Sociology*. New York: Random House, 1970. This volume is a lengthy (1,000 page) compilation of essays by sociologists concerning every facet of urban sociology, including theory and approaches, urbanism and urbanization, urban ecology, urban planning, and urban change. A useful source.

McKelvey, Blake. *The Emergence of Metropolitan America, 1915-1966*. New Brunswick, N.J.: Rutgers University Press, 1968. McKelvey presents an interesting history of the development of the metropolitan United States. Particularly useful is chapter 2, which discusses the growth of American cities in the 1920's.

McKenzie, Roderick D. *Roderick D. McKenzie on Human Ecology: Selected Writings*. Edited by Amos H. Hawley. Chicago: University of Chicago Press, 1968. A collection of separate essays by McKenzie on the topic of human ecology, the field pioneered by McKenzie and his colleagues at the University of Chicago in the 1920's and 1930's.

Park, Robert E., Ernest W. Burgess, and Roderick D. McKenzie. *The City*. Chicago:

University of Chicago Press, 1925. This volume (reprinted in 1967) consists of a series of essays written by several sociologists of the Chicago school of the 1920's and 1930's. Included is Burgess' chapter entitled "The Growth of the City: An Introduction to a Research Project," in which he first lays out his concentric circle hypothesis.

Roebuck, Janet. *The Shaping of Urban Society.* New York: Charles Scribner's Sons, 1974. This is a thorough examination of the development of urban society in all its forms and functions. Particularly useful are the chapters on the industrial city and the foundations and forms of the modern city.

Lisa Langenbach

Cross-References

Cities: Preindustrial, Industrial, and Postindustrial, 253; Industrial Societies, 953; Suburbanization and Decentralization, 2010; Urban Planning: Major Issues, 2109; Urbanization, 2129.

CONCEPTUALIZATION AND OPERATIONALIZATION OF VARIABLES

Type of sociology: Sociological research
Field of study: Basic concepts

Conceptualization and operationalization are essential processes in the development and testing of a theory. Conceptualization refers to the creation, labeling, and definition of ideas ("concepts"), which are abstract units of reality. Operationalization refers to the "operations" used to measure those ideas. Such measures must be empirical in nature.

Principal terms

CONCEPT: an abstract idea that mentally categorizes a recurring aspect of concrete reality by identifying its key components and thereby defining it

EMPIRICAL: perceptible or measurable by means of sensory evidence; observable

HYPOTHESIS: a statement predicting a relationship between variables; it is a theoretical statement that has been operationalized

INDICATOR: a measurable characteristic that is selected to provide information about the existence or degree of occurrence of a given variable

MEASUREMENT: the process of developing specific indicators of variables for the purpose of testing hypotheses, developing theory, and discovering the incidence of variables

QUANTITATIVE AND QUALITATIVE: types of measurement using numerically based indicators of variables (quantitative) versus more subjective indicators not reducible to mathematical properties (qualitative)

RELIABILITY: characteristic of an indicator which, after repeated attempts at measuring a given variable in a variety of situations, gives consistent results

SCALE: a series of indicators that together attempt to measure a given variable

VALIDITY: characteristic of an indicator that accurately measures a given variable

VARIABLE: a particular type of concept that varies in degree—that is, has a range of values associated with it

Overview

The ultimate goal of any scientific endeavor is to develop a body of knowledge that describes and/or explains some aspect of concrete or empirical reality. This body of knowledge is called "theory." Being abstract, it is bound neither by time nor by space, as it applies to that aspect of reality of interest to a researcher. The basic building blocks of theory are called "concepts." Concepts are abstract representations of units of reality of interest to the scientist that are labeled and defined. Thus, in social science, there are such concepts as minority group, social stratification, family, and love. Each has a definition and directs one to look at a particular thing or part of concrete reality. These concepts may or may not exist to varying degrees, thus the distinction between variables and nonvariables. For example, a family either exists or does not depending on this definition; however, social stratification (the system of ranking of categories of people) may vary as to its presence depending on the amount and distribution of such things as power, wealth, and prestige among the members of the society being studied.

The means by which social scientists identify units of reality important to a scientific endeavor and label and define those units is called the process of conceptualization. It, in fact, is the same logical process used daily by each of us that helps us to make sense of our world, the process called induction. In order to understand empirical reality, we must simplify it. We do this by categorizing units of reality that are similar, defining those units by a definition that indicates their shared elements, and giving the units labels. This process moves us away from the multiplicity of unique concrete elements themselves to a more abstract grouping of them that emphasizes the similarities among the units and ignores their dissimilarities. Such a "concept" may vary in abstractness, or the degree to which it is directly observable in reality. For example, one could conceptualize a "family" as an adult male, an adult female, and their offspring legally bound together by law. As such, one could fairly easily identify families in order to study them, because this concept is of a low order of abstraction. One cannot as easily observe human emotions such as love or hate, however, since they cannot be observed directly. One cannot see love or hate per se.

The process of conceptualization is as essential in the scientific process as it is in day-to-day functioning. The major difference is the specificity demanded by science to ensure that there is a common understanding of what is being identified and how it is being defined. Once concepts have been developed, scientists want to know how they relate to one another in order to develop an understanding of how reality operates. Thus, using the examples above, they might say that "the less love in a family, the higher the chance of divorce occurring." This might seem a reasonable statement, given day-to-day observations, but this abstract, theoretical statement must be tested to see if the degree of love existing is indeed related to the occurrence of divorce. In order to do this, the scientist must activate the process of operationalization.

The process of operationalization involves identifying the existence of the concept in reality or, in the case of a variable, the degree to which it exists in reality. One must move from an abstract level to a concrete, measurable level of analysis. Thus, using the example above, one must be able to identify families (a relatively easy thing to do, since that concept is of a low order of abstraction) as well as the existence of love, or the degree to which it exists. Since love is of a high level of abstraction, the scientist must state precisely what must be examined, what empirical information must be collected (an indicator or indicators), in order to say that love exists and to what degree it exists. Once it is stated what specific information must be collected and how one is to go about collecting it, one says that the concept (love, in this case) is operationalized. There are many ways in which this or any concept could be measured. For example, one could ask the adults in a family whether they love each other, or one could specify what behaviors (either their presence or absence) to look for—such as touching, amount of leisure time spent together, and so forth.

Two major problems emerge in the process of operationalization. One has to do with what is called validity, and the other has to do with reliability. Validity is the determination of the extent to which the measures or indicators (how the concept has been operationalized) do indeed measure a concept or accurately reflect its existence. Reliability refers to the degree to which a given measure of a concept, when used over time, will consistently arrive at the same results. Ideally a researcher wants a concept's measure to have both a high level of validity and reliability; there are various ways to ensure this.

Finally, how one measures a concept can range from the simple to the complex. For example, one can combine a number of reasonable measures of a concept and give quantitative scores to reflect the existence of the concept. For some concepts there are various complex measurement tools called "scales" available; for others, there are simple measures. Thus, one could use an existing measure or develop one's own as needed in order to measure a variable.

Applications

Use of the processes of conceptualization and operationalization is not limited to science. They are used by individuals and organizations in every sphere of life and activity in attempts to know, understand, and measure reality. Thus, educators want to know how well students are absorbing the knowledge and skills being taught; manufacturing firms want to know the quality of the products they are producing; retailers want to know how satisfied their customers are; social programs want to know how well their programs are meeting their program goals; and so on. In each of the above cases, respectively, what is meant by "how well," "quality," "satisfaction," and "meeting goals" must be made meaningful through the conceptualization process. Then appropriate information must be identified that will adequately measure each (the process of operationalization). Two cases can be used to illustrate these processes. In the first, the focus is on theoretical development; in the second, it is on application.

In 1897 French sociologist Émile Durkheim published a book entitled *Le Suicide: Étude de sociologie* (*Suicide: A Study in Sociology*, 1951). In it he examined the relationship between the nature of society and the personal act of suicide. He was convinced that the structure of society could have an influence on the suicide rate of its population. In examining different societies, he believed (conceptualized) that the closeness of the relationships of the members of a society could be important in preventing suicide. He labeled this closeness "social integration" and recognized it as a concept that could vary in degree (a variable) from low to high. The idea of suicide (the concept) was already in common use, and a count was kept of the number of deaths attributed to suicide in most European countries. (In fact, suicide was already operationalized, with each state identifying what should be looked for in a death that would indicate it as a suicide as opposed to an accidental or natural death.) With a recognition that he would have to operationalize the concept of social integration, Durkheim proposed that the higher the rate of social integration, the lower will be the rate of suicide. He already had the suicide rate by country; now he needed to operationalize "social integration."

Durkheim recognized that the concept to be operationalized was highly abstract and that a number of different measures could be used to indicate the degree of its existence. Therefore, he developed several measures (different ways of operationalizing) that he applied separately to determine the rate of integration. The following focuses on only one of those measures (another example is the use of marital status to measure the degree of social integration).

Durkheim thought that the prevalence of the Roman Catholic religion as opposed to the Protestant religion in any country would be indicative of a high degree of integration. His reasoning was that the Catholic faith reflected much greater control in society than did the Protestant. Protestantism placed heavy emphasis on the individual and was much less authoritarian in regard to beliefs and practices than Catholicism. Thus, Catholicism, to a much greater degree, insisted on and enforced a common basis of beliefs and practices that in essence gave the people something to share that "held them together." This operationalization of the concept was very simple but effective, although it does have flaws (or problems of validity). It allowed Durkheim to compare rates of suicide for countries that were primarily Protestant with countries primarily Catholic. His finding was that Catholic countries did indeed have lower rates of suicide; therefore, he concluded that the greater the degree of integration, the lower the suicide rate. Durkheim's research added to knowledge of the causes of suicide and has been useful in giving some hints as to what a society could do to lower suicide rates.

The second example is one with which everyone is familiar, so it will not be as detailed as the Durkheim example. The example is that of educational testing. Every test given in school is a measure of something learned, whether it be knowledge of history dates, an understanding of the causes of the French Revolution, the skill of adding fractions, or the formulation of a research paper. Quite often, the process of conceptualization need not come into play because the ideas already exist as a body of knowledge (geometry, for example). What the instructor must do, however, is design (operationalize) a test that will accurately (validly and reliably) reflect the knowledge gained by the student. The test must be based on the information provided; the problems or questions presented must be clear and complete; and the grading must be complete, objective, and consistent. If the test has been properly designed to reflect the knowledge (operationalized), the application of the test might indicate one of several things, all of which call for some action by the instructor or school. Scores may indicate that the instructor is or is not teaching what needs to be taught, that the students are or are not prepared to learn the material being taught, or that the teaching style and method are or are not appropriate for the students.

The processes of conceptualization and operationalization are a part of everyday life, practiced and not focused upon, yet essential to everyone's ability to know and to function as a human being. The processes are also essential to the formal operations of organizations, in which goals are expected to be met, and to science, in which knowledge is produced. In the latter case, these processes are a matter of great significance and concern and must be performed with precision and accuracy.

Context

The emergence of sociology as a discipline is generally associated with the writings of August Comte in the 1830's. Comte was interested in studying society—its nature and change—by use of the scientific method. Yet he never went beyond the point of trying to describe society based upon his personal experiences and reading. Thus, one might say that he never went beyond conceptualization, since he never systematically and clearly attempted to operationalize and test his ideas. Many of the early "sociologists" have been termed "armchair theorists" because they were more interested in developing ideas than in testing them.

Émile Durkheim, mentioned earlier, is generally credited with completing the first major scientific work in the discipline with the 1897 publication of his work on suicide. The work is a classic of conceptualization and operationalization within the framework of a scientific study. His careful analysis, including both theoretical development and scientific methodology, is worth a careful reading.

With the twentieth century, the process of conceptualization advanced with the emergence of new areas of interest. There was also a greater development of ideas concerning the nature of theory and the types of concepts used in theory. Talcott Parsons, for example, is well known for his detailed analysis and explication of the nature of the social system, using highly abstract and complex concepts. During the same period, operationalization continued to advance. Through the early and middle twentieth century there was a clear movement toward greater quantification of data. This was given a boost through the introduction of computer analysis, which promised complex and rapid analysis of data.

As part of the quantification process, the methodology related to the development of scales advanced; several measures of the same concept could be incorporated to reach a measure more reflective of the complex nature of some concepts. Other forms of measurement important to operationalization were developed as well. Unobtrusive measures were designed and used—measures that did not involve the "obvious" collection of data (such as observing the neatness of books on library shelves to determine topic areas most referenced). Further, advances in the design and use of questionnaires and interview schedules occurred, as did the refinement of the process of direct observation. Advances in operationalization will continue as sociology and the other social sciences struggle with the continuing challenge of creating better measures for the concepts they use.

Bibliography

Babbie, Earl. *The Practice of Social Research.* 4th ed. Belmont, Calif.: Wadsworth, 1986. Babbie's work is a standard textbook in social research. Chapters 5 and 6 discuss in detail the processes of conceptualization and operationalization.

Bonjean, Charles M., Richard J. Hill, and S. Dale McLemore. *Sociological Measurement: An Inventory of Scales and Indices.* San Francisco: Chandler, 1967. An inventory of measures that have been used in social research. The measures are listed by subject area, and references are provided so that readers can review the work in which each measure appeared.

Durkheim, Émile. *Suicide: A Study in Sociology.* Edited by George Simpson. Translated by John A. Spaulding and George Simpson. New York: Free Press, 1951. This book, first published in French in 1897, is considered the first example of the use of the scientific approach in sociology. It provides a classic presentation of conceptualization and operationalization in an attempt to determine the conditions leading to suicide.

Goldenberg, Sheldon. *Thinking Methodologically.* New York: HarperCollins, 1992. An introduction to social science methodology, placed in the context of the positivistic-interpretivist debate: Can social science be modeled after the objective approach of the physical sciences, or must it take into account the fact that human beings are self-aware and always interpreting the world around them? One's stand on this issue significantly affects one's choice of methods.

Miller, Delbert C. *Handbook of Research Design and Social Measurement.* 5th ed. Newbury Park, Calif.: Sage Publications, 1991. Miller's work not only gives an overview of the entire research process but also provides a list of measures used in social research along with their descriptions. Examines how valid and reliable they are, their place of publication, and references to research in which they have been used.

Webb, Eugene, Donald Campbell, Richard D. Schwartz, and Lee Sechrest. *Unobtrusive Measures: Nonreactive Research in the Social Sciences.* Chicago: Rand McNally, 1966. This book is a discussion of the nature and types of unobtrusive measures, and it includes examples and references for each type.

Charles J. Karcher
Barbara C. Karcher

Cross-References

CONFLICT PERSPECTIVES ON DEVIANCE

Type of sociology: Deviance and social control
Fields of study: Social implications of deviance; Theories of deviance

The conflict perspective views conflict as a normal part of social life deriving from competition among groups for society's resources. Conflict perspectives on deviance define issues of deviance as issues of power; they address questions of inequity and inequality in the creation of definitions of deviance, in the application of those definitions, and in the resulting sanctions regarding deviance.

Principal terms
CAPITALISM: an economic system based on private ownership of property and the means of production; the guiding principle is maximization of profit
DEVIANCE: behavior that violates some basic values and norms of society; deviance is present in all societies and may therefore be seen as functional
ELITE DEVIANCE: illegal or unethical behaviors engaged in by members of the upper class, primarily in various aspects of business and industry; white-collar or corporate crime
HEGEMONY: the preponderance of influence and power that is held by society's formal leadership; governments and major religions tend to be the most predominant hegemonic structures in societies
IDEOLOGY: a system of beliefs and values; a dominant ideology is assumed to exist and be reflected in a society's laws and regulations, but in actuality, many ideologies coexist
LABELING: the process of naming deviance and deviants; a label "sticks" when it is bestowed by those in power
MASTER STATUS: a deviant label that, once applied, is very difficult to shed (for example, child molester)
MORAL ENTREPRENEURS: persons who attempt to define behavior as deviant; some have official power (legislators, clerical leaders), but others do not
NORMS: behavioral expectations of societies, some of which are codified into laws
POWER: the ability of a person or group to force its will on others, even in the fact of explicit (or implicit) opposition

Overview

The conflict perspective on deviance explains deviance in relation to issues of power. It articulates instances of inequity and inequality in defining deviance, applying those definitions, creating sanctions for engaging in deviance, and formulating reactions to the processes of deviance.

Sociologists within the conflict tradition are often labeled "radical" or "Marxist" sociologists. The former term came about because at the time these theorists were first publishing their ideas, anyone who criticized the status quo of capitalism was generally considered radical (if not heretical); the latter comes from the fact that conflict theory has its origins in the work of Karl Marx, in which the ideology of capitalism is viewed as an exploitive and materialist system that produces class conflict and inequitable economic relationships. From this foundational perspective, the existence of deviance and crime is viewed as a predictable and natural product of the domination of the working classes by the elite class. The elite class owns the means of production in a system characterized by competition and conflict over scarce resources. Thus, economic disadvantage and the resulting inability to meet basic human needs lead to offenses—historically, often crimes involving property. Meanwhile, the economic advantage of the elite class historically has meant that the elite class can utilize clandestine deviant measures to maintain its advantage and privilege.

According to many sociologists (among them Gresham M. Sykes, Jeffrey H. Reiman, and Richard Quinney), the essence of the conflict perspective on deviance is the existence of a political state apparatus controlled by an elite ruling class. With such control, the ruling class is able to influence the making and enforcement of laws to its own advantage; thus the ruling class is a group of very powerful moral entrepreneurs. Law, it is argued, appears to be a social institution that assists the ruling class in the rationalization and support of economic benefits. Following this line of thinking, Allen E. Liska, Mitchell B. Chamlin, and Mark Reed state that law is a weapon of the ruling class used to maintain the status quo.

A fundamental assumption of any social system that seeks to call itself "just" is the existence of nondiscriminatory laws. From the conflict theory perspective, however, because there is a process in place in which one class seeks to protect its interests, the ruling class gets to make the laws. The ruling class also has the power to determine what and who is defined as deviant, and—equally important—what the sanctions are and how the deviance is to be "fixed." Thus, conflict theorists argue that laws are far from nondiscriminatory.

Many laws and public policies are a direct result of the ruling class working its influence on lawmakers, who themselves are also part of the elite ruling class. The result of such influence is the differential (discriminatory) treatment of different segments of the population in terms of deviance. For example, vagrancy laws are much more likely to be applied to certain classes of people than others (youth, under-represented persons, and the poor). The labels which are used to describe and categorize people also reflect class differences; for example, groups of under-represented males (and sometimes females) are called "gangs," while groups of more well-to-do youth, male or female, are called "cliques." Similarly, a group of lower-class boys who overturn a visiting school's bus parked in a school parking lot are said to have engaged in vandalism. A group of middle-class football players who overturn a visiting school's bus, on the other hand, may be said to have been carried away by healthy rivalry, engaging in "boys will be boys" behavior. Errors (innocent or otherwise) related to the payment of income taxes by middle- or lower-class citizens are often met with seizure of property, whereas income tax errors and evasions by members of the upper classes are often dealt with through consultations regarding ways to remedy the "error." Robbery and burglary are often harshly punished, while violations of antitrust laws, selling products known to be harmful to people or the environment, and business practices documented as dangerous to employees are many times leniently punished (if there is indeed any punishment at all). Such inequities, from the conflict theory perspective, clearly illustrate the protection of the interests and practices of the elite and ruling class.

The major discussions of conflict theories of deviance occur within the contexts of law and economic interest groups. While the conflict perspective of deviance, to many, makes its case articulately and well, others are critical of it. Many critics do not believe, for example, that there is one American "ruling class." Many critics also do not believe that, even if there were a ruling class, it could exert the kind of control and power that the conflict theorists posit. Conflict perspectives on deviance are also criticized for being impossibly utopian in their visions of application of the theory to "correct" the causes of deviance they articulate.

Applications

A number of factors have influenced the degree to which conflict theory views of deviance have resulted in practical applications. These factors include the view, held by many laypersons as well as some scholars, that conflict theorists are "radical," perhaps even dangerous or communistic because of their criticisms of the capitalist economic structure. Also, many people view as heretical (or simply untenable) the following set of propositions important to the conflict perspective: the existence of an elite ruling class; the hegemonic power of that elite ruling class, resulting in inequity and inequality in the definitions of deviance; the creation of laws based on those definitions; and the differential application of those laws. Nevertheless, the conflict view of deviance has had a noticeable impact on sociology, if only because of the reactions it has engendered from other scholars.

One of the most well-known applications of the conflict perspective of deviance involves the labeling perspective, developed by Howard S. Becker. The labeling perspective describes a process by which both deviance and conformity are thought to be a result of people being defined (labeled) by others and then acting accordingly. More specifically, the labeling perspective takes into account the power of some individuals or groups to label others and have those labels "stick," while succeeding in deflecting negative labels themselves. Those to whom labels have been applied often do not have the power to resist or negate those labels. Those groups with power, who succeed in assigning labels and thus definitions of deviance to others, are acting as moral entrepreneurs. Labeling theory helps to explain why groups of lower-class males may be called "gangs" while groups of upper-class males may be "cliques"; why women who provide sexual services to lower-class men are "whores" and women who provide sexual services to upper-class men are "escorts" or "call girls." Labeling is said to produce deviance because those to whom a label of deviance is applied do not have the power to deflect the label; they accept the label and engage in behaviors that are now defined as deviant. While the labeling perspective has been used most often to define and label the actions of individuals, more generalized conflict theories of deviance have been applied to analyses of elite deviance, notably corporate and white-collar crime.

Primarily, conflict theories of deviance have been used to raise questions about the apparent discrepancies in the creation and application of definitions of criminal behavior. Conflict theory raises questions about the ability of the powerful to define as "criminal" such things as some types of art, which the powerful may define as pornography, and loving someone of the same gender, which is defined as homosexuality. In another example, gambling is legal in Atlantic City and Las Vegas, and jaunts to those cities are labeled acceptable entertainment, but bingo games to raise funds for churches, temples, or schools are illegal in some states, as is betting on sports events.

Conflict theorists of deviance also apply their work through various types of activism—exposing abuses of power and advocating reform. Conflict theorists analyze such social and political issues and events as embezzlement, stock fraud, Watergate, the Iran-Contra affair, and abusive "medical" tests and experiments (one well-known example is the "Tuskegee experiment," in which prisoners with syphilis were purposely not treated so that the effects of the disease could be studied), many of which have been kept under cover by government agencies. The conflict perspective of deviance asks why and how such events could have happened as well as why such large-scale violations of human rights continue to occur, given the public outcry raised over crimes against a single person or property crimes committed by individual perpetrators. The answer, from the conflict perspective, lies in the power of the elite class to influence the creation and enforcement of laws and the ability of the elite class to protect itself from prosecution.

Many conflict theorists suggest that nothing short of a complete, radical transformation of society would help alleviate the social problems noted above. This transformation is deemed necessary because the "cause" of deviance is seen to reside not in the individual but in the social structure itself—its laws and customs—and especially in capitalism. Such a transformation would need to restructure the political and economic order as well as class relationships; the goal would be a more equitable treatment of all persons, resulting in more equitable definitions and applications of labels of deviance.

Context

The first clearly recognized development of the notion of deviance can be traced to Émile Durkheim's work "The Normal and the Pathological," in *Les Règles de la méthode sociologique* (1895; *The Rules of Sociological Method*, 1938). Durkheim's writing formed the foundation for the functionalist theories of deviance. Functionalism, the first major theoretical framework of sociology, views societies as consisting of interrelated institutions and groups that together help a society work (function) smoothly enough to meet its members' needs.

Many theories of deviance were developed in the United States in the first half of the twentieth century. There was an initial focus on biological, psychological, and social psychological explanations. Then sociologists began to identify more specifically social factors (such as massive immigration, urbanization, industrialization, and, later, processes of social interaction) that were theorized to produce deviance.

The 1970's, probably as a result of the sociohistorical turbulence and changes of the 1960's, saw substantial development of conflict theories of deviance. These theories, with their roots in the work of Karl Marx, recognized power and class as two significant—and heretofore largely neglected—social facts to be recognized in definitions of deviance. This explication of power and class as important factors caused some scholars to reformulate or even reject earlier theories of deviance and social control. Conflict theories of deviance (also called, by critics, "critical" or "radical" theories) raised questions about the labeling of "secret" deviance (such as consensual same-gender relationships and extramarital relations), victimless crimes (such as gambling and prostitution), and the apparent lack of response to elite (corporate and white-collar) deviance. Many of these theories focused on the general area of crime.

The appearance of conflict theories of deviance marked a significant shift in sociological thinking about deviance. Early theories explained the causes of deviance as existing within the individual; later theories focused attention on the social circumstances of the deviants as the causes of deviance. With conflict theories, however, the focus shifted to the larger social context in which the so-called deviant lived; it looked at the structures of power and hegemony that defined what was deviant and determined how the behaviors so defined would be treated.

Bibliography

Becker, Howard S. *Outsiders: Studies in the Sociology of Deviance*. New York: Free Press, 1963. A readable classic in the field of deviance that raises a number of critical issues, such as whose rules determine what will be defined as deviant and who gets so labeled. Recognizes and discusses the issue of power in regard to creating definitions and bestowing labels. Highly recommended.

Chambliss, William J. "Toward a Political Economy of Crime." *Theory and Society* 2 (1975): 149-170. Addresses the position that there is a powerful class that is able to influence the creation and execution of laws through manipulation of the criminal justice system, a process which then benefits the powerful and makes the powerless more vulnerable to application of the laws. One of the foundational works in the area of conflict theories of deviance.

Hartjen, Clayton A. *Crime and Criminalization*. New York: Praeger, 1974. An analysis of the administration of justice that addresses a very important question about the differential application of justice. Examines why some laws are largely unenforced while others are enforced with a vengeance.

Liazos, Alexander. "The Poverty of the Sociology of Deviance: Nuts, Sluts, and Perverts." *Social Problems* 20, no. 1 (1972): 103-120. An outstanding article addressing the history of deviance and social problems and noting how the focus of sociology in these areas has been on individual acts and "dramatic" forms of deviance. The article points out how this process very noticeably neglects studying acts of deviance committed by those with power.

Liska, Allen E. *Perspectives on Deviance*. Englewood Cliffs, N.J.: Prentice-Hall, 1981. The theme of this work is that definitions of deviance reinforce the superiority of the ruling class. The only way to eliminate class superiority, says Liska, is to transform society completely, eliminating institutions which contribute to class hierarchies.

Quinney, Richard. *Class, State, and Crime: On the Theory and Practice of Criminal Justice*. Englewood Cliffs, N.J.: Prentice-Hall, 1985. An important reading in the conflict perspective on deviance, and one often cited as containing the most explicit statement of the utopian ideals of the conflict perspective.

Reiman, Jeffrey H. *The Rich Get Richer and the Poor Get Prison*. 2d ed. New York: John Wiley & Sons, 1984. An overview of the conflict perspective on deviance as it addresses crime control in the United States. Articulates and highlights the inequities and disparities in the treatment of criminals from the lower and upper classes.

Simon, David R., and D. Stanley Eitzen. *Elite Deviance*. 2d ed. Boston: Allyn and Bacon, 1986. A good look at power in society. Makes the point that few enforcement resources are directed at elite deviance, despite its enormous costs—financial and human—compared with all other types of crime.

Spitzer, Steven. "Toward a Marxian Theory of Deviance." In *Criminal Behavior: Readings in Criminology*, edited by Delos H. Kelley. New York: St. Martin's Press, 1980. This work articulates a social-conflict theory of deviance. Its major premise is that certain categories of people, defined as "problem populations" (those seen to be threatening to the way capitalism works) are labeled as deviant. Based on Marx's classic analysis of the relationship of classes, norms, and economic systems.

Sykes, Gresham M. "Criminology: The Rise of Critical Criminology." *The Journal of Criminal Law and Criminology* 65 (June, 1974): 206-211. Addresses a fundamental assumption of the conflict perspective on deviance, namely that the state is a political and economic entity controlled by the ruling class for its own advantage. Also identifies the strengths of the conflict perspective in relation to deviance, which are related to systemic, endemic structures and hegemonies.

M. F. Stuck

Cross-References

Capitalism, 191; Conflict Theory, 340; Crime: Analysis and Overview, 373; Deviance: Analysis and Overview, 525; Deviance: Biological and Psychological Explanations, 532; Deviance: Functions and Dysfunctions, 540; Social Stratification: Analysis and Overview, 1839; Social Stratification: Modern Theories, 1859; White-Collar and Corporate Crime, 2179.

CONFLICT THEORY

Type of sociology: Origins and definitions of sociology
Field of study: Sociological perspectives and principles

Conflict theory is the sociological perspective that focuses on tension, competition, and division in society. It assumes that no society is devoid of conflicts of interest and that in the process of struggling for scarce and valuable resources groups develop strategies to maximize their rewards and minimize their losses.

Principal terms

CONFLICT: the tension, hostility, or competitiveness that exists among groups in society as they struggle to obtain social resources and improve their positions in the social system

ELITES: those groups in society that manage to control the largest amount of social resources and obtain a privileged position in relation to other groups

NORMS: sets of shared patterns of conduct that provide a group with the guidelines for acceptable and nonacceptable behavior

SOCIAL CHANGE: the ongoing process of societal transformation, caused by the constant struggle among groups for scarce resources or rewards

SOCIAL RESOURCES: the desirable or valuable cultural items (such as power, prestige, and property) that empower their holders to achieve an elite status within the social system

SOCIAL STRATIFICATION: the hierarchical ranking of groups and individuals in society, determined in accordance with the amount of resources they hold within the social system

Overview

The discipline of sociology contains a number of major theoretical frameworks within which sociologists examine social processes and institutions. Three perspectives that are generally considered of central importance are functionalism, conflict theory, and interactionism. Functionalism places an emphasis on the operation of a society in meeting the needs of its members; it therefore emphasizes the factors that are necessary for society to operate—or function—effectively.

Conflict theory, on the other hand, focuses on the tension, hostility, competition, and division in society. This perspective assumes that all valuable social resources or rewards—such as power, prestige, and property—are scarce in human groups. This scarcity generates conflict, since several groups must vie for control of the resources and for the privileged positions in the social system. Given that no society has managed to achieve an equal distribution of resources among all its members, it seems safe to assume that no society is devoid of conflicts of interests and that, in the process of struggling for scarce and valuable resources, groups develop strategies to maximize their rewards and minimize their losses.

To conflict theorists, the struggle for social resources never happens under equal or fair conditions. Some groups begin the race with additional opportunities, privileges, and advantages. Depending on which social resource one is studying, certain groups and individuals always seem to have an edge on the competition—an edge that may be the result of merit, skills, and hard work, or a consequence of shrewdness, opportunism, timing, trickery, and whatever other methods may be devised to gain an advantage over the competition. Those groups and individuals who manage to gain control over a large amount of social resources obtain a privileged status within the social system; they are the elite groups of the society.

Elite groups are not necessarily defined as only the wealthy in a given society; they may be any group in control of advantages in a field of scarce resources. They can be groups of famous artists, athletes, intellectuals, or scientists; they may be powerful generals, politicians, or business leaders. They may be at the top of the social hierarchy according to one measure of social stratification (education, income, class, or occupation) but not necessarily according to all measures. For the sake of a more precise analysis, however, some conflict theorists prefer to define elite groups more narrowly as those few at the top of the social stratification system who seem to benefit most from the status quo in society.

Conflict theorists document how elite groups manage to take control of scarce resources in society and maintain that control at the expense of all other groups. Their assumption is that in the process of becoming elites, certain groups fashion the social institutions, laws, and norms of a society for the purpose of maintaining their own privileged positions. Since the elite groups have more resources, they also have greater coercive power: They have the ability to use the system to push the rest of the population into compliance and conformity with their vision of the status quo. A good example of that ability is a society's laws governing the inheritance of wealth or property, according to which the affluent are able to transmit the scarce resources they have amassed to their offspring. Another example is the structure of higher education. Prestigious private universities, in catering to the children of the powerful, help them transfer their privileged position to their offspring by guaranteeing better social opportunities for their graduates.

According to conflict theorists, elite groups not only control the social system but also develop an ideology of domination that justifies their privilege. To maintain order, elite groups must convince other social groups that their subordination either is temporary or is in the best interests of the society as a whole. The ideology that the elite groups create in order to accomplish this must either give other groups the impression that the system is open (and that it is therefore possible to improve one's position) or give other groups the impression that subordination is necessary because of their lack of ability or because of the "natural" order of things. To the extent that other groups accept the elites' ideology, the stability of the system is guaranteed, and its patterns of domination and subordination remain unchallenged.

The work of three European scholars—Karl Marx, Max Weber, and Georg Simmel—provided a basis for the development of conflict theory. Karl Marx provided conflict theorists with the most critical evaluation of Western society. He believed that social systems distribute scarce resources unequally and that certain groups in society appropriate greater amounts of resources at the expense of all others, thus contributing to conflict among classes. To Marx, the end of class conflict could only come with a reorganization of the social system under which egalitarian patterns of resource distribution would be put in place.

Weber added to Marx's insights by insisting that class alone is not sufficient for identifying the privileged in society. Although wealth and ownership of the means of production are important signs of privilege, status is also derived from prestige, breeding, and other social categories. Weber believed that the stratification of privilege in modern societies is more complex than Marx had presented in his model. Weber also pointed out more clearly the connection between ideology and distribution of resources.

Simmel further enriched the theoretical base of conflict theory by suggesting that conflict serves as a source of both integration and dissention. Intragroup conflict, for example, helps integrate society by serving as a safety valve for built-up hostility; if workers are fighting one another, they will not organize and unify to challenge their employers. Another good example of the power of conflict to promote societal integration is the fact that conflict with outside groups may lead to increased levels of social solidarity within the group being attacked—thus, in a country at war, dominant and subordinate groups might suspend their hostility for the sake of fighting a common enemy.

American sociologists C. Wright Mills and Lewis A. Coser each made significant contributions to conflict theory. Drawing on the insights of the classical theorists, Mills was one of the early conflict theorists in American sociology. He laid considerable groundwork for the perspective in two controversial books. In *White Collar* (1951), he identified a privileged occupational category and delivered a highly critical analysis of its dominance in American society. In *The Power Elite* (1956), Mills expanded the notion of a privileged group to encompass the business leaders, politicians, and military leaders who, in his opinion, personified the unified, all-powerful group that controls the United States. Mills's work was characterized by his effort to show that conflict is not an occasional or accidental aspect of society but rather an integral part of it.

Coser provided conflict theory with its next important contribution. In his book *The Functions of Social Conflict* (1956), Coser documented how conflict plays a role in preserving society as much as consensus does. For example, he shows how, in large, modern societies, the practice of democracy creates cross-conflicts by bringing together under the umbrella of large parties a variety of ethnic, economic, political, and regional groups who otherwise might be divided by basic, irreconcilable differences. Coser shows how conflict may serve also to bring some isolated individuals into active roles for change and may clarify the positions and boundaries of antagonistic groups so that they become better aware of their relative strengths and of possible means to create peaceful accommodation.

Applications

Conflict theory provides a means of understanding the dynamics of power and privilege in society. By identifying the groups who benefit from present social arrangements and studying the process by which they reached their present conditions, one can understand not only their privileged position but also the strategies they used to reach their goal and the ideology that has been employed to sustain the status quo. One application of the perspective comes in the area of gender stratification. Here, an ascribed trait or status (gender) is used to limit the access of one segment of society to available social resources. Studies of inequality of power, prestige, and property between the sexes show that the patterns of domination and subordination existing between men and women in the United States cannot be totally explained by either the merits of males or the inability of females.

For example, using insights from conflict theory, one can show that as late as 1991 very few women held powerful positions in American politics (two senators, four governors, and about 6 percent of members of Congress), which limited women's future ability to gain power or to create policy that would correct the situation. Furthermore, the lack of political power may have more to do with what might be termed the rules of the game (the regulations controlling elections, the funding of successful campaigns, and the willingness of voters to deem women reliable and competent leaders) than with an absence of capable women to run for office. The distribution of prestige and property seems no different from the distribution of power. In the early 1990's, the gender wage gap in the American marketplace (on average, full-time working women earn between 65 and 72 cents for every dollar earned by full-time working men) and the sex segregation of occupations (men-dominated occupations draw higher pay scales than women-dominated occupations) had more to do with the barriers and regulations created by the dominant group than with the amount of training, experience, or competence of female workers.

According to the Bureau of the Census, whereas women accounted for 45 percent of the labor force in 1988, they represented only 7 percent of engineers, 9 percent of dentists, 20 percent of physicians, and 20 percent of lawyers and judges. In a comparison of median annual earnings for full-time employment, the Bureau of the Census found that in 1987, female executives were making an average of $21,874 a year, compared with $36,055 for their male counterparts; accountants made $22,960 (females), compared with $34,867 (males); engineers made $32,506 (females), versus $40,309 (males). The principle seems to hold true for most professions. Furthermore, studies of gender stratification show how sexism has been used as an ideology of domination to justify the level of privilege enjoyed by males in American society.

Another area that has benefited from conflict theory's insights is the study of race relations. Although prejudice may be considered a result of individual bigotry, stereotyping, and false and incomplete information related to minority groups, discrimination is the process by which social structures are set in place by a dominant group to treat people of different racial background unequally and inequitably. In doing so, discrimination helps sustain the privileged conditions of the dominant group.

The resistance to changing segregation laws in the United States during the 1950's is well documented and was responsible for the growth of one of the largest mass movements in modern American history—the Civil Rights movement. Under legal segregation, an ascribed trait (perceived racial identity) was used to keep a distinct segment of the population from having access to social resources. Through segregated schools, housing, and job opportunities, the dominant majority managed to impose living conditions on the minority that benefited the status quo at the expense of the minority's well-being.

To this day, the effects of such discrimination are still felt nationwide. Race discrimination studies show that, even taking into account education, experience, training, and all other variables that represent merit, African Americans are barred from valuable resources in society because of norms that sustain the barriers against members of their ethnic group. In 1989, 25.9 percent of African American households had an annual income of less than $10,000, compared with 7.7 percent of white American households. At the other end of the spectrum, 13.8 percent of African American households earned an annual income of $50,000 or more, compared with 23.9 percent of white households. In 1987, about one African American in three lived below the poverty line, compared with one in ten white Americans. Unemployment rates for young African American men were three times higher than for young white men. Two of every three white households owned their own homes, compared with fewer than half of all African American households. Studies of race stratification have indicated that the dominant group supports its control through promulgating an ideology of racism to justify or explain the status quo.

Context

Conflict theory emerged in mainstream American sociology as a reaction to, and criticism of, functionalism. Functionalism was the leading theoretical approach in American sociology for a large part of the 1940's and 1950's. Led by Talcott Parsons, functionalists adopted an organic conception of society, one which placed a premium on social consensus, stability, and order. Using the metaphor of society as an organism, functionalists dissected society into its constituent parts, studying and explaining each part in terms of its contribution to the existence, operation, and survival of the larger whole. Every element of society was seen as functional in the stability of the whole, with society being held together by the harmony and cohesion that stemmed from the shared values, norms, and beliefs of its members.

To conflict theorists, society is anything but a balanced, harmonious organism. Many of the early theorists were frustrated with functionalism's inability to explain the tensions, hostilities, and cleavages they perceived in the social system. Assuming that the study of harmony and consensus explained only part of social reality, they began to emphasize the need for a study of tension and disagreement. Drawing on the work of European scholars Marx, Weber, and Simmel, American conflict theorists such as Mills and Coser produced a more critical appraisal of society when they highlighted the struggles and dissensions witnessed in the interaction of social groups with unequal access to resources.

Building on the work of Mills, Coser, and others, American sociologists continued to refine conflict theory. In *Conflict Sociology* (1975), Randall Collins summarized the contributions of conflict theory to American sociology. Drawing on the works of his predecessors, Collins defines conflict theory, explains its major premises, and explores how it helps sociologists to understand and study racial and ethnic cleavages, gender inequality, age inequality, religious dissension, and political antagonisms in modern society. Collins makes explicit the notion that social resources are scarce and valuable and that therefore their distribution creates the conflict of interests that leads to a hierarchy of privilege and power in modern society.

Jonathan Turner, in his book *The Structure of Sociological Theory* (1982), provides another treatment of conflict theory. Defining conflict as a process of events that leads to varying degrees of violence between parties, Turner outlines the outbreak of violence in nine steps. According to him, conflict takes place when social groups who do not receive a proportionate share of resources in a society begin to question the legitimacy of the system. As those groups become more aware that it is in their interest to challenge the system of resource allocation, they may rise to confront the status quo. Becoming better organized as hostility grows in intensity, they struggle until there is an outbreak of violence which ultimately defines the resolution (whether favorable or unfavorable to their cause) of the situation.

Bibliography

Bradley, Harriet. *Men's Work, Women's Work*. Minneapolis: University of Minnesota Press, 1989. An overview of the social processes through which occupations become segregated by sex and opportunities to obtain social resources are divided across gender lines.

Carmichael, Stokely, and Charles V. Hamilton. *Black Power: The Politics of Liberation in America*. New York: Random House, 1967. This book provides the reader with an incisive application of conflict theory's most basic insights. Written during the time of the urban riots in the United States, it provides an incisive analysis of group dominance and the importance of its ideology of domination.

Collins, Randall. *Conflict Sociology*. New York: Academic Press, 1975. Collins' book is one of the best overall presentations of conflict theory as a sociological perspective. In it one finds not only a discussion of previous works in the field but also an effort to present a synthesis—a unified description of the field that may aid in the understanding of different social cleavages in society.

Coser, Lewis A. *The Functions of Social Conflict*. Glencoe, Ill.: Free Press, 1956. Following in the footsteps of Simmel, Coser provides the reader with the most thorough exploration of how conflict can be a source of integration in society.

Mills, C. Wright. *The Power Elite*. New York: Oxford University Press, 1956. In this book, Mills expands the concept of privileged group to identify the members of a unified American power elite. According to him, the power elite represents the interests of three major sectors in society: business groups, political leaders, and military leaders.

_____ . *White Collar.* New York: Oxford University Press, 1951. Mills's critical analysis of white-collar workers as a privileged occupational group in American society. The book discusses the creation and maintenance of the white-collar occupation as a class and the justification for its position in the system.

H. B. Cavalcanti

Cross-References

Age Inequality: Functionalist versus Conflict Theory Views, 34; Conflict Perspectives on Deviance, 334; Education: Conflict Theory Views, 579; The Family: Functionalist versus Conflict Theory Views, 739; Functionalism, 786; Gender Inequality: Analysis and Overview, 820; Religion: Marxist and Conflict Theory Views, 1610; Social Change: Functionalism versus Historical Materialism, 1779; Social Stratification: Marxist Perspectives, 1852; The History of Sociology, 1926; Sociology Defined, 1932.

CONFUCIANISM AND TAOISM

Type of sociology: Major social institutions
Field of study: Religion

Confucianism and Taoism are the two major belief systems indigenous to China. Together with Buddhism, they make up the "Three Teachings of China." Both Confucianism and Taoism have, throughout history, profoundly influenced Eastern culture.

Principal terms
CONFUCIANISM: a philosophy founded by Confucius in sixth century B.C.E. China
RECTIFICATION OF NAMES: according to Confucius, this process involved reconciling language with reality and was vital to the establishment of a virtuous society
TAOISM: a belief system that may include both religious and philosophical aspects and which developed out of indigenous Chinese culture
TAO-CHIA: Taoism as a philosophy
TAO-CHIAO: Taoism as a religion

Overview

Taoism and Confucianism developed from indigenous religious beliefs and philosophies which predate both by several millennia. These traditional religious practices involve veneration of ancestors and honored deceased, and they recognize several deities, including many nature spirits. Ancient philosophies explain the universe in terms of two polar forces: Yin and Yang. Yin encompasses darkness, passivity, and destruction; it is considered the female half of the duality. Yang embodies light, activity, and construction; it is associated with the male aspect. Wisdom is found through understanding and acceptance of these forces at work in the world. Elements of these older beliefs pervade the doctrines of both belief systems.

Taoism as a philosophy (Tao-chia) teaches a way to live in harmony with the unnameable, inexplicable force that pervades every aspect of life. This force may be referred to as the Ultimate, the One, the Universe, or any other all-inclusive designation. It surpasses human understanding, however, and therefore is limited by any attempt to define or label it. Roughly translated, "Tao" means a path or road. Tao, in its highest sense, then, is the Way—the way of acting in accordance with this higher force. "Te" is virtue. One of the most important and universally accepted Taoist texts, the *Tao Te Ching*, would then be "The Virtue of the Way."

The Way is characterized by belief in the unity of all things; one who achieves this unity transcends all dichotomies and sees beyond them to the source of all things. Taoists also seek harmony with nature, both in an external and internal sense. In addition to reverence for the natural world, Taoists believe in the purity of inner nature.

Everything, people included, possesses a natural state. Attempting to alter this condition is an action against universal principles. A Taoist therefore avoids influences contrary to these goals and seeks to act according to inner nature. The way to do this—or, perhaps, the result of achieving this—is expressed in the concept of *wei wu wei*: "to do without doing" or "to act without acting." When people follow the Way, their actions will be spontaneous, natural, and unselfconscious and therefore will be virtuous and meaningful.

Confucianism developed in the sixth century B.C.E. when its founder, Confucius, consolidated and edited the teachings of the ancients, organizing this knowledge into the six books of the *Classics*: the *Book of Poetry*, the *Book of History*, the *Book of Rites*, the *Book of Music*, the *Book of Change* (the *I Ching*), and the *Spring and Autumn Annals*. Along with these ancient teachings, Confucius incorporated his own views in the *Analects*, which comprises his sayings and deeds and was compiled sometime after his death. It is usually taken as the most reliable source of his teachings.

Like Taoists, Confucianists believe that attaining virtue is the highest goal for which a person can strive. In Confucianism, however, metaphysical considerations serve primarily insofar as they explain or parallel worldly matters. Its view of the universe is much more pragmatic than Taoism's. Therefore, instead of emphasizing transcendence and emptiness as the highest forms of virtue, Confucianism focuses on the qualities that exemplify the good or virtuous person. Confucius recognized the existence and importance of higher powers but was more concerned with their practical applications: "I study things on the lower level but my understanding penetrates the higher level," he says in the *Analects*. In this respect, Confucianism might be understood as a mirror image of Taoism. Taoists contemplate the One and gain understanding of all things contained within it. Confucianists understand the One primarily through its secular applications.

Both systems began as philosophies. Only later did they become religions, incorporating aspects of traditional worship with philosophy. As a religion, Confucianism calls for adherence to the traditional indigenous beliefs. Veneration of deities and the deceased is an important part of Confucius' philosophy, and although most of his philosophy deals with worldly issues, he does speak of the importance of religious observation in the *Analects*. Similarly, Taoism, when practiced as a religion, includes elements of the traditional beliefs, along with some Buddhist influences.

To label the complete system of either Confucianism or Taoism as a religion is to ignore the history of the Chinese traditions and religions that preceded them. In the first place, Confucius was not regarded as a prophet by his people, and he never considered himself to be one. In addition, he emphasized secular issues much more than transcendental considerations. Finally, while he did advocate traditional religious practices, these were beliefs and rituals that antedated him by many centuries. Therefore, he could hardly be considered the founder of a religion. To think of him as such is a purely Western interpretation. The same might be said of Taoism. As is true of Confucianists, people who consider themselves Taoists may embrace the philosophy but not the religion, or they may adhere to both.

Applications

Although not primarily a social philosophy, Taoism teaches that civilization and its practices often seek to corrupt our true natures. Withdrawal from worldly, material things is vital to attaining the Taoist ideal of virtue. Since in the Taoist ideal people act in harmony with the world, themselves, and one another, little government, if any, should be needed to maintain order. It is against the natural way to impose civilization, morals, and practices on people. Governments, unfortunately, often attempt to do just that. Doing so eventually results in chaos because by doing so one attempts to circumvent natural processes. Therefore, the government that governs least (or that governs in accordance with natural principles) usually governs best.

Confucianism, like Taoism, generally assumes that human nature is good and that virtuousness is the highest state a person can achieve. Consequently, both have in common the belief that a society governed by virtue rather than force is the ideal; also, when the people of a state are virtuous, its rulers need not exercise their authority. Since Confucianism is much more a social system than Taoism, Confucianism's view of a person's relationship to society differs greatly from Taoism's. In Confucianism, civilization is natural and desirable. Society makes possible the spread, development, and reinforcement of good values. While an individual should strive throughout life to achieve the highest possible virtue, government's role is to encourage and promote this development—to reward virtue with virtue and wickedness with justice.

According to either philosophy, an individual's purpose in life is to become as virtuous as possible. Confucianism differs from Taoism in its methods of and purposes for attaining this ideal state. Each aspect of virtue should be applied, foremost, in service of the state—practiced for the benefit of all. In the *Analects*, Confucius outlined the components of virtue. A virtuous person is benevolent, wise, honest, and courageous; fulfills all filial duties and responsibilities; is dependable and reliable in all promises, words, and actions; and is reverent and respectful in both word and action. He or she also has the ability to assess situations and act properly in accordance with these qualities.

For the Confucian ideal of government to function efficiently, a leader should exemplify legitimacy and virtue. In this, a leader would effectively serve the state and would be a model for the people to emulate. The same is true of administrations. Fairly selected members would ideally compose a professional aristocracy of capable, honorable persons, all dedicated to serving the people and their state. The best and most worthy should naturally rise to positions of authority. Most important, officials should gain the trust and confidence of the people. Under such conditions, the common people follow the model established by the elite. Proper leadership, then, can engender moral behavior in citizens.

Unlike Taoism, Confucianism does not require that the individual have an understanding of the larger principles behind it. While the rulers and sages should fully understand the laws of heaven, it is not necessary that the lower classes grasp such esoteric principles. As long as those in the upper class do, and as long as the common citizens follow their lead, the government will function effectively. Confucianism therefore suggests a trickle-down method of establishing virtue. Government officials provide the model for citizens to emulate. The system honors and rewards virtuous behavior and therefore produces virtuous citizens. This is quite unlike Taoism's emphasis on individual enlightenment.

Strong family relationships further establish and regulate acceptable behavior. Filial piety parallels the ideal government-citizen relationship. Parents provide and protect, and they expect in return honor and obedience; this translates itself into good citizenship—respect for rulers and government—as the child becomes an adult. Religion is an equally important influence. Just as proper family relationships establish a hierarchical system, assigning roles of leadership or obligation, so does adherence to religious practices. Religion, as a symbol of the relationship between humans and God, can be easily extended as a parallel between citizens and the state, further affirming the social hierarchy and power structure.

When asked what he believed to be the first step in correcting an administration's or society's problems, Confucius asserted the principle that has come to be known as the "Rectification of Names": "Let the ruler *be* a ruler, the minister *be* a minister, the father *be* a father, and the son *be* a son." Confucius said that to reconcile the meaning of words with reality was to put language in accord with truth and to put duty in accord with action. With such abstracts clearly defined, it becomes easier to explain, understand, and engender the virtues specific to each person.

Context
Confucianism began as one of many philosophies in China's "Hundred Schools" period and emerged as the official teaching in 136 B.C.E. With the appearance of Taoism and Buddhism, Confucianism was temporarily eclipsed around the second century C.E.; in reaction to this, Neo-Confucianism began to develop during the T'ang dynasty. It continued to be an influence for the next thousand years. Confucianism spread to Japan in the sixth and seventh centuries and continues to be an influence on modern Japanese society.

Because Taoism is a development and extension of ancient philosophy, it is impossible to determine precisely when it evolved. Taoism as a religion (Tao-chiao) grew out of Taoism as a philosophy (Tao-chia). The history of the philosophy—so intrinsically tied to the older systems—is lost somewhere in antiquity.

In China, the Yellow Emperor is credited with formally establishing Taoist philosophy, which would place its development between 2697 and 2597 B.C.E. Legend says that he learned it from a sage and passed it down to the people. Other reports have the philosophy developing among Chinese tribes who lived more than seven thousand years ago; these tribes were driven into Korea around 3000 B.C.E. and carried Taoism with them. It is easier to approximate the date of Tao-chiao's formalization. Chang Tao Ling, a first century C.E. Taoist philosopher, and his followers combined elements of Buddhism, traditional Chinese beliefs, and Taoist philosophy into an organized religion.

With the establishment of Confucianism as the state school of China, the *Classics* became a standard part of the educational system; they continued to be so until the twentieth century. Although it did not have the same degree of state support, Taoism continued to flourish as well. Contact with the West, however, beginning in the seventeenth century, resulted in profound changes in Eastern worldviews and beliefs. By the 1920's, the Chinese Republic, which exalted science, technology, and social development, overthrew the last of the imperial dynasties. The Communist regime, instituted in 1949, substituted secularism for religion. Later, the Cultural Revolution of the 1960's and 1970's attempted to displace Confucianist hierarchical structures and the intellectual, aristocratic ruling class. It attacked Confucianism and all other traditional practices.

Consequently, much of the religious practice involved in these philosophies ceased in China proper. Yet in other Chinese regions, such as Hong Kong and Taiwan, traditional practices continue. Confucianism survives as an ethical philosophy in Japan; Taoism and Confucianism, as philosophies, both continue to influence aspects of Chinese culture.

Bibliography

Chan, Wing-Tsit, comp. and trans. *A Source Book in Chinese Philosophy*. Princeton, N.J.: Princeton University Press, 1963. Chan examines Taoism, Confucianism, and Buddhism; he offers translations and discussions of ancient, medieval, and modern texts alike. His information is thorough, extensive, detailed, and easily understood. A valuable source for those interested in any aspect of Chinese philosophy.

Chang, Carsun. *The Development of Neo-Confucian Thought*. 2 vols. New York: Bookman Associates, 1957, 1962. Chang provides a comprehensive view of the development of Confucianism, focusing especially on Neo-Confucianist philosophers. He also includes interesting and helpful comparisons of Confucius' teachings and Western philosophies.

Cleary, Thomas, ed. and trans. *Vitality, Energy, Spirit: A Taoist Sourcebook*. Boston: Shambhala, 1991. Cleary offers translations and interpretations of both classical and modern Taoist writings. He also includes fables, stories, and historical information on and excerpts from traditional texts.

Hoff, Benjamin. *The Tao of Pooh*. New York: Penguin Books, 1983. Presents an easily understood illumination of Taoist principles by using Winnie-the-Pooh and the rest of A. A. Milne's characters. The text is both enlightening and practical, regardless of the reader's level of philosophical experience. It is especially helpful for those who feel themselves unable to understand the scholarly notes and jargon that usually accompany translations or discussions of philosophical texts. A valuable supplement to any translation of the *Tao Te Ching*. Hoff seeks to portray the depth and beauty of Taoism, which is often lost in more academic treatments of the philosophy.

Rozman, Gilbert, ed. *The East Asian Region: Confucian Heritage and Its Modern Adaptation*. Princeton, N.J.: Princeton University Press, 1991. This text contains several essays on Confucianism's continuing influence. In addition to Rozman's introduction ("The East Asian Region in Comparative Perspective"), the text includes Patricia Ebrey's "The Chinese Family and the Spread of Confucian Values," JaHyun Kim Haboush's "The Confucianization of Korean Society," Martin Collcutt's "The Legacy of Confucianism in Japan," Rozman's "Comparisons of Modern Confucian Values In China and Japan," and Michael Robinson's "Perceptions of Confucianism in Twentieth Century Korea."

William Nelles
Stephanie Pierrotti

Cross-References

Buddhism, 165; Christianity, 231; Islam and Islamic Fundamentalism, 1022; Judaism, 1029; Religion: Beliefs, Symbols, and Rituals, 1598; Religion: Functionalist Analyses, 1603; Religion: Marxist and Conflict Theory Views, 1610; The Sociology of Religion, 1952.

CONQUEST AND ANNEXATION OF RACIAL OR ETHNIC GROUPS

Type of sociology: Racial and ethnic relations
Field of study: Patterns and consequences of contact

Conquest and annexation are two processes by which one group may be subordinated to another following contact. To maintain social stability, the subordinate or minority group must either be excluded from or integrated into dominant society. Societal control is maintained by a continuum of forms from destruction to absorption of the subordinate group.

Principal terms

DOMINANT GROUP: the group that exercises control over societal resources

ETHNIC GROUP: a group classified according to national origins or cultural characteristics shared by its members, such as language, religion, food habits, and folklore

MINORITY OR SUBORDINATE GROUP: a group distinguished by recognizable physical or cultural characteristics which become the basis for unequal treatment and less access to power; it may or may not represent a numerical minority

RACIAL GROUP: an ethnic group whose members are classified according to certain physical differences that a society deems significant; the characteristics used to assign people to different races vary from one society to another

SOCIAL STRATIFICATION: the structured ranking of entire groups of people that perpetuates inequalities in power and treatment

SUBORDINATE GROUP FORMS: relatively stable, but not necessarily permanent, relationships between dominant and subordinate groups

SUBORDINATING PROCESSES: the processes through which one group becomes dominant over another group following contact

Overview

The types of relations that exist between racial or ethnic groups in culturally diverse societies depend on how the various groups are brought into contact with one another and on how their cultural distinctiveness relates to gaining access to resources and power. Race or ethnicity is often the basis for social stratification. Barriers to the full societal participation of racial or ethnic subordinate groups include attitudes of prejudice, the practice of discrimination, and the existence of institutional structures and norms which limit the options of subordinate groups. Such systemic barriers are referred to as institutional discrimination.

Two major ways sociologists attempt to explain the maintenance of such stratification are through functionalist theories and conflict theories. In the former, the focus is on how stratification systems maintain stability and social order. In the latter, the focus is on the struggle for power and resources and the means by which the powerful maintain and enlarge control. These two types of explanations are not mutually exclusive. They can reflect different points in historical time or different perspectives of the same experience of social inequality. In South Africa, for example, dramatic social stratification has existed, with the dominant white society (a numerical minority) controlling most of the land and mineral resources, technology, and the military. Elaborate laws have controlled the freedom of movement of black South Africans and ensured the availability of a black labor force. From the dominant white perspective, a stable system has existed, one that has been justified by an ideology which historically has been grounded in a belief of white superiority. From the black South African perspective, the structural injustices have maintained unequal access to food, health care, education, and jobs; this lack of access has prohibited social mobility. Both nonviolent resistance and violent confrontation have resulted as blacks have struggled for access to resources and self-determination.

A variety of processes can lead to the formation, annexation, or conquest of racial or ethnic subordinate groups. These subordinating processes can be distinguished from one another according to the degree to which the racial or ethnic group participates voluntarily and according to whether migration is involved. Voluntary migration characterizes immigrant groups that may be seeking greater access to personal freedoms and economic resources. It also characterizes refugee groups that may be fleeing armed conflicts, persecution, or natural disasters. Involuntary migration characterizes the experience of slaves or indentured servants. In annexation, once-dominant peoples may become subordinate without migrating from their homelands. This occurs when nations expand their borders to incorporate neighboring lands and their inhabitants. Finally, colonization occurs when a foreign power usurps and maintains political, social, economic, and cultural domination over land and peoples without annexing them into its national structure. Even following a country's independence from a colonial power, it may be controlled by that power because of economic and social dependence on the former colonizer. This is referred to as neocolonialism.

The relationship of racial or ethnic groups to the dominant group in a society can take on a variety of subordinate forms. These forms vary according to the degree to which the racial or ethnic group maintains a distinct identity and the degree to which these subordinate groups experience intergroup contact with the dominant group. Genocide is the ultimate loss of racial or ethnic identity coupled with separation from the dominant group. This may be a deliberate and systematic killing of group members with the intent of obliterating them, as was Adolf Hitler's policy toward Jews in Nazi Germany. Genocide also may be less intentional but no less complete. Disease and brutal treatment by the Spanish wiped out the indigenous Indians of what is now the West Indies. This loss of a forced labor pool required that the Spanish begin to import African slaves. Expulsion describes the subordinate form in which a racial or ethnic group's identity is maintained but the group is completely forced from the lands conquered by the dominant group. The Bosnian Serb "ethnic cleansing" of Bosnian Muslims during the early 1990's is a contemporary example of expulsion. Through massacre, rape, and the razing of villages, Muslim people were forced to flee their country. Segregation describes the subordinate form in which group identity is maintained and separation from the dominant group occurs; however, complete removal of the racial or ethnic group from its homeland does not necessarily follow. Segregation may be voluntary, as with Amish Christian communities in Pennsylvania. It may be involuntary and enforced by law as was the case for African Americans in the southern United States until the 1960's, or it may be involuntary and enforced by social norms, as continues to be the case for African Americans, particularly for those living in poverty in urban settings.

A number of subordinate forms exist in which substantial interaction occurs between members of subordinate and dominant groups. In assimilation, racial or ethnic groups relinquish their distinct identities to take on characteristics of the dominant group. Sociological theory often distinguishes between cultural and structural assimilation. In the former, a racial or ethnic group adapts the cultural patterns of the surrounding society without necessarily being fully accepted into that society. In the latter, a racial or ethnic group enters into close relationships with members of the dominant group and full participation in mainstream society. Amalgamation or fusion describes the combining of a racial or ethnic group with the dominant group to form a new group. The mestizos of Latin America are an amalgamation of Spanish and indigenous Indian peoples. Societies in which this is a predominant occurrence are sometimes described as melting pots. Finally, cultural pluralism describes societies in which ongoing intergroup contact occurs but ethnic or racial groups maintain distinct identities.

Applications

Subordinating processes and forms are dynamic, and more than one may reflect the experience of a racial or ethnic group over time. Two examples of subordinating processes and forms will be presented here. The first is from the United States and reflects the experience of an American Indian people. The second is international and reflects the experience of black Jamaican people.

Before the arrival of the "white man," the Cowlitz Indians of what is now southwestern Washington state were a powerful and independent dominant group. In the early 1800's, explorers, trappers, and traders provided the Cowlitz with their first contact with whites, who were moving westward and annexing more and more land. By the 1830's, the white settlers' numbers, technology, and access to military support (as well as the effects of their diseases on the native population) permitted them to become the dominant group, while the Cowlitz were transformed into a subordinate group. Land and other natural resources were no longer adequate to support both the dominant white economy and the Cowlitz aboriginal economy. From a conflict model perspective, a struggle for power and resources now characterized the relationship of the Cowlitz (and other American Indians) to the white settlers. This struggle led to armed conflicts, with white society ultimately retaining control. A plethora of treaties followed in the 1850's, with some tribes being segregated on reservations located in their ancestral lands. All treaties presented to the Cowlitz, however, required that they be expelled from their lands. Consequently, the Cowlitz refused all treaties. With continued encroachment of white society, the Cowlitz lost their land base and could no longer maintain their aboriginal economy. They were forced to enter the mainstream economy of the white society to survive.

The early 1900's was a time in which the dominant white society, both formally through law and informally through social norms and social censure, attempted to force assimilation on the Cowlitz. The Cowlitz were pressured to change their names, to cease practicing their cultural ways, and to speak English. In the mid-1900's, the Bureau of Indian Affairs of the United States government administratively terminated the tribe on the grounds that the Cowlitz people were completely assimilated and no longer constituted a distinct cultural group. This termination cut the Cowlitz off from those services and resources reserved for American Indians by the United States government.

In reality, the Cowlitz have not assimilated. Although their lack of land base forced them into the economy of the dominant society, they have retained their ethnic identity and tribal government. They still gather socially as a tribe, own acreage on the Cowlitz River as a tribe, and regularly represent Cowlitz perspectives on local and state issues relevant to their ancestral lands. They and the white society within which they live form a plural culture. The Cowlitz have petitioned the United States government for recognition of their tribal status.

Spain first colonized Jamaica in 1494 and ruled for the following 161 years. During this period Spanish disease and brutality resulted in genocide of the indigenous Arawak Indians, and the importation of black Africans as slaves began. The British captured the island in 1655 and ruled in a variety of capacities until independence was claimed in 1962. Under British colonial rule, an artificial society was created for the sole purpose of making money for British landowners. The island was populated by continual importation of slaves, indentured servants, prisoners sent over from Britain, buccaneers, and other white settlers.

Black slaves provided the necessary labor force for sugar production. They lived segregated from their white overseers and masters, who implemented policies designed to disrupt individual and group ethnic identities. Blocking the continuation of African traditions and hindering the formation of family or community ties among slaves, white landowners practiced a form of ethnocide—cultural destruction. Their purpose was both to increase the perceived disparity between their power and the powerlessness of the slaves and to ensure that slave energy was focused on plantation production. In fact, until the slave trade was abolished, it was considered more economical to work a slave to death and purchase a new one than to support bringing up a new generation of slaves from birth. From the dominant white perspective, a stable system existed; however, even under these circumstances slaves devised methods to retaliate and exercise some control over the slave overseer. "Quashee" behavior (purposely stupid, bungling, and inefficient performance) provided a means for slaves to frustrate the overseer intentionally and thoroughly. Slaves also fomented rebellions.

Emancipation occurred in 1834; the new free black population consisted of peasants and unskilled workers who continued to be dominated and denigrated by white society. They did have one obvious mechanism of control over the white landowners: They could withdraw their work, and they did so sporadically as a mark of their freedom. In the years following emancipation, first as a British Crown colony and then as an independent nation, progress was made in government, health, education, and social services. This permitted a black professional class to emerge and gain social and political power even in the midst of race-related prejudice, discrimination, and institutional racism. Today over 90 percent of Jamaicans are of African descent, and they with their compatriots of European or Asian backgrounds form a somewhat plural society. Social stratification continues to exist, however, since the vast majority of black Jamaicans are poor. As with many countries in the developing world, Jamaica suffers massive international debt, trade imbalances, and domestic economic crisis. These economic difficulties perpetuate a neocolonial dependency, particularly on the United States.

Context
Social problems associated with race and ethnicity were omnipresent during the early years of American sociology at the beginning of the twentieth century. Former slaves and new generations of African Americans born into freedom were living in poverty, with many migrating to the more industrialized and urbanized northern states. Great influxes of European immigrants filled urban settings and worked at low-paying jobs. Some of the earliest sociological work on race and ethnicity was conducted by African American W. E. B. Du Bois, who addressed racism and social problems in his now-classic *The Philadelphia Negro: A Social Study* (1899).

In the first decades of the 1900's, sociological theory moved from racial determinism (viewing race as the basis of intellect and personality) to social or cultural determinism. In the 1920's, while society attempted to control immigration and the eugenics movement sought to control procreation of certain racial or ethnic groups, sociology argued that it was social conditions and social structures which facilitated or hampered the social mobility of racial or ethnic groups. Sociology also argued that assimilation of ethnic groups was natural, inevitable, and desirable; in fact, it was during this period that the seminal race relations cycle of assimilation was presented by sociologist Robert E. Park.

During the periods of the Great Depression and World War II, sociological theory focused on cultural differences between racial or ethnic groups and on race relations. Reformist efforts decreased during the period between 1945 and 1960, as sociology was dominated by functionalism, with its emphasis on stable social systems and a renewed call for value-neutral and objective scientific methods. Internationally, the period following World War II was characterized by anticolonialism and nationalism, and sociologists became interested in the new relations between former colonizers and indigenous peoples. By the 1960's, sociologists refocused attention on the persistence of prejudice and discrimination, and they developed the concept of institutional discrimination. They were compelled to do so because, in spite of the Supreme Court ban on segregation in schools, the Civil Rights movement, and the Civil Rights Act of 1964, social inequality continued in the United States. Not surprisingly, explanations based in conflict theories began to dominate. Also during this period, increasingly complex, multidimensional models of assimilation were being proposed; sociologist Milton Gordon's foundational analysis of cultural and structural assimilation emerged.

Today, with subordinate or minority groups together becoming the numerical majority in the United States, increased specialization is occurring in the study of race and ethnicity (for example, Hispanic sociology and Asian American sociology). Models that address social inequality among racial or ethnic groups are increasingly focusing on the economic and political resources of the groups and their competitors. Finally, the persistence or resurgence of racial or ethnic group differences and conflicts around the world, vast movements of refugees, and continual immigration are leading American and international sociologists to investigate how modernization is affecting ethnic mobilization—how ethnic groups take collective action to advance their purposes.

Bibliography

Berry, John W. "Psychology of Acculturation: Understanding Individuals Moving Between Cultures." In *Applied Cross-Cultural Psychology*, edited by Richard W. Brislin. Newbury Park, Calif.: Sage Publications, 1990. An internationally renowned cross-cultural theorist and researcher, Berry comprehensively presents his widely cited model of acculturation. Written from the perspective of social psychology, this chapter is an excellent companion to the more structural sociological models of culture contact.

Brown, Dee. *Bury My Heart at Wounded Knee*. New York: Pocket Books, 1981. First published in 1974, this is a documented account of the conquest of American Indians and the annexation of their lands in the American West during the second half of the nineteenth century. Written in a captivating style from the perspective of the Indian peoples. Includes photographs from the period.

Casas, Bartolome de las. *The Tears of the Indians*. Translated by John Phillips. Stanford, Calif.: Academic Reprints, 1953. A truly remarkable eyewitness account of the Spanish conquest, enslavement, and genocide of the indigenous people in the West Indies and parts of Latin America. Written during the first half of the 1500's, the accounts were compiled in support of Casas' position strongly advocating humane treatment of the Indians.

Gordon, Milton M. *Assimilation in American Life: The Role of Race, Religion, and National Origins*. New York: Oxford University Press, 1964. A classic work in sociology in which Gordon presents a multidimensional view of assimilation. Many of the concepts he proposed have since passed into general application—most notably cultural and structural assimilation. Challenging reading level.

Patterson, Orlando. *The Sociology of Slavery*. Rutherford, N.J.: Fairleigh Dickinson University Press, 1975. A comprehensive and fascinating analysis of Jamaican slave society existing on an island chiefly populated by people brought against their wills. Patterson provides insights into social institutions of both masters and slaves, as well as into patterns of social control and resistance.

Schaefer, Richard T. *Racial and Ethnic Groups*. 5th ed. New York: HarperCollins, 1993. An accessible introductory textbook surveying theories and research on race and ethnicity. Includes full chapters on the major racial or ethnic groups in the United States, a comprehensive bibliography, and extensive suggestions for further reading.

Williams, Vernon J. *From a Caste to a Minority: Changing Attitudes of American Sociologists Toward Afro-Americans, 1896-1945*. New York: Greenwood Press, 1989. Readable and well documented historical analysis of American sociology's first fifty years of investigation into race and ethnicity, with a particular focus on African Americans. Argues that the application of assimilationist theory transformed sociology into one of the most progressive of social sciences.

Mícheál D. Roe

Cross-References

Annihilation or Expulsion of Racial or Ethnic Groups, 92; Apartheid, 127; Cultural and Structural Assimilation, 405; Internal Colonialism, 1015; Minority and Majority Groups, 1219; Pluralism versus Assimilation, 1374; Poverty and Race, 1472; Racial and Ethnic Stratification, 1579; Segregation versus Integration, 1707; Slavery, 1754.

CORPORATIONS AND ECONOMIC CONCENTRATION

Type of sociology: Major social institutions
Field of study: The economy

Corporations have proved to be a successful form of business organization. This success has sparked a lively debate between those who worry about the extent of the economic power that is held by some corporations and those who defend the rights of corporations to wield economic power.

> *Principal terms*
>   ANTITRUST: refers to government action to prevent private businesses
>   from undermining competition
>   CONCESSION THEORY OF THE CORPORATION: the theory that the
>   corporation's unique legal status is a governmental creation
>   EGALITARIANISM: the theory that justice requires the equal distribution
>   of goods to all members of society
>   INDIVIDUAL RIGHTS: moral/political principles stating every individ-
>   ual's control over his or her own life, including the liberty to use his
>   or her person and property as he or she sees fit
>   INHERENCE THEORY OF THE CORPORATION: the theory that the corpora-
>   tion's unique legal status arises from contractual agreements among
>   private individuals who are exercising their rights to liberty,
>   property, and association
>   LIMITED LIABILITY: an owner's legal status of being responsible for a
>   business's financial obligations only to the extent of his or her
>   financial investment

Overview

One of the major organizational innovations in the history of business was the development of the corporation. In the United States in the nineteenth century, a rising population, new industrial technologies, and stable political and legal environment made possible the existence of large-scale, long-range business organizations. The corporation evolved as the business form best suited for the new economic circumstances. The success of the corporate form is indicated by the fact that in the twentieth century, virtually all of the largest and longest enduring businesses have been corporations.

Corporations are distinguished from the two traditional forms of business organization (the single proprietorship and the partnership) by four features: organizational separation of ownership and management, legal limitation of owners' liability to the amount of their investment, entity status, and perpetual life.

Entity status means that the corporation is considered legally to be an individual that can sue and be sued in its own name. A proprietorship or a partnership is not able to do these things; its owners can sue or be sued only as individuals. Perpetual life means that the corporation's existence is not tied to the existence of any of its particular owners. In a proprietorship or partnership, by contrast, the business is automatically dissolved upon the death of the proprietor or either of the partners. Entity status and perpetual life have contributed to the popularity and success of the corporate form: Entity status makes it easier for any lawsuits to be brought and resolved, and perpetual life makes it easier for the corporate business to continue functioning upon the death of any of its owners. The other two features, however—the separation of ownership and management, and limited liability—have been more instrumental to the corporation's success.

In a single proprietorship or a partnership, typically the owner also manages the business (though hired managers and "silent" partners can also exist). In a corporation, ownership and management are organizationally separate. The separation has proved to be enormously beneficial to both owners and managers, since it brings together those who have managerial skills but not necessarily capital and those who have capital but not necessarily sufficient skills, time, or interest to run a business. The separation has thus been instrumental in bringing together the assets and skills necessary for large-scale business operations.

Finally, limited liability has been important. In a single proprietorship or a partnership, the owners' (the proprietor's or the partners') nonbusiness assets are liable for any losses incurred by the business. This means, for example, that if the business goes bankrupt, the bankruptcy court may require that the nonbusiness assets of the owners be used to settle any amounts owed to the business' creditors. In a corporation, by contrast, the nonbusiness assets of the owners (the shareholders) are not liable for losses incurred by the business. Limited liability has made available to corporations increasing amounts of capital: Those who provide the capital are legally liable for the actions of management only to the extent of their investment, so they are more likely to be willing to invest as owners in a corporation than in a proprietorship or a partnership.

Thus, in the corporate form of business, there are four features that contribute to making possible large-scale, long-term business enterprises: perpetual life contributes to longevity, entity status contributes to more easily settling legal difficulties, separation of ownership and management contributes to bringing together individuals with complementary assets, and limited liability contributes to making larger amounts of capital available. For these reasons, the corporation has been a popular and successful form of doing business.

The success of the corporation has brought a flood of criticism. In fact, during the past century, the bulk of the criticism of business has focused on the corporation. Most large businesses are corporations, which means that the greatest concentrations of private wealth tend to be found in corporations. Accordingly, criticisms of large-scale business have tended to focus upon the corporation.

Most fears and criticisms of the corporation are based on the fact that many corporations succeed in acquiring great economic power. Traditionally, concentrations of power have been viewed with suspicion, since power can be abused, and economic matters have often been viewed with suspicion, since many people have ambivalent attitudes toward wealth.

One category of fears and criticisms of corporate power is primarily economic. Included in this category are worries about the effects on the economy in general and a corporation's employees in particular when a large corporation fails or relocates. Also included in the economic category are fears that the relatively large size of some corporations gives them some immunity from competitive market forces and thus gives them an unfair competitive advantage over other businesses. A corporation that succeeds in capturing a large share of a market may attempt to charge higher prices to its customers; sometimes this practice is called "monopolistic pricing." A large corporation may cut its prices in order to undersell a smaller competitor; sometimes this practice is called "cutthroat pricing." Two or more corporations may agree to sell to their customers at the same price; sometimes this practice is called "price fixing." In all these cases, the fear is that the large corporation is abusing its economic power by undermining competition.

A second category of fears about the concentration of economic power in some corporations is political. In the twentieth century, American politics evolved from a principled free enterprise separation of politics and economics to become a more pragmatic mixture of free enterprise and government regulation. In a mixed economy, special-interest groups lobby the government to adopt legislation that advances their interests. The mixture of economic freedom and government regulation changes as different special-interest groups win the ongoing lobbying competitions. In a mixed economy, corporate lobbyists become just another special interest competing for the government's favor against lobbyists representing other corporate and business interest groups, labor interest groups, consumer interest groups, farming interest groups, environmental interest groups, and so on. In such a system, political health is defined in terms of one interest group's not having more influence than any other interest group, so that the lobbying competition is conducted by players of roughly equal strength. With players of roughly equal strength, one can expect that each interest group will win a roughly equal number of competitions, and the system as a whole will evolve toward a healthy balance between the competing interests. To the extent, therefore, that any one interest group acquires greater lobbying influence than any other, the fear arises that the system will become unbalanced in the direction of favoring that one group's special interests. In a mixed economy, large corporations have an opportunity to turn their economic power into political power: They can use their wealth to convince politicians and those who elect them to pass legislation that protects their interests, provides them with special advantages, damages their competitors' interests, or does all these things. Accordingly, the growth of corporate economic power comes to be seen as giving corporations unfair political advantages over the other special interest groups and therefore is perceived as a threat to the political health of the system.

A third category of worry about the economic power of corporations is more broadly social. Some corporations have achieved great economic success, while others have achieved modest success, struggled, or gone bankrupt. The inequalities of wealth in the corporate world are a microcosm of society as a whole: Some have great wealth, while many have a moderate amount or little. The worry comes from those committed to "egalitarianism"— the view that in a just society great inequalities of wealth will not exist. Some egalitarians hold that equality is a fundamental moral concept by which all social arrangements are to be judged; inequalities according to this view, are intrinsically immoral. Other egalitarians are opposed to inequalities on more pragmatic grounds, arguing that great inequalities cause widespread envy and resentment among the members of society, which in turn undermine social harmony and stability. From either egalitarian perspective, the corporation's ability to create large amounts of wealth is a vice (or at best a mixed blessing), since not all people share that wealth.

Applications

Those who worry about corporate economic power fear that corporations will abuse their power in the economic or political realms, or believe that the concentration of economic power contradicts the social goal of economic equality.

Accordingly, there have been many social and political efforts to prevent perceived abuses of corporations' economic power and to spread their wealth more broadly. Political efforts have resulted in a broadening of the scope of governmental involvement in the economy. To lessen or stop the negative consequences of a large corporation's failure or relocation, governments have, for example, used tax dollars to bail out failing or bankrupt corporations, mandated that corporations give earlier notice to their employees of their intent to close, and used tax dollars for unemployment insurance. To prevent corporations from charging prices that it deems improperly higher than, lower than, or the same as the prices charged by its competitors, the federal government has established "antitrust" laws. To spread corporate wealth more broadly, governments have enacted taxes. For example, corporate income is taxed twice: Because of its entity status, the corporation is viewed as an individual and thus pays taxes on predividend income, and the corporation's owners (the shareholders) pay taxes on the dividend income that they receive from the corporation.

Complementing these political efforts to curb and control corporations' economic power have been social efforts. A major element in these efforts has been the advocacy of corporate "social responsibility." Whereas governments enforce their rules by force, the thrust of the social responsibility movement has been to get corporations voluntarily to check their economic power and to spread their wealth more broadly. For example, a "socially responsible" corporation will voluntarily divert larger portions of its earnings toward charity and philanthropy, will voluntarily limit its attempts to advance its interests in the political arena, and will voluntarily accept the idea of an increasing role of government participation in its affairs as a "partner."

The concept of "partnership" between government and corporation has also been defended by means of the "concession theory of the corporation." The concession theory argues that the corporation owes its very existence to the government. The corporation enjoys entity status, perpetual life, and limited liability, all of which, according to the concession theory, are special legal standings and protections that the government chooses to give to corporations but not to other businesses. Therefore, the concession theory concludes, the corporation is a creature of the government. Thus, the government is in a position to ask for and receive something from the corporation; namely, the use of some of the corporation's economic power to advance public interests.

Context

The foregoing discussion has emphasized the concerns that lead to the conclusion that, in general, corporate economic concentration is bad. These concerns most often arise within the context of analyzing the corporation either from a broadly socialist perspective—in which case the concentration of power in corporate hands is bad because it leaves in private sector power that should be in public, governmental hands—or from a mixed economy perspective, in which case concentrations of power in the hands of any one segment of society are bad because they unbalance the system. In either case, the proposed solutions are to call for increased government regulation to limit the use of corporate economic power and to request of corporations the voluntary nonuse of their economic power in certain areas.

In contrast to the broadly socialist and mixed economic perspectives is the free enterprise or capitalist perspective on corporations. Free enterprise emphasizes the rights of individuals to their liberty and property, and analyzes corporations in terms of the rights of the individuals who make them up.

Advocates of capitalism argue that business enterprises, even large ones, are voluntary associations of autonomous individuals who think they can do better for themselves if they work together cooperatively. According to this view, individuals are in charge of their own lives and seek to make their own lives fulfilling and enriched. Exercising their rights to freedom of association, they form business organizations to make more money. They manufacture and market a product. If they find enough customers who are willing to buy at their prices, they make a profit. If not, they lose money. In either case, the economic power concentrated in a business is equivalent to its ability to satisfy its customers.

Corporations, in this view, are simply a special case of business organization. It is true that corporations enjoy special legal standings—entity status, limited liability, and so on—that other business organizations do not, but advocates of free enterprise reject the concession theory in favor of the "inherence theory," which holds that all of the corporation's features can be analyzed in terms of private contractual agreements among the owners, employees, customers, and creditors of the corporation. Robert Hessen has offered an analogy to the marriage relationship in an attempt to make clear the difference between the concession and inherence theories. It is true that a married couple enjoys a special legal relationship, but it would be odd to argue that therefore marriage is a governmental concession or that therefore married couples have special obligations to use their assets for public ends. Marriage is a private, voluntary, contractual arrangement that is entered into by individuals for mutual, private benefit; it is a relationship that is recognized, not created, by the government. As with a marriage, the members of a corporation and those who deal with them have the right to pursue their own ends, to associate with one another or not as they see fit, and to keep and use the wealth they acquire, so long as they respect the rights of other individuals.

Bibliography

French, Peter A., Jeffrey Nesteruk, and David T. Risser, with John Abbarno. *Corporations in the Moral Community*. Fort Worth: Harcourt Brace Jovanovich, 1992. An introduction to corporate business ethics written by a team of philosophers and political scientists. Chapter 6 is of special relevance to the issue of corporations and economic concentration in a mixed economy; the authors defend a mixed system and propose changes in the direction of limiting corporate power by limiting, for example, corporations' rights to freedom of speech and privacy.

Gunderson, Gerald. *The Wealth Creators: An Entrepreneurial History of the United States*. New York: E. P. Dutton, 1989. An engaging survey by an economic historian of what made possible the growth of large business firms in the United States from Colonial times to the twentieth century. Chapters 5 to 9 are especially informative: They focus on the latter half of the nineteenth century's new national markets, the forces leading to horizontal and vertical mergers of businesses, size and economies of scale, the effect of antitrust legislation, the nature of economic power, and the thesis of the "robber barons."

Hessen, Robert, ed. *Does Big Business Rule America? Critical Commentaries on Charles E. Lindblom's "Politics and Markets."* Washington, D.C.: Ethics and Public Policy Center, 1981. An interdisciplinary collection of eight responses to Lindblom's *Politics and Markets*.

——————. *In Defense of the Corporation*. Stanford, Calif.: Hoover Institution Press, 1979. A detailed, scholarly response to the case for the federal chartering of corporations. Includes discussion of the corporation's historical roots and a philosophical account of the corporation's moral basis. Of special relevance is Hessen's defense of the "inherence" theory of the corporation (the view that the corporation's distinctive features arise through contract) against the "concession" theory of the corporation (the view that the corporation's distinctive features are a special creation of the government).

Lindblom, Charles E. *Politics and Markets*. New York: Basic Books, 1977. An influential treatise by a political scientist, arguing that corporations have an undue influence on contemporary politics and proposing the replacement of the current "polyarchic" (democratic) political and free market economic institutions with polyarchic political and centralized economic institutions. It would be instructive to read this book in conjunction with Hessen's *Does Big Business Rule America?*

Nader, Ralph, Mark Green, and Joel Seligman. *Taming the Giant Corporation*. New York: W. W. Norton, 1976. Consumer advocate Nader and two colleagues defend the concession theory of the corporation and propose that the power of corporations be limited through a system of federal chartering and control.

Rand, Ayn. *Capitalism: The Unknown Ideal*. New York: New American Library, 1967. An influential philosophical defense of capitalism on the basis of individual rights to liberty and property. Of special relevance to the issue of corporations and economic concentration is Federal Reserve Chairman Alan Greenspan's essay "Antitrust."

Stephen R. C. Hicks

Cross-References

Capitalism, 191; Deindustrialization in the United States, 462; Industrial and Postindustrial Economies, 940; The Industrial Revolution and Mass Production, 946; Industrial Societies, 953; Marxism, 1127; Monopolies and Oligopolies, 1248; Multinational Corporations and the Third World, 1268.

THE COURTS

Type of sociology: Deviance and social control
Field of study: Controlling deviance

Courts first interact with a criminal defendant when probable cause for arrest is reviewed at a preliminary hearing. Defendants can plead guilty thereafter, often in return for sentencing concessions, or await a trial by a jury. With procedures based both on the common law and the constitution, the courts of the United States are comparatively fair, but are uncertain dispensers of "just deserts" for crime.

Principal terms
ADVERSARIAL SYSTEM: a court system in which opposing attorneys are supposed to present the most vigorous cases possible for their clients; truth is intended to emerge from the clashing views
INDICTMENT: an accusation by a grand jury charging a defendant with specific criminal conduct
INQUISITIONAL SYSTEM: the European court system, in which investigation and questioning are the responsibilities of the presiding judge, who is charged with finding the truth
PROBABLE CAUSE: reasonable ground for believing that a specified crime has been committed by a specified person; the basis for arrest
VENIRE: a panel of prospective jurors drawn from a presumably representative list of citizens
VOIR DIRE: a pretrial inquiry in which the judge and opposing attorneys question prospective jurors to determine possible biases
WARRANT: an order issued by a judge that authorizes the search of a described place or the arrest of a particular suspect based on stated probable cause

Overview

The courts are judicial bodies that serve society's need for impartial mediators empowered to resolve conflicts by applying agreed-upon rules. When conflicts occur between private citizens, the courts apply a set of rules called the civil law. Other rules, considered so basic that their violation puts one in conflict with society itself, constitute the criminal law.

The system of courts in the United States is adversarial in nature and hierarchical in organization. Parallel systems exist at the state and the federal levels. In this adversarial system, the truth is expected to emerge from the competitive views of the prosecution, which seeks evidence indicating the guilt of the criminal defendant, and the defense attorney, who seeks to establish reasonable doubt about guilt. The system is hierarchical in that procedures and decisions of trial courts can be reviewed by appellate courts and occasionally by the state or the U.S. Supreme Court. The Supreme Court of the United States selects from the cases referred to it those that raise important constitutional issues. U.S. Supreme Court decisions, as well as legal precedents from the common law, have been crucial in protecting the rights of individual suspects.

Most criminal cases which try offenses against the state begin and end in state trial courts. Once a criminal act, either a misdemeanor (less serious) or a felony (punishable by a prison sentence of greater than a year), has been committed, the first step is that of investigation by police. Eyewitness accounts are sought; physical evidence is gathered and preserved; any suspects are interrogated. Suspects must be informed of their constitutional protection against self-incrimination (a process known as the Miranda warning), and searches for evidence held privately must be initiated by warrants stating specific reasons for the search.

Once the evidence is clear enough to establish probable cause, an arrest may be made. The suspect must be brought before a magistrate within a relatively short period of time, and a preliminary hearing is held. The evidence is reviewed and evaluated, the suspect is again informed of his or her rights, and the conditions of awaiting trial are established. The suspect may be allowed to post bail (forfeited if the suspect does not appear for trial), or compelled to remain in custody. For felony charges in many jurisdictions, the prosecutor must once again submit evidence to a grand jury for an indictment. The specific charges are read to the suspect in a formal hearing called an arraignment.

Between the formal accusation and the trial, a number of important events occur. Evidence is subpoenaed; sworn testimony is gathered. Motions are filed that set the terms of the trial to come; motions to exclude evidence illegally gathered, motions of discovery based on the right of the accused to have knowledge of the evidence against him, and motions *in limine* seeking advance rulings concerning issues that will emerge during the trial are especially common. In more than 80 percent of all criminal cases, the waiting period concludes with a plea of guilty that is negotiated by the defense attorney in exchange for concessions.

Finally, for the cases that remain, there is the constitutionally guaranteed trial by jury. As the first step in selecting a jury, a panel of candidates representative of the community is selected (a *venire*). The final set of jurors is drawn up after a process of inquiry into attitudes that appear relevant to the case (the *voir dire*). A juror displaying bias may be discharged. Each attorney can exclude a limited number of the remaining prospective jurors without citing reasons. The traditional jury consists of twelve citizens, but smaller juries are constitutionally permitted.

The trial itself proceeds in an orderly series of stages: opening statements, presentations of evidence by each side, summary statements, the judge's instruction to the jury, jury deliberations, verdict, and posttrial proceedings.

The trial commences with an opening statement by the prosecution, which bears the burden of proof. The defense usually exercises its right to an opening statement. Such opening statements outline the case to be presented. Then the actual evidence is presented, first by the prosecution (the plaintiff in a civil case), then by the defense; finally, the prosecution or plaintiff has the opportunity to present rebuttal evidence. After each presentation, the adversarial side has the right to cross-examine witnesses.

The attorney for each side concludes its case by summarizing the evidence and organizing it persuasively. Finally, the judge instructs the jury as to the law to be applied to the case.

Jury deliberations take place in private, and precautions are taken to shield the jury from outside influences or pressure. If the jury returns a verdict of "not guilty," the case ends. The accused cannot be tried again for the same offense. If a verdict of "guilty" is returned, the defense may appeal based upon specific errors in the proceedings. The defendant is sentenced most often by the judge, often after he or she has gathered presentencing reports by social workers and recommendations by the attorneys.

Applications

Each of the constitutional principles protecting the rights of accused citizens has been implemented by judicial procedures and practices. For example, preliminary hearings are held to ensure that confessions are truly voluntary; also, the defendant may file motions to exclude any evidence obtained by an illegal search based upon the "exclusionary rule." Yet in other instances, the implementation of constitutional protections appears far different from that originally envisaged.

Nowhere is the disparity greater than between current court practices and the "speedy and public trial by an impartial jury" guaranteed by the U.S. Constitution. To begin with, only a small fraction—by most estimates, fewer than 10 percent—of all criminal cases even reach the trial stage. Most are resolved by pretrial negotiations between defense and prosecution attorneys, in some jurisdictions with the participation of the judge. Such negotiations (plea bargaining) involve the exchange of a guilty plea for a reduction in the number and nature of the charges against the defendant. This extra-constitutional arrangement has become popular as the volume of criminal cases and the time consumed by the average trial have both increased exponentially. Savings in expense; in the time of lawyers, police, potential witnesses, and jurors; and in the overall burden on the courts are considerable.

On the other hand, plea bargaining, however efficient, offers an inducement to waive a fundamental right guaranteed by the Constitution. Defendants may feel, sometimes with reason, that they will be penalized if they demand a trial. In some cases, the impression of a negotiated compromise is an illusion. Many prosecutors, judges, and defense attorneys are quite aware of the "going rate" for particular offenses, and some of the charges reduced may have been introduced as bargaining chips in the first place. Cases also sometimes occur in which an admitted criminal avoids prosecution in return for testimony about accomplices.

Even in the small percentage of cases that reach the stage of jury trial, the application seems rather different from the theory of an impartial jury of peers who are apprised of the relevant facts, which they objectively evaluate in the context of the law. Trial lawyers do not really want an impartial jury, but rather one sharing biases favorable to their case. To select such a positively biased jury, trial lawyers exercise a sort of folk wisdom concerning the correlates of pro-defense (or pro-prosecution) biases.

Furthermore, juries seem to remember and process the facts that emerge at a trial quite selectively. An especially effective opening statement by either side can set the stage for all that is to come (psychologists refer to this as the primacy effect). Information made especially salient (as, ironically, by a judge's instructions to disregard it) can be given particular importance. Once many jurors become convinced of the guilt or innocence of the defendant, attention may lag. Judicial instructions on the pertinent law are often not entirely understood. Jury deliberations usually veer in the direction of the original majority view (the polarization effect).

Punishment, which can include fines, probation, incarceration of varying lengths, or even death, is decided by judicial sentencing in most states, by a jury in a few. It is subject to review by appellate courts. According to some views, fairness requires the certainty of a consistent sentence for a specific criminal offense. The thrust of sentencing reforms in the last two decades of the twentieth century has been toward consistency in sentencing implemented by uniform sentencing codes. Federal judges, in particular, are supposed to stay within the guidelines of the sentencing codes.

Investigations of actual sentencing practices, however, find that judicial discretion still results in a variation in penalties for the same legal offense. Such variations do not always appear unfair. Repeated felons, for example, are more likely to be given prison terms and longer prison terms that those who commit an offense for the first time. Other factors, however, seem to add a considerable chance factor to sentencing decisions. Judges who have served as district attorneys tend to give harsher sentences than judges who have not; judges who construe the purpose of penalties as retribution or deterrence tend to give harsher penalties than judges who are optimistic about rehabilitative possibilities; judges in general give harsher sentences than juries. All in all, the greatest sentencing discrepancies take place when there are both aggravating factors ("the well-to-do CPA didn't have to embezzle") and mitigating factors ("it's his first offense").

Context

Courts have been evaluated both according to the fairness of their procedures and according to the fairness of their outcomes. Most of the principles mandating procedural fairness and fairness in assuring the guilt of punished defendants emerged from procedures in the English Common Law and were transplanted to the United States as part of the Bill of Rights of the Constitution. The efficiency with which courts dispense "justice," in the sense that the consequence of every offense is punishment proportional to this offense, forms a third standard. The eighteenth century English philosopher Jeremy Bentham argued that the rationale for a criminal justice system is to assure that the penalties inflicted upon lawbreakers are severe enough to outweigh any profit or pleasure derived from the offense. This would discourage repetitions of the offense by the lawbreaker or by others who might otherwise follow his or her example. The rationality of the social order is thus preserved.

Most observers evaluate the U.S. court system rather high on procedural fairness when realistic standards are applied. State trial courts are more scrupulous in observing constitutionally mandated procedural requirements than such courts were a century ago. Not uncommonly in 1900, evidence acquired through illegal searches and pressured confessions was used to convict criminal defendants who appeared without legal representation before a jury consisting only of white males. This jury might have already listened to several other cases the same day. As a result of a series of Supreme Court decisions, many since 1950, constitutionally mandated rights were given a broad interpretation and applied to the state courts. Coerced confessions and evidence improperly seized (as without a properly specific warrant) were held to be inadmissible; impoverished defendants accused of felonies had a right to court-appointed attorneys; a jury of one's peers must fairly represent all segments of the community. Although the high incidence of plea bargaining is often held to be a departure from the constitutional standard, it should be remembered that the negotiations that result in such bargains occur within the context of the probable outcome of a trial in which these constitutional protections are observed.

Compared with the inquisitional systems of many other countries, where the judge supervises the investigation of the case and questions witnesses, American defense attorneys, as legal adversaries of the prosecution, have been shown to be notably more successful in uncovering obscure evidence favorable to defendants. When comparisons are made, the American system is perceived, even by defendants, as fairer.

Assessing the U.S. courts by the standard of fair outcomes is more difficult. Such a standard demands that innocent defendants be acquitted and guilty defendants be convicted and given penalties in proportion to their crimes. There are on record documented cases of innocent citizens who have been convicted of felonies and imprisoned, most frequently based on mistaken eyewitness identification. Such cases are, however, the exceptions; most felons eventually admit their guilt. The high proportion of criminal defendants who plead guilty is probably attributable in part to the improved ability to identify physical evidence such as fingerprints and DNA samples and to conduct detailed forensic examinations. Courts are mostly correct about guilt as well as innocence.

The question of whether the guilty are assigned penalties that fit their crimes can be answered a number of ways. If one is asking whether fixed penalties are mechanically assigned to specific, legally defined offenses, then the answer is clearly "no." From the investigating police officer who may not arrest to the plea-bargained sentence, administrative discretion is an important factor throughout the process. Much of this discretion is not, however, arbitrary. Almost every criminal act involves aggravating and mitigating circumstances that properly modify the degree of punishment considered just. Few people, for example, would equate a husband who helped end the life of his wife afflicted with the pain of terminal bone cancer with the husband who kills his wife to collect on a large insurance policy—both are similar premeditated murderers under the law. Rehabilitative possibilities again complicate the picture. The possibility of successful rehabilitation may make a short prison term and a long parole a rational penalty for a nonviolent first-time offender. Unequal sentences for the same offense, as legally defined, are not always unjust.

The most common criticisms of the outcomes of the criminal justice system are simply that many crimes are unsolved and that for many years the incidence of crime, particularly of violent crimes, has continued to increase. The fact is, however, that the incidence and detection of crime are influenced greatly by social trends beyond the control of the courts. Family instability, educational failures, unemployment, geographic and social mobility, and the availability of guns have all been identified as major factors in the incidence of crime. Some of the young, impulsive thrill seekers most prone to criminal careers may not be deterred by long-term consequences, however severe.

Perfect justice, like any other abstract ideal, is unobtainable in a world of real people. Yet those criminal cases that reach the U.S. courts are subject to a process that is surprisingly efficient and fair. Compared to the courts of other times and places, one might say that the United States has achieved a system of less imperfect justice.

Bibliography

Brown, Stephen, Finn-Aage Esbensen, and Gilbert Geis. *Criminology: Explaining Crime and Its Context*. Cincinnati, Ohio: Anderson, 1991. Describes in detail the many types of crime, their correlates in biological, social, and cultural conditions, and competing theories explaining crime. Includes a one-chapter summary of the criminal law.

Davis, Kenneth Culp. *Discretionary Justice: A Preliminary Inquiry*. Westport, Conn.: Greenwood Press, 1969. Documents the extensive role of discretion in courts and administrative agencies. Treating this as a problem, the author offers suggestions to "confine, structure, and check" this discretion.

Horowitz, Irwin A., and Thomas E. Willging. *The Psychology of Law: Integrations and Applications*. Boston: Little, Brown, 1984. A good account of the functioning of the courts in applying both the criminal and the civil law. A scholarly treatment of the relevant historical and philosophical context.

Kalven, Harry, and Hans Zeisel. *The American Jury*. Boston: Little, Brown, 1966. An exhaustive classic work concerning the functioning of juries. Includes some major empirical studies.

Wrightsman, Lawrence S., Michael T. Nietzel, and William H. Fortune. *Psychology and the Legal System*. 3d ed. Pacific Grove, Calif.: Brooks/Cole, 1994. Offers a detailed review of the criminal justice system from the investigation of a crime to the incarceration of the offender. Offers recommendations for reform.

Thomas E. DeWolfe

Cross-References

CRIME: ANALYSIS AND OVERVIEW

Type of sociology: Deviance and social control
Fields of study: Forms of deviance; Social implications of deviance; Theories of deviance

Crime may be considered deviant behavior against which a society has passed laws. Modern societies have created elaborate systems to measure, understand, dissuade, and punish criminal behavior. A number of categories have been created to describe crime; among them are violent crime, professional theft, white-collar or corporate crime; organized crime, and crimes against the public or moral order ("victimless" crimes).

Principal terms

BIOLOGICAL THEORIES: explanations of criminality that emphasize constitutional or genetic variables to differentiate between criminals and noncriminals

CRIME: behavior that violates laws that prohibit such behavior and that mandate punishment for committing it

CRIME RATE: the number of crimes committed in a particular geographic area during a particular time period divided by the number of people living in that area

CRIMINALITY: stable differences across individuals in their tendency or likelihood to commit criminal acts

CRIMINOLOGY: the branch of sociology that scientifically studies the various aspects of crime

NATIONAL CRIME SURVEY: data gathered on six major crimes (rape, robbery, assault, household burglary, larceny, and motor vehicle theft) by the Bureau of the Census

PSYCHOLOGICAL THEORIES: explanations of criminal behavior that focus on characteristics of the individual (for example, seeing crime as a rational choice between alternatives)

SOCIOLOGICAL THEORIES: explanations of criminal behavior that emphasize group processes and social behavior

UNIFORM CRIME REPORTS: a yearly compilation of crime based on a count of nine "index" crimes by local police forces and published by the Federal Bureau of Investigation

Overview

Crime refers to the commission of behavior that violates laws intended to prohibit such behavior and to punish it when it occurs. Crime is a short-term and circumscribed behavior in which particular individuals use force or fraud to commit deviant or antisocial acts.

Underlying this straightforward definition is a diverse range of behaviors that are influenced by many variables. First, crime expresses itself in many different ways. Robert F. Meier, in 1984, distinguished nine major forms of crime. The first is homicide and assault, wherein the perpetrator uses, respectively, lethal or nonlethal force and violence on the victim. Second is forcible rape, in which a sexual act is forced upon a victim (almost always female) without her consent. This is also called sexual assault. Third is occasional property crime, in which one party damages or illegally transfers to himself or herself another person's property. Fourth is crimes against the public or moral order, including prostitution, drug abuse, and illegal gambling; these require the participation of a "customer" who purchases the opportunity to engage in that behavior. Fifth is political crime; resistance (dissent, evasion, disobedience, or violence) by members of society to those in power. Sixth is white-collar and corporate crime, which is an economic offense (such as antitrust offenses, bribery, and bank embezzlement) committed by means of fraud, deception, or collusion. Seventh is gang delinquency, in which a group of individuals, numbering from a few to several thousand, engage in criminal activity as part of the group's norms. Eighth is organized crime, wherein a syndicate of individual criminals organize themselves in order to promote their criminal activity and protect themselves from legal authorities. The Mafia is the most notorious example. Ninth is professional theft; this refers to individuals who make a livelihood or occupation of crime, much like any legal profession or job. Pickpocketing, burglary, shoplifting, forgery, extortion, and confidence swindling are typical behaviors. Two other forms of crime can be added to Meier's list. Kidnapping and abduction consist of crime wherein a person is illegally seized and detained for purposes of ransom or illicit sex, or in order to regain a child lost in a custody action. Finally, hate crimes are directed against persons of a particular race (60 percent of all hate crimes), religion (20 percent), ethnic orientation (10 percent), or sexual orientation (10 percent). The specific offenses involved in this category include many of the previously listed forms of crime (such as assault, vandalism, robbery, and arson).

The frequency of crime is most extensively assessed by two annual measures. The National Crime Survey interviews sixty thousand random households to see if they have been victims of six of the crimes listed above. The Uniform Crime Reports collects data from sixteen thousand law enforcement agencies nationwide about nine of those crimes. Before examining some of these data, it should be noted that not all crimes are measured. According to James Q. Wilson and Richard J. Herrnstein, at least half of all serious crime goes unreported or undetected; therefore, these measures underestimate the true frequency of crime. According to the 1993 Uniform Crime Reports, in 1992 one criminal offense occurred every two seconds, one violent crime every twenty-two seconds, and one property crime every three seconds. A total of 14,438,191 crimes occurred in 1992 (a crime rate of 5,660 per 100,000 people). Of these crimes, burglary represented 20.6 percent of the total, aggravated assault 7.8 percent, robbery 4.7 percent, forcible rape 0.8 percent, murder 0.2 percent, motor vehicle theft 11.1 percent, and larceny-theft 54.8 percent. The total figure represents an increase in known offenses of 4 percent from 1988 but a decrease of 3 percent from 1991.

If these data are examined further, a number of interesting and possibly significant findings emerge. Most criminals are males who are young and live in large cities. The peak age of criminals is seventeen, and the crime rate declines significantly around the middle twenties to early thirties and thereafter. Evidence suggests that when trivial crimes (such as stealing a candy bar) are excluded, persons from the lower socioeconomic classes are more likely to have committed a serious crime than persons from upper socioeconomic classes. As average household income increases, the crime rate in that area decreases. African Americans are significantly overrepresented among persons arrested, convicted, and imprisoned for committing a crime. Most violent crimes (80 percent) are committed by strangers. Victims of personal crime are overwhelmingly male, young, low-income, and disproportionately minority— basically they have the same profile as the typical offender.

Criminal behaviors seem to be interchangeable rather than repeated in a pattern. In other words, if a person commits a robbery, it is no more likely that the person will commit another robbery than engage in another criminal act such as assault, rape, or drug use. The larger the number of children in a family, the more likely that each of them will commit a crime. Criminal tendencies arise early in life, and crime tends to run in families. Geographic area, population density, degree of urbanization, stability of the population, modes of transportation and the highway system, climate, quality of law enforcement, and availability of guns and drugs influence the incidence of crime. Past criminal behavior is indicative of future criminal behavior. Michael R. Gottfredson and Travis Hirschi concluded in 1990 that crime is not a highly profitable alternative to law-abiding behavior. It is primarily a petty activity that is of little significant benefit to the perpetrator.

There are certainly exceptions to each of these facts; for example, some elderly people and women do commit crimes, and some crimes are very profitable. When viewed as trends, however, these facts and the statistical data on which they are based are significant for understanding why crime occurs and perhaps for finding effective ways to cope with it.

Applications

The ultimate value of the information gathered about crime is that it may possibly be applied to finding effective means of curtailing criminal activity. These data can be applied, for example, to three important issues in coping with crime: how to deal with criminals, the effectiveness of gun control; and the effectiveness of increasing the number of police officers.

Since the 1980's incapacitation has been emphasized as the preferred method of controlling crime. Rehabilitation proved to be a failure, and deterrence never caught the interest of policy makers. Incapacitation is based on the simple idea that if criminals are in prison they cannot be in society committing crimes. Resources are focused on habitual or chronic offenders or career criminals. Numerous studies have shown that a small percentage of individuals commit most crimes. By imprisoning these chronic offenders rather than stressing crime prevention for the whole population, it is argued, a significant reduction in the rate of crime could be achieved. The public appears to be sympathetic toward incapacitation; a survey by the newspaper *USA Today* in October, 1993, revealed that 75 to 82 percent of the sample want posting bail and being released on parole made more difficult and favor more severe sentences.

As Gottfredson and Hirschi point out, however, the criminal justice system already uses prior criminal record as a major criterion for severity of sentencing. Thus it is not immediately apparent how an already highly selective system could be improved upon. One could try to identify those chronic offenders who currently evade notice of the system. Yet by the time such individuals will have been apprehended and imprisoned they will be adults, and, as noted, the likelihood of criminal behavior declines drastically in the mid-twenties. It is therefore less likely that these individuals would be continuing to commit criminal acts even if they were not incarcerated. For such an approach to be effective, chronic offenders would have to be identified in their early teens, prior to the age of rapid onset and peaking of crime—about age seventeen. This cannot be reliably accomplished, however, because a significant portion of first-time (about 50 percent) and second-time (about 33 percent) offenders do not commit a subsequent crime. By the time persons have committed enough crimes to be unequivocally judged chronic offenders, they would be adults and would be less likely to commit further crimes. This suggests that specialized "career criminal" units in police departments, in spite of their popularity among police, politicians, and the media, may be a waste of time and money that could be better spent elsewhere.

Regarding the efficacy of gun control, there seems to be a positive correlation between levels and frequency of criminal violence and an increasing arsenal of firearms. According to some research, firearms kill more people between the ages of fifteen and twenty-four (roughly the decade of peak crime rates) than do all natural causes combined. Gun deaths, including suicides, exceeded thirty-seven thousand in 1992, and handgun homicides reached about thirteen thousand. The homicide rate is about ten deaths for every 100,000 Americans. According to New York City police commissioner Raymond W. Kelly in 1993, the number of guns privately owned in the United States doubles about every twenty years. There were about 200 million guns in circulation in 1993, compared with 54 million in 1950. In contrast, in countries with strict gun control laws the homicide rate is significantly lower. In Britain in 1990 there were only twenty-two handgun homicides. In Canada and Japan, respectively, the homicide rate is five and less than one for every 100,000 people. The American public seems in sympathy with increased gun control. The *USA Today* survey revealed that 64 percent of the sample advocate stricter gun laws.

Such laws would probably significantly lessen instances of domestic violence and personal injury; however, some researchers argue that gun control laws would not have any effect on criminal offenders. These individuals tend to buy their weapons through the underground economy or black market, where a vast supply and variety of weapons exist and where middlemen purchase them for criminals. These critics doubt that gun control laws, which are aimed at the legitimate market, would significantly affect criminals' purchasing of weapons.

It would seem sensible that one way to cope with crime effectively would be to increase the size of police forces. President Bill Clinton, in the crime bill he submitted to Congress in 1993, advocated funding to hire an additional eighty thousand police officers. Gottfredson and Hirschi argue, however, that there is no evidence that a substantial decrease in crime rate can be achieved simply by increasing the number of police. Some have argued that the police are not an important consideration in the great bulk of robberies, burglaries, assaults, homicides, thefts, or drug deals. The perpetrators do not know or care about the probability that they will come under police scrutiny. Also, some police perceptions about crime run counter to what data suggest. For example, the police tend to concentrate on hardened adult criminals, whereas most offenders are youths. The police create specialized units to combat particular types of crime, whereas criminal acts are interchangeable, and criminals are versatile in their behavior.

Public demands for more police, gun control, and incapacitation reflect legitimate concerns of the citizenry about crime, especially violent crime. According to the Uniform Crime Reports, the rate of violent crime increased nearly 20 percent between 1988 and 1993; crime has become a dominant political issue. Yet the public perception of how to deal with crime, as well as the perceptions of many politicians and professionals, does not necessarily square with the evidence. Research shows that what appear to be reasonable and commonsense solutions would probably not be effective and would drain resources and money away from more productive solutions.

Context

Connections can be drawn between criminal law, criminal behavior, and statehood, as suggested by their simultaneous appearance in human history. Crime was first addressed by rules forbidding it, which were enacted by authorities representing the state. (Strictly speaking, prior to the creation of states there was no crime.) Members of society demanded from their government that they be protected in exchange for their permission to be governed. The various central political authorities identified those behaviors that were inimical to the best interests of the individual and society. Formal rules (laws) that prohibited these behaviors (crime) were written, and an elaborate apparatus was constructed to enforce these rules (law enforcement agencies and the criminal justice system). Criminology is the branch of sociology that scientifically studies crime in the hope of understanding why it occurs and of finding effective means for coping with it.

For most of its history, criminology has focused on the institutions, social arrangements, and customs of society; however, general dissatisfaction over the failure of these sociological theories to account adequately for criminal behavior led to an emphasis on individual differences. Such theories stress the concept of criminality—studying the differences among individuals that are correlated with a tendency to commit criminal acts. Whatever social factors contribute to crime must all affect individual behavior if they are to affect crime. To understand crime is to understand the variables that control individual behavior.

For example, Wilson and Herrnstein believe that crime results from how a particular pattern of variables such as constitutional factors, gender, intelligence, personality, and conscience affects what a person considers to be a rational choice among alternatives. Thus, commission of a crime may be chosen because the criminal perceives it to be preferable to the other available alternatives; this might happen if, for example, the likelihood of reward is greater than the likelihood of punishment.

In contrast, Gottfredson and Hirschi believe crime to be more a result of low self-control. Certain individuals seek short-term pleasures and do not weigh the long-term consequences of their behavior. They act impulsively and take risks, are indifferent to the concerns of others, and are relatively unconcerned about delayed punishment (incarceration) for their actions. Low self-control originates during the first six to eight years of life, when a child is primarily under family supervision but is also influenced by schools and peer relationships. These influences are critical in developing restraint and self-control and, thus, law-abiding behavior. According to this view, the future criminal falls outside of these influences during the critical formative years. Thus, focusing resources on making particular criminal acts more difficult will be of only limited value. Rather, the most effective focus would be on facilitating the family's capacity to socialize its children as the only realistic long-term social policy with any hope for significantly reducing crime.

Bibliography

Denno, Deborah W. *Biology and Violence*. New York: Cambridge University Press, 1990. A detailed treatment of the biological features of criminal behavior. Includes chapters on developmental factors, intelligence, case studies, how biology and responsibility are related, and predicting criminal behavior on the basis of biological and environmental variables.

Federal Bureau of Investigation. *Crime in America*. Washington, D.C.: U.S. Government Printing Office, 1993. A detailed and comprehensive statistical treatment of major types of crime (murder, forcible rape, robbery, aggravated assault, burglary, larceny-theft, and motor vehicle theft). Published annually, it is important for any student of crime.

Gottfredson, Michael R., and Travis Hirschi. *A General Theory of Crime*. Stanford, Calif.: Stanford University Press, 1990. An interdisciplinary analysis of crime which argues that current traditional theories are inadequate. The authors posit a theory of crime based on lack of self-control. A carefully researched and convincing account.

Laufer, William S., and Freda Adler, eds. *Advances in Criminological Theory*. New Brunswick, N.J.: Transactions, 1990. Volume 2 of a serial publication that discusses issues in criminological research. This volume contains articles on corporate crime theory, comparative cross-cultural research, and the media and crime.

Meier, Robert F., ed. *Major Forms of Crime*. Beverly Hills, Calif.: Sage Publications,

1984. Various authors discuss nine major forms of crime in terms of what each is and how often it occurs, theories, social and legal reaction to the crime, characteristics, and future directions for research.

Tonry, Michael, and Norval Morris, eds. *Crime and Justice: An Annual Review of Research*. Chicago: University of Chicago Press, 1990. This serial volume, like the Laufer and Adler book, explores issues of interest in crime. This volume, number 12 in the series, discusses the neuropsychology of juvenile delinquency, continuity and change in youth gangs, and developmental factors in crime.

Wilson, James Q., and Richard J. Herrnstein. *Crime and Human Nature*. New York: Simon & Schuster, 1985. The authors do an admirable job of organizing and analyzing a massive and wide ranging amount of criminological and psychological literature. They stress individual factors as well as social variables and theorize that crime results from individual choice. Well written, scholarly, filled with relevant information, and controversial.

Laurence Miller

Cross-References
The Courts, 367; The Criminal Justice System, 380; Cultural Transmission Theory of Deviance, 424; Deviance: Analysis and Overview, 525; Deviance: Biological and Psychological Explanations, 532; Deviance: Functions and Dysfunctions, 540; Gangs, 792; Organized Crime, 1322; Prostitution, 1526; Uniform Crime Reports and Crime Data, 2090; White-Collar and Corporate Crime, 2179.

THE CRIMINAL JUSTICE SYSTEM

Type of sociology: Deviance and social control
Field of study: Controlling deviance

In order for a society to maintain itself and survive, it must provide for the safety and security of the members of that society and their possessions. This responsibility is assumed by the criminal justice system. This system consists of five divisions linked together in a sequential progression as a person passes through it (laws, law enforcement, courts, correctional institutions, and rehabilitation).

Principal terms
COURTS: duly constituted organizations responsible for determining the length and type of punishment for those persons convicted of committing a crime
CRIME: behavior that violates a law which specifically prohibits such behavior, as, for example, illegally taking or selling certain property or committing acts of violence
CRIMINAL CORRECTION SYSTEM: a group of duly constituted organizations responsible for housing and supervising persons convicted of crimes by means of confinement in prisons or parole
CRIMINAL LAWS: legal and formal prohibitions of certain behaviors and the specification of penalties for committing those behaviors
FELONY: a serious crime such as murder, selling drugs, or auto theft
LAW ENFORCEMENT AGENCIES: duly constituted organizations responsible for the investigation and apprehension of persons who have committed crimes
MISDEMEANOR: a minor, less serious crime such as petty theft, vagrancy, or small-time gambling
RECIDIVISM: the commission of a criminal act by a person who has previously been convicted for criminal activity and served time
REHABILITATION AGENCIES: duly constituted organizations that facilitate the return of certain criminals to society with the aid of social workers or probation and parole officers

Overview

In order to provide protection and security for the personal well-being and possessions of the collective members of society, modern states have developed criminal justice systems. In the United States, the system consists of five components. First, laws prohibit certain behaviors. The next three components are the three social institutions that implement these laws: Second, law enforcement agencies are responsible for apprehending lawbreakers. Third, courts determine the length and type of punishment for those found guilty. Fourth, the criminal correction system isolates and incarcerates the criminal population in penal institutions. Additionally, in the belief that some criminals can be successfully reformed and integrated into society, rehabilitation agencies have been created.

The distinctive features of criminal law, according to Michael D. Bayles, are the strict prohibitions of certain behaviors and the imposition of penalties of varying degrees on offenders. The distinctive penalty is imprisonment. Besides enunciating specific penalties for violations, criminal laws serve to deter people from committing criminal acts, to exact retribution for wrongdoing, to condemn behavior contrary to accepted social values, and to educate through the process of condemnation.

Criminal law is based on three fundamental principles. The principle of innocence does not permit knowingly punishing innocent persons and provides protections against mistakenly punishing innocent persons. The principle of pollution, derived from ancient codes stating that certain acts "pollute" society, emphasizes that the state has the responsibility of formulating and enforcing laws. Laws can be enacted only by Congress, state legislatures, or local authority. The principle of proportionality states that punishment must be proportional to the seriousness of the crime. By making the punishment fit the crime, a distinction between constructive and destructive retribution is established.

The responsibility for enforcing laws resides with various governmental enforcement agencies. These agencies are empowered to investigate the commission of criminal acts and to arrest and detain the alleged perpetrators for possible prosecution. Law enforcement agencies operate under four different jurisdictions: city, county, state, and federal government. Each agency is responsible to its own division of government. City and county police are responsible for preventing and investigating crime and apprehending offenders only within that state or county. State police officers sometimes help city and county police in addition to their main duty of maintaining law and order on the state highways. Federal agencies (the Federal Bureau of Investigation, Drug Enforcement Administration, Coast Guard, Immigration and Naturalization Service, Secret Service, and Bureau of Alcohol, Tobacco and Firearms) become involved in especially serious crimes—those that cross local or state jurisdictions or are beyond the capacity of other agencies. Examples are bank robberies, assassinations, kidnappings, bombings, firearm violations, smuggling, and moving and selling illegal drugs.

The determination of the guilt or innocence of a person accused of and prosecuted for a crime and the nature and length of punishment for that crime if the person is convicted are the responsibility of the courts. The judiciary in the United States is a dual court system; that is, each state and the federal government has its own set of courts. The federal judicial system is composed of the Supreme Court, eleven courts of appeal, and thirteen district courts. The courts of appeal and district courts each serve specified geographic locations in the United States. District Courts have original jurisdiction in federal criminal cases. All cases originate here once an indictment from a federal grand jury is handed down. Convicted defendants have the right of appeal to the court of appeal in their jurisdiction. If the appeals court upholds the district court's conviction, the conviction may be appealed to the Supreme Court, the final arbiter. The Supreme Court has the discretion to consider or not consider the case; the great majority of cases are not heard.

State courts can be separated into four levels. Most criminal cases are handled in trial courts of limited jurisdiction. These encompass about 90 percent of all state courts and include municipal and juvenile courts. Their jurisdiction is limited to minor cases such as infractions and misdemeanors. Trial courts of general jurisdiction include district, circuit, and superior courts, and they handle the more serious criminal cases (felonies). Intermediate appellate courts hear appeals from the trial courts. Courts of last resort (supreme courts) can review appeals from the appellate courts if they choose. They are the final arbiter.

The criminal correction system operates on the same four levels as government: national, state, county, and local. The federal prison system incarcerates men, women, and juveniles who have broken federal laws. These institutions are either maximum security penitentiaries for the most violent and dangerous criminals, medium security facilities for prisoners who are not violent or who have demonstrated good behavior; minimum security facilities for those convicted of lesser offenses such as income tax evasions, forgery, or minor theft; and prerelease centers, much like halfway houses, which hold prisoners whose term is nearly up and who are permitted to interact with the community. State prison systems have all the divisions of the federal system; each state runs its own particular system. County and local institutions are generally jails rather than prisons. Jails serve primarily as holding areas for prisoners awaiting trial, although offenders convicted of a misdemeanor may serve their terms there. Other individuals may be put into pretrial release programs which permit them to remain in the community under supervision. Still others are permitted to go free after posting monetary bail as a guarantee that they will appear later for trial.

In the belief that some offenders can be rehabilitated or can live productive lives without being incarcerated—and in an effort to relieve overcrowding in prisons—rehabilitation programs have been instituted. Social workers work within the prison and develop programs to help prisoners learn and adjust; for example, group therapy programs encourage prisoners to share their concerns and feelings in order to understand themselves better. Parole may be granted to a prisoner who has served part of his or her term. A person may also be granted probation instead of being incarcerated. In both parole and probation, the person lives in society rather than in prison. Such individuals are supervised in varying degrees of closeness by parole and probation officers. They obey any court orders and demonstrate they are living as law-abiding citizens. Violation of the conditions of probation or parole may result in imprisonment.

Applications

In order to appreciate how the five components of the criminal justice system mesh together and operate, it is instructive to follow a case through the state system. A crime is committed. The police investigate, gather evidence, and then arrest a suspect, who is taken to jail and booked. An initial hearing is held before a judge to determine whether the suspect will be released until trial or held in jail. The suspect may be released on his or her own recognizance (a written pledge to return for trial), or he or she may have to post monetary bail which will be forfeited if he or she fails to appear for trial (about 90 percent of those released appear for trial). Bail can be denied if the suspect has a prior criminal record, is believed to pose a threat to the citizenry, or is deemed likely to skip bail.

Next, the police present their evidence to the district attorney's office, which decides if the evidence is sufficient to establish guilt "beyond a reasonable doubt" and can therefore justify prosecution. If not, the case is dropped, and the suspect is released from jail or bail is returned. If the crime is minor (vandalism, for example) the accused might be diverted to a social service agency. If the district attorney decides to prosecute, a document called an information is filed in some states, with the court citing the charges. In other states and in federal court, a grand jury hears evidence and determines whether there is enough evidence for a trial. If there is, an indictment is issued that specifies the charges.

A date is then set for the trial. The accused is represented by a defense lawyer; representation is a right of any person charged with a crime. The defendant can hire his or her own attorney; if he or she cannot afford to pay one, a court-appointed public defender is assigned. After indictment, a preliminary hearing is held before a judge. The prosecution presents evidence to establish a basis for going to trial. The defense may refute this evidence or raise procedural questions. The judge can dismiss the case or bring it to trial, at which the prosecuting and defense attorneys face each other before a neutral judge and jury. This adversarial system presumably brings out the facts that determine guilt or innocence while protecting the rights of the accused. Rather than facing trial, however, the defendant may decide to plead guilty after the preliminary hearing (or at any time prior to the jury's verdict) by negotiating a plea bargain with the prosecutor. The defendant pleads guilty in exchange for a lesser sentence than might have been received if the case had gone to trial. About 80 percent of cases are handled in this way, avoiding costly and time-consuming trials.

If the case goes to trial, a jury must first be selected. When the trial begins, opening statements are made by each attorney. The prosecution then calls witnesses to support its case, and the defense cross-examines the witness in an attempt to undermine their credibility. The defense then calls its witnesses, if it so chooses, and the prosecutor in turn may cross-examine them. After each side has presented its case, final arguments are delivered—each attorney interprets the evidence as he or she hopes the jury will view it. The jury then deliberates and attempts to reach a verdict. If this proves impossible, a hung jury (a mistrial) is declared, and the prosecution must decide whether it wants to retry or dismiss the case. The great majority of cases end in a verdict, and the verdict is guilty in about 75 percent of cases.

In a few states, the jury recommends or even determines the punishment, but this is most often done by the judge. The judge may assign probation if the offense is not too grave or it is a first offense; the convicted person is allowed to live in his or her community under strict supervision for a determined time. The judge may impose a prison sentence for a determined period of time at a particular type of correctional facility. The convicted person may appeal the conviction to a state or federal appeals court while free on bail or while serving the sentence. In appellate proceedings the court reviews the trial transcript to determine whether there are sufficient grounds to reverse the conviction. If the appeals court upholds the conviction, a further appeal may be made to the state supreme court or the federal Supreme Court. These supreme courts are the final arbiters.

If all appeals are lost, the sentence must be served. If the person is a model prisoner who behaves properly, the length of the sentence may be reduced ("time off for good behavior"). In some cases, prisoners may be granted parole, which is like probation, after having served a certain minimum sentence. In other cases, the sentence may specifically deny any opportunity for parole, and the full length of the sentence must be served.

Context

The criminal justice system occupies a prominent position in sociology. First, the criminal justice system is a massive and extensive system that pervades all levels of society and directly or indirectly affects the life of every citizen. There are thousands of state and federal laws whose purpose is to regulate daily conduct. More than sixteen thousand local police forces and three federal government departments (the Department of Justice, the Department of the Treasury, and the U.S. Postal Service) are responsible for enforcing those laws. A formalized hierarchical state and federal court system determines guilt or innocence and appropriate punishment for the guilty. State and federal penal institutions house and care for many of these guilty individuals. A rehabilitation system attempts to integrate offenders back into society. The second reason for sociology's interest in the system is that the criminal justice system is directly concerned with the prevention and management of deviant behavior. Crime is a type of deviant behavior. Edwin M. Schur defined deviant behavior as that which is viewed as involving a personally discredible departure from the normative expectations of a group. Such behavior produces a collective response directed at isolating, treating, correcting, or punishing individuals who engage in such behavior. All societies produce deviance, and therefore all societies must cope with deviance. The criminal justice system is the United States' method of coping with crime.

As Victoria L. Swigert observed, a criminal justice system, criminal behavior, and statehood are all inseparably joined. Crime is conduct that is forbidden by rules that are enforced by the authoritative representatives of the state. Therefore, states had to be created before crime could exist. Thus, a centralized state authority, crime, and a criminal justice system all appeared at the same time in human history.

The criminal justice system evolved from demands of the citizenry. In exchange for their consent to be ruled by the state, the state had to reciprocate and provide for the personal security of the citizenry and the protection of their possessions. Survival of the society demanded that such provisions be fulfilled. The criminal justice system is thus intimately linked to the well-being of society. This linkage places the criminal justice system in a prominent position in the context of the sociological study of deviance.

There is no reason to expect that the study of the criminal justice system will ever lose its central position in sociology. Attorney Alan Dershowitz has commented that the adversary system in criminal courts generally produces accurate results while safeguarding the rights of the accused. This same comment generally characterizes the other four components of the system as well. Yet this should not obscure the many problems and inefficiencies that need to be studied and modified so that the system can more fairly and accurately serve the best interests of society. A small sample of the many issues that need to be addressed includes wrongful convictions, racial bias in the system, police brutality, the negative effects that enforcement of existing drug laws is having on the apprehension of violent criminals, the place of juveniles in the system, overcrowding in prisons, the rising rate of violent crime, the high rate of recidivism for certain crimes, the changing roles of women in the system, and the extreme expense and amount of time involved in prosecuting certain cases.

Bibliography

Bayles, Michael D. *Principles of Law*. Boston: Reidel, 1987. Bayles discusses a number of types of laws; he includes an extensive and thorough chapter on criminal law. Well written, scholarly, and informative.

Carp, Robert A., and Ronald Stidham. *The Federal Courts*. 2d ed. Washington, D.C.: Congressional Quarterly, 1991. A comprehensive presentation of the various aspects of the federal judiciary. Covers history, jurisdiction and workload, personnel, decision making, and policy making. Well written, easy to read, and informative.

_____ . *Judicial Process in America*. 2d ed. Washington, D.C.: Congressional Quarterly, 1993. This volume presents much of the same coverage of the federal judicial system as the authors' previously cited volume. This volume also contains a good presentation of the state court system.

Cohen, Paul, and Shari Cohen. *Careers in Law Enforcement and Security*. New York: Rosen, 1990. The authors present a clear and complete description of the organization and function of the various federal and state law enforcement agencies. Includes information about parole and probation.

Sullivan, Larry E. *The Prison Reform Movement: Forlorn Hope*. Boston: Twayne, 1990. A complete history and discussion of the rationale for prisons, the changing beliefs in what prisons should try to accomplish, and the various attempts at reforming perceived defects. A most readable and interesting treatment of the prison system.

Weiss, Ann E. *Prisons: A System in Trouble*. Hillsdale, N.J.: Enslow, 1988. An excellently written and perceptive description of prison life, the problem with prisons, and alternative solutions. Much of the book is written in an involving "You-are-there" style.

Laurence Miller

Cross-References

CROSS-SECTIONAL VERSUS LONGITUDINAL STUDIES

Type of sociology: Sociological research
Fields of study: Basic concepts; Data collection and analysis

Cross-sectional and longitudinal studies are two methods of collecting information for research purposes. Depending on the research questions one wishes to answer, either method of data collection may be appropriate. These two methods represent the two most common data-collection methods used by social scientists.

Principal terms
COHORT: a mutually exclusive group of individuals as defined by an experimenter; members of a specific cohort are assumed to have experienced the same historical conditions at approximately the same time
CROSS-SECTIONAL STUDY: a type of study in which different cohorts are compared at the same point in time
DEPENDENT VARIABLE: the observed, consequent, or outcome variable; this variable is the one on which the effects of the independent variable are observed
INDEPENDENT VARIABLE: the treatment, antecedent, or causal variable; cohort membership is often used as an independent variable
LONGITUDINAL DESIGN: a type of study in which a single cohort is compared over some (usually extended) period of time

Overview

Broadly speaking, social scientists are faced with two problems when conducting research. One problem is that of discovering the measurement properties—that is, the reliabilities and validities—of various research instruments, such as questionnaires, assessments, and treatments. The other problem is that of establishing causal relationships among independent and dependent variables. The scientific method is generally considered the only acceptable method of demonstrating cause in the social and physical sciences. Social scientists Paul B. Baltes, Hayne W. Reese, and John R. Nesselroade define the scientific method as "careful observation under known conditions." This definition is useful in that it suggests that many methods of careful observation exist. Cross-sectional and longitudinal studies are two such methods of careful observation. These two methods provide slightly different, though equally important, information about the relationships among variables. Consequently, these two methods are used quite commonly in the social sciences to discover causal relationships among variables.

A cross-sectional study is a type of study in which different groups of individuals, often called cohorts, are compared at one point in time. Cohorts may be different age groups, different ethnic groups, or even different countries. In fact, any mutually exclusive collection of individuals that the experimenter clearly defines may be used to define a cohort. The intent of this type of study is to compare cohorts in terms of the features that differentiate them (such as age, cultural backgrounds, or political systems). Thus, the focus of cross-sectional studies is often said to be on interindividual differences—that is, the differences between individuals—as a function of cohort membership.

A longitudinal study, on the other hand, is a type of study in which a single cohort is studied over time. For example, one might study the self-concepts of a group of children as they go through puberty, or the changes in Asian Americans' ethnic identity as they become assimilated to the larger culture, or the development of capitalism in an emerging democracy as it matures. The intent of this type of design is to compare the cohort with itself as it changes or ages. Thus, the focus of longitudinal studies is often said to be on intraindividual change—changes within the individuals who make up the cohort—as a function of time. In cross-sectional studies, different groups of individuals are studied, whereas in longitudinal studies, the same individuals are studied repeatedly. Figure 1 is a representation of cross-sectional and longitudinal studies.

		Time of Testing		
		1980	1990	2000
	1920		70	
	1930		60	
	1940		50	
Birth Cohort	1950		40	
	1960		30	
	1970		20	
	1980		10	

FIGURE 1a. EXAMPLE OF A CROSS-SECTIONAL DESIGN. Values in the figure are ages at which groups of individuals were interviewed. Thus, individuals born in the 1980 birth cohort who were interviewed in 1990 were 10 years old.

		Time of Testing		
		1980	1990	2000
	1920			
	1930			
	1940			
Birth Cohort	1950	30	40	50
	1960			
	1970			
	1980			

FIGURE 1b. EXAMPLE OF A LONGITUDINAL DESIGN. Values in the figure are ages at which the same group of individuals was interviewed. Thus, individuals born in the 1950 birth cohort were interviewed in 1980, 1990, and 2000, at ages 30, 40, and 50, respectively. (Adapted from Rybash, John W., Paul Roodin, and John Santrock, *Adult Development and Aging*. 2d ed. Dubuque, Iowa: Wm. C. Brown, 1991.)

Often, because of the complexity of social phenomena, the relationships among variables are unclear and the causal mechanisms ambiguous. Thus, the task for social scientists is to gather the information in such a way that this ambiguity is reduced as much as possible. The scientific method is one way of reducing ambiguity and establishing clear evidence regarding the relationships among variables. In their book *Quasi-Experimentation: Design and Analysis for Field Settings* (1979), social scientists Thomas D. Cook and Donald T. Campbell note that well-designed experiments reduce ambiguity; they do not eliminate it completely. The proposition that ambiguity is not eliminated completely may be traced to two sources. First, social scientists often use probabilistic rules of inference (inferential statistics) when making conclusions about relationships among causes and effects and therefore are never certain in an absolute sense about the results of experiments. Second, ambiguity arises because for any one experiment, a large number of plausible explanations exist for the observed relationships among suspected causes and their putative effects. Thus, social scientists try to anticipate each so-called rival explanation and design experiments so that the plausibility of each may be assessed. The goal is to discover the most plausible explanation and thus to establish the causal relationship among variables.

Merely performing an experiment does not guarantee that causal relationships among variables can be demonstrated. In fact, the method by which information is collected has substantial impact on the validity of scientists' claims about cause. The essential aspect of designing experiments is reducing the number of alternative interpretations of the cause-effect relationship to a minimum.

In general, no single universally accepted research design exists that yields unambiguous information about the relationship among variables. This is true of both cross-sectional and longitudinal studies. It is possible, however, to evaluate different research designs with regard to their internal validity. Studies in which little ambiguity surrounds the causal relationship between independent and dependent variables are said to be high in internal validity, whereas studies in which considerable ambiguity surrounds the causal relationship are said to have little internal validity.

Applications

If a researcher wanted to study the development of intelligence over the life span, he or she might be interested in examining the effects of age (the independent variable) on scores on an intelligence test (the dependent variable). The researcher may collect information about age differences in intelligence by using either a cross-sectional or longitudinal design. In a cross-sectional study, the social scientist would interview several groups of individuals of different ages and would give each age group the same intelligence test. Subsequently, the researcher would compare the different age groups' performance on the test in the hope of making some conclusions about the developmental changes in intelligence over the life span.

The major advantage of this type of study is its efficiency. All the information could be collected within a few weeks or months. Moreover, this type of study allows one to compare developmental differences across a wide range of ages. For example, one could compare the performance of ten-year-olds with that of seventy-year-olds, a range of sixty years, in order to understand the developmental differences in intelligence (see Figure 1a). The efficiency of cross-sectional studies accounts for their frequent use in the social sciences.

What degree of internal validity do cross-sectional designs possess? That is, to what extent are they plagued by alternative explanations for the observed differences among age groups? The most salient rival explanation in cross-sectional studies is selection. In the present context, this threat to internal validity refers to the numerous differences between groups of individuals (disregarding developmental differences) that might influence the dependent variable, intelligence. Thus, while the researcher may observe differences in intelligence scores associated with age group, it is unclear the extent to which these differences are entirely attributable to development. Age groups differ not only in age, but also in the amount and nature of their formal education, the presence and severity of chronic health problems, the familiarity with and anxiety about testing situations, among a number of other features. Many of these differences are associated with birth cohort but are unrelated to the developmental course of intelligence, and each may reasonably be expected to affect performance on an intelligence test. For example, social scientist Paul B. Baltes noted in 1987 that successive generations have attained increasing levels of formal education and that education is positively related to intelligence quotient (IQ) scores. Moreover, each succeeding generation has benefited from advances in medicine that have eliminated or reduced the effects of many diseases known to affect cognition (perhaps most important among these is hypertension).

Thus, selection differences mimic age differences because the features that make groups "select" vary with age. It is critical to realize that such differences may not be "true" developmental differences, but rather may be selection differences. When comparing age groups in a cross-sectional study, researchers are simultaneously comparing different birth cohorts as well, which makes unambiguous statements about age effects difficult.

Consider next a longitudinal study of intelligence. In this study, the researcher would follow a single birth cohort over several years as it ages (see Figure 1b). At every time of measurement, the researcher would give the same individuals the same intelligence test. Subsequently, the researcher would compare the cohort's performance on this test at each time of measurement in the hope of drawing some conclusions about the developmental changes in intelligence over the life span. The major advantage of this type of study is that it affords a more precise representation of intraindividual change in intelligence. Because the researcher limits the study to a single cohort, no confounding of birth cohort and age is possible. This design is not without its shortcomings. One practical limitation is the time required to complete the study. Using Figure 1b as an example, twenty years would have to pass before the scientist could collect all the information. When compared to cross-sectional studies, the decreased efficiency of longitudinal designs reduces their appeal to researchers.

Second, the internal validity of this type of design is threatened by testing. In the present context, this threat refers to the changes in test scores that are attributable to completing the same test repeatedly. For example, if a teacher were to give students the same test repeatedly over the school year, scores could be expected to improve simply because of students' increasing familiarity and comfort with the test. The same effect can occur in longitudinal studies even though the testing occurs over a longer time span. Therefore, although longitudinal studies do afford the opportunity to observe intraindividual change, it is unclear what proportion of that change is attributable to intraindividual change and what proportion is attributable to repeated exposure to the test.

Another threat to the internal validity of longitudinal studies is mortality. This threat refers to the loss of participants over the course of a study because of time conflicts, lack of interest, and even death. Using Figure 1b as an example, it is very likely that some participants interviewed in 1980 will not participate at subsequent times of testing for a variety of reasons. The threat to validity arises because those participants who decide to drop out do so for specific reasons, and those who remain in the study also do so for specific reasons. It has been observed that those with chronic health conditions, low income, less formal education, and lower levels of motivation tend to drop out of longitudinal studies. In the example of intelligence testing, such mortality affects a study in important ways. Those subjects who return for subsequent testing tend to have higher IQ scores than those who do not return for subsequent testing, not because IQ has increased over time, but because it is the best performers who complete the subsequent tests. As a consequence, the picture of the change in intelligence provided by a longitudinal study may be an overly optimistic one, because primarily those with high levels of education, motivation, health, and intelligence itself remain in the study.

Thus, testing and mortality mimic age changes because testing and mortality exert their influence over time just as age does. It is critical, however, to realize that such differences may not be true developmental differences, but rather may be testing and/or mortality differences. When comparing the same cohort over time in a longitudinal study, social scientists who are not aware of the influence of testing and mortality will end up with ambiguous results regarding age change.

Context

The elements of modern experimentation began appearing in published research early in the twentieth century. The use of control groups and the development of inferential statistics in the late 1800's and early 1900's paved the way for modern forms of social science research. Moreover, the language of experimentation came into its own shortly after the middle of the twentieth century with the publication of Donald T. Campbell and Julian C. Stanley's *Experimental and Quasi-experimental Designs for Research* (1963), a publication now considered to be a classic.

By the middle of the twentieth century, sociological theories were devoting attention to cohorts as units of analysis. Sociologists, cultural anthropologists, and social psychologists began to study the processes by which cohorts exert influence on, and are themselves influenced by, society. Concern with the impact on the individual of the rapid social change of industrialized countries made cohort analysis a compelling area of research to social scientists, and this interest has continued. In the 1960's and 1970's, designs incorporating combinations of cross-sectional and longitudinal designs were first discussed and implemented in research. These hybrid designs overcame many of the limitations of simple cross-sectional and longitudinal designs, and they integrated research findings from sociology, psychology, and demography.

A science is only as good as the information it encompasses. Research designs—cross-sectional and longitudinal studies among them—can provide the accurate and valuable information essential to good science. The value of the information derived from research depends greatly on the sensitivity of the scientist to the strengths and weaknesses of research methods.

Bibliography

Baltes, Paul B, Hayne W. Reese, and John R. Nesselroade. *Life-Span Developmental Psychology: Introduction to Research Methods.* Monterey, Calif.: Brooks/Cole, 1977. This book covers the strengths and weaknesses of experimental designs common in the social sciences.

Campbell, Donald T., and Julian C. Stanley. *Experimental and Quasi-experimental Designs for Research.* Boston, Mass.: Houghton Mifflin, 1963. This work is considered by many to be the classic source on experimental design. It includes the first discussion of sources of internal invalidity.

Cook, Thomas D., and Donald T. Campbell. *Quasi-experimentation: Design and Analysis Issues for Field Settings.* Boston, Mass.: Houghton Mifflin, 1979. This work is an updated version of the 1963 Campbell and Stanley book. Includes additional coverage of experimental designs, inferential statistics, and the language and logic of experimentation.

Rosenthal, Robert, and Ralph L. Rosnow. *Essentials of Behavioral Research: Methods and Data Analysis.* 2d ed. New York: McGraw-Hill, 1991. This exhaustive source covers research issues for social scientists in the fields of sociology, cultural anthropology, and psychology. Extensive discussion of the logic and philosophy of experimentation supplements the chapters on research methods and data analysis.

Schaie, K. W. "A General Model for the Study of Developmental Problems." *Psychological Bulletin* 64, no. 2 (1965): 92-107. In this somewhat technical work, Schaie discusses the disadvantages of cross-sectional and longitudinal designs and suggests new designs to overcome these weaknesses.

Frank H. Jurden

Cross-References

CROWDS AND CROWD DYNAMICS

Type of sociology: Collective behavior and social movements

A crowd is a group of people who engage in face-to-face interaction at the same time and place. Sociological theories of crowd dynamics emphasize the spontaneous, extrainstitutional, and unorganized aspects of crowd behavior.

Principal terms

CIRCULAR REACTION: an exchange of emotional responses among crowd members; emotions intensify as they are shared

COLLECTIVITY: a group of people who share a common interest; may be compact (a crowd) or diffuse (a public)

EXTRAINSTITUTIONAL: outside the normal patterns of social relations

HOMOGENEOUS: possessing similarity or sameness; early theories of crowd dynamics portrayed members as having "one mind"

NORM: a rule of social behavior

SANCTION: a reaction to normative or non-normative behavior; in other words, a reward or punishment

Overview

Collective behavior is characterized by spontaneous, unstructured, extrainstitutional activity performed by a group of individuals. One type of group that may engage in collective behavior is the crowd. A crowd is a compact collectivity with members involved in face-to-face interaction, together at the same time and place. The crowd contrasts with the public, which is a more diffuse and scattered group of individuals who share interest in a common issue. According to sociologist Erich Goode in *Collective Behavior* (1992), "while a given individual can—and always does—belong to several publics simultaneously, one can belong to only one crowd at a time."

Sociologist Herbert Blumer identified four types of crowds: casual, conventionalized, expressive, and acting. The casual crowd is loosely organized—for example, a group of people who are milling around a concert hall, waiting to enter. The conventionalized crowd is less fleeting and more strongly organized, such as a group of spectators at a sporting event who clap and exclaim spontaneously yet within a fixed set of appropriate norms. The expressive crowd is best characterized as a joyous collectivity; for example, a crowd at a religious revival. The acting crowd is one with a specific objective or goal. It is often depicted as angry, violent, and irrational.

Collective behavior theorists tend to focus on Blumer's concept of the acting crowd. Early theories of crowd dynamics often depicted the members of a crowd as irrational, deviant, or even "mad." Popular writer Gustave Le Bon promoted this idea of the hysterical, angry crowd in his seminal work *Psychologie des foules* (1895; *The Crowd: A Study of the Popular Mind*, 1986). Le Bon wrote from an elitist position and supported the aristocracy of his native France. He saw members of crowds as inferior beings, and his work had strong racist and sexist connotations.

Despite the biased point of view from which Le Bon wrote, he is considered to be the principal precursor of contagion theory. The basic idea of contagion theory is that crowds generate an excitement which is contagious in a way that is similar to an infectious disease. Sociologist Robert Park, an early contagion theorist, viewed crowd dynamics as an interactive social psychological process, dominated by the power of suggestion. In *The Crowd and the Public and Other Essays* (1904), he wrote, "people under the influence of a collective stimulus often carry out actions which as individuals they neither could nor would do."

Blumer also considered crowd behavior to be directed by suggestive influence, accompanied by a state of social unrest. He characterized crowd dynamics as a process of circular reaction in which members transmit feelings to one another. As feelings of anger, fear, and excitement are shared, they intensify, and people become irrational and psychologically unstable, leading them to commit acts that they normally would not.

Like contagion theorists, convergence theorists emphasize the homogeneity of crowds. Convergence theorists assert that people who come together in a crowd have a predisposition to do so. The crowd gives people the opportunity to express their "true selves" in a way that they would not or could not as individuals. In other words, people are drawn to participate in crowds because of the kinds of people they are.

More developed forms of convergence theory focus on specific characteristics of individuals that impel them to participate in certain forms of crowd activity. Erich Goode, for example, applies convergence theory to the phenomenon of crowds of teenagers yelling and screaming at a rock concert. Convergence theory would suggest that they engage in this behavior as an extension of their everyday selves, as an outgrowth of emotional adolescence.

In *Frustration and Aggression* (1939), psychologist John Dollard and his colleagues focused on frustration as a convergent characteristic. They suggested that a prolonged state of frustration generates aggression that can lead to violent crowd activity. When the crowd cannot strike out at the actual or perceived source of its frustration, members will direct their aggressive behaviors toward something or someone that is readily available and that does not pose a threat.

Both contagion and convergence theories emphasize the unanimity of crowds. Emergent norm theory, in contrast, recognizes the diversity of crowd members and goes against the notion that they are driven to irrationality. According to this perspective, first put forth by sociologists Ralph Turner and Lewis Killian in 1957, people acting within crowds are not necessarily deviants; in other words, they do not purposefully violate generally held norms. On the contrary, groups of people in ambiguous and uncertain circumstances often generate new rules of social behavior, what the authors refer to as "emergent norms."

Emergent norm theory recognizes the diversity of crowd membership. For example, sociologist Jerry M. Lewis, in his 1972 analysis of the 1970 Kent State University demonstration, noted that the crowd consisted of an "active core," "cheerleaders," and "spectators." Emergent norm theory emphasizes that although individuals act in relation to one another in a crowd, they do not necessarily all perform the same activity.

Turner and Killian suggest that people generally want to do the right thing in any given circumstance and that they look to others for confirmation that their behavior is appropriate. When a particular situation is unclear or confusing, conventional norms may not apply. People within the crowd attempt to define the situation so that they will receive approval from others and not suffer from any negative social sanctions.

Applications

Contagion and convergence theories are rarely used to explain crowd dynamics in contemporary sociology, though elements of these approaches still persist. More common is the application of emergent norm theory to crowd phenomena such as disasters, riots, looting, and panics.

Looting after a disaster or riot is defined as a criminal activity and therefore is a violation of conventional social norms. Although it is popularly perceived that looting after disasters is a common occurrence, it is actually quite rare. When looting does occur after a disaster, it is usually perpetrated by individuals from outside the community in which the disaster took place.

Looting is more common during civil disturbances and riots. In these situations, looting is a crowd activity in which community members break into stores, often in their own neighborhoods. Those who engage in this activity are diverse in terms of sex, race, age and social class; people generally work in pairs, family units, or other small groups. Additionally, looting in this context is a public event in which people do not generally attempt to hide their actions. Looting behavior may seem random and irrational to the outsider, but it actually has a pattern which can be explained with emergent norm theory.

In their research article "Property Norms and Looting: Their Patterns in Community Crises" (1970), sociologists E. L. Quarantelli and Russell R. Dynes explain that in the civil disturbances of the 1960's, the most commonly looted stores were those that sold groceries, furniture, apparel, and liquor; crowds collectively defined which stores to loot. For example, Quarantelli and Dynes found that in Newark, New Jersey, nearly half the stores looted fell into one of these categories, while many other businesses remained intact.

In the context of a civil disturbance, property norms become redefined. The new norm of property is an emergent one. Through the process of collective redefinition, looting behavior becomes normative, the socially acceptable thing to do. Quarantelli and Dynes point out that although looters substitute one emergent norm for a conventional one, looters tend to obey other traditional social norms, such as traffic regulations. Consequently, Quarantelli and Dynes maintain that crowd behavior is not completely unstructured.

Sociologists who study crowd dynamics are also interested in the study of panics. Sociologist Neil Smelser distinguished between fearful panics and acquisitive panics. In a fearful panic, people rush to escape a perceived catastrophe. For example, a crowd in a motion picture theater rushes to escape if someone yells, "Fire." In a fearful panic, the crowd is in a state of terror and ignores the presence of others to save themselves from the source of fear.

In an acquisitive panic, the crowd rushes toward something desirable that the individuals all try to get for themselves. The acquisitive panic is an intensified "craze" in which people ignore the safety of others. A good example of an acquisitive panic is a situation in which a very popular toy, such as the Cabbage Patch Kids dolls of the mid-1980's, is in very high demand and short supply. When such a shortage occurs, crowds of people may rush into a store that they perceive has the object of their desire. In the process, they may ignore conventional norms of manners and safety.

Theories of crowd dynamics that emphasize homogeneity, such as the contagion and convergence approaches, predict that in a panic, all members of the crowd will act in the same way. Contagion theory portrays the crowd as irrational, destructive, and highly emotional. Convergence theory emphasizes the "kinds of people" likely to be present at a certain type of panic. For example, only certain types of people are likely to desire a Cabbage Patch doll so intensely (for themselves or their children) that they would rush to the department store to compete—even fight—with others to buy one.

In his study "Panic at 'The Who Concert Stampede': An Empirical Assessment," sociologist Norris Johnson suggests that panic reactions within crowds are quite rare. He analyzed data regarding the concert of the Who on December 3, 1979, when eleven young people were crushed to death while waiting to enter Riverfront Coliseum in Cincinnati, Ohio, where the rock concert was being held. Local newspapers characterized the incident as an acquisitive panic, in which young people presumably pushed, shoved, and even trampled one another in order to get the best seats.

In his analysis of police records and interviews with people present at the incident, Johnson found that the depiction of the event by the local press was inaccurate. Intensive crowd density and a lack of sufficient ticket checkers meant that most people were completely unable to move. Once the doors finally opened, the crowd surged forward and about twenty-five people fell. As the push of the crowd continued, people fell on top of those already on the concrete. The "stampede" by the Who's audience was not an acquisitive panic, as depicted by the media, but an "escape panic," characterized here by people trying to get out of the overcrowded situation.

Johnson uses emergent norm theory to explain the helping behavior that occurred during the situation, but he notes that this theory does not account for the variety of behaviors performed by crowd members. In other words, in a unique situation, more than one emergent norm may develop.

Context

The earliest works on crowds tended to emphasize their psychological dimensions. The first major treatise on crowd behavior, *Memoirs of Extraordinary Popular Delusions and the Madness of Crowds* (1841), by Charles McKay, emphasized the crowd's irrational aspects. Studies such as this, as well as Le Bon's work, were concerned with why people seem to lose their individual motives, morals, and "sense" once they take part in such a group. They were particularly concerned with ways in which revolutionary mobs disturb the social order. Since these authors were concerned with protecting the status quo, they portrayed crowd members very unfavorably.

A basic principle of sociology is that social behavior is patterned in some way. This principle has presented a unique difficulty in the study of crowds, because to the outsider, crowd activity often seems completely chaotic and without order. Early researchers such as sociologist Herbert Blumer and social psychologist Floyd Allport examined crowd behavior more empirically, yet they held to the notion that the emotionality of crowds impels individuals to do things they normally would not.

In the 1960's, researchers became more concerned with how to explain rioting activity associated with the Civil Rights movement. At this time, traditional ideas about the nature of crowds began to change, and earlier theories were seen as perpetuating stereotypes about people who engage in crowd activity in situations such as riots, disasters, and panics. Sociologist Carl Couch examined ten of these stereotypes and concluded that the reason it is difficult for sociologists to find patterns of behavior in crowds is that the stereotypes (of emotionality, irrationality, and so on) are unfounded. In fact, the term "crowd" itself is so infected with past stereotypical meaning that many researchers prefer to use sociologist Clark McPhail's alternative term, "temporary gathering."

What has emerged in sociology is recognition of both the diversity of crowds and the rationality of their members. It is recognized that within a crowd, not everyone engages in the same behavior; in an emergency, for example, some people are helpers, while others are onlookers. Some people choose to be crowd members, while others do not. Other research, such as that by Adrian Aveni, acknowledges that while crowds are composed of diverse individuals, friendship groups within crowds also have an impact on behavior. In any case, the influence of the rational-calculus approach in sociology suggests that people seek to maximize rewards and to minimize costs regardless of their individual roles in the crowd environment. This is a popular approach to explaining behavior in sociology, and it is becoming increasingly important to the study of crowds.

Bibliography

Blumer, Herbert. "Collective Behavior." In *Principles of Sociology*, edited by Alfred McClung Lee. 3d ed. New York: Barnes & Noble, 1969. A classic chapter (originally published in 1939) in which the author puts forth his version of contagion theory, "circular reaction." He also delineates a typology of crowds that sociologists still use today. Although theoretical in nature, this chapter is very readable.

Couch, Carl. "Collective Behavior: An Examination of Some Stereotypes." *Social Problems* 15 (Winter, 1968): 310-322. An excellent critique of the impact of contagion and convergence theories on the study of collective behavior. The author provides a comprehensive analysis of the stereotypical characteristics of crowds perpetuated by these theories, such as irrationality, suggestibility, and spontaneity.

This critique is well suited for college students.

Goode, Erich. *Collective Behavior*. Fort Worth, Tex.: Harcourt Brace Jovanovich, 1992. A comprehensive text of the study of crowds and social movements. It includes end-of-chapter readings by other authors, as well as a bibliography at the end of each chapter. A good, basic overview.

Johnson, Norris. "Panic at 'The Who Concert Stampede': An Empirical Assessment." *Social Problems* 34 (October, 1987): 362-373. A research article on panic. The author uses emergent norm theory to dispel the myth that crowds are irrational in crisis situations. Gives the reader insight into how crowd dynamics theory can help to explain real-life events.

Le Bon, Gustave. *The Crowd: A Study of the Popular Mind*. New York: Penguin Books, 1977. Originally published in 1895, and published since in many various editions, this now-classic work is the basis for the development of contagion theory and, essentially, all study of crowd behavior. Although dated, it is well worth reading.

McPhail, Clark. *The Myth of the Madding Crowd*. New York: Aldine De Gruyter, 1991. An in-depth analysis of contagion, convergence, and emergent norm theories as well as an introduction to the author's reframing of crowd dynamics theory as an "assembling process." Contains an extensive bibliography.

Turner, Ralph H., and Lewis M. Killian. *Collective Behavior*. 2d ed. Englewood Cliffs, N.J.: Prentice-Hall, 1972. A classic, well-written text, highly recommended for both college students and general audiences. This text is the original source for the authors' discussion of emergent norm theory. Turner and Killian also incorporate segments of many research articles into the text, giving the reader insight into the breadth of collective behavior research.

Wright, Sam. *Crowds and Riots: A Study in Social Organization*. Beverly Hills, Calif.: Sage Publications, 1978. Focuses on the different types of group structures formed in crowds. Contains a useful chapter on how one might conduct a participant observation study of crowd behavior.

Donna Maurer

Cross-References

Collective Behavior, 291; Cultural Norms and Sanctions, 411; Mass Hysteria, 1134; Mobs, Riots, and Panics, 1226; Revolutions, 1641; Rumors and Urban Legends, 1667.

CULTS

Type of sociology: Major social institutions
Field of study: Religion

Cults are religious organizations that have their roots outside the dominant religious traditions of a society. The meaning of this concept is widely debated and applied in various ways. Because of the negative connotation of this label and the controversy surrounding these religious organizations, many scholars prefer to use the term "new religious movement" (NRM).

Principal terms

CHURCH: a large religious organization that considers itself uniquely legitimate and existing in a positive relationship with society

CULT: the beginning stage of a new religion

CULTURE: the beliefs, values, behavior, and material objects shared by a group

NEW RELIGIOUS MOVEMENTS: groups that either encourage or discourage social change through their system of beliefs, values, symbols, and practices related to the sacred

ORGANIZATION: a group guided by specific goals, rules, and positions of leadership

RELIGION: a set of symbols, beliefs, values, and practices related to the sacred that provides believers with a meaning system

SECT: a group that has broken away from an existing religious body, usually to maintain its traditional roots

SECULARIZATION: a decline in the influence of religious beliefs, symbols, values, and practices

SOCIETY: a grouping of people who share a culture and a social structure

THEORY: an interrelated set of ideas that provides explanations for behavior

Overview

There is an ongoing debate in the social sciences as to the meaning and usage of terms that describe religious organizations. Four major concepts (church, denomination, sect, and cult) have been used by social scientists to define and discuss religious groups. These four terms are often referred to as "ideal types." An ideal type is the pure form of a phenomenon one is studying or analyzing. Ideal types are rarely found in social reality. Churches and denominations are organizations that are accepted by and reflect mainstream society and culture. A sect is a religious organization that experiences tension with mainstream society and culture. Sects attempt to maintain the traditional foundations of their religious identity. The cult is also a religious organization that experiences tension with mainstream society and culture. Sociologically speaking, cults are the starting point of new or alternative religions, whereas sects break away from established religions. Social scientists generally agree that a cult is an alternative way of "doing" religion. Cult members adhere to a faith perspective that is distinctly different from the dominant ones in their respective cultures, and they are frequently followers of charismatic leaders.

In his book *Alienation and Charisma: A Study of Contemporary American Communes* (1980), sociologist Benjamin Zablocki defines a charismatic leader as one whose authority is based on the shared belief that he or she is the representation of the collective self of the group. The late Swami Prabhupada of the Hare Krishna movement, Sun Myung Moon of the Unification Church, Bhagwaan Rajneesh of the former Rajneeshees (Rajneesh Foundation International), the late David Koresh of the Branch Davidians, and Elizabeth Clare Prophet of the Church Universal and Triumphant are often identified as charismatic leaders. Many cults experience a difficult transition upon the departure or death of a charismatic leader; some even cease to exist.

Church historian J. Gordon Melton considers the term "cult" a pejorative label that has been applied to a wide variety of religions, especially non-Western religions. Melton notes that social scientists tend to be the least pejorative in their use of cult, whereas the anticult movement is the most pejorative. Anticultists often refer to new religions or alternative religions as "destructive cults" that hypnotize and brainwash prospective members. Anticultists also believe that cults are pseudoreligious organizations (false, deceptive religions that have deviant and criminal tendencies). Increasingly, social scientists prefer to use the term "new religious movement" (NRM) to emphasize the sociological understanding of the cult as a type of religious organization.

In the introduction to his book *Social Science and the Cults: An Annotated Bibliography* (1990), sociologist John Saliba briefly discusses the variety of cults that exist in American society and the problems that come with studying and classifying them. Social scientists insist that overgeneralizing (assuming that all cults are the same) about cults, alternative religions, or new religious movements distorts understanding of their belief systems, social structures, and relationships with society. In his volume *The Encyclopedia of American Religion* (1978), Melton groups all religions into one of seventeen families, based on heritage, theology, and lifestyle. Contemporary cults fit into six of these family groups: Pentecostal, communal, metaphysical (supernatural), psychic and new age, "magick," and Eastern and Middle Eastern. Melton's classificatory scheme implies a sense of continuity between contemporary cults and other alternative religions in the history of Christianity.

Historians of religion Robert Ellwood and Harry Partin classify cults based largely on their philosophical and religious traditions. They group contemporary cults into five divisions: Theosophical (speculation about the nature of the soul) and Rosicrucian (study of religious mysticism) traditions, spiritualism and unidentified flying object (UFO) groups, initiatory groups, neopaganism, and Eastern traditions. Ellwood and Partin agree with Melton that contemporary new religious movements are not necessarily new phenomena. Sociologist Eileen Barker has constructed a classification scheme for new religious movements based on ideological and theological differences. She developed four categories: those deriving from the Christian tradition, those that have their origins in the Eastern traditions, parareligious groups rooted in the human potential movement, and esoteric (mysterious) groups such as those rooted in witchcraft, satanism, paganism, and the occult.

Sociologist Roy Wallis offers a sociological framework for understanding new religions. Wallis identifies three analytical types of movements based on their orientation to the world: world-rejecting, world-affirming, and world-accommodating. These classifications are based on how the cult defines itself in regard to the mainstream society and culture. A second sociological classificatory scheme was developed by sociologist Bryan Wilson. Wilson lists seven categories that he considers to be deviant responses to the world: conversionist, revolutionist, introversionist, manipulationist, thaumaturgical (magical), reformist, and utopian. These categories were originally labels for divisions within Christianity, but they have since been adopted for classifying new religious movements.

Sociologists Rodney Stark and William Sims Bainbridge, in their book *The Future of Religion: Secularization, Revival, and Cult Formation* (1985), classify cults into audience cults, client cults, and cult movements. Audience and client cults are not full-fledged religious movements. They offer members services such as publications and magical practices but do not require commitment and conversion to the group. Cult movements are full-fledged organized religious organizations that provide a variety of services for their members.

Applications

The International Society for Krishna Consciousness (ISKCON, or Hare Krishna), founded by A. C. Bhaktivedanta Swami Prabhupada, and the Holy Spirit Association for the Unification of World Christianity (the Unification Church or "Moonies"), founded by Sun Myung Moon, are two cults (new religions) that have been highly visible and immersed in controversy since their arrival in the United States.

Swami Prabhupada emigrated from India in 1965 and settled in New York City. By the early 1980's there were fifty Hare Krishna centers in the United States. The main center in the United States is located in Los Angeles. ISKCON is a conservative form of Hindusim that centers on the practice of bhakti yoga (devotional practices). The Hare Krishna lifestyle is ascetic and semimonastic. Local centers support themselves by selling Hare Krishna publications and incense.

Hare Krishna beliefs and practices, such as observing a strictly vegetarian diet, chanting the mantra (a sacred formula), males shaving their heads, dressing in traditional saffron-colored robes, soliciting money at airports, and breaking off ties with nondevotees appear to be at odds with the dominant values of society. Thus they create tension between ISKCON and others, especially the family members of devotees.

The Unification Church was started in Korea in 1954. It began its activities in the United States in 1959, but did not become prominent until the early 1970's. It blossomed with the arrival of Sun Myung Moon from Korea in 1973. An international headquarters was established in New York City, and centers were opened around the country. Moon said that when he was sixteen Jesus appeared to him and selected him to complete Jesus' unfulfilled mission. In 1972 Moon stated that he received a message from Jesus telling him to move to the United States. Moon has asserted that he has now completed the unfulfilled mission of Jesus by marrying and having twelve children.

Members of the Unification Church believe that they are building the kingdom of God on Earth and that they are accomplishing this through the physical salvation initiated by Moon. According to Moon, Jesus fulfilled only half of his messianic mission and offers his followers only spiritual salvation. Moon's followers believe that Moon has provided them with the opportunity for physical salvation. The central beliefs of the Unification Church center on the principles of creation, fall, and restoration. The principle of restoration involves a member aligning himself or herself with the Messiah. This is done through sacrificial work and celibacy. After a period of sacrificial work and celibacy, church leaders find a suitable mate for the member (one usually not known by the member) and they are married.

A number of theories have attempted to explain the significance and rise of new religious movements. According to the functionalist sociological perspective, cults fulfill basic human needs that are not being met by other sources of religious meaning. Other viewpoints emphasize different aspects of cults. Some scholars view cults as a response to the secularization of Western society. In secularized and "demystified" American society, notes theologian Harvey Cox, new religious movements respond to moral ambiguity with moral absolutes. Some sociologists point to the roles that political disenchantment and rapid social change may play in encouraging the formation and growth of new religious movements. Others have described cults as indicators of a "new humanism" originating in the emphasis of Eastern traditions on the inherent subjective nature of the divine.

A small number of social psychologists and psychiatrists support the belief that cult formation is based on brainwashing and that those who join cults do not do so voluntarily. The majority of social scientists, however, see a mixture of sociocultural phenomena linked to the emergence of new religious movements. They do not believe that brainwashing or coercive persuasion are viable explanations for the emergence and growth of new religious movements. The American Psychological Association has refused to recognize the existence of "brainwashing" in new religious movements. Psychiatrist Marc Galanter and psychotherapist Robert L. Moore indicate that what is often reported as nonconventional behavior of new cult members is actually normal behavior because the new member is adapting to the norms (rules) of the group.

Context

Sociologist Thomas Robbins argues that the study of new religious movements has revitalized and transformed the sociology of religion. Historically, sociologists focused primarily on Western forms of religion, neglecting the Eastern traditions. For all practical purposes, the study of religion was in essence the study of Christianity. The scholarly literature on new religious movements constitutes probably the largest share of scholarship being conducted today in the sociology of religion.

Nevertheless, the study of new religious movements, often referred to in the literature as sects or cults, has always been present in the sociology of religion. Theologian H. Richard Niebuhr, in his book *The Social Sources of Denominationalism* (1929), discusses the work of sociologist Max Weber and theologian and church historian Ernst Troeltsch, who identified the differences between church and sect and the social correlates of these concepts. Niebuhr's book is a classic study of the social organizational origins of theological and religious differences.

The study of religious organizations is still in its infancy, and much more theoretical development is necessary. In the 1970's social scientists focused their attention on the overall phenomenon of new religious movements and examined both the social aspects of religion and religious ideas. More recently, social scientists have investigated the controversies surrounding the recruitment strategies of new religious movements. More sociologists of religion are also examining the conflicts and controversies relating to church-state tensions.

Sociologist Roland Robertson argues that the most important sociological aspect of new religious movements is the changing conceptions of the relationship between the individual and society. The major focus for sociologists of religion, according to Robertson, should be to analyze the way in which religion as a social phenomenon is produced, reproduced, and transformed.

Bibliography

Beckford, James A. *Cult Controversies: The Societal Response to New Religious Movements*. New York: Tavistock Publications, 1985. Discusses four of the more controversial cults: the Unification Church, Scientology, the Children of God, and the Hare Krishna. The author examines recruitment and disengagement processes of cults.

Bromley, David G., and Phillip E. Hammond, eds. *The Future of New Religious Movements*. Macon, Ga.: Mercer University Press, 1987. A collection of articles prepared by scholars from various disciplines. The articles were delivered as papers at a conference on the future of new religious movements held in Berkeley, California, in October, 1983. Highly recommended.

Bromley, David G., and Anson D. Shupe, Jr. *Strange Gods: The Great American Cult Scare*. Boston: Beacon Press, 1981. A very readable and objective book that attacks the myths about cults generated by the anticult movement.

Galanter, Marc. *Cults: Faith, Healing, and Coercion*. New York: Oxford University Press, 1989. Written by a psychiatrist, this book focuses on the nature of charismatic groups. Galanter uses a systems approach to analyze group structure and functioning. Contains a useful bibliography.

Glock, Charles Y., and Robert N. Bellah, eds. *The New Religious Consciousness*. Berkeley: University of California Press, 1976. A collection of sixteen essays examining the religious dimension of the youth culture of the 1960's. The San Francisco Bay area was the setting for the research that generated these essays.

Melton, J. Gordon. *Encyclopedia Handbook of Cults in America.* New York: Garland, 1992. A handy reference book that should be in the reference section of any good library. Sections are devoted to identifying and discussing established cults and newer cults. Good bibliography.

Melton, J. Gordon, and Robert L. Moore. *The Cult Experience: Responding to the New Religious Pluralism.* New York: Pilgrim Press, 1982. Appendix A is a useful guide that provides descriptions of the major alternative religions. Offers guidelines for family and friends to help them understand and deal with the tension that often accompanies membership in an alternative religion.

Robbins, Thomas. *Cults, Converts, and Charisma: The Sociology of New Religious Movements.* Beverly Hills, Calif.: Sage Publications, 1988. A summary of the scholarly literature on new religious movements. Excellent bibliography.

Saliba, John A. *Social Science and the Cults: An Annotated Bibliography.* New York: Garland, 1990. A concise and well-written introductory chapter on social science and cults. The annotated bibliography contains 2219 citations. An extremely useful resource on cults for scholars and nonscholars alike.

William L. Smith

Cross-References

CULTURAL AND STRUCTURAL ASSIMILATION

Type of sociology: Racial and ethnic relations
Field of study: Theories of prejudice and discrimination

Sociologist Milton Gordon made a major contribution to assimilationist theory by clearly distinguishing two types of assimilation: cultural assimilation, sometimes referred to as acculturation, and structural assimilation, which refers to the integration of minority groups into all aspects of social life.

Principal terms

ACCULTURATION: the process whereby a minority group takes on the values, language, and behavior of the dominant cultural group; also the process by which culturally distinct groups understand, adapt to, and influence each other's culture

ETHNIC GROUP: a group that is united by a common and distinctive cultural heritage, language, and history

RACE: a group that is socially defined on the basis of real or perceived physical characteristics, nationality, and ethnicity

RACIAL DISCRIMINATION: individual and institutional behavior, practices, and policies that result in harm, whether intended or not, to individuals on the basis of race

RACIAL PREJUDICE: the dislike and fear of others based on real or perceived physical differences

SOCIAL INSTITUTIONS: social arrangements and interactions that order familial relations, religious beliefs and practices, governance, economic relationships, education, and culture in society

SOCIAL STRUCTURE: the relations among individuals and groups to social institutions such as the economy, the government, educational systems, families, religion

Overview

According to Milton Gordon in *Assimilation in American Life* (1964), the study of how groups are incorporated into American society has been plagued by two major problems. First, the American legal system does not distinguish groups on the basis of race, religion, or nationality. Instead, all individuals are simply considered Americans. In contrast, Gordon says, the social reality is that there are distinct subgroups in American society, organized and identified on the basis of race, religion, and nationality. Since the legal system ignores this, the reality is hidden.

The second problem that Gordon defined lies in the manner in which the social sciences have dealt with the reality of diversity in American life. Gordon claims that social scientists prior to him focused primarily on the cultural behavior of individuals and groups and on studying the extent to which various ethnic racial groups had adopted the values and behavior of the dominant group in society—Anglo-Americans. They also focused on studying the attitudes of the dominant group, examining the extent and basis of racial prejudice. This is problematic, according to Gordon, because it ignores the issue of how so many diverse groups are incorporated into the social structure. Furthermore, neither social scientists nor policy makers have made clear what the goals of assimilation are—whether the United States would like to see total assimilation into one culture (a "melting pot" composed of a blend of cultures) or whether groups should maintain distinct cultures (a view sometimes referred to as cultural pluralism). To Gordon, the major question is: What is the impact of racial, religious, and national diversity on social relations and social institutions in a democratic industrial society such as the United States? To answer this question, Gordon argued, sociologists must clearly define assimilation and the various types of outcomes that might emerge from intergroup contact. Consideration of both cultural issues and the social structure must be included.

Gordon was the first to distinguish assimilation from acculturation and to propose two distinct types of assimilation: cultural assimilation (or acculturation) and structural assimilation. Generally, acculturation requires a change of culture on the part of the "out-group" in order to adapt to the dominant group. Structural assimilation requires that the out-group enter into the clubs, groups, and social institutions of the core group, thereby establishing primary relationships with individuals in the core. Ultimately, total assimilation implies that there are no cultural differences and that out-groups can no longer be distinguished from anyone else.

Gordon defines total assimilation as a process that may require seven steps toward its ultimate conclusion, the blended society. Step one is acculturation, in which an ethnic group changes its cultural patterns to those of the core group (in the United States this process is often referred to as Anglo-conformity). Step two is structural assimilation, in which the out-group establishes primary relations with the core group and enters the social structure of the core. The third step is marital assimilation, in which the out-group intermarries with members of the core and produces children. Step four is identificational assimilation, in which ethnic groups stop identifying with their ancestral ethnic group and identify with the core. The fifth step is attitudinal reception, in which the core is no longer prejudiced against members of the out-group. Step six is behavioral assimilation, in which the core stops discriminating against members of the out-group, and step seven is civic assimilation, in which the out-group has no value conflicts with the core group over governance.

According to Gordon, although acculturation is likely to be the first step, it may take place without leading to the other steps toward total assimilation. A group may acculturate itself to the norms of the dominant group without that acculturation being followed by any further acceptance or integration for a prolonged period of time. In other words, a group's successful acculturation neither guarantees its entry into the subsociety of the core nor guarantees that the core group will stop being prejudiced toward them or discriminating against them. Thus, the process of total assimilation requires cooperation from both sides: The entering group must adapt itself to the core group, and the core group must come to accept the entering group and treat its members on the basis of their individual merit rather than on the basis of their ethnic, religious, or national heritage.

Although Gordon did not believe that acculturation would ensure other forms of integration into the core's society, he did think that structural assimilation was the key to the remaining stages in the process toward total assimilation. For example, once the out-group has entered into close, or primary, relationships with the core group by entering their cliques, clubs, and institutions, Gordon believed that it followed "naturally" that individuals would form close relationships, fall in love, and marry outside their group. It would be "inevitable," following the formation of close ties with the core, that members of an out-group would begin to identify with the core subsociety, because they would lose their own ethnic identity. By this time, they would have taken on the appearance, dress, and behavior of the core group, so there would be no basis for prejudice against them. Once prejudice declines, it follows—for Gordon—that negative discriminatory behavior will cease. Since the formerly distinct group would now be completely accepted into the subsociety of the core, and would be identified with it, the group's members would experience no value conflicts with the core group in civic affairs.

Applications

Gordon applied his seven-stage theory of assimilation to an analysis of several diverse ethnic, religious, and racial groups in American society to examine variations in the assimilation process. Generally, he believed that the mode of acculturation in the United States is one of Anglo-conformity. In other words, if groups are to be considered acculturated, they must conform to the behavioral patterns and norms of those whose ancestors migrated from England. In fact, he believed that Anglo-conformity had largely been achieved in terms of acculturation. Gordon said that acculturation was very successful with the children of immigrants because of their immediate contact with public schools and the mass media. In cases in which acculturation was weak, as in the case of American Indians and African Americans, he claimed that factors existed which retarded the process of acculturation for these groups. In other words, he claimed that acculturation was still happening, but at a slower pace. In the case of American Indians, their ongoing ethnic identification with ancestral tradition, coupled with their isolation on reservations and special status as sovereign nations, mitigated against acculturation. Gordon said that, for blacks in the rural South, slavery and the long years of exploitation and discrimination which followed had led to the development of a subculture whose behaviors and values were so distant from Anglo culture that prejudice and discrimination remained intense. For those blacks who migrated to urban industrial centers, acculturation was also retarded because of prejudice and discrimination.

Generally, however, despite the failures of some groups to move speedily through the assimilation process, Gordon maintained the belief that assimilation would eventually occur. To the extent that he saw the development of a black middle class, he saw barriers breaking down, providing evidence that discrimination would have only a delaying effect on assimilation.

Contemporary applications of Gordon's theory have diverged, in part, from the earlier ideological concepts that called for Anglo-conformity. This can be seen particularly in the area of education. Curriculum reform has been directed toward multicultural education, with its goal of appreciating diversity. Many educators argue that when individuals come to appreciate the contributions various ethnic, racial, and religious groups have made to American society, they will come to appreciate and identify with one another. This is seen as an important step toward ending prejudice and discrimination. At the same time, however, many educators stress that it is important for immigrant children to learn English—an important step, Gordon acknowledged, toward acculturation on the basis of Anglo-conformity.

School desegregation programs also can be interpreted as applications of Gordon's concepts of acculturation and structural assimilation. Many—not all—social scientists argue that when children of different racial and ethnic backgrounds can go to school together, play sports together, and know one another intimately, they will grow up without prejudice and discrimination. Furthermore, school desegregation programs are expected to break down the isolation of groups. Residence has remained distinctly organized around race (in particular) and ethnicity. School busing programs, many of which were instituted in the 1970's and 1980's, promoted desegregation and structural assimilation by forcing children across the boundaries of their racial or ethnic communities. In many cases, these programs have operated without the support or cooperation of the core subsociety—Anglo-Americans.

Generally, scholars find that white ethnic groups have been more likely to be assimilated than have groups of other races. For example, in a study that Stephen Steinberg cites in his text, *The Ethnic Myth* (1981), Richard Alba found that rates of intermarriage had increased among six different European ethnic groups. Steinberg claims this as evidence for the occurrence of amalgamation, but only among European ethnic groups.

Context

Sociologists prior to Gordon, following the tradition of Robert Park, tended to define assimilation in terms of acculturation, amalgamation, or both. Generally, they defined acculturation as a process through which ethnic groups come to share a common culture and individuals are regarded on the basis of merit, without encountering prejudice. Amalgamation refers to a biological process, implying intermarriage between individuals of diverse backgrounds that leads to a biological blending through the offspring of those relations. Gordon claims, however, that sociologists did not clearly indicate whether acculturation should or does imply a reciprocal process whereby various ethnic groups take on attributes of one another's culture, resulting in a melting pot. It might imply a process in which groups are expected to conform to the values and behaviors of the dominant ethnic group, which he refers to as the host or core ethnic group (Anglo-Americans are the core group in American society).

Furthermore, Gordon claims that acculturation may not be complete; one outcome might be cultural pluralism, under which groups remain distinct yet share in the social structure.

Gordon is considered one of the more sophisticated assimilationist theorists, and assimilationist theory was the forerunner of more recent sociological theories of race and ethnicity. Gordon has been criticized, however, for holding the same assumptions as other assimilationists. A major criticism evolved around the notion of "delayed" assimilation, or what some scholars refer to as a "lag" in full assimilation. Generally, this notion is applied to racial groups, who remain furthest behind in total assimilation. Scholars such as David Wellman, in his 1977 book *Portraits of White Racism*, argue that prejudice by whites is not predicated upon the cultural differences of racial minorities. Rather, Wellman argues, white racism—which embodies discrimination— is a rational defense of the privileges that have been accorded to whites and denied to people of color. He also argues, as does Robert Blauner in *Racial Oppression in America* (1972), that assimilationist scholars fail to distinguish between ethnic and racial groups, expecting that both kinds of groups can be (and are desired to be) fully accepted into the society dominated by Anglo-Americans. Wellman and Blauner also question the assumption of assimilationist scholars that all groups are willing to drop their own cultures and take on that of the core. More important, they separate prejudice from discrimination, so that prejudice is not viewed as a cause of discrimination. As evidence, they point to polls which indicate that prejudiced attitudes are declining among whites, even while racial minorities continue to have significantly less income, wealth, and political power than whites. Contemporary sociologists are more prone to focus on the relations between ethnic and racial groups and the larger social structure than to maintain the focus on explaining prejudice that was dominant in earlier decades. This trend has been spurred by the notion that American society is not, in reality, open to all, nor is it a meritocracy in which individuals are rewarded on the basis of merit rather than on the basis of race, ethnicity, religion, or national origin. In the early 1990's, prominent attention was given to works such as Andrew Hacker's *Two Nations: Black and White, Separate, Hostile, Unequal* (1972), which argue that American society is a dual society divided by race. Such works place emphasis on the notion—implied by Gordon's distinction between cultural and social structure—that regardless of whether individuals change their culture or maintain it, they may not be accepted in American society, particularly if they are people of color. The notion that race, not ethnicity, is the most significant factor emerges strongly in Michael Omi and Howard Winant's *Racial Formation in the U.S.* (1986). Omi and Winant argue that race is a central and persistent feature in American social structure. These types of arguments tend to mitigate against an ongoing commitment to the assimilationist thesis in sociological thought.

Bibliography

Blauner, Robert. *Racial Oppression in America*. New York: Harper & Row, 1972. In this influential book, Blauner criticizes predominant trends in the sociology of race relations, particularly assimilationist theories, and counters their focus on race prejudice with an analysis of racial privilege as embedded in a system of internal colonialism.

Feagin, Joe R. *Racial and Ethnic Relations*. 3d ed. Englewood Cliffs, N.J.: Prentice-Hall, 1989. This introductory text on the sociology of race relations examines sociological theories against the background of extensive case histories of various ethnic and racial groups in the United States. Bibliographies for each group can be found at the end of each chapter.

Gordon, Milton. *Assimilation in American Life*. New York: Oxford University Press, 1964. Gordon assesses previous theories of assimilation and explains his own seven-stage theory of assimilation, distinguishing between cultural and structural assimilation as well as giving three models of assimilation outcomes: Anglo-conformity, the melting pot, and cultural pluralism.

Steinberg, Stephen. *The Ethnic Myth*. New York: Atheneum, 1981. An introductory text on race and ethnic relations. Ethnicity and the contemporary interest in ethnicity are reexamined in terms of the social structure, with a focus on economic institutions. Theories of race relations are presented and reviewed in the light of specific historical cases of racial and ethnic groups.

Wellman, David. *Portraits of White Racism*. New York: Cambridge University Press, 1977. Wellman presents an excellent critique of assimilationist perspectives on race relations, offering his own theory of white racism to counter the notion that prejudice is responsible for discrimination. He then presents case studies based on interviews with white individuals of varied ages and backgrounds to explain the dynamics of white racism.

Sharon Elise

Cross-References

Assimilation: The United States, 140; Individual Discrimination, 547; Ethnic Enclaves, 682; Institutional Racism, 996; Internal Colonialism, 1015; The Race Relations Cycle Theory of Assimilation, 1572; Racial and Ethnic Stratification, 1579; Racism as an Ideology, 1586; Social Stratification: Analysis and Overview, 1839.

CULTURAL NORMS AND SANCTIONS

Type of sociology: Culture
Field of study: Components of culture

Cultural norms are rules or expectations regarding how people should behave; sanctions are rewards or punishments for behaving or not behaving appropriately according to the norms. A variety of sanctions are used by individuals, organizations, and institutions to encourage compliance with their norms. While some sanctions are more effective than others, they generally act to sustain cultural values.

Principal terms
CULTURE: the shared knowledge, values, beliefs, norms, and sanctions of a particular group of people
DEVIANCE: the violation of cultural norms
INTERNALIZATION OF NORMS: the process of making compliance with cultural norms an automatic part of one's personality
LAWS: norms that have been formally included in a written legal code
MULTICULTURAL EDUCATION: educational programs recognizing and showing respect for the cultural diversity within a society
SOCIAL CONTROL: methods used to ensure conformity to cultural norms; these usually include the application of positive and negative sanctions
SOCIALIZATION: the social learning process through which people develop their personalities and internalize cultural values and norms
SUBCULTURE: a group that shares some values and norms of the dominant culture but that also has its own distinctive values and norms

Overview

When people share cultural norms, they not only have guidelines for their own behavior but also have some ability to predict the behavior of others. Formal norms, usually written rules, and informal norms, or unwritten rules, often are derived from the shared values and beliefs of a society. Sociologists recognize that societies have a large variety of formal sanctions (such as report cards and pay raises) and informal sanctions (such as frowns and praise) to encourage compliance with their norms. A positive sanction is a reward for compliance, while a negative sanction is a punishment for noncompliance.

To understand many of the social controversies within a culturally diverse society such as the United States, it is important to be aware of its different cultures and subcultures as well as of their sometimes conflicting components. Contrary norms exist not only between different cultures but within each culture. Most societies have one dominant culture. Sociologist Robin M. Williams noted in 1970 that the dominant culture of the United States has between fifteen and twenty core or central values. Other sociologists have pointed out that the core values and related norms in the United States change over time. Interpretations of values also can change.

To see how norms often are derived from a culture's values, four values identified by Williams may be considered: success, progress, freedom, and patriotism. Related norms include the ideas that one should strive to do well in school to become successful later; that the government should support scientific research to help society progress; that citizens should exercise their freedom to vote; and that it is a patriotic duty to rally around the president if the country is threatened with war. An example of a change in the interpretation of one of these core values is that, in the early years of the United States, freedom to vote included only white men who owned property, so the norm was that only these people were expected to vote.

The most reliable method of ensuring compliance with cultural norms involves the internalization of norms. In other words, people must be taught or socialized in such a way that they automatically want to comply with cultural norms. For example, the norm that students should study hard may be internalized. Initially, the reason a child may study hard could be the expectation of parental praise. Eventually, the child may feel enough self-esteem (an internal sanction) for studying hard that an external sanction, such as parental praise, is no longer necessary to encourage compliance with the norm. If the child occasionally does not comply with the now internalized cultural norm, he or she may feel guilty. Such an unpleasant feeling can be a negative sanction that reinforces the internalized norm. In other words, it could make the child's desire to study hard stronger in the future.

Social groups, organizations, and institutions seek to socialize people into internalizing norms. For example, some people willingly donate money to charity; some people do not cheat when paying taxes. In these cases, charity organizations and the government, respectively, may have successfully convinced them that such uses of their money will make them feel good about themselves.

Such socialization of people is an easier and more reliable method of ensuring norm compliance than either having to provide an external positive sanction each time norm compliance has occurred or applying external negative sanctions after people have violated norms. (It would be extremely difficult for the government to reward people each time they obeyed a law.) Moreover, research has shown that prison sentences (an external negative sanction) often do not convert criminals into law-abiding citizens upon their release from prison. Nevertheless, often people believe, correctly or incorrectly, that external sanctions must be used to force compliance with certain norms. Usually these are norms that are considered especially important to supporting a group's interests, cultural values, and sense of social order.

Norms that are believed to have moral significance to individuals or society, such as "One should not cheat on one's spouse" and "One should not steal," are called mores by social scientists. Sometimes, such mores and other norms considered especially important to a society are codified into laws. The seriousness of the negative sanction or punishment imposed following the violation of a more or a law suggests how important the underlying norm is to the culture. Violating a law resulting in a twenty dollar fine signifies a less significant form of cultural deviance than a crime resulting in a twenty-year prison sentence.

Another type of norm is a folkway. Sociologist William Graham Sumner coined the term "folkway" in his book *Folkways* (1907). Folkways refer to those norms of a cultural group that have little or no moral significance (for example, that one should wear proper clothes to a wedding). Rules of etiquette concerning eating are other examples of folkways. In the United States, for example, it is commonly expected that people place one hand under the table while eating, whereas the folkway in German culture entails placing both hands on the table. Even though parents might consider it very important that children internalize a culture's rules regarding "proper" eating and other "good manners," for most people violations of these and other folkways do not represent an important form of cultural deviance. If external sanctions are imposed at all, they generally will be mild; people might frown if someone wears shorts to a formal wedding, but they would not impose a fine or jail sentence.

Applications

Sociologists have observed how highly authoritarian forms of government ensure compliance with their cultural norms concerning social order: They often apply strong negative sanctions to punish people who violate mores and laws. When Chinese soldiers brutally attacked university students demonstrating in Tiananmen Square in 1989, much of the world was horrified to learn how far the Chinese government would go to reinforce its norms. Killing protestors was the government's approach to preventing others from challenging government rules and regulations.

Sanctioning of cultural norms by more democratic governments can also be severe, as when the National Guard attacked protesting university students at Kent State University in Ohio in 1970. In that case, an agency of the federal government was reacting against those who did not believe that the United States should be fighting a war in Vietnam. Cultural norms embodied in most governmental policies and programs in the United States are promoted through milder sanctions, yet even these can be quite effective in promoting the cultural norms of those in power. Since these norms sometimes clash significantly with the values and norms shared by members of some subcultures in culturally diverse American society, some critics have referred to the government's attempts to enforce compliance with its policies as "social engineering."

For example, educational policies of public schools sometimes become quite controversial because members of an ethnic, political, or religious subculture do not share the cultural norms being promoted by state, federal, or school board policies. While a state policy may require teachers to educate children about sex, some parents believe that sex education should be solely a family responsibility. Other controversies have involved whether students should be required to pledge allegiance to the flag, to learn another language, to have a "moment of silence," to learn evolution, to learn creationism, to celebrate religious holidays, to learn about the history of ethnic groups other than their own, to read certain books, or to be bused to distant schools for the purpose of desegregation.

Governments and school boards have used a variety of negative and positive sanctions in order to force compliance with their policies. If a policy is only a recommendation (say, to raise student awareness about the dangers of drugs), then schools may not experience any negative sanctions for not complying with that policy. Violations of stricter governmental policies, however, have resulted in strong negative sanctions. Examples include cases in which lawsuits were filed against school districts or in which federal troops were called in to force desegregation. On the other hand, positive sanctions come into play when teachers and administrators who comply with cultural norms embodied in state or federal policies are rewarded. For example, schools may receive extra funding for offering drug awareness programs that the government recommends.

Efforts to increase multicultural education in higher education and to increase cultural diversity among university faculty have been resisted by some professors and others in higher education. University or government policies that seek to introduce new norms regarding what should be taught in the classroom or which people should be hired and promoted conflict with some professors' traditional subcultural norms. Generally, professors value academic freedom and independence highly. These values have become embodied in norms such as "We should be able to hire and promote whomever we believe is most qualified to become a professor," and "We should be able to teach whatever we believe is important." Proposed policies calling into question traditional hiring and teaching practices are often seen as outside interference and can be strongly resisted by these professors.

Controversies over traditional versus new cultural norms have resulted in numerous negative sanctions being applied by opposing sides within universities. On some campuses, budget cutbacks have served as a justification for cutting the funding of relatively new multicultural education programs that often employ minority group members. Some professors also have supported "reverse discrimination" lawsuits in instances when they felt forced to hire an affirmative action candidate that the administration selected instead of a white male whom they believed was better qualified. When such negative sanctions are effective in punishing people (or programs) seeking to introduce new cultural values and norms, these sanctions support the traditional norms regarding hiring, promotions, and curricular content. Students are also affected by such actions. They may have fewer opportunities to take multicultural courses, and there may be fewer requirements that they take them.

On the other hand, strong opposition to the norms of the traditionalists also has arisen. For example, negative sanctions have been used against professors resisting change—they may be shunned by some students and colleagues, and letters criticizing them and their views may appear in the press. When powerful administrators of a university have strongly supported new multicultural norms, they have applied positive sanctions to support multicultural programs and personnel. These have included special funding for professors engaged in research promoting multicultural education.

Context

Research about norms and sanctions has been important to analyses of societies ever since sociology became a discipline. Anthropologists and sociologists have long used functionalist theoretical perspectives to analyze how norms, sanctions, and other parts of a culture affect a cultural system and function to meet the needs of the society. Anthropologist Marvin Harris, for example, noted that a seemingly irrational religious norm in India, the taboo against eating beef, actually serves India's impoverished economy well. Cows can more efficiently be used to produce milk and butter, oxen for plows, and manure for fertilizer, fuel, and flooring material than to provide beef to the masses. From this perspective, it would be dysfunctional for India to sanction the eating of beef.

In the 1950's and early 1960's, functionalist approaches dominated sociological analyses of society in the United States. Talcott Parsons, the most prominent American functionalist, explained how major American values and norms function: They maintain the country's social order while serving the needs of the people. For example, when people share the traditional belief that mothers ought to be the main providers of emotional support to family members, then society has an established method of providing emotional support in times of crises.

The views of C. Wright Mills and other conflict theorists who opposed functionalism began to be voiced more widely among sociologists in the United States beginning in the late 1960's. Social scientists and the general public were becoming increasingly aware of ways that the country's relatively powerless people, such as its ethnic and political minorities, were being harmed when values and norms benefiting only those in power were sanctioned by societal institutions such as the government, the economy, the media, and the educational system. Acts of civil disobedience and inner city riots brought attention to the racism built into the country's laws and economic practices. Instead of focusing on how society is held together by common values and norms, conflict theorists pointed to the many conflicting interests and values of people within it. Functionalists, they complained, focused only on the values and norms of the dominant culture.

They also criticized functionalism for being a politically conservative perspective in that it suggested that people who protest against or even criticize the culture of the powerful and its unjust norms are engaging in behavior that is dysfunctional for society. Functionalists were also seen as supporting negative sanctions, such as jail sentences, being used to punish people who violate unjust laws and other norms.

Today, most sociologists in the United States accept certain of the insights of functionalism, such as its recognition of the effects of cultural values, norms, and sanctions on the rest of society. Yet they also recognize the inherent conflicts that exist within a multicultural society and do not assume that positively sanctioning all the values and norms of the dominant culture is functional for the entire society.

Bibliography

Banks, James A. *Multiethnic Education*. Boston: Allyn & Bacon, 1988. This book clearly outlines what educators can do to encourage students' appreciation of cultural diversity. For example, the author suggests specific programs that promote respect for the values and norms of students coming from diverse ethnic groups.

Gove, Walter R., ed. *The Labelling of Deviance*. Beverly Hills, Calif.: Sage Publications, 1980. The labeling perspective suggests that violations of cultural norms result in a deviant label mostly for relatively powerless people. Nine articles examine different social reactions for violations of criminal and noncriminal norms.

Lappe, Frances Moore. *Rediscovering America's Values*. New York: Ballantine Books, 1989. The author raises probing questions regarding certain American norms derived from such cultural values as choice, opportunity, and responsibility. Especially interesting is the question of how seriously Americans take these values in the light of poverty, illiteracy, hunger, homelessness, and other social problems.

Moffat, Michael. *Coming of Age in New Jersey*. New Brunswick, Conn.: Rutgers University Press, 1989. This highly readable book is an ethnographic study of the subculture of students at a state university. It includes students' own accounts of their values, norms, and sanctions regarding topics of interest to them, including friendships, racism, and sex.

Sumner, William G. *Folkways*. Boston: Ginn, 1907. This sociological classic introduced the concepts of folkways and mores, providing numerous examples of cultural differences. Topics include cannibalism, sexual mores, blood revenge, and primitive justice. Other examples of cultural variation involve norms concerning marriage, sports, drama, and education.

Grace M. Marvin

Cross-References

Culture: Material and Expressive Culture, 430; Culture and Language, 436; Culture and Technology, 443; Deviance: Analysis and Overview, 525; Deviance: Functions and Dysfunctions, 540; Subcultures and Countercultures, 2003; Values and Value Systems, 2143.

CULTURAL RELATIVITY VERSUS ETHNOCENTRISM

Type of sociology: Culture
Field of study: Cultural variation and change

Cultural relativism refers both to an attitude that one should avoid judging the ways of other people without first understanding their culture and to a doctrine that prohibits the judging of another culture under any circumstances. Ethnocentrism is an attitude that the values, beliefs, and norms of one's own culture are superior to those of other cultures and can be used to evaluate the cultures and behaviors of other peoples.

Principal terms
ABSOLUTISM: the belief that there is only one clear standard by which behaviors can be judged as either right or wrong
ASSIMILATION: the blending of two or more cultures, usually reflecting cultural adaptation to the culture of the more powerful group or groups
CULTURE: the shared values, beliefs, norms, ideologies, customs, and technological knowledge of a social group
ETHNIC GROUP: a group of people distinguished principally by their common cultural heritage
ETHNOGRAPHY: the study of the culture of a social group
MELTING POT: an image of the United States in which the cultural diversity of its various immigrant, ethnic, and minority groups melts into a new American culture
PLURALISM: the maintenance of social equality and respect for the cultures and peoples of different ethnic groups living in the same society
SUBCULTURE: the culture of a subgroup that has much in common with the culture of the larger society but that also has its own set of norms, beliefs, and values
VALUES: standards used to evaluate what is good or bad, right or wrong, beautiful or ugly

Overview

In their efforts to explain the behaviors of social groups, sociologists and other social scientists have studied cultures and subcultures throughout the world. Sociologists generally seek to understand the role of an individual cultural element, such as a particular ritual or religious belief, within an entire cultural system and to avoid making a judgment about it without taking the entire sociocultural system into account. This attitude, called cultural relativism, arose partly because social scientists have seen how the social and cultural characteristics of different cultures and subcultures often can be explained by those cultures' very different historical, environmental, economic, and political conditions. Maintaining such an attitude also suggests that one will not be quick to judge one culture as superior or inferior to the culture of any other group.

This "open-mindedness" is assumed to be the opposite of ethnocentrism, a normal tendency to believe that the values, beliefs, norms, and customs of one's own culture are superior to those of others. Most people unwittingly are socialized into becoming ethnocentric; for example, they are not aware of how strongly they may have become influenced by their parents and schools to believe that their own society's culture is the one against which all others should be judged. Moral absolutism often is a part of ethnocentrism. Moral absolutists believe that their culture's definition of good and bad behavior sets the standard by which anyone else's behavior should be judged. The ethnocentric person is less likely than a cultural relativist to try to understand how the wider sociocultural context of another group may help explain its particular beliefs, behaviors, and values.

Some social scientists and philosophers distinguish between maintaining an attitude characterized by cultural relativism and holding a doctrine of cultural relativism. Recognizing the differences between the attitude and the doctrine helps explain some controversies surrounding the concepts of cultural relativism and ethnocentrism. Because they want to show respect for cultural differences, most sociologists, anthropologists, and others who study culture support research methods that reflect an attitude of cultural relativism. That is, they believe that to produce valid and reliable studies of a culture, researchers should develop some empathy for its members. By placing themselves in the situation of people from another culture, researchers can better understand why people relate to the world in ways that may be quite foreign to the researcher.

Participant observation is one research methodology that a sociologist might choose in order to examine a group's culture. In order to understand the group better, a participant observer becomes part of it, engaging in the same activities as the group members. Such a method allows the sociologist to collect data about the beliefs, values, and customs of a group of people; in addition, as a participant observer he or she may be able to develop a better appreciation of the group's entire cultural system than an "outside" researcher such as a survey researcher could. With enough data and understanding, the participant observer has the material to produce an ethnography, sometimes called an "insider's view of a culture."

A sociologist holding an attitude of cultural relativism may or may not support a doctrine of cultural relativism. According to Melvin Tumin in *Patterns of Society* (1973), such a doctrine "holds that no judgments of comparative value or worth can be made about different culture patterns, because each has its own integrity and rationale for its members." A doctrinaire cultural relativist may go so far as to say that no matter how repulsive an action that occurs in some other culture may be to an outsider, it is wrong to judge the ways of that culture.

Many sociologists have dismissed cultural relativism when it is presented as a doctrine because it assumes that there are no basic moral values shared by nearly all peoples. Most social scientists point to certain morally intolerable behaviors that they believe reflect universal values; that is, there are some acts that most good people across different cultures believe to be morally inexcusable. One commonly used example of such an act is genocide—the attempt to exterminate an entire population, as was practiced against Jews in Nazi Germany and against various tribal groups in colonial American days.

To the many sociologists who cannot accept a doctrinaire cultural relativism, a limited degree of ethnocentrism may sometimes be considered appropriate. For example, according to this approach, if the sociologist's own culture incorporates what is assumed to be an almost universally respected moral absolute (that genocide is evil, for example), then this absolute could be used as a standard to evaluate other cultures or their components. Thus, genocide would deserve condemnation anywhere that it is found. It is not always clear, however, what constitutes a universal moral value. This is one reason why trying to understand the broader cultural context of an alien custom remains important to most sociologists. Cultural relativism—contrasting with most people's normal tendency to be ethnocentric—is the attitude that sociologists generally promote as teachers, researchers, writers, and activists.

Applications

Even the wisest of people often find it difficult to distinguish clearly between attitudes of cultural relativism and ethnocentrism in settling the cultural conflicts that underlie some contemporary social issues. Such conflicts can arise from cultural differences between societies or from differences within a society. Examples include debates over how a poor society should develop economically and over the proper goals of bilingual education in the United States.

Economic development is not proceeding as rapidly today for Third World countries—the poor "developing" countries of Latin America, Asia, and Africa—as it did for the "now rich countries," such as the United States, Germany, and Japan, when they underwent industrialization. In fact, many developing countries actually are falling behind, with masses of people becoming ever poorer. Development experts often adopt a purely economic perspective, arguing that many Third World people will have to become "more Westernized" by changing their beliefs, values, and customs for their societies to become as economically productive as the now rich countries. For example, government programs in Kenya and Tanzania have attempted to force nomadic tribes to become settled ranchers. Such attempts have also been applied to poor groups living within rich countries, such as the American Indians in the United States, who were forced to learn the dominant culture's language, attend its schools and churches, and work in the market economy.

The policies of industrialized nations and of multinational organizations often promote programs that could be called ethnocentric, since they strongly encourage or force people to give up their cultures and to adopt the lifestyle more common to industrialized countries. The United Nations, the United States, the World Health Organization, and other nations and organizations with an interest in Third World development have forced Third World peoples with traditional subsistence economies to relocate from traditional lands in attempts to "help" them. This has occurred in India and the Philippines, for example, in order to allow the development of hydroelectric projects.

An industrialized country providing aid to poor societies also might require peasants or natives to use technologically advanced farming practices that are not a part of its traditional culture. In Micronesia, for example, the customs and traditional subsistence gardening practices of native Micronesians were seen by outsiders as impeding their economic progress. Thus, in the 1950's, the United States introduced new governmental, farming, educational, housing, and public service programs in an attempt to force an end to the native subsistence economy.

The history of the United States—and of many South and Central American countries—reveals numerous governmental efforts to eliminate the native custom of sharing common lands. Governments divided communal property, allowing only individuals to possess land. In the process, other customs of tribal groups were destroyed as well, with natives becoming increasingly dependent on each country's dominant economy. Cultural relativists decry the ethnocentrism of such government practices, arguing that the affected peoples themselves should be allowed to determine the degree to which their farming and other customs should be changed. Broader issues have also been raised, such as the argument that modernization may not be nearly as beneficial as the ethnocentrists believe. For example, if greater agricultural productivity entails replacing human labor with machines, a resulting increase in the country's production may not justify greater unemployment and poverty among the poorest classes. An environmentally conscious cultural relativist might even ask whether peasant farmers' way of life should be valued more highly than that of an agribusiness; the traditional culture may well be more ecologically sustainable, and thus more economically productive, in the long run.

Another example of a culture conflict within the United States that raises questions about ethnocentrism and cultural relativism involves contemporary immigration issues. California has the largest amount of immigration among the fifty states, with more than half of its immigrants coming over the border from Mexico. Many of California's public schools now provide bilingual education in which immigrants are taught both in English and in their native language.

There are numerous controversies over the goals and methods of such bilingual education. Parents, educators, and the public at large disagree, for example, over what the goals of bilingual education should be. Some people argue that the aim should be biculturalism or multiculturalism, whereby native English speakers and non-English-speaking students alike develop a greater understanding of languages and cultures other than their own. Others argue that the aim should be cultural assimilation, whereby children whose native language is not English become increasingly "Americanized." In other words, the goal of bilingual education should be enabling students eventually to learn how to communicate exclusively in English and to adopt the rest of American culture as well. This view is supported by those who believe that the

United States should be a "melting pot"—a country where culturally diverse people learn to blend into one American dominant culture.

An emphasis on Americanization certainly suggests an ethnocentric attitude. Some advocates argue that if too much diversity is allowed, then a country cannot function effectively: Citizens must learn a common culture, they say, if only to promote a shared sense of civic duty. Moreover, they argue, the government has more important ways to spend money than to provide bilingual or multilingual street signs, social service personnel, voting instructions, and other public documents. A cultural relativist might point to a number of events in the history of the United States as a counterargument: Ethnocentric definitions of Americanization have led to scandalous examples of discrimination (not to mention violence) against ethnic groups, such as laws limiting voting eligibility, and to a refusal to recognize how many different cultures have contributed to the United States' heritage.

Context

Ethnocentric attitudes were common among Western social scientists before the twentieth century, with anthropologists adopting the doctrine of cultural relativism only in the second quarter of the twentieth century. Eventually, cultural anthropologists' comparative studies led them to believe that a Eurocentric view of the world (an ethnocentric view based on European cultural standards) could no longer be justified.

The doctrine of cultural relativism has nineteenth century roots, however, and can be seen in the ideas of Auguste Comte. Comte can also be called a cultural determinist, because he believed in the primacy of cultural and social phenomena over all else: People can discover reality, including moral values, he held, only through the symbols that each culture creates. Moreover, since humans are creatures of culture, they are not justified in making comparative moral judgments. In contrast to this doctrine of cultural relativism is the view of many social scientists today: They view nature, not culture, as the basic foundation of reality, with culture playing a mediating role.

Historical and comparative studies of cultural change reveal that throughout history societies have forcefully demonstrated ethnocentric attitudes toward other societies, resulting in cultural changes benefiting the conquerors; European colonists, for example, despite their rationalizations, generally exploited foreign peoples and natural resources to benefit only themselves. Gerhard Lenski and Jean Lenski, in *Human Societies* (1991), developed a theory that helps explain and predict these and other processes of global cultural change. The Lenskis view one component of culture, technological expertise, as especially significant in determining which societies have been (and will be) the most powerful in shaping the cultures of other societies. This theory is not ethnocentric, since it does not assume that cultures with either lesser or greater technological advancements are superior to other cultures. Instead, the theory simply describes how cultural change, for better or worse, generally has taken place.

For example, the cultures of most hunting and gathering peoples were abandoned or destroyed as the more productive horticultural practices and more powerful horticultural societies came into being. The ways of life of most horticultural societies, in turn, were abandoned or destroyed as societies practicing agriculture became more powerful. Then, industrial societies came to dominate; in the world today, agricultural societies are still struggling for survival in the face of tremendous pressure from industrialized nations.

Just as theorists try not to make ethnocentric judgments in describing cultural change processes, researchers attempt to avoid ethnocentrism and cultivate an attitude of cultural relativism. One area where this is crucial is within the growing field of applied sociology. Applied sociologists must avoid accepting government and business contracts for developing social change programs that will have detrimental effects on a culture. To prevent ethnocentrism, sociologists can refer to codes of ethics—such as the code of the American Sociological Association—that provides clear guidance.

Bibliography

Bodley, John H. *Victims of Progress*. 3d ed. Mountain View, Calif.: Mayfield, 1990. An excellent paperback that describes the devastating effects of ethnocentric policies of governments, churches, and individuals on tribal groups throughout the world. It is captivating and ultimately very disturbing reading. Geared to college students and the general reader.

Brewer, Marilynn B., and Donald T. Campbell. *Ethnocentrism and Intergroup Attitudes*. Beverly Hills, Calif.: Sage Publications, 1976. This is based on a ten-year study of tribal interactions and perceptions in East Africa based on questionnaires and interviews. The book concludes with a discussion of a unified theory of ethnocentrism. The orientation of the research is social psychological.

Donnelly, Jack. *Universal Human Rights in Theory and Practice*. Ithaca, N.Y.: Cornell University Press, 1989. Donnelly examines human rights from a variety of non-Western and Western perspectives bridging social science, foreign policies, and philosophy in today's world. Three chapters devoted to human rights and cultural relativism are of special interest to those interested in exploring the possible existence of universal moral values. Contains an extensive bibliography.

Kephart, William M., and William Zellner. *Extraordinary Groups: An Examination of Unconventional Life-Styles*. New York: St. Martin's Press, 1991. A fascinating examination of subcultures within the United States, exploring a range of cultural beliefs and values. Groups covered include the Old Order Amish, the Shakers, the Mormons, and others.

Reynolds, Vernon, Vincent Falger, and Ian Vine. *The Sociobiology of Ethnocentrism*. Athens: University of Georgia Press, 1987. This book contains fifteen articles exploring both genetic inheritance and socialization as factors in xenophobia, discrimination, racism, and nationalism. Explores how morality, ideology, history, and culture have either reinforced or overridden the predisposition to be ethnocentric.

Scharfstein, Ben-Ami. *The Dilemma of Context*. New York: New York University Press, 1989. The author argues that total relativity is not possible and seeks a practical solution somewhere between relativism and absolutism. Explores the cultural contexts of groups as diverse as American Indians, Hindus, and criminals. This book, containing both an impressive index and bibliography, is directed at social scientists and philosophers but is accessible to college students as well.

Grace M. Marvin

Cross-References

Assimilation: The United States, 140; Cultural and Structural Assimilation, 405; Cultural Norms and Sanctions, 411; Culture: Material and Expressive Culture, 430; Pluralism versus Assimilation, 1374; Social Change: Sources of Change, 1786; Values and Value Systems, 2143.

CULTURAL TRANSMISSION THEORY OF DEVIANCE

Type of sociology: Deviance and social control
Field of study: Theories of deviance

Cultural transmission theory postulates that deviance is sociologically transmitted from one generation to the next when communities or neighborhoods develop cultural traditions and values that tolerate or encourage deviant conduct and rule breaking. This theory offers explanations of why some communities persist in having high rates of deviance, such as crime and delinquency.

Principal terms

CULTURE: a total way of life, consisting of values, beliefs, norms, and modes of conduct

NORMS: the social rules of a society or group; they include both formal laws and informal customs

SOCIAL CONTROL: the formal and informal techniques used by society and groups to regulate conduct

SOCIAL DISORGANIZATION: a breakdown in the social control system that regulates behavior

SOCIALIZATION: the process by which a person is molded into a social being through learning the values and norms of society

SUBCULTURAL THEORIES OF DEVIANCE: a group of theories that use subcultures as a medium for explaining deviance; for example, delinquent gangs or drug subcultures

SUBCULTURE: a group that holds different values, beliefs, norms, and behavior from those of the dominant culture; for example, ethnic, age, or social class groups, drug subcultures, and delinquent gangs

Overview

Cultural transmission theory, which is an outgrowth of studies of urban crime and delinquency, is given its most systematic statement by sociologists Clifford R. Shaw and Henry D. McKay. The central tenet of cultural transmission theory is that deviance can be passed down from generation to generation because of community traditions and values that are either permissive toward or supportive of violating conventional rules of conduct, including criminal laws.

According to cultural transmission theory, in communities in which traditions that are permissive toward deviance have become relatively fixed over time, children are socialized into deviance by learning values and beliefs that tolerate or condone violating conventional rules. Even though the residential population in the community may change over time, deviant behavior patterns persist, to the extent that these subcultural traditions and values remain. Thus, cultural transmission asserts that deviance not only can be sociologically inherited from one generation to the next but also persists in a community after the succession of new residents.

Some communities or neighborhoods are more likely than others to develop subcultural traditions that tolerate deviance and law breaking. This is especially true of inner-city districts, which are often transition areas for ethnic groups and immigrants. Rapid changes in residential composition can lead to community difficulties in adjusting to the diversity of cultural backgrounds. An influx of new businesses and industry can also introduce disruptive elements by bringing in new workers and by radically altering the social and physical environment of a community. These changes can create value conflicts and otherwise weaken informal, as well as formal, social controls. Thus, if a community is unable to accommodate these changes, social controls break down. This process is called social disorganization. When a community does not function effectively as a medium of social control, deviance becomes tolerated, if not accepted, and community residents become more susceptible to deviant behavior patterns.

The rationale of cultural transmission theory is best illustrated by Shaw and McKay, who investigated variations in crime and delinquency rates over a fifty-year period in metropolitan Chicago. In their books *Social Factors in Juvenile Delinquency* (1931) and *Juvenile Delinquency and Urban Areas* (1942), Shaw and McKay observed that delinquency rates vary widely by neighborhood. The highest rates tend to be nearest the central business and industrial districts, decreasing as one moves from the city center to the edge of the city. Although the racial and ethnic composition in high delinquency areas changed almost completely over a period of several decades, delinquency rates remained virtually unchanged. These "delinquency areas" tend to be characterized by physical deterioration, economic insecurity, family disintegration, conflicting cultural standards, and little concerted action by the community residents to solve common problems. Shaw and McKay interpreted these phenomena as symptoms of social disorganization.

Shaw and McKay also observed that when communities went into decline, more prosperous families would relocate as soon as it was feasible to other neighborhoods or suburban areas. This had the effect of intensifying social disorganization, since the remaining ethnic groups were often slow to integrate into the community. Because family socialization patterns are also undermined by social disorganization, which promotes family disharmony and frustration, the play and peer groups of juveniles take on new social meaning by offering order to their daily lives. This process creates social circumstances that give rise to delinquent gangs. When these gang subcultures become rooted in the community, successive generations of children are socialized to norms that encourage delinquent behavior.

In his books *The Jack-roller: A Delinquent Boy's Own Story* (1930), *The Natural History of a Delinquent Career* (1931), and *Brothers in Crime* (1938), Shaw examined three case studies of juvenile delinquents that trace how delinquency is socially transmitted and how youngsters are socialized into deviant conduct. Differential association theory, proposed by sociologist and criminologist Edwin H. Sutherland, offers a more precise statement of this socialization process by specifying how criminal, delinquent, or deviant behaviors are learned. In this respect, cultural transmission and differential association are closely related.

A variation of cultural transmission can also be seen in subcultural theories—a group of theories that emerged beginning in the 1950's. Subcultural theories of deviance, most of which focus on explaining crime and delinquency, are based on the assumption that people are socialized into the values and norms of the groups to which they belong. If the immediate values and norms are at odds with the dominant culture, the resulting behaviors may be deviant, even illegal. Thus, subcultures are the medium for transmitting deviant values and beliefs. Subcultural theories have been developed to explain violence, sexual deviance, drug addiction, and other forms of deviance.

Applications

Cultural transmission theory, together with related subcultural theories of deviance, has had a major impact on both scholarly and lay thinking about the causes of crime, delinquency, and other forms of deviance. In a general sense, cultural transmission theory has helped to sensitize the public, community leaders, and policy makers to the social problems that come from neighborhoods that fall into decline. The works of Shaw and McKay point to reasons that the quality of community life must be protected and enhanced by carefully planned and implemented social policies and programs.

Informed by the concepts of cultural transmission and the results of his research studies, Shaw took an active part in shaping programs in slum neighborhoods that could restore natural social controls within the community and that could reduce crime and delinquency. In 1932 he began the Chicago Area Project, which established twenty-two neighborhood centers in six areas of Chicago. Shaw used committees of local residents instead of an outside or centralized staff to control community center activities. Members of the neighborhood were employed as staff. His project was a pioneering effort in using theory and research to inform the design and implementation of community-based programs in which local residents themselves play active, often leading roles in protecting their welfare and in enhancing the quality of neighborhood life. Tenant organizations in public housing projects that confront the classic ills of slum neighborhoods, such as crime, delinquency, narcotics trafficking, and prostitution, are extensions of the concepts of community involvement and democratic decision-making that Shaw advocated and implemented in the Chicago Area Project. In addition to reducing community problems, participation in these activities rejuvenates interest among residents in safeguarding the welfare of their community. Shaw and McKay's work can be seen as contributing to an American tradition of empowering people to solve their own problems as well as an example of tapping the knowledge and insights of local residents to develop policies and programs for themselves and their communities.

The logic of cultural transmission and its corollary, subcultural theories, is also connected to delinquency prevention programs. For example, if local cultural traditions and delinquent subcultures function to socialize youngsters to delinquent values and to encourage deviant conduct, then programs that neutralize or disrupt this socialization process are potentially useful as preventive measures. Historically, this rationale has been popular in many government and community prevention programs. Such programs have tried to redirect delinquent gang behaviors into constructive activities. This approach, extensively utilized in Chicago, Boston, New York, and Los Angeles, uses well-trained street workers who establish relationships with gang leaders and organize their members into clubs; they provide opportunities for recreation and access to jobs and education.

A similar rationale can also be seen in the numerous government-funded and privately funded drug education programs. By educating children (particularly those growing up in communities with a firmly established drug subculture) to the social and personal consequences of drug use, programs can help to neutralize the subcultural forces that attract young people to drugs in peer group settings.

Implications of Shaw and McKay's cultural transmission theory and of their analyses of crime and delinquency in communities suggest that the stability of neighborhoods, especially those in transition, can be fragile. Shaw and McKay recognized that the expansion of industry and business disrupts the social stability of surrounding neighborhoods as well as the social controls that promote conformity among residents. Although their Chicago Area Project focused on curbing delinquency, rather than on empowering the community to protect itself from invasions by business and industry, their work pointed to the importance of designing sound local government and zoning policies to safeguard the quality of residential life.

Context

Cultural transmission theory is closely tied to a school of sociological thought and to an approach to the study of social life that began in 1914 at the University of Chicago's Department of Sociology. Often called the Chicago school by sociologists, it was led by Robert Park, who had previously been a Chicago newspaper reporter and had investigated social conditions in the city for twenty-five years. Park borrowed ideas from the field of ecology, a branch of biology in which animals and plants are studied in relation to one another and to their natural habitat. Park reasoned that there is also an ecology to the organization of human communities. Using concepts such as "symbiosis," which refers to how organisms of different species can live together to their mutual benefit, he formed a theory of human ecology.

This theory became a dominant intellectual influence that shaped the scholarly thinking and research conducted by University of Chicago sociologists for the next fifty years. In 1928, Ernest W. Burgess, guided by Park's concepts of human ecology, pointed out that there are patterns of ecological growth in cities. Cities, he noted, not only grow around their edges but also have a tendency to expand radially from the center in concentric circles. This pattern can be likened to the circles created by a rock that is tossed into a still pond. Each circle gradually expands outward. Burgess observed that social life and activities differed in each concentric zone or circle. Zone 1, for example, was the central business district; zone 2, an area of transition with typically poor families and ever-changing by expanding businesses from zone 1.

Zone 3 was typically working-class neighborhoods and was followed by residential and commuter zones. This viewpoint of city growth clearly influenced Shaw and McKay, who in 1945 advanced a different concentric-zone model of the city.

At the time Shaw began his work in the 1920's, the United States was engulfed in a crime wave because of resistance to the Eighteenth Amendment (Prohibition), which outlawed the manufacture and distribution of alcoholic beverages. Crime and delinquency problems were particularly severe in Chicago. Shaw, who worked as a probation and parole officer, believed that the delinquency problem was attributable to juveniles' detachment from conventional groups. After his appointment to the Institute for Juvenile Research in Chicago, Shaw developed a plan to study delinquency, using Park's human ecology theory to guide his work. Later joined by McKay, his research used court records to pinpoint the residences of delinquents. Using "zone maps," the two were able to identify problem neighborhoods and to compare prevalence of delinquency by zones. Because not all youths in problem neighborhoods were in court records, Shaw also compiled extensive life histories from juvenile delinquents to ascertain influences from their social environments.

Other theories, such as differential association and subcultural theories of crime and deviance, utilize frameworks and concepts that are related to cultural transmission theory. Nevertheless, Shaw and McKay's work can be set apart from most theories of deviance in that their ideas and research findings served in part as a blueprint for a specific community program—the Chicago Area Project.

Bibliography

Cohen, Albert K. *Delinquent Boys: The Culture of the Gang*. New York: Free Press, 1955. This is a classic theory of delinquent gangs and subculture that links the theories of Émile Durkheim and Robert K. Merton to elements of the work of Shaw, McKay, and Sutherland. This book is relatively easy reading for those with an elementary background in sociology or criminology.

Jack-roller, the, Jon Snodgrass, et al. *Jack-roller at Seventy*. Lexington, Mass.: Lexington Books, 1982. Written shortly before the Jack-roller's death and long after Shaw's death in 1957, this book completes the story begun in Shaw's 1930 book *The Jack-roller*. It also contains additional sections on related issues written by James Short, Gilbert Geis, and Solomon Kobrin.

Shaw, Clifford R. *The Jack-roller: A Delinquent Boy's Own Story*. Introduced by Howard S. Becker. Reprint. Chicago: University of Chicago Press, 1966. Unlike Shaw's statistical studies, this book (first published in 1930) is a case study of a jack-roller—a thief or "mugger" who commits personal robbery—that has come to be a classic in sociology. Shaw traces the subject's life history so that readers can see the influences shaping his life and his delinquent career. The study provides evidence presumed to support cultural transmission theory. Recommended for those with little or no background in sociology.

Shaw, Clifford R., and Henry D. McKay. *Juvenile Delinquency and Urban Areas*. Rev. ed. Chicago: University of Chicago Press, 1969. A revised edition of Shaw and

McKay's original 1942 book reporting findings from their study of crime and delinquency in Chicago. The authors identify variations in delinquency rates by city districts, using zone maps of the city to plot data. The book contains an excellent introduction by James Short that addresses the significance and impact of Shaw and McKay's work. Contains a useful bibliography.

Symposium on Juvenile Delinquency, University of Chicago, 1972. *Delinquency, Crime, and Society*. Edited by James F. Short, Jr. Chicago: University of Chicago Press, 1976. A series of essays summarizing and discussing the contributions of Shaw and McKay, with special emphasis on their delinquency area studies, the Chicago Area Project, and cultural transmission theory. This book also discusses Shaw and McKay's importance within the University of Chicago research tradition. Recommended for those with at least a moderate background in sociology. Contains a useful bibliography.

Vold, George B., and Thomas J. Bernard. *Theoretical Criminology*. 3d ed. New York: Oxford University Press, 1986. Chapter 10, "The Ecology of Crime," includes a discussion of Shaw and McKay's research work and cultural transmission theory; also see chapter 11, "Strain Theories," for summaries of subcultural theories. Recommended for students. Contains a good bibliography.

Gerald R. Garrett

Cross-References

Anomie and Deviance, 100; Conflict Perspectives on Deviance, 334; Crime: Analysis and Overview, 373; Delinquency Prevention and Treatment, 476; Deviance: Analysis and Overview, 525; Deviance: Biological and Psychological Explanations, 532; Deviance: Functions and Dysfunctions, 540; Juvenile Delinquency: Analysis and Overview, 1036; Labeling and Deviance, 1049; The Medicalization of Deviance, 1178; The Structural-Strain Theory of Deviance, 1990.

CULTURE: MATERIAL AND EXPRESSIVE CULTURE

Type of sociology: Culture
Field of study: Components of culture

The material and expressive products of culture are valuable resources for sociologists interested in different social groups and in the processes of social and cultural definitions. Material culture is the physical manifestation of a society; it includes, among other things, works of art, the ways people produce and process food, and ritual objects of various sorts.

Principal terms
AESTHETICS: the critical study of the creation, appreciation, and philosophy of the beautiful
CULTURAL MATERIALISM: a controversial anthropological explanation of human behavior developed by Marvin Harris
CULTURAL STUDIES/CRITICISM: a theoretical and methodological perspective which treats all cultural products as symbolic "texts"
CULTURE: socially transmitted rules for human behavior involving both physical and mental processes
EXPRESSIVE CULTURE: cultural products which are created to communicate emotion, transmit social information, or satisfy some physical need; usually given meaning in some public context within different taste cultures
MATERIAL CULTURE: tangible, usually everyday, objects whose production, variation, use, and forms may be investigated across time and space

Overview

The terms "material culture" and "expressive culture" are rather cumbersome phrases for elements of society and culture which are produced by human hands and illustrate the powerful connection between physical objects and human behavior. Other collective nouns often used for such products are "objects," "things," and "artifacts." "Artifact," however, often contains an unspoken assumption of artistic value or merit. Visual and decorative arts, architecture, literature, and film are all examples of artistic expressions which have traditionally been the interest of aestheticians and scholars of the humanities. The modern Western idea of art—sometimes called "art with a capital 'A'"—is essentially a bourgeois concept, derived from a strong emphasis on individualism. It emphasizes the expression and reception of pleasure in ways that often illustrate hierarchical social relationships. As a result, much of the study of expressive culture has depended on, or reflected, specific classification systems and power structures rather than examining the values that artifacts and objects have for individuals or groups in society.

The study of art from a social science perspective demands concepts and methods that are value-neutral. Therefore, the definitions of the terms "expressive culture" and "material culture" may be more flexible and broad, and less bound by artificial distinctions, than one might originally expect. Particularly in the social sciences, the term "material culture" is often used as an umbrella term—as a general term for the products (material and expressive) of culture and society that illustrate the process by which form is given to conceptual thought.

Careful and informed study leads to consideration of the complicated interactions that take place among creators, audiences, and their cultures. Artifacts and things reveal social and creative processes which illustrate continuities and differences both among people and their societies and among cultures across time and space. Material and expressive culture can be studied as records that provide valuable information about people's lives, ideas, attitudes, and behaviors.

Objects reflect and influence the mental constructs intrinsic to culture. No things exist in vacuums; all are parts of systems. Therefore, the creation and exploitation of artifacts leave a kind of cultural "fingerprint" which a researcher can use to organize a comprehensive picture of social life and meaning. Each member of society makes or uses objects of different sorts. Through these activities, human beings surround themselves with objects which conform to individual and social identities, requirements, and desires. Individuals use accessible resources and technologies and adapt them as circumstance and custom dictate. Investigation of how people define their aesthetics and display their artistic efforts, how they organize the world around them, and how they develop and manifest their attitudes and beliefs about their environment, both natural and social, allows researchers to both record behaviors and infer their meanings.

The cultural worlds in which people live are both individually and socially constructed. People are socialized to the rules and requirements of their environments, but they also repeatedly revisit and rediscover the world on their own. Expressive artifacts—including art, architecture, crafts, clothing, and foods—act as records and symbols of the tangible and intangible relationships of cultural life. The most significant quality of things is their physicality, their concreteness. People tend to associate objects with certain time periods and experiences, particular social groups and situations, and specific locations and landscapes. Material and expressive cultures, then, reveal the connection between the mind and behavior, between goods and social and political life, and between individuals and society.

As elements of social systems, things are accessories to group memories and affiliations; they make the connections between people tangible and external. Artifacts can give the past a physical reality in the present, embodying events, people, and values central to the social group. Things can function as social bonds; gifts, for example, indebt the receiver to the giver.

Things also embody ideologies. Physical and expressive cultural artifacts can convince or convert. Artifacts give ideas, attitudes, and social experiences compelling and tangible presences in people's lives. Things help people place themselves in a broad spectrum of social, ideological, and economic categories. Things can symbolize an individual's sense of place in the world by embodying status, taste, and attitudes. In important and significant ways, people are what they make, own, use, and see.

Applications

The study of material culture combines the insights of several disciplines, including art, architectural, and decorative arts history; cultural anthropology; archaeology; folk life studies; cultural geography; and social and cultural history. Ethnography and archaeology are both sociological subdisciplines which, perhaps because of their connections to the humanities, have traditionally dealt with material cultural processes and products.

Material culture needs to be understood both in its "natural" context and in relationship to its makers and users. Material and expressive cultural objects are more than artifacts, they are conduits to the connections between human existence and expression. Things inform the study of people and their constructed realities. Thus, researchers in material culture look for universals; at the same time, they note patterns and preferences peculiar to an individual or group.

Generally, material culture study emphasizes group commonalities such as ethnicity, race, religion, region, and occupation. People generally use objects in planned ways that express group identities situationally. The researcher in material culture collects and interprets objects and artifacts peculiar to a group in order to examine the durability and vigor of particular groups. Folk life studies often include racial and ethnic material culture. For example, Robert Thomas Teske's "Living Room Furnishings, Ethnic Identities, and Acculturation Among Greek-Philadelphians" (1979) surveyed living room and parlor furniture and accessories as indicators of assimilation into mainstream American life. In another example, Mihalyi Csikszentmihalyi and Eugene Rochberg-Halton, behavioral scientists at the University of Chicago, developed a survey, interviewed people about their furnishings and special mementos, and collected their findings in an important book, *The Meaning of Things: Domestic Symbols and Self* (1981).

Material culture related to one's job, age, or sex has been given less attention than that of folk, ethnic, or racial groups. One important and suggestive work in this area is Lizabeth A. Cohen's article "Embellishing a Life of Labor: An Interpretation of the Material Culture of American Working-Class Homes, 1885-1915" (1980). Cohen is a historian interested in the everyday social (rather than political or occupational) lives of working-class Americans. This article uses domestic settings and the objects in them to document the lives of a group who left little in the way of standard historical documents. Cohen's conclusions are an elegant melding of sociological theories, social historical perspectives, and material culture studies methodology.

Understanding and investigating artifacts and objects as part of a society's culture has had significant impact on scholars of the sociology of art as well as on students of material culture. Vera L. Zolberg, in *Constructing a Sociology of the Arts* (1990), illustrates the primary importance of contextualizing art in terms of time and space, both in a general sense and in a specific way, so that training, rewards, institutional norms, and support systems are taken into account. Her argument enlarges the meaning and importance of expressive and material culture objects by keeping them at the theoretical center of a research problem while acknowledging that they are parts of larger sociocultural networks.

It is in this area that material culture study and sociological study of the institutions and artifacts of the arts offer their greatest contributions to students of the social sciences. Material and expressive culture objects can provide researchers with rich sources of information about social life, depending on the combination of purposes and perceptions that are brought to them. Objects may hold many meanings, depending on where they are, who uses them, and who looks at them. Objects represent meanings and ideas, processes and behaviors, and statements about culture and society.

Context

Because material and expressive artifacts are the result of human motives and activities, they are extremely useful in the study of human life and society. Particularly since the 1960's, scholars in a variety of disciplines have discovered the power of artifacts as subjects of and tools for research. Studying things enhances traditional areas of inquiry such as history; interest in physical and expressive artifacts has also given researchers new insights into the lives of ordinary people and nonliterate cultures, the subtle workings of the mind, and the social significance of materialism.

Individuals and groups whose experiences are not recorded through written records can be accessed through their material and expressive culture. For such groups as the working class, the poor, women, and people of color, artifacts, no matter how modest, are important resources for historians and scholars. In the 1960's, historiography underwent a significant change under the influence of what came to be called the "new social history," whose primary interest was including ordinary people in the historical record.

Structuralism and semiotics were also developed in the 1960's, as scholars in a variety of disciplines were influenced by new theories and methods in anthropology and linguistics. From these perspectives, artifacts can be investigated to gain insights into how the human mind works. As products of thought, artifacts can provide links between the internal structures of the mind and the external constructions of the world. Visual thinking, while most highly developed in artists, designers, and architects, is a modality common to all human beings. One of the best ways to understand it is through the study of the products of visual thought. Meaning resides not in things themselves but in the minds of the people who create them.

Things, in and of themselves, however, do shed light on materialism. In a materialistic society, things are an end in themselves. For example, in American society, goods have a heightened significance, and the American Dream is tied to a life filled with material abundance. Things are central to such a system, and the only way to understand its functionings and symbolism is through examination of its significant objects.

Yet sociologists have spent much less time and effort investigating material or expressive culture than they have on many other subfields of sociology. This may be largely attributable to a historic tension between sociology and the humanities, which have been seen as the "natural" custodian of art studies. There have been slow but steady developments in the sociology of the arts since the 1960's, probably as a result of the growth of interdisciplinary studies, theories, and methods since the end of World War II. While some of this change may be attributed to a realization that the arts must be understood and studied within a social context, this change in attitude may also reflect an increase in the status of the arts in American society.

Arguably one of the most important developments in the sociology of the arts was the publication of a collection of essays entitled *The Sociology of Art and Literature: A Reader* (1970). Although intended as a classroom text, the anthropology also promoted an institutional approach. Each of the book's three editors contributed an important essay. Milton C. Albrecht introduced the reader to the idea of art as an institution, expanding the meanings of the term "art" to include visual, musical, and literary products. James H. Barnett reprinted his synthetic essay of 1958, "The Sociology of Art." Mason Griff, drawing on his empirical study of art students in Chicago, presented an important and creative article on the recruitment and socialization of artists.

Beginning in the 1970's, the sociology of art began to solidify its disciplinary base and to formalize its theories and methods. Increasing sociological interest in the mass media, popular culture and arts, and visual communication contributed to a period of growth and activity. The production of culture became an issue of concern to sociologists, and material and expressive objects became increasingly significant to sociological research. The meaning of things began to be reevaluated in such works as Marvin Harris' *Cultural Materialism: The Struggle for a Science of Culture* (1980), and the symbolic importance of artifacts began to be defined by their environments and the changing circumstances in which they played a part rather than by their physical properties alone.

There is no real consensus as to the "meaning" of art, and therefore there is no consistency to definitions of the sociology of art. Perhaps because the field is still open to influences and insights from various other disciplines, the social sciences have much to offer to the study and understanding of the material and expressive elements of culture. As the barriers between traditionally humanistic and social scientific methods and theories weaken and blend, the study of material and expressive culture will continue to be a rich resource for a variety of approaches, including the sociological.

Bibliography

Albrecht, Milton C., James H. Barnett, and Mason Griff, eds. *The Sociology of Art and Literature: A Reader*. New York: Praeger, 1970. An early but still significant resource. Divided into six subject sections: artists, distribution and reward systems, forms and styles, history and theory, methodology, and tastemakers and publics.

Becker, Howard S. *Art Worlds*. Berkeley: University of California Press, 1982. A seminal theoretical work on art as collective action.

Cohen, Lizabeth A. "Embellishing a Life of Labor: An Interpretation of the Material Culture of American Working-Class Homes, 1885-1915." *Journal of American Culture* 3-4 (Winter, 1980): 752-775. A social history that uses material culture to discover patterns of sociability and social identity in the urban working class at the beginning of the twentieth century.

Csikszentmihalyi, Mihalyi, and Eugene Rochberg-Halton. *The Meaning of Things: Domestic Symbols and Self.* New York: Cambridge University Press, 1981. An unusual and interesting look at material objects in the home and their meanings for their users from a behavioral point of view.

Foster, Arnold W., and Judith R. Blau, eds. *Art and Society: Readings in the Sociology of the Arts.* Albany: State University of New York Press, 1989. A well-executed collection of essays showing the range of subjects and approaches in the field.

Gowans, Alan. *Reading the Visible Past: Social Function in the Arts.* Ann Arbor: UMI Research Press, 1990. Entertaining, informative examination of social contexts in the visual arts and architecture by an iconoclastic art historian and scholar.

Harris, Marvin. *Cultural Materialism: The Struggle for a Science of Culture.* New York: Vintage Books, 1980. Provocative and controversial work of cultural anthropology which applies Darwin's biological theories to cultural evolution in combination with Marx's ideas about a cultural dialectic, materialism, and social evolution.

Schlereth, Thomas J., ed. *Material Culture Studies in America.* Nashville, Tenn.: American Association for State and Local History, 1982. Excellent introductory text, with a fine essay on the history of material culture studies in the United States and essays by practitioners arranged as statements about theory, method, and practice.

Teske, Robert T. "Living Room Furnishings, Ethnic Identity, and Acculturation Among Greek-Philadelphians." *New York Folklore* 5, nos. 1-2 (1979): 21-31. An ethnic material study that demonstrates the positive results the method can offer to careful practitioners.

Zolberg, Vera L. *Constructing a Sociology of the Arts.* New York: Cambridge University Press, 1990. An unusual methodology and a cogent statement of theory enliven this study of patrons, patronage, and avant-garde art forms.

Jackie R. Donath

Cross-References

CULTURE AND LANGUAGE

Type of sociology: Culture
Field of study: Components of culture

Culture and the language that expresses it are intertwined to such a degree that no one has yet been able to determine which has more influence over the other. The debate continues regarding whether a culture's perception and ordering of the world is determined by its language or whether a culture's language is solely a result of the way the society orders its world.

Principal terms

CULTURE: human traditions and customs that are transmitted through learning between generations; the learned and shared beliefs of a society

DIALECT: a variety or subset of a language used by a group of speakers set off socially or geographically from the main or original body of the speakers of that language; a dialect may or may not be intelligible to other speakers of the parent language

ETHNOLINGUISTICS: the study of the relationship between a language and the cultural behavior of the speakers of that language

HONORIFICS: linguistic markers that signal respect toward the addressee

JARGON: a specialized vocabulary or means of speech specific to a particular group or activity

LANGUAGE: in this work, verbal symbolic communication including a vocabulary and system for its use; language is symbolic in that the sound representing an item or idea is not necessarily related to that item or idea

LINGUISTICS: the study of human speech, including the units of which the language is made as well as its grammatical structure and history

NATIVE LANGUAGE: that language acquired by a person during the early years of development, which is that person's first language of thought and communication

SOCIETY: organized life in groups, especially among humans; members of a society generally share the same cultural characteristics

Overview

Language and culture are expressions of the world that are found in all societies. The nature of their interrelationship and influence on each other is not easily grasped. For the social scientist, the study of language within a culture is a means of looking at that culture's social structure and interpersonal relationships, since it is language that expresses the various aspects of culture, such as labeling, kinship, actions, and beliefs.

The terms "language" and "dialect" are often used interchangeably, although such usage is inaccurate. A language is a communication system that may include a number of variations, known as dialects. In this work, the term "language" will be used to indicate the spoken communication of a cultural group.

Language is the means by which most human thought is communicated. Also, much of social and cultural behavior is expressed by the means of the spoken word. Language is a cultural universal: It appears in all cultures throughout the world. Within each language are universals: greetings, farewells, formal language, and politeness. Language is an oral expression of concrete forms that also carries symbolic meaning; what one says may not be what one means. Thus, in addition to naming the world, language expresses relationships among things. This means that although a word such as "tomorrow" may be translatable from one language to another, it may not have the same meaning in both languages. In one, "tomorrow" may mean "the next day," while in another "tomorrow" may mean "some time in the future."

Culture is the overt and covert expression of the behavior and beliefs of a group of people. It is expressed in the traditions and customs of that people. It includes but is not limited to knowledge of the physical world, beliefs and rituals, moral direction, law, and artistic expression, including graphic arts, dance, music, and so forth. One of the most important aspects of culture is that it gives order to the world in which its participants live. Colors, actions, kinship, and familial relationships are all a part of culture. These relationships are expressed by language, although they may be expressed differently in each cultural setting. In one setting, cats and snakes may be grouped together, since both have similar eye types, large mouths with fangs, and slithery bodies, and both make hissing sounds. In another setting, there may be no relationship between the two creatures.

Language, as a means of communication, has a twofold role in a society. Language is a source of information about a culture and a society (it shows how a group of people label the world), and it is a means by which members of a society socialize or interact. Linguist Irving M. Copi discusses the three basic functions of language within a culture as being, first, to communicate information; second, to express emotion (to communicate feelings); and third, to give commands or requests. He states that these three groups of expression are not necessarily mutually exclusive. The interaction that is facilitated by language use enables individuals in a society to work together more effectively and eases social pressure.

The nature of the relationship between language and culture is not entirely understood. Ronald Wardhaugh has suggested at least four possible correlations of language and culture: (1) social structure may influence linguistic structure (for example, there may be gender-based differences in speech); (2) linguistic structure may determine social structure (it is the language itself, not the speakers of the language, that is gender-biased); (3) language and societal influences are bidirectional—that is, they may influence each other; (4) there is no relationship between language and culture. Most ethnolinguistic studies have eliminated the possibility that the last relationship is valid. They hold that there must be some relationship between language and culture.

The remaining correlations are fuel for debate among ethnolinguists. Preceding Wardhaugh, Benjamin Whorf (1897-1941), an insurance adjuster turned linguist, pursued the idea that language had the greater effect on culture. He proposed that the world is experienced differently by different language communities and that these differences are caused by different cognitive associations as expressed by the language.

During the 1960's and 1970's, British sociologist Basil Bernstein suggested that although the relationship of language and culture is reciprocal, culture has the greater influence on language. According to this theory, it would be the speakers of the language, not the language, who were gender-biased.

The study of the relationship between language and culture is valuable in leading to an understanding of the cognitive processes of various societies. Since each language is the medium by which its speakers express their organization of the world, each language system must be equally valid. One language is not "better" than another. Each language is valid because it expresses complex relationships in the world of its speakers. The "simple, primitive" language does not exist.

Applications

Language has many functions within each culture. It is the primary means of the retrieval of sociocultural knowledge for each group. Language is also the agent of socialization within a culture, teaching each member his or her place within that society. In addition, language is used as an agent of power, distinguishing social rank, which is slightly different from simply socialization. Finally, as world communication develops and languages become less isolated, language planning is coming into prominence as a means of adaptation to increasing lingual and cultural encounters.

A child in any society usually grasps the main aspects of the primary language before the age of five years. The babbling of infants includes the sounds of many human languages, some of which do not occur in the language of the child's family or society. Positive reinforcement encourages the child to continue certain sounds and delete others from the babbling repertoire. Later learning extends to grammar, meaning, and symbolism. All this is achieved without formal instruction.

Language, however, is not culturally bound. A person is not born with a genetic tendency to speak a language. A person of Yakima Indian ancestry does not "naturally" speak the Sahaptin language. If he or she has learned English as a primary language, his or her genetic structure does not make the learning of Sahaptin any easier.

The sociocultural knowledge of a group includes not only daily instructional activities but also the more subtle communication of humor, slang, figures of speech, proverbs, and so forth. An American child who is not fully enculturated into English-speaking society may not understand figures of speech. A child relating a made-up story to an adult while sitting on the adult's lap may be told, "You're pulling my leg." The child may reply, "No, I'm not. I'm sitting on your lap." The same difficulty exists with proverbs. Although a Westerner might understand the Arabic proverb "one bird in the hand is better than ten on a tree," he or she might find it more difficult to understand the proverb "he does not know the difference between an 'alif' and a minaret."

In addition to rules of grammar, a child learns the appropriate social use of language, including his or her place in society. Often this relationship is indicated by "honorifics." Honorifics include terms of address to others that vary by gender, age, and family position, and terms that indicate social distance to those persons outside one's family. In English, social distance is indicated, for example, by the use of Mr., Mrs., and Ms. in combination with the surname of the addressee. A person addressing a close acquaintance would generally use a given name or nickname to identify the person. Social distance may be maintained by persons of differing age groups, social status, duration of acquaintance, or kinship. In Spanish and other languages, other formal terms of address are used in addition to a formal or informal version of the language. A person of high social status may speak to a person of lower social status in the familiar form of address (for example, *tu* in Spanish), while the person of lower status must speak to a superior in the formal form (*usted* in Spanish). As one increases in age and/or social status, one's linguistic patterns change in accordance with the culture's standards.

While power as expressed in verbal communication in society may be related to social distance and rank, it also has a broader application. Language as a means of social power occurs in groups that use "jargon," or a specialized vocabulary or way of speaking. Black English is sometimes included in such a category; persons outside the "in" group may not be able to understand what is being said. Even more frequent are those terms used by particular academic or business groups. Many computer-illiterate people have walked into a computer store and been overwhelmed by the "bits," "bytes," and other technical terms that are used with ease by the computer professional. Other professional groups with specialized vocabularies include physicians, lawyers, academics in various fields, and religious professionals. A visit to a physician, attorney, or cleric can be particularly intimidating, since these individuals not only use language specific to their training but also have power by virtue of their positions.

As a result of increasing world communication and the demise of language isolation, language planning is becoming a concern in many societies. Language planning is not a new idea. The inception of the "dictionary" was an early attempt at planning that resulted in some degree of standardization of spelling and pronunciation. As modern technology becomes widespread, the sharing of words between societies introduces ideas that are foreign to the adopting culture. For example, ethnolinguist George Herzog has noted terms used to describe a car among the Pima Indians of Arizona before 1941. The automobile is described with a Pima term meaning "moves by itself." The pistons are "arms," the wheels are "legs," and the tires are "shoes." As new technological vocabularies were introduced from the West to Japan, Western theories and technologies were included. Philosophies and relationships alien to the Japanese culture were included in these vocabularies—ideas that could not be expressed within the Japanese language. In order to communicate, the Japanese language had to be changed to include words and expressions that were able to incorporate the new technologies.

As language and culture interact, it is possible to see language as a means of ordering culture in the areas of knowledge acquisition, societal roles, and power. Language also functions adaptively as a means of assimilating new ideas and technologies.

Context

The question of the interrelatedness of language and culture has been debated since at least the eighteenth century. During the late 1700's, two German scholars considered this problem. Johann Gottfried von Herder declared that the origin of language is in human nature and that knowledge is possible only through language. Wilhelm von Humboldt stated that the character and structure of a language expresses culture and individuality, and that people perceive the world through language.

During the late nineteenth century, the Swiss linguist Ferdinand de Saussure asserted that language was a product of culture and that the individual was a passive participant in an established language system. Saussure maintained that language was immutable and not subject to change. The next great sociolinguist was Edward Sapir, who is considered to be the founder of the field of ethnolinguistics. He was influenced in his thinking by both Wilhelm von Humboldt and the noted anthropologist Franz Boas. Sapir proposed that human perception of the world occurs mainly through language. This explains the diverse behavior among people of different cultural backgrounds. Sapir's most noted student was Benjamin Whorf, a fire-prevention inspector for an insurance company. Whorf's experiences in "habitual thought," or word patterns that lead people to act in a certain fashion, caused him to question these word patterns. He proposed that humans see and hear and experience the world in a given way because the language habits of the community predispose certain choices of interpretation.

Concurrently, but separately from Sapir and Whorf, the Soviet linguist V. N. Volosinov developed very similar views about the interconnectedness of language and culture.

Following Sapir and Whorf, Noam Chomsky asserted that language is a universal innate facility. He produced some seminal works in the field of ethnolinguistics (*Reflections on Language*, 1975). More recently, British sociologist Basil Bernstein has been interested in the role of language in the socialization process. He examines the ways in which members of various social groups develop language dialects as a means of communicating with one another. He suggests that it is culture that has the greater effect on language.

Ethnolinguistics seems to be moving toward a concern for language planning and political correctness as they affect the identity of citizens and society. The trend toward linguistic and cultural pluralism can be seen in the demise of the Soviet Union and Czechoslovakia and the rise of ethnic (and linguistic) states. Issues of bilingual education—the adoption of English as the official language in the United States, the use of French in Quebec, the acknowledgment of formerly low-status languages in

Africa—are coming to the fore as studies in ethnolinguistics. Such issues as these affect the view that each individual in the societies involved has of himself or herself, and they may direct the focus of ethnolinguistics.

Bibliography

Anderson, Wallace L., and Norman C. Stageberg. *Introductory Readings on Language.* New York: Holt, Rinehart and Winston, 1966. This collection of essays includes a reprint of Edward Sapir's 1921 article "The Nature of Language." It is a good overview of the field of ethnolinguistics (sociolinguistics).

Baugh, John, and Joel Sherzer, eds. *Language in Use: Readings in Sociolinguistics.* Englewood Cliffs, N.J.: Prentice-Hall, 1984. A selection of classic papers in sociolinguistics from the 1970's and 1980's. Included are "Linguistic Diversity of Social and Cultural Context," "Language in Social Interaction," "Language and Speech in Ethnographic Perspective," and "Social Bases of Language Change."

Bonvillain, Nancy. *Language, Culture, and Communication.* Englewood Cliffs, N.J.: Prentice-Hall, 1993. A comprehensive text on the subject of sociolinguistics. This book discusses not only the relationship between language and culture but also means of communication between individuals, communities, and nations.

Chomsky, Noam. *Reflections on Language.* New York: Pantheon Books, 1975. This volume is a compilation of lectures and essays from Chomsky's wide-ranging career. It is a general and nontechnical summary of some of the basic questions regarding language and human activity.

Saussure, Ferdinand de. *Course in General Linguistics*, edited by Charles Bally and Albert Sechehaye. Translated by Wade Baskin. New York: Philosophical Library, 1959. This is the only existing collection of the work of Ferdinand de Saussure. Based on lectures given to students in Geneva, it was published after Saussure's death by his students Bally and Sechehaye. This work is considered by many to mark the beginning of twentieth century linguistics.

Spier, Leslie A., Irving Hallowell, and Stanley S. Newman. *Language, Culture, and Personality: Essays in Memory of Edward Sapir.* Menasha, Wis.: Sapir Memorial Publication Fund, 1941. A collection of essays that are considered classics in the field of ethnolinguistics. This book is a good example of the status of the field at the time of its publication.

Wardaugh, Ronald. *An Introduction to Sociolinguistics.* New York: Blackwell, 1986. This introductory text covers most of the topics discussed in a sociolinguistics course. It requires little previous knowledge and includes questions for discussion.

Weinstein, Brian, ed. *Language Policy and Political Development.* Norwood, N.J.: Ablex, 1990. This collection of papers on language policy is the result of the efforts of fourteen political scientists and linguists from Europe, North America, and India who met to discuss language policy and language planning. It contains good examples of language policy and planning from throughout the world.

Susan Ellis-Lopez

Cross-References

Cultural Norms and Sanctions, 411; Cultural Relativity versus Ethnocentrism, 417; Culture: Material and Expressive Culture, 430; Culture and Technology, 443; Gender Socialization, 833; Interactionism, 1009; The Sociology of Knowledge, 1946; Symbolic Interaction, 2036.

SURVEY
OF
SOCIAL
SCIENCE

ALPHABETICAL LIST

SOCIOLOGY

CATEGORY LIST

ORIGINS AND DEFINITIONS OF
SOCIOLOGY

POPULATION STUDIES OR
DEMOGRAPHY

RACIAL AND ETHNIC
RELATIONS